Research Methods in Practice

Strategies for Description and Causation

Second Edition

Dahlia K. Remler • Gregg G. Van Ryzin

Baruch College and The Graduate Center, City University of New York

Rutgers University, Newark

Los Angeles | London | New Delhi
Singapore | Washington DC

Los Angeles | London | New Delhi
Singapore | Washington DC

FOR INFORMATION:

SAGE Publications, Inc.
2455 Teller Road
Thousand Oaks, California 91320
E-mail: order@sagepub.com

SAGE Publications Ltd.
1 Oliver's Yard
55 City Road
London EC1Y 1SP
United Kingdom

SAGE Publications India Pvt. Ltd.
B 1/I 1 Mohan Cooperative Industrial Area
Mathura Road, New Delhi 110 044
India

SAGE Publications Asia-Pacific Pte. Ltd.
3 Church Street
#10-04 Samsung Hub
Singapore 049483

Acquisitions Editor: Vicki Knight
Associate Editor: Katie Guarino
Editorial Assistant: Jessica Miller
Production Editor: Libby Larson
Copy Editor: Melinda Masson
Typesetter: C&M Digitals (P) Ltd.
Proofreader: Scott Oney
Indexer: Karen Wiley
Cover Designer: Rose Storey
Marketing Manager: Nicole Elliott
Cover Art: Hanna Mandelbaum (HannaJanePaints.com)

Printed in the United States of America

Library of Congress Cataloging-in-Publication Data

Remler, Dahlia K.

Research methods in practice : strategies for description and causation / Dahlia K. Remler, Baruch College, City University of New York, Gregg G. Van Ryzin, Rutgers University, Newark.

pages cm
Includes bibliographical references and index.

ISBN 978-1-4522-7640-3 (pbk.)
ISBN 978-1-4833-1239-2 (web pdf)

1. Research—Methodology—Study and teaching (Graduate)
I. Van Ryzin, Gregg G. (Gregg Gerard), 1961- II. Title.

LB2369.R46 2014
378.1'70281—dc23 2014000280

This book is printed on acid-free paper.

14 15 16 17 18 10 9 8 7 6 5 4 3 2

Brief Contents

Detailed Contents

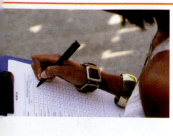

Preface

This book began on a Saturday morning in the spring of 2004, when Dahlia came to visit one of Gregg's executive master of public administration classes. It was a chance simply to observe, get feedback, and share ideas about how to teach research methods. We had each taught this kind of course for years in different programs, but this opportunity arose because we were about to become members of the same faculty in the fall.

We are rather different from each other. Dahlia is an economist with a keen interest in economic theory and causal research. Gregg is a psychologist by training with a background in survey research and program evaluation. Dahlia works on issues related to health care and more recently education. Gregg works on issues related to urban services and public opinion. Our teaching and writing styles—even our personalities—are quite different.

But we hit it off immediately. We realized that our differences in training and experience complemented and reinforced each other. We discovered that we both had a deep commitment to trying to teach research methods well—with clarity, rigor, and purpose. We shared a strong belief that research methods matter—not just to those who plan to become researchers, but to decision makers and practitioners preparing to tackle some of society's toughest problems. We also shared a belief in the value of interdisciplinary research. And we were both increasingly disappointed in the books available to assign to our students.

The standard research methods books we were using had a strong sociology flavor, yet our students came from diverse fields and had more policy-related interests. We wanted a more interdisciplinary approach and more examples of applied social and policy research across various substantive areas (such as public management, education, criminal justice, public health, urban planning, social work, and other areas).

Some of the standard books were initially published several decades ago, and—although new editions were coming out—they seemed to us to be a bit old-fashioned. Research methods and statistics have advanced very rapidly over the past few decades—not only technologically but intellectually—with important influences coming from economics, psychology, political science, epidemiology, statistics, and various other disciplines. We wanted a book that better reflected current thinking.

We also found that the books we were using did not cover causation sufficiently—despite the fact that causal research is essential to understanding the origins of social problems and the effectiveness of proposed solutions. When books did discuss causation, they focused heavily on experiments rather than the observational studies (with control variables or matching), quasi experiments, and natural experiments that modern social and policy researchers mostly depend on to examine causal questions in the real world. We wanted a book that would help students think seriously about causation and recognize and assess the actual research strategies used most often to try to get at it.

Many books describe the abstract concepts of the scientific method and the technicalities of specific methods, but we wanted a book that also gave a feel for the realistic trade-offs, uncertainties, habits, and also excitement that constitute the research experience. To do so, the book we envisioned would contain plenty of in-depth, real-world examples of a wide range of studies that would serve not only to illustrate key methods and ideas but also to demonstrate the value of research to public policy and practice. Research is not perfect—often far from it. Still, we believe that it provides the best hope we have for truly improving the world we live in.

Finally, we also wanted a book that worked for our diverse students, who differ tremendously in their quantitative and research backgrounds—and vary a great deal in what they want to use research for. Some students already have experience doing research, while others have no prior knowledge at all. Some students have backgrounds in quantitative fields like engineering or finance, while others have backgrounds in humanistic fields like history or the arts. Yet all of our students—indeed, we would argue all practitioners and even all citizens—face a deluge of research, analysis, and statistics and must learn to interpret findings, recognize misrepresentations, and make judgments about the strength and relevance of the evidence.

One of the challenges in writing about research methods for such a diverse audience is whether and how to introduce some of the more advanced or technical topics. Rather than leave out important topics, we decided to provide at least short conceptual introductions, avoiding the technical details and emphasizing a more intuitive approach. This way, readers would be able to recognize such techniques when used in studies, and those learning to do their own research would have some initial ideas about the aims and possible applications of more advanced techniques. That is just one of the ways we tried to design a book that will be useful for our readers for years to come as they develop in their careers.

By the end of that morning (probably it was the early afternoon by the time we finished our coffee and discussion), we decided to begin writing our own research methods textbook. We started gradually, using a few draft chapters as supplements to the standard textbooks we were using. As we wrote and taught with our emerging book, we found new ways to explain key ideas, experimented with the best order of topics, dug up interesting examples, and worked to clarify and simplify the often confusing terminology of research methods. As the full book took shape, we had many discussions and debates about ideas and worked long hours revising and rearranging the chapters into a logical, clear, and coherent whole.

We have been extremely gratified by the positive reactions—from students, instructors, and independent readers—to the first edition. Perhaps most gratifying is to discover that those who appreciate our book seem to range so widely in their fields of interest and especially their backgrounds, from experienced researchers to students just starting their training in—and perhaps a little fearful of—research methods.

We both learned a tremendous amount in the process of writing this book and in making revisions for the second edition. We hope that the book helps students and others learn a great deal as well.

How the Book Is Organized—and Why

We organized the book broadly around what we see as the two main kinds of research: strategies for description (Chapters 4 to 7) and strategies to get at causation (Chapters 11 to 15). Descriptive research questions ask about *what is*—the characteristics and patterns that exist in the social world. Causal research questions ask about *what if*—how things in the social world would be different if we made a change. Both are essential in most basic and applied fields, yet it is critical to recognize this distinction when doing or assessing studies (and not, for example, assume that a descriptive study demonstrates causation).

Before getting into the details of descriptive and causal research, some foundational concepts and tools (Chapters 1 to 3) are essential. These include the nature of research and of the scientific method, and, importantly, the foundational role of theory, the tool of path models, and core concepts (such as variables and relationships) that appear in almost all forms of research. We also cover qualitative research (Chapter 3) as foundational because it often serves as an exploratory method and because it helps generate theory and identify causal processes. Introducing qualitative methods early also allows later, more quantitative chapters to incorporate and integrate the qualitative perspective so that we can present more of a mixed-methods approach to most topics.

Although we kept the order of topics fairly traditional, similar to other research methods books and courses, we have situated some chapters differently and introduced novel ones. We put the chapter on qualitative research early in the book for the reasons just mentioned. We cover sources of secondary data (Chapter 6) before primary data (Chapter 7), because many students will work mostly with secondary data (both in their classes and in their careers) and because of the burgeoning availability of secondary data on the Internet.

We placed the chapters on statistical analysis (Chapters 8 to 10) between Part II (Strategies for Description) and Part IV (Strategies for Causation) because the tools of statistical analysis (including statistical inference) are largely descriptive—statistics alone do not establish causation—and because certain statistical tools are needed for some of the most widely used strategies for causation (such as control variables). We have given the statistical analysis chapters their own part (III) also to emphasize that they are tools that can be used for many purposes, separate from the conceptual and methodological issues covered in other parts of the book—and to give readers and instructors flexibility in how much statistics to delve into. For those with a background or recent course work in statistics, Part III can be used for review or even skipped entirely. For those needing to learn statistics along with research methods, the chapters of Part III provide a choice of learning levels from basic data analysis and interpretation (Chapter 8) to statistical inference (Chapter 9) and more advanced multivariate techniques (Chapter 10). Although we envision most readers as having had at least some prior course work in basic statistics, the book is nonmathematical and written to be accessible to those without prior course work in statistics.

In Part IV on strategies for causation, we have a somewhat novel chapter at the start focused on the issue of causation itself (Chapter 11)—what it is, why it is important, and how to begin identifying it. We have found that probing these questions in depth provides motivation and background for learning the logic and methods of various real-world causal research strategies. Instead of presenting randomized experiments right away, the "gold standard" for determining causation, we first cover observational studies with control variables (Chapter 12, which provides the intuition) and how to implement this strategy using multiple regression (Chapter 13, which provides additional statistical details for courses with a more quantitative focus). We cover observational studies first because they are the most numerous in social and policy research and thus the ones students are most likely to encounter in their studies and in their careers. But more important, understanding the limits of observational studies illuminates the need for and logic of randomized experiments, which are covered next (Chapter 14). Following the chapter on randomized experiments, we have another somewhat novel chapter on natural and quasi experiments (Chapter 15) that covers a variety of real-world strategies that emulate the advantages of experimental research for answering causal questions. Natural and quasi experiments, along with observational studies, represent the vast majority of research used to inform policy and practice. The order of chapters in Part IV aims to facilitate understanding of these types of studies.

In Part V, we conclude the book with some consideration of the broader context and communication of research, including the politics and production of research, additional ethical issues, and some practical advice on finding, reviewing, and communicating research.

We recognize, to be sure, that different instructors and programs have different styles and requirements. Some courses must be completed in just a quarter, for example, while others take place over a semester or even an academic year. So to the extent possible (in a linear medium such as a book), we have tried to allow the chapters to be used in a different order or to be taught in parts. For example, some instructors may wish to combine, or omit, selected chapters, in particular the chapters in Part III on statistics (which may not need to be covered in some courses) or Chapter 13 on using multiple regression to estimate causal effects (which is a bit more statistical). Still, we have put much thought and a good deal of class testing into this book, and so we encourage instructors to at least consider the general logic of presentation suggested by our table of contents.

What's New in the Second Edition?

Writing a book like this requires many decisions about coverage, organization, terminology, and style. Although we worked hard on the first edition to get it right, we have continued to think about ways to improve the book. And we have received a great deal of helpful feedback since the book's publication from instructors, students, and reviewers. The main changes to the second edition attempt to improve the book and respond to this feedback in several key areas.

To begin with, we have provided more in the way of explicit guidance for those planning or doing their own research project or thesis. This includes a revised discussion of formulating a research question, which has been moved from the end of the book up to Chapter 2, where it links with the discussion of theory and model building. We provide new guidance on determining sample size in Chapter 5 (and also Chapter 9). And we have added a new section on doing a literature review in Chapter 17. At the end of most chapters, we have also added tips on doing your own research study. Although the book continues to view research methods as important for many people, not just researchers, these revisions aim to give more explicit guidance to students and others involved in doing their own research.

We substantially expanded coverage of research ethics, which is now introduced more prominently and fully in Chapter 1 as well as discussed in subsequent chapters covering the various methods of research. In Chapter 16, we also provide more guidance on the ethical review process, practical advice on writing informed consent forms, keeping data confidential, and other aspects of performing ethical research, as well as a discussion of ethical dilemmas in research. Although some instructors might prefer to see ethics covered all in one place, we continue to believe that many ethical issues arise—and make the most sense—in the context of discussing particular methods, such as qualitative research, surveys, or experiments. We hope our additional coverage provides a fuller understanding of research ethics, while continuing to show how ethical issues permeate most aspects of the research process.

We have also made a number of organizational changes in this edition regarding the coverage of statistics, which is always a tricky balance. Although the ideas and techniques of statistics are integrally connected to research methods, we have tried in this edition to better separate out the more mathematical topics to give instructors and readers greater flexibility in how much statistics to cover. For example, we moved the more mathematical aspects of sampling (such as calculation of standard errors and confidence intervals) out of Chapter 5 on sampling and into a new Chapter 9 that deals with statistical inference. And we separated out the discussion of using multiple regression to estimate causal effects into a new Chapter 13, leaving Chapter 12 to introduce observational studies at a more conceptual, intuitive level. This allows topics like sampling and observational studies (with control variables) to be approached either with or without the mathematical equations and details. We also created a new Part III that contains most of the statistical topics, including basic data analysis and interpretation (Chapter 8), statistical inference (Chapter 9), and multivariate statistics (Chapter 10). The extent to which statistics is or is not taught as part of research methods, or is or is not a prerequisite, varies a great deal across disciplines and programs. We hope these changes make our book more useful for a variety of pedagogical approaches.

In addition, we have made numerous more specific yet important revisions to nearly every chapter of the book. These revisions were aimed at clarifying and refining concepts, improving our explanations, changing or updating examples, improving figures and creating new ones, updating and adding references, and so on. We added a list of learning objectives at the start of each chapter, inserted margin questions to help readers review the material along the way, and provided a list of key terms as well as additional exercises at the end of the chapter.

Finally, we have revised and expanded the supplementary materials for students and instructors, which are available on SAGE's companion website for this book at **www.sagepub.com/remler2e**. These supplementary materials include flashcards, quizzes, and SAGE Journal articles for students; and for instructors, test banks, PowerPoint slides, sample syllabi, and an instructor's manual.

When our editor at SAGE, Vicki Knight, asked us to work on a second edition, we both agreed with the aim in mind of simply updating things and fine-tuning the book in a few necessary places. We clearly failed, producing instead a rather substantial rewrite of what many told us was already a very good book. We hope we have done much more good than harm to the book—and that instructors, students, and others will appreciate and benefit from the improvements in this second edition.

Acknowledgments

The students who read draft chapters of the book in our various classes gave us comments, as well as the opportunity to directly observe what aspects of the chapters did and did not work. Their feedback was critical to the book, and we thank them.

We are very grateful to our editor at SAGE, Vicki Knight. She saw potential in our book at an early stage, provided valuable encouragement and criticism as the book took shape, and shared with us her extensive experience in the craft and business of textbook publishing. She is also a joy to work with. We thank Lauren Habib at SAGE, who helped us a great deal with the first edition of the book, and Kalie Koscielak and Jessica Miller, who helped with the second edition. We also thank Katie Guarino for her work, particularly on the supplements. We also express our gratitude to all those who helped in the production of the second edition. We especially want to thank Melinda Masson, our copyeditor, for her attentive and very thoughtful work on the manuscript. And we are very grateful to Libby Larson, our production editor, for her vision and skill in producing a beautiful new edition of the book.

Hanna Mandelbaum (HannaJanePaints.com) created the original cover art for this second edition, titled "Travectories," as well as the cover art for the first edition. We thank her for finding two beautiful ways to illustrate different aspects of complex causal relationships.

We are grateful to our professors, mentors, colleagues, and students who have furthered our thinking and learning about research methods over the years. Dahlia would particularly like to thank Deborah Balk, Gregory Colman, Allison Cuellar, David Cutler, Sherry Glied, Claudia Goldin, Jessica Greene, Michael Grossman, Katherine M. Harris, Ted Joyce, Lawrence F. Katz, Sanders Korenman, Joseph Newhouse, and Katherine Swartz. Gregg would particularly like to thank Frank Andrews, Etienne Charbonneau, Steve Dietz, Donna Eisenhower, Martin Frankel, Ashley Grosso, Steven Immerwahr, Robert Kaestner, Mirae Kim, Sanders Korenman, Cecilia Lavena, Rom Litwin, John Mollenkopf, Doug Muzzio, Leanne Rivlin, Susan Saegert, Ann Schnare, Carroll Seron, and Gary Winkel.

Finally, we would like to thank those who read and commented on individual chapters, the detailed outline, or in some cases the entire book for the first edition:

Philip Alberti, *New York City Department of Health and Mental Hygiene*

Howard Alper, *New York City Department of Health and Mental Hygiene*

Deborah Balk, *Baruch College and The Graduate Center, City University of New York*

Martin Frankel, *Baruch College and The Graduate Center, City University of New York*

Ted Joyce, *Baruch College and The Graduate Center, City University of New York*

Sanders Korenman, *Baruch College and The Graduate Center, City University of New York*

Cheryl Merzel, *Albert Einstein College of Medicine, Yeshiva University*

Matthew Neidell, *Columbia University*

Suzanne Piotrowski, *Rutgers University, Newark*

Pauline Rothstein, *New York University*

Alan Sadovnik, *Rutgers University, Newark*

Arloc Sherman, *Center on Budget and Policy Priorities*

Dorothy Shipps, *Baruch College, City University of New York*

Robert C. Smith, *Baruch College and The Graduate Center, City University of New York*

Jeanne Teresi, *Columbia University and Research Division, Hebrew Home at Riverdale*

We would also like to thank SAGE's outside reviewers who read and commented on the initial proposal and on drafts of the various chapters for the first and second editions:

Adam Atherly, *University of Colorado Denver, Colorado School of Public Health, Health Systems, Management, and Policy*

Sarah Baird, *George Washington University, Global Health*

Jim Banta, *Loma Linda University School of Public Health, Public Health*

Anthony Bertelli, *University of Southern California, Public Administration and Policy*

David Daniel Bogumil, *California State University, Northridge, Sociology*

Colleen Chrisinger, *University of Oregon, Planning, Public Policy, and Management*

Amita Chudgar, *Michigan State University, Educational Administration*

Matthew Cooper, *Ealing, Hammersmith & West London College, Business Administration*

Alaster Scott Douglas, *University of Roehampton, London, Education*

Michael D. Grimes, *Louisiana State University, Sociology*

Mara Fuertes Gutiérrez, *Leeds Metropolitan University, United Kingdom, Languages*

Kristen Hopewell, *University of Michigan, Sociology*

Osarumwense Iguisi, *London Millennium College/University of Benin, Nigeria, Business and Management*

Douglas Jackson-Smith, *Utah State University, Sociology, Social Work, and Anthropology*

W. Jake Jacobs and Sacha Brown, *University of Arizona, Psychology*

Mark Kovic, *Midwestern University, Health Sciences*

Gary Langford, *Naval Postgraduate School, United States, and the Defence and Systems Institute, University of South Australia, Australia, Engineering and Applied Science*

Sue Lillyman, *University of Worcester, Health and Society*

Nasser Mansour, *University of Exeter, United Kingdom, Education*

Dave E. Marcotte, *University of Maryland Baltimore County, Public Policy*

Khadijah O. Miller, *Norfolk State University, Interdisciplinary Studies*

Stephen S. Owen, *Radford University, Criminal Justice*

Chester Robinson, *Tennessee State University, Public Administration*

Michelle Rogerson, *University of Huddersfield, Applied Criminology*

Jennifer Shea, *San Francisco State University, Public Affairs and Civic Engagement*

Sevil Sőnmez, *University of North Carolina Greensboro, Marketing, Entrepreneurship, Hospitality, and Tourism*

Richard Tardanico, *Florida International University, Global and Sociocultural Studies*

Craig Tollini, *Western Illinois University, Sociology and Anthropology*

Gwen Urey, *California State Polytechnic University, Pomona, Urban and Regional Planning*

Pavlos A. Vlachos, *The American College of Greece, Marketing*

Marc D. Weiner, *Bloustein Center for Survey Research, Rutgers University, Planning and Public Policy*

Xiaohe Xu, *University of Texas at San Antonio, Sociology*

Glenn A. Zuern, *Albany State University, Criminal Justice*

About the Authors

Dahlia K. Remler is a professor in the School of Public Affairs at Baruch College and the Department of Economics at The Graduate Center, both of the City University of New York. She is also a research associate at the National Bureau of Economic Research.

Dahlia has been in an unusual mix of disciplinary and interdisciplinary settings. She received a bachelor of science in electrical engineering from the University of California at Berkeley, a doctorate in physical chemistry from Oxford University—while a Marshall Scholar—and a doctorate in economics from Harvard University. During the Clinton administration's health care reform efforts, Dahlia held a fellowship at the Brookings Institution to finish her dissertation on health care cost containment. She then held a postdoctoral research fellowship at Harvard Medical School, followed by assistant professorships at Tulane's and Columbia's Schools of Public Health, prior to joining the faculty at Baruch. She enjoys comparing and contrasting how different disciplines see the same issues.

Dahlia has published widely in a variety of areas in health care policy, including health care cost containment, information technology in health care, cigarette tax regressivity, simulation methods for health insurance take-up, and health insurance and health care markets. She has also recently started working on higher education and media issues. Her work has appeared in the *Journal of Policy Analysis and Management*, *Health Affairs*, the *Quarterly Journal of Economics*, the *American Journal of Public Health*, *Medical Care Research and Review*, and many other journals. She blogs on health care policy, higher education, and other topics at DahliaRemler.com.

Dahlia lives with her husband, Howard, in New York City, where they enjoy the city's theaters, restaurants, and parks—and Dahlia enjoys being a complete amateur dancer in some of the city's superb dance studios.

Gregg G. Van Ryzin is a professor in the School of Public Affairs and Administration at Rutgers University, Newark. He received his bachelor of arts in geography from Columbia University and his doctorate in psychology from the City University of New York. During his doctoral training, he worked as a planner for a nonprofit housing and community development organization in New York City, and he completed his dissertation on low-income housing for the elderly in Detroit. He next worked in Washington, DC, for ICF Inc. and later Westat Inc. on surveys and program evaluations for the U.S. Department of Housing and Urban Development and other federal agencies. In 1995, he joined the faculty of the School of Public Affairs at Baruch College, where he directed the Survey Research Unit for eight years. In that role, he helped develop and direct the New York City Community Health Survey, a large-scale behavioral health survey for the city's health department, and also played a key role in shaping and conducting the city's survey of satisfaction with government services. He has spent time in Madrid, collaborating with researchers there on the analysis of surveys about public attitudes toward Spanish government policy.

Gregg has published many scholarly articles on housing and welfare programs, survey and evaluation methods, and public opinion about government services and institutions. His work has appeared in the *International Review of Administrative Sciences*, the *Journal of Policy Analysis and Management*, the *Journal of Public Administration Research and Theory*, the *Journal of Urban Affairs*, *Nonprofit and Voluntary Sector Quarterly*, *Public Administration Review*, *Public Management Review*, *Public Performance and Management Review*, *Urban Affairs Review*, and other journals.

Gregg lives in New York City with his wife, Ada (a history professor at NYU), and their daughters Alina and Lucia. They enjoy life in their Greenwich Village neighborhood, escaping on occasion to Spain, Miami, Maine, Cuba, and other interesting places in the world.

PART I

FOUNDATIONS

Learning about research methods requires motivation, a sense of purpose, and some ideas about how to begin. This first part of the book aims to introduce you to research and its many uses in the real world, hopefully motivating you to want to learn more. It also covers the theories, models, and research questions that guide researchers' thinking and that the methods covered later in the book help to test or answer. And this part of the book introduces you to qualitative research, which is an important starting point for exploring the social world as well as a useful method for developing theories and models. Together, these chapters provide a foundation for your developing knowledge of research methods.

Thousands of studies have looked at global warming.

Source: © 2009 Jupiterimages Corporation.

Overview: In this chapter, you will learn why research methods matter—not just for those who do research but for those who apply it to policy and practice. Research provides a fact base for decisions and helps win arguments; and sometimes (if you're not careful), research misleads. Knowing research methods also provides a foundation for understanding performance measurement, program evaluation, and the push for evidence-based policy and practice in many fields. You will begin to see how descriptive ("what is") questions differ from causal ("what if") questions and what defines research and the scientific method more generally as a way of knowing about the world. And you will learn about the ethics of doing research with human participants—ethics that shape social and policy research. This chapter aims to spark your interest in research methods—and to help you approach the rest of the book with an open and informed perspective.

Objectives

Learning Objectives

After reading this chapter, you should be able to

- Find examples of research applied to policy or practice
- Understand the character of research as a form of knowing
- Appreciate the limitations of research
- Distinguish causal and descriptive questions
- Describe key ethical principles of human subjects research and appreciate how they shape social and policy research

1 Research in the Real World

Do Methods Matter?

We want to do things in our lives and in our work to make a difference in the world—to educate children, treat or prevent sickness, reduce crime and violence, promote the arts, develop innovative products, feed the hungry, house the homeless, and improve our workplaces and our communities. We share a desire to do something meaningful, to leave our mark in the world. But doing so requires a base of evidence beyond our own personal knowledge and experience—evidence about how things really are, and evidence about how to make things better.

We need such evidence not only to enhance our own understanding and decision making but also to convince others—those with the authority and resources that we need to accomplish our aims, or those with opposing points of view who stand in our way.

Good Evidence Comes From Well-Made Research

The best evidence comes from good research. Good research can appear in the form of a study published in a journal, but it can also be an internal analysis of administrative data, a government or foundation report, a performance measurement brief, a program evaluation, a needs assessment, or a client or employee survey. Government agencies collect and disseminate a great variety of empirical evidence on many important topics, such as health services and outcomes, educational attainment, labor market characteristics, crime victimization and punishment, housing conditions, environmental air and water quality, and so on. (To get a flavor of all that is available from the U.S. federal government, visit *data.gov;* or for United Nations data, visit *data.un.org*. Most national governments and many international organizations and regional governments have similar sites.)

Because of the Internet and modern communications technology, we now live and work in a world in which an abundance of studies and statistics swirl all about us and hover within easy grasp—provided we know what to choose, how to make sense of it, and where to apply it.

Good research—just like a good car or a good pair of shoes—must be well designed and well made. But we cannot simply rely on brand names (although knowing that research comes from a respected scientific journal or reputable research institution does provide some assurance). Still, each study is unique, and each has unique strengths and weaknesses. So we need to understand how research is made—that is, research methods.

Research methods are the techniques and procedures that produce research evidence, such as sampling strategies, measurement instruments, planned comparisons, and statistical techniques. So we need to understand research methods to judge the quality of a study and the evidence it provides. Research methods are what this book is all about.

May the Best Methods Win

We also need an understanding of research methods to attack evidence that hurts our cause or defend evidence that helps it.

Consider the controversy over abstinence-only sex education for teenagers. Some communities feel strongly that teens should be discouraged as much as possible from engaging in sexual activity and that comprehensive sex education (which can involve distributing condoms and instructing teens in their use) sends the wrong signal. Others warn that the abstinence-only approach does little to change the reality of teenagers' lives, leaving them vulnerable to unwanted pregnancy and sexually transmitted diseases (including AIDS).

Sex education in schools has spurred controversy—and research.

Source: © iStockphoto.com/IsaacLKoval.

As is often the case with a controversial public policy issue, both sides can point to studies to bolster their arguments. A review by Douglas Kirby (2007) uncovered 115 studies of various pregnancy prevention programs targeting U.S. teens, including abstinence and comprehensive programs. So neither side can win just by pointing to "*a* study" that supports their position.

Instead, we must struggle over how well made the conflicting studies are—meaning their methods. The argument may be won by having a better made study—or lost by having a poorly made one. So, although the war may start from a substantive policy disagreement, such as how best to provide sex education to teens, the battles often rage over research methods.

Research-Savvy People Rule

Some of you may be training to become researchers or analysts—and so doing research will be (or already is) part of your job. Clearly, knowing research methods is important to you. But many of you are (or plan to be) practitioners, doers—implementing programs, delivering services, managing people, or leading organizations. Why do you need to know research methods? We've already suggested a few reasons: Good research provides a fact base for decisions and wins arguments, and the quality of research often hinges on the methods used. But knowing research methods can help your career more directly as well.

We live and work in an "information age" in which the ability to find, understand, and make use of complex sources of information—such as research—represents an important skill. An explosion of data of all kinds—from governments, businesses, and virtually every other institution or activity in our lives—means that those who know how to handle, analyze, and interpret data have great value to organizations and employers. Organizations regularly commission research, and so their top leaders or managers must know how to make sense of and apply research findings to improve policies and programs. Funding agencies and legislative bodies demand "evidence-based"—meaning research-based—programs and management reforms. To win funding for your program or organization, you need the ability to demonstrate an understanding of research in your field of policy or practice.

So without a grasp of research methods, you will be at a disadvantage in applying for jobs, advancing into leadership positions, and attracting financial and political support for your program or cause. With a good understanding of research methods, you can do more and go farther in your career.

Research, Policy, and Practice

Research has become an essential element of modern public policy and management in the form of performance measurement, program evaluation, and the push for evidence-based policy and practices.

Performance Measurement

In many fields these days, there has been much emphasis put on **performance measurement** and performance management. The idea is sensible: We should measure how well we're doing and ideally manage to improve it. New York City's CompStat program—a data-driven effort to closely track crime and hold managers accountable for controlling it—is an often-cited example. And the push to measure performance is big in education, business, health care, and many other fields. The mass of data available today, thanks to the information revolution, fuels this trend. Performance measurement has now become a pillar of contemporary policy and practice in the public and nonprofit sectors (Hatry, 2007; Kaplan & Harvard Business School, 2009; Poister, 2003).

In the following chapters, you will see how logic models can help you figure out what to measure. You will learn what makes for valid and reliable measurements. And you will be introduced to various sources of data to measure outputs and outcomes, including both existing data and original surveys. All this material is critical to understanding and implementing performance measurement and management.

Evaluation Research

Much **evaluation research** aims to answer these questions: Did a program or intervention have an impact? Did it improve or change things? Other program evaluations seek to describe the process of implementing the program. Evaluation research is now a standard requirement of most government or foundation grants and contracts. Most new policy or management initiatives demand some form of evaluation as well. So evaluation research, too, has become a pillar of contemporary policy making and management in the government, the nonprofit sector, and even the business world (Rossi, Lipsey, & Freeman, 2003; C. Weiss, 1997).

But how can we know if a program or initiative is having its intended effect? Later chapters will introduce you to the basic ideas involved in thinking about cause and effect. They will cover strategies for estimating causal effects, including the use of control variables, randomized experiments, and various forms of what are called natural and quasi experiments. These are the major strategies for conducting evaluations of program impact.

Evidence-Based Policy and Programs

As suggested earlier, governments, businesses, and nonprofit organizations increasingly favor evidence-based policies and programs—strategies that have proven their effectiveness with research. It's not enough any-more to have a few heartwarming testimonials or a plan that just looks good on paper. The trend toward evidence-based policy and practice now permeates many fields (Davies, Nutley, & Smith, 2000). Even political campaigns now make much greater use of data and evidence-based approaches to gathering votes (Scola, 2012).

Due to limited resources, policy makers and practitioners must often choose between effective programs. Therefore, comparing the effectiveness of different programs is crucial, as is comparing *cost-effectiveness*—the outcome obtained relative to the cost of the program. Such comparisons require evidence about the magnitude of a program's effect—how large an influence a program has on the outcome.

The chapters that follow will give you tools to identify and assess evidence that supports or can improve your program or initiative. And it will help you understand how to produce good research evidence to support your aims.

Evidence Can Mislead

On top of all that we've mentioned so far about the importance of research methods, it can be embarrassing to be wrong—and sometimes, if you're not careful, evidence can mislead.

What examples have you seen of performance measurement, program evaluation, or a focus on evidenced-based policy in your work or area of interest?

Misleading Measurements

No Child Left Behind (NCLB) was signed into law in 2002, setting in motion a wave of reform in schools all across the United States that became suddenly preoccupied with high-stakes testing, worried about closing the race gap, and apprehensive about the need to demonstrate rapid gains in test scores. NCLB won support in part because of the "Houston miracle," the fact that this large, diverse city had itself demonstrated remarkable gains in reading and math scores, especially for Black and Hispanic students—at least according to scores on the Texas Assessment of Academic Skills (TAAS). If Houston could do it, so could the rest of the nation.

But scores on another test—the Stanford Achievement Test—taken by the same Houston students during the same school years showed a much different picture, according to an analysis by the *New York Times* (Schemo & Fessenden, 2003). Scores on the Stanford test, which is used nationwide, showed little or no gain overall in Houston and little or no narrowing of the race gap. Several well-known experts in education statistics, asked by the *New York Times* to review the discrepancy, concluded that the TAAS had considerably overstated the progress made by Houston students. Standardized tests do not necessarily provide a consistent measure.

Misleading Samples

In response to a U.S. Supreme Court decision on gun control, a *USA Today* (2008) quick poll asked visitors to its website, "How many guns do you own?" About 30,000 people die in the United States each year from gun-related accidents or violence (Centers for Disease Control and Prevention, 2008), so many are concerned about gun ownership in the U.S. population. But how high is the rate of gun ownership? A total of 1,987 people responded to the *USA Today* quick poll, and the results showed that fully 89% owned a gun—suggesting gun ownership is nearly universal. But the quick poll relied on a voluntary sample—website visitors who found the article online and decided to participate in the poll.

When the General Social Survey (GSS) asked a sample of 1,996 adults if they owned a gun, only 35% reported that they did. Which survey do we believe? The GSS uses much better methods—including careful random sampling—to produce its results. The true rate of gun ownership in the United States is certainly much closer to 35% than it is to the strikingly high figure of 89%. The flawed methods of the *USA Today* quick poll grossly overstated gun ownership in the United States. The solid methods of the GSS get us closer to the truth.

Fluoridated water is associated with weakened bones, but is it a cause?

Source: Can Stock Photo Inc./Elenathewise.

Misleading Correlations

Many cities and towns add fluoride to the water supply because it helps prevent tooth decay in children. Other cities do not add fluoride. Some people worry that ingesting fluoride can have adverse effects on older people, in particular, weakening their bones and leading to debilitating and painful hip and other bone fractures. This fear comes from studies that show that older people living in cities and towns with fluoridated water tend to have higher rates of bone fractures as compared with older people living in cities and towns with untreated water (Jacobsen et al., 1990). In other words, there is a correlation between fluoride in the water and bone fractures. Should cities stop the practice of adding fluoride to municipal water supplies?

People living in cities that add fluoride to the water may be different from people living in cities that do not. A study in the United Kingdom (Hillier et al., 2000) used methods to take individual differences in characteristics (age, sex, and body weight) and lifestyle (physical activity, smoking, and drinking alcohol) into account. When they did, the correlation between exposure to fluoridated water and bone fractures disappeared. This study suggests that the original correlation many people worried about was probably due to these other factors—it was a **spurious correlation**. In other words, it would be misleading to interpret the correlation between fluoridated water and bone fractures as showing that fluoridated water causes bone fractures to increase—and so we shouldn't change municipal water treatment policy because of it.

QUESTION

Can you think of any other examples of a misleading measurement, sample, or correlation?

What Is Research?

This book is about research methods—but what is research? We can define research as a social and intellectual activity that involves systematic inquiry aimed at accurately describing and explaining the world. But it helps to get a bit more specific.

Secondary and Primary Research

People often "research" a topic at the library or on the Internet. Such information searches and syntheses are best referred to as **secondary research**—the search for published sources describing the results of research or information provided by others. While secondary research is an important skill that we cover in the last chapter (Chapter 17), it is not the focus of most of what we cover in this book, nor is it what we mean when we use the word *research*.

Rather, we use the term *research* to refer mostly to original research, or **primary research**—the original collection or analysis of data to answer a new research question or to produce new knowledge. In journals, such studies are referred to as original contributions. What gets confusing is that original or primary research can involve **primary data** collection—collecting *new* data to provide a description or explanation of the world. But it can also involve the original analysis of **secondary data**—data collected by others, such as existing government surveys, administrative records, or transcripts. Indeed, much primary research gets done using secondary data.

Unfortunately, the term *data* can be a bit confusing. When we look up a few published facts or even a table of statistics online or in the library, we sometimes refer to this as finding "data" on a topic. But in this book, we use the term **data** to refer to largely unprocessed observations—a data set or raw data, they're sometimes called.

QUESTION

In your own words, explain the differences between primary and secondary research and between primary and secondary data.

We now turn to some of the key features of research, particularly as it applies to policy and practice.

It Comes in Various Shapes and Sizes

As you will see from the many examples throughout the chapters in this book, research comes in a surprisingly wide variety of shapes and sizes:

- Large-scale studies of broad populations
- Small-scale studies of one locally situated group
- Snapshots in time
- Studies of outcomes or events that occur over many periods of time
- Laboratory experiments
- Naturalistic observations of real-world settings
- Carefully planned interventions
- Theoretical analyses
- Opportunistic discoveries of unplanned events
- Informal research conducted for the purpose of organizational strategy or management

One of the important points to realize about research, and about researchers, is that inventiveness and creativity are an important part of the process. Good research often involves the imaginative application of new methods, innovative techniques, or clever strategies to learn about the world. It is this creative aspect of research methods that makes the topic so interesting to those familiar with it. We will try to give you a flavor of this variety and creativity in the chapters to come.

It's Never Perfect

Research, like everything else that is human, is not perfect—far from it. Every study has weaknesses, as you will see in this book. It is important to spot these shortcomings and understand their implications.

But it is also important not to entirely discard a study because it has some methodological or other shortcomings. We don't want to throw the baby out with the bathwater. Every study has strengths, too—or at least most studies do. There is often something to be learned from almost any study, and the perfect study is just not possible—especially in social and policy research. A good consumer of research can both spot the weaknesses and recognize the strengths.

It's Uncertain and Contingent

Many think of research as providing certain and universal conclusions. But research evidence often includes a large dose of *uncertainty*, typically expressed in the form of probability statements or qualified conclusions. Thus, researchers talk about the results "indicating" this or that, "suggesting" that something is true, or showing that an outcome was "likely" due to a presumed cause. In part, this comes from the language of modern statistics, which uses the laws of probability to make inferences about unknown populations or causes. But this way of speaking and writing also reflects the inherent uncertainties involved in making firm statements or conclusions about complex human and public affairs.

Social and policy research is also **contingent**—bounded in space, time, and context. A study that finds evidence for the effectiveness of an education reform in one school district, for example, may not hold true in other districts with different children, teachers, budgets, and administrative structures. A mental health intervention that is shown to be effective with affluent suburban adults may not have the same effect on poor, inner-city adults living much-different lives. The motivations found to encourage productivity in one organization may not be the same as the motivations that matter in another organization.

It Aims to Generalize

Generalizability is the ability to take the results of research and apply them in situations other than the exact one in which the research was carried out. Although we just noted that research is often contingent, researchers nevertheless strive at the same time to make their work generalizable. This is quite important: If the research results only apply in the exact setting (time, place, circumstances) in which the study was conducted, then they cannot be used to inform policies or practices in other situations.

For example, a study might examine a policy of requiring out-of-pocket payments for emergency visits to the hospital and find no impact on health outcomes for patients. But say the study is done using data from one insurance plan that covers mostly younger, healthy workers with good incomes. Do the results apply to insurance plans that cover older, less healthy individuals with low incomes? Probably not: Such individuals might well behave differently if required to make payments for their emergency visits. So the study has limited generalizability. We might even worry that the study is only relevant for that one particular insurance plan and the population it serves, making it of little use to anyone else. While generalizability is always a goal, real-world research is often less generalizable than we would like.

This is not to say that social and policy research has little to offer—on the contrary. But you do need to be realistic and appreciate the limits, as well as the rewards, of research.

Bits and Pieces of a Puzzle

It's also true that a single study is almost never definitive. Rather, empirical evidence on a topic is cumulative. Research produces a *body* of evidence, and researchers talk about arriving at a scientific *consensus* within the bounds of what is likely to be true (or not).

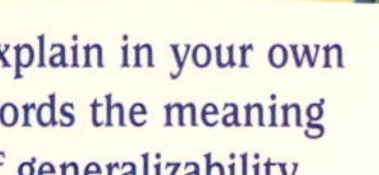

Explain in your own words the meaning of generalizability.

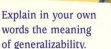

Consider global warming—is the world really heating up, and if so, is global warming natural or manmade? There have been thousands of individual studies of various aspects of global warming over the years, from tracking the melting of the polar ice caps to observing animal species, mapping storms and rainfall, sampling the level of ozone and other pollutants in the atmosphere, and so on. None of these studies alone definitively proves that human activity is causing the earth to get hotter—indeed, some contradict this hypothesis. To help establish a consensus—particularly given the monumental economic costs and political complexities involved in responding to global warming—the United Nations (UN) and the U.S. federal government each established scientific panels to review the research evidence. The UN's Intergovernmental Panel on Climate Change (2007) concluded that the earth had probably gotten warmer over the past 100 years and that human activity was "very likely" the cause. The U.S. government's panel also said it was likely that global warming had been caused by human activity (U.S. Global Change Research Program, 2009). But to arrive at this conclusion took many years of research and thousands of individual studies—not to mention much political debate. And the process goes on.

The same kind of process of accumulating evidence, engaging in scientific debate, and searching for consensus characterizes most areas of research. Of course, most topics of research do not inspire as many studies or the establishment of large national or multinational scientific panels to search for a consensus. Nevertheless, something similar happens on a smaller, quieter scale in the various journals, research conferences, and institutions where studies on a topic are presented and debated. And consensus is not always, or even often, possible: Too much is unknown, and more research remains to be done.

It Involves Competition and Criticism

The process of research is also one of continual competition and criticism—the continuous testing of the consensus. There are researchers who doubt aspects of the man-made global warming hypothesis, for example, and they are busy conducting and gathering evidence to challenge, or at least refine, the consensus. Conclusions that withstand this kind of competitive onslaught become what we consider to be established knowledge (for the time being).

The formal expression of this critical attitude is the process of **peer review**. Most research journals, as well as research funding programs, use a peer-review process in which the studies or proposals are reviewed and approved (or rejected) by a group of peers—other researchers in the same field—who render a judgment on the methods and worth of the paper or proposal. This process is usually blind (neither the researcher nor the reviewer knows who is who) to rule out favoritism and to encourage reviewers to be honest and forthright in their criticism. You, too, should think in this honest, critical way as you hear or read about research (although, of course, sometimes even the best and most experienced researchers struggle to keep an open mind).

It Can Be Quantitative, Qualitative, or a Mix of Both

Much research involves numerical measurement and statistics, but research can also involve language, images, and other forms of expressing meaning that researchers then interpret. The former is referred to as quantitative research, the latter qualitative research. Qualitative studies involving the interpretation of language can be done rigorously—despite the lack of scientific-looking tables and formulas. Numbers do not make a study good or scientific.

These days, social and policy research often uses mixed methods that combine the advantages of both quantitative and qualitative techniques. Because social phenomena are so difficult to pin down, researchers often use multiple methods to confirm a finding, a process sometimes referred to as triangulation.

Although most of the chapters in this book are devoted to topics typically thought of as part of quantitative research, we discuss the role and contribution of qualitative methods in all of the chapters. And we devote an early chapter (Chapter 3) to qualitative research because we consider it to be foundational. In an important sense, good quantitative research is based on good qualitative research. The two perspectives enhance one another.

It Can Be Applied or Basic

Research can be **applied**—done because we have a practical need to know. For example: How many people are currently unemployed? Would smaller classes improve learning? Does adding police officers reduce crime? Applied research typically has direct implications for policy and practice. Many of the examples in this book focus on applied research.

But research can also be **basic**—the pursuit of knowledge for its own sake, rather than being based on an immediate practical need. Basic research in a given field also tends to focus on more abstract or fundamental processes of nature or society. For example, we might be interested in studying how people make decisions involving uncertainty, how the human body responds to long-term exposure to stress, how children acquire a language, or the evolutionary basis of human cooperation. Basic research also advances policy and practice by providing a solid foundation of knowledge. But the link is less direct.

Descriptive and Causal Research

Research sometimes aims simply to describe the world—how things are. At other times, its goal is to provide a causal explanation—how would things be different if we changed something? This basic distinction is fundamental to thinking about and conducting research and provides a road map of sorts for the rest of this book.

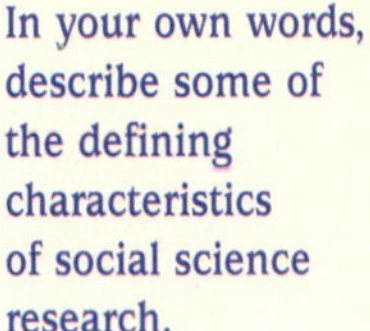

QUESTION

In your own words, describe some of the defining characteristics of social science research.

Description: What Is the World Like?

Concern about autism has been growing for some time, and parents and other advocates have pressed for services to help autistic children and for more research about the disease. In evaluating how to react to autism, policy makers and practitioners need to know how many people (and particularly children) with autism there are in the population. They need to know if the rate of autism is growing—and, if so, how quickly. They need to know whether autism is more concentrated in certain places or groups in the population. They need to know the severity and forms of autism. In other words, policy makers and practitioners need a good *description* of autism to address the problem.

The goal of **descriptive research** is to paint an accurate picture of the way the world is. Descriptive research includes describing just one variable—such as the rate of autism in the population. It also includes describing **relationships**—how two different variables are related (see Chapter 2). Relationships are often referred to as associations or correlations. For example, autism rates have been growing, so time and autism are related. Or at least it seems so—researchers worry that perhaps we have simply gotten better over time at identifying people with autism and that this enhanced ability to identify the disease accounts for the upward trend. Autism and geographical region are also related—the disease is more common in California, for example, than in other parts of the United States. But it turns out that this description is not so certain—perhaps autism is not consistently identified everywhere. Descriptive research can be harder than you might expect.

What is known about autism?

Source: © iStockphoto.com/ Tramper2.

Before figuring out what to do about a problem like autism, the problem must be described. Knowing the lay of the land is important before deciding where to go. But once practitioners have described the problem, the task of tackling and solving it has just begun. After all, we want to figure out how to make things better—not just sit around and watch things happen. In the case of autism, policy makers and practitioners want to figure out how to prevent and hopefully cure, or at least ameliorate, the disease.

Causation: How Would the World Be Different If Something Changed?

The goal of **causal research** is to answer "what if" questions to find out how to make things happen. Specifically, if we change one thing, will other things (outcomes we care about, such as autism) change? And if they do change, by how much?

For example, what would happen to the severity of the disease if children with autism stopped eating gluten? Would it change at all? If so, by how much? Or what would happen to autism rates if children stopped being vaccinated?[1] More generally, we want to know what factors have caused the growth of autism over time (if indeed the trend is real and not just an artifact of better identification techniques).

Descriptive and causal research are both important in practice, but answering causal questions is especially central to the work of practitioners. Public policies, social programs, and management initiatives aim to do things—to make something happen. So answering questions such as "What will happen if we do X?" is essential.

Description of a Correlation Is Not Proof of Causation

It is easy to confuse correlation, the description of a relationship, with causation. If more educated mothers are more likely than less educated mothers to have children with autism—a correlation—then it is easy to conclude that something about educated mothers causes autism. However, that may not be so. Think about the earlier example of fluoridated water and fractured bones. When researchers, policy makers, or practitioners naively assume that a correlation implies causation, grave errors can be made.

For example, because autism rose over the same period that vaccine use rose, and because autism symptoms start at about the same time that toddlers receive many vaccines, many people concluded that vaccines cause autism. Many parents started to reject vaccines, causing some outbreaks of previously suppressed illnesses.

One of the most important skills you will gain from this book is how to distinguish a correlation, the description of a relationship, from evidence of a causal effect. We address this in Chapter 11, our chapter on causation. Another, perhaps even more important, skill is how to judge the quality of evidence of causation and how to do research that provides evidence of whether a causal effect exists and how big it is.

What is the difference between descriptive and causal research?

Because distinguishing description from causation is so important, we have organized this book around that distinction. Part II of the book covers strategies for description, while Part IV covers strategies for causation. We will stress again and again the distinctions between description and causation and between correlation and causation.

Epistemology: Ways of Knowing

How much do you weigh? How do you *know* that's how much you weigh? Probably you used a scale and remember the result. You measured your weight—an elementary act of research. How high is Mount Everest? If you know, how do you know? Did you measure it? If you don't know, how might you try to learn how high Mount Everest is? You will probably turn to other sources, perhaps searching the Internet and examining a

[1] See the chapter "Vaccines and Autism?" in the book by Arthur Allen (2007), which addresses this controversy. There is no good evidence that vaccines cause autism and some evidence that they do not.

website that you trust (secondary research). But of course you should consider how the website got its information.

We have many ways of knowing—what philosophers of science call **epistemologies**. Sometimes we directly learn something ourselves. But we can't do that about most things in the world. Often, we just accept what some trusted authority says is true. Sometimes, we rely on knowledge that comes from our cultural or religious traditions. We know other things through intuition or common sense.

The Scientific Method

There are many ways of knowing things, but in modern society the scientific method is a privileged way of knowing. Most of the ideas and techniques presented in this book are based on the scientific method.

Obviously, you cannot directly research everything you need to know on your own. So this book will teach you not only how to do research but how to critically assess and make use of the research produced and published by others. It will also help you judge knowledge that comes from authority, tradition, and common sense more effectively by using the standards of the scientific method.

The **scientific method** can be defined as an approach to acquiring and correcting our knowledge about the world. It has several key characteristics:

- Systematic observation—or measurement of various features or behaviors in the world (including qualitative observation).
- Logical explanation—in the form of a theory or model that makes sense according to basic rules of logic and accepted facts.
- Prediction—in the form of a hypothesis, based on a theory, of what we will observe if the theory is true. (This is seen as superior to after-the-fact, or ex post facto, explanations, which are not falsifiable.)
- Openness—meaning the methods used to produce evidence are clearly documented and made available for review. This allows for replication—repeating the study to see if the results hold (and in what contexts).
- Skepticism—researchers scrutinize and critique each other's work, a process referred to as peer review, in search of possible shortcomings or alternative explanations.

In sum, the scientific method is a privileged form of knowing because it is generally transparent, logical, and fact based. But scientific evidence can be misrepresented or misused, so you still need to question scientific knowledge just as you would question common sense, tradition, or authority. Also, it is important to point out that there are varying understandings of what constitutes the scientific method, and that this understanding has changed over time and across scientific fields (Godfrey-Smith, 2003).

Is There One Truth in Social Science?

The scientific method originated with the natural sciences. Newton's physics, Galileo's astronomy, Lavoisier's chemistry, and Mendel's genetics are early examples. But the social world is different from the physical or biological worlds, due to factors such as human consciousness, culture, history, and politics. And social phenomena vary by place and time much more than do physical or biological phenomena.

As a result, knowledge produced by the social sciences, such as how markets work or how children learn, is more contingent and less generalizable than is knowledge produced by the natural sciences. Moreover, how we interpret social phenomena is shaped in part by language and culturally constructed categories. These categories even influence the kinds of social objects or actions we observe, and our social constructions also vary from time to time, from culture to culture, and from political perspective to political perspective. So even when we try to be objective, our interpretations will be influenced by our categories of subjective experience and judgment.

Because social ideas and facts are constructed in this way, some people reject the relevance of the scientific method to the study of society and public policy. Indeed, others even reject the idea that an objective truth, even a contingent truth, exists for social phenomena outside of our various subjective, socially constructed vantage points. This skeptical view is generally referred to as *antipositivism*, because it is opposed to so-called **positivism**, the approach of social researchers who pattern their work after the natural sciences. However, positivism has a more precise meaning in the philosophy of science, where it refers to a rather strict form of empiricism (such as behaviorism in psychology). We acknowledge that ideas and even observations about social phenomena are inevitably influenced by social constructions, particularly by history and culture. Nonetheless, we believe that the scientific method, broadly defined, provides the most pragmatic approach to understanding and solving many of the pressing social problems we face today.

Our perspective in this book can be described generally as **scientific realism** (Bunge, 1993; Godfrey-Smith, 2003): "realism" because we believe that the social world, although profoundly shaped by human history and culture, is still part of an objective reality that exists outside of our thoughts and perceptions, and "scientific" because we believe it is possible to use the scientific method—or methods modeled on the scientific approach—to learn about and understand the social world. We do not mean to minimize the practical problems of applying scientific approaches to social phenomena, but we consider them to be *practical*, not existential, problems. When studying policy and society, the scientific method can serve as an ideal—even if social and policy research does not always live up to this ideal.

Induction and Deduction

There are several ways in which researchers employ the scientific method to tackle a problem or curiosity, as illustrated in Figure 1.1. One approach is to begin by doing systematic observation of the world, and then develop a logical explanation (theory) to account for what they see—an approach referred to as **induction**. In anthropology, for example, researchers typically observe people in a community for some time before developing an explanatory theory. Qualitative research, described in Chapter 3, is often inductive. Induction also happens in quantitative research when many possible relationships between variables are explored before an explanatory theory emerges from the observed patterns.

The other approach is **deduction:** The researcher moves straight to the development of a logical explanation or theory and only later gathers evidence to test the theory. For example, rational choice theorists in economics and other fields approach many problems with the fundamental assumption that people or institutions will seek to maximize their gains and minimize their losses. Starting from this assumption, they then generate hypotheses and predictions about not only economic decisions but also such things as racial discrimination, marriage, and voting (Becker & Becker, 1998). In social research, some researchers called **structuralists** insist that social research must always start with theories and test these with empirical predictions.

Most researchers, however, practice a combination of induction and deduction. They have a theory, gather data to test it, but then also examine the data in other ways to develop new theories.

Proof Requires Fresh Data

While most researchers practice a combination of induction and deduction, even in a single study, the structuralists have a point that applies broadly in research: *Data cannot be used to both develop a theory and definitively confirm it.*[2] Fresh data are required to truly test a theory or support a hypothesis. Think of your favorite detective novel. Detective X uses induction to come up with a theory of the crime that fits all the existing

---

[2]We cover this issue in more detail in Chapter 9. It is related to issues of statistical power in hypothesis testing.

Figure 1.1 Induction and Deduction

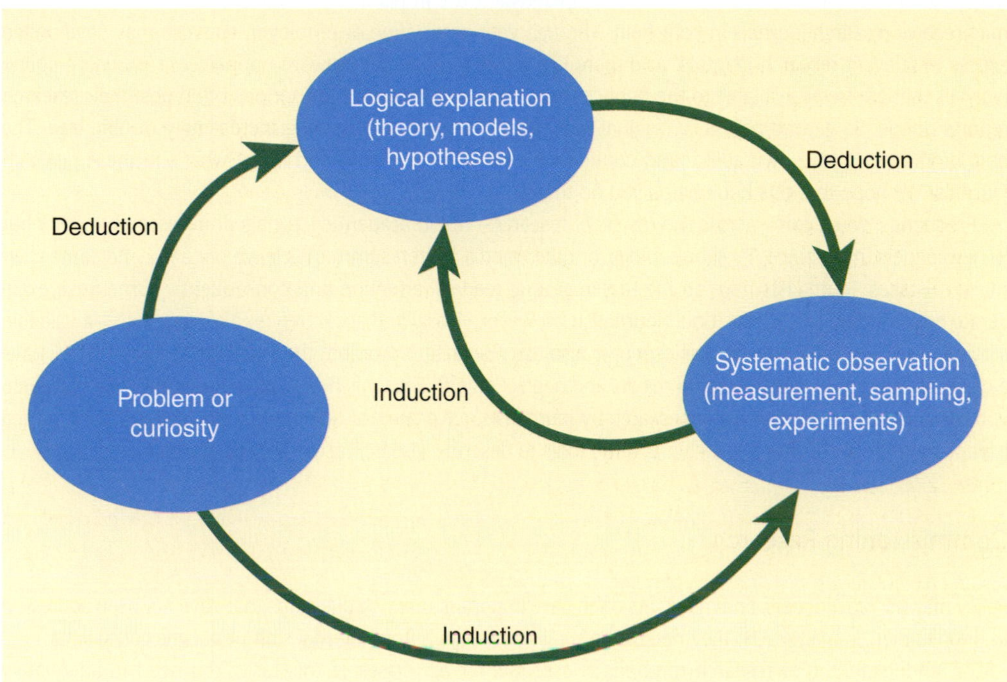

clues. The theory suggests some previously unknown and unsuspected fact—mud on the perpetrator's evening dress, for example. If the prediction matches the fact, the perpetrator's guilt appears much more likely. Prediction provides powerful proof.

In social and policy research, some studies strive to generate theory, while others aim to test theories. Research is often an iterative process in which deduction and induction alternate (as Figure 1.1 illustrates).

Approaching Research From Different Angles

You may encounter research from various angles: as a consumer of research findings in news articles, government reports, or journal articles; as someone who commissions research to satisfy a pressing information need; or as someone who conducts research on your own or as part of a team. This book addresses all of these perspectives.

Consuming Research

Research appears in many forms—in journal articles, government papers, foundation or advocacy reports, internal memos, articles posted on the Internet, blogs, and various summaries in print and electronic news media. An important goal of this book is to help you become a better consumer of research evidence—to take what's valuable and useful from available research and apply it to the task of solving important problems and improving people's lives. We hope that this book sparks your curiosity about what's out there ("I wonder if someone has done a study about . . . ") and that it gives you the skills and confidence to go directly to the source. There is much to learn from reading an original study (even though such research is not always written in a very user-friendly style, something researchers need to work harder at, in our view).

QUESTION

Describe in your own words some of the key characteristics of the scientific method.

Many of you are members of or will join professional associations—in public administration, education, management, public health, social work, criminal justice, urban planning, or other fields. As members, you may receive research journals in your field. Through your association or employer, you also may have online access to relevant research journals. And there is a growing movement toward open-access journals—online journals that are freely available to the public. Governments and other organizations often post their research reports online. So getting access to original studies in your field is becoming increasingly trouble free. The only hindrance is your own ability and confidence to read, understand, and apply what's in these research journals. We hope that this book helps you do that.

Frequently, you'll come across the results of research—not in academic journals or in research reports but in newspapers, magazines, TV shows, blogs, or other media. Often summaries leave out a lot, and some even make mistakes. Journalists have an interest in getting readers' attention and consequently sometimes exaggerate or sensationalize results. Good journalists, however, clearly and accurately explain research—a valuable service to society. Advocates and salespeople also use research to promote their cause or product. They have a clear incentive to exaggerate some results and neglect others. The tools that you'll learn in this book will help you critically examine accounts of research by journalists, advocates, or advertisers. And if you aspire to be a part of the media, this book will give you the tools to describe research accurately to your audience.

Commissioning Research

Policy makers, practitioners, and managers often have important research questions that have not been addressed in prior studies or analyses. So they need to commission research from internal staff or outside consultants.

An understanding of research methods is essential for all phases of this task. You need to adequately frame the initial research question and discuss it with the research team. You need to approve the team's proposal or work plan, for example how it will sample, measure, and draw analytical conclusions to help answer your question. As the client, you will be called on to make decisions or sign off on changes as the research unfolds (nothing ever goes perfectly as planned). You will be the main reviewer of briefings and draft reports. And most likely you will participate in the presentation of the final research results in meetings with organizational leaders, in testimony before legislative bodies, or in press conferences with the media.

Who is selected to do the research will, of course, have a critical influence on its quality—so hire or choose your research team wisely. But you, as the client who commissioned and managed the research in the first place, are just as important a part of the process. This book will help you become a better purchaser and manager of research.

Conducting Research

When we think of a researcher, we tend to envision a professor in a university or a white-coated scientist in a laboratory. If this is your calling, then of course you must know research methods especially well. Indeed, a solid grasp of research methods can help a new scholar or scientist become more productive, succeed at publishing, and participate more fully in his or her field of study.

But not everyone who conducts research these days fits this traditional mold. On the contrary, increasingly, applied research of various kinds is being conducted in large and small government agencies, nonprofit organizations, businesses, foundations, advocacy groups, the news media, and a growing industry of consulting firms that support the research needs of public, nonprofit, and business organizations. Some of these applied researchers have PhDs or other doctoral degrees, but many do not. Indeed, there are quite a few master's and even undergraduate programs that provide research and analysis skills sufficient to begin a career as an applied researcher or policy analyst.

Moreover, there are many situations in which practitioners engage in informal research. Examples include doing your own survey of employees or clients; making comparisons using performance measures;

examining the effectiveness of a new program or management initiative using administrative data; and doing qualitative interviews or focus groups for purposes of internal strategy, marketing, or decision making. These activities are research, too, even though the people doing them do not aim to publish in peer-reviewed journals or release results in official research reports. Knowledge of research methods can dramatically improve one's ability to do informal research well.

Ethics of Research

Social and policy research raises important ethical issues because it deals with human beings—their health, living conditions, rights, and well-being. These ethical concerns shape and constrain the designs of research studies, providing a context for the research methods you will learn about in this book.

Poisoned by New York's Best Restaurants

In an effort to study how firms deal with customer complaints, a professor of business at Columbia University sent the same complaint letter to 240 fine restaurants in New York City (Kifner, 2001; Sieber & Tolich, 2013, p. 149). In the letter, he stated that he had just dined at the restaurant with his wife, a special anniversary dinner, only to spend the night suffering from the symptoms of food poisoning. "Our special romantic evening became reduced to my wife watching me curl up in the fetal position on the tiled floor of our bathroom between rounds of throwing up," the letter complained (Kifner, 2001), also noting that he had no desire to contact regulatory agencies but only wrote "in anticipation that you will respond accordingly" (Sieber & Tolich, 2013, p. 149). The restaurateurs who received the letter were dismayed and distraught, believing they were responsible for a grave error that could ruin their reputations and even put them out of business. Some restaurant employees were fired. When it turned out that the letters were faked, as part of a study, the restaurateurs were outraged at the researcher and the university and later even tried suing for damages (Fried, 2004).

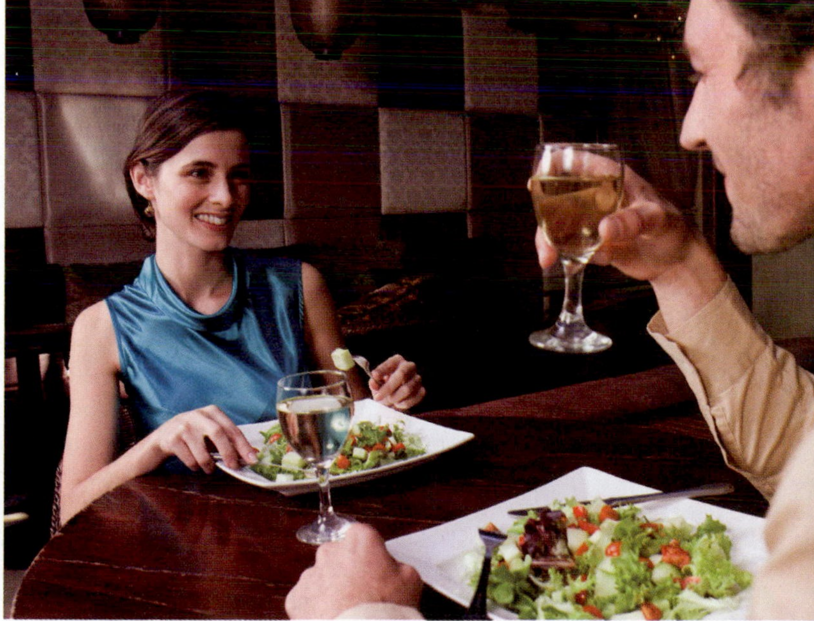

Restaurateurs did not consent to be research subjects.

Source: © 2009 Jupiterimages Corporation.

Was the food poisoning research unethical? If so, why? Did it matter that the restaurateurs never willingly agreed to participate, that they were deceived, or that they suffered emotional distress? Does the value of the research—or lack of value, according to some—make this study more or less ethical? Does it matter whether or not an alternative, less risky approach to the same research question was possible?

From a legal perspective, the courts found no financial damage to the restaurants, although they did find potential for emotional distress. Most of the court cases were dismissed (Fried, 2004), and the remaining ones were presumably settled. Still, the university had to apologize profusely and the professor was sanctioned for failing to follow the university's procedures for human subjects research. The university reacted by providing all business professors with the same training and information about ethical human subjects research routinely required of biomedical researchers and many social scientists.

This example clearly illustrates that researchers these days cannot just go out and do any study that they want to, that there are ethical rules and limitations on their research. But what are these principles and procedures of ethical human subjects research, and what are their origins?

History of Human Subjects Abuses in Research

The history of research involving human beings includes many instances of unethical practices, sometimes extremely troubling practices. Early medical experiments were performed on prisoners, racial minorities, or poorhouse residents, often without their consent or even knowledge. During the Nuremberg trials, it was revealed that the Nazis had a program of profoundly inhumane medical experiments on Jews imprisoned in concentration camps during World War II.

In the United States, the U.S. Public Health Service ran the notorious Tuskegee syphilis study from the 1930s through as late as the early 1970s. In the study, researchers recruited African American subjects (mostly poor sharecroppers) with late-stage syphilis into the study and then followed them for many years to observe the course and consequences of the disease. The participants were never treated for the disease, suffered painful and debilitating symptoms, and eventually died from the disease (Jones, 1993).

The most clearly egregious abuses of human research subjects occurred in biomedical research, and as a result many early regulations stemmed from these cases (Israel & Hay, 2006, p. 40). However, ethical concerns have been raised by research in the social sciences as well, particularly with regard to social experiments. In Stanley Milgram's (1974) obedience-to-authority studies of the 1960s, subjects were asked by an authority figure to give (phony) electrical shocks to another individual sitting behind two-way glass. Some subjects complied with the request to the point of administering what they believed were fatal shocks to an actor behind the glass—a disturbing experience for someone who simply agreed to participate in a campus psychology experiment.

Milgram's experiment became an emblem of the ethical problems that can arise in social experiments. Sieber and Tolich (2013, pp. 52–57), however, note the important insights from Milgram's experiment and wonder if the strong condemnation of it was due less to the deception, which is not necessarily unacceptable, than to the unpleasant truths it revealed about ordinary Americans. They argue that the experiment could have been made ethically acceptable with modifications, for example allowing disturbed subjects to withdraw at some point, rather than repeatedly saying, as was done, that "the experiment must go on."

Some nonexperimental social science studies were also controversial. In 1966–67, Laud Humphreys (1975) investigated impersonal male-male sexual activity in public toilets by serving as a lookout (a participant observer). He then surreptitiously followed participants to their cars, noted their license plate numbers, looked up their addresses, and then later interviewed them in their homes, pretending they had been randomly chosen. Humphreys discovered that many of the men outwardly lived as married heterosexuals, and he gained valuable insights into their motivations, attitudes, and complex identities. But Humphreys was heavily criticized for ethical lapses, and he even lost his job because of it. Sieber and Tolich (2013, p. 69), however, argue that Humphreys's research, like Milgram's, revealed information that would be hard to learn in other ways and that it was more ethical and respectful of its participants than is often assumed. As in Milgram's work, the fact that the findings of the study were disturbing to many people played a role in the ethical backlash against it.

Whatever the ethical drawbacks of particular pieces of social science research in the past, the potential for abuse was greater then because researchers worked without clear ethical guidelines or procedures to review and approve the ethics of their studies. Where did the principles and procedures that shape current social and policy research come from?

Principles of Ethical Research Emerge

The abuses of biomedical research drove the establishment of the first formal principles for ethical human subjects research. The Nuremberg Code of 1947, stemming from the trial of Nazi doctors and scientists, outlined various principles of ethical conduct in research, among them informed consent, voluntary participation, no harm to subjects, and beneficence.

The 1964 Declaration of Helsinki of the World Medical Association adopted the same key principles, which have now become the foundation of contemporary research ethics in most countries around the world.

The outrage in the United States over the Tuskegee syphilis study, together with an influential publication showing widespread violations of the Nuremberg Code in medical research (Beecher, 1966), led to the Belmont Report[3] of 1979, which provided the framework for current U.S. ethics regulations (known as 45 C.F.R. Part 46). These regulations require the establishment of institutional review boards (IRBs) composed of researchers and laypeople who review and approve the ethics of all federally funded research involving human subjects. Among other requirements, approved research must satisfy principles summarized by three standards:

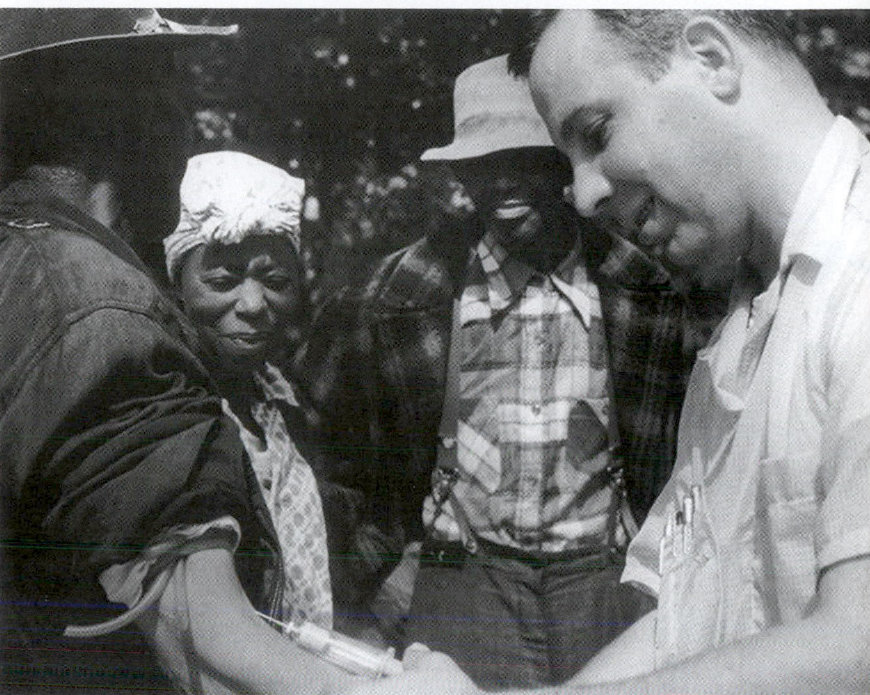

The Tuskegee syphilis study had serious ethical problems.

Source: © The U.S. National Archives and Records Administration.

- **Respect for persons** dictates that people used as the subjects of research provide informed consent and are not coerced into participating in research.
- **Beneficence** dictates that people who participate in research are not harmed and, indeed, that they should realize some benefit from the research.
- **Justice** requires consideration of equity among subjects and fairness in regard to who becomes a research subject.

Several Commonwealth countries, particularly the United Kingdom, Canada, Australia, and New Zealand, as well as many Western European countries, developed ethical principles and procedures similar in many ways to the United States (Israel & Hay, 2006). Certainly all of these countries and others now have ethical review organizations like U.S. IRBs, although not all countries regularly make social research subject to formal ethical oversight. Still, approaches to regulating research ethics do vary across countries, particularly in whether the approaches are top down, as in the United States, or more bottom up, as in the United Kingdom.

What Constitutes Informed Consent?

Although ethical principles and procedures have been established across the globe, deciding the ethical standards in particular research situations is not always clear. Consider the example of informed consent, which lies at the foundation of current research ethics. Being informed means not only understanding what the research entails but being competent to give voluntary consent (Faden & Beauchamp, 1986). So there can be tension between providing full information about the research procedure and doing so in a way that subjects can genuinely understand. Studies have shown that comprehending many informed consent forms requires a high reading level (Israel & Hay, 2006, chap. 3). Language and cultural barriers can also complicate genuine understanding.

[3]The Belmont Report is available from the U.S. Department of Health and Human Services at www.hhs.gov/ohrp/humansubjects/guidance/belmont.html

Consent should be given voluntarily, but what this means is not always clear, particularly when people have limited power or choices in their lives. For example, Fontes (1998; cited in Israel & Hay, 2006, p. 65) describes two conflicting views about the use of incentives in research on Brazilian street children: Offering to pay the children to participate is potentially coercive, but not paying them is potentially exploitative. Or consider a government benefit program that wants to assess clients' experiences in a survey. Even if given assurances, will clients fear that refusal to participate in the survey could jeopardize their benefits? And consider the issue of data gathered for nonresearch reasons, such as ordinary administrative data or the information about people's online behavior. Is informed consent required to use such data for research?

QUESTION

How does the requirement of informed consent embody some of the key principles of ethical research?

Ethical Issues Depend on Research Form and Context

Although all research on human subjects shares certain common ethical issues, principles, and procedures, a great deal also depends on the type of research and the context. Data should be kept confidential, but what confidentiality means, and how one ensures it, would be much different for a statistical study using administrative health data than an in-depth interview study about sexual abuse in childhood. Issues like informed consent, confidentiality, or the acceptable use of deception arise to different extents and in different ways depending on the form and context of the research.

As a result, in the chapters to come, we will return often to the issue of ethics in the context of discussing the various methods of social research. In particular, we will cover ethical issues and approaches for

- qualitative research, including ethical issues related to qualitative interviews, focus groups, participant observation, and existing qualitative data, on pages 87–88 in Chapter 3;
- measurement, in particular the length of questionnaires and the burden on subjects, on page 131 in Chapter 4;
- secondary data, including the confidentiality and consent issues that arise in using administrative data, public use surveys, and matching data, on page 191, pages 203–204 in Chapter 6;
- primary data collection, with a particular focus on the ethics of survey research, on pages 231–232 in Chapter 7;
- laboratory and controlled experiments, and ethical issues in causal measurement in general, on page 370 in Chapter 11;
- randomized experiments, which by design involve denying potentially beneficial treatments to a control group, on pages 455–458 in Chapter 14; and
- quasi and natural experiments, which resemble randomized experiments but have their own unique ethical issues, on pages 492–494 in Chapter 15.

We will also return to research ethics in Chapter 16, where we look at ethical issues that arise in applying research to policy as well as give some more practical guidelines about how to navigate the IRB review process for your own research.

Conclusion: The Road Ahead

The ideas and concepts of research methods come from many different disciplines—sociology, economics, the health sciences, and education, to name a few. As a result, it is less a neatly ordered landscape than a somewhat tangled and overgrown woods. So as you travel the road ahead, we will try to clear away the brush along the way—yet still preserve the variety of ideas and concepts that you will find in the many disciplinary journals and reports of research. It might comfort you to know that even experienced researchers, talking across disciplinary boundaries, often do not understand one another because of the many dialects of research methods. This communication gap is unfortunate, of course, but it is part of the real world of research. Thus, an important skill to have, both as a researcher and as a consumer of research, is to be able to see through the tangle of terms and to get a good view of what issue or idea is really at stake.

We begin our journey in the next chapter with an introduction to *theory, models, and research questions*—the conceptual tools researchers use to think about the world and to begin to figure out how to study it.

Chapter Resources

Key Terms

- Applied research
- Basic research
- Beneficence (in research ethics)
- Causal research
- Contingent
- Data
- Deduction
- Descriptive research
- Epistemology
- Evaluation research
- Generalizability
- Induction
- Justice (in research ethics)
- Peer review
- Performance measurement
- Positivism
- Primary data
- Primary research
- Relationships
- Research methods
- Respect for persons (in research ethics)
- Scientific method
- Scientific realism
- Secondary data
- Secondary research
- Spurious correlation
- Structuralists

Exercises

Battleship Research

1.1. You saw in this chapter how research is used in battles over controversial public policies, such as sex education or global warming. Can you think of other important policy debates in which opponents use research to support their arguments? How do research methods play a role in these debates?

Research in the Corner Office

1.2. We made the case in this chapter that the ability to judge and apply research evidence is an important qualification for top management and leadership positions. Identify this kind of position in an organization or agency in your area of interest. In what ways does the person in this job use or commission research? If possible, interview the person.

Following the Trends

1.3. In your area of interest, think of an example for each of the following:

- A performance measure
- A program evaluation
- An evidence-based policy or practice

Misleading Evidence

1.4. Most studies have their critics. Search for a news article on the Internet using the key words *study* and *criticized* and find one that interests you. Or find any news article that summarizes the findings of a recent study (most journalists will mention at least a few criticisms). Do the criticisms of the study have to do with misleading measurements, misleading samples, or misleading correlations? If so, explain how in your own words.

Descriptive Versus Causal Research

1.5. The distinction between descriptive and causal questions is a fundamental one in research. Think about a social problem or issue that people are talking about these days. What are some descriptive questions that research could help answer? What are some causal questions?

Ways of Knowing

1.6. Go to Wikipedia.org and find an entry on a topic that you know about through personal experience, such as a sport or hobby in which you participate. You may need to restrict yourself to a short part of an entry.

(a) Can you tell where the information provided comes from? (Wikipedia aims to have information in its entries come from authoritative sources and not primary research by the contributor or personal experience.)

(b) How did cited sources learn the information? What are the various ways they could learn information?

(c) Does the information agree with what you know from personal experience?

(d) Is there anything you would like to add from personal experience? How do you know the information you would like to add? Could you find a citation that would satisfy Wikipedia's official (though far from always met) standards?

1.7. Read an entry from the *FiveThirtyEight* blog (found at www.fivethirtyeight.com with older entries at http://fivethirtyeight.blogs.nytimes.com), such as Nate Silver's "Do Presidential Polls Break Toward Challengers?" (2012a). Using the criteria that define the scientific method, determine the extent to which the author is employing the scientific method. Find your favorite source of political commentary. To what extent is the analysis there employing the scientific method?

Ethical Research: Informed Consent

1.8. Find a journal article or research report on a social or policy issue that interests you. Does the research use human subjects? If so, what ethical issues are involved? If not, how does the researcher explore social or policy issues without human subjects?

1.9. Think of a research question that you would like to explore by interviewing people. How can you ensure that the project satisfies the criteria of respect for persons, beneficence, and justice? What information should the informed consent document include?

Student Study Site

Visit the Study Site at **www.sagepub.com/remler2e** to

- test your knowledge with the self-quiz
- check your understanding of key terms with the eFlashcards
- explore helpful resources that relate directly to this chapter

Like architects, researchers build models to represent the real world.

Source: © Aping Vision / STS / Getty Images.

Overview: Theories emerge in response to questions about how the world works. In this chapter, you will learn how researchers use a theory to explain an outcome of interest—and how they use a model to express a theory. You will understand the parts of a model—variables, relationships, and causal mechanisms—and gain practice using path diagrams to work out the logic of a theory. And you will appreciate the usefulness of theories and models for explaining social problems and for evaluating programs or interventions. Finally, you will learn how to generate and focus a research question to motivate your own research.

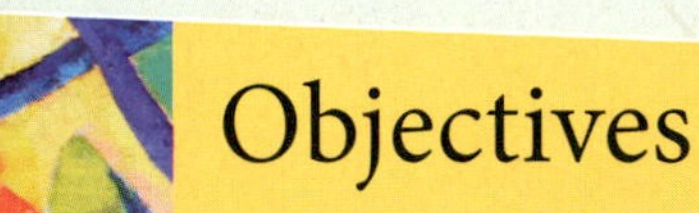

Objectives

Learning Objectives

After reading this chapter, you should be able to

- Recognize the key features of a middle-range theory
- Understand the following basic concepts: variable, variation (cross-sectional and longitudinal), relationship (positive and negative), hypothesis, and unit of analysis
- Identify the independent and dependent variables in a theory—and the causal mechanism that connects them
- Produce a model using a path diagram
- Recognize logic models and how they are used to represent a program or intervention and its mechanism(s)
- Generate and focus a research question

Theory, Models, and Research Questions

Fighting Crime in New York City[1]

"One unrepaired broken window is a signal that no one cares," wrote George L. Kelling and James Q. Wilson in a 1982 *Atlantic* article, "and so breaking more windows costs nothing." Thus, going after small, seemingly petty disorders such as vandalism, graffiti, or public drunkenness may help prevent more serious crime from occurring. "We decided to apply this concept to crime in the subways," recalls William Bratton, then chief of New York City's transit police. "Fare evasion was the biggest broken window in the transit system. We were going to fix that window and see that it didn't get broken again." When Mr. Bratton became commissioner of the city's regular police force in 1993, he began a "quality of life" initiative that took aim at the very "broken windows" Kelling and Wilson wrote about: vandalism, graffiti, panhandling, loitering, and public drinking.

The broken windows theory was used to fight crime in New York's subways.

Source: © Can Stock Photo Inc. / littleny.

Crime in New York City fell dramatically throughout the 1990s and beyond. Many police chiefs and criminologists credited the "broken windows" theory for New York's success and sought to replicate it in other cities. Others, however, doubted the theory and pointed to other factors—the end of the crack epidemic, demographic change, and the growing economy at the time—for the drop in crime in New York City and other urban areas. Knowing why crime fell in New York City—which theories are true—can help us effectively make crime policy decisions in the future.

This chapter begins by defining theory and models and introducing the basic notions of variables, relationships, and causal mechanisms—the building blocks of theory in social and policy research. It then shows how to

[1]This example is based on D. W. Miller (2001).

work with these ideas in the form of path diagrams, which will also become important later in the book for applying methods demonstrating causation. And the chapter will illustrate how theory, in the form of a logic model, can become a useful tool for planning, managing, and evaluating programs. The chapter concludes with some advice about coming up with your own questions and ideas for research.

What Is a Theory?

The term **theory** can mean different things to different people in the social sciences, but most of the time it refers to a logical idea or conjecture about how a particular corner of the world works. This is what Robert K. Merton (1967) called **middle-range theory**. King, Keohane, and Verba (1994) provide a general definition: "A social science theory is a reasoned and precise speculation about the answer to a research question, including a statement about why the proposed answer is correct" (p. 19). Thus questions—both research and (we would add) practical or policy questions—prompt us to seek plausible answers, to propose theories.

Theories can describe a large-scale occurrence, such as the start of a war between nations, or a relatively small-scale event, such as the ability of a child to sound out a word. A theory is practical because it provides insight on how to change the world. If we know what causes war, perhaps we can find a way to prevent it. If we know what makes a child recognize parts of a word, perhaps we can help children read better. Of course, a theory is not necessarily correct—it must stand up to questioning and empirical testing.

Theories Identify Key Variables

Theories serve a number of important purposes in research. The broken windows theory, for example, directs our attention to a key concept or variable, disorder, as a possible factor in the occurrence of crime (another variable). This illustrates one of the essential functions of a theory: It tells us what variables matter in the explanation of a given outcome or behavior. Perhaps we hadn't considered disorder (such as vandalism and graffiti) as a distinct concept before—or as an especially important factor in more serious crimes. In this way, a theory helps us identify and take notice of key variables that we should measure or observe.

Theories Tell Causal Stories

Inherent in a scientific theory is the notion of *causation*. A theory proposes a causal process or mechanism that produces an outcome of interest. According to the broken windows theory, disorder in a neighborhood, such as vandalism and rowdy behavior, *causes* crime because it signals that no one cares, that rules can be broken with impunity. This encourages criminals to act freely. In a sense, a theory provides a causal story of *how* things happen. Of course, proving causation—proving that the story is true—can be difficult. That is what the chapters of Part IV in this book are all about.

A Cause, One of Many

The broken windows theory says that disorder causes crime, but what we really mean is that it is *a* cause—*one of many* causes. The alternative theories suggested earlier—jobs, crack cocaine, and demographic change—are also possible causes, as are the weather, popular culture, and a host of other factors. Most policy and social outcomes have many causes. But the fact that an outcome has many different causes in no way undermines a theory that focuses on just one particular cause. Social phenomena are complex, and we cannot study everything all at the same time.

The many causes and other contingencies involved, however, mean that theories in social and policy research are *probabilistic*—they predict how things are *likely* to turn out, on average. But they do not guarantee a predicted outcome every time. This is because the other causes will be at work, too, in a given setting, often in conflicting and complex ways. So even if our theory remains true, reducing disorder will not necessarily reduce crime the same way in every location—or maybe it will not be effective at all, in some places. It may lead to a reduction in crime in most precincts, but not all; the strategy may work in New York and Los Angeles, but not Chicago.

Theories Explain Variation

Theories also aim to explain *variation*—the changes or fluctuations in an event or behavior, such as crime. Figure 2.1 shows the variation in the murder rate in New York City from 1980 to 2010, and you can see that it goes up and down. This kind of variation over time is referred to as **longitudinal variation**.

A theory could also explain variation *across* individuals, organizations, or places at the same point in time. For example, we could look at large U.S. cities and see that some are higher and others lower in crime in the same year (say 2010), as in Figure 2.2. This is referred to as **cross-sectional variation**.

Explaining the causes of variation—why crime rises and falls over time, or why some cities have more crime at the same time as others have less—is what theory in social and policy research is mostly about. And if we have a good theory to explain the causes of such variation, perhaps we can find ways to influence it and thus, for example, help lower crime.

Figure 2.1 Longitudinal Variation: New York City Murder Rate, 1980 to 2010

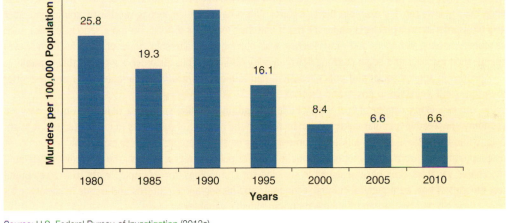

Murders per 100,000 Population
25.8
19.3
30.7
16.1
8.4
6.6
6.6
1980
1985
1990
1995
2000
2005
2010
Years

Source: U.S. Federal Bureau of Investigation (2013a).

Figure 2.2 Cross-Sectional Variation: Murder Rates in Large U.S. Cities in 2010

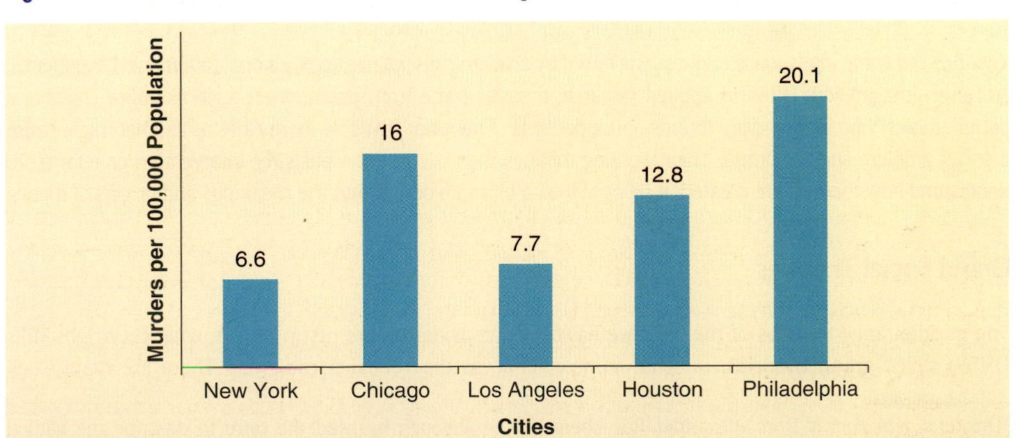

Source: U.S. Federal Bureau of Investigation (2013b).

QUESTION

Life expectancy is a basic indicator of the health and well-being of a country's population. What does it mean to talk about *cross-sectional variation* between countries in life expectancy? What does it mean to talk about *longitudinal variation* in life expectancy for a country or region?

Theories Generate Testable Hypotheses

Good theories should have *observable implications* (King et al., 1994). In other words, they should generate **hypotheses**—predictions of what will happen if our theory is correct. The hypotheses can be compared with the facts, making the theory potentially *falsifiable* (a critical feature of a scientific theory, according to Popper, 1959). A vague statement, a claim that is impossible to verify, or a truism does not qualify as a scientific theory.

In our example of the broken windows theory, we should expect to see *more* crime in neighborhoods with vandalism and graffiti and *less* crime in neighborhoods that do not have these symptoms of disorder. Or better: We would predict that if we took specific steps to reduce vandalism and graffiti in a neighborhood, the rate of more serious crimes would go down. A hypothesis is thus a prediction of what will happen—an observable implication of a theory—that we could compare with facts and data.

So a theory—even if it makes logical sense—is not necessarily true. A theory proposes one possible way that things work. Empirical observations must be made to test this theory against reality—and alternative theories must be tested as well. Only after our theory survives the gauntlet of empirical testing and competition from other theories do we begin to develop confidence that it might truly describe and explain reality.

Theories Focus on Modifiable Variables

As we've noted, there are many causes of a complex outcome such as crime. Many of these we cannot influence, but some we can. For example, perhaps patrol officers have been neglecting vandalism, graffiti, and other acts of disorder in their precincts under the belief that their real job is to focus on more serious felonies, such as robbery, assault, auto theft, and gang violence. With training and leadership, however, the officers could well change their behavior and begin cracking down on petty disorders. Thus, disorder is a **modifiable variable**.

QUESTION

A theory serves a number of purposes in social and policy research. What are some of these purposes of a theory?

Theories in applied social and policy research tend to focus on *modifiable* variables because these offer the most useful guidance to policy and practice.

In contrast, other causes of crime may be largely **nonmodifiable**, such as a downturn in the national economy, the weather, popular culture, or an increase in the number of teenagers in the population. It might help to know how these factors influence crime and thus be able to predict when to expect the next jump (or drop) in crime. But from the standpoint of public policy or police practice, at least, these remain largely nonmodifiable variables. Still, basic research in sociology or criminology, for example, might well develop and test theories of how such general cultural, economic, and demographic patterns and trends in society influence crime. So theories can and do focus on nonmodifiable variables as well.

Where Do Theories Come From?

Theories can come in response to questions raised by academic disciplines, exploratory studies, lived experience, and even imagination. Often in applied research, theories come from practitioners such as police chiefs and patrol officers, who in their daily rounds notice patterns of behavior that give them clues as to what might cause a social problem such as crime. Their working theories then become the basis for intervention or reform. To understand how theories are created, it helps to look a bit more deeply into the meanings and origins of theory.

Grand Social Theories

The middle-range theories of the kind we have been considering are distinct from what C. Wright Mills (1959) called **grand theories**, or what some refer to as theoretical paradigms.[2] There are many such

[2]The term *paradigm* is from Alexander Rosenberg (2012), although he used the term to describe the natural sciences.

grand theories or paradigms in the social sciences, including structural functionalism, symbolic interactionism, rational choice theory, sociobiology, Marxist historical materialism, Freudian psychoanalysis, critical theory, feminism, and postmodernism (A. Rosenberg, 2012; Seidman, 2012). As we noted earlier, the term *theory* can mean different things to different people in the various disciplines and branches of the social sciences.

These grand social theories or paradigms can shape a researcher's view of what variables and mechanisms are needed to explain human behavior, and in this way become a source of the kind of middle-range theories that interest us here. To give one example, a rational choice theorist might seek to explain crime in terms of the opportunistic pursuit of self-interest in situations where the rewards of committing the crime (money, pleasure) outweigh the costs (possibility of arrest and punishment). But some grand theories, like critical theory and postmodernism, are more antipositivist, questioning notions such as causation and empirical testing when applied to human behavior. Thus their versions of middle-range theories (to the extent this term can still be applied) look much different than the configurations of variables, relationships, and causal mechanisms we focus on here (Godfrey-Smith, 2003; A. Rosenberg, 2012). The type of theory presented in this chapter (and in this book), therefore, applies to many—but not necessarily all—research traditions in the social sciences.

Academic Disciplines

Academic disciplines also shape the kind of theories formulated by researchers. For example, economic theories often center on individuals making rational choices to optimize their well-being (*Homo economicus*); sociological theories often focus on how institutions or social structures in society condition the actions of individuals; and psychological theories often focus on conscious and unconscious processes of thought and emotion that influence our behavior. Indeed, most disciplines have foundational principles or perspectives that establish frameworks for their theories. So if you go further into the theory of any particular discipline, you will need to learn much more about how that discipline develops and evaluates its theory. Such disciplinary theories provide additional insights, although they can sometimes blind researchers to alternative forms of explanation and understanding. Indeed, many important advances in theory these days have come from people who cross disciplinary boundaries.

Induction and Deduction

As we saw in Chapter 1, theories can come from a process of induction—building up theory from scattered pieces of empirical evidence and experience. Theories can also come from a process of deduction—starting from initial ideas or logical principles and then testing these with empirical observations. In practice, theories often come from a mix of both thought processes.

When testing a theory, however, the distinction between induction and deduction is especially important: *You cannot test a theory using the same data or set of facts that inductively produced the theory.*

Testing a theory with the same facts that generated the theory amounts to a sure thing—a test whose answer you know already in advance. It does not permit you to be wrong (it is not *falsifiable*). So you need a new set of data or facts, another study, to test an inductive theory. Because a deductive theory starts first with ideas or logical principles, before collecting data, you do not have the same problem. But, of course, you still need to go out and gather a set of data or facts to test your deductive theory.

QUESTION

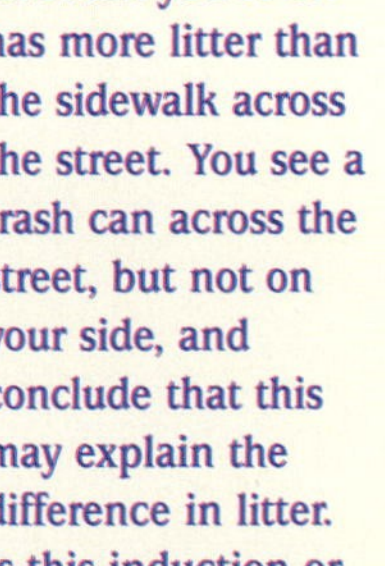

You notice the sidewalk you're on has more litter than the sidewalk across the street. You see a trash can across the street, but not on your side, and conclude that this may explain the difference in litter. Is this induction or deduction? What would you need to do to test your theory?

Exploratory and Qualitative Research

Theory emerges also from attempts to tie together the strands of empirical evidence in a particular field of research, such as criminology. Prior studies may contribute individual pieces of empirical evidence concerning the factors associated with crime, but much is gained when a theory emerges that fits the pieces together into a coherent whole.

Qualitative research, such as participant observation or in-depth interviews (discussed in Chapter 3), is another very important source of theory. Qualitative research provides insight into the processes and influences at work in a particular social setting, such as a high-crime neighborhood. Insights may suggest variables, such as social control, that help prevent crime and that can become the targets of policy intervention.

Theories, Norms, and Values

Scientific theories are **positive**—describing how things are; they are not **normative**—describing how they should be. The broken windows theory does not convey the wishes or dreams of its promoters for how people *ought* to behave, in some ideal sense, or how society should function. Rather, the debates about the correct theory of crime focus on what variables and processes actually *do* produce crime in the real world, in all its often-unflattering glory.

But be aware that, in another sense, scientific theories are not value free. Different theories focus on different causes that imply quite different policy alternatives—get tough with petty criminals, instead of creating economic opportunity in poor neighborhoods, for example. Therefore, the motivations driving the promoters of a theory, like the motivations for much that is human, do involve beliefs and values. But a scientific theory must stand up to the test of empirical observation and competition from other theories.

Theories can be based on underlying assumptions that are not always obvious. The underlying assumptions can be associated with a discipline or school of thought, such as economists basing their theories on the belief that individuals behave rationally. Or the underlying assumptions can stem from a researcher's culture or political beliefs. Whatever their origins, implicit assumptions often shape theories. When you interpret a theory or create your own theory, try to become aware of these underlying assumptions and make them explicit.

What Is a Model?

A **model** serves to articulate and communicate a theory. It is a representation that is specific and clear, in the same way that a miniature model of a building represents clearly and precisely what an architect plans to build. Models may at first seem like unnecessary abstractions, but in fact they help a great deal to make sense of complex phenomena, and they force us to think clearly.

A model is typically either graphical (a picture) or mathematical (an equation). In this book, we will mostly use graphical models to express theory, specifically, **path diagrams** (also called **path models**). Figure 2.3 is a path diagram that expresses the broken windows theory of crime. It expresses the idea, presented earlier, that seemingly trivial acts of *disorder* trigger more serious *crime*. (We will make use of path diagrams often in this book.)

Variables and Relationships

A model, such as the path diagram in Figure 2.3 of the broken windows theory, is made up of two components: variables (the ovals) and relationships (the arrows). The plus sign (+) indicates the direction of the relationship, which we have more to say about shortly.

A **variable** is something that can take on different values or assume different attributes—it is something that *varies*. Figures 2.1 and 2.2 demonstrate that the murder rate takes on different values over time and across cities—so it is a variable. Our theory aims to explain this variation, the highs and the lows, by way of another variable—disorder. Variables must be able to move—to *vary*—in both directions: up and down.

The **relationship** between crime and disorder is represented by the arrow pointing from disorder to crime, showing that changes in disorder cause changes in crime. In a theory, as discussed earlier, we are interested in

Figure 2.3 Path Diagram of the Broken Windows Theory

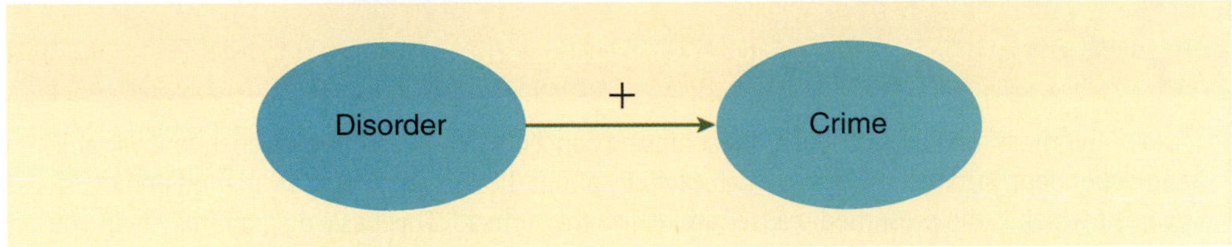

causal relationships (hence the arrow showing the *direction* from cause to effect). A **causal relationship** refers to how change in one variable produces or leads to change in another variable. Cracking down on vandalism and graffiti, for example, produces a reduction in more serious crimes (according to the theory).

Independent and Dependent Variables

In the model shown in Figure 2.3, *disorder* is the **independent variable**, and *crime* is the **dependent variable**. The independent variable is the *cause*, the dependent variable the *effect*. By convention, the independent variable is symbolized by *X*, while the dependent variable is symbolized by *Y*. Just as cause comes before effect, and *X* comes before *Y* in the alphabet, the independent variable comes before the dependent variable in the causal order of things. Here is a very helpful little diagram for thinking clearly about independent and dependent variables:

Various terms are used by different researchers to describe independent and dependent variables, as Box 2.1 explains (see also Box 2.2). For example, in program evaluation and health research, the independent variable is often a *treatment* and the dependent variable an *outcome*.

To practice these ideas, see if you can identify the independent and dependent variables implied in each of the following statements:

- In an effort to reduce traffic accidents, the city government lowered the posted speed limit on all of its streets and thoroughfares.
- Researchers have found a link between climate change and civil unrest (including war), particularly in developing countries.
- Allowing employees a flexible schedule increases productivity, according to management experts.
- A news article reports that students who use Facebook get lower grades in college.

So which is which? In the first statement, the speed limit is the independent variable, and traffic accidents are the dependent variable. Lowering the speed limit is a policy change or intervention (a manipulable variable), and often this can serve as a clue to the independent variable. In the second statement, climate change is the independent variable and civil unrest the dependent variable. Here there is no clear intervention or manipulable variable (although perhaps climate change can be mitigated by public policy—or so we hope). But it is clear that the cause-effect arrow can point in only one direction: Wars, riots, and other civil disturbances cannot influence the climate. So it must be that climate change is the possible cause (independent variable) and civil unrest the effect (dependent variable). The third statement has no reference to research but makes clear that flexible schedules are the cause (independent variable) and productivity the effect

BOX 2.1
Independent and Dependent Variables

Two of the most fundamental yet often confusing concepts in research are independent variable and dependent variable. It helps to think carefully about the sequence of the variables and to ask yourself which is the presumed "cause" and which the "effect." This basic diagram may help you sort things out:

Symbols:	***X***	→	***Y***
Meaning:	"Cause"		"Effect"
Name:	**Independent**		**Dependent**
Other names:	Explanatory		Response
	Treatment		Outcome
	Program		Outcome
	Predictor		Predicted
	Regressor		Regressand
	Explanans		Explanandum

As shown, researchers refer to independent and dependent variables by many different names, which is another source of confusion. And in some situations, it is not entirely clear which variable is "cause" and which is "effect," as Chapter 11, on causation, will explain.

(dependent variable). In the fourth statement, the news article implies that Facebook is the independent variable and grades the dependent variable, but here the causal order is more ambiguous (perhaps students turn to Facebook for consolation after getting low grades). Stating or implying that X is the independent variable and Y the dependent variable does not necessarily make X the cause and Y the effect in the real world, a topic we will cover in depth in Chapter 11.

Causal Mechanisms

QUESTION

Can you turn the saying "practice makes perfect" into a relationship between variables, using the example of a schoolteacher?

Because theories express causal relationships, change in the independent variable is presumed to *cause* change in the dependent variable. Thus, there must be some notion of how this happens—the **causal mechanism**—underlying the causal relationship. Disorder in a neighborhood signals that no one cares, that rules are not enforced; criminals read these signals and become emboldened to commit crime. This is the causal mechanism in the broken windows theory.

Although it is a critical component of the broken windows theory, notice that this causal mechanism does not appear in Figure 2.3 as such. To provide a full description of the theory, therefore, we need to accompany the path diagram with a statement of the process or mechanism that explains *how* change in the independent variable causes change in the dependent variable.

We will see shortly that we can, in fact, make this causal mechanism more explicit by adding **intervening variables** to the model. Intervening variables represent steps in the causal process leading from the independent to the dependent variable. If these intervening variables can be measured and incorporated in a test of the model, much is gained: We can see not only whether X and Y are related, as predicted by our theory, but whether they are related through the intervening variables that represent the theory's causal mechanism.

BOX 2.2

Equations as Models: Right-Hand Side and Left-Hand Side Variables

In this book, we mostly use path diagrams for our models. However, models in the form of equations are also used. By convention, as noted previously, Y often symbolizes the dependent variable, and X often symbolizes the independent variable. An equation modeling the relationship can have many forms but will often look something like this:

$$Y = a + bX,$$

where a and b can be specific numbers, such as 5.4 or − 9. Notice that the convention with respect to placement of the independent and dependent variables on the page is reversed from the path diagram: The dependent variable (Y) is on the left, while the independent variable (X) is on the right. Indeed, those who use equations as models frequently refer to independent variables as *right-hand side* variables and dependent variables as *left-hand side* variables.

Direction of a Relationship

As mentioned, the plus or minus sign along the arrow in a model indicates the direction of the relationship. In Figure 2.3, there is a **positive (+) relationship** meaning that disorder (independent variable) and crime (dependent variable) move in the *same* direction. If disorder goes up, crime goes up, and if disorder goes down, crime goes down. Therefore, in general, *high* values of the independent variable (disorder) are presumed to result in *high* values of the dependent variable (crime), and correspondingly, *low* values of the independent variable result in *low* values of the dependent variable. In other words, we would expect cities with low levels of disorder to have low levels of crime and those with high levels of disorder to have high levels of crime. Figure 2.4 illustrates this pattern.

In a **negative (−) relationship**, in contrast, the independent and dependent variables move in *opposite* directions. So *high* values of the independent variable tend to occur with *low* values of the dependent variable. For example, we might expect that the level of income in a city and the rate of crime are negatively related: more income in a community, less crime committed; less income, more crime. In an X–Y graph, a negative relationship is downward sloping (see Figure 2.4).

Specifying the *direction* of a relationship between the independent and dependent variables is an important part of making a theory precise. Just saying that disorder and crime "are related" in some way is not much of a theory. We need to explain in what way they are related. Specifying the direction of the relationship allows for observable implications—hypotheses that can be tested with data.

Relationship Directions for Categorical Variables

It may be hard to describe the direction of a relationship for some variables—in particular categorical variables that do not have any numerical value, order, or direction (also called nominal variables). For example, suppose a city is divided into four districts—Northside, Southside, Westside, and Eastside—and we have a

Figure 2.4 Positive and Negative Relationships

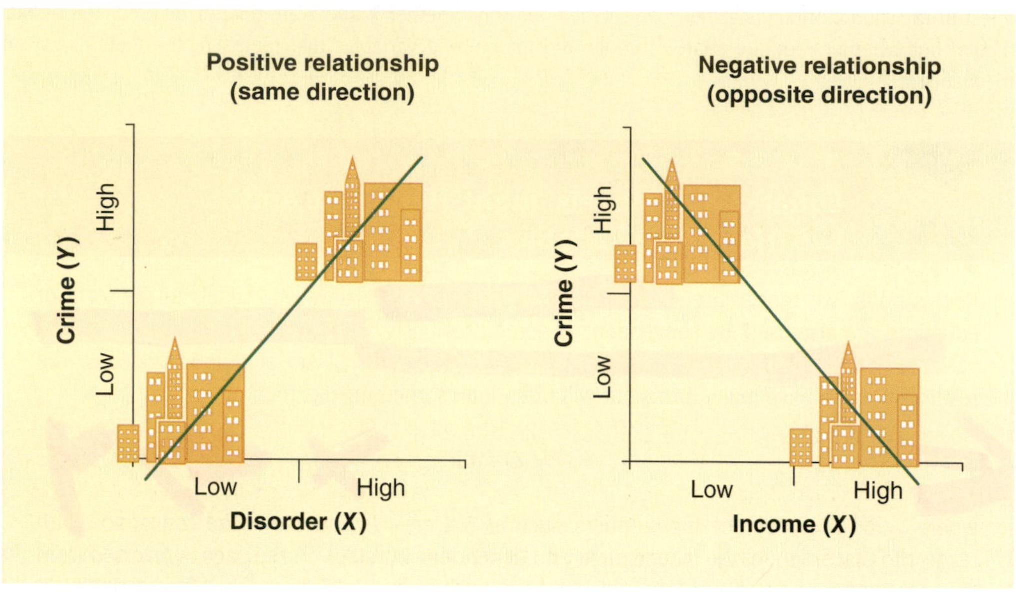

theory that something unique to each of the districts influences its crime rate. Clearly, we cannot really specify the direction of the relationship between *district* and *crime* as being either positive or negative.

However, a variable that has just two categories—such as having a neighborhood watch group and not having a neighborhood watch group—does have an order to it: *Up* is having a watch group; *down* is not having one. We might hypothesize that the relationship in this case would be negative (assuming a watch group helps deter crime). Such variables are called *dummy* (or indicator) variables. Chapter 4 covers the topic of levels of measurement, including categorical, quantitative, and dummy variables. It is sufficient at this point just to be aware that it can be a bit tricky sometimes to show categorical variables in a path diagram—but possible if they are made into yes/no variables.

QUESTION

What is the direction of the relationship between poverty and life expectancy? What is a possible causal mechanism?

Naming Variables

Variables must be able to take on different values, so it's best not to think about or name variables in a model in a one-sided or directional manner. Moreover, giving variables a directional name creates confusion when interpreting the model.

For example, say we have a theory that *more* income in a neighborhood causes *less* crime. Good enough—and it works alright to put things this way in a sentence. But often, we are tempted to translate these words directly to a path diagram, like this:

More income → Less crime

At first glance, this might make sense, but we still need to specify the direction of the relationship—an important aspect of the theory, as we've just seen. Is it positive—higher levels of *more income* leading to higher levels of *less crime*? Or is it negative—higher levels of *more income* leading to lower levels of *less crime?* As you can tell, these questions are not at all clear grammatically or logically. Let's try using nondirectional variable names instead, like this:

Income → Crime

This makes the task of specifying the direction of the relationship clearer—even though you may think at first glance that it looks wrong (how does having income cause crime?). But according to our theory, *more* income leads to *less* crime—a negative relationship. So the direction of the relationship should be expressed in the arrow—not in the variable labels. We just need to add a minus sign (–) to the arrow connecting income to crime to complete the picture.

$$\text{Income} \xrightarrow{-} \text{Crime}$$

To summarize: When drawing a model, the variable names should be nondirectional, and the direction of the relationship should be indicated by a plus or minus sign on the arrow.

Models With Multiple Causes

To keep things simple, we have been focusing thus far on models that involve a single independent variable—a single cause. This is in part because, as we noted earlier, theory often centers on one independent variable at a time, even though real-world outcomes such as crime often have many causes. But you should know that, in most social and policy research, models—especially statistical models used for purposes of data analysis—often include multiple causes, multiple independent variables. This is typically the situation in multiple regression analysis, for example, perhaps the most widely used statistical technique in social and policy research (a technique we will cover in Chapter 10 and also in Chapter 13).

There are two main reasons to include multiple causes in a model. First, other causes of the outcome may be correlated with the independent variable of interest, and thus it is necessary to separate out the unique effect of the key independent variable of interest from these other causes. We will have much more to say about this topic in Chapters 12 and 13, where we discuss control variables. Second, in some situations, the theory itself identifies multiple causes of the outcome. For example, we may have a theory that views crime as a complex result of key economic and demographic forces in society.

Children's shoe size and reading level are related because of their age.

Source: © iStockphoto.com/a-wrangler.

Causal and Noncausal Relationships

We've been thinking a lot about causal relationships, but it is important to point out that not all relationships in the real world are causal. Any kind of correlation or association is, properly speaking, still a *relationship*—but not necessarily a *causal* relationship.

Variables can be correlated with each other for other reasons, such as the presence of a third, common cause that ties them together—a *spurious* correlation. For example, in a group of elementary school kids, there is a correlation between shoe size and reading level, but only because shoe size and reading level are influenced by age. Older kids both have bigger feet and read better.

In other cases, variables can be related just by coincidence. For example, you might find that you have more fun on Saturdays with an odd-number calendar date than Saturdays that have an even-number calendar date. Superstitions often get started by people observing chance correlations.

Although causal and noncausal relationships look the same on the statistical surface—patterns of positive, or negative, correlation between variables, as in Figure 2.4—they are fundamentally different. Later in this book, we discuss how to distinguish a causal relationship from a mere correlation or just a chance coincidence. For now, simply remember that a straight arrow in a path diagram refers to a causal relationship. We will represent a **noncausal relationship** in a path diagram by a curved dotted line with no arrowheads at all, as shown in Figure 2.5. (Some choose to represent noncausal relationships using a curved line with arrowheads.)

Figure 2.5 Noncausal (or Spurious) Relationship, Shown With a Dotted Line

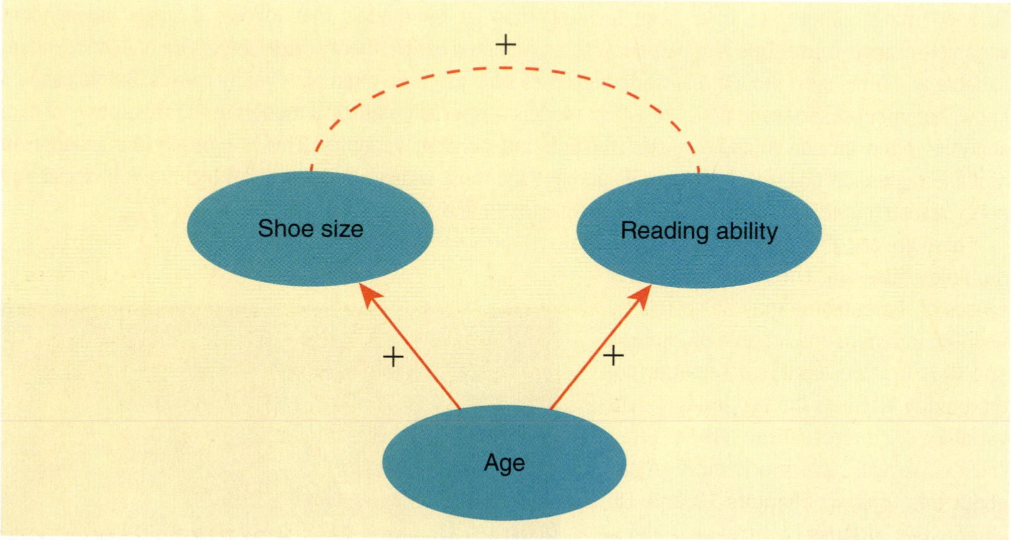

Unit of Analysis

The variables in a model describe something—people, places, or things. *Income*, for example, is a variable that could describe the income of a person, the combined income of a household, or the median income of a neighborhood, a city, or even a nation. The objects or things described by the variables in a model are referred to as the **unit of analysis**. The unit of analysis can also be thought of as the level of aggregation, or disaggregation, of the data that will be used to test the model.

Table 2.1 illustrates what data (perhaps in a spreadsheet) would look like when the unit of analysis is *individuals:* Each row of the spreadsheet is a different individual, and the variable *income* describes these individuals. Table 2.2 illustrates what the data would look like when the unit of analysis is *cities:* Each row is a different city, and the variable *median income* describes the cities.

Same Theory, Different Unit of Analysis

In the case of the broken windows theory, we might use neighborhoods or precincts as the unit of analysis. Neighborhoods can have more or less disorder (vandalism and graffiti), as well as more or less crime. But the

Table 2.1 Data With Individual as Unit of Analysis

Individual[3]	Income ($)
Joe	44,800
Bill	59,100
Sue	31,500
Ramon	17,200

Table 2.2 Data With City as Unit of Analysis

City	Median Income ($)
New York	39,300
Chicago	38,800
Los Angeles	39,100
Houston	37,400

unit of analysis could be something larger—a whole city. Cities can have more or less disorder, as well as more or less crime. Or it could be something smaller—a city block. Ultimately, crimes are committed by individuals or small groups of individuals, which are even smaller units of analysis. A theory might really operate at the level of the individual—or at a broader community level. But as a practical matter, the data in our example of the broken windows theory may be available only for geographic units, such as blocks, precincts, or cities. Table 2.3 shows various units of analysis that might be used to test the theory.

Table 2.3 Different Units of Analysis and Corresponding Variables

Unit of Analysis	Independent Variable	Dependent Variable
Cities	Citywide disorder rate	Citywide crime rate
Neighborhoods	Neighborhood disorder rate	Neighborhood crime rate
Blocks	Block-level disorder rate	Block-level crime rate
Individual persons	Perception of disorder	Decision to commit a crime

When explaining variation over time (longitudinal variation), the unit of analysis must include the time period also. For example, disorder could refer to the level of disorder in a city *in a particular year*. In that case, the unit of analysis would be the *city-year*.

The unit of analysis is important to keep in mind when specifying a theory, interpreting variables, and seeking ways to test the theory. The unit of analysis will also become important later when we cover other topics in the book, such as measurement, sampling, sources and methods of gathering data, and statistical analysis.

[3]Real data would generally contain an ID number and no names to protect the anonymity of those studied. See the discussion of the ethics of administrative data in Chapter 6.

The Aggregation Problem and the Ecological Fallacy

It is important to point out that relationships that hold at one unit of analysis may not hold at more aggregated levels, a phenomenon referred to as the *aggregation problem*. In some cases, the direction of the relationship may even be reversed, a phenomenon referred to as the **ecological fallacy**. Such reversals of direction typically occur when there is some other influential variable that is not included in the analysis.

For example, the term *ecological fallacy* was invented in a study examining the relationship between literacy and immigration at both the state and the individual level in 1930 (Robinson, 1950). Looking across states, researchers found a positive correlation between the share of the population who were immigrants and the literacy rate. But looking across individuals, there was a negative correlation between literacy and immigrant status. Thus, although individual immigrants were less likely to be literate, immigrants moved to states with more literate populations.

Although the aggregation problem and the ecological fallacy matter in some situations, quite often relationships that appear at an individual unit of analysis also hold when the data are aggregated. There is a technical literature about the conditions under which aggregation is possible (e.g., Blundell & Stoker, 2005). Thus, aggregated data often can and do provide insights into individual behavior.

Let's turn now to the application of theory and models—in the form of logic models—to the tasks of planning, managing, and evaluating programs.

QUESTION

New studies have directly measured happiness using large surveys from around the world. Can you think of several different units of analysis for studying happiness?

Logic Models

In many areas of policy and practice these days, you will hear about **logic models** that describe how programs or interventions produce desired outcomes. Logic models (which are also referred to as *program theories, outcome-sequence charts*, or *theories of change*) are increasingly required by government agencies and foundations for program management, funding, and evaluation (W. K. Kellogg Foundation, 2004). As the definition in Box 2.3 makes clear, a logic model is much like a path diagram—what we have been discussing all along in this chapter, but applied to a particular program or intervention.

BOX 2.3
What Is a Logic Model?

A logic model's purpose is to communicate the underlying "theory" or set of assumptions or hypotheses that program proponents have about why the program will work, or about why it is a good solution to an identified problem. Logic models are typically diagrams, flow sheets, or some other type of visual schematic that conveys relationships between contextual factors and programmatic inputs, processes, and outcomes.

Logic models can come in all shapes and sizes: boxes with connecting lines that are read from left to right (or top to bottom); circular loops with arrows going in or out; or other visual metaphors and devices. What these schemata have in common is that they attempt to show the links in a chain of reasoning about "what causes what," in relationship to the desired outcome or goal. The desired outcome or goal is usually shown as the last link in the model.

Source: Schmitz & Parsons (1999).

We will now illustrate the idea of a logic model with an extended, real-world example focused on class size and learning.

Do Smaller Classes Help Kids Learn?

Smaller classes may improve learning in many different ways.

Source: © iStockphoto.com/Neustockimages.

The Jackson, Mississippi, Public Schools (JPS) began a class-size reduction program, committing $1.8 million in funds to hire 32 new teachers for 26 schools in Grades 1 through 3. According to JPS (2004), "studies indicate that smaller classes reduce discipline problems and increase the time a teacher spends in instruction." Teacher Kescher Love explained, "That's because with fewer students teachers had more time to give to each student. Smaller classes are an important factor" (JPS, 2004). JPS hoped the program would increase the percentage of students passing its third-grade "exit test" (required for them to move on to fourth grade) as well as improve students' final classroom grades and daily attendance. Initial anecdotal evidence appeared encouraging. According to Smith Elementary Principal Gailya Porter, the additional money reduced the average size of her school's third-grade classes to 22 students—well below the state-mandated ceiling of 27 students. "We saw our retentions [the number failing the exit test] in the third grade drop to only four students," Mrs. Porter said (JPS, 2004).

You might recognize that underlying Jackson's class-size reduction program is a theory—a set of assumptions about how reducing the number of students in Grades 1 through 3 will produce improvement in Jackson's third-grade exit test scores and other outcomes. Let's build a logic model to express the program's theory, first simply expressing the basic model and then elaborating the causal mechanisms through which it works.

Figure 2.6 shows the simplest model: Class size is related directly to academic achievement, as measured by test scores.[4] It is often a good idea to begin a logic model in this simple form, with just the independent and dependent variables.

Figure 2.6 Path Model of the Class-Size Reduction Program

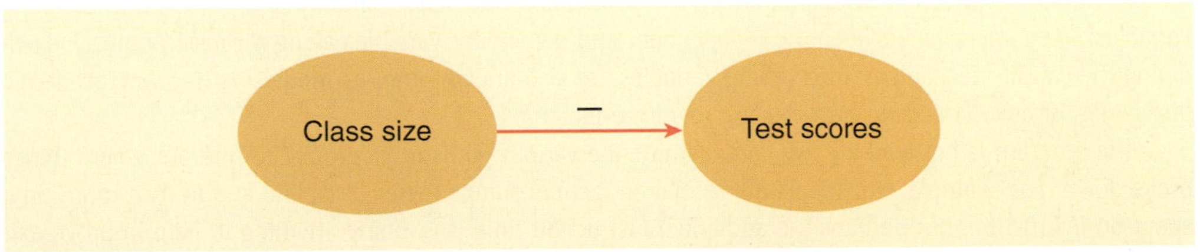

But this basic model is incomplete, because it provides only limited information. Suppose, as the anecdotal evidence suggests, that the exit test scores improve after the program's implementation. That's good news for Jackson and its students, of course, but we don't know *how* the program accomplished its success—just that

[4]There are, of course, many ways to express educational achievement, and test scores may or may not be a good method, but this is not our focus quite yet. See Chapter 4 on measurement for more on this issue.

it did (or at least seems to have done so). Perhaps we could find ways to make the program even more successful if we knew more about how class size influences test scores. But let's suppose that a more systematic evaluation reveals that the program, after all, does little to improve exit test scores—despite the initial, encouraging anecdotes from principals and others. What went wrong? Why isn't the program working as we hoped?

Intervening Variables

A more detailed logic model, such as Figure 2.7, might help us unravel the mystery. Recall that JPS pointed to research and the experience of teachers to suggest that smaller class size leads to fewer discipline problems (i.e., more discipline) and, as a result, more time spent on instruction. Smaller class size also may result in more individual attention to students. These factors in turn help students do better on the exit test.

Figure 2.7 Logic Model With Intervening Variables

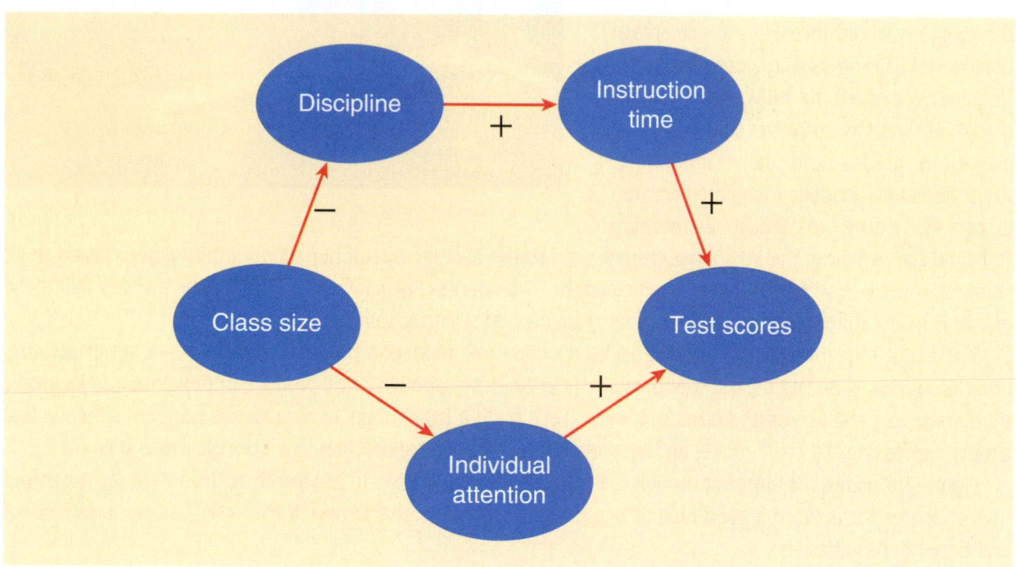

The variables such as individual attention, discipline, and instruction time in Figure 2.7 are intervening variables: They *intervene* between the independent and dependent variables along a causal pathway, elucidating the causal mechanism. Intervening variables are also known often as **mediators** in many academic disciplines, or as *intermediate outcomes* in program evaluation.

Speed bumps are a traffic safety intervention aimed at protecting pedestrians. What is an *intervening variable* (or *mediator*) that explains how speed bumps work to improve pedestrian safety?

If the program is not working, we can examine the various paths in Figure 2.7 to find out where things broke down. For example, smaller class size may in fact encourage better discipline and in turn more time spent on instruction, but perhaps the additional instruction time isn't doing anything to help improve exit test scores. A fresh look at how well the curriculum prepares kids for the exit test may be needed.

You'll notice in the more complex Figure 2.7 that if you follow along the causal pathways, using the rules of multiplication, you will get the original negative relationship specified in the simple, two-variable model shown in Figure 2.6. For example, the pathway class size → discipline → instruction time → test scores includes one negative and two positive relationships. Multiplying a negative by a positive and again by another positive results in a negative relationship ($-1 \times 1 \times 1 = -1$). In other words, if class size is negatively related to test scores, then the pathway class size → discipline → instruction time → test scores should also be negative. This is a good way to check if a logic model is indeed logical and internally consistent.

What About Other Causes?

We've illustrated the presumed *mechanisms* through which class size is expected to affect test scores. This is of particular interest if we want to understand or illustrate the logic of the program, if we need to fine-tune the program, or if we seek to evaluate how the program is working. However, test scores have lots of other causes, and we could flesh out our model further by including them. As you will see in later chapters of this book, some of these other causes may need to be taken into account in order to accurately estimate the true effect of the program. They may be needed as control variables, which we will cover in Part IV of the book (particularly, Chapters 12 and 13).

For example, say Jackson third graders are increasingly coming from families of lower socioeconomic status (SES), resulting in lower test scores. Since this change in student SES may result in more students failing the exit tests, scores might come down despite the class-size reduction program. At the same time, suppose Jackson is also putting an emphasis on recruiting good, experienced third-grade teachers from nearby districts, part of the same push to do better—but quite a different approach than class-size reduction. The new teachers might well be helping more kids pass the exit test, again apart from the effects of the class-size reduction program.

Figure 2.8 shows these additional factors at work influencing exit test scores along with class-size reduction. Even when concentrating on a single independent variable such as class size, therefore, including other important causes in the model can be valuable in thinking about the program and planning the analysis.

Figure 2.8 Logic Model Showing Other Causes and Intervening Variables

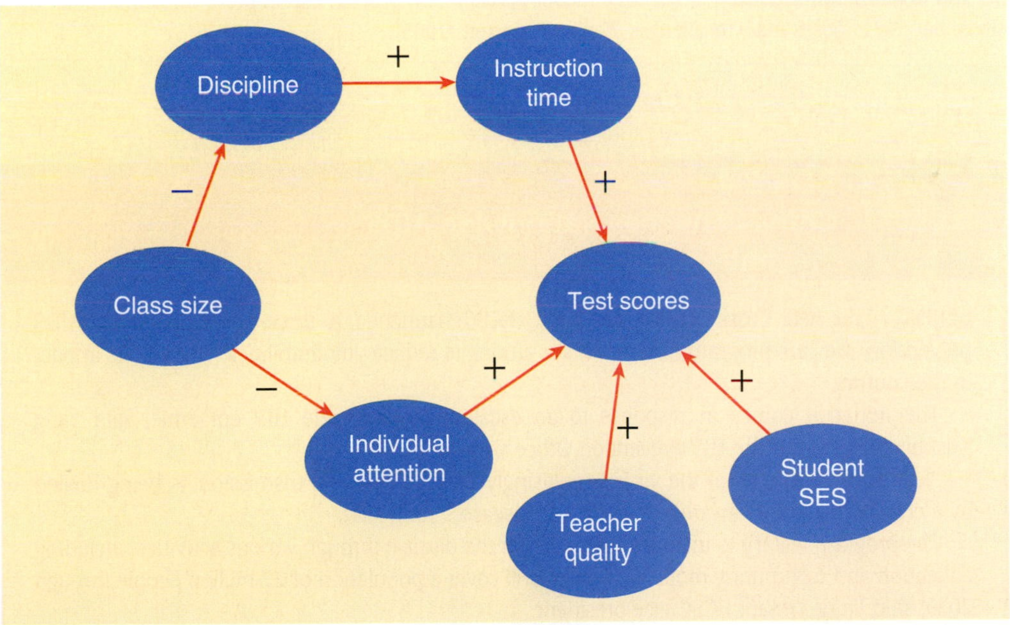

Usefulness of a Logic Model

Logic models serve several useful purposes. To begin with, a good logic model identifies important, sometimes previously unrecognized variables to track. It thus contributes a great deal to the task of establishing relevant *performance measures*, or *performance indicators*, to monitor the program. A good logic model helps similarly in the design of a *program evaluation*, calling attention to important intervening variables to measure as part of the evaluation, in addition to longer-term outcomes.

But a logic model can still be useful by itself even if performance measures and program evaluations are not available, or when planning a program, because it can expose logical weak links in the program theory. To give an example, suppose Westside hospital proposes a public advertising campaign to increase its volume of heart surgery patients. The basic program theory looks like this:

Marketing program → Patient volume

This seems logical at first glance, but we need to consider how the marketing program will increase the volume of heart surgery patients, the causal mechanism. We can do this by adding intervening variables to the model. Suppose the theory behind the program is that the marketing campaign will enhance the perceived reputation of the hospital in the eyes of prospective patients, these patients will then come to prefer Westside for heart surgery, and thus the volume of patients will increase. Here is the expanded logic model:

Marketing program → Perceived reputation of hospital → Patients' preference for hospital → Patient volume

This expanded model forces us to consider more explicitly the logic of each link. What about the last link? How important are patient preferences, really, in the decision about where heart surgery takes place? Do patients even get to decide? Perhaps not, as often doctors are the final decision makers. At the very least, the logic model has forced us to think through the logic of the program more carefully. Engaging many stakeholders and organization members in the logic model development process can improve implementation decisions, but it also poses many challenges (Kaplan & Garrett, 2005).

BOX 2.4 China Launches Nationwide AIDS Prevention Program

BEIJING—The Red Cross Society of China (RCSC) launched a three-year nationwide AIDS prevention and care program here on Friday, aiming to reduce vulnerability to HIV and its impact in the country.

The initiative comes in response to an escalating nationwide HIV epidemic, said Yang Xusheng, director of the HIV Prevention Office with the RCSC.

"It's clear the spread of the virus, increasingly through sexual transmission, is being fuelled by a continuing lack of awareness about the disease," Yang said.

The program will try to increase awareness of the disease through various activities, including education and community mobilization that will cover a population of 27 million people through 2010, said Jiang Yiman, RCSC vice president.

He said the program would also provide home-based support and care to 90,000 HIV infected people and their family members.

The program is aimed at preventing further infection of the disease and reducing discrimination to HIV carriers in the society.

Source: "China launches nationwide AIDS prevention program." (n.d.). Retrieved July 23, 2009, from http://www.chinadaily.com.cn/china/2008-03/28/content_6574756.htm.

Tips for Creating a Logic Model

The examples thus far in this chapter have illustrated how to develop a logic model for a program. Now, we lay out several specific tips for doing this yourself. To practice, we will use the example of an AIDS prevention program in China (Box 2.4).

Tip 1: Start with a single dependent (*Y*) variable or outcome. Real-world programs often have several outcomes, but it helps to focus on one at a time. The AIDS-prevention program in China, for example, aims both to prevent further infection *and* to care for those who have the disease (and also suffer from discrimination). These different outcomes might well be influenced by different variables, so each may require a somewhat different logic model. Again, it helps to start with one dependent variable at a time. We focus on the incidence of AIDS.

Tip 2: Next, add a single independent (*X*) variable representing the program. Many real-world programs have more than one channel or treatment—in effect, more than one independent variable. The AIDS-prevention program in China involves some form of mass-media campaign (such as radio ads and billboards) but also a more grassroots, community-based effort. It is likely that these two channels or treatments operate in much different ways and may even have distinct outcomes (at least distinct intermediate outcomes).

Tip 3: Put the program (the *X* variable) on the left side of the diagram and the outcome (the *Y* variable) on the right. Draw the program and the outcome each in one place and one place only in the diagram. Leave space in between for the intervening variables. For example,

Program ⟶ AIDS

(Of course, the relationship is negative, since the program is expected to decrease AIDS.)

Tip 4: Add *intervening variables* to the model—and think carefully about whether the intervening variables represent distinct pathways or instead steps along the same causal pathway. For example, say the community-based component of the AIDS-prevention program involves *distributing condoms* and also holding education sessions to build *knowledge* of the disease. We might at first draw it like this:

Program → Knowledge → Access to condoms → AIDS

But that is not correct. Knowledge of AIDS does not *cause* access to condoms (or vice versa). Rather, each is a separate channel or path through which the program influences risk.

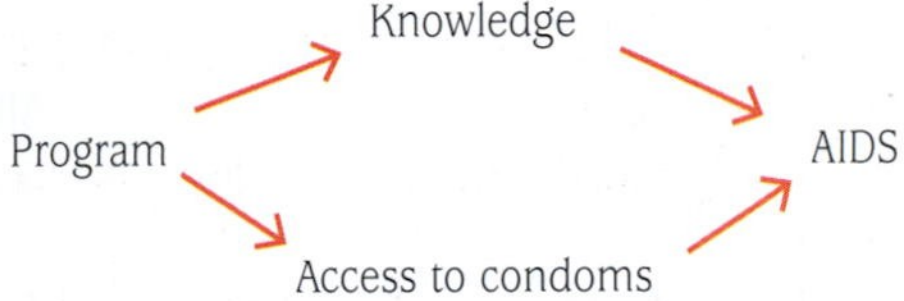

Tip 5: On the other hand, if something really is an intervening variable (along the causal pathway), don't draw it as a separate causal pathway. For example, if the program's distribution of condoms increases access to condoms, and this in turn increases the use of condoms, then access and use are not separate causal pathways. In other words, don't draw the diagram like this:

Rather, these intervening variables are steps along the same causal pathway, like this:

Program → Access to condoms → Use of condoms → AIDS

Tip 6: To make your theory really convincing, look at each link in isolation and make sure that you can explain every link in your theory. If a link between one variable and another is not obvious or does not make intuitive sense, then you may need to add intervening variables to explain the connection. You want your model to be largely self-evident for it to be truly convincing to a funder or policy maker. It is not completely obvious how knowledge about AIDS reduces incidence of the disease. To make it obvious one would specify knowledge of how risky sexual behavior increases the chance of getting AIDS and then a reduction in risky sexual behavior.

Knowledge → Risky Behavior → AIDS

Tip 7: As explained earlier in this chapter, avoid giving the variable names a direction. For example, name the variable not "Increased knowledge" but rather just "Knowledge." Express the direction of the relationship between variables by adding + or – signs next to the arrows. Keep in mind that not all variables necessarily will have a direction, particularly some categorical variables.

Tip 8: Finally, be aware that different levels of detail in a logic model are appropriate for different purposes. When you are trying to show the big picture of a complex, multipart program that aims to influence many outcomes, it will be necessary to simplify the logic model and leave out some detail. You see below a streamlined version of the program logic model, suitable for a proposal, and below that a more detailed version, what would emerge from an effort by program developers to figure out if and how the program would actually work.

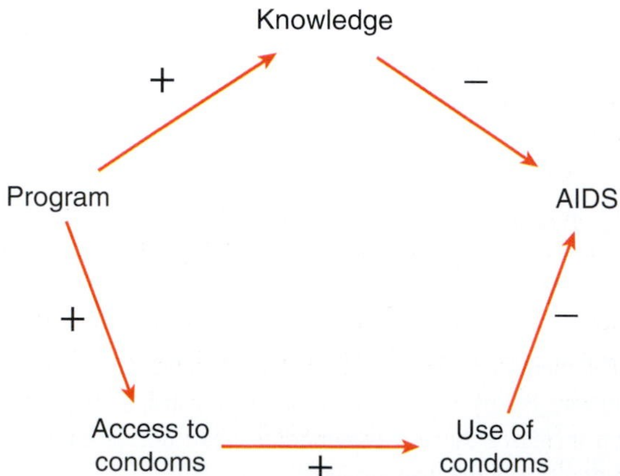

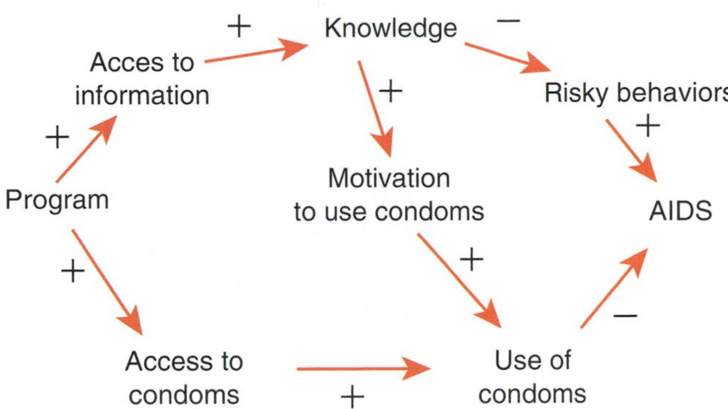

We stressed earlier that theories must stand up to empirical evidence. Ideally, each link in your logic model would have empirical evidence backing it. In reality, you are unlikely to be so lucky. It is still important to clearly spell out each important link in your theory, as described in Tip 6, so that its plausibility can be assessed. When possible and appropriate for your audience, describe what evidence exists to support your theory, as well as where evidence is lacking.

Inputs, Activities, Outputs, and Outcomes

Some logic models are focused purely on causal mechanisms—much like the models we have been considering so far. But often, logic models include a focus on the implementation of the program as well, including program inputs, activities, and outputs. **Inputs** are the financial, human, and material resources required by the program. **Activities** include training, counseling, marketing, and other tasks that make up the work of implementing the program. And **outputs** are the immediate products of these activities, such as people trained, brochures distributed, vaccinations given, or citations issued. Inputs, activities, and outputs lead in turn to **outcomes**. It often helps to further separate these into *short-term* outcomes, *intermediate* outcomes, and *long-term* outcomes.

Figure 2.9 provides an example from a Centers for Disease Control and Prevention guidebook. It illustrates a logic model for a high blood pressure (HBP) reduction program that emphasizes chronic care management (CCM). The model shows the program's inputs (funding and clinic partners), activities (education and training), and outputs (clinic teams being educated and trained) that in turn set in motion a causal sequence of outcomes. The immediate short-term outcomes are more appropriate treatment of patients and more chronic care management. This leads to the intermediate outcome of more patients who keep their high blood pressure under control and, in turn, the long-term outcome of less heart disease and fewer strokes. Logic models such as this provide both a managerial perspective, showing how program implementation happens, and a causal theory of how the program produces outcomes that matter to funders, policy makers, and society.

When drafting logic models such as these, it is important not to get so immersed in diagramming the details of implementation—inputs, activities, and outputs—that the model fails to clearly articulate how the program produces desired outcomes. After all, doing something about these outcomes is the whole point of the program. For example, make sure that the logic model includes the ultimate outcome and that the causal mechanism is clear and convincing.

Figure 2.9 Logic Model of High Blood Pressure (HBP) Reduction Program That Emphasizes Chronic Care Management (CCM)

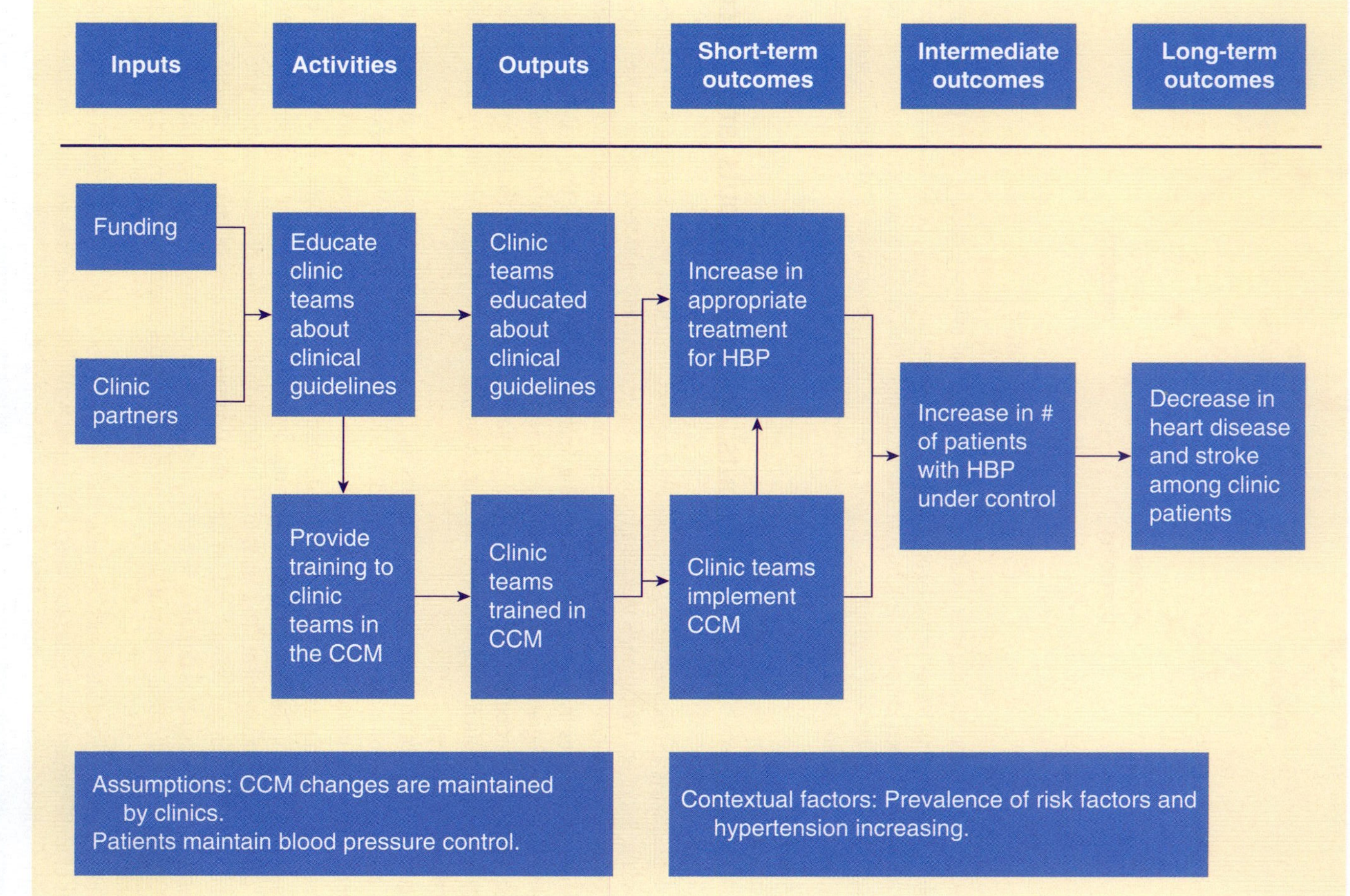

Source: Centers for Disease Control and Prevention (n.d.).

Additional Issues in Theory Building

There are some additional issues that are important to consider when building a theory, beginning with some alternative views of the form and function of theory in social and policy research.

Interpretivist Theory

We have presented a somewhat narrow view of theory—portraying it primarily as a matter of variables and causal relationships. This view of theory is the norm for quantitative research, but qualitative research (the topic of the next chapter) also uses other types of theories. Moreover, our view of theory—middle-range theory—is associated with the scientific realism perspective of this book. **Interpretivism,** associated with antipositivism, has very different sorts of theories, which focus on the interpretation of the meanings and intentionality of human actions (A. Rosenberg, 2012). These theories focus on an intersubjective understanding of people rather than an empirical explanation of their objective behavior. Rather than articulating causal relationships, the aim of interpretivist theory is to comprehend people's norms, values, and symbols—to make sense of people on their own terms and how they experience their world. In this way, theory does not always take the form of variables, relationships, and causal mechanisms as we have said. We will have more to say about the interpretivist perspective in the next chapter.

Does Theory Shape Observation?

We have said that theory must stand up to observation, and this would seem to imply that observations (measurements, data) occupy an entirely separate realm, independent of the theory and models being tested. But in an important sense, observations are theory laden (Kuhn, 2012). Take the example of survey research (Chapter 7), which starts off with a blank page—what questions should we ask respondents? Say we are interested in public attitudes toward genetically modified foods. Using our models and hypotheses, we write out specific questions to measure our variables. But people may not know much or have well-formed views on genetically modified foods, or many other important issues. Still, when we ask them about it in a survey, they readily comply—by essentially forming an opinion or making up an answer (Zaller, 1992). Even the wording of a question can introduce an idea, or stimulate an attitude, that may not have existed in the person's consciousness prior to hearing the question. In this way, a theory can shape the observations used to test it.

Theories of the Independent Variable

Our focus has been on theories of what variables drive the dependent variable. However, in later chapters, we will need to focus on theories about what drives the *independent* variable as well. This may seem strange and even contradictory. After all, we defined the independent variable as the cause and the dependent variable as the effect. However, when we start to use empirical evidence, things get more complicated.

For example, people may observe that precincts with more disorder have more crime, and thus conclude that disorder causes crime. But another possible theory, consistent with the evidence, is that disorder and crime are partly symptoms of the same underlying malady—such as social and economic disadvantage. In other words, perhaps *both* disorder and crime are effects caused by another variable, disadvantage, as shown in Figure 2.10. If so, attacking disorder in the hope of reducing crime may be less effective than we initially thought.

This is a tricky issue that Part III will address more fully. Nonetheless, as further motivation for practicing your theory-building skills, keep in mind that figuring out the theory of the independent variable is very important for applying the empirical methods we will learn later in this book for sorting out causal effects.

Figure 2.10 Common Cause of the Independent Variable and Dependent Variable

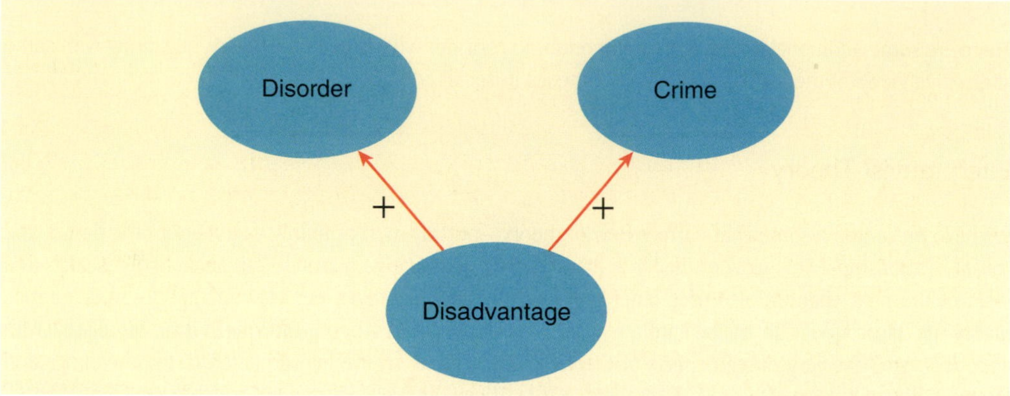

Moderators

Sometimes a variable in a model is believed to influence not another variable but the *relationship* between two other variables. For example, in our class-size model, the effect of instruction time could depend on how experienced the teacher is. The increase in test scores due to more instruction time could be even higher if there is a more experienced teacher in the room. In this example, teacher experience is said to moderate the effect of instruction time on test scores—thus, teacher experience is a **moderator variable**. In some disciplines, much the same idea is referred to as an *interaction*.

In a path diagram, a moderator variable is depicted by an arrow coming from the moderator and pointing toward the relationship (the middle of the arrow) that it influences, as shown in Figure 2.11. Later chapters will have more to say about how to analyze and interpret moderator (or interaction) effects.

Figure 2.11 Moderator Depicted in a Path Diagram

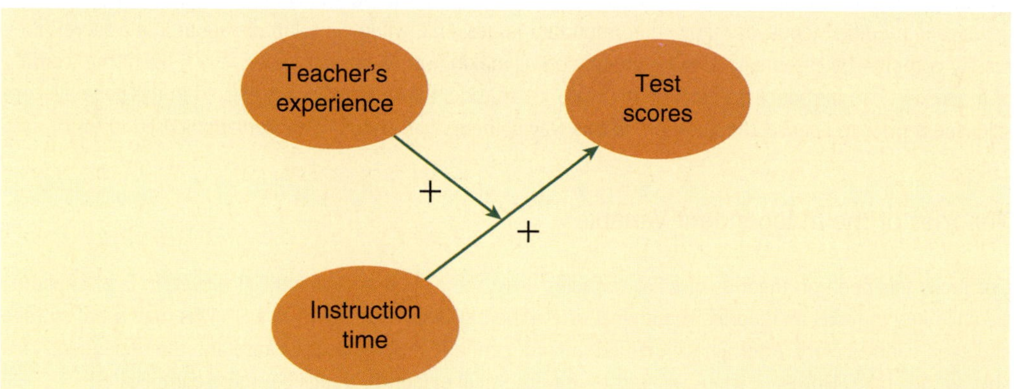

Hierarchical (Multilevel) Models and Contextual Variables

Some models—called **hierarchical models**, or **multilevel models**—describe relationships between variables at different units of analysis. For example, a model of student test scores that uses the student as the unit of analysis might also include classroom-level or school-level variables, such as the qualifications of the classroom teacher or the amount of financial resources the school expends per pupil. Higher-level variables such as these are sometimes referred to as *contextual variables*. We discuss this issue a bit more in Chapter 10 on multivariate analysis.

Theoretical Research

Most research is *empirical*, involving observation or experimentation, but some research is purely theoretical. That might seem like an oxymoron, and certainly any full investigation of a topic must include empirical evidence. Nonetheless, thinking theoretically is an important part of the greater research endeavor, particularly when mechanisms and relationships are complicated or not intuitively obvious. As a result, you will find articles and books in most fields devoted entirely to proposing or developing theory or models. Indeed, the Kelling and Wilson (1982) article on the broken windows theory is an example of sorts.

But much theoretical research involves making predictions about new or complicated situations by combining and applying a large group of well-established theories. For example, Rosen (1981) used well-accepted economic theories applied to several linked markets to show how technological changes, such as music recording, which allowed many people to consume the talents of a single opera singer, resulted in much higher earnings for just a few stars instead of the many more ordinary singers who previously earned a living by performing live opera. Rosen has extended his theory (as have others since then) to predict and explain growing inequality in many fields due to other technological changes.

Examining complex and interrelated systems using already existing theories can help predict consequences of particular policies. For example, Christensen and Remler (2009) combined existing economic theories from other areas to show that rapid adoption of electronic medical records could leave providers locked into systems that use relatively backward technologies and do not communicate well with other systems. Theoretical research combines known empirical evidence and established theories to gain insight, make predictions and recommendations, and suggest directions and hypotheses for future empirical research.

How to Find and Focus Research Questions

As we saw at the start of this chapter, theory can be defined as "a reasoned and precise speculation about the answer to a research question" (King et al., 1994)—but what is a **research question**? Roughly speaking, we can say it is the question that motivated the researcher to do the study. But what exactly makes for a good research question, and how do you come up with one?

If you go by what you read in a research article or report, you get the sense of an orderly process: The research question follows directly from a review of the literature or theory in a field, and it precedes the collection and analysis of data. But the tidy picture provided by a published study masks a great deal of messy exploration, backtracking, and second-guessing that goes on behind the scenes. Often a researcher begins with only a vague sense of a question. It even happens that a researcher starts with one question, only to switch to another (more interesting or more answerable) question in midstream. Sometimes the data come first, for example when a researcher working with a survey conducted for one purpose realizes it can be used to study something else entirely. A study looks neatly crafted on the printed page, but it is often produced on a rather messy workbench.

This section on research questions is especially important if you need to begin your own study, perhaps as part of a research project or thesis. But it is also of interest if you mainly seek to understand and apply research to policy or practice; it is always important to be aware of the motivation that led a researcher to conduct a study.

Applied Research Questions

In applied research, the questions often arise from practical concerns of policy makers and practitioners: Do smaller classes help kids learn better? If we allow employees to work from home, will they be more or less productive? Will lowering the speed limit on roadways reduce traffic fatalities? Organizations and decision makers all over the world have many questions like these, and they often commission or sponsor research to answer them. More generally, society as a whole has many such practical questions, and thus independent researchers

Research looks neat on the printed page, but it is often produced on a messy workbench

Source: © istockphoto/ EasyBuy4u.

(such as university students or professors) can use these as inspiration for the research questions guiding their own work.

But to be viable and useful for research, the practical question must be clarified and focused. One way to do this is to use the model-building tools we have been discussing in this chapter. In a study of a program or intervention, for example, the researcher needs to define the intervention (independent variable) and precisely what outcomes are expected (dependent variable), including perhaps unintended consequences. And the researcher must inquire about relevant intervening variables or mechanisms. Take, for example, the following question:

- Do smaller classes help kids learn?

In the case of the Jackson Public Schools, we might need to focus this a bit:

- Does the JPS class-size reduction program improve scores on the third-grade exit test? And if so, through what mechanisms (instruction time, individual attention) does class size influence test scores?

We might go on to add a question about unintended consequences:

- Does the JPS class-size reduction program reduce the resources available for other services (such as the library, art and music classes, or the after-school program)?

As this example illustrates, a single study can seek to answer more than one question. It also illustrates that formulating a research question and specifying a model are interlinked activities. Questions lead to theory and a model, but a theory and model also help refine and even reshape the original question or questions.

Questions You Ideally Want to Answer, and Those You Really Can

Another important aspect of refining and clarifying your research question is to make it answerable. Often researchers find that the question they started with is not feasible, as a practical or ethical matter, and so they must settle for an answer to a related question—an approximation of sorts. But it is better to have an approximate answer than none at all.

Suppose you're interested in increasing voting among young adults in the country. You want to know how interested they are in politics, and how often they vote. Ideally, you would probably like to study a representative sample of young adults from across the country. But for practical reasons, you might have to settle for college students on your campus whom you can more easily interview. You might ask them in a survey about their interest in politics, but what about their voting behavior? You could ask them about the last election, but some students may have been too young to vote then (and besides, what you really want to know is how their *current* interest in politics predicts their *future* voting behavior). You could try to follow up with the students just after the next election, to see if they voted or not, but this would require waiting months if not years for data, plus the difficulties of recontacting people. So instead you add a question to your survey about their *intentions* to vote, or not, in the next election. In this way, your question has morphed into something answerable, if a bit less grand: How interested are students on my campus in politics, and do they intend to vote in the next election?

Even the best researchers must make compromises. Consider another example that has been studied a great deal: Does divorce have long-term detrimental effects on children, psychologically or educationally? Because we cannot rewind the clock and see what would have happened to these children had their parents not divorced, this question is hard to answer directly. We could compare differences between those whose parents divorced and those whose parents did not, as in a study by Huurre, Junkkari, and Aro (2006). But because these groups may be different in important ways, this comparison answers a different, but still valuable, question. A study by Gruber (2004) used changes over time in state divorce laws to determine the long-term effects on children of making divorce easier. But this, too, is a slightly different question from our ideal question, because we still aren't sure if the detrimental effects on children can be attributed to divorce itself or perhaps some other consequence of the changes in law. And Gruber's study was unable to consider some of the psychological outcomes observed by Huurre and colleagues (2006). Flexibility and compromise are required when translating your ideal question into a doable research question.

Know If Your Question Is Descriptive or Causal

Throughout this book, we make a distinction between descriptive research (that answers "what is" questions) and causal research (that answers "what if" questions). We view this distinction as fundamental to understanding research. When coming up with your own research question, you should be clear about this distinction as well. Do you want a *description* of voting behavior—*what is* the rate of young voter turnout, and has it changed over time? Or do you want a *causal explanation* of voting behavior—*what if* we lowered the cost of voting (in terms of time, travel, and effort); would young voter turnout increase? These are two very different kinds of questions, requiring different research strategies. So it is important to clarify which type of question, descriptive or causal, will be the main focus of your study.

Make Your Question Positive, Not Normative

We've seen already that theories are positive—about how the world really is—and not normative—about how we want the world to be. Similarly, your research question will lead in a more productive direction if you frame it as a positive and not a normative question.

Again focusing on the idea of getting more young people to vote, suppose you come up with a research question such as this: *Why aren't more young people interested in politics and more willing to vote in elections?* This question implies a normative framework (that people *should* care about politics and *should* vote). We might well agree with these values, but a researchable question needs to be more positive—for example, *how interested are young people in politics? How often do they vote? And does interest in politics influence people's voting behavior?* These questions get at the same basic issue, but they are more positive, less normative, and thus more answerable by empirical research.

Generating Questions and Ideas

Although pressing social or practical problems often suggest questions, sometimes researchers (particularly in academic settings) must come up with their own ideas for research in a more abstract way. You may be asked to do this for a class project, a thesis, or a dissertation. So what exactly should you do?

One answer is to review the scholarly literature in your field and look for anomalies or unanswered questions. In Chapter 17, we give some guidelines on how to find and review published research. The course work you do in substantive areas is an obvious place to look for topics of interest to you—and the corresponding unanswered questions and anomalies. (Research methods courses, unlike substantive area courses, typically focus on *how* to do research, but not *what* to do it on.) For applied research, the relevant policy and practice discussion—in trade literature, news stories, conferences, social media, and everyday conversations—is useful not just for supplying existing questions like "Do smaller classes help students learn?" but also for highlighting problems and new phenomena. A researcher can combine concern about middle school students and electronic devices with knowledge of psychology to develop new research questions, such as "Does the plethora of electronic devices harm the development of concentration skills among middle school students?"

It is also important to read widely, outside your field, as this can introduce you to new ideas or a new perspective on your area of interest. Find books or articles from other disciplines that interest you, especially those written for a more general audience. Newspapers, magazines, and blogs can also help you think broadly about your topic. Don't be afraid to use your own personal life experiences, as these can give you a unique perspective and motivation. In doing all of this, be sure to keep a notebook of your ideas for research. Jot down everything that comes to mind. Most experienced researchers have such a notebook (either paper or electronic), and they typically have a dozen ideas written down for every one that eventually turns into a full-blown study.

Heuristics

Andrew Abbott (2004) has identified certain *heuristics*—intellectual tricks or moves—good researchers often use to generate interesting and productive research questions. To illustrate, let's say you are interested in the issue of declining voter turnout and political participation in modern democracies. Why do some people vote, while others do not?

This is a well-worn question, but one heuristic you could use to liven it up is to make an *analogy*. What if you tried viewing voting as an economic transaction (Dubner & Levitt, 2005)? How much does it cost people to vote (in time, travel, effort)? Has the cost of voting gone up in recent years (more complications, higher opportunity costs)? And what is the payoff from voting (in terms of benefits from preferred politicians and policies)? Was the payoff better (patronage jobs, more competitive elections) in the past than it is now? As Abbott (2004) points out, this can also allow you to *borrow a method* (another heuristic move) from one discipline (economics) and apply it to the problems of another (political science).

Yet another heuristic move is to make a *reversal*—turn things around. "It might be worthwhile to stand this problem on its head," Dubner and Levitt (2005) of Freakonomics fame write, "and instead ask a different question: considering that an individual's vote almost never matters, why do so many people bother to vote at all?" This kind of reversal may make you think quite differently about the topic of voter turnout and political participation. Abbott's (2004) book provides many more such heuristics (problematizing the obvious, changing context, stopping and putting in motion, etc.), but the larger point is to look for ways to free up your imagination so that you can think about a problem or issue in a new light.

Conclusion: Theories Are Practical

According to Webster's dictionary, the adjective *theoretical* can mean "concerned primarily with theories or hypotheses rather than practical considerations" (Babylon, 2013). Many people have a similar association when they hear the word *theory*. Practitioners often think that they do not want to become too theoretical or spend too much time thinking about theory.

We hope that this chapter has convinced you that theories are practical. As we saw, New York Police Department Commissioner Bratton, not the kind of person you'd think of as being lost in the clouds, focused the largest police force in the United States around the broken windows theory. Theories come from police chiefs and criminologists who strive to prevent crime and save property and lives.

We have seen two ways in which a theory is practical. First, theories can help us understand the causes of a social problem or condition we care about. Understanding the causes of crime, for example, helps shed light on what police departments and other institutions in society might do to prevent it. We often welcome theories that help us explain and understand urgent social problems, giving us clues about what programs or interventions are most likely to work.

Second, logic models can help us understand how a program or policy works—how it achieves, or fails to achieve, its intended result or outcome. Such understanding can be used to improve a program or policy if it isn't working well. In other words, it is often not enough to know *that* a program works or doesn't—we need to know *why* it works (or doesn't).

For both of these uses of theories, path diagrams are valuable tools. As we move on to later chapters of the book, path diagrams will continue to be essential tools, particularly in Part IV, on causation. Once you get used to thinking in terms of path diagrams, you'll be surprised how useful they can be.

BOX 2.5
Critical Questions to Ask About Theory, Models, and Research Questions

- What is the theory being tested in a study?
- What is the independent variable? What is the dependent variable? And what is the causal mechanism that links them?
- What is the unit of analysis?
- Was the theory developed inductively or deductively? Did it come from practical experience, exploratory or qualitative studies, a grand social theory, a discipline, or something else?
- What is the theory behind a program or intervention?
- Is there a logic model that describes how the program works? Does it make sense?
- What is the question that motivates the study? Is it an applied or policy question, or a more academic question?

BOX 2.6
Tips on Doing Your Own Research: Theory, Models, and Research Questions

- Use the advice in this chapter to identify and focus your research question. Try writing out the question in a clear, simple sentence or two.
- Is your research question mainly descriptive or mainly causal? If it is causal, can you state the main hypotheses (predictions) that stem from your theory?
- Create a path model to represent your theory; clearly identify the independent variable, the dependent variable, and key intervening variables or causal mechanisms. Also be sure to specify the directions of the relationships. Try showing and explaining your model to friends or colleagues—is it clear? Does it make sense to them (and to you)?
- What unit of analysis would you use to test the theory? Think about the kind of data you could actually find or gather, as this often determines the answer to this question.
- Think about how you would analyze the data, including specific statistical techniques, since the feasibility of the data analysis often restricts the research question. (See Part III of the book)
- After developing the model, and considering the limitations on finding or gathering and analyzing data, go back to your research question. Does it correspond to the model? Is answering the research question really doable? Does the question need to be revised, refined, or restricted in any way?
- Try repeating the steps above for a related or even different research question—often you need to come up with several research ideas in order to find one that would be interesting and feasible for you to carry out.

Chapter Resources

Key Terms

- Causal mechanism
- Causal and noncausal relationships
- Cross-sectional variation
- Ecological fallacy
- Grand theory (theoretical paradigm)
- Hierarchical (multilevel) models
- Hypothesis
- Independent and dependent variables
- Inputs, activities, outputs, and outcomes
- Interpretivism
- Intervening variable (mediator)
- Logic model
- Longitudinal variation
- Middle-range theory
- Model
- Moderator variable
- Modifiable and nonmodifiable variables
- Path diagram (or path model)
- Positive (+) and negative (−) relationships (direction of a relationship)
- Positive and normative
- Relationship
- Research question
- Theory
- Unit of analysis
- Variable

Exercises

Make a Theory

2.1. Make a basic theory to explain each of the following outcomes. Keep it simple—think of the most obvious and intuitive explanation. Use a path model to represent your theory, which should have an independent variable (which you identify) and a dependent variable (which is the outcome itself). Supplement your model with a brief description in words, including the causal mechanism (this is very important).

- Traffic fatalities (on highways)
- Smoking (among teenagers)
- Litter (on sidewalks)
- Attendance (at a local art museum)

Identifying Independent and Dependent Variables

2.2. Identify the independent and dependent variables implicit in the following quotes:

a. "The key to a good, high-paying job is education."
b. "Oatmeal is an important part of a heart-healthy diet."
c. "Passing out condoms to teenagers just encourages sexual activity."
d. "To reduce youth violence, we need more after-school programs."

Positive and Negative Relationships

2.3. Identify the most likely direction (positive, negative) of the following relationships:
   a. Age and health (of individuals)
   b. Work experience and earnings (of individuals)
   c. Traffic volume and air pollution levels (of cities)
   d. Gender inequality and female life expectancy (of countries)

Unit of Analysis

2.4. This chapter discussed a class-size reduction program in Jackson, Mississippi. The most basic model of the program looked like this: Class size → Test scores. What are some possible units of analysis for this model? Specify an independent and dependent variable for each of the various units of analysis (as in Table 2.3).

Logic Model of a Program (Project-Length Exercise)

2.5. Consider a policy or social program that actually exists or that you would like to propose. Something that really interests you and that you know something about is best. Prepare a description of the theory of how your program works.

Make sure that you include the following:

   a. What are the outcomes (dependent variables) the program is designed to affect? If there are many outcomes, restrict your analysis to one outcome or to a few closely related outcomes.
   b. What is the unit of analysis that the variables describe?
   c. Describe your program. Be as explicit as possible: Do not use vague generalities.
   d. Using a path diagram and a narrative description, describe your theory of how the program is supposed to work. Both the path diagram and the narrative description should make clear the *mechanism(s)* through which the program will affect the outcome. So, if a link is not obvious, break it down into the steps along the way, illustrating the intervening variables. There can be many mechanisms through which a program works. If so, pick only a couple and just note that there are other mechanisms. This section should illustrate to your readers why they should believe that the program will work—will affect the outcome(s). It will also make clear what the weak linkages are.

Developing a Research Question

2.6. Choose a topic in your field or in an area of interest to you and try developing it into a research question using the following steps:
   a. Jot down as many questions as you can think of related to your topic.
   b. Pick the question that interests you the most.

c. Is your question primarily causal, or descriptive? Edit your question if necessary to clarify this.
d. Make sure your question is positive (and not normative). Again, edit it accordingly (even though you may have a moral or political interest in the topic).
e. Try developing a simple theory, in the form of a path model, to represent a plausible answer to your question. (Note: This step applies only to causal questions, not descriptive questions.)
f. Think about how you would answer your question. Fine-tune your question so that it is something you really could answer with the resources available to you.

Student Study Site

Visit the Study Site at **www.sagepub.com/remler2e** to

- test your knowledge with the self-quiz
- check your understanding of key terms with the eFlashcards
- explore helpful resources that relate directly to this chapter

Qualitative research often involves the interpretation of language and texts.

Source: © istockphoto/tigermad.

Overview: This chapter introduces you to qualitative research—an important approach to social inquiry that is especially useful for generating theory as well as other research purposes. You will learn how qualitative research differs from quantitative research, how these two approaches can be combined, and the role each plays in the research process. You will get a feel for basic types of qualitative studies or methods, including in-depth interviews, focus groups, participant observation, and case studies, as well as the analysis of documents and many other forms of existing qualitative data. You will also learn about selecting cases for qualitative research, coding qualitative data, and software for qualitative data analysis. This chapter begins the discussion of qualitative research, but later chapters—although focused on traditionally more quantitative topics—provide further details about qualitative research and further illustrations of its usefulness.

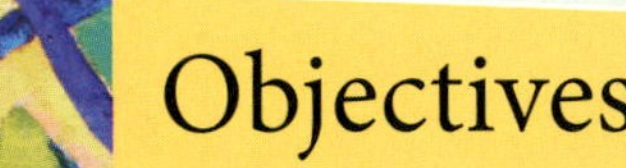

Objectives

Learning Objectives

After reading this chapter, you should be able to

- Identify qualitative research and to recognize its advantages for certain research purposes
- Describe how qualitative research differs from quantitative research, and some of the issues involved in the qualitative-quantitative debate
- Know the different types of qualitative interviewing and techniques for conducting and recording interviews
- Recognize the main features and advantages of the focus group method, participant observation, and case study research
- Describe the steps involved in qualitative data analysis, including coding and the use of qualitative software
- Appreciate some of the unique ethical issues raised by qualitative research

3 Qualitative Research

Fighting Malaria in Kenya

The World Health Organization (WHO) estimates that malaria kills nearly 1 million people each year, mostly children living in sub-Saharan Africa (WHO, 2009). Malaria is the fourth leading cause of death for children in developing countries (following birth complications, respiratory infections, and diarrhea, according to the Centers for Disease Control and Prevention [CDC], 2009a). In an effort to combat the disease, which is transmitted from person to person by mosquitoes, governments and private organizations have invested billions in the development and testing of new drugs to treat malaria.

Artemisinin-based combination therapy (ACT) has emerged as an effective approach to treating the disease and saving lives. WHO issued a recommendation that governments use ACT in place of older therapies that are failing because the malaria parasite has grown resistant to them. In response, the Ministry of Health in Kenya supplied ACT and provided training on its use to government health dispensaries in the country, especially those in rural villages threatened by malaria. The ministry expected these steps to lead to the widespread use of ACT to treat malaria patients.

But a follow-up survey of workers in health dispensaries found that far less than half of the patients with malaria were being treated with the new drug therapy. Most of the health workers said that they had received the training and had ACT in stock, but still they were not proving the therapy to sick children in rural Kenya. Why? The answer to this question matters: All the investment in research and development to combat malaria are worth little if frontline health workers cannot, or will not, deliver effective new treatments to sick people.

To find an answer, Kenyan health researcher Beatrice Wasunna and colleagues conducted a series of in-depth qualitative interviews with 36 health workers who had training and supplies of ACT but were not administering the therapy according to official guidelines (Wasunna, Zurovac, Goodman, & Snow, 2008). By in-depth qualitative interviewing we mean that they talked at length with individual health care workers and listened to their explanations, in their own words, for why they were not administering ACT to sick patients.

Here is what the findings from the interviews revealed (all quotations are from Wasunna et al., 2008):

- Health workers knew that ACT was expensive medicine, and they feared that the Kenyan government, although it had supplied health dispensaries with an initial stock, would not be able to do so in the future. As one interviewee put it, "We are always sure that we will run short of it in due course. That's why we try to ration." Many said that they reserved their stocks of ACT for the neediest, most deserving patients.

- At about the same time Kenya's drug agency was distributing ACT, the same agency also sent even larger stocks of an older antimalarial drug, amodiaquine. This created much confusion among workers in the local health dispensaries. As one person explained, speaking of his coworkers, "They are asking why the government is still supplying so much of it [amodiaquine], if they are not supposed to use it?"
- The training health workers received on the use of ACT gave inconsistent messages, leaving many with the impression that special testing was mandatory before prescribing ACT. Moreover, the health dispensaries often did not have the microscopes or kits required to do the testing. According to one health worker, "In the first place when we got this [ACT] we were told not to use them unless we get those kits."
- Health workers reported being pressured by patients for the older antimalarial, amodiaquine, because it was more familiar and also because it was simpler to use. "You know the mothers are used to amodiaquine syrup so they usually complain that they have to crush too many [ACT] tablets," explained a health worker.
- Finally, the interviews suggested that most dispensaries were understaffed, with high turnover and lack of supervision. As one health worker describes the problem,

> We were told to give quality care, it is one thing saying but another doing. Sometimes you just give quantity care because I'm all alone here. I have 2–3 community health workers and they are not conversant with the new treatment policy . . . If there could be additional health workers, then we can give the patient quality care.

These interview findings suggest possible reasons why health workers in Kenya did not switch to the new therapy—the possible causes of the problem.

Theory, Causes, and Qualitative Research

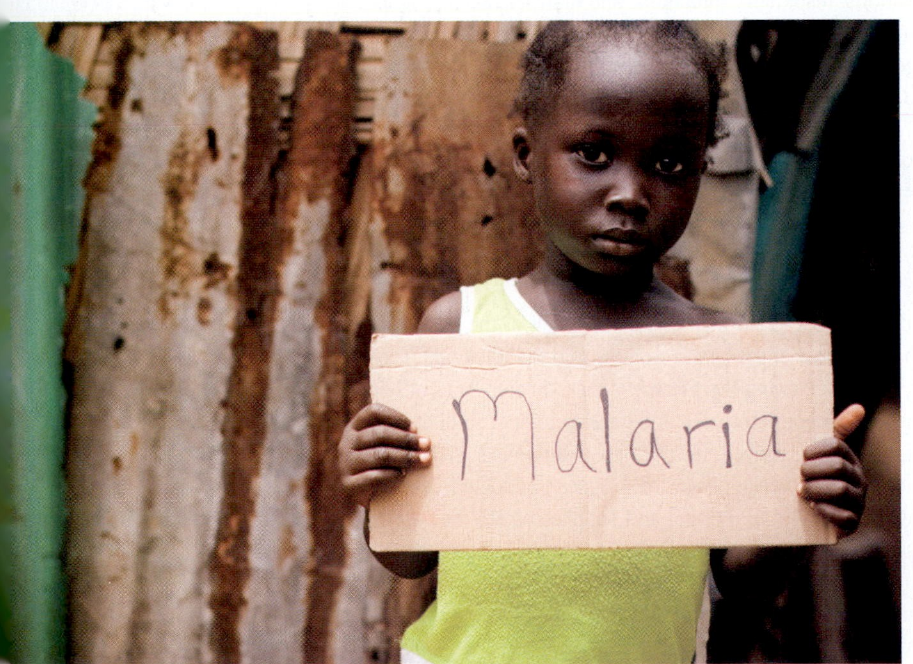

Malaria is a leading cause of death in developing countries.

Source: © iStockphoto.com/MShep2.

The Kenyan malaria study illustrates well the nature and value of *qualitative research*. Sometimes the best way to find out an answer to a pressing public policy or management problem is to go directly into the field, observe conditions on the ground, and ask the people involved—in their own words—for their interpretation of what is happening and why.

Qualitative research is particularly useful and well suited to discovering important variables and relationships, to generating theory and models, particularly uncovering possible causes and causal mechanisms. We often get ideas about possible causes from case studies or qualitative observations. And qualitative methods do an especially good job of uncovering and documenting causal processes or mechanisms. Glaser and Strauss (1967) coined the term **grounded theory** to refer to this theory-generating aspect of qualitative research. And George and Bennett (2005) employ the notion of *causal process tracing* to explain how good qualitative research uncovers causal mechanisms.

The findings from the in-depth interviews in Kenya, for example, suggested possible causes of the reluctance of health workers to prescribe ACT: lack of trust that ACT supplies would be maintained, continued distribution of older drugs, patients who preferred the older drugs and resisted switching, misunderstandings picked up from the trainings, and lack of staff and resources at the dispensaries. Health officials could use these qualitative findings to come up with a program theory—a logic model—of variables that encourage, or hinder, the use of ACT. Indeed, qualitative studies such as this frequently provide the insights needed to construct the kinds of models we saw in the previous chapter.

It is because of this theory-generating, model-building aspect of qualitative research that we introduce the topic at this point in the book. Qualitative methods also play an important role in other aspects of research, such as developing measures, pretesting surveys, or following up on experimental findings, as we will discuss in later chapters. But qualitative methods are important in their own right as a way of generating research knowledge. Indeed, many studies and even whole fields of investigation rely solely on qualitative methods.

In this chapter, we focus on the various approaches and methods of qualitative research. We begin by defining qualitative research and contrasting it with quantitative research.

What Is Qualitative Research?

Qualitative research can be defined in terms of the kind of data it produces and in terms of the form of analysis it employs. Some also argue that qualitative research involves a different logic of inquiry as well, a point we will return to shortly. In terms of data, qualitative research involves various kinds of nonnumerical or **qualitative data**, such as interviews (oral communication), written texts or documents, visual images, observations of behavior, case studies, and so on. The malaria study in Kenya, for example, was based on data from in-depth interviews of 36 health workers. The tape recordings and transcripts of these interviews, together with whatever notes or observations the researchers made when they visited the rural health dispensaries, constitute the data for this qualitative study.

In terms of analysis, qualitative research relies on various methods of *interpretation*. Because qualitative data are often spoken or written language, or images that have symbolic content, making sense of the data involves interpreting their meaning. Moreover, qualitative analysis relies on the fact that the objects under investigation are human beings and that language provides a unique window into the thoughts, experiences, and motivations of others. Thus language allows for **intersubjectivity**—the ability to stand in someone else's shoes, as it were, and see the world as it appears from their perspective.

QUESTION

In your own words, how would you define qualitative research?

Thus, qualitative researchers rely on this human potential for intersubjectivity, achieved through interpretation of language and other symbolic systems (such as body language or images), to explain human behavior. The Kenyan research team listened to the health workers, interpreted their stories, and drew conclusions about why ACT was not being prescribed as intended.

Contrasting Qualitative With Quantitative Research

To understand what distinguishes qualitative research, it helps to contrast it with **quantitative research.** In quantitative research, investigators often observe the world using instruments (including structured questionnaires) that produce quantitative measurements, or numerical data, representing various characteristics, behaviors, or attitudes. They also retrieve data that are already in numerical form, such as prices. Quantitative researchers analyze the numerical data using the tools and techniques of statistics, from simple graphs and tables to sophisticated multivariate techniques.

Quantitative research can investigate characteristics thought of as qualitative, including emotions, beliefs, or other intangible variables. For example, there is a great deal of quantitative research on topics such as happiness, religious beliefs, self-esteem, and trust of other people. What makes these studies quantitative is that they use instruments that produce numerical data, and these data are analyzed using statistics. So it is not the topic of the research that makes it qualitative or quantitative—the distinction lies in the nature of the data and methods of analysis.

Focus on Cases Rather Than Variables

As we saw in the previous chapter, theories are mostly about variables and how they are related to one another. This perspective is associated primarily with quantitative research. But qualitative research often does not start with variables. Rather, it focuses on **cases**—individuals, groups, or institutions.

We will have more to say about the case study method later in this chapter. A basic motivation for this approach is that by examining cases in their full complexity, the relevant variables can be identified and tested (George & Bennett, 2005). This is another way to appreciate how qualitative research generates theory and helps build models.

A Configuration of Causes

Another way qualitative research contrasts with quantitative research is its approach to causation, a topic we will have much more to say about in Chapter 11. Quantitative studies often aim to isolate a single cause at a time, and then to measure its average effect across many individuals or cases. Qualitative research, however, often aims to come up with a unique configuration of diverse influences or causes at work in a particular setting (Ragin, 2008). The result is what is sometimes referred to as an ideographic explanation, meaning an explanation that pays attention to the distinctive set of circumstances or conditions that brought about an event or behavior. In the Kenya study, the causes of the failure to dispense the new malaria treatment were found to be many, including hording (because of worries about the lack of supplies), staff misunderstandings about the required testing, a preference for the old medication on the part of mothers, and so on. In other words, the study found the problem stemmed from a configuration of causes that were unique to the situation in rural Kenya at the time.

Small-n Studies and Purposive Sampling

Quantitative research typically involves probability (random) selection of people or cases and a large sample size, or a "large *n*" (*n* refers to the *number* of people or cases in the sample). We discuss the ideas and issues of sampling fully in Chapter 5.

Qualitative research, in contrast, most often involves **purposive** or **theoretical sampling** and a "small *n*." In qualitative research, in other words, people or cases are chosen for a specific purpose, or to generate theory, and the number of people or cases is necessarily limited because of the more intensive, time-consuming character of qualitative data collection and analysis. To this extent, qualitative research involves trading off the generalizability that comes with large, random samples for the ability to do more in-depth (thick) description and to select cases of theoretical importance.

The Kenyan study of malaria included $n = 36$ qualitative interviews, but it was based on responses from a prior, quantitative survey of $n = 227$ health workers. Many qualitative studies involve even fewer people or cases (a case study of $n = 1$ even). In contrast, many quantitative surveys involve samples of thousands of people. Here is how the Kenyan researchers describe the basis for selecting their sample:

> Four criteria were applied to these health workers to qualify for inclusion in this qualitative study: 1) they must have received training on the new treatment guidelines; 2) they were working at health facilities where [ACT] was in stock on the day of the survey; 3) they were routinely involved in the diagnosis of malaria at their facility; and 4) during the 2006 facility-based assessment they prescribed [ACT] for less than 40% of patients for whom they made a routine diagnosis of malaria. This group was selected deliberately because of their degree of non-adherence, and the lack of other obvious reasons for this. (Wasunna et al., 2008, p. 3)

In this way, the health workers selected for qualitative interviewing were chosen purposively for an important theoretical reason: to find out why health workers with both training and access to ACT were not prescribing the new therapy to their patients with malaria.

The qualitative sampling in this study from Kenya focused on a particular group of theoretical interest. Another qualitative sampling strategy is to select people or cases to produce theoretically interesting variation.

Say, for example, you want to study leadership styles in nonprofit organizations, and your initial theory or model suggests that leadership style reflects both the size of the organization and the gender of the director. You would then want variation on both these theoretically key dimensions, as in Table 3.1. Selecting cases to fill the four cells of this purposive sampling table would help ensure that your study had theoretically interesting variation.

There are many forms of purposive or theoretical sampling for qualitative research. Patton (2002), for example, lists and discusses 16 different strategies, including sampling typical cases, sampling extreme or deviant cases, snowball or chain sampling (also called respondent-driven sampling), sampling cases that both confirm and disconfirm the theory, sampling politically important cases, and so on. We will return to many of these methods in Chapter 5 on sampling.

Schools of Thought in Qualitative Research

Because qualitative methods originated from various academic disciplines—including anthropology, sociology, psychology, philosophy, and linguistics—there are various schools of thought or intellectual traditions in qualitative research.

For example, one important tradition is *hermeneutics,* which is a philosophy and method of interpretation that originated in the work of 19th-century scholars concerned with deciphering the meaning of ancient or religious texts (Palmer, 1969). Because what people say and do in the social world can be thought of as a "text" of sorts, hermeneutics became an influential approach to the task of interpretation in qualitative social research (Bauman, 2010). Another important tradition in qualitative research is *phenomenology,* which is a philosophy that prioritizes subjective experience and seeks to carefully describe and explain the structure and flow of consciousness (Sokolowski, 1999). Because human beliefs, intentions, and perceptions are often the focus of social research, the phenomenological approach has been adopted by many qualitative researchers as a way to understand the social world (J. Smith, Flowers, & Larkin, 2009).

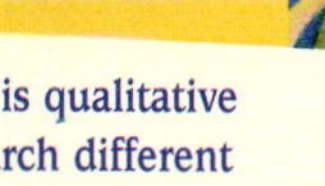
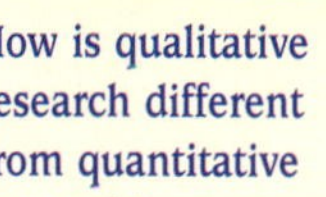

QUESTION

How is qualitative research different from quantitative research?

These are just a few examples of qualitative schools of thought. Qualitative researchers may also describe their work as ethnomethodology, grounded theory, narrative analysis, semiotics, and so on. Sometimes these labels refer to a method as well as a school of thought, but at other times two researchers using an apparently similar method (such as interpreting interviews) will use much different concepts to describe what they are doing. Patton's (2002) comprehensive book on qualitative research methods provides a more in-depth discussion of these various schools of thought. Table 3.2, which is adapted from Patton's book, provides a useful summary of the foundational questions, disciplinary roots, and key thinkers associated with each of these schools of thought.

Although we cannot examine each of these schools of thought in detail, we can make several key points. Qualitative researchers come from different philosophical and epistemological perspectives, often rooted in their disciplinary training. And some schools of qualitative thought argue that qualitative research represents a distinctly different logic of inquiry or epistemology, one that is more humanistic, socially critical, and

Table 3.1 Purposive Sampling of Nonprofit Directors

	Female Director	Male Director
Large nonprofit	Case A	Case B
Small nonprofit	Case C	Case D

skeptical of traditional scientific notions of objectivity and causation (Lincoln & Guba, 1985; Patton, 2002). But throughout this book, we approach qualitative methods as an integral part of the scientific tradition, broadly defined, rather than as a separate approach. At the same time, we recognize that some schools of thought in the qualitative tradition might not agree with our approach.

Advantages of Qualitative Research

We have already emphasized the theory-generating, model-building advantages of qualitative methods. And we have mentioned how qualitative methods can help us understand or uncover causal processes or causal mechanisms at work in a setting. But there are some other specific situations in which qualitative methods are especially useful:

Table 3.2 Qualitative Epistemologies or Schools of Thought

School of Thought	Foundational Questions	Disciplinary Roots	Key Thinkers and Writers
Ethnography	What is the culture of this group of people?	Anthropology	Malinowski, M. Mead, Lévi-Strauss, and Geertz
Ethnomethodology	How do people make sense of their everyday lives?	Sociology	Garfinkel
Grounded theory	What theory emerges from a setting and is grounded in the observations made?	Sociology	Glaser and Strauss
Hermeneutics	How can the original intention of the author of a text, or the producer of a cultural artifact, be interpreted and understood?	Theology, philosophy	Gadamer and Ricoeur
Narratology (narrative analysis)	What does this narrative or story reveal about the person or group that created it?	Literature	Foucault, Bal, and Genette
Phenomenology	What is the meaning and structure of the lived experience of a given phenomenon for this person or group?	Philosophy	Husserl, Schutz, and Merleau-Ponty
Semiotics	How do signs (words, symbols) carry and convey meaning in particular contexts?	Linguistics, literature	Barthes
Social constructivism	How have people in this setting constructed their beliefs and views?	Sociology, philosophy	Berger and Luckmann, Searle
Symbolic interactionism	What common set of symbols and understandings give meaning to people's interactions?	Psychology	G. H. Mead, Cooley, Blumer, and Goffman

Source: Adapted from Patton (2002). Used with permission from Sage Publications.

- Exploratory studies of new or only vaguely understood social or organizational behaviors
- Rapid reconnaissance in situations where time does not permit more structured, quantitative research
- Understanding important individuals, such as leaders of an organization, or unique cases, such as a government agency reacting to a crisis (this is because statistical techniques offer little advantage when only one or a few cases are involved)
- Understanding small groups and group dynamics
- Understanding cultures or subcultures, in large part because cultures are expressed with language and other symbolic systems
- Analyzing visual images or communication
- Analyzing historical or archival texts

Qualitative research has its limitations as well: It is not good for producing precise measurements of variables, estimating characteristics of a large population, calculating the magnitude of relationships between variables, or providing statistical evidence of a cause-effect relationship—although it is good at uncovering possible causes when these are largely unknown, as noted above.

In the sections that follow, we take up the discussion of the various methods and sources of data available for conducting qualitative research for policy and practice. So let's now look more closely at some of these—beginning with already existing qualitative data.

Existing Qualitative Data

Qualitative data can be produced from interviews, focus groups, or other methods of original data collection to be discussed shortly. But a great deal of qualitative data already exist in the form of published and unpublished documents, transcripts, testimonies, tape recordings, official records, correspondence, news articles, and reports, as well as a host of cultural artifacts, such as movies, television, music, art, and so on. In addition, websites, blogs, social media, and other online sources provide a virtual universe of existing qualitative data.

A good example of the use of existing qualitative data is a study done by Harpster, Adams, and Jarvis (2009) about verbal indicators of guilt in 9-1-1 calls involving a reported homicide. Using existing tape recordings of 100 calls made to law enforcement agencies across the United States, the researchers looked for indications of the callers' guilt or innocence. They then compared the indications with the callers' actual guilt or innocence, as established by the courts.

One such indication they found is whether the caller began with a plea for help (a sign of innocence) or merely reported the crime without asking for help (a sign of guilt). Consider the following two calls:

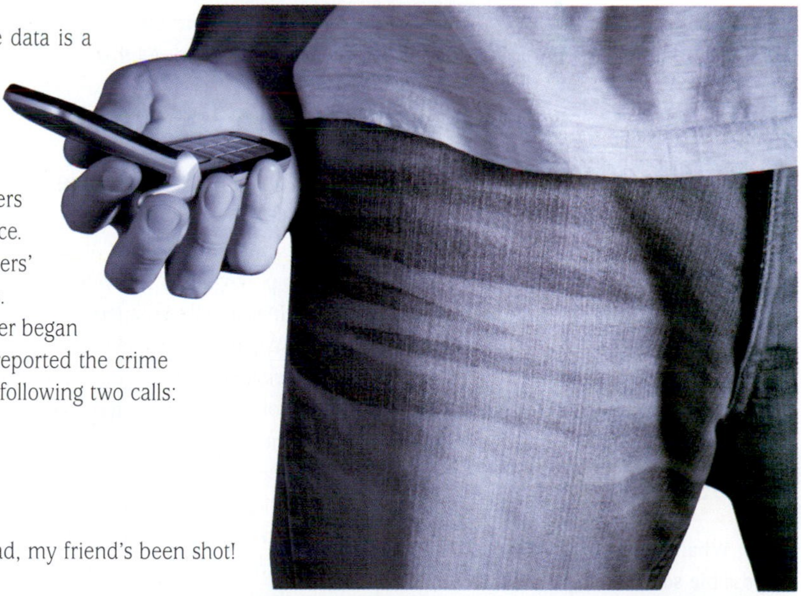

Call 1

Dispatcher: 9-1-1, what is your emergency?

Caller: Get an ambulance to 4200 Dryden Road, my friend's been shot!

Call 2

Dispatcher: 9-1-1, what is your emergency?

Caller: I have an infant, he's not breathing.

Sometimes, people call 9-1-1 to report their own crimes.

Source: © iStockphoto.com/AdamG1975.

In the first case, in which the caller asks for help, the person who made the call was innocent. In the second case, in which the father making the call does not ask for help for his child, a later autopsy revealed that he had in fact shaken his infant son to death. Some of the other key verbal indications of guilt discovered by this study include providing extraneous information, stating conflicting facts, and being inappropriately polite ("Hi, I've been shot, and my husband has been shot").

The findings of this qualitative study have important implications for police investigation of suspected homicides. The study also involved some statistical analysis, which is not uncommon in qualitative studies that involve coding and content analysis. We will address coding and content analysis a bit later in the chapter.

Archival and Other Written Documents

A great deal of information is written down in various texts and official records stored in physical or electronic archives. Historical research can be thought of as a form of qualitative research based largely on finding and interpreting these archived texts and records. But documents represent an important and widely useful form of existing qualitative data for more contemporary issues and problems as well. Some relevant types of documents include the following:

- Testimonies made at hearings or trials
- Legislative floor debates
- Minutes of meetings held by various types of organizations
- Language contained in laws and regulations
- Mission statements or strategic plans
- Official correspondence from elected officials, government administrators, or businesses
- Notes on clients or patients kept in clinical logs
- Letters of inquiry or complaint sent by customers or citizens

In addition, of course, there are the many published sources—newspapers, magazines, books, journals, professional newsletters, and so on. All these various sources of written material or texts can serve as data for qualitative research.

Visual Media, Popular Culture, and the Internet

Thus far, we have dealt mostly with forms of written or oral language. But qualitative data also come in the form of images such as photographs and videos. Sometimes the images come from published or broadcast sources, such as magazines and newspapers, television, movies, and music videos.

A study by Theresa Webb and colleagues, for example, examined popular movies rated PG-13 to assess the level of exposure to violence that is typical of movies frequented by adolescents. They found that violence permeated nearly 90% of the movies in their sample and that nearly 50% contained acts of lethal violence (T. Webb, Jenkins, Browne, Afifi, & Kraus, 2007).

What are some possible sources of existing qualitative data?

As more and more social behavior occurs online, increasing amounts of qualitative data are available on the Internet. Social media, such as Facebook and Twitter, have especially transformed the way in which people communicate and interact socially and professionally. These newly available sources of secondary qualitative data have given rise to a whole new field of inquiry, referred to variously as virtual anthropology, online ethnography, webnography, and netnography (Kozinets, 2009).

Although plenty of qualitative data already exist, often researchers find that they need to collect their own, original qualitative data. One of the most direct means of doing so is to interview people.

Qualitative Interviews

Interviewing is a basic methodological tool in qualitative research, one that can be used alone or as part of participant observation or case studies (discussed a bit later on). Qualitative interviews involve **open-ended questions** that allow people to respond in their own words and that encourage detailed and in-depth answers. In this way, they differ from the highly structured, largely closed-ended (check-the-box) questions characteristic of most surveys (discussed in Chapter 7). Qualitative interviews can be described as either unstructured or semistructured.

Unstructured Interviews

Unstructured interviews have no predetermined set of questions. An unstructured interview can seem much like an ordinary conversation, but there are important differences. As Robert Weiss (1994) explains in his book *Learning From Strangers,*

> In an ordinary conversation, each participant voices observations, thoughts, feelings. Either participant can set a new topic, either can ask questions. In the qualitative interview the respondent provides information while the interviewer, as a representative of the study, is responsible for directing the respondent to the topics that matter to the study. (p. 8)

Weiss (1994) gives an example from an interview of a 66-year-old woman conducted as part of a study of how people adjust to retirement after a lifetime of work. The topic of the study provides a general framework for the discussion, but much of the interview centers on what the woman has to say about her everyday life and, in particular, her isolation and withdrawal from society. The interviewer's questions are not scripted but rather arise spontaneously in response to what the woman says during the interview. For example, at one point in the interview, the woman mentions that her daughter recently encouraged her to volunteer. In response, the interviewer asks, "Could you walk me through that conversation with your daughter where she made the suggestion to volunteer?" (Weiss, 1994, p. 6). A fairly long and detailed response follows.

Unstructured interviews are typical of participant observation or ethnographic research in which the researcher is embedded in a setting for an extended period of time, sometimes years. A good example is Robert Smith's (2005) ethnography of Mexican immigrants in New York City. Participation over a long period helps establish the trust needed to conduct in-depth, unstructured interviews of informants, such as recent immigrants, who may be much less forthcoming in more structured, one-shot interviews.

Sometimes, however, qualitative researchers need to conduct interviews that are more structured—semistructured interviews as they are called. But it's important to understand that all qualitative interviewing involves some structure and that, in practice, the distinction is often more one of degree than one of kind.

Semistructured Interviews

The study of treating malaria in Kenya involved **semistructured interviews** of workers in local health dispensaries. Here is how Wasunna and colleagues (2008) describe their data collection method:

> Since the study was addressing the sensitive topic of nonadherence to guidelines, individual in-depth interviews (IDIs) were selected as the most appropriate data collection tool to investigate opinions and reasons underlying such behavior. A semi-structured interview guide was developed which allowed for flexibility within the discussions, and explored health worker perceptions about the new treatment policy and reasons underlying their decisions not to prescribe [ACT]. The influence of perceived severity of

illness on prescribing practices was explored through a case vignette methodology in which health workers were asked to respond to a specific case management scenario. (p. 3)

Notice that the in-depth interviews followed a semistructured **interview guide**. A semistructured interview guide is a set of open-ended questions, sometimes accompanied by probes, that help guide or structure the discussion. It helps ensure that each interview covers substantially the same topics, although the guide is meant to be a flexible tool and not a standardized script. Some respondents may have a lot to say about certain topics and less about other topics, and the order in which topics come up during the course of the interview may vary. A good qualitative interviewer does not read from a script.

In the Kenyan study, the researchers also presented a vignette (a short, written description) of a malaria case and asked the health workers how they would respond to the case. Presenting respondents with a vignette, a photograph, or some other kind of written or visual information can help prompt discussion, as well as vary the pace of an in-depth interview that can last 2 hours or more.

To get a sense of what a semistructured interview guide looks like, let's consider another health study involving rural parents in Canada (N. Miller, Verhoef, & Cardwell, 2008). These researchers were interested in understanding how rural parents acquired and used health information to make decisions about immunizing their children. Figure 3.1 presents the semistructured interview guide Nancy Miller and her colleagues followed in their interviews with parents.

QUESTION

What are the differences between an unstructured interview and a semistructured interview?

Notice first that there are only 11 questions, yet the interviews likely took at least an hour or more. Semistructured interview guides typically have fewer than 20 questions, sometimes fewer than 10. This is because the questions are intentionally open-ended—meaning they ask for an explanation rather than just brief answers. Asking many "what" or "how" questions tends to help in this regard; for example, "What information did you need and/or want to know?" When a yes/no question is asked, it is followed by an open-ended probe. For example, "Did you use information in the decision? If yes, what role did the information play?" Although it appears simple, it takes time and careful thought to craft a good semistructured interview guide.

Figure 3.1 Semistructured Interview Guide Used to Study Immunization in Rural Canada

1. Could you tell me about the journey/process you went through in making a decision about immunizing your child?
2. Did you use information in the decision? If yes, what role did the information play? Were there other influences in your decision about immunizing?
3. What were the sources of information you used? Where did you look? Please tell me if you found information readily available to you.
4. What information did you need and/or want to know?
5. Did you find information from the sources you used conflicting or confusing? If so, how did you handle it?
6. In your opinion, what makes up good information?
7. Credibility criteria:
    - How did you determine what kind of information was going to be helpful?
    - How did you decide who to believe and trust as sources of information?
    - How did you determine they were experts?
    - What specifically made the information reliable from your perspective?
8. Health professionals:
    - Did you find the information given you by health professionals addressed your concerns/questions adequately? Please explain.
    - Did they give consistent information about immunization or were there differences?

9. What is your preference in how you receive information?
10. Do you have any ideas/recommendations of how information can be conveyed to parents more effectively?
11. Do you have any recommendations for health professionals in how they provide and share information to parents about immunization?

Source: N. Miller et al. (2008).

Asking Truly Open-Ended Questions

Writing questions that are truly open-ended takes practice. Say, for example, we are interested in studying leadership in a nonprofit organization and want to hear from middle managers. We might include in our interview guide a question such as this:

Do you consider your executive director to be a good leader, or not?

Fair enough. But because middle managers tend not to want to talk too much about their executive director, especially if they have something unflattering to say, we might not get much discussion going. "I guess he's OK—better than the last one," we might hear, but that doesn't give us much information or insight. But we can use "what" and "how" to ask the question another way:

Tell me how your executive director is, or is not, a good leader.

Or perhaps better:

What makes your executive director a good leader—or what makes him not such a good leader?

These questions are more open-ended—they do not let the respondents off the hook, as it were, so easily. The respondents must explain their answer—*how* he is a good leader (or not) and *what* makes him a good leader (or not).

The Power of Probes

Experienced interviewers have a certain touch—getting people to talk, to open up. Think of a good TV or radio talk show host—many of them have this skill. For example, Terry Gross of National Public Radio, host of the show *Fresh Air,* is well known for her skillful questioning. Her in-depth interviews with authors, artists, politicians, and others can be heard online at www.npr.org/programs/fresh-air. You'll notice several things if you listen carefully: (1) She does not talk much—the airspace, as it were, is carefully reserved for the respondent; (2) at the same time, she keeps the interview from wandering off topic and helps focus it and move it along; (3) she uses truly open-ended questions that encourage thoughtful expression; and (4) she uses simple probes in a surprisingly effective manner at key moments in the interview. Here are some common probes she and other experienced interviewers tend to use to good effect:

- Say more about that.
- Explain that to me.
- Why is that important to you?
- Tell me what happened.
- Can you give me an example of that?
- What was that like for you?

- What did that mean to you?
- What made you think of that just now?
- What led up to that?
- What happened next?

This kind of open-ended probing is part of what makes in-depth, qualitative interviewing different from the structured, mostly closed-ended questioning typical of quantitative survey research.

Some Practical Considerations When Doing Interviews

There are a number of practical considerations in doing interviews. To begin with, should the interview be conducted in person, on the telephone, or some other way? In-person interviews are generally favored as they show respect, establish rapport, allow for visuals or handouts, and capture body language and voice tone. In-person interviewing sometimes allows the researcher to visit the location where the respondent lives or works, permitting direct observation of the setting. However, sometimes an in-person visit is not practical, so interviewing by telephone, Skype, video call, or even e-mail is an option.

Another practical consideration is whether to use audio (or video) recording, or just take notes, and whether recordings should be transcribed. The answers depend on the available resources, the timeline, the sensitivity of the topic, and the importance of capturing exact wording for later analysis and reporting. Most researchers make an audio recording of the interview, provided the respondent agrees and that the recording does not inhibit a candid discussion.

Another decision is whether to interview respondents once (a cross section) or on several occasions over time. Depending on the nature of the research, it may be useful to interview the same respondent on multiple occasions over a period of time. This will allow for information about changes or temporal dynamics.

Another decision is how much to tell the respondent in advance about the topics of the interview. For some studies, it may even be helpful to send the outline of topics in advance so that the person can review them and prepare for the interview. Revealing the questions in advance can be necessary sometimes for getting the person to agree to do the interview. But more often, it is sufficient simply to describe the purpose, sponsorship, and general topic of the interview.

Let's turn now to another type of interview—a group interview called a focus group.

Focus Groups

Focus groups are one of most widely used, and widely useful, methods of qualitative research—especially applied research for policy and practice. The method consists essentially of a group interview typically involving 6 to 12 people. The number of participants should be enough to make the discussion lively, but not so many that the size of the group inhibits engagement. The participants sit around a table, along with a **moderator** who asks questions and guides the group discussion. An audio and sometimes video recording of the discussion is made for later analysis. An assistant moderator sits off to one side, and often observers watch the discussion from behind a two-way mirror. Figure 3.2 presents a typical layout of a focus group facility. Although firms rent out specialized focus group facilities that look like this, it is quite possible to hold focus groups in an ordinary conference or meeting room.

Typically a focus group study involves at least 2 or 3 separate focus groups to allow for the possibility of confirming or replicating findings. Some studies can comprise 20 or more separate focus groups, with much depending on the number of subgroups of interest in the study. A school system, for example, may want to hear from parents, students, and teachers to get ideas about a new program or initiative. But the discussion would be less open if we mixed these three subgroups together. Instead, it is preferable to hold separate focus groups of parents only, students only, and teachers only. To feel confident that we have represented the views

Figure 3.2 Layout of a Typical Focus Group Facility

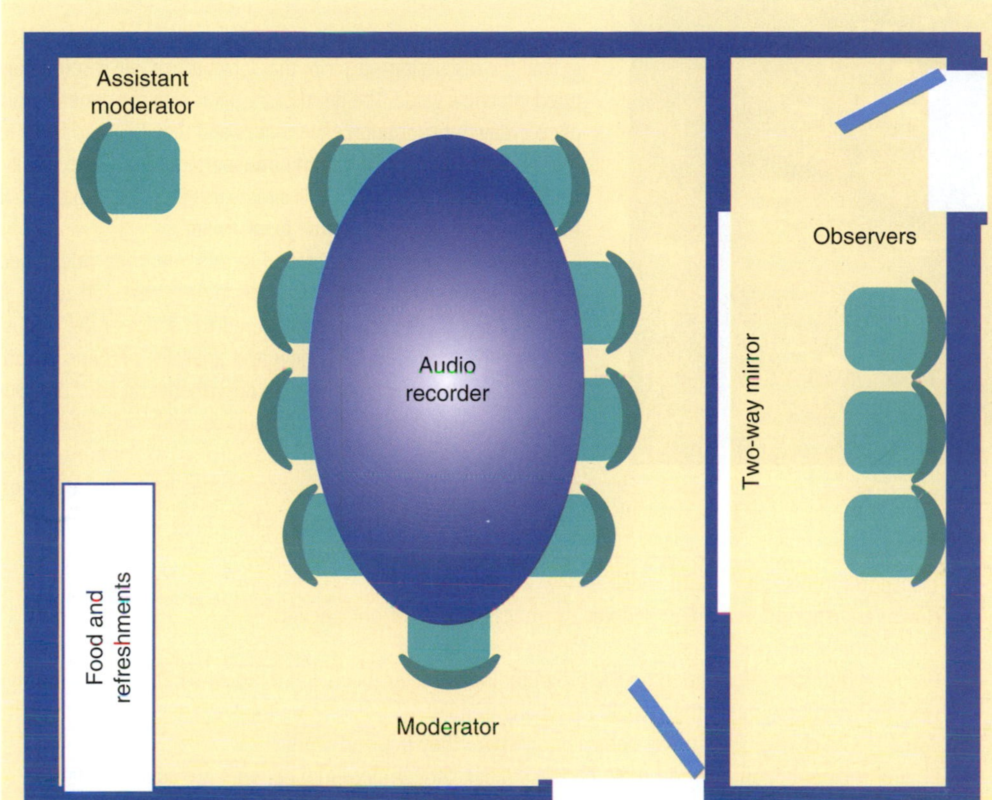

of each subgroup adequately, however, a study like this would require at least six to nine separate discussions—two to three for each subgroup.

It is generally best to organize focus groups of people who do not know each other too well, as sometimes prior issues or personal relationships can inhibit or distort the discussion. But this may not always be possible, for example when studying an organization, a neighborhood, or a professional network.

What Do People Think of Congestion Pricing?

To get more into the details of the focus group method, let's consider an example. The U.S. Federal Highway Administration commissioned a focus group study of public attitudes toward congestion pricing for the use of roads and highways during peak times (Petrella, Biernbaum, & Lappin, 2007). The study consisted of four focus groups in the northern Virginia suburbs of Washington, DC (representing a fast-growing metro area) and four focus groups in the Philadelphia area (representing an older, slow-growth metro area). In each area, two of the four focus groups were made up of the general driving public, while the other two were composed of small business owners and representatives of shipping and transportation companies.

This selection of locations and of different user groups illustrates well the purposive nature of qualitative sampling. Typically, an incentive payment is offered to help ensure that participants will show up as scheduled at the focus group facility and to compensate them for their time. Often focus group participants are recruited by telephone, from lists or from random dialing, but then screened for certain experiences or characteristics.

Focus groups can help reveal what people think about important issues, like congestion pricing.

Source: © iStockphoto .com/egdigital.

Moderating a Focus Group

The moderator of these focus groups follows a moderator's guide to lead the discussion—a script that looks much like a semistructured interview guide. The discussions open with the general topic of everyday transportation experiences and then begin to focus in more on the question of funding transportation and, specifically, congestion pricing. Figure 3.3 illustrates this focusing-in pattern of the discussion (hence the name *focus group*).

The discussions are audiotaped (and sometimes videotaped as well) for later review and analysis by the research team. If time and resources permit, a full typed transcript of the discussion may be produced for review and analysis, perhaps including coding and content analysis (as described a bit later on). But often the audio recordings alone suffice, with only illustrative quotes transcribed verbatim. The aim is to capture major themes or insights. Here are some themes from the report on congestion pricing (Petrella et al., 2007, p. 8):

- Transportation issues: "Traffic dictates how we live our lives"
- How is transportation funded: general awareness, but short on specifics
- Congestion-based pricing: they get it, for the most part
- People want more information on the program; in particular they want to know what their tax savings would be and how much they would be paying in tolls
- Some would change their travel behavior, or where they live and work
- Environmental benefits not on most people's radar, though potential benefits are acknowledged

Figure 3.3 General Flow of a Focus Group Discussion

Open with an easy, general discussion:
"What are some of the transportation issues or concerns you have in your everyday life?"

Steer the discussion toward the topic:
"How is transportation funded–how should it be funded?"

Focus on the topic:
"What do you think of the idea of congestion pricing?"
- Probe
- Test ideas

Confirm/validate main points

Why a Focus Group? Why Not Individual Interviews?

You might be wondering, "What are the reasons for having a focus *group* discussion, as opposed to a series of *individual* interviews?" There are several reasons:

- As a practical matter, the research team can interview 6 to 12 people at one time and place rather than having to schedule and conduct that many individual interviews.
- But more important, individuals in the group cue or prompt each other in ways that an interviewer—even an experienced and well-prepared one—is not able to do in a one-on-one interview. This within-group cuing and prompting can spark an animated discussion and help uncover important issues.
- People will agree or disagree on topics, thus allowing the researcher to see what views are widely shared versus views that are more idiosyncratic. In this way, it helps the researcher better understand the generalizability of qualitative findings.
- Many important issues or topics in social life are influenced by group processes or how others around us view and discuss the matter. Focus groups mimic this social process of knowing or thinking about an issue.

There are reasons not to have focus group discussions as well. The method does not work well for personal or sensitive topics that people do not feel comfortable discussing among a group of strangers. As indicated earlier, focus groups often do not succeed with groups of people who already work together or know each other well (because prior issues and relationships tend to overshadow or distort the discussion). And focus groups do not provide depth on any one individual's experiences.

Telephone and Online Focus Groups

Recruiting participants to show up at a facility at a given time and place can require much effort and inconvenience. Moreover, there are situations in which the potential participants reside in such geographically dispersed locations that they cannot assemble for an in-person discussion. As a result, some studies conduct focus groups by telephone or online.

In a telephone focus group, the respondents use a dial-in conference calling service to connect with each other and the moderator at an agreed-on time. As in a regular focus group, the moderator leads the discussion following a semistructured guide, and the discussion is recorded (most conference calling services can do this for a fee). Because of the lack of visual cues and call quality issues with multiple parties on the line, it is often better in a telephone focus group to have fewer participants (4 to 6, rather than 6 to 12). The length of the discussion tends to be shorter as well (about 60 minutes rather than the 90 minutes or more that is typical of in-person focus groups).

QUESTION

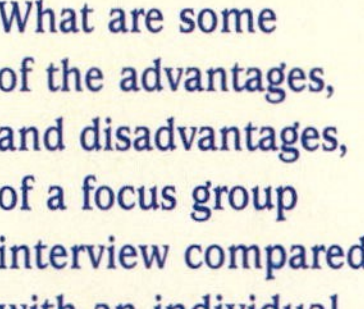

What are some of the advantages, and disadvantages, of a focus group interview compared with an individual interview?

Online focus groups are another possibility these days, and indeed a number of market research firms specialize in organizing and conducting focus groups on the Web. Web conferencing services, such as WebEx, GoToMeeting, or even Skype, provide Web-based software that can be used to conduct your own online focus group. Some companies, such as GroupQuality and VisionsLive, offer more specialized online focus group software. Using the Web for focus groups is especially suited to situations in which participants need to respond to visual materials, such as ad copy, a video clip, or a slide presentation. Obviously, online focus groups work only with participants who have ready access to the Internet and are comfortable with using Web-based communications.

Qualitative Observation

Qualitative research sometimes involves direct observation of behavior. Rather than interview people, the researcher directly observes a setting or behavior and takes notes or records the observations using still or video photography. Capturing the observations in this way allows for later, more careful, review and interpretation.

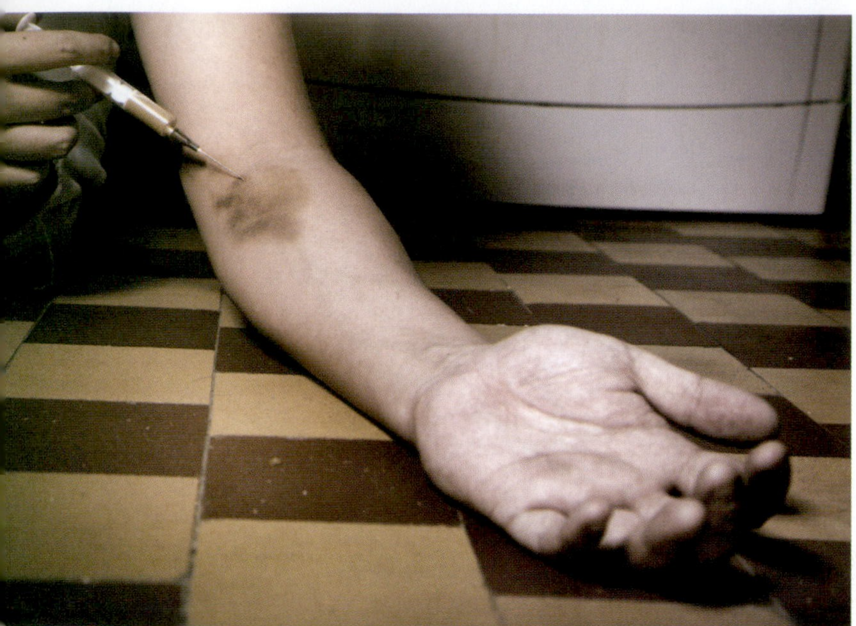

Injection drug users can spread hepatitis C.
Source: © iStockphoto.com/ Zhenikeyev.

Take for example a study of hepatitis C prevention by Treloar and colleagues (2008), who videotaped the injecting episodes of drug users in a medically supervised clinic in Sydney, Australia, to study risky practices. An analysis of the videos identified 27 risky practices, such as not washing hands or swabbing the injection site, injecting against the direction of blood flow, and using fingers to stop the bleeding or even licking blood off the injection site. As the authors conclude about their findings,

> The strength of this study relies on the use of video recordings of injecting episodes. . . . It is very difficult to accurately record the behaviours observed in this study using self-report or even during real-time observation: we viewed each video multiple times to accurately record practice. (Treloar et al., 2008, p. 64)

Photography and videography are used in similar ways to study a wide range of behaviors, including classroom interactions in a school or the behavior of suspects and officers during a police interrogation.

Participant Observation and Ethnography

Sometimes to understand a group or social situation, you must join it—that is the essential idea behind **participant observation** (Jorgensen, 1989). The method is associated with **ethnography**, bringing to mind the image of an anthropologist like Margaret Mead living among indigenous people like the Samoans in remote corners of the world (Mead, 1971). But participant observation can be useful for social and policy research in settings closer to home as well.

Why Do the Homeless Refuse Help?

Often homeless individuals with psychiatric problems refuse offers of help despite their desperate need for food, housing, and medical care. Why? Tanya Marie Luhrmann (2008) provided some answers to this question based on more than 1,000 hours of participant observation over 3 years in one Chicago neighborhood. As she describes her method (talking about herself in the third person): "She spent most of her time in the drop-in center but also met with women she knew from the drop-in center in local shelters, parks, and restaurants. These meetings were casual, unscripted, and dominated by the subject's concerns" (Luhrmann, 2008, p. 15). One of her key findings was that many of the women wanted to avoid the designation of being "crazy" provided by a diagnosis of psychiatric disability, which was often a condition for receiving housing and other benefits.

Notice how the study took many hours and required a fairly long period of involvement of the researcher in the setting. This is typical of ethnographic studies. Such studies are especially well suited to broad, complex, and open-ended research questions (such as why homeless people refuse much-needed assistance). As the research is conducted, important themes and topics emerge.

Notice too how ethnography tends to make use of unstructured interviews, particularly once the trust of participants has been gained. Indeed, the long-term involvement of the researcher in the setting and with the lives of participants greatly facilities access to people and encourages more open, in-depth, and revealing discussions. This is one of the key advantages of ethnography.

Why do some homeless people refuse help?

Source: © iStockphoto .com/skyak.

Levels on a Participation-Observation Continuum

The researcher may participate in and interact with the setting to a greater or lesser extent. As a result, qualitative researchers often think in terms of a participation-observation continuum of possible roles, following Gold's (1958) original categorization:

Complete participant, in which the researcher takes on a central role in the setting—for example, becoming a teacher's assistant in order to study a disadvantaged school

Participant as observer, in which the researcher spends significant time in the setting, joining in important activities or events, but does not assume an actual role as such (Luhrmann's [2008] study of homeless people in Chicago is a good example.)

Observer as participant, in which the researcher visits the setting, typically only on one of just a few occasions, to conduct interviews with people and make observations

Complete observer, in which the researcher attempts to remain unobtrusive and does not interview or engage with people in the setting—for example, sitting in an emergency room waiting area in order to observe the interactions of patients and staff

The level of active participation versus unobtrusive observation depends on the setting, the research aims, and the relationship the researcher has with the setting. And there are trade-offs. Participation provides a unique, firsthand perspective many times, but it also risks influencing the very behaviors that you are trying to observe. Participation is also time-consuming and can create ethical dilemmas, as described at the end of the chapter.

Secret Shopping and Audit Studies

In consumer studies, researchers sometimes use a form of participant observation called the *secret (or mystery) shopping method*—playing the role of a customer to experience service quality. But the same approach can be used to evaluate welfare offices, emergency rooms, visitor information centers, 3-1-1 help lines, libraries, and so on. For example, a team of field-workers might visit library branches to make standard requests for information and assistance, making notes afterward about various aspects of their visit.

QUESTION

In what ways is a study based on participant observation different from one based on qualitative interviews?

A related example is *audit studies,* which have been used to investigate discrimination in employment, housing, and lending (Struyk & Fix, 1993). In an audit study of job discrimination, for example, matched pairs of auditors who are similar in most job-related characteristics (and given the same résumé and coaching)—yet differ in race—visit an employer to apply for a job. Discrimination is inferred if there is a systematic difference in job offers. Audit studies are primarily a form of randomized experiment (covered in Chapter 14), but the auditors also observe the setting and how they are treated. Thus, audit studies are—in a very real sense—a form of short-term participant observation.

As the examples of secret shopping and audit studies illustrate, at times, participant observation can involve the observer going underground, as it were, and disguising himself or herself to experience or test the setting. This raises ethical issues that we discuss later in this chapter. But more often in participant observation, including ethnography, the researcher identifies himself or herself as a researcher, and then proceeds to join the setting to observe and interview people.

Case Study Research

As we mentioned earlier, qualitative research is grounded in the in-depth study of cases, such as people, groups, or organizations. So in one sense, it would seem that most qualitative research could be defined as case study research. But the term **case study** tends to be reserved for research that focuses on one case or just a few complex cases.[1] Case studies also typically involve a larger, aggregate-level case—such as an organization, a neighborhood, or a nation-state—rather than an individual person. In clinical research, however, there are case studies of individual patients with a particular condition or disease. And in leadership studies, case studies of individual leaders are not uncommon.

Maryland's Gun Violence Act

To get the flavor of a case study, let's consider the following abstract from an article by Frattaroli and Teret (2006) in the journal *Evaluation Review*:

> The Maryland Gun Violence Act, enacted into law in 1996, explicitly authorized courts to order batterers to surrender their firearms through civil protective orders. It also vested law enforcement with the explicit authority to remove guns when responding to a domestic violence complaint. In order to assess how these laws were implemented, we designed a case study and collected data from in-depth, key informant interviews, court observations, and relevant documents. We present findings from this study and recommend how to increase the likelihood that policies designed to separate batterers and guns are implemented in a way that will result in greater protections for victims of domestic violence. (p. 347)

The study found that ambiguities in the language of the law left police officers uncertain about how to carry out the new policies in specific domestic violence situations. And it revealed that leadership commitment to the new policies within police departments influenced how fully and aggressively police officers applied their new authority.

This case study uses many of the qualitative methods discussed earlier—in-depth interviews, participant observation in courtrooms, and the analysis of existing documents. In this sense, the case study is not a different method of qualitative data collection but makes use of several qualitative data collection methods. Moreover, case studies can even involve quantitative methods—a survey of employees within one organization,

[1]Research case studies should not be confused with teaching cases, although both are in-depth analyses of one particular organization or situation. The practice of teaching cases began in business schools but has spread to many public policy schools and other applied programs.

for example—and frequently a combination of qualitative and quantitative data (mixed methods). The case study uses as many methods as needed to get the fullest possible picture of a particular case.

Note that although the study investigates one law in Maryland, it aims to uncover aspects of implementation that can be applied to similar policies and programs in other places or contexts. The individual case, in other words, provides an opportunity to discover generalizable knowledge. The aim is to gather enough details of the particular case to learn about variables, mechanisms, and patterns that would be relevant to other cases and contexts.

Selecting a Case to Study

Given that a case study often involves just one case, how should we make the selection? There are several approaches. *Paradigmatic* case selection involves selecting an average case that offers the greatest generalizability, revealing what is typical. For example, we might want to study the typical role of leadership in public schools by picking a school with average student characteristics and test scores. However, it might be preferable for some research purposes to select an *extreme* case. For example, we might want to study the role of leadership in a particularly successful school, one that has exceptional test scores and is well above average. Another approach is to choose *critical* cases, cases that exhibit particular characteristics that have theoretical or practical significance. Continuing with our example, we might want to study the role of leadership in a school that has dramatically improved, going from failing to succeeding in terms of test scores (or other measures of educational performance).

Robert Yin's (2008) book *Case Study Research* explains case selection and also provides a good starting point for learning more about case study design and methods more generally. (For more technical approaches to case selection, see also Seawright and Gerring [2008].)

QUESTION

In what ways does case study research overlap with other methods of qualitative data collection? In what ways is it a different approach?

Comparing Cases

Although many case studies involve just a single case, like the study in Maryland, *comparative case studies* involving two or more cases often provide additional analytical leverage. Specifically, the researcher can employ cross-case analysis in addition to within-case analysis to uncover influential factors or explanations. This is an approach traditionally found in history and comparative politics (Lijphart, 1971; Skocpol & Somers, 1980). Certainly, the choice of cases to compare becomes critical, as it substantially shapes the contrasts that will emerge from the findings. Comparative case studies often involve only two or three cases, but sometimes they can involve a larger number of cases (but still fewer than a typical quantitative study).

Qualitative Data Analysis

The raw data from qualitative research typically take the form of field notes, interview transcriptions, video or audio recordings, or documents. *Qualitative data analysis* involves the organization and interpretation of these materials. There are three main steps involved in qualitative data analysis (from Creswell, 2006):

- Preparing and organizing the data
- Reducing and summarizing the data, possibly through a process of coding
- Presenting the data, in narrative form, figures, and/or tables

Simply reading, reviewing, and thinking about the data is an essential aspect of qualitative data analysis. But researchers also employ various strategies and tools to organize and interpret qualitative data, which we will discuss shortly. But it helps to begin with a few general points about qualitative data analysis and how it differs from quantitative analysis.

Integration of Analysis and Data Gathering

Qualitative analysis often happens not just at the end of data collection, as with quantitative analysis, but simultaneously with the collection of interviews or other qualitative data. As the researcher conducts interviews or makes observations, patterns and interpretations occur to the researcher, and these influence the course of further data collection. In this way, qualitative analysis is often an integral part of qualitative data collection, as Figure 3.4 illustrates. Notice from this figure that one way to decide how many interviews, focus groups, or observations are "enough" in a qualitative study is that this process of data, analysis, more data, more analysis, and so on reaches a point of **saturation:** Few new questions or issues arise that have not already been discovered.

The process of analysis and interpretation in qualitative research largely occurs within the mind of the researcher. Therefore, it can be easy to conflate or confuse an objective observation with a subjective interpretation. (This problem, by the way, is not unique to qualitative research and can happen also in more quantitative analysis.) Good qualitative researchers learn to approach their subjects with an open mind, to be transparent in their methods, to look for cases that disprove as well as prove their assumptions, and to support their conclusions with evidence.

Figure 3.4 General Flow of Qualitative Analysis

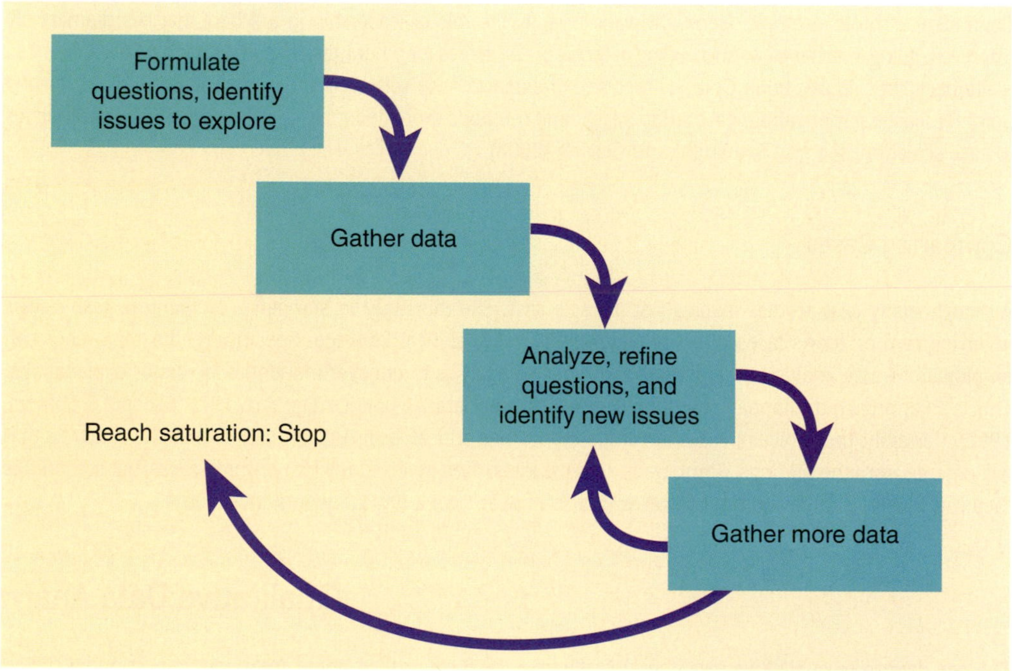

Tools of Qualitative Analysis

Analyzing qualitative data, such as a batch of interviews or focus groups, can be a daunting task. Interviews or focus groups are often lengthy and wide ranging, and the ambiguities of language (particularly spoken language) can make it difficult to decipher what people mean. It can also take a few hours to carefully read or relisten to even a single in-depth interview or focus group, which of course implies that the task of analyzing a dozen or more interviews or focus groups can take days if not weeks. Qualitative data analysis is a time-consuming process. What tools and techniques do qualitative researchers use to make this task manageable and to make sense of their data?

One important tool is to debrief after each interview, focus group, or period of participant observation. *Debriefing* involves writing down (or voice recording) your immediate impressions or ideas while they are fresh in your mind. Thus, it is important to allow time for this as part of the data collection process. These debriefing notes provide a head start on the development of codes and themes and thus save time later during the analysis stage. Because the collection of qualitative data takes place typically over many weeks or months, many qualitative researchers also keep a journal to record more general ideas and interpretations that occur over the course of their fieldwork. Such a journal helps a great deal to organize and focus the later task of analysis.

Qualitative data itself begins with carefully reading or listening to the transcribed or recorded interviews or focus groups, describing or summarizing what people have said, and adding annotations or memos to the data. As part of this task, it is especially important to look for links or connections among interviews or ideas as well as more general themes or patterns. Some of the more specific tools of qualitative data analysis include the following (from Creswell, 2006):

- Sketching ideas
- Making notes or memos
- Summarizing observations or interviews
- Creating codes
- Counting the frequency of codes
- Reducing codes into themes
- Relating themes to each other
- Relating themes to relevant literature or theory

The specific tools and techniques employed in any given qualitative data analysis vary greatly depending on the method and purpose of the study. For example, analyzing unstructured interviews or participant observation is a much different process than analyzing a batch of more structured interviews. And a qualitative study for an academic dissertation is bound to be much more detailed than a rapid reconnaissance done for an administrative or other applied purpose.

There is a growing literature on the many different techniques of qualitative data analysis (Corbin & Strauss, 2007; Grbich, 2012; Miles & Huberman, 1994). But perhaps the most general tool for analysis of qualitative data is coding, so let's look more closely at how this is done.

Coding and Content Analysis

Coding refers to a process of tagging the text or other qualitative data using a system of categories, a *coding scheme*—essentially the creation of variables. Coding enables sorting, counting, and other quantitative analysis, but it can also be used without any quantitative analysis—simply as a way to facilitate interpretation of a body of qualitative data. This process of coding and analyzing qualitative data is also referred to as **content analysis**.

To illustrate, recall the earlier example of the study of 9-1-1 calls for indications of innocence or guilt. The raw data for this study consisted of 100 recordings of 9-1-1 calls made to various police and sheriff's departments across the United States to report a homicide. The researchers developed a set of 8 verbal indicators of innocence and 12 verbal indicators of guilt—codes—drawing on theory and prior research. They then examined each call to see if each of the 20 indicators applied or not. So each call had 20 codes, one for each indicator.

Let's try applying some of the categories or codes used in this study. Here are some of the verbal indicators of guilt:

A. Resistance in answering

B. Repetition

C. Conflicting facts

D. Extraneous information

E. Inappropriate politeness

F. Insulting or blaming the victim

G. The "huh?" factor (being caught off guard when asked a simple question)

Now let's consider the transcripts of several calls. For each call, see if you think that any of the codes apply.

Call 1

Dispatcher: Do you know what's wrong with your daughter?

Caller: Not a clue.

Dispatcher: Has she taken any medications?

Caller: She might have—she's very, very sneaky. She threw a huge temper tantrum earlier; she might have taken something.

Call 2

Dispatcher: 9-1-1, what is your emergency?

Caller: Hi, I've been shot, and my husband has been shot.

Call 3

Dispatcher: 9-1-1, what is your emergency?

Caller: I just came home, and my wife has fallen down the stairs! She's hurt bad, and she's not breathing!

Dispatcher: How many stairs did she fall down?

Caller: Huh?

As you can see, determining which codes apply to a segment of text like this takes some thought. You have to read the call carefully, perhaps reread it a few times, review the available codes, and decide which applies.

As it turns out, Call 1 is an example of Code F, insulting or blaming the victim. Call 2 is an example of Code E, inappropriate politeness (saying "Hi" does not seem quite right when reporting that you and your husband have been shot). And Call 3 is an example of Code G, the "huh?" factor, being caught off guard by a simple question. This example involves only short verbal exchanges and a relatively simple coding scheme. The task of coding many in-depth interviews, with a more elaborate coding scheme, can take many, many hours.

The consistency with which codes are applied to the text becomes an important issue in coding and content analysis—sometimes referred to as **intercoder reliability**. We will have more to say about the concept of reliability in the next chapter on measurement, but the basic idea is that if you repeat the coding of a particular text, it should result in a consistent category or score. If two coders both assign Code F to Call 1, in other words, this is evidence that the coding of the data is reliable. Even if just one person does all the coding, his or her own consistency in coding should be examined. Researchers sometimes pick interviews or observation to code a second time, just to check their own consistency.

Where Do Codes Come From?

Coding schemes can be developed deductively or inductively, and typically the coding scheme develops and changes as it is used. Codes may be created deductively from just thinking about a topic, from theory, or from prior studies. But codes also arise inductively from reading and interpreting the qualitative data. As such, the coding scheme typically evolves and changes as the analysis proceeds. Codes can be renamed, clarified, collapsed together, split apart, and otherwise reorganized. In an important sense, the development and refinement of a coding scheme itself sheds much light on the interpretation of the data. As we will see next, the task of developing, changing, and refining a coding scheme is greatly facilitated by the use of qualitative analysis software.

To Code or Not to Code?

Not all qualitative research involves coding, and some researchers use coding only as a supplement to more interpretive methods. Coded data can be analyzed quantitatively, but some feel that doing so sacrifices many of the advantages of qualitative research—its rich, thick description and focus on cases, rather than variables. But the decision to code does not mean that other forms of qualitative analysis cannot also be done. And coding can be done purely to better organize qualitative data for later in-depth interpretation, without any intention of doing statistical analysis.

Qualitative Data Analysis Software

With advances in technology, computer software programs have been developed to help with the tasks of qualitative data analysis. Increasingly, qualitative data—including audio and video recordings, photos, and documents—are now readily digitized and can be stored, organized, and analyzed in electronic form. Moreover, the capabilities of qualitative analysis software have improved and now accommodate qualitative data in many different formats, including both text and PDF, digital photographs, MP3 and other audio files, and digital video files.

The software includes tools to segment, tag, and categorize the content of these various files so that they can be sorted and analyzed. While software is particularly valuable for coding and content analysis, it can also be valuable purely for data management and organized note taking.

Some of the more widely used qualitative analysis software programs are NVivo, Atlas.ti, and Ethnograph. There are some freeware programs as well, including AnSWR and EZ-Text (both provided by the CDC), as well as RQDA (which runs in the R open-source statistical computing package). Figure 3.5 shows a screenshot of NVivo to give you a flavor of what this kind of software looks like. Qualitative analysis software allows researchers to do many things that are difficult or impossible to do by hand, including the following:

- Store and organize qualitative data in electronic form, including text, images, and audio files
- Search interviews or field notes for key words or phrases
- Create coding categories, as well as flexibly edit or rearrange categories as the analysis proceeds
- Apply codes to segments of text, images, or audio files
- Accommodate multiple coders and provide information on intercoder reliability
- Use codes to retrieve or gather selected segments of text, images, or audio files
- Group or combine codes together into themes
- Track or count the co-occurrence of categories or themes
- Visualize qualitative data as graphs or models

Although it provides many efficiencies and new capabilities, qualitative data analysis software is not a substitute for careful, thoughtful interpretation. It is a useful tool, but it does not do the thinking for you. And in some situations, such as a small focus group study or rapid reconnaissance of a situation, it may not be worth the time and effort required to transcribe, code, recode, and analyze the data using software.

Figure 3.5 Screenshot of NVivo Qualitative Analysis Software

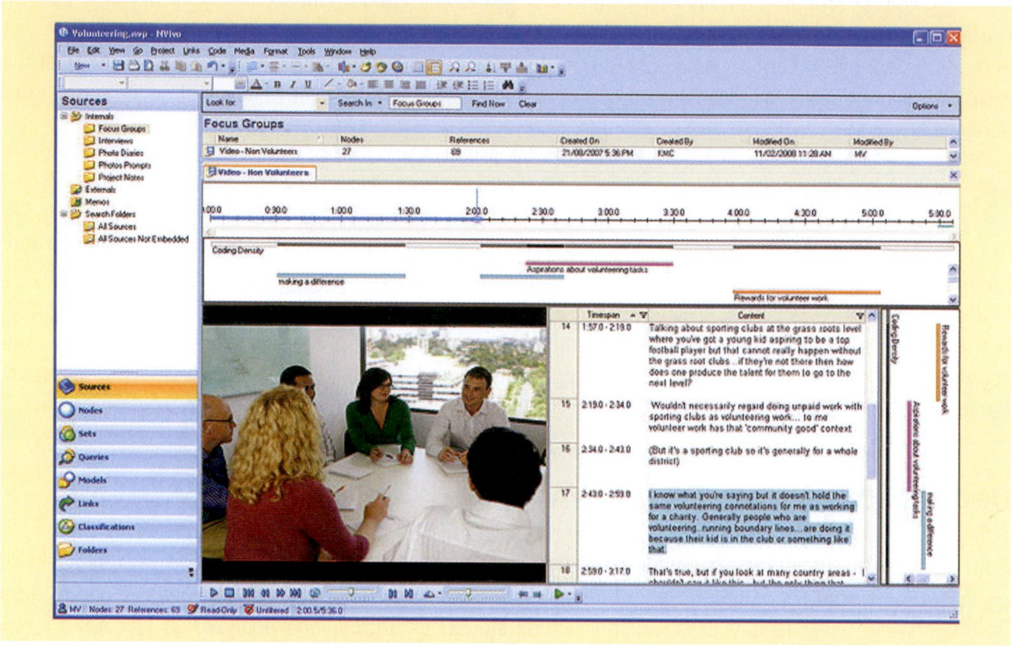

Source: QSRInternational.com.

The Qualitative-Quantitative Debate

Earlier we defined qualitative research in contrast with quantitative research. As it turns out, much debate has gone on in the social sciences between qualitative and quantitative researchers.

A Brief History of the Debate

QUESTION

What are some of the key steps involved in qualitative data analysis?

The social sciences originated in a more qualitative vein in the late 19th and early 20th centuries with, for example, the psychology of William James, the anthropology of Franz Boas, and the sociology of the Chicago School (Ernest Burgess, George Herbert Mead, Robert Park, and Louis Wirth)—all of whom relied on interpretive, ethnographic, or case study methods. In Europe, there had been an established tradition of interpretative approaches to social science coming from figures like Max Weber, Georg Simmel, and Wilhelm Dilthey. During World War II, Robert Merton developed the focused interview to study wartime propaganda films, a technique that developed into what we today call focus group research (discussed above).

But a movement to model the social sciences on the hard sciences (particularly physics and biology), coupled with rapid advancement in statistics, led to a *quantitative revolution* in various branches of the social sciences. Although with 19th-century roots in the "social physics" of Auguste Comte and the early positivism of Émile Durkheim, this quantitative turn gathered strength in the period after World War II with continuing advances in statistical methods and in computing capabilities. Paul Lazarsfeld was an influential figure in sociology during this period, and important influences came from postwar advances in econometrics and epidemiology. Social science journals of various kinds also proliferated, and the format of many of these journals favored quantitative research.

Qualitative researchers began to push back, pointing out the limitations of quantitative methods. A literature criticizing the quantitative or "positivist" approach emerged, and efforts were made to develop and refine qualitative methods. Antipositivist schools consolidated around a focus on human subjectivity, the social construction of reality, and a critical stance toward existing social relations. Books and journals about qualitative methods have since proliferated. Graduate programs in many of the social sciences now offer courses in qualitative methods to balance their courses in quantitative methods. But some disciplines (such as economics) remain predominantly quantitative, while others (such as anthropology) remain predominantly qualitative.

Some see the qualitative-quantitative divide in the social sciences as fundamental and enduring. At one level, there are good reasons for this: The interpretation of subjective intensions underlying human action is a fundamentally different exercise than the testing of causal explanations of objectively measured behavior. However, others—especially applied researchers—have come to view the two approaches as more often complementary in practice than conflicting. They recognize that in some situations, qualitative research provides the best approach to answering a pressing policy or practice question. In other situations, quantitative research is needed. Indeed, many researchers today recognize the advantages of mixed-methods studies. **A mixed-method study** combines qualitative and quantitative approaches (Creswell & Clark, 2006).

Blurring the Lines: How Qualitative and Quantitative Approaches Overlap

Although qualitative and quantitative methods tend to be viewed as distinct categories, in the actual practice of social research, they often overlap. Sometimes, the analysis of qualitative interviews or observations, for example, involves *counting* words or behaviors. Qualitative analysis software for content analysis, discussed above, can be used in this way. And coded qualitative data can be analyzed quantitatively using a variety of methods. Moreover, quantitative research is often qualitative too: In statistical studies of numerical data, researchers typically include a section labeled "interpretation" in which they bring qualitative judgments or evidence to bear on the meaning of their statistical findings.

Table 3.3 illustrates this overlap between qualitative and quantitative data and analysis (Bernard, 1996). Some studies do involve entirely interpretive analysis of texts or interviews (Box A), and other studies can involve entirely statistical analysis of numerical data (Box D) with very little qualitative interpretation. But many studies fall in Boxes B and C—quantitative studies with substantial elements of qualitative interpretation, or qualitative studies that include statistical analysis of coded or categorized themes, images, or meanings.

Earlier we mentioned that quantitative studies in social and policy research often investigate intangible constructs such as perceptions, emotions, and attitudes—constructs that are essentially qualitative in lived experience. This suggests another way in which qualitative and quantitative methods overlap. Take the example of *social support*—the other people in our lives who are there for us in times of need. We appreciate when we have such support, and feel alone without it, but we experience it qualitatively, not quantitatively, as might happen when we measure our weight or calculate our income. But social scientists have found ways to quantify social support (called a *construct*) by putting numbers to *indicators* of the experience, as illustrated in Figure 3.6. (The scores for family, friends, and significant others are each composed of multiple questions on a questionnaire.) In this way, many of the measures found in quantitative social and policy research are essentially numerical representations of qualitative experiences. We discuss these issues further in Chapter 4 on measurement.

A Qualitative-Quantitative Research Cycle

It can help to think about qualitative and quantitative approaches as contributing to a cycle of research, as shown in Figure 3.7. When confronted with a new social problem or management challenge, such as a

Table 3.3 Qualitative and Quantitative Data and Analysis

	Data	
Analysis	**Qualitative**	**Quantitative**
Qualitative	A Interpretive studies of texts, interviews, images, or qualitative observations	B Interpreting the meaning of numerical findings, or using qualitative evidence to illustrate statistical results
Quantitative	C Turning words or images into numbers—such as word counts or content analysis	D Statistical studies based on surveys or other numerical data

Source: Adapted from Bernard, H. R. (1996). Qualitative data, qualitative analysis. *Cultural Anthropology Methods Journal* 8(1): 9-11. Copyright © SAGE Publications, Inc.

Figure 3.6 Quantitative Indicators of Qualitative Constructs

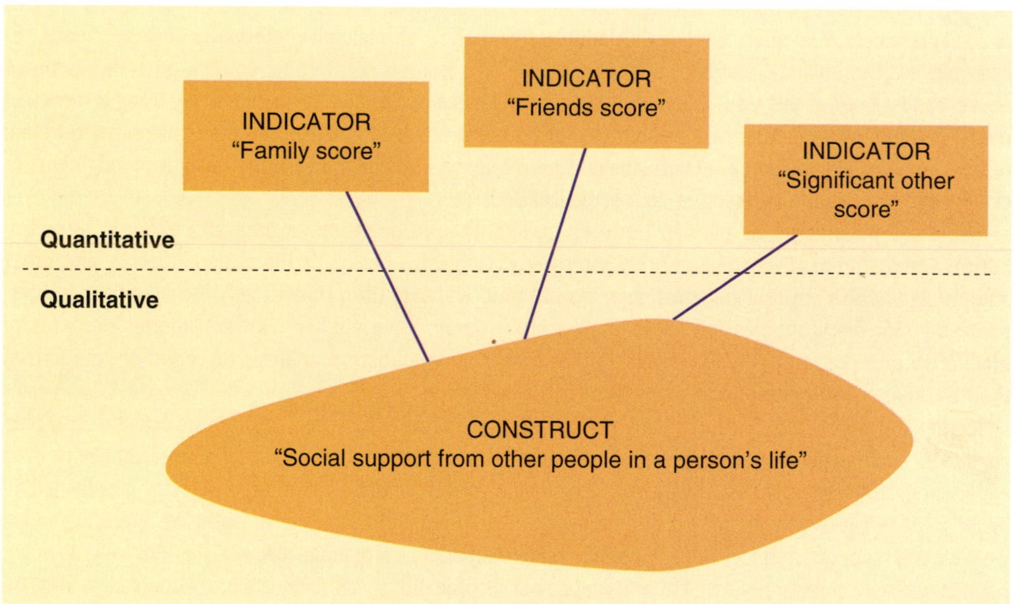

breakdown of morale in a work organization, often the first step is to explore the situation and discover key variables and relationships. Qualitative research is especially well suited to this task. We might decide, for example, to commission a series of in-depth interviews or focus groups to get ideas about what is troubling employees. This initial phase of exploration/discovery also can suggest theories or models to explain what is happening.

Next, it is useful to more systematically measure the key variables and estimate relationships. Based on our initial qualitative findings, for example, we might commission a more structured employee satisfaction survey across the organization, one focused on measuring the key variables uncovered by the initial interviews or focus groups. Data from the survey would then be analyzed statistically, including testing the relevant models.

Finally, the statistical findings may be ambiguous in places, or the data may not fully confirm the model. Moreover, unanticipated relationships between variables may be uncovered by the statistical analysis. In this way, quantitative research too can be exploratory. So we may decide to follow up our survey with more interviews or focus groups, this time with an emphasis on understanding the nature of relationships evident in our quantitative results. For example, we can explore or seek confirmation of the causal mechanisms—the social, institutional, or psychological processes that produce the statistical relationships we see in our quantitative results.

The same cycle often characterizes academic research as well. For example, a doctoral student doing a dissertation on how public schools handle children with learning disabilities may begin by visiting a few schools; interviewing teachers, parents, and students; and observing the daily classroom routines. These qualitative observations, combined with background literature on the topic, provide a foundation for conducting a survey or gathering existing data (from school records or other sources) for statistical analysis involving many schools. After reviewing the statistical findings, the doctoral student may need to return to a few particularly successful, or unsuccessful, schools to gain a more in-depth understanding of her results.

Large government surveys or program evaluations, even large randomized field experiments, also tend to follow this cycle. Initial qualitative research is used to develop questionnaires, determine site logistics, and carefully design experimental procedures. The survey or experiment is then carried out, producing quantitative data for statistical analysis. But then qualitative follow-up investigation is often required to gain a fuller understanding and produce a better interpretation of the quantitative results.

Figure 3.7 Cycles of Research

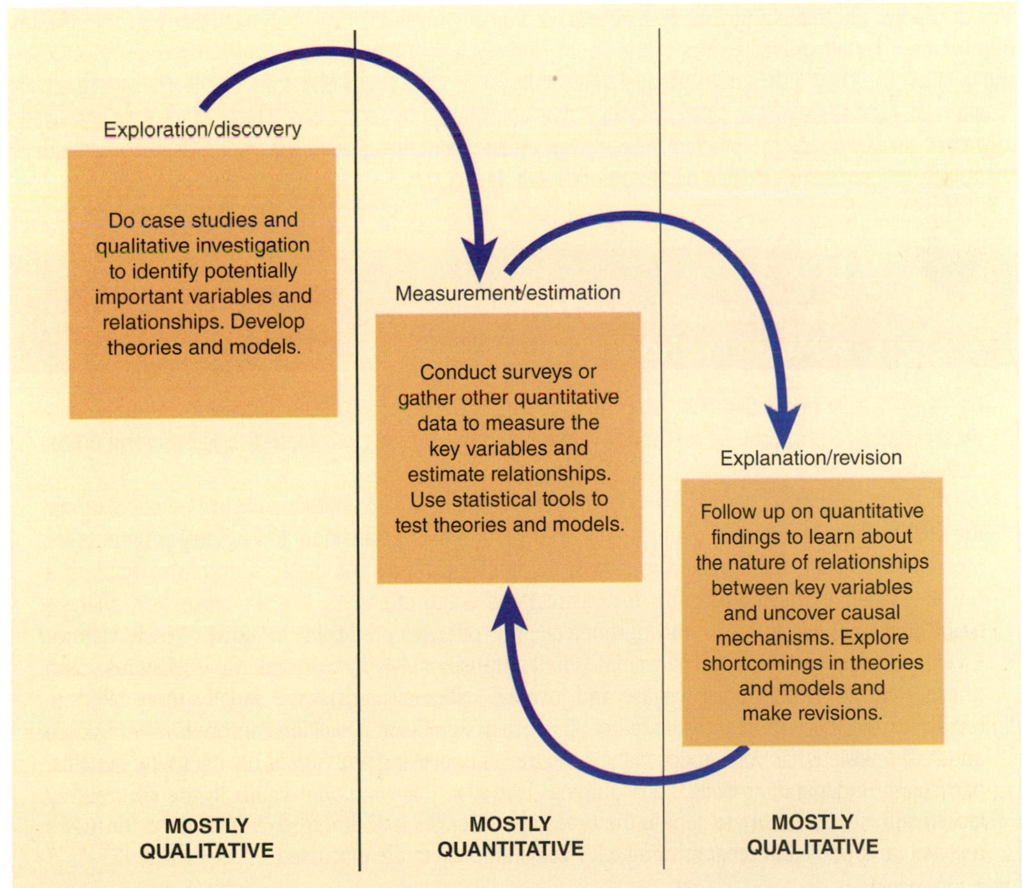
Exploration/discovery
Do case studies and qualitative investigation to identify potentially important variables and relationships. Develop theories and models.
Measurement/estimation
Conduct surveys or gather other quantitative data to measure the key variables and estimate relationships. Use statistical tools to test theories and models.
Explanation/revision
Follow up on quantitative findings to learn about the nature of relationships between key variables and uncover causal mechanisms. Explore shortcomings in theories and models and make revisions.
MOSTLY QUALITATIVE
MOSTLY QUANTITATIVE
MOSTLY QUALITATIVE

Mixed-Methods Research and Triangulation

The fact that qualitative and quantitative approaches each have unique strengths, as well as limitations, has led many researchers to favor *mixed-method* studies (Creswell & Clark, 2006). For example, the *New York Times* and other large organizations that do public opinion research often conduct follow-up qualitative interviews to accompany their quantitative surveys. In a poll conducted in early January 2013, in the wake of the shooting at Sandy Hook Elementary School, the *New York Times* found that the percentage of Americans supporting stricter gun laws had risen sharply to 54%, from just 39% several months earlier. The article then quoted from a follow-up interview with a 64-year-old woman from Atlanta who is a gun owner:

> I'm from a rural area in the South, I grew up in a gun culture, my father hunted. However, I don't believe being able to have a gun keeps you from thinking reasonably about changes that would keep someone from walking into a school and being able to kill 20 children in 20 seconds. I think that we can say, O.K., we want the freedom to have guns in this country, but there are rules we can all agree to that will make us all safer. (Cooper & Sussman, 2013)

The quantitative polling results, combined with the qualitative quote, give a fuller picture of the large shift that occurred in the public's mood on this controversial issue. **Triangulation** is the term often used to describe how multiple sources of evidence, from both quantitative and qualitative methods, can converge on a finding or confirm (or refute) a theory.

Box 3.1 provides another example of mixed-method research from an evaluation of transition services for incarcerated youth. In this study, the researchers used quantitative statistical analysis to estimate the relationship between certain characteristics of the youth (such as age of first arrest and number of prior offenses) and recidivism. They also employed qualitative interviews with youth and staff of the transitional living program to gain additional insight on factors that contributed to recidivism. These qualitative interviews suggested that, although the program helped with independent living skills, the youth faced overwhelming challenges on their return to their neighborhoods and peers.

BOX 3.1
Transition Services for Incarcerated Youth: A Mixed Methods Evaluation Study

By Abrams, Laura S., Sarah K. Shannon, & Cindy Sangalang. (2008). Transition services for incarcerated youth: A mixed methods evaluation study. *Children and Youth Services Review, 30*(5), 522–535.

Abstract: Despite a considerable overlap between child welfare and juvenile justice populations, the child welfare literature contains sparse information about transition and reentry programs for incarcerated youth. Using mixed methods, this paper explores the benefits and limitations of a 6-week transitional living program for incarcerated youth offenders. Logistic regression analysis found that only age at arrest and number of prior offenses predicted the odds of recidivism at 1-year post-release. Youth who participated in the transitional living program and dual status youth (those involved in both child welfare and juvenile justice systems) were slightly more likely to recidivate, but these differences were not statistically significant. Qualitative interviews with youth and staff revealed that both groups viewed the transitional living program as having many benefits, particularly independent living skills training. However, follow-up with youth in the community lacked sufficient intensity to handle the types of challenges that emerged. Implications for future research and transition programming with vulnerable youth are discussed.

Ethics in Qualitative Research

Qualitative research raises a variety of unique ethical issues—issues that can sometimes be more difficult to anticipate and handle than those that arise in quantitative research.

Presenting Qualitative Data

Presenting data in the form of extended quotes, photographs, or video recordings can make individuals clearly identifiable. Moreover, in-depth interviewing, case studies, participant observation, and other qualitative methods frequently reveal many details about the people or places in the study. These things can make it hard to provide anonymity or ensure confidentiality, even if only quotes as text are presented. Thus, presenting qualitative evidence without identifying the people or places involved can be a challenge.

QUESTION

In what ways do qualitative and quantitative research overlap? In what ways are they fundamentally different?

Can You Obtain Informed Consent?

The usual approach to informed consent requires a formal written explanation of the study and the participant's signature. This can be difficult to implement in some qualitative studies, such as participant observation. When a researcher simply observes public behavior, written informed consent is usually not required. But there can still be ethical quandaries if the researcher conceals his or her true identity and role as a researcher from participants in a setting. For example, a researcher may spend time in an emergency waiting room, pretending to be just another patient, to unobtrusively observe the behavior and interactions of patients and staff. People in this setting may well say things or behave in ways they might not have done otherwise, had they been fully informed that they were being observed as part of a research study.

The problem is even greater when the researcher participates in settings that are not public. Think about the ethical dilemmas of observing a private political meeting, a self-help group, a religious ceremony, or even a workplace. Should you observe such settings without disclosing your role as a researcher? At what point should you make a disclosure, and to whom? What should you do when your participant observation leads you into an unstructured interview and people begin confiding in you?

It is difficult to give ready-made answers to such ethical questions because much depends on the context, topic, and procedures of the research. That is why each study must undergo its own individual ethical review. Informed consent and voluntary participation remain key elements of ethical research, but sometimes these standards can prove difficult to implement in participant observation and related forms of qualitative research.

Should You Help People With Their Problems?

The open-ended nature of qualitative research, particularly in-depth interviews, means that sensitive topics may arise in the course of the interview that emotionally upset participants—an adverse event, as it's called in research ethics. Sometimes the interview also uncovers important unmet needs of the person for services or assistance. As a result, in some qualitative studies, it may be necessary to plan for such events and be ready to give social service referrals. This is particularly important when the topic is innately sensitive, such as domestic violence or substance abuse.

But it is difficult to predict or control what comes up in any qualitative study, no matter what the topic. For example, in a study of subsidized housing one of us (GVR) conducted, an elderly woman being interviewed about her need for subsidized housing began reflecting on her childhood. She then revealed that she had been abused as a young girl and that this experience had complicated many aspects of her adult life, eventually resulting in her need for subsidized housing in old age. Although this was a study about a housing program—not child abuse—a description of child abuse ended up on the recording. In-depth interviews often uncover sensitive topics, such as corruption in an organization, abuse of power, or private information about the respondent or other people in the setting.

What should the researcher do with this information? In some circumstances, more confidentiality than initially promised may be required. In other cases, the researcher may have an ethical duty to act. Providing a referral to social services may be the most ethical thing to do. But sometimes it can be more difficult to know how to respond. What action should the researcher take upon learning about ongoing domestic abuse if the victim, promised confidentiality, does not wish to seek help? In a case like this, ethical principles can conflict.

Should You Empower People?

These various ethical quandaries of qualitative research have led some to call for qualitative research to be action oriented, emancipatory, and empowering (Fetterman, Kaftarian, & Wandersman, 1995; McIntyre, 2007; Stringer, 2007). This view is sometimes associated with the approach of **critical theory** (Agger, 2006). The idea, in brief, is that researchers should not just study people and settings but use their intimate knowledge, along with their privileged position, to help transform and improve the situation. Often this involves a critique of the institutions or structures of economic, political, or social power that oppress participants. Although this perspective is not strictly limited to qualitative research, it does arise more in situations where the researcher has intimate knowledge of the setting and a sustained, personal relationship with the people being studied.

Conclusion: Matching Methods to Questions

This chapter has introduced you to qualitative research—an important and widely useful approach to research, especially for generating theory, building models, and uncovering causal processes. You will learn other, more traditionally quantitative methods in the chapters that follow. But we will also regularly revisit the qualitative perspective in these later chapters to emphasize how qualitative and quantitative approaches complement each other and work well in combination.

In closing, it is important to realize that no single approach to research can answer every important policy or practice question. The initial quantitative survey in Kenya, for example, did not reveal *why* some health workers did not provide ACT to all patients. Even if the researchers had followed up with another survey to learn more, they would probably have had to guess at the reasons and causes, possibly missing some important ones. Also, the limited range of responses typical in a quantitative, closed-ended survey would have provided less detail and nuance. So a survey alone would not have fully answered their question about why health workers in the field were not prescribing ACT to their malaria patients.

On the other hand, if the Kenyan study had only relied on a few in-depth interviews, it would not have allowed an estimate of the overall usage of ACT to begin with—possibly leading researchers to miss the very problem the qualitative study helped address. For getting representative estimates of the extent of a problem, more quantitative methods of measurement and sampling are needed—the topics of the next two chapters. In all research, it is important to match the method to the question, but that is particularly true for choosing between qualitative and quantitative approaches. Often both approaches are needed to provide a complete answer.

BOX 3.2 Critical Questions to Ask About a Qualitative Study

- Why did the researchers choose to use qualitative methods?
- What qualitative method did they use—interviews, focus groups, case studies, textual analysis, mixed methods, or something else?
- Were the methods of data collection and analysis explained clearly and in sufficient detail to understand what was done?
- How were people or cases selected? Were cases chosen theoretically or in a purposive way to further the specific research questions?
- Does the study provide sufficient evidence to support its claims—for example, quotes or results of a more formal content analysis?
- Was the research done in such a way that theories or expectations could potentially be disproven? Does it consider contradictory evidence and alternative explanations?
- Did the researchers clearly distinguish what was observed from how the observations were interpreted?

BOX 3.3 Tips on Doing Your Own Qualitative Research

- Be aware of the advantages, as well as the limitations, of qualitative research—choose a qualitative approach with purpose.
- Decide what qualitative method(s) to use—such as interviews, focus groups, participant observation, or case studies—depending on your topic, context, and constraints.
- Have a clear sampling or recruiting strategy to find the people you want in your study; check to see that your sampling strategy provides a sufficient variety of people and perspectives.
- If you are doing interviews, you will need to decide how structured or unstructured to make them; this often depends on your topic and on how much involvement or interaction you will have with respondents. Develop an interview guide with the appropriate level of structure (such as probes for semistructured interviews) and make sure that the interview will address your research questions.
- Determine what means you will use to record your interviews or other qualitative data and acquire the related technology, such as an audio or video recorder; be sure also to have a plan for storing and securing your qualitative data (whether written notes or electronic files).
- Decide whether, and to what extent, you will transcribe your interviews for analysis—this is a time-consuming process that is often underestimated.
- Determine if you will use qualitative data analysis software to code and analyze your data, and make sure you are familiar with the software and its capabilities.
- Establish procedures for recording and reporting data in a way that provides anonymity or confidentiality to participants; also have a plan for responding to people's needs or problems that might emerge in your study, particularly if participants are from a vulnerable population.

Chapter Resources

Key Terms

- Case
- Case study
- Coding
- Content analysis
- Critical theory
- Ethnography
- Focus group
- Grounded theory
- Intercoder reliability
- Intersubjectivity
- Interview guide
- Mixed-method study
- Moderator (of a focus group)
- Open-ended questions
- Participant observation
- Purposive (or theoretical) sampling
- Qualitative data
- Qualitative research
- Quantitative research
- Saturation
- Semistructured interview
- Triangulation
- Unstructured interview

Exercises

More Qualitative Evidence About Injection Drug Use

3.1. In this chapter, we described a study by Treloar and colleagues (2008) that used video to document risky practices of injection drug users. Below is an abstract from another study using qualitative interviews that provides additional insight on this same topic. Using this abstract, can you come up with a model—including several variables and relationships—of the possible causes of risky injection practices?

> We report the findings of an in-depth interview study conducted with 45 female injecting drug users in Britain. Women described experiences of injecting themselves and being injected by others, including instances of bodily harm and pain. Cleanliness when injecting was an issue of particular importance. An interesting division ("line of decency") occurred between opinions on sharing needles versus sharing injecting equipment. Partnership dynamics were important and partners sometimes had a pervasive influence on women's drug use and injecting practices. Narratives of risk showed that some women understood the risk of blood-borne viruses and outlined practical risk-prevention strategies. Some women did not perceive themselves to be at particular risk. Moral opinions were voiced about the risk behavior of others. Notions of risk were highly contextual and depended on a woman's immediate injecting situation. This article reports the inherent complexity resident in women drug users' decisions surrounding their injecting behavior. (Sheard & Tompkins, 2008)

Is It Qualitative or Quantitative?

3.2. Below are short descriptions of studies. For each one, decide if you think it is best described as a qualitative or quantitative study, and explain why.

- Researchers use data from a survey to study the correlation between people's self-reported *happiness* and their belief in *life after death.* They find that 52% of those who believe in life after death are "very happy," compared with only 39% of those who do not believe in life after death.
- As part of a program evaluation, a team of government auditors visits program grantees and interviews directors at length about their ability to draw down and expend grant funds on schedule. The interviews reveal that few have expended any funds at all. The directors attribute the problem to excessive delays and complications in executing grant agreements with the agency. The auditors also observe that the directors seem to lack knowledge of the government contracting process.

Should You Use Qualitative or Quantitative Research?

3.3. Below are some research questions. For each one, decide if you think it is best answered by qualitative or quantitative research, and explain why.

- Bullying is an important problem, particularly in middle schools, but not much is known about how students who are the targets of bullying deal with the problem. What strategies do they use to avoid or confront bullies? To whom do they turn for help? How does bullying affect their life inside and outside of school?
- Bullying is an important problem, especially in middle schools, but not much is known about the true extent of the problem. What percentage of children experience bullying? Are there differences in rates of experienced bullying by gender or race?

Making It Qualitative, Making It Quantitative

3.4. Below are several research topics that might be addressed by either qualitative or quantitative studies. For each one, think of what a qualitative study of the topic might look like. Then think of what a quantitative study of the same topic would look like.

- Teen drug use
- Morale in a work organization
- Teaching effectiveness in elementary school math education
- Police-community relations

Existing Qualitative Data

3.5. Identify a public program, service, or agency of interest to you. What forms of existing qualitative data might there be for studying this program, service, or agency? How would you obtain these data, and what might the data tell you?

Interviewing a Friend

3.6. Conduct an unstructured interview with a classmate, friend, or family member on a simple but fairly interesting topic. Some possibilities include voting, recycling, exercising, saving money, and commuting. Spend at least 30 minutes doing the interview and try using the power of probes and "what" or "how" questions (as explained in this chapter). Be sure to record the interview or take notes. Write a paragraph or two about what you learned about the topic and the person from the interview.

Planning a Focus Group

3.7. Think of a problem or issue that you are familiar with from work or from your community. Then outline a plan for a focus group study of the issue, including the following:

- The topic of the focus group
- The target population
- How many focus groups to hold—and if there are important subgroups
- Where you would hold the focus groups
- A list of five to seven open-ended questions that would guide the focus group discussion

Observing a Setting

3.8. Identify a simple public setting of interest, such as a park, a post office, a bus stop, or a traffic intersection. Observe the setting for at least 15 minutes, taking occasional notes. Find another similar setting and observe it also for 15 minutes. Write a paragraph or two describing what you observed and learned about each setting.

Developing a Coding Scheme

3.9. StoryCorps.org is a project that records short oral histories from the lives of ordinary people. Find two related stories that interest you, listen to them, and try creating a simple coding scheme that you can use to summarize and compare the stories. You will probably have to listen to the stories several times to fully develop your coding scheme. (The stories are organized by category on StoryCorps.org, which will help you find two stories that are fairly closely related.)

Student Study Site

Visit the Study Site at **www.sagepub.com/remler2e** to

- test your knowledge with the self-quiz
- check your understanding of key terms with the eFlashcards
- explore helpful resources that relate directly to this chapter

PART II

STRATEGIES FOR DESCRIPTION

Accurately describing the world is an important task of research. We need to know what conditions look like, for example how extensive a problem really is in a population, before we can take meaningful action. This part of the book covers various research strategies for description, including measurement, sampling, obtaining secondary data, and conducting surveys as well as other primary data collection. These strategies provide an important window to reality—they allow us to observe many critical conditions and important trends that would otherwise remain hidden or only dimly perceived.

Measurement involves instruments and systematic observation.
Source: © iStockphoto.com/wragg.

Overview: This chapter will introduce you to the key ideas and issues involved in measurement—the systematic observation and recording of features of the world that matter to us. You will learn how to conceptualize and operationalize a measure and how to think about and assess the validity of a measure. You will learn about measurement error and measurement reliability too. And you will learn about the level of measurement and its implications for data analysis. The trustworthiness of research often hinges on how well the measures used capture the key concepts under investigation. And measurement—in the form of performance measurement—also has become an integral part of public policy and management.

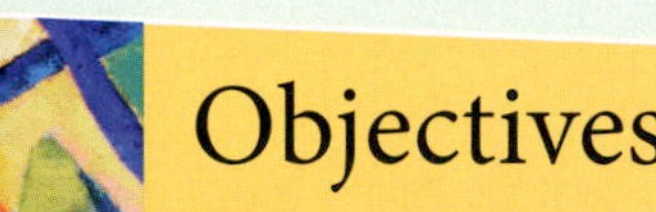

Objectives

Learning Objectives

After reading this chapter, you should be able to

- Identify how a given measure is conceptualized, including its dimensions
- Recognize how a measure is operationalized, including the use of instruments, proxies, and scales
- Judge the validity of a measure, especially in the context of its purpose or application
- Understand the issue of measurement error, and be able to judge the reliability of a measure (along with the implications of unreliability for data analysis)
- Identify the level of measurement of a variable, particularly the distinction between quantitative and categorical variables
- Recognize the trade-offs involved in measurement, including cost and ethical limitations

Measurement 4

The U.S. Poverty Measure

President Lyndon B. Johnson announced a "War on Poverty" in his 1964 address to Congress "to pursue victory over the most ancient of mankind's enemies." A plethora of new programs targeted the problem of poverty in America, including job training, Head Start preschooling, Medicare and Medicaid, housing assistance programs, and food stamp expansion. The U.S. welfare state assumed its full form during the 1960s, with the War on Poverty as its key mission.

The problem was no one quite knew how to measure poverty. So how was the government to know if its War on Poverty was being won or lost?

In this chapter, we will look at how researchers and practitioners create and carry out measurements—translating concepts that we care about, such as poverty, into recorded observations that can be organized and analyzed. The trustworthiness of research often hinges on how well this translation gets made—how well the measurements capture the key concepts under investigation. And measurement too has become an integral part of delivering public services, evaluating program outcomes, and managing organizations.

What Is Measurement?

Measurement refers to the process of systematically observing some feature or characteristic of the world and then recording it in the form of a number or category. We make observations of the world all the time, but when we make those observations systematic in a form that allows analysis, we've begun doing *measurement*. Once measured, the characteristic can be more effectively organized and understood.

Think about sitting on a park bench and observing people strolling by. This is observation, certainly, but not measurement. But imagine you were to take out a pad of paper and begin tallying up the passersby in order to count up how many people enter the park? You would then be doing measurement—systematic observation and recording. You might record your tally in categories: children versus adults, for example. Or you might organize your tally into time intervals (every half hour, let's say) to see how the number of park-goers rises and falls with the time of day.

Measurement can be as simple as a head count using a pad of paper, or it can be much more operationally complex. To count the number of people in the United States each decade, the Census Bureau engages in years of planning, employs tens of thousands of workers, and spends billions of dollars. (For a history of social measurement, see Duncan, 1984.)

Measurement in Qualitative Research

By most definitions, the term *measurement* implies a process of counting and quantification. And indeed the concepts and methods of measurement in social and policy research come mostly from the quantitative research tradition. However, measurement happens also in qualitative research, in particular, when content analyzing and coding qualitative data (as discussed in the previous chapter). Thus, many of the topics in this chapter apply equally to the process of coding qualitative data. More broadly, qualitative observation attempts to be systematic also. So the core concepts researchers use to think about measurement—such as conceptualization, validity, and reliability—are relevant to all forms of qualitative observation, whether coded or not. We will return to this point later in the chapter.

Performance Measurement

The need for measurement—like the need to measure poverty—begins often from a practical need to take account of some aspect of the world in order to better understand or influence it. Indeed, **performance measurement**—the use of measurement for administrative purposes or leadership strategy—is increasingly important in many areas of public, nonprofit, and business management these days (as mentioned in Chapter 1). Performance measurement focuses on measuring the activities, outputs, and outcomes of programs, initiatives, or even entire organizations (Hatry, 2007; Holzer & Yang, 2004; Poister, 2003). It can be thought of also as the application of the theory and practice of measurement to professional practice and public accountability. As such, our discussion of key measurement concepts in this chapter has direct application to performance measurement as increasingly practiced by government, nonprofit, and business organizations.

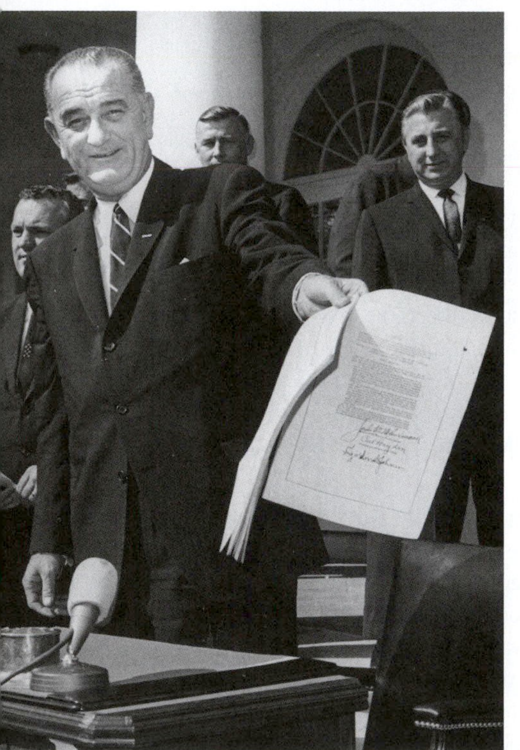

Lyndon B. Johnson launched the War on Poverty.
Source: Arnold Sachs/Hulton Archive/Getty Images.

Measurement: The Basic Model and a Road Map

To organize the chapter that follows, it helps to visualize a basic model of measurement (Allen & Yen, 1979), shown in Figure 4.1. Using this model, we can lay out the big picture of measurement and what this chapter will cover.

Measurement begins with a **construct** (or **trait**)—the concept or thing that we seek to measure. Clearly and precisely defining our constructs requires careful conceptualization. Next, we must devise or identify an empirical **measure**, or indicator, of the construct. This is the task of operationalization. We will discuss both conceptualization and operationalization in the following pages.

Real-world measures almost never fully capture the construct, and random errors inevitably happen in measurement processes. The arrow leading from the construct to the observed measure represents the idea of measurement validity—the correspondence with the original concept we want to capture. The arrow leading from the random error term to the measure represents the idea of measurement reliability—how much noise, or inconsistency, turns up in our measure. We will cover validity, measurement error, and reliability in detail in this chapter.

With this basic model of measurement in mind, let's turn to the task of conceptualization—that is, figuring out what it is we want to measure in the first place.

Figure 4.1 Basic Measurement Model

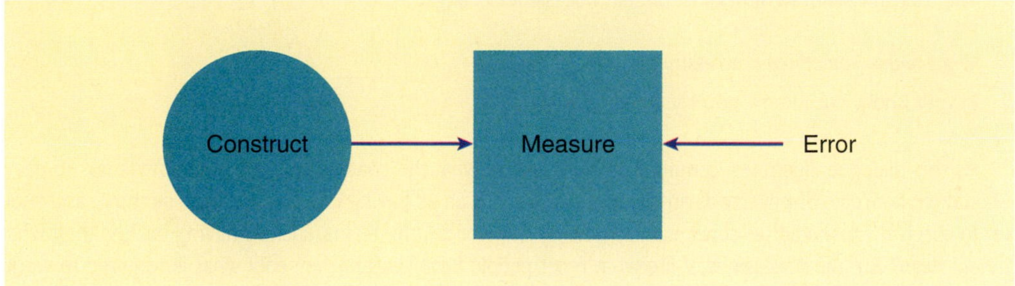

Conceptualization

A first—although sometimes overlooked—step in the measurement process is to be clear about what it is you want to measure. How should we define the *construct* (or trait) that we aim to capture through a measurement process? Answering this question is the challenge of **conceptualization**: defining carefully and precisely what it is you seek to measure.

Defining Can Be Difficult

Conceptualization can be fairly straightforward, as when measuring something uncomplicated like the number of people in a park. To be sure, this requires some conceptualization—what constitutes the park boundaries, what period of time to use, what counts as being *in* the park (staying for at least a few minutes, perhaps), and so on. Similarly, outcomes such as births, deaths, body mass (weight), traffic volume, ozone levels, consumer spending, and a host of other constructs that matter in public policy and in research present relatively manageable conceptual challenges, even though they may be technically or logistically difficult to measure.

QUESTION

When an airline sends you a survey that asks you to rate a recent flight you took on a 1–10 scale, what construct (or trait) are the researchers trying to get at? What is the empirical measure (or indicator)?

But other concepts of interest to researchers and policy makers cannot be so directly or unambiguously defined. This often makes it much more difficult to agree on what it is we are trying to measure. Consider the following dialogue about the concept of *poverty:*

What does it mean for people or households to be in poverty?

Well, it means that they don't have enough.

But how much is enough and enough of what?

They don't have the necessities: enough to eat, decent housing, and so on.

What's decent housing? Does it include indoor plumbing for toilets and showers?

Definitely!

What about in the 18th century, when even the king of England did not have indoor plumbing? Was he poor?

No. Things were different then. Nobody had that, no matter how rich.

So poverty depends on what other people have.

I guess so.

So if most people become better off and I don't, then I become poor.

That doesn't seem right. It must be that necessities change.

What makes something a necessity?

I don't know, but I know poverty when I see it.

As this dialogue illustrates, coming to agreement on what the concept of poverty means is not so easy. Should we conceive of poverty as an *absolute* standard, such as having just enough food, clothing, and shelter to survive? Or should we conceptualize poverty in more *relative* terms, such as having far less than what others have? Are the necessities of life what most people have? Or are they only what is required to work, maintain basic health, or even just survive?

Value Judgments and Politics in Measurement

Another reason that such concepts can be difficult to define conceptually is that they require value judgments. Defining someone as *poor, motivated, reading at grade level, at risk, intelligent,* and so on requires agreement not only about what these concepts mean, but also about what values or standards ought to be reflected in the acceptable levels we set for these measures. Establishing such standards is more of an ethical or political question than a scientific one.

Differences in conceptualization complicate the task of doing international comparisons of poverty (see Box 4.1)—as well as unemployment, crime, educational achievement, and other important research and policy issues.

Where Do Conceptualizations Come From?

The notion of poverty extends far back into ancient history. But the need to make the notion into a fleshed-out construct—the need to fully conceptualize it—stems from public policy initiatives and practical programs,

BOX 4.1
Is Poverty the Same Thing the World Over?

Mollie Orshansky, the inventor of the U.S. poverty measure, understood that poverty was a controversial and political concept, and so she chose to conceptualize poverty in narrow terms: as having less than the minimum income required by a family to get by. As Orshansky explained, "If it is not possible to state unequivocally 'How much is enough,' it should be possible to assert with confidence how much, on an average, is too little" (quoted in Fisher, 1992). Orshansky's conceptualization is an absolute definition of poverty, in the sense that she set an absolute or fixed minimum standard of basic food and other essentials (which, apart from being adjusted for inflation, has remained the same since the 1960s).

This contrasts with the conceptualization of poverty in Europe where a *relative* measure of poverty, defined as some fraction (60%) of the typical (median) income of a population, is more often employed (European Commission Directorate-General for Employment, Social Affairs & Inclusion, 2011). In Europe, in other words, poverty is conceptualized in terms of *having an income that is less than 60% of the typical income of others in the society.* The United Nations measures poverty using survival and education measures, as well as economic security (Human Development Reports, n.d.).

such as the War on Poverty. Thus, constructs arise sometimes from policy initiatives or demands for attention to pressing problems, with initial conceptualizations found in the language of legislation, regulations, and policy debates. Constructs can also come from management initiatives, such as an organization that decides to improve, let's say, its customer service. The corresponding mission statements or strategic plans might include a conceptualization of what "customer service" means to the organization. Typically, however, the conceptualizations contained in legislation, mission statements, or other background documents must be refined and specified further to guide measurement.

Importantly, constructs also come from *theory*. As we saw in Chapter 2, theories propose causal stories about how things happen and get expressed typically in models made up of variables and relationships. The variables in a model are constructs. They are specific traits, behaviors, or characteristics that we hope to measure in order to test the theory. So theories—or more precisely theoretical research and writing—serve to help identify and define the constructs to measure. Indeed, clearly defining key constructs—conceptualization—is an important aspect of specifying a theory.

And in the case of logic models—the application of theory to program design and evaluation—the activities, outputs, and short-term and long-term outcomes in the model are constructs too. As such, logic models similarly serve as tools for identifying and defining important constructs to measure. The exercise of producing a logic model typically includes a narrative explanation of the logic model, including conceptualizations of the constructs. But again, these initial conceptualizations usually must be refined to develop an actual measure of the construct.

QUESTION

How latent or manifest are these educational constructs: attendance, writing skills, reading comprehension?

Manifest and Latent Constructs

Some constructs are more directly observable than others. For example, we can pretty well directly observe a child's height and weight, but we cannot so directly observe his or her knowledge of mathematics or language arts. A child's self-esteem is even more hidden. In measurement theory, height and weight are referred to as **manifest constructs** of the child, while self-esteem and knowledge of mathematics or language arts are **latent constructs**. A key part of conceptualization is determining how manifest or latent a construct is.

The field of **psychometrics** deals with the measurement of latent traits or constructs, mostly using composite measures made up of multiple *items*—related manifest measurements, such as agreement with statements about your personality or answers on a language arts test, that provide indicators of a latent construct (Furr & Bacharach, 2008; McIver & Carmines, 1981). We will learn how items, indicators, and composite measures are used to capture latent constructs later in the chapter.

IQ tests measure multiple dimensions of intelligence.
Source: © iStockphoto.com/KLH49.

Dimensions

Some concepts are inherently multifaceted. Consider the concept of health—many would agree it includes being free of pain, able to move easily, not fatigued, mentally alert, and upbeat. Yet these are not necessarily the same things—you could be free of pain but still fatigued or able to move about easily enough but feeling down. Health is complex and multifaceted. As researchers say, the concept of health contains multiple **dimensions** (also referred to as **domains**). To fully define such concepts, one must first describe all their dimensions.

One of the most widely used overall measures of health is the SF-36 (Short Form-36), a 36-item questionnaire developed by the RAND Corporation (2010; Ware & Donaldson Sherbourne, 1992) for a large study of health outcomes. The SF-36 has the following eight dimensions:

1. Physical functioning (running, lifting, climbing stairs, etc.)
2. Role limitations (not working or getting things done) due to physical functioning
3. Role limitations (not working or getting things done) due to emotional problems
4. Energy/fatigue (feeling worn out or tired)
5. Emotional well-being (feeling down, nervous, or unhappy)
6. Social functioning (health interfering with normal social activities)
7. Pain (severity and interference with functioning)
8. General (self-reported) health

QUESTION

Say you are interested in measuring consumer satisfaction with a new product, such as a smartphone. What are some dimensions of satisfaction you should consider?

Other health measures have similar, but not identical, dimensions.

Intelligence is perhaps even more abstract than health—and certainly more controversial. It too has been conceptualized as having different dimensions. For example, the extensively used Stanford-Binet measure of intelligence, devised originally in the early 1900s to classify French schoolchildren for remedial education, has five dimensions: (1) fluid reasoning, (2) knowledge, (3) quantitative reasoning, (4) visual-spatial processing, and (5) working memory.

Dimensions can be made into distinct measures. Alternatively, or in addition, the dimensions can be incorporated into a single, composite measure of the construct. The SF-36 does both. Controversies surrounding a measure are often due to the emphasis on, or exclusion of, some dimensions over others. Thinking about a construct's dimensions is a particularly important step in conceptualization.

Operationalization

After defining conceptually what to measure, researchers must then figure out *how* to measure it. This is the task of **operationalization**: the specific procedures (operations) a researcher carries out in making and recording a measurement. Let's look at how the U.S. poverty measure is operationalized.

Birth of the U.S. Poverty Measure

At the time President Johnson announced his War on Poverty, Mollie Orshansky was at work in a small office in the Social Security Administration on the development of a practical poverty measure (Fisher, 1992). An economist with prior experience in the Agriculture Department, she conceptualized poverty as an absolute measure—and specifically as "less than the minimum income required by a family to get by" (see Box 4.1). That still left the problems of defining what it means to "get by" and figuring out what income that would require.

The Agriculture Department had developed a so-called Economy Food Plan to provide basic nutrition when family funds were low. This was the least costly food plan that a family could use and still maintain its health and well-being (if it shopped and cooked wisely). At the time, the Agriculture Department also had survey data on household food expenditures, but the government did not collect information on the various other costs of living (housing, clothing, transportation, health care, etc.).

The share of a family's income spent on food had long been considered a useful gauge of economic well-being. (The higher the fraction of income spent on food, the poorer the family.) Orshansky observed that, on average, families in the United States at the time spent about one third of their income on food and two thirds on everything else in life. So this became a good, rough guess as to what the other essentials of life must cost.

Thus, a family with income less than three times this basic minimum food expenditure could be classified as *poor*. Further refinements are made to reflect family size, and the poverty threshold gets updated each year to reflect changes in prices. Box 4.2 details this operational definition of the U.S. poverty measure.

Operationalizing poverty measurement involves many details of procedure, data, and calculation. We consider next some other common features of operationalization: instruments; protocols and research personnel; proxies and indicators; and scales and indexes.

Mollie Orshansky, the inventor of the U.S. poverty measure.

Source: SSA History Archives.

Instruments

To operationalize a measure, researchers often use **instruments**—tools that help measure something. For example, in the criminal justice field there is the breathalyzer (for measuring blood alcohol) and the radar gun (for measuring the speed of cars on roadways). In the environmental protection field, there are passive and active air samplers (for measuring air pollutants) and the dosimeter (for measuring

BOX 4.2 Operational Definition of Poverty in the United States

It often surprises people to learn how the U.S. official poverty measure is operationalized:

- Establish the baseline poverty threshold (base year is 1966):
  - The cost of an Economy Food Plan devised by the United States Department of Agriculture (USDA)
  - A multiplier (3), based on survey estimates of what typical families spend on food versus other essentials
  - An adjustment for family size
- Update the poverty threshold to present day:
  - An inflation factor (the Consumer Price Index [CPI]) to update the thresholds to current dollars
- Determine whether particular families or individuals are in poverty as well as the poverty rate:
  - Collect current data on the incomes and family size in the U.S. population from one of the established federal surveys (the Current Population Survey [CPS]).
  - A family (and all its members) can be classified as "poor" if its income is below the poverty threshold for a family of its size.
  - The percentage of people in poverty can be calculated for the nation, states, or other geographic areas.

noise). In medicine, we find numerous instruments, such as the thermometer, the sphygmomanometer (for measuring blood pressure), the glucometer (for measuring blood sugar), and so on. When planning or evaluating research, considering the advantages and drawbacks of the instruments used for measurement is important. In some biomedical studies, even the make and model of the instruments are mentioned in published studies.

Questionnaires Are Instruments

Questionnaires used in surveys of individuals, households, or firms are also thought of by researchers as instruments. Similarly, coding sheets or observation forms used with qualitative data are viewed as instruments as well. And query protocols of computer programs that extract data from computerized databases are also instruments of a kind. Although they are not mechanical or electrical devices that record physical characteristics, questionnaires and coding forms are indeed tools that help researchers operationalize measurements. Thus, they are instruments—and researchers refer to them as such.

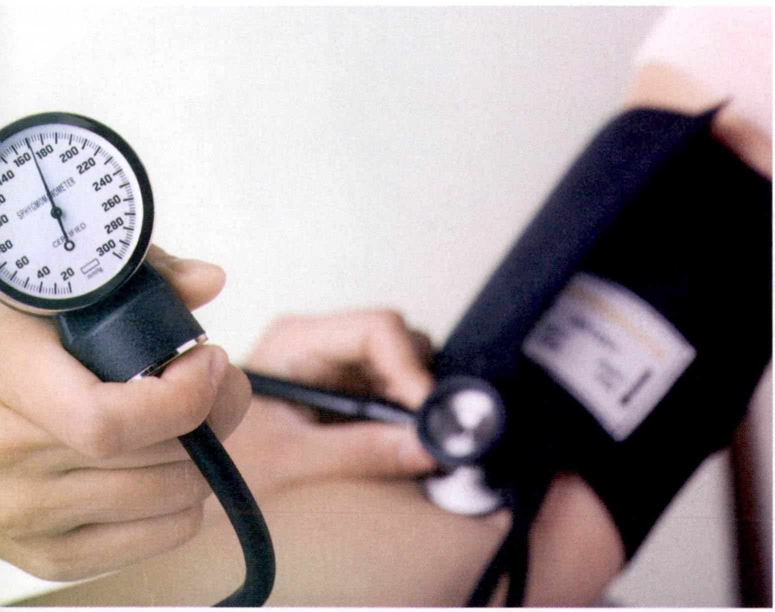

Measuring blood pressure with a sphygmomanometer.
Source: © iStockphoto.com/nycshooter.

Protocols and Personnel

Measurement also involves **protocols** or carefully specified procedures for using the instruments properly. These protocols are an important part of the operationalization of a measure. When measuring your height, for example, a medical assistant will ask you to take off your shoes, stand up straight, look forward, and relax your shoulders. Most instruments have protocols like this that guide the person using the instrument to obtain a consistent, accurate reading. Similarly, a questionnaire includes various explanations and instructions that help the respondent answer the questions as completely and accurately as possible.

Often, *technicians, interviewers,* or *trained observers* are required to carry out the measurement. These *research personnel* are also a key part of the operationalization of a measurement, so their selection, training, and supervision become important considerations. In some fields, such as psychological testing in education, only trained and licensed school psychologists can administer the tests or instruments used to measure students. Similarly, some mechanical or electrical instruments can be used only by specially trained people (such as medical technicians) or require licenses or certification. This is because the people using the instruments to carry out the measurement become a critical factor in how well the measurement gets made.

Proxies and Indicators

Sometimes a construct is too difficult or costly to measure directly, or it is not measured in existing data sets available for analysis. In such cases, researchers may operationalize a construct by using a **proxy**—a measure that substitutes for another, unavailable measure. For example, education researchers using existing school records might employ reduced-price lunch eligibility as a proxy for the parents' socioeconomic status. Or a criminologist might record the percentage of houses in a neighborhood with bars or gates on the windows as a proxy for the residents' fear of crime.

Proxies have their drawbacks, and sometimes they can mislead. But the clever use of proxies in the hands of a careful researcher can often produce interesting and insightful research findings, despite resource or data limitations.

Proxy Respondents and Proxy Reporting

Sometimes in surveys, respondents report on behalf of someone else in the household or organization. There are a variety of reasons for this. Adults, for example, are often asked to report on behalf of children in the household, as are family members or caretakers on behalf of those without the cognitive or physical abilities to answer for themselves. Or the desired respondent may simply be too difficult to contact. And in some situations, one representative of a firm or agency may be asked to report on behalf of all employees of the organization. For the CPS, the U.S. Bureau of Labor Statistics interviews one respondent in each household yet asks the respondent to report on the working status and earnings of all household members. In all these cases, the respondent is referred to as a **proxy respondent**, and the information gathered on others is *proxy reporting*. In turn, the answers that the respondents provide are *proxies* for the answers the individuals would have provided themselves.

Indicators

We've seen already how some constructs are latent and can be measured only indirectly through various indicators—which are proxies of a kind. But researchers reserve the term *proxy* as such for situations when, as a matter of economy or convenience, they must use a clearly different measure than what might ideally be used. **Indicators**, in contrast, aim to capture a construct that is not measurable in any other way.

Indicator is a term that comes from psychometrics, and it usually refers to a questionnaire item administered as part of a survey or test. For example, self-esteem is indicated by the extent of agreement with the statement "I feel that I'm a person of worth, at least on an equal basis with others" (M. Rosenberg, 1965). However, to represent latent constructs such as self-esteem well, researchers use multiple indicators and combine them into a composite measure (such as a scale), as we describe next.

Composite Measures: Scales and Indexes

QUESTION

Describe the similarities and differences between proxies and indicators.

Composite measures—scales and **indexes**—are measures composed of multiple items. When used to measure latent (not directly measurable) constructs, the items are called indicators. Composite measures are widely used in social and policy research. The use of multiple items serves several purposes: It ensures fuller coverage of the content of a construct; it better captures the range of intensity or difficulty of the construct; and it helps average out measurement error and thus enhance reliability—issues we'll cover in more detail later in the chapter.

Consider a construct such as *self-esteem*—someone's sense of personal self-worth, which many people believe is a critical factor in problems such as teen pregnancy, drug and alcohol abuse, and dropping out of school. Morris Rosenberg (1965) developed a self-esteem scale using respondents' ratings of their level of agreement with 10 statements (reversed items are flagged with an asterisk):

1. I feel that I'm a person of worth, at least on an equal basis with others.
2. I feel that I have a number of good qualities.
3. *All in all, I am inclined to think I'm a failure.
4. I am able to do things as well as most other people.

5. *I feel I do not have much to be proud of.
6. I take a positive attitude toward myself.
7. On the whole, I am satisfied with myself.
8. *I wish I could have more respect for myself.
9. *I certainly feel useless at times.
10. *At times I think I'm no good at all.

You can see how these statements, the *indicators,* all seem to get at the basic view people have of themselves. Self-esteem is latent, an internal self-perception, but we can infer its intensity or level from a person's pattern of responses to these statements.

Figure 4.2 graphically depicts a measurement model of the Rosenberg self-esteem scale. The arrows leading from the construct to the indicators suggest that a person's manifest scores on the indicators are, in a sense, caused by his or her latent (but real) self-esteem (the construct). The indicators also reflect some amount of measurement error (or noise), perhaps from the way the statement is worded, presented, or interpreted by the respondent.

The measurement model in Figure 4.2 illustrates how researchers think about scales and indeed measurement more generally. When looking at data or statistics, all we ever see are the indicators—such as the distributions of responses to questions on a questionnaire. But it is important to realize that researchers think of these indicators as reflecting a mix of the underlying construct as well as some idiosyncratic component,

Figure 4.2 Model of a Self-Esteem Scale

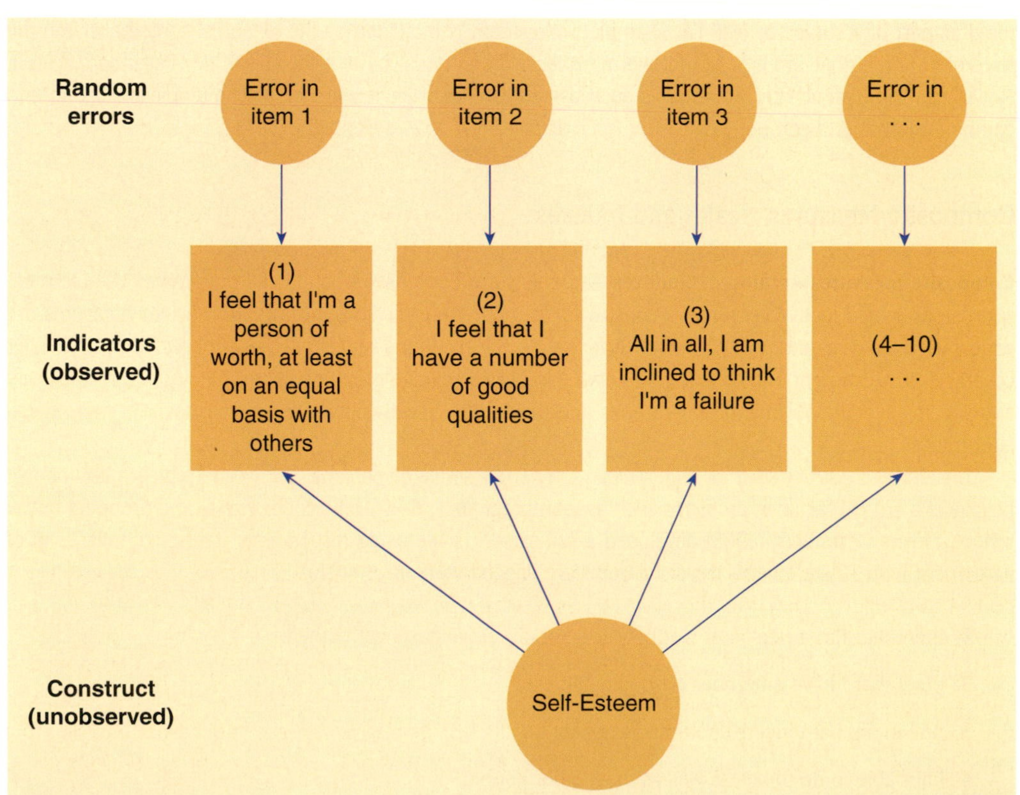

the error or noise that is unrelated to the construct. One of the advantages of composite measures (multi-item scales), as opposed to single-item measures, is that they permit the underlying construct and error components to be separated statistically. Statistical techniques, such as confirmatory factor analysis and structural equation modeling (discussed in Chapter 10), are used, with models like Figure 4.2, to implement that separation and more clearly represent the construct. More simply, researchers will often just sum up the items to form a scale, allowing the random measurement errors to cancel each other out.

Response Formats

The items listed for the self-esteem scale are statements to which respondents would indicate their level of agreement. But to completely describe the items, we must also specify the **response format**—the categories or range people are given in order to register their response to a question or statement. A response format might consist of two possible responses: *Agree* and *Disagree.* Or it might consist of five possible responses: *Strongly agree, Somewhat agree, Neither agree nor disagree, Somewhat disagree,* and *Strongly disagree.* This last format is associated with a *Likert scale,* named after the psychometrician Rensis Likert, who introduced this response format (see Box 4.3).

BOX 4.3
What Is a Likert Scale?

Rensis Likert was one of several pioneers of *psychometrics*—the measurement of intangible, psychological traits or attitudes using multi-item scales (Furr & Bacharach, 2008; McIver & Carmines, 1981). Likert introduced the agree-disagree response format, which became very widely used to create scales and in survey research more generally. Some refer to a single survey question with an agree-disagree response format as a Likert scale. It is more correct to call an individual question such as this either an item with a Likert response format or, more simply, an agree-disagree item or question.

True Likert scales—the composite measures—are composed of multiple agree-disagree items that have been carefully selected and empirically tested to reflect the same latent trait. Some incorrectly refer to all rating scales, regardless of the response format, as Likert scales. Other major innovators, particularly Louis L. Thurstone (Thurstone scaling) and Louis Guttman (Guttman scaling), developed different kinds of scales using different kinds of response formats. For an introduction to the construction of such scales, see Spector (1992).

Is It a Scale or an Index?

Although the terms *scale* and *index* are sometimes used interchangeably in social and policy research, people do often distinguish them. The defining features of scales and how they differ from indexes, however, can vary among disciplines, researchers, and situations.

The term *scale* often refers to a multi-item measure formed of intercorrelated items that reflect a latent construct. To be considered a good scale in this sense, the items must be highly correlated. The 10 items of the Rosenberg self-esteem scale, for example, are all highly correlated with each other and thus plausibly reflections of a single, latent construct (Gray-Little, Williams, & Hancock, 1997). Sometimes researchers use the term *Likert scale,* as discussed in Box 4.3, to refer to this type of scale.

Correspondingly, researchers may reserve the term *index* for composite measures in which the items are not necessarily well correlated. For example, the U.S. government's Consumer Price Index is composed of the prices of many different goods and services, weighted by their share in typical consumers' purchases. Of course, prices of food and prices of clothing may not be highly correlated, but they still belong in the CPI since consumers purchase both.

A related way of distinguishing scales and indexes is to use the term *scale* to refer to a multi-item measure that has been previously tested or validated and reserve the term *index* for a more ad hoc composite measure.

Finally, a scale can be defined more narrowly as a composite measure in which the items are chosen not because of their intercorrelation, but because they have a logical order that captures a *scale* of intensity of a construct being measured. For example, the original Bogardus (1933) social distance scale is composed of seven items judged to have a particular order showing decreasing intensity of social acceptance of someone from another race or ethnic group:

1. Would marry
2. Would have as a regular friend
3. Would work beside in an office
4. Would have several families in my neighborhood
5. Would have merely as a speaking acquaintance
6. Would have live outside my neighborhood
7. Would have live outside my country

Notice that these items represent more than just indicators of a latent construct; they aim to represent degrees of social distance. Many academic achievement tests are designed as scales in this sense, with items of increasing difficulty (see Box 4.4). Guttman scaling and Thurstone scaling are variations of this kind of measurement (see DeVellis, 1991). If *scale* is defined this way, then the term *index* would be used for a Likert-type scale (like the Rosenberg self-esteem scale) because the items are interchangeable indicators and do not fall in a definite order of intensity (as they do in the social distance scale).

QUESTION

When measuring a latent construct such as self-esteem, what are some of the advantages of using a composite measure composed of multiple indicators?

The term *index*, however, is perhaps most widely used to refer to various aggregate measures developed to track social or economic characteristics over time, such as the CPI. Stock indexes provide another well-known example, such as the S&P 500 index in the United States or the FTSE ("footsie") 100 index in the United Kingdom, both of which are aggregates of the diverse stock prices of the largest publicly traded companies in each country. The Consumer Sentiment Index, a measure of consumer confidence, is another well-known example (see Figure 4.3).

The different meanings of the terms *scale* and *index* can be subtle. Researchers use them differently or even interchangeably, depending on field and context, as we noted earlier. The most important thing is to focus on how a particular composite measure is constructed and how good it is—how valid and reliable. We turn to this topic next.

Validity

We hope that the measurements we use get at the truth—this is the intuitive notion of *measurement validity.* The **validity** of a measure refers to how well the measure actually represents the true construct of interest—the thing we are trying to measure. It turns out to be surprisingly hard to establish whether a measure is valid or not.

BOX 4.4
Using Items That Vary in Difficulty: Item Response Theory

Item response theory (IRT) is a psychometric approach that makes use of item difficulty in measuring an underlying trait (see Chapter 13 of Furr & Bacharach, 2008). Consider the example of a test to measure "math ability." The test could be made up of all equally difficult items so that the probability of a correct answer (for someone with a given level of math ability) is the same for each question. Alternatively, items could vary in difficulty (as they do in most tests) so that the probability of a correct answer would depend on both item difficulty and individual math ability. In this way, IRT uses variation in item difficulty to get at the underlying trait.

Although IRT is most easily understood in the context of educational testing, it can be applied in other contexts as well. In the self-esteem scale (discussed earlier in this chapter), consider substituting the new item "I often think I'm no good at all" for the original item "At times I think I'm no good at all." Both clearly get at the same underlying trait, self-esteem. But to agree with the newer item requires a lower level of self-esteem than to agree with the earlier one—it is "more difficult" in the language of IRT.

IRT is the basis of *computerized adaptive testing* (CAT), in which test takers can receive quite different items, tailored to their ability. CAT begins with an item of average difficulty. If the individual answers correctly, the next item is of higher than average difficulty. If the individual answers incorrectly, the next item is of lower than average difficulty, and so on. CAT is much more efficient and precise than conventional tests, because item difficulties are targeted toward exploring the relevant range of the trait for each individual.

Is the U.S. Poverty Measure Valid?

The answer, according to many people, is *no*—but not always for the same reasons (Blank, 2008). To get a feel for the idea, let's look at why different people view the official U.S. poverty measure as invalid.

The 1960s-era U.S. poverty threshold is updated by adjusting for inflation using the CPI. It is the same for all parts of the United States, so it does not reflect local differences in the cost of living—even the striking differences in housing costs across the United States. In 2013, for a family of four (with two adults and two children), the poverty line was about $2,000 a month. Using Orshansky's basic formula, that works out to $667 for food and $1,333 per month for shelter, clothing, transportation, and everything else.

Most people today spend less than a third of their income on food, because the price of food, adjusted for inflation, has fallen. But the real price of housing, for example, has increased dramatically. So many contend that the income needed to afford the necessities of life these days is far more than three times the price of a basic food plan.

On the other hand, in the mid-1960s, poor people had only their own incomes with which to purchase necessities. Following the War on Poverty, programs such as food stamps, Medicaid, and public housing provided in-kind benefits. In the 1990s, the Earned Income Tax Credit (EITC) put cash directly in the hands of poor families. The definition of income in the U.S. poverty measure does not count these in-kind benefits or the EITC rebate. So some argue that the official poverty measure overestimates poverty.

While the U.S. poverty measure wasn't a bad attempt in 1966, its validity in today's world is highly questionable. Building on extensive prior analysis, the Census Bureau created a Supplemental Poverty Measure (SPM) that attempts to address all the concerns described above, plus others (Short, 2011). But the same political reasons that made it difficult to switch poverty measures for so many years (Blank, 2008) mean that

QUESTION

Is the frequency of attending religious services a valid measure of the strength of someone's religious beliefs? How, and how not?

the SPM will likely be used for research purposes only, with the long-standing U.S. poverty measure remaining the government's official poverty gauge. Moreover, the SPM has been challenged, particularly for its construct of "material" poverty, excluding health care and health insurance, and the view that the corresponding operationalization undermines the validity of the SPM, even as a measure of material poverty (Korenman & Remler, 2013). In the end, it is just very difficult to create a valid measure of something as complex as poverty.

There are many approaches to establishing validity and therefore many different types of validity (Carmines & Zeller, 1979). The terminology can get confusing, so we will focus more on the logic and ideas. One class of approaches involves empirical strategies for testing or demonstrating validity, referred to as *criterion-related validity* (Trochim, 2001), which we will get to in a bit. But first, we discuss nonempirical, essentially judgmental assessments of how well a measure represents a construct.

Face Validity

To judge validity, we often look at what is called the **face validity** of the measure: Just based on looking at the measure, on the face of it, how well does the measure get at what we want to measure?

The polygraph—or lie detector—is supposed to measure whether a person is lying or telling the truth. In fact, it measures heart rate, perspiration, and other physiological manifestations of nervousness. The concept of a lie is translated into nervousness, which in turn is translated into the physiological manifestations of nervousness.

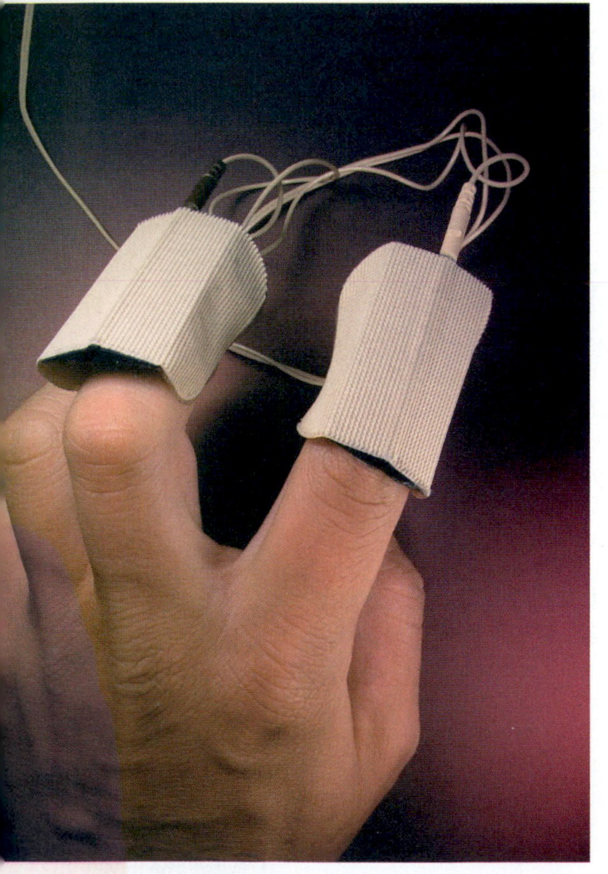

A polygraph attempts to measure if someone is lying.
Source: © iStockphoto.com/MummuMedia.

On the one hand, this has some face validity—people telling lies are often nervous. On the other hand, it lacks face validity because being nervous and telling a lie are not the same thing and do not always coincide.

Do Self-Reported Measures Have Face Validity?

Many measures work by asking people to report what they did—called **self-reporting**. For example, exit polls ask people how they voted, and behavioral health surveys ask people how much they smoke or drink alcohol. On the one hand, such measures appear to have face validity because they directly ask what we want to measure. On the other hand, what people do is not the same as what they say they do, so the face validity of such behavioral self-reports can be questioned, especially when they involve sensitive or socially undesirable behaviors. Moreover, we will see later on that self-reports of certain subjects have poor criterion-related validity.

Content Validity

A good measure should include all the important dimensions of the construct, which is the idea of **content validity**. For example, a measure of suffering, or not suffering, from pain would not be a valid measure of *health* because it would miss so many other dimensions of health, such as illness (which may or may not cause pain), physical limitations, fatigue, emotional well-being, and so on. So even if our measure accurately captured pain, it would lack content validity as a measure of general health.

The content validity of a measure also depends on whether it captures the full range of *variation* in the construct. A yes/no question about pain on a survey might be able to differentiate between "no" pain and "some" pain, but it would not be able to differentiate between "moderate" pain and "severe" pain.

High-Stakes Educational Tests: Do They Miss Some Dimensions of Educational Achievement?

Standardized educational tests are the subject of much debate these days. Some criticize them, saying that they leave out many dimensions of education, focusing only on math and some English language skills. The tests often do not include history or science or a variety of other important topics. Moreover, they are mostly multiple-choice tests that do not gauge students' ability to write an essay or to solve a multifaceted, real-world problem. Such criticisms amount to saying that the content validity of such tests is low, because some dimensions of educational achievement are missed.

Others, however, are strong supporters of standardized tests. They note that empirically the test results predict later academic performance, a form of criterion-related validity known as predictive validity, which we cover shortly. The two views are not inconsistent: Standardized tests could do a good job of capturing some dimensions of education, dimensions that are important for later achievement, while simultaneously missing other dimensions. Few measures capture all dimensions of a complex construct.

Standardized tests measure some, but not all, dimensions of learning.
Source: © Can Stock Photo Inc. / cmcderm1.

Valid for What Purpose?

Because no measure is perfect in all ways, validity should be assessed based on the purpose for which the measure is used. For example, if today's educational tests are viewed as a measure of fundamental skills, they could be valid. But as a measure of all that we might expect from our public schools, many believe that they have limited content validity due to important dimensions being missed.

Consider the concept of happiness, which sometimes gets measured in surveys with the following question:

Taken all together, how would you say things are these days—would you say that you are very happy, pretty happy, or not too happy?

1. *Very happy*
2. *Pretty happy*
3. *Not too happy*

It turns out that this very simple kind of self-reported happiness measure works pretty well—it is valid—for very broad studies of general populations, such as comparing happiness levels across nations or for populations over time (Layard, 2005). But it would not be valid for a clinical diagnosis of depression. For this, psychologists use a much more detailed measure such as the Beck Depression Inventory, a scale that has 21 multiple-choice questions. So the validity of a measure depends on how it is used.

QUESTION

Explain the concepts of face validity and content validity in your own words.

Content validity, face validity, and other nonempirical methods of assessing validity are the first and perhaps the most fundamental forms of validity to assess. But it is hard to prove validity in these ways; it remains primarily a matter of subjective judgment. Sometimes, we would like to have objective ways to test or demonstrate validity.

Criterion-Related Validity

To demonstrate the validity of a measure—to validate it, as researchers sometimes say—it is often necessary to turn to empirical evidence. This is referred to broadly as **criterion-related validity**, and there are various forms of it.

Self-Reported Drug Use: Is It Valid?

Suppose we want to measure people's illegal drug use. This is not too conceptually difficult: We know pretty well what it means to take illegal drugs. Operationally, we might measure this by directly asking people about their drug use—in other words, *self-reported* drug use. This has some face validity, but will people tell the truth?

To find out, we need to compare the self-reported measure with some other, more objective measure of drug use. For example, chemical analysis of urine and hair can reveal recent drug use. Using this method in a validity study of steel plant workers in the United States, researchers found that the rate estimated from urine and hair analysis was about 50% higher than self-reported drug use on a questionnaire (R. Cook, Bernstein, Arrington, & Andrews, 1997).

The National Center for Health Statistics (NCHS) uses surveys to estimate that about 9% of the U.S. population 12 years of age and older used illegal drugs in the past month (NCHS, 2011), representing about 20 million people. The steelworkers study, however, suggests that this figure could perhaps be much higher.

If a measure agrees with another contemporaneous measure of the same concept, it is said to have **concurrent validity**. Clearly, self-reported drug use has poor concurrent validity. Demonstrations of concurrent validity are only as good as the concurrent measure, however. If hair and urine analyses turn out to be faulty measures of recent drug use, then this validity test does not tell us as much as we might hope.

When asked in surveys, people tend to underreport illegal drug use. *Source:* © iStockphoto.com/Fitzer.

Does the Measure Predict Behavior?

Another approach to validity is to test how well our measure predicts some future behavior or variable that is a logical consequence of the thing we are trying to measure. So if we want to validate a measure of job satisfaction, for example, we might test to see if those who score low on our measure are more likely to quit their job in 12 months than those who score high on the measure. If so, we can say our measure of job satisfaction has **predictive validity**—it predicts something that logically should follow in the future from the thing we hope we are measuring.

Does Consumer Confidence Predict Economic Activity?

The University of Michigan conducts a monthly survey to measure consumer confidence, officially known as the *Consumer Sentiment Index*. As the name suggests, the index (composed of five survey questions) aims to measure how positive or negative consumers feel about the economy and, thus, how likely they will be to spend. Consumer spending constitutes about two thirds of the $17 trillion U.S. economy, so the Consumer Sentiment Index is a widely watched indicator.

How well does the Michigan index predict actual economic activity? Figure 4.3 shows the pattern over the past several decades, with the periods of economic recession shaded in. The Michigan index trends downward going into recessions and moves back up coming out of recessions. So it seems to have predictive validity—it predicts something that a measure of consumer confidence logically should: consumer spending and in turn economic activity.

Does the Measure Relate to Other Variables as Expected?

In many situations, researchers must use other, less direct strategies to assess validity. One such strategy is to make comparisons with other variables that theoretically or logically should be related to our measure of interest. Often, these variables are part of the same survey or other data set, rather than future behaviors. And they are not alternative measures of the same thing, as in concurrent validity. It's helpful to consider an example.

The European Social Survey (ESS)—a random sample survey of 40,000 people from more than 30 countries—includes a self-reported measure of health, which asks people to rate their health from 1 = *very bad* to 5 = *very good*. This is interesting and potentially very useful data—but how valid is the ESS measure of health? It is impossibly expensive to obtain current medical records or clinical health exams for so many survey respondents. And we are unlikely to be able to track these individuals into the future to observe their health outcomes. But we do know that older people everywhere suffer more from health problems than do younger people, and the ESS has a measure of age as one of a number of standard demographic variables. So logically we should expect the ESS health measure (if it is a valid measure of health) to be negatively

Figure 4.3 The Consumer Sentiment Index

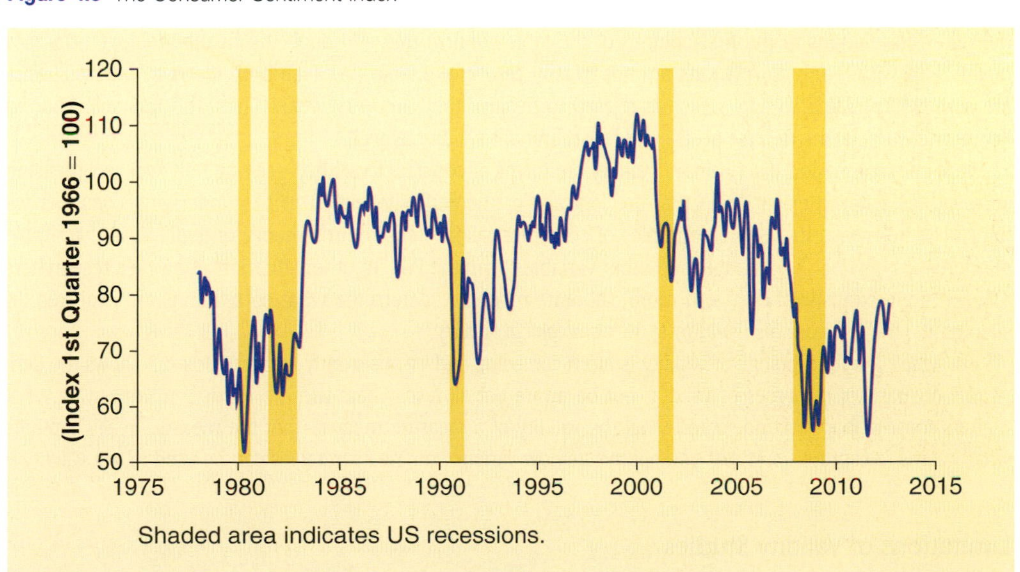

Source: Survey Research Center, University of Michigan; Federal Reserve Bank of St. Louis.

Table 4.1 Correlations From the European Social Survey (ESS)

	Health	Age	Ideology (Left-Right)	Religiosity
Health	1			
Age	−.36	1		
Ideology (left-right)	.03	.07	1	
Religiosity	−.05	.19	.17	1

Source: The European Social Survey (ESS).

correlated with the ESS age variable (negatively correlated in the sense of more age, less health). Let's calculate the correlation (r) and see what we find:

$$r_{\text{age-health}} = -.36$$

The result is encouraging: The ESS self-reported measure of health is, indeed, negatively correlated with age as we logically and theoretically expected. And $r = -.36$ is a moderately strong correlation, which also makes sense. The ESS health measure behaves as we expect the construct of health to behave.

The correlation with age confirms that the ESS health measure has what researchers call **convergent validity** because it converges (correlates) with variables we'd expect it to be related to.

Similarly, we can also look to see if the ESS measure of health is *not* related to other measures that it should have little or no logical connection with, such as ideology. This is called **discriminant validity**. Too strong a correlation with other, logically unrelated things indicates that a measure is perhaps capturing something other than what it was intended to measure.

Researchers often consider convergent and discriminant validity together by looking at a correlation matrix as in Table 4.1.

Table 4.1 again shows the moderately strong negative correlation with age, $r = -.36$, suggesting that the ESS measure has convergent validity. But the ESS health measure should *not* be related to many other things, such as political ideology (left-right) or religiosity (how religious people consider themselves to be). Indeed, the other correlations in the first column of the table confirm this. Although the health-ideology (.03) and health-religiosity (−.05) correlations are not exactly zero in the table (because both ideology and religiosity are somewhat related to age, which is related to health), they are very weak. Thus, the ESS self-reported health measure seems to have pretty good discriminant validity as well.

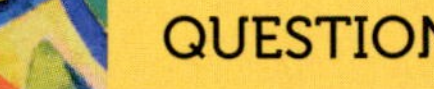

QUESTION

Suppose one college aptitude test is considered more valid than another because it is more strongly associated with students' later GPA in college. What kind of validity is being assessed?

Both convergent and discriminant validity are forms of **construct validity**—seeing how well our measure corresponds with other variables that are logically or theoretically related to the underlying construct we purport to be measuring. Some examples of construct validity require little theory or logic, as in the simple relationships between health, age, and other variables from the ESS. In other situations, however, researchers rely on more extensive theory and more elaborate models to determine what correlations are expected. In such cases, the tests are also said to show *nomological validity*.

But again, the terminology of validity is often confusing and inconsistently applied. Box 4.5 shows the definitions of many of the types of validity, but be aware not all researchers use the terms the same way. What matters most is that you understand what the validity of a measure means—that the measure really captures what it aims to capture—and that you appreciate how various empirical strategies can be used to test validity.

Limitations of Validity Studies

When researchers and others say a measure has been *validated,* they generally mean that some effort has been made to empirically study the properties or characteristics of a proposed or established measure. Curiously, often

BOX 4.5
The Various (Measurement) Validities

Researchers refer to many different types of validity and not always with consistency. The terms are less important than the big ideas and a feel for what validity means and how it can be demonstrated. However, just in case, here is a fairly complete list of the various validities and their definitions (adapted from Carmines & Zeller, 1979):

Face validity	Does the measure look like it gets at the construct, on the face of it? Does it seem to make sense?
Content validity	Does the measure include all the important dimensions of the construct? Does it capture the full range of the construct?
Criterion-related validity	How well does the measure relate, empirically, to various criteria that can demonstrate its validity?
Concurrent validity	Does the measure concur or agree with other established classifications or test scores?
Predictive validity	Does the measure predict logically related outcomes or behaviors in the future?
Convergent validity	Does the measure correlate with other, closely related measures in the same data set?
Discriminant validity	Is the measure independent of (not correlated with) other measures in the same data set that it does not logically relate to?
Construct validity	Does the measure behave in a statistical model in a way that would be expected, based on theory and prior research?
Nomological validity	Does the measure behave as it should in a more complex theory with a system of other variables?

Importantly, all these terms refer to the validity of *measures.* The term *validity* is also applied to *studies*—for example, the internal and external validity of a study—as we explain in other chapters.

so-called validity studies turn out, on closer reading, to be primarily *reliability* studies—studies that look at the test-retest consistency or internal consistency of indicators that make up a measure (as will be discussed shortly).

True validity studies seek to show how well a measure reflects the construct it aims to represent through one or more of the criterion-related validity strategies discussed above, such as concurrent validity, predictive validity, convergent validity, or discriminant validity. Box 4.6 describes a genuine validity study. But a validity study is not an all-or-nothing proposition—often the evidence is less than completely convincing.

Moreover, many measurements in use in research and public policy have not been empirically validated at all; the researchers or policy analysts simply claim or assume their measures are valid. Often this can be because there is no clear criterion of validity.

And as we have seen, a measure can be valid for one purpose but not another. A simple one-question measure of happiness might be valid for a large social survey but not for clinical diagnosis of depression. Therefore, you can't simply accept the validity of a measure because it was tested in one particular context

BOX 4.6
Example of a Validity Study

By Spencer, Elizabeth A., Appleby, Paul N., Davey, Gwyneth K., & Key, Timothy J. (2007). Validity of self-reported height and weight. *Public Health Nutrition, 5*(4), 561–565. Reproduced with permission.

Objective: To assess the validity of self-reported height and weight by comparison with measured height and weight in a sample of middle-aged men and women, and to determine the extent of misclassification of body mass index (BMI) arising from differences between self-reported and measured values.

Design: Analysis of self-reported and measured height and weight data from participants in the Oxford cohort of the European Prospective Investigation into Cancer and Nutrition (EPIC–Oxford).

Subjects: Four thousand eight hundred and eight British men and women aged 35–76 years.

Results: Spearman rank correlations between self-reported and measured height, weight and BMI were high ($r < 0.9$, $p > 0.0001$). Height was overestimated by a mean of 1.23 (95% confidence interval [CI] 1.11–1.34) cm in men and 0.60 (0.51–0.70) cm in women; the extent of overestimation was greater in older men and women, shorter men and heavier women. Weight was underestimated by a mean of 1.85 (1.72–1.99) kg in men and 1.40 (1.31–1.49) kg in women; the extent of underestimation was greater in heavier men and women, but did not vary with age or height. Using standard categories of BMI, 22.4% of men and 18.0% of women were classified incorrectly based on self-reported height and weight. After correcting the self-reported values using predictive equations derived from a 10% sample of subjects, misclassification decreased to 15.2% in men and 13.8% in women.

Conclusions: Self-reported height and weight data are valid for identifying relationships in epidemiological studies. In analyses where anthropometric factors are the primary variables of interest, measurements in a representative sample of the study population can be used to improve the accuracy of estimates of height, weight and BMI.

and with one use in mind. If you intend to use the measure for something else, even having a published validity test may not help you.

Validity is obviously an important quality in a measure. We want to know that our measures capture what they were designed to capture. But there is another aspect of a good measure that also matters: *reliability*—or the consistency of the measure. Indeed, discussions of validity and reliability often go hand in hand. But to understand reliability, it is helpful to first consider the concept of measurement error.

Measurement Error

Error is an inherent part of the measurement process. The old carpenter's adage, "measure twice, cut once," expresses our common understanding that any one measurement of something—even something as simple as a length of wood—is likely to be off the mark, even if only just a touch. Measurement error comes from the imperfections of our instruments (or questionnaires), from the imperfections in our use of the instruments, and from the nature of how people respond to being measured.

Bias

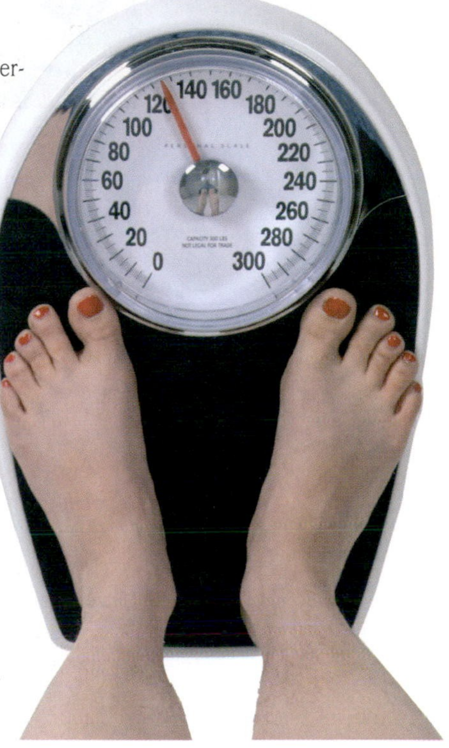

All measurements have errors.

Source: © iStockphoto.com/twilightproductions.

It helps to distinguish two forms of measurement error: those errors that are random and average out to zero, referred to as **random measurement error** or **noise**; and those errors that are systematic and on average bend the measure in a particular direction, referred to as **systematic measurement error** or **bias**. Let's consider systematic measurement error or bias first, as this is what most people have in mind when we think about an "error" in a measurement—although it is often not what researchers and statisticians mean by measurement error.

Say your bathroom scale has not been well calibrated and that, when no one is standing on the scale, the needle rests at +2 pounds instead of zero. Each morning when you weigh yourself, then, the reading will be 2 pounds more than your actual weight. This is a *systematic* error—a 2-pound *bias* (upward) in the measurement of your weight.

Bias is closely related to the idea of validity—although the term typically has a narrower and mostly quantitative meaning. Bias in measurement usually refers to a systematic upward or downward distortion in the level of a measurement. Validity of a measure, in contrast, refers to the broader definition and meaning of what we aim to measure.

Bias in social and policy research comes from different sources, for example from the wording or order of questions on a questionnaire or from the tendency of people to give socially desirable answers. Hence researchers talk about *question wording bias*, *social desirability bias*, and other types of measurement bias. And be careful not to confuse measurement bias with other forms of bias in research, such as sampling bias or bias in estimating causal effects, which are covered in separate chapters. Box 4.7 provides more explanation of the various types of bias and related terminology.

Also, be aware that the term *bias* in research methods and statistics does not mean the same thing as the term *bias* when speaking of a person's actions or behavior, although they are related. When a person prejudges or makes unfair conclusions about an issue, a person, or a situation, we say they are biased—for example, a male boss may be biased in his evaluation of the work done by female employees in the organization. Bias in this sense is understood as a characteristic of a person's viewpoint or thought processes. In research, bias is a characteristic of the procedures (such as measurement) that produce evidence—independent of the researcher's thought processes or intentions. However, bias in the more psychological sense remains a factor also in research, particularly when people interpret their findings and draw conclusions.

Random Error—Noise

Random measurement error, or *noise,* is a bit more difficult to visualize, but it's a very real and important issue in research. Let's return to our simple example of the bathroom scale. Imagine your scale is a bit old and has a slightly bent needle that doesn't quite rotate as smoothly as it once did. So the needle gets a bit stuck each time it settles, although sometimes it gets stuck above the true mark and sometimes below it. But these errors are random—over many mornings, in the long run, they do not make you appear systematically heavier or lighter than you really are. In other words, the average of these errors over many, repeated measurements (of the same object, you) is zero. This is what researchers mean by random error or noise.

Random error or noise is a very real part of research, as all measurements have some degree of unpredictable or uncontrollable errors that happen in the process of doing the measurement. Mechanical instruments have flaws; questionnaires can be ambiguous or unclear; research workers may use instruments

BOX 4.7
Bias, Bias Everywhere

Bias—systematic error—has many causes and appears in many forms in research, beyond just measurement bias. There can be bias in sampling (which we cover in Chapter 5) and bias in the estimation of causal effects (which we cover in the chapters in Part IV). But in all cases, bias refers to a systematic difference between what one is trying to estimate (body weight, the level of poverty in a community, or the effect of class size on test scores) and the truth or real value. And bias always refers to systematic errors (estimates that are too high, or too low) as distinguished from random errors (which tend to average out).

And even measurement bias can come from a variety of sources, some of which we will discuss when we cover surveys in Chapter 7:

Interviewer or observer bias: distortions or systematic bias attributable to the particular interviewer or observer who is collecting the data.

Instrument bias: refers to results that are inaccurate or distorted by a faulty or uncalibrated scientific or other instrument.

Question order bias: responses influenced by the form or content of preceding questions.

Question wording bias: responses that are distorted by how the question is worded.

Response bias: a broad term that refers to various ways in which respondents alter their answers because of the format or context of the study.

Social desirability bias: the tendency to respond in a socially, morally, or politically correct way.

inconsistently; interviewers or observers may mistakenly record an observation; respondents to a survey can get impatient or distracted; the machines, or workers, that enter data into a database can make keypunch errors; and so on. All these things can combine to produce random error or noise in our measurements.

Realize that both types of measurement error—bias and noise—can be present at the same time in a measurement. You can forget to calibrate your bathroom scale, so that it systematically adds 2 pounds to your weight, while at the same time the needle gives inconsistent readings each time you weigh yourself. In fact, real measurements often include some degree of both systematic error (bias) and random error (noise).

Bias and Noise in the U.S. Poverty Measure

As we've already seen, some consider the U.S. poverty measure to be biased downward, that it underestimates the real level of poverty in the U.S. society. The formula for calculating the poverty line (three times the USDA Economy Food Plan) is out of date, because the cost of food has declined while housing, transportation, health care, and other necessities are more expensive. Others point out that the U.S. poverty measure may be biased upward, that it may overstate poverty because it fails to take into account housing subsidies, food stamps, subsidized child care, tax credits, and other such benefits that were not available in the 1960s. Both are right in many ways—and the debate quickly moves to the broader validity issues involved in measuring a difficult concept such as poverty.

But what about the question of random error, or noise, in the official U.S. poverty measure? To think about this kind of measurement error—the kind of measurement error that researchers and statisticians often have in mind—we need to consider the actual sources of data the U.S. government uses to measure income and family size.

The government, as it turns out, uses several sources of information on household income to calculate poverty. Let's focus on the CPS, the major source of income data for the regular annual poverty estimates that appear most often in the news or research reports. Random measurement error, or noise, comes from the procedures used to carry out this survey.

The CPS is a labor force survey conducted mostly by telephone as well as in-person interviews with more than 75,000 households. (This is the sample size of the Annual Social and Economic Supplement, which provides the data for annual poverty estimates.) A single respondent in each household is asked a series of questions about his or her employment and income as well as the employment and income of other members of the household who are 16 years of age or older. Some 1,500 interviewers are needed to carry out the CPS, and although they receive careful training and supervision and now use computer-assisted interviews, they undoubtedly make occasional mistakes in asking questions and recording answers.

Respondents undoubtedly make mistakes too, as it is difficult to recall and report one's own income flawlessly during a long, live interview. Moreover, respondents to the CPS must report on the income of other members of the household too (proxy reporting), which is even more difficult for people to do without making at least some errors.

The various sources of household income recorded by the CPS are then added up, and total household income is reported—say $23,820 for the family with ID number 27031 in the data set. Imputation, methods for filling in values when income questions are unanswered or otherwise left blank, provides yet another source of error. Suppose this family has four members, as recorded by the CPS. (However, this number could also involve an error as both respondents may misreport or interviewers may erroneously record the real number of family members.) We then compare the family's income with the poverty line ($23,550 for a family of four) and classify our case with ID number 27031 as "not poor."

You can see how this classification could quite easily be mistaken—it could involve error. And in the CPS, there are undoubtedly many cases that lie close enough to the poverty threshold that random errors in the CPS measurement of income (or family size) could lead to numerous misclassifications—one way or the other (random measurement error).

QUESTION

Explain why data entry errors are a form of random error or noise.

Bias and noise are a part of every process of measurement, from weighing yourself on a bathroom scale to tracking poverty in the U.S. population. For a more formal treatment of bias and noise, known as *classical test theory*, see Box 4.8.

BOX 4.8
Classical Test Theory

The following equation or mathematical model of measurement, which comes from classical test theory, can provide another way to think about the issue of errors in measurement:

$$X_i = T_i + B_i + N_i$$

X stands for the observed value of our variable, for example, the total income of a given family i. The equation alerts us to the fact that the observed or *measured* income of the family, what we come up with from some measurement procedure, such as the CPS, is really a combination of T, the *true* income of the family, plus perhaps some *bias, B*, and certainly at least some *noise, N*. Ideally, we would like B and N to be zero—and thus X to be a pure reflection of T, the true value we are trying to measure. But unfortunately, that is not the case with most real-world measurements. To illustrate, here is a snapshot of a segment of some raw data:

(Continued)

(Continued)

i	*X*
1	45,737
2	19,074
3	32,911
4	16,987

Again, *i* stands for individual, so this table is showing the first four individuals in a data set of many such measurements. *X* again stands for the variable, in this case household income (in dollars per year). Individual 2, for example, has an annual family income of $19,074.

But notice that we directly observe neither *T, B,* nor *N* in our data—only *X,* which reflects some unknown combination of all three of these elements ($X_i = T_i + B_i + N_i$). In practice, the extent of bias *B* or noise *N*—in place of the true score *T*—remains for the most part a matter of judgment and debate. To actually observe *B* or *N,* special validity or reliability studies—some discussed earlier in this chapter—need to be carried out.

Reliability

Measurement **reliability** refers to the consistency of a measure—and it is directly related to the concept of random error or noise. If our measure has little noise, it will produce few random errors each time we take a measurement. It will be a consistent measure with good reliability. If the measure contains a lot of noise, however, it will be full of random errors, and we'll get inconsistent results—even if we measure essentially the same object. It will have poor reliability. Figure 4.4 illustrates good and poor reliability graphically.

A reliable measure is not necessarily a valid one. This is why Figure 4.4 does not include the *construct*—the trait or attribute that we are trying to measure in the first place. Indeed, we can have a very reliable measurement that misleads—such as a bathroom scale that consistently gives the wrong weight. Thus, a measure can have little or no noise but still be seriously biased or reflect something quite different from what we intended to measure.

Why Reliability Matters

But reliability still matters. And it matters in different ways, depending on what purpose we have in mind. There are at least three main ways in which measures get used in research and in practice.

Calculating Averages

Measures can be used to produce averages (means or proportions) over a group, such as determining the share of U.S. families in poverty. Provided the sample is large enough, a high degree of reliability may be unnecessary because the random measurement errors cancel each other out and thus have little effect on the average. But large random errors do increase the variability of the measure—and in turn confidence intervals (or margins of error) as explained in Chapter 9.

Figure 4.5 shows some made-up data in which the same generic *X variable* is graphed, with each depiction adding larger random errors to the original variable. Even as the reliability gets worse, and the noise

Figure 4.4 Good and Poor Reliability

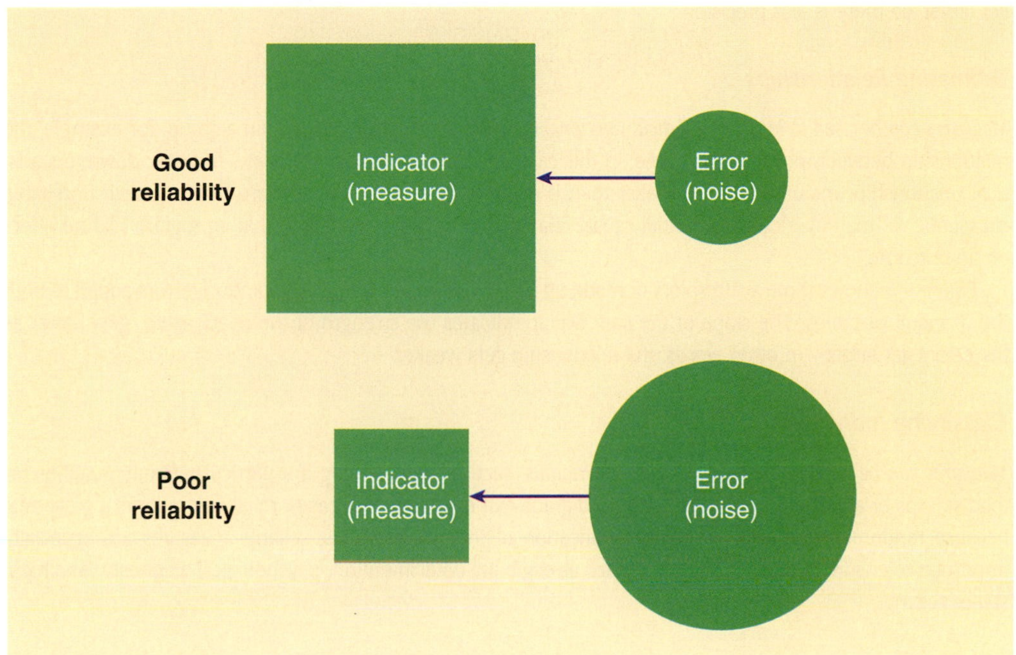

Figure 4.5 As Reliability Gets Worse, Averages Change Very Little

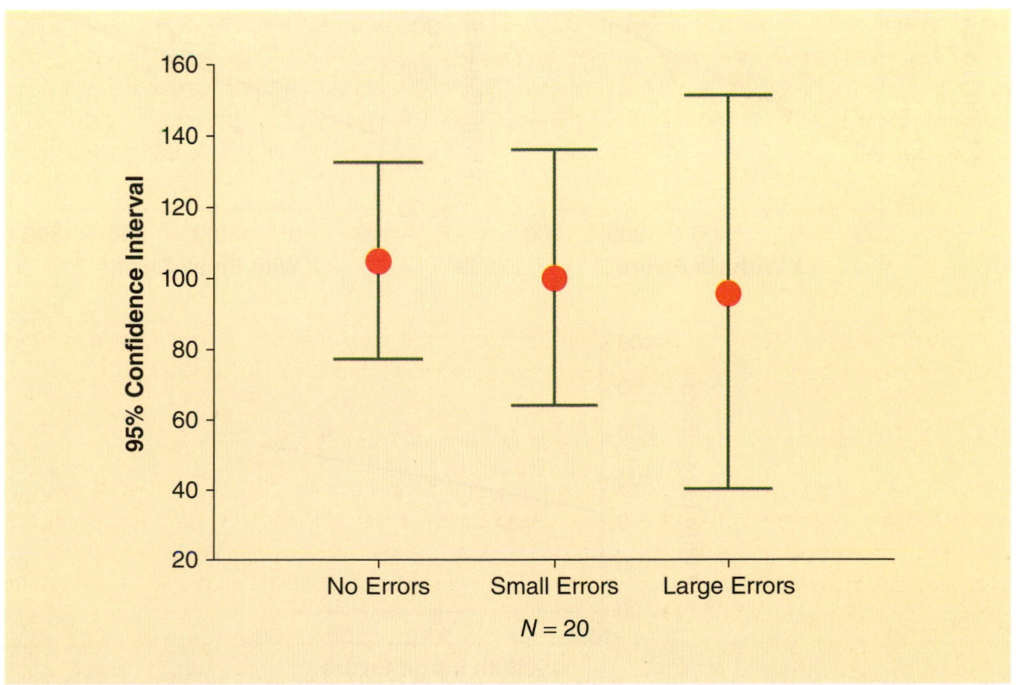

increases, the averages change very little and remain close to 100. But notice that the confidence intervals get larger, so there is less precision.

Estimating Relationships

Measures can be used to look at statistical relationships (such as correlations) within a group, for example, the relationship between poverty and crime. In this case, random errors can attenuate, or water down, a statistical relationship, making it seem weaker than it really is. This can be a problem because, with unreliable measures, we may overlook a potential causal relationship or falsely conclude that a program had no effect on an outcome.

Figure 4.6 shows three scatterplots of made-up data, with increasingly large random errors added to both the *X* and *Y* variables. The slope of the line, which indicates the strength of the relationship, gets flatter as the errors get larger—in other words, the relationship gets weaker.

Classifying Individuals

Measures can be used to target or classify individuals, such as determining if a particular family qualifies for food stamps or a particular child passes a third-grade exit exam. In such cases, reliability matters a great deal because random errors imply the misclassification of individuals. Thus, reliable measures are especially important to ensure fairness in situations such as eligibility determination, psychological diagnoses, and high-stakes testing.

Figure 4.6 As Reliability Gets Worse, Relationships Get Weaker

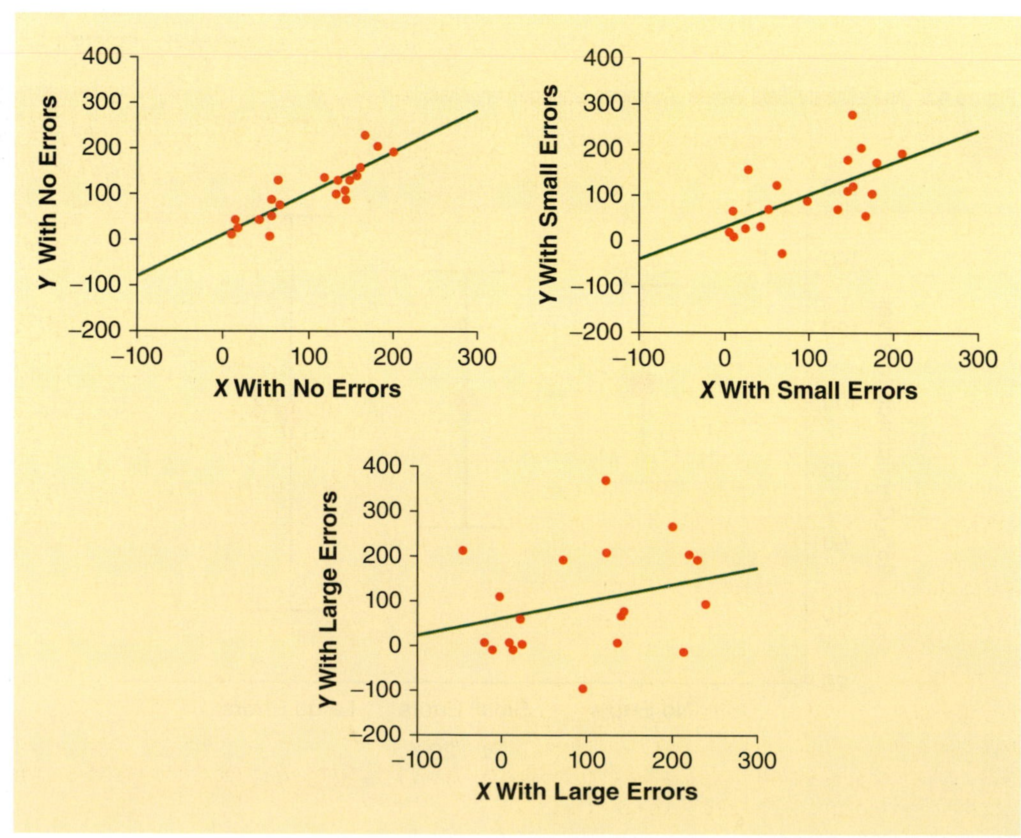

Tracking Changes Over Time

The growing emphasis on accountability and performance measurement means that more and more organizations are being assessed by their improvement over time, including schools, police departments, hospitals, businesses, and many more. And often methods used to establish the effectiveness of programs or interventions also rely on measuring changes over time. But repeating a measurement procedure in a consistent, reliable way can prove difficult to do in practice, especially as technology and conditions change. And mistaking a random fluctuation for a real gain, or decline, in an outcome can lead to faulty decisions for policy and practice.

Although we would like always to have good reliability, there are real costs to achieving it.

Many Ways to Tell If a Measure Is Reliable

Reliability is easier in some ways to demonstrate than validity—because we don't have the construct, the "truth," to worry about. We just need to show that a measure consistently gives the same result when applied to the same object or reality. Repeating a measurement and observing its consistency is a good way both to think about and to test reliability. Within that broad basic idea, there are a variety of methods for determining reliability.

Test-Retest Reliability: Measuring the Same Thing Twice

The most basic approach to determining reliability is to measure the same thing twice—what researchers call **test-retest reliability**. For example, an education department might hope that its new fifth-grade language arts test is reliable, that it does not contain too much noise or random error. So when developing the test (often under contract to specialized educational testing companies), the department will give the test to a group of students and, after a period of time, will test the same students again. The correlation of the first test results with the second test results provides a gauge of the reliability of the new language arts test.

However, because people learn from taking tests the first time, scores the second time around can reflect this. Test-retest reliability makes a lot of sense for a relatively stable physical characteristic, such as someone's weight on a given morning, but it is more problematic when people can learn or when the intrinsic construct we are measuring changes over time.

Errors can be made in determining eligibility for benefit programs.

Source: © iStockphoto.com/pixeljar.

Interrater Reliability: How Consistent Are the Research Workers?

As we've seen, often measurements get carried out by people, raters or interviewers, hired and trained to do the measurement. So another type of reliability that we should worry about is how similar the scores of the raters or interviewers are when they measure the same person or object. This is called **interrater reliability**. Obviously, we want the scores to be the same (or at least very similar) and not too dependent on the particular views, personalities, or habits of the research workers.

For example, we could ask four street cleanliness raters, working for a city sanitation department, to rate the same 20 blocks selected from across a sanitation district. The correlation of the four raters' scores with each other would serve as our gauge of reliability. We could work to improve the habits of those raters whose scores did not match closely with the others.

Reliability of Scales: Split-Half Reliability and Internal Consistency

When the measure is a scale composed of multiple indicators, such as the SF-36 health scale or the 10-item Rosenberg self-esteem scale, reliability can be gauged through the **internal consistency** of the various indicators. Do the indicators or items go together—do they paint a consistent picture?

One way to gauge this is to calculate a measure of the *split-half reliability*: Divide the items randomly into two halves, say an SF-18a and an SF-18b, and then look at the correlation between the two halves. Correlations range from 0 to 1, so a higher correlation indicates a more internally reliable scale (see Chapter 8 for more explanation of statistical correlation).

A more sophisticated and more often used measure of internal consistency is *Cronbach's alpha* (named after Lee Cronbach, the educational psychologist who invented it). Cronbach's alpha (sometimes reported as just alpha [α]) is the average of all possible split-half correlations. So it still measures how one half of a test corresponds with the other, but it averages out the variation due to the luck of the draw, as it were, in the split-half method.

Alpha ranges from 0 to 1, with .70 sometimes used as the minimally acceptable level of reliability (Spector, 1992). But as we pointed out earlier, much depends on the purpose of the measure. An alpha just above .70 is not nearly good enough for purposes of psychological diagnosis or high-stakes tests applied to individuals, for example.

The more correlated the responses to the scale items are with each other, the larger the alpha. And the more items we include in the scale, holding constant the degree of correlation, the larger the alpha. So researchers can improve the internal consistency of their scales by selecting items that go well together and by using more items. This is one reason psychological tests have so many items—the Beck Depression Inventory has 21 items, for example—because the more items, the greater the reliability.

In a sense, you can think of internal consistency as similar to interrater reliability—if you imagine that the items or indicators are in a sense like "raters" who are rating the same object or concept.

In your own words, explain how the test-retest and split-half methods both get at the basic notion of reliability.

Parallel Forms Reliability: Did Educational Test Scores Really Go Up?

In the United States and around the world, standardized tests are increasingly employed to evaluate students and schools. Newspapers and politicians claim success if the scores go up or look for blame if they go down—but are these year-over-year differences real?

For obvious reasons, the questions on educational tests cannot be the same each year. But are tests using different questions really comparable? This is a reliability question, sometimes referred to as **parallel forms reliability**. Test scores may go up or down this year for a variety of reasons—the students taking the test each year are a different group of individuals, schools improve or decline, teachers and principals move in and out of the system, and so on. But the test itself changes too.

Validity and Reliability: Contrasted and Compared

A measure can be valid but not reliable, or reliable but not valid—or it can be both (the best result), or neither (the worst). The analogy of shooting at a target helps illustrate this idea, as shown in Figure 4.7. The lower left target shows a shooter who is reliable but not valid—her shots are highly consistent but off the mark. The upper right target, in contrast, illustrates a shooter who is valid but unreliable—on average his shots center on the bull's-eye but are wildly dispersed (lots of random errors). The lower right target illustrates the best shooter—the shots are both consistent (reliable) and on the mark (valid). Finally, the upper left shooter is the worst, as the shots are both widely dispersed and off the mark. Picturing this bull's-eye analogy often helps in learning and applying the distinction between validity and reliability.

Figure 4.7 Bull's-eye Illustration of Possible Validity and Reliability Combinations

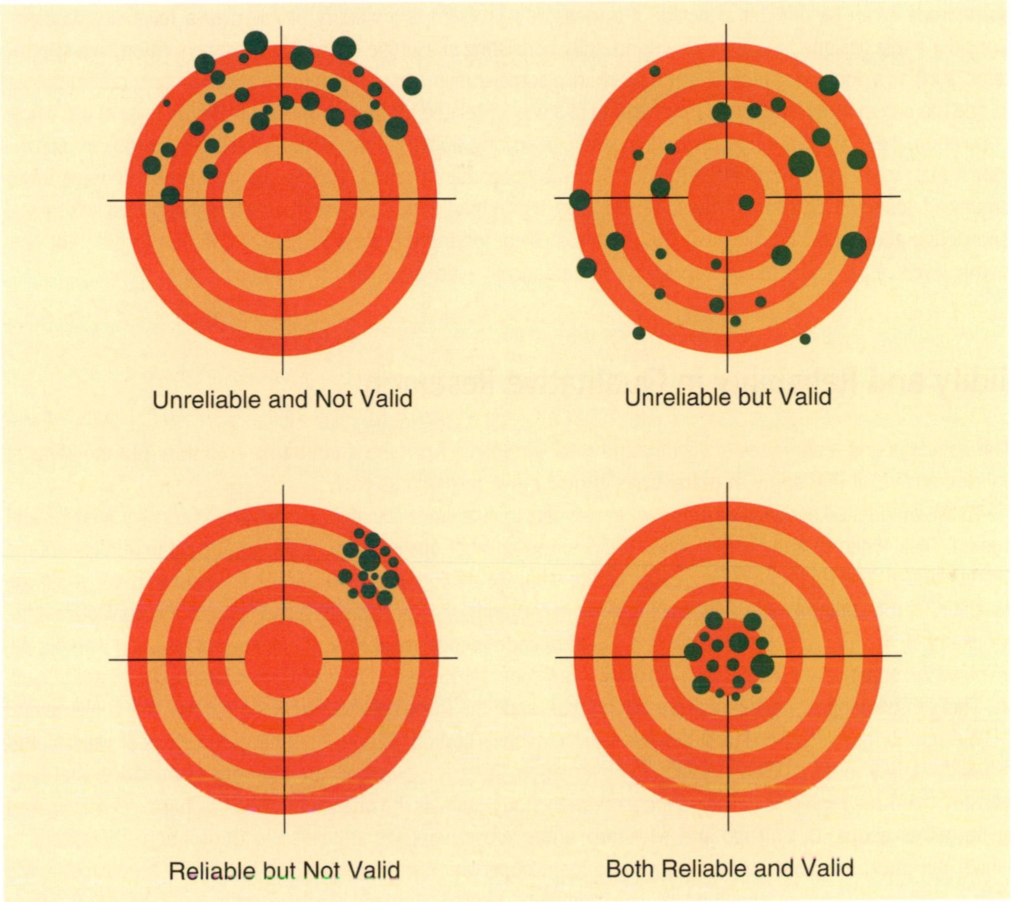

Source: http://assets.sbnation.com/assets/988678/560px-Reliability_and_validity.svg.png.

Distinguishing Validity and Reliability in Job Performance Measures

To get a feel for how to apply the ideas of validity and reliability, consider the example of measuring job performance. Organizations face this task and hope to use measures that are both valid and reliable—measures that truly gauge employees' effectiveness on the job as well as their contribution to the organization's success. One option is to ask employees to rate their own job performance in a confidential survey. But such self-reported measures may not be valid: Employees are likely to systematically overestimate their job performance, both because it is in their interest to do so and because most people see themselves (or seek to present themselves) in a favorable light. A further validity problem is that employees may lack the knowledge to evaluate their contribution to the organization's overall success. Nevertheless, such self-reported job performance measures may still be very reliable—employees may be quite consistent in how they overrate themselves.

Another option is to instead ask supervisors to evaluate employees' job performance. This helps get around the biases inherent in self-reporting and is perhaps a more valid measure of an employee's actual job performance. But here we might worry about reliability. Would different supervisors make the same assessment? Are they consistent in how they rate employees who perform equally well?

Distinguishing Validity and Reliability Can Depend on Context

Sometimes it can be difficult to decide if a measure's problem is a validity problem or a reliability problem. Consider a test designed to measure writing skills, consisting of a single essay that must be written on a specific topic, such as a hobby or political event. By chance some students may know more about or be more interested in one topic than others, affecting their writing in a way unrelated to their writing skills. At the level of the whole population, these are random errors in a measure of writing skills that cancel out—a reliability problem. But the topics may work systematically better for one subgroup than another. Poorer children probably have fewer organized activities. They may have fewer hobbies, which they must organize themselves, or at least less formal knowledge about their hobbies. For the purposes of comparing the writing skills of children at different economic levels, a particular essay test may be systematically biased—a validity problem.

Validity and Reliability in Qualitative Research

The concepts and techniques of validity and reliability come from the quantitative tradition. But the ideas of validity and reliability apply in many ways to qualitative research as well.

As we mentioned earlier, measurement occurs also in qualitative research, particularly in content analysis and coding. Thus, when creating and applying codes to text or other qualitative data, it is important to think about the validity of the codes—do the codes really capture what we think they do? And it is important to think about the reliability of the coding process—is it being done consistently? It is possible to recode part of the qualitative data, for example, in order to establish what can be called **code-recode reliability**. When several research workers are involved in coding, it is also possible to examine intercoder reliability, which is directly related to interrater reliability. This can be done by having the research workers code the same text and then comparing their consistency.

But not all (or even most) qualitative research involves coding. Still, the fundamental ideas of validity and reliability apply to all types of qualitative observation. Take, for example, the in-depth observation that happens in an ethnographic or participant observation study, such as the one mentioned in Chapter 3 that looked at homeless people in Chicago and why they often refuse help. We still need to think about the extent to which the interpretations derived from participant observation in this study are valid—do they capture the real experiences and motivations of the homeless people studied? And we still need to think about reliability—are the interpretations consistent? Would repeating the participant observation, or would another participant observer, yield similar interpretations and conclusions?

Finally, empirically testing the validity and reliability of qualitative observation presents unique challenges and may not be possible in many qualitative studies. Much the same holds true in many quantitative studies as well. The validity and reliability of measures and observations must be considered as part of all types of research.

Levels of Measurement

Measurements produce *variables* that can be analyzed. For quantitative data, the variables take the form of numbers, but not all numbers have the same meaning. In particular, sometimes numbers represent categories, while at other times they represent actual quantities of something. Thus, researchers distinguish two broad types, or **levels of measurement**:

- **Quantitative variables** in which the numbers refer to actual quantities of something. For example, in a housing survey, we might find a measure of the number of rooms in the housing unit (1, 2, 3, or 4 rooms, etc.).
- **Categorical variables** in which the numbers stand for categories. In a housing survey, for example, we might find the type of heating in the housing units recorded as either 1 = *electric*, 2 = *gas*, 3 = *oil*, or 4 = *other*.

The level of measurement is important for the analysis of data. Certain statistical methods require quantitative variables, while other techniques are appropriate for categorical data.

To give a simple example, it would be meaningless to calculate a mean (average) for the type of heating (say 2.3) because the numbers in this measure are really just codes for categories of heating, and averaging them tells us nothing. In contrast, it would be useful to find that the mean number of rooms is (say) 4.6 because this number expresses a true quantitative average of something (rooms). In fact, much of the variety and complexity one encounters when learning statistics stems from the fact that different statistical tools get used with different levels of measurement. We will learn more about this in Chapters 8, 9, and 10.

Quantitative Measures

It is perhaps best to begin with quantitative measures or variables, as these are measures in which the numbers refer to real quantities of something. For example, in social research we often measure things such as age (in years), income (in dollars, euros, etc.), hours of work in a typical week, or weight (in pounds or kilograms). When these measurements get recorded in these units, they are quantitative measures or variables.

The **unit of measurement**—the precise meaning of the numbers that appear in a data set—is critical. For example, income in U.S. surveys is often recorded in thousands of dollars, rather than in dollars, so that a value of "26" in the data set means 26,000 dollars of income. If weight appears in the data set as "91," we need to be careful to notice if this means 91 pounds or 91 kilograms. Quantitative data are useless and cannot be interpreted or analyzed unless we know the units of measurement. (See Box 4.9, which clarifies the difference between the unit of measurement and similar sounding, but quite different, concepts.)

Care must be taken to spot measures or variables that may look like they are quantitative, but on closer inspection are not. For example, here is the ESS codebook's description of the measure of household income of some 40,000 people living in more than 20 different countries (ESS, n.d.):

HINCTNT: Total household income from all sources

1. *Less than €1,800*
2. *to under €3,600*
3. *to under €6,000*
4. *to under €12,000*
5. *to under €18,000*
6. *to under €24,000*
7. *to under €30,000*
8. *to under €36,000*
9. *to under €60,000*
10. *to under €90,000*
11. *to under €120,000*
12. *€120,000 or more*

Although the measure refers to household income in euros, it records income in 12 broad categories. Often, surveys ask for income in this way because respondents are unable, or unwilling (because of privacy concerns), to report their exact income. As a result, this kind of measure of income is categorical, not quantitative.

BOX 4.9
Unit/Level of Measurement/Analysis?

Unfortunately, research terms sometimes sound too much alike and start to blur together in our thinking. Here are the distinctions between three similar-sounding terms:

1. *Level of measurement:* This refers to the distinction between quantitative and categorical variables, to what some call the ladder of measurement: nominal, ordinal, interval, and ratio.
2. *Unit of measurement:* This refers to units, such as dollars of income or kilograms of body weight, that define the quantitative variable. If a variable takes the value of 66, for example, the unit of measurement is the answer to the question 66 what? These are often just called units.
3. *Unit of analysis:* This refers to the objects or things described by the variables. Do the variables in the study describe people, households, neighborhoods, nations, organizations, or something else? To avoid confusion, note that "unit" in *unit of analysis* has a completely different meaning than "unit" in *units (of measurement)*.

QUESTION

State the unit of analysis, unit of measurement, and level of measurement in the following case: a data set of households, with the variable being annual income in dollars.

In some discussions of research methods, you'll find quantitative measurements further classified into *interval* and *ratio* measurements. Most quantitative measures you'll come across are in fact ratio measurements—they have a meaningful 0 point, such as €0 of income, or 0 years of work experience or age. (Even though in a real data set you may not have someone with 0 years of age, a newborn, this variable still has a meaningful 0 point.)

Interval measurements are not as common, but good examples in research are scales or indexes that have rather arbitrary units of measurement. For example, the Stanford-Binet IQ test scores used often in educational assessment range in practice from a low of about 50 to a high of about 150, with 100 as the mean (the standard deviation is 16). This is a quantitative measure, but it does not have a true 0 point; thus it is an *interval*-level measurement. However, interval measures still have the feature that the difference between 50 and 60 is the same as the difference between 70 and 80. The size of the interval does have meaning.

For most statistical analyses, the distinction between interval and ratio levels of measurement does not matter much. But the distinction between the quantitative level and the categorical level of measurement does matter.

Categorical Measures

A *categorical* measure or variable is one in which the numerical values in the data set serve to classify the people or objects being measured into categories. There are two kinds of categorical measures or variables:

1. **Nominal:** Measures or variables in which the numbers refer to categories that have no inherent order to them, so the categories can be arranged in any order.
2. **Ordinal:** Measures or variables in which the numbers refer to categories that do have an inherent order to them, and thus the numbers convey that order.

Let's look at the Global Attitudes Project, a survey organized by the Pew Research Center that interviewed more than 38,000 people in 44 nations on a wide range of global issues. Consider first the following example of a *nominal* question or measure:

Here is a list of five dangers in the world today. In your opinion, which one of these poses the greatest threat to the world?

1. *Spread of nuclear weapons*
2. *Religious and ethnic hatred*
3. *AIDS and other infectious diseases*
4. *Pollution and other environmental problems*
5. *Growing gap between the rich and poor*

This measure is *nominal* because the numbers 1 to 5 stand for categories that do not have any inherent order to them. In other words, we could easily rearrange the categories, along with their corresponding numeric codes, without really changing the meaning of the measure:

1. *Growing gap between the rich and poor*
2. *Pollution and other environmental problems*
3. *Spread of nuclear weapons*
4. *Religious and ethnic hatred*
5. *AIDS and other infectious diseases*

Again, the codes 1 to 5 just tag the categories and do not imply that the categories follow any particular order.

Ordinal measures, in contrast, are categorical measures that do follow an order. Here is another example from the 44-nation survey of the Global Attitudes Project:

There has been a lot of talk about globalization these days. Do you think that globalization is a very good thing, somewhat good, somewhat bad, or a very bad thing?

1. Very good
2. Somewhat good
3. Somewhat bad
4. Very bad

This measure is *ordinal* because the numerical codes 1 to 4 not only represent categories but also express the *order* of the categories, from “very good” to “very bad.” We could not, for example, so easily rearrange the categories as we did before:

1. Very bad
2. Somewhat good
3. Very good
4. Somewhat bad

This ruins the meaning of things—we need the categories to remain in order. Of course, we could reverse the order, so that 1 = *very bad* and 4 = *very good*, but this simply illustrates again that the categories do, indeed, have an order.

QUESTION

In a data set of individuals, what is the likely level of measurement for the following variables: Annual Income in Dollars; Race; Life Satisfaction?

With an ordinal variable, we can't be sure that the distance, say, between *very bad* and *somewhat bad* is the same as that between *somewhat bad* and *somewhat good.* So we need to use caution applying certain statistics—such as means or correlations—that assume a regular, quantitative distance between intervals. Still, in practice, researchers do often treat ordinal measures as if they are quantitative. And researchers have come up with a few ways to convert their categorical measures into quantitative ones.

Turning Categorical Variables Into Quantitative Ones

The desire to convert categorical variables into quantitative ones crops up often in social and policy research. This is due to the fact that (1) categorical measures appear often in surveys, and (2) researchers like to use advanced analytical tools for quantitative data (regression, factor analysis, etc.). Various techniques can be used to upgrade the level of measurement.

Dummy Variables

Dummy variables (also called **indicator variables**) are categorical variables that have only two values, 0 and 1. For example, the variable "Employed" indicates if the individual is employed or not; the variable "Female" indicates if the individual is female or male (not female). Dummy variables can be treated sometimes as quantitative variables because they represent a single *unit* of something, such as "employment."

Dummy variables are extremely convenient for analyzing and interpreting data. If a data set has a dummy variable "employed," the mean of that variable will tell us the share (proportion) of the population that is employed. Dummy variables can also be used for nominal variables with more than two categories, such as "race," which might have the categories of White, Black, Hispanic, Asian, and Other. In this case, we convert each category into a separate dummy variable, such as White (1 = *yes,* 0 = *no*), Black (1 = *yes,* 0 = *no*), and so on.

Dummy variables are often used in correlation and regression analysis, especially as independent variables. And dummy variables often get used to represent programs or treatments—specifically whether a person or case is in the treatment group (coded 1) or the control group (coded 0).

Midpoint Approximation

For ordinal measures of an underlying construct that is intrinsically quantitative, such as income, it is possible to approximate a quantitative measure by substituting a midpoint for the original category codes. Returning to the example of the ESS (n.d.), we can recode the income categories to midpoints as shown below:

	Total Household Income From All Sources		Midpoint
1.	Less than €1,800	→	€1,200
2.	€1,800 to less than €3,600	→	€2,700
3.	€3,600 to less than €6,000	→	€4,800
4.	€6,000 to less than €12,000	→	€9,000
5.	€12,000 to less than €18,000	→	€15,000
6.	€18,000 to less than €24,000	→	€21,000
7.	€24,000 to less than €30,000	→	€27,000
8.	€30,000 to less than €36,000	→	€33,000

	Total Household Income From All Sources		Midpoint
9.	€36,000 to less than €60,000	→	€48,000
10.	€60,000 to less than €90,000	→	€75,000
11.	€90,000 to less than €120,000	→	€105,000
12.	€120,000 or more	→	€130,000

The ESS's household income question is essentially ordinal, as the values 1 to 12 in the data set represent income categories, not quantities of euros. But if we recode these values as shown—substituting the midpoints of the income ranges (shown above) for the categories 1 to 12—we can approximate a quantitative measure of income in euros.

Notice that we cannot take the midpoint of the bottom and top categories, and so we have to use our judgment about what value to use.

Multi-item Scales

Adding up ordinal items or indicators representing a scale, such as the agree-disagree items of Rosenberg's self-esteem scale, produces a composite score that researchers often view as quantitative. Even if the individual items or indicators remain ordinal, the sum of many such indicators produces a fairly continuous set of values that can be treated as a quantitative variable.

Endpoint Scales and Thermometers

Another technique for turning an ordinal measure into at least a semiquantitative measure is to present questions on a 1 to 7 or 1 to 10 scale with only anchoring statements at the ends of the scale, rather than labeling only a few categories. For example, a standard way to ask people about their happiness in life is this question:

Taking all things together, would you say you are . . .

1. Not too happy *2. Pretty happy* *3. Very happy*

But by adding a few more categories, and only labeling the endpoints, we can ask the question this way:

Taking all things together (on a 1–7 scale), would you say you are . . .

Not too happy						*Very happy*
1	*2*	*3*	*4*	*5*	*6*	*7*

Because the numbers do not have labels, except at the endpoints, some researchers argue that the distance between numbers can be interpreted as equal intervals (of happiness on a 1–7 scale). Also, the equal spacing of the numbers visually reinforces this meaning. This idea becomes even more apparent with a 10-point scale:

Taking all things together (on a 1–10 scale), would you say you are . . .

Not too happy									*Very happy*
1	*2*	*3*	*4*	*5*	*6*	*7*	*8*	*9*	*10*

Going still further, survey researchers sometimes use what they call a *feeling thermometer,* an imaginary 0 to 100 quantitative scale to rate political leaders, groups, or institutions in society. Figure 4.8 presents results from the American National Election Studies showing the public's feelings toward gays and lesbians in U.S. society.

This graph shows a gradual "warming" of attitudes toward gays and lesbians in U.S. society (from 30 to 46 "degrees" over the 18-year period shown), although the thermometer still remains in "cool" territory. Similar feeling thermometers have been used to quantify attitudes toward racial and ethnic groups, political candidates, government institutions, other nations, and so on.

Units of Analysis and Levels of Measurement

We have been thinking mostly in terms of measures of individual people, or sometimes families, but variables can describe larger units of analysis as well. Recall that the *unit of analysis* refers to the objects or things described by the measure (people, firms, neighborhoods, etc.). For example, much demographic and policy data get reported and analyzed at various geographic levels, such as cities, counties, or regions. Education data often get reported at the level of schools, not individual students. This matters for the level of measurement because often variables that are categorical at the level of an individual person, student, or household become quantitative at a larger geographic or organizational unit of analysis.

Let's return to our example of poverty. If we are measuring an individual person or household, using the U.S. government's official poverty measure, we classify the individual as either "poor" or "not poor." Thus, at the individual level, poverty is a categorical variable. But if we look at poverty at the level of, say, census

Figure 4.8 Feeling Toward Gays and Lesbians in the United States

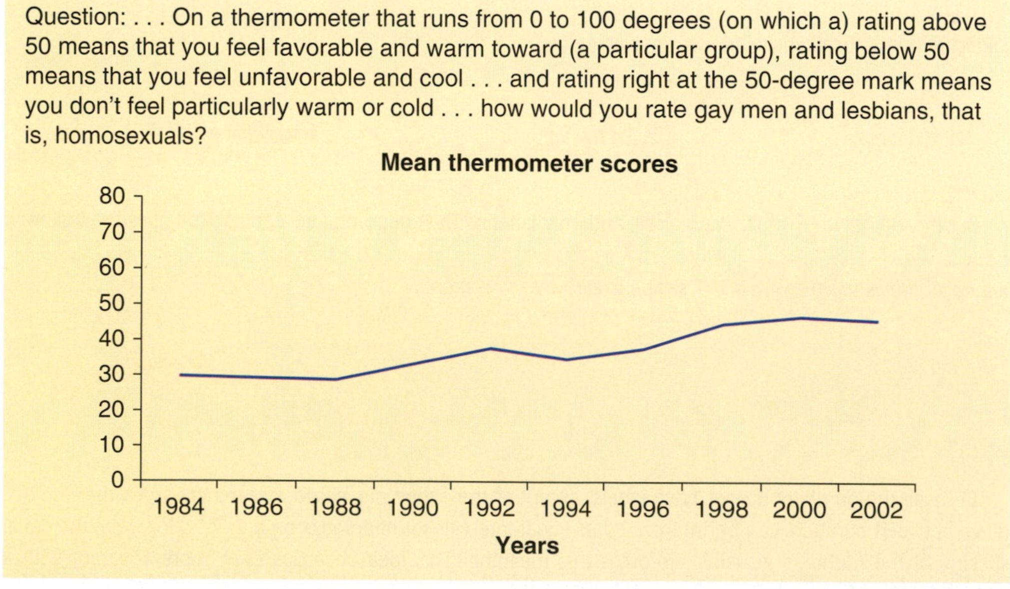
Question: . . . On a thermometer that runs from 0 to 100 degrees (on which a) rating above 50 means that you feel favorable and warm toward (a particular group), rating below 50 means that you feel unfavorable and cool . . . and rating right at the 50-degree mark means you don't feel particularly warm or cold . . . how would you rate gay men and lesbians, that is, homosexuals?
Mean thermometer scores
80
70
60
50
40
30
20
10
0
1984 1986 1988 1990 1992 1994 1996 1998 2000 2002
Years

Source: Egan & Sherrill (2005); Data from the National Election Studies, conducted by the Center for Political Studies at the University of Michigan.

tracts or counties, then most often we will be dealing with a poverty *rate,* or the *percentage* of people (or households) living in poverty. This percentage might well range from as low as 2%, 3%, or 4% to 20%, 30%, or 40% or more. Thus, at the level of a census tract or county, poverty clearly is a quantitative measure. So to determine the level of measurement, you need to consider the unit of analysis as well.

Measurement in the Real World: Trade-offs and Choices

In this chapter, we have covered many ideas involved in measurement—the systematic observation and recording of features of the world that matter to us. In an ideal world, we would like to create and use the best possible measures, measures that are highly valid and highly reliable. But in the real world, measurement involves trade-offs and choices. To conclude this chapter, it is helpful to consider some of these real-world trade-offs and choices that we must face when doing measurement.

What Will It Cost?

Everything has its price—including the validity and reliability of measurement. We know, for example, that self-reported measures of health, spending, drug use, and other behaviors are not as valid as more direct, objective methods of measurement, such as clinical exams, obtaining bank records, or taking hair and urine samples. But these other, more direct measurement methods often cost a lot more, so in practice we sometimes must settle for self-reported measures that we know are less valid.

Reliability is enhanced by the number of indicators, as we have seen, and the use of multi-item scales produces variables that have a more quantitative level of measurement. But the length of questionnaires or observation forms increases the cost of data collection. Interviewer time, printing and mailing costs, data processing effort, and time in the field—all are affected by the length of our questionnaires or instruments. To economize, we often opt for shorter measures, for example, using one question to measure a construct rather than a scale, even when realizing that the reliability of a single-item measure is less good and that the lower level of measurement may restrict analysis.

Is It Ethical?

Long questionnaires also impose a burden on respondents—raising ethical concerns. We shouldn't ask or expect people to complete hours-long interviews or book-size questionnaires, just because having more indicators gives us more reliability and results in a higher level of measurement.

In an effort to achieve validity, we could always deceive people or violate their privacy. For example, we could ask people for a lock of hair during an in-person interview to take back to a lab for analysis of drug use. We could make up some harmless excuse for what we're doing ("Hair samples tell us how much healthy sunshine people around here are getting this time of the year"). This would be a more valid measure than asking for self-reported drug use. But tricking people into giving us a hair sample would be unethical.

How Will It Affect the Quality and Rate of Responding?

If an interview or questionnaire is too long, respondents will drop out or fail to respond in the first place. So although from a reliability or level-of-measurement perspective it might be best to have long, multi-item measures for every construct in a study, the length of an interview or questionnaire affects the response rate and thus the generalizability of the sample. We will learn more about these sampling issues in Chapter 5.

Very long tests, observation forms, or interviews also tend to be completed less carefully than shorter ones. Respondents, observers, or interviewers may engage in *sufficing* behavior—rapidly completing the interview or observation form just to satisfy the researcher but without giving much care to the task. This kind of carelessness in responding or observing introduces new sources of bias and noise into the measurement process—working against our original aims.

Validity-Reliability Trade-off

Many standardized tests work by giving students a battery of multiple-choice questions, which is good for reliability (the more items, the more reliable the measure). And it might help in the task of creating a truly quantitative test score. But this may not be the most valid assessment of an ability—such as English language arts. We might like to know if students can read a substantial text, understand it, and then evaluate and react to it in the form of a carefully organized and well-written essay.

In fact, New York State now measures students' English language arts ability by requiring them to spend an entire test day on a single essay, with other days devoted to more traditional multiple-choice questions. Grading these essays, however, is extremely time-consuming and expensive, requiring many extra hours by a team of teachers, and it is difficult to do consistently (think about the *interrater reliability* problem discussed above).

Inventing a measure is tempting, but it has its drawbacks.
Source: © iStockphoto.com/BartCo.

Moreover, there is surely random error or noise in using just one essay as an indicator of writing ability. For example, the topic that happens to be chosen for the essay one year is surely more familiar and interesting to some students than to others. Ideally, we would like to have several essays each year to capture students' writing ability across a range of topics. This would help us average out the random errors or noise. But it is not feasible for a school system to administer and grade several days' worth of essay writing—having one long essay to score is difficult enough. Thus, in an effort to get a more valid indicator, such as a long essay, we must sacrifice reliability.

This validity-reliability trade-off is widespread in research. Indeed, it helps explain some of the tension and disagreement between those who favor in-depth, *qualitative* observation and those who prefer more standardized and systematic, but perhaps more superficial, *quantitative* methods of measurement. In a sense, qualitative researchers can be thought of as more focused on validity, while quantitative researchers tend to emphasize reliability.

To really get at a construct, it is tempting to create an entirely new and original measure—something that is just right for our particular research or policy goal. But using established measures—measures developed, tested, and applied in previous studies—often provides better assurances of validity and reliability.

Moreover, measures are often used to make comparisons over time, examining trends or focusing specifically on changes over time. Creating a new measure—even if it is more valid—makes it hard to make comparisons across time. This is an issue that is constantly faced by large annual surveys sponsored by governments and other organizations.

For example, the U.S. Bureau of Labor Statistics (BLS) has a long-standing annual survey about employee benefits, including health insurance. However, the form of health insurance has changed dramatically over the past several decades—and it is in the process of further structural changes. Does the BLS try to ask questions about health insurance that allow for comparisons over time? Or does it ask questions that create the most valid measures of the type and value of health insurance people have today? Like most agencies, the BLS tries to do some of both, balancing the two concerns.

Incentives to stick with an established measure are part of why we continue to have the flawed U.S. poverty measure. Related political issues, discussed in Chapter 16, are also part of the problem.

High Stakes? Gaming and Other Behavior Responses

As accountability pressures in health, education, and other sectors grow, the measurement of improvement—or how outcomes change over time—has become an increasingly high-stakes issue. For example, in the United States, for some patients, health care organizations can be "paid for their performance"—for improvements in quality measures, including patient outcomes (McClellan et al., 2010). Such high-stakes performance measurement can lead to behavior changes that interfere with the validity of measures themselves. At one extreme, there is the problem of the incentive for outright fraud and cheating. For example, in Atlanta in 2013, dozens of teachers and administrators were indicted for helping students answer tests and also falsifying test results in an effort to win funding bonuses from the federal government.

But legitimate efforts by people or organizations to better their scores can also cause inconsistent and even biased increases over time. For example, hospitals can improve their information technology systems and clinical record keeping in ways that make their outcomes look better. Another example comes from New York State, where math scores on a high-stakes test increased much more rapidly than scores on a no-stakes national test administered at the same time. Among the factors driving differences, education analysts found three interrelated practices: making all past test questions available to teachers and students, creating new test questions very similar to past ones, and the widespread practice of coaching students with past test questions. Such coaching likely meant that learning was concentrated not only on test material but also on recognizing patterns in the test items themselves so that students could give correct answers "without necessarily understanding the underlying math" (Green, 2009). This example is part of a broad set of behavioral responses that undermine measures used for accountability described by Koretz (2005) for education but applying more broadly.

Use Multiple Measures for Multiple Dimensions—or Aggregate to One Measure?

Aggregating many different dimensions of a construct into a single measure simplifies and reduces the information, making it easier to use. But think about poverty: One can have enough to eat and a decent place to live but still have inadequate education and health care. For this reason, some advocate multiple measures, a kind of dashboard approach, which provides a fuller picture (Blank, 2008; Citro & Michael, 1995). Indeed, while the European Union (2011) has a "headline indicator" of poverty (less than 60% of median income), it considers that one measure to be incomplete, so it also uses a wide array of other indicators, such as lacking four or more "deprivation items," things like keeping the home adequately warm (European Commission Directorate-General for Employment, Social Affairs & Inclusion, 2011).

Others, however, emphasize that the realities of the policy process—together with the limited ability of both the public and policy makers to make use of multiple measures—argue for one single best number (Bernheim, 1998). Ideally, there could be both separate measures for each dimension and a summary aggregate. But resources and attention are limited. Moreover, any aggregate will inevitably emphasize some dimensions over others, making the aggregate inappropriate for some purposes or perspectives. The United Nations has both separate measures for health, education, and living standards as dimensions of poverty and an aggregate poverty index (Human Development Reports, n.d.). However, Ravallion (2011) notes that the weights used for aggregation are inevitably ad hoc.

Conclusion: Measurement Matters

The topic of measurement, with its sometimes arcane and confusing jargon, can seem to have little practical relevance. We hope that the examples in this chapter have convinced you, however, that this is not the case. Measurement matters—it is how we track critical social and economic problems, inform policy debates, and evaluate outcomes we care about. Measurement also plays a key role in the management of organizations and in the provision of public services. Knowing how to think about and evaluate measurement, therefore, is an important skill whether you are a researcher or a practitioner. But like all skills, it comes mostly with practice. So we encourage you to ask questions about the measures you encounter, to dig beneath the surface. How was the measure defined or conceptualized? How was it operationalized—that is, what are the details of how the measurement was carried out? Does it get at what we think it measures—is it valid? Is the measurement consistent—is it reliable? The more you ask and try to answer these questions, the more skill you will gain in interpreting, doing, and using measurement.

BOX 4.10
Critical Questions to Ask About Measurement

- What is the purpose of the measure—where and how did it originate? (Knowing the history of a measure—such as the U.S. poverty measure—not only is interesting but also provides insight on its usefulness and limitations.)
- What is the conceptual definition of the construct that the measure aims to capture? Are there dimensions to the construct, and if so, what are they? Is there debate, or confusion, about the meaning of the construct?
- How is the measure operationalized? What instruments (including questionnaires), personnel, and protocols (procedures) are used to carry out measurement of the construct? Does the measure involve one item or indicator, or is it a multi-item scale? Is it a proxy measure? Does it involve proxy reporting?
- How valid is the measure? Does it have face validity? Does it capture the dimensions and variation of the construct (content validity)? Is there any empirical evidence about the validity of the measure (criterion-related validity)? If so, what kind of evidence is it (what kind of criterion-related validity is it)—and how convincing is the evidence?
- How reliable is the measure? Is there any evidence for the reliability of the measure? If so, what kind of evidence is it (what kind of reliability test)—and how convincing is the evidence?
- What is the level of measurement of the variable?

BOX 4.11
Tips on Doing Your Own Research: Measurement

- Identify the key variables in your study. This is best done using a path model—see the Tips on Doing Your Own Research at the end of Chapter 2.
- First develop a clear, conceptual definition of what you are trying to measure—including any dimensions. Pay attention to how the measure will be used.
- Look to see if established measures exist for your key variables—these may be standardized questions used on previous surveys, or a published scale composed of multiple items. Assess how well the existing measures fit your conceptualization.
- Think about how to operationalize your measure—that is, what instruments (including questionnaires), personnel, and protocols (procedures) you will need to use.
- Decide if you will use just one item or indicator, or whether you might need a composite measure built from multiple items (which can be more reliable, but take more time and other resources).
- If you are using secondary data, you may need to consider relying on proxy measures for some of your constructs—but choose your proxy measures carefully (as they are often open to interpretation).
- Anticipate ways to test the validity and reliability of your measures, for example by doing a correlation analysis or (for multi-item scales) an internal consistency analysis. For established measures, look to see what other researchers have to say about their validity and reliability.

Chapter Resources

Key Terms

- Bias (in measurement), or systematic measurement error
- Categorical variable
- Code-recode reliability
- Composite measure
- Conceptualization
- Concurrent validity
- Construct
- Construct validity
- Content validity
- Convergent validity
- Criterion-related validity
- Dimension (domain)
- Discriminant validity
- Dummy variable, or indicator variable
- Face validity
- Index
- Indicator
- Instrument (of measurement)
- Internal consistency
- Interrater reliability
- Latent construct
- Level of measurement
- Manifest construct
- Measurement
- Nominal categorical variable
- Operationalization
- Ordinal categorical variable
- Parallel forms reliability
- Performance measurement

- Predictive validity
- Protocols
- Proxy
- Proxy respondent
- Psychometrics
- Quantitative variable
- Random measurement error, or noise
- Reliability
- Response format
- Scale
- Self-reporting
- Test-retest reliability
- Trait
- Unit of measurement
- Validity (of a measure)

Exercises

What Does Poverty Mean to You?

4.1. This chapter discussed absolute and relative ways to conceptualize poverty. Which conceptualization do you agree with most? Explain why.

How Would You Measure . . . ?

4.2. There are many possible things you might be interested in measuring. Below are a few examples. For each one, do the following: (1) Write a conceptual definition of the construct; (2) come up with a list of 5 to 10 observable indicators of the construct; and (3) decide if your indicators can be grouped into two or more dimensions.

- Life skills
- Civic engagement
- Urban blight
- Organizational politics

Measuring Consumer Confidence

4.3. Given below are the five questions the University of Michigan uses to compute its Consumer Sentiment Index, based on a random sample of about 500 adults each month. Do you see any dimensions in this measure? Does this measure have good face validity? Does it have good content validity?

a. We are interested in how people are getting along financially these days. Would you say that you (and your family living there) are better off or worse financially than you were a year ago?

b. Looking ahead, do you think that a year from now you (and your family living there) will be better off financially, worse off, or about the same as now?

c. Turning to business conditions in the country as a whole, do you think that during the next 12 months we'll have good times financially or bad times, or what?

d. Looking ahead, which would you say is more likely: that in the country as a whole we'll have continuous good times during the next 5 years or so or that we will have periods of widespread unemployment or depression, or what?

e. About the big things people buy for their home—such as furniture, a refrigerator, stove, television, and things like that. Generally speaking, do you think now is a good or a bad time for people to buy major household items? (University of Michigan, 2009)

How Clean Are the Trains?

4.4. A mass transit agency is considering two proposed methods for rating the cleanliness of its trains. One proposal is to have raters count the number of pieces of trash in the centermost car of each train as it arrives at the end of the line on Wednesday evenings at 8. Another proposal is to have observers ride the trains several different times a week, at different locations, and describe their cleanliness in a written report using their own words. Which measure is more reliable? Which measure is more valid?

Is the Vocabulary Test Culturally Biased?

4.5. A *picture vocabulary test* is one way to assess language ability in young schoolchildren. Suppose the test asks U.S. children to come up with the vocabulary words for the pictures below:

A

B

How might this test be culturally biased? What might it be measuring other than language ability? Can you think of some pictures to use that would make the test less culturally biased?

A Healthy Snack—or Not?

4.6. In this exercise, you will use the following 4-star system to rate the healthiness of some common snack foods:

****	Healthy
***	Somewhat healthy
**	Somewhat unhealthy
*	Unhealthy

With another person (or in a small group), rate the snack foods in List A below—with each person doing independent ratings. When you are done, share and discuss your ratings with each other: How similar or different are they? Why did you give each snack food the rating that you did? How could you make your ratings more reliable (consistent)?

Next, repeat the exercise with List B (again, with each person doing independent ratings). Again when you are done, share and discuss your ratings with each other: Have your ratings become any more reliable? Why, or why not? What does this exercise illustrate about the task of assessing and improving the reliability of a measure?

List A	List B
Banana	Apple
Chocolate bar	M&M's
Cookies	Brownie
Cupcake	Doughnut
Frozen yogurt	Low-fat ice cream
Nuts	Raisins
Potato chips	Corn chips
Pretzels	Saltine crackers
Tangerine	Orange
Yogurt	Cheese stick

Assessing Performance Measures

4.7. Identify a performance measure that would be useful in your current work, your past work, or an area that interests you—or a performance measure that is in fact used in any of those situations. Then, do the following:

- Describe how valid you think the measure is—and why.
- Describe how reliable you think the measure is—and why.
- Given that there are limited resources available, is there a tension between trying to improve both the validity and reliability of the measure? Explain your answer.

Assessing Educational Effectiveness

4.8. Consider two tests that could be used to evaluate a university's effectiveness at teaching critical thinking and communication skills to undergraduates. The first test is a multiple-choice test with questions on reading comprehension, language, and math, similar to the SAT in the United States. The second test provides the students with a single real-world case involving practical issues and data, including quantitative data, from several sources. The product that students produce for the second test is a memo, which must suggest a particular response to the case and support the decision with evidence and analysis. The second test is graded using specific criteria on critical thinking and communication (a rubric).

- Discuss the validity of each test for assessing the *level* of critical thinking and communication skills of students. Compare and contrast the two tests in terms of validity.
- Discuss the reliability of each test for assessing the *level* of critical thinking and communication skills of students. Compare and contrast the two tests in terms of reliability.

Relative Poverty—Relative to Whom?

4.9. The European Union (EU) uses as its main poverty measure having income less than 60% of the median income in the country—a measure of relative poverty. But this raises important issues about the conceptual definition of poverty and the purpose of the poverty measurement. The countries of the EU differ dramatically in income and other measures of their standard of living. Richard Burkhauser (2009) showed that if the EU instead used a measure based on the median income of the entire EU population, poverty rates would become dramatically different: Lithuania's 20% poverty rate would become 68% and the United Kingdom's 19% poverty rate only 4%. He also showed how poverty rates in the United States would look very different if the measure was relative poverty *within* a state.

- For what purposes is a relative poverty rate more valuable than an absolute poverty rate?
- What group is the relevant reference group for a relative poverty measure? Those in the same country? Region? Neighborhood? The entire world? How does the relevant group depend on the conceptualization and purpose of the poverty measure?
- Has the revolution in communication, which brings the Internet and television into poor, remote corners of the world, changed the relevant group for particular purposes?

Student Study Site

Visit the Study Site at **www.sagepub.com/remler2e** to

- test your knowledge with the self-quiz
- check your understanding of key terms with the eFlashcards
- explore helpful resources that relate directly to this chapter

Sampling often aims to represent large populations.

Source: © Can Stock Photo Inc./photostocker

Overview: In this chapter, you will learn about sampling—the selection of people or elements to include in a study. The chapter begins with the idea of generalizability—projecting from one limited study to a larger reality, which is the primary aim of sampling. You will then find out about basic sampling concepts, the issues of coverage and nonresponse bias, and the use of volunteers and other nonprobability samples. Next, you will be introduced to the theory and methods of random sampling—one of the most important inventions of modern social science and a vital tool for public policy and practice. Finally, you will become familiar with the motivations and methods for more complex forms of random sampling developed to implement the ideas of random sampling in the real world.

Objectives

Learning Objectives

After reading this chapter, you should be able to

- Assess a study's generalizability from its sampling approach and other aspects of the study
- Describe basic sampling concepts, such as population, sample, census, and inference
- Know the basic steps involved in selecting a sample
- Determine whether a sampling approach has problems of coverage and nonresponse, as well as whether these problems lead to bias—and, if so, the direction of the bias
- Recognize forms of nonprobability sampling, along with their uses and limitations
- Understand the logic and importance of probability sampling, including the relation of sample size to precision (confidence intervals)
- Recognize some of the more complex forms of probability sampling used in real-world social and policy research

Sampling 5

Gauging the Fallout From Hurricane Katrina

Hurricane Katrina hit the Gulf Coast of the United States on August 29, 2005, near the city of New Orleans. As most of the world watched in horror, the storm and its aftermath became one of the deadliest and costliest natural disasters in U.S. history. In early September, CBS News conducted a poll of 725 adults nationwide and reported that 77% of the country felt that the federal government's response to the disaster was inadequate, with fully 80% believing that the government did not act as fast as it could have (CBS News, 2005).

At about the same time in early September, a team of public health researchers at an emergency Red Cross shelter in Austin, Texas, set up to accommodate the hordes of evacuees from New Orleans and surrounding areas questioned 132 shelter residents about their experiences during the disaster. The researchers discovered that it took these survivors 4 full days on average to be evacuated from the city, during which time 63% had sustained injuries, 81% were separated from family members, and 63% reported being directly exposed to corpses. The authors of the study, published in the *American Journal of Public Health,* concluded that "Katrina-related trauma and its psychological sequelae will remain a significant public health issue for years to come" (Mills, Edmondson, & Park, 2007, p. S116).

Both the CBS telephone poll and the emergency shelter study involved **sampling**—the process of selecting people (or elements) for inclusion in a research study. In this chapter, we'll see how the CBS poll of only 725 randomly sampled individuals can represent several hundred million people in the U.S. population. But we'll also consider the many practical difficulties and limitations that often produce bias in telephone polls and other sampling situations. And you'll learn that useful research can be done also with nonrandom samples, such as the public health study of evacuees in just one Red Cross shelter in Texas, although there are important limitations as well. Sampling is part of the broader issue of *generalizability*—the extent to which the findings of a study can be projected, or generalized, to other people, situations, or time periods. We begin first with this fundamental notion of generalizability.

Generalizability

We often find research interesting or useful not because of what it uncovers about the people or elements that happen to be in the study, but because of what the findings mean for the larger world we live in. In the

Researchers used sampling to understand the effects of Hurricane Katrina.

Source: © David J. Phillip/Corbis.

CBS poll, for example, we really don't care particularly about what the 725 people in the poll think about the U.S. policy response to Katrina. What matters is what they tell us about the thinking of the whole nation (a few hundred million people). Similarly, with the 132 shelter residents, their experiences are of interest primarily because they shed light on what happened to the tens of thousands of people like them who fled New Orleans. This illustrates the concept of **generalizability**—the ability to project the results of one study to a much larger reality.

Generalizability is also called **external validity**—the extent to which a study's findings hold true outside of (external to) the particular context of the research (Shadish, Cook, & Campbell, 2002). But because of the many other "validities" in the lexicon of research jargon (measurement validity, internal validity, etc.), we prefer to use the more descriptive term *generalizability.*

Several factors make a study more or less generalizable.

Population of Interest, Sampling, and Generalizability

Every study has a **population** of interest—the population the study aims to investigate in the first place. The CBS poll aimed to study all U.S. adults, while the shelter study aimed only to study those evacuated from New Orleans. And every study aims to investigate at least one or more **parameters**—characteristics or features of the population of interest. The CBS poll aimed to learn the proportion of the U.S. population who saw the government's response to Katrina as inadequate. The shelter study aimed to learn the proportion of New Orleans evacuees in shelters who had sustained injuries and the average number of days it took for them to be evacuated. The closer a study's results get to the true parameters—the true characteristics of the population of interest—the more generalizable the study.

Moreover, the broader the population of interest—the more geographic areas, the more periods of time, the more groups of people—the more generalizable the results. If a study is done at one point in time, it may provide just a snapshot of events or behaviors that can fluctuate a great deal. Public opinion about the government's response to Katrina certainly changed over the days and weeks during which the disaster unfolded and was covered by the news media. But if a study is done over many points in time, the results tend to be more generalizable. Similarly, if a study is done in just one place, it may capture local idiosyncrasies and not the wider reality. Katrina evacuees fled to many different cities in nearby states and beyond, not just to Austin, Texas (and not just to Red Cross emergency shelters). If a study is done in many places, its results can be more broadly generalized. But not all studies seek to represent a broad national or international population: Sometimes, we wish to capture a snapshot of a particular time or place, or study a unique or specialized group.

A random sample (or probability sample), in which participants are chosen randomly from a population, is often much more generalizable than other, nonprobability forms of sampling. In fact, a small random sample often beats a much larger nonprobability sample in terms of generalizability. The CBS telephone poll, based on a small random sample, is much more representative than, say, an effort by CBS to have millions of its viewers call the network to express their views. This kind of **voluntary sample**, in which participants simply volunteer to be part of the study, will likely produce less representative and therefore less generalizable results. But it is often difficult to select a true random sample in the real world, as we will see shortly.

A **convenience sample**, in which researchers rely on the most readily available participants, such as the Red Cross shelter study, will also be less generalizable. In fact, it is not totally clear what population the people in the Red Cross shelter are supposed to represent: All New Orleans residents? Just those who fled to shelters, rather than to family, friends, or hotels? Or just those who fled to this one particular shelter in Austin, Texas? It's difficult to know for sure how representative those in this shelter are of any of these larger groups; hence, our ability to generalize is uncertain.

QUESTION

What are some of the features of a sample that make it more or less generalizable?

We will learn much more about random (probability) sampling, as well as nonprobability forms of sampling (such as voluntary and convenience sampling), later on in this chapter. Generalizability, however, is not simply a matter of aiming to represent broad populations and employing probability sampling. It is more subtle and complex than this.

Are Experiments More Generalizable?

Many basic biological, psychological, or even economic processes or behaviors can be shown to be fairly universal—highly generalizable, in other words—even when the studies use relatively small and unrepresentative samples of volunteers, usually in the context of a controlled experiment. Experiments are used to determine causal relationships—answers to "what if" questions—and we will have much more to say about them in Chapters 11 and 14.

Consider, for example, the fact that most drug or medical trials—experiments that test the effectiveness of treatments we all depend on—come from samples of clinical volunteers. (See, for example, ClinicalTrials.gov for information about ongoing clinical trials.) Psychological experiments have discovered important laws of perception, cognition, and behavior using only small numbers of volunteers, often undergraduate psychology majors at one university. Similarly, experimental economists have demonstrated some basic structures of economic behavior (such as altruism and risk aversion) by running small-scale experiments such as the *ultimatum game* or the *prisoners' dilemma,* typically involving only a handful of volunteers. Thus, despite the unrepresentativeness of study participants, important and often generalizable findings come from good experimental research. The reason is that experiments often test well-specified theories and do an especially good job at demonstrating causation.

Of course, not all experiments and causal relationships generalize from idiosyncratic volunteer samples to a broader population. Moreover, experiments have often been criticized for restricting their population of interest to fairly homogeneous groups. For example, many of the experimental studies done on the prevention of heart disease have included mostly or only men (Melloni et al., 2010), despite the fact that the risk factors and thus prevention strategies for heart disease in women may be different. Such practices can undermine the generalizability of research evidence. So generalizability is still a concern for experiments.

Replicating Research and Meta-Analysis

Replication refers to repeating a study with a different sample; in a different place, time period, or policy context; and with a different study design. Replication dramatically enhances the generalizability of small experimental studies done on nonrandom samples. Many of the experimental studies in medicine, psychology, and economics referred to above have been replicated many times. Thus, although a particular study might have limited generalizability on its own, it may fit together with a growing pattern of similar results that accumulate across many related studies. This is why research with small, confined, or highly self-selected samples can still be important—it may be part of a broader field of research that leads, eventually, to generalizable knowledge.

Is daily mortality linked to air pollution?

Source: © iStockphoto .com/Daniel Stein.

Since replication is critical to generalizability, it is helpful to be able to systematically combine different studies. **Meta-analysis** is a method for pooling together multiple smaller studies to get a much bigger, combined study. Formally, meta-analysis is a set of statistical techniques for integrating the separate effects reported in many studies into a single, more generalizable estimate of the effect of a given treatment, or variable, on an outcome of interest (Lipsey & Wilson, 2001).

For example, meta-analysis was used to join more than a dozen studies of the relationship between air pollution and daily mortality in urban areas around the world, showing that airborne particle concentrations are a significant risk factor for mortality (Schwartz, 1994). Another meta-analysis looked at 124 experiments conducted from 1953 to 2002 to test the efficacy of second-generation antipsychotic drugs for treating schizophrenia, finding that only some were more effective than earlier drugs (Davis, Chen, & Glick, 2003). Meta-analysis is applied these days in many areas of research, including health, education, social work, criminal justice, job training and employment, and more.

Are Relationships More Generalizable? Health and Happiness in Moldova

Relationships among variables are often more generalizable than descriptive findings such as percentages or means. To illustrate this fact, let's look at some data from the World Values Survey, one of the largest social surveys of its kind, involving more than 50,000 interviews in nearly 100 different countries. Table 5.1 shows the means of a measure of self-reported health and happiness for all nations in the survey and for the small Eastern European nation of Moldova, the country that happens to have the lowest scores for both health and happiness.

Clearly, the levels of health and happiness in Moldova do not generalize well to other countries—Moldovans rate their health and happiness much lower than the overall average. As it happens, Moldova's per capita gross domestic product (GDP) is less than $3,000 per year, and *The Economist* rated it 99th out of 111 countries on its world quality-of-life index ("Moldova," 2009).

Now let's consider the *relationship* (correlation) between health and happiness—are healthier people happier? Table 5.2 shows the health-to-happiness correlations—indices of the strength (from 0 to 1) and direction (+ or –) of the statistical relationships—for all nations and for just Moldova. (See Chapter 8 for help with interpreting correlations.)

Table 5.1 Health and Happiness Means (World Values Survey)

Means	All Nations (n = 55,356)	Moldova (n = 974)
Health (0–100 scale)	71.8	50.4
Happiness (0–100 scale)	69.1	50.9

Table 5.2 Correlation of Health and Happiness (World Values Survey)

Correlation	All Nations (n = 55,356)	Moldova (n = 974)
Health and happiness	.333	.337

The positive .333 correlation for all respondents to the World Values Survey (n = 55,356) implies that, across the globe, healthier people are, as we might expect, happier—but the relationship is surprisingly similar for just the 974 people surveyed in Moldova. By the way, for the Nigerians in the survey (n = 2,021), who perhaps somewhat surprisingly rate their health and happiness among the *highest* of all the nations (86.8 and 85.9, respectively), the correlation of health and happiness is .359, quite similar again to Moldova and to the correlation for all nations. So if we wanted to study the connection between health and happiness, we might do fairly well even with access only to data from the small landlocked nation of Moldova. The relationship we have discovered seems to be fairly generalizable to many other peoples and parts of the world.

Indeed, one of the reasons why small experiments of volunteers can produce generalizable findings is that experiments—randomized experiments—are designed precisely to produce good evidence of true (unbiased) causal relationships, as we will learn in Chapter 14. And relationships, as we have just seen, tend to be more generalizable.

QUESTION

What makes experiments and statistical relationships often reasonably generalizable, even when based on limited and relatively unrepresentative samples?

Generalizability of Qualitative Studies

Qualitative research (discussed in Chapter 3) is typically done on small nonprobability samples and, therefore, is not generalizable in the sense of statistical representativeness. However, qualitative research can produce generalizable theories ("hows" and "whys") without trying to copy the sampling methods of quantitative research (Small, 2009). A qualitative researcher acquires, over a long period of detailed observation, an in-depth familiarity with a group of people or social setting that can allow the researcher to sort out the more universal, or *generalizable,* features of a setting from its more individual ideographic aspects. But a lot depends on how much time and effort is devoted to qualitative observation as well as the openness and judgment of the researcher (Lamont & White, 2005).

Having considered the foundational issue of generalizability, we can turn now to the more specific concepts and methods of sampling.

Basic Sampling Concepts

As we have said, sampling refers to the process of selecting people or *elements* from a population for inclusion in a research study. Researchers do sampling because limited resources and time often prevent them from studying an entire population. But their aim is still to produce findings that are generalizable. Let's begin by looking at some basic sampling concepts (see also Henry, 1990; Kalton, 1983).

Population, Sample, and Inference

When doing sampling, a **sample** is selected from a population of interest—but the word *population* (or *universe*), as researchers and statisticians use the term, does not necessarily mean the general human population of a society (or the universe of stars and galaxies). For example, environmental scientists monitor the quality of air in urban areas by taking daily *samples* of air, using special monitoring equipment, from the

Figure 5.1 The process of sampling and making an inference

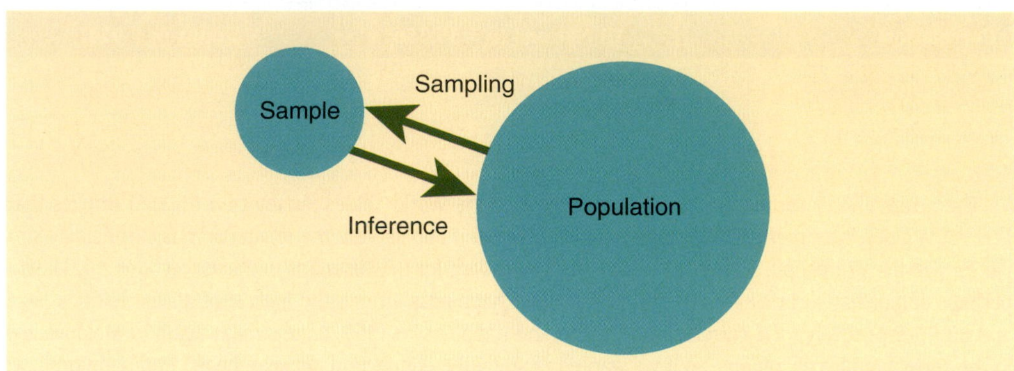

population of air surrounding a city (the airshed). Or auditors might take a *sample* of reimbursement records from a *population* of all travel reimbursements made by an organization during a given fiscal year. Researchers then use their samples to make *inferences* about the population.

Figure 5.1 illustrates the process of sampling in order to make an **inference** from a sample to a population. Specifically, this involves using a *statistic* calculated from the sample to make an inference about the *parameter* of the population. Although data are collected on the sample, you must be very clear about the conceptual and operational definition of the population to make a proper inference.

Who Is Included in the Eurozone Unemployment Rate?

For example, Agence France-Presse (2012) announced the following headline: "Eurozone Jobless Rate Hits New Record of 11.7 Percent." What is the population this statistic refers to? It takes a little investigating to come up with a precise answer. First, the Eurozone includes the 17 nations that have adopted the euro as their national currency—not all 27 European Union (EU) nations (e.g., the United Kingdom and Denmark use their own national currencies, even though they are members of the EU). Moreover, the 11.7% unemployment rate refers to the *labor force,* not to the general population, or even the working-age population. As economists define the labor force, it excludes those who are unavailable to work—for family, health, or other reasons. Even more important, it excludes those who are not actively seeking work because they are discouraged or otherwise don't want or need to work. This latter definition means that the official unemployment rate does not mesh with some individuals' intuitive use of the term *unemployment rate.* In fact, less than half (48%) of the more than 325 million people in the Eurozone are active in the labor force (OECD.Stat Extracts, 2013). So to answer our question, the 11.7% unemployment rate refers just to those in the labor force of the 17 EU nations that use the euro.

Whose Opinions Does an Oklahoma Poll Tell Us About?

Consider another example: What is the population in the following poll reported by the Associated Press (2008)?

> TULSA, Okla. (AP)—A recent poll finds Oklahoma voters support pay raises for teachers even if that means no state income tax cuts. The survey of 757 likely voters found 54% say they prefer bringing teacher salaries up to the regional average instead of a merit pay system. Thirty-eight percent prefer developing a merit pay plan. And 57% say they would rather see a teacher pay raise than a cut in state income tax rates.

The population in this poll is "likely voters who live in Oklahoma"—but let's consider what this really means. Of Oklahoma's 3.7 million total "population" at the time (U.S. Census Bureau, 2013a), only 2.6 million were eligible to vote by age and citizenship status. And of these, only 1.5 million actually *did* vote in the last general election (United States Elections Project, 2012). Likely voters in an election yet to occur are even harder to pin down. Different pollsters use different criteria to determine if someone is a likely voter. Even conceptually, whether or not someone *is* a likely voter depends on *how* likely. So the population in this case is much smaller and more specific than it might at first appear.

These examples illustrate that you must be precise in thinking about the *population* for a particular study and thus what the *sample* and statistics that come from it represent. Many mistakes of inference and interpretation get made by researchers, and often by users of research findings, from not paying careful attention to the precise definition of the population.

Census Versus Sample

When data are collected on the entire population, rather than a sample, this is referred to as a **census**. The U.S. Census and other censuses conducted in various countries around the world attempt to count and assess the characteristics of everyone in the society (the population). This is such a large undertaking in the United States, with its 300 million people, that the government attempts it only once every 10 years. But again, as researchers and statisticians use the term, *census* refers more generally to any study in which you have data on an entire population.

For example, thanks to the convenience of electronic records, auditors may analyze records of *all* reimbursements by an organization during a fiscal year, not just a sample. If you survey all 800 employees in an organization about their job satisfaction, not just a sample of employees, then you are doing a *census* survey of the population of employees. To take another example, a study titled "Fatal Outcomes From Liposuction: Census Survey of Cosmetic Surgeons" involved contacting all 1,200 actively practicing North American board-certified plastic surgeons to ask about deaths after performing the procedure (Grazer & de Jong, 2000).

With small populations, a census is not difficult to do—and in fact there is little to be gained from sampling. Sometimes, however, a sample is better than a census—even when you can do both—as the case of crime statistics illustrates.

How Many Rapes in the United States?

Rape is one of the major forms of violent crime and a continuing problem in modern societies. According to the FBI's Uniform Crime Reports, a total of 85,593 cases of forcible rape (including attempted rape and sexual assault) were recorded in the United States in 2010. The Uniform Crime Reports are a kind of a *census*—an attempt to count *all* crimes by gathering reports made (usually by victims) to law enforcement agencies across the nation (U.S. Federal Bureau of Investigation, 2013a).

The U.S. government also conducts the National Crime Victimization Survey (NCVS)—a *sample* of the population (12 years of age and older)—to estimate the number of crimes and crime victims in the United States in a given year. About 40,000 households are sampled as part of the NCVS each year. According to estimates from the NCVS, projected to the population, there were 268,574 rapes or sexual assaults in the United States in 2010 (U.S. Bureau of Justice Statistics, 2013)—182,981 *more* cases of rape and sexual assault than were reported to the FBI.[1]

Why are the two estimates so different, and which is more accurate? Intuitively, one might imagine that the complete census of all reported crimes nationwide and tallied by the FBI would be best. But the FBI's

[1]Although there are some differences in how the FBI and NCVS measure or count rape, most of the 182,981 difference is due to the fact that rape often goes unreported to the police and in turn to the FBI. The crime reports suffer from much greater nonresponse bias than the NCVS sample does.

QUESTION

What is the difference between a census and a sample? How can a sample sometimes be more accurate than a census?

census consists of only *reported* rapes. Many rape victims are afraid, embarrassed, or otherwise unwilling to report rape or attempted rape to the police.

The NCVS, on the other hand, asks about crime victimization of various kinds, including rape, in the context of a carefully planned, confidential interview that is conducted in private for research purposes only. Thus, respondents often feel more willing and able to say what happened to them, although it is quite likely that rape gets somewhat underreported to NCVS interviewers as well. Still, the reason the U.S. government spends the substantial resources needed to conduct the NCVS on just a sample of households is that it provides a better estimate of many crimes—even though it is based on just a sample of the U.S. population—than the census of reported crimes gathered each year by the FBI.

Thus, sometimes a sampling approach works better than trying to carry out a population census. So it is often wise to devote more resources—more planning and attention—to getting good data on a small *sample* than to spread resources too thinly on trying for a census of the entire *population*.

How to Select a Sample: Sampling Frames and Steps

How do you actually select a sample—what are the steps involved? Assuming that you have defined your population of interest, one of the most important first steps is to identify some kind of list, map, or other operational representation of the population from which the sample can be selected—a **sampling frame**, it is called. For example, a membership mailing list serves as a sampling frame for the population of members of a voluntary organization. Today, with almost every organization having an e-mail list of its employees, members, clients, customers, donors, students, and so on, sampling frames for organizational members or affiliated individuals have become much easier to obtain.

For broader populations, however, other sampling frames must be used. Local governments sometimes use lists of registered voters, or property tax records, as a sampling frame for the population of community residents. Maps showing regions, cities, towns, or districts are also used as sampling frames. In telephone surveys, the sampling frame is typically the system of area codes and exchanges used to assign telephone numbers. The sampling frame can also be a procedure that enumerates a population. For example, exit polls are based not only on a list of established polling stations but also on a visual tally of people leaving selected polling places on Election Day.

Using the sampling frame, the researcher then selects a subset of units or elements to be included in the sample. This usually involves one of several methods of random selection, which will be explained later in the chapter. People, households, establishments, or other units must then be contacted and invited to participate in the study. In the exit polling example, researchers might select every 20th person leaving the polling place and ask him or her to participate in the poll. Responses or observations are then recorded, and finally the findings are used to draw conclusions (inferences) about the population.

To summarize, here is a list of the basic steps involved in sampling:

- Define the population of interest for the study.
- Identify a sampling frame that represents this population.
- Select a subset of units (people, households, establishments, etc.) from the frame to be included in the sample.
- Contact the sampled people or units and request their participation.
- Record their responses or make observations.
- Summarize the findings and draw conclusions (inferences) about the population.

How Large Does My Sample Need to Be?

To fully answer the question of how large your sample needs to be, it is necessary to have some statistical foundations that we will get to later in this chapter. But we can provide a few initial guidelines.

First, and most importantly, how large a sample size you need depends on how much statistical precision you want or can afford. **Precision** refers to the amount of random error in the statistics computed from a sample (such as means or percentages), due to the fact that each sample differs just by chance from the population. The larger the sample, as you might guess, the less random fluctuation and hence the more precision there will be in the sample statistics—and thus the more closely the sample will mirror the population.

QUESTION

What are the steps involved in selecting a sample?

Second, how large a sample you need depends on how much you plan to cut up your data into subgroups, such as men versus women, for separate analysis. For a given level of precision, it is the sample size of the subgroup that matters—not the overall sample size. So if you plan on analyzing men and women separately, you would need about twice the sample as you would need to analyze them together.

Third, the sample size you need does *not* depend on the size of the population—for a given level of precision, you need the same size sample for a large population (such as the entire U.S. adult population) as you do for a small population (such as the adult residents of Smalltown, USA). These guidelines will make more sense, as noted, when we get to the statistical foundations of sampling.

Problems and Biases in Sampling

With the basics of sampling in mind, we turn now to two major difficulties in getting a truly random or representative sample, even when we use probability sampling. The first problem is whether the sampling frame adequately covers the population of interest. The second problem stems from the difficulties involved in contacting and getting people (or organizations) to actually respond or participate in the study. Both of these problems can cause **sampling bias**—a sample that gives systematically different results, because of shortcomings in the sampling process, from what would be obtained by studying the whole population.

Note that sampling bias, which produces results that are systematically too high or too low (relative to the population), is different from the issue of precision, which reflects only random sampling error in the results. This is analogous to the distinction made in Chapter 4 between measurement bias (which is systematic) and measurement error (which is random). Let's look now at how to think about and judge the potential for sampling bias in a study.

Coverage Problems

Ideally, the sampling frame *covers* the entire population of interest, the target population that the study aims to understand. In practice, however, the sampling frame is necessarily something available, concrete, and often limited. **Coverage bias** occurs when the members of the sampling frame are systematically different from the target population in a way that influences the results of the study.

Coverage is a growing problem in telephone surveys. Listed telephone numbers (such as you find in a city's phone directory) fail to provide a good sampling frame for most telephone surveys because so many households remain unlisted. And listed households may well be different (older, male, higher-income, longer-time residents, etc.) than unlisted households, resulting in potential coverage bias. For this reason, another sampling frame based on creating a list of phone numbers from random digits (called **random digit dialing**, or **RDD**) must be used instead. (We will explain more about the details of RDD sampling later on in this chapter.) However, not all households have traditional landline telephones, as increasing numbers of people rely only on cell (mobile) phones, and telephone pollsters cannot as easily call cell phones. Cell phone–only households are likely to be younger, unmarried, and more mobile than other households. So there are growing coverage problems and potential coverage bias with the RDD method of sampling as well.

Coverage problems arise not only from a sampling frame missing groups who are in the population but also from erroneously including those who are not in the population. Traditional RDD methods assumed that people lived in the region that corresponded to the area codes and exchanges of their phone numbers. Today, people can transfer those numbers, particularly mobile phone numbers, when they move. Consequently, a survey aimed at people in one city may get people in another city, due to coverage problems. Thus, it is important to investigate the nature of the list or other sampling frame for a study, consider how well it covers the population of interest, and think about the potential for coverage bias.

Nonresponse Problems

Nonresponse and the potential bias it can produce in a study are important factors in most research these days—whether it involves a census or a sample, and whether it is quantitative or qualitative. The **response rate** to a survey or other data collection effort is the result of two factors:

- **Contact rate**—how successful the researchers are at contacting people or units
- **Cooperation rate**—how willing the contacted people or units are to participate

To arrive at the response rate, these two factors are multiplied: Thus, *response rate = contact rate × cooperation rate.* For example, suppose that in a telephone survey, 50% of households on a list answer the phone after several call attempts (contact rate), and 70% of those who answer agree to be interviewed (cooperation rate). So the response rate would be .50 × .70 = .35, or 35%. Be aware that sometimes research reports will call the cooperation rate a "response rate," and the contact rate will be ignored. So it is important to look at the details of what was actually done.

Nonresponse is a growing problem in surveys, particularly telephone surveys such as the national poll about the government's response to Katrina. Most polling organizations won't even reveal their response rates, in large part because they are low and getting lower. In fact, even in well-done telephone surveys these days, the response rate is often less than 50% (sometimes much less), in part because many people screen incoming calls or don't answer their phones (contact rate) and because, increasingly, people do not welcome or trust pollsters enough to consent to an interview (cooperation rate). The respected Pew Research Center (2012a), one of the few survey organizations to honestly discuss and publish its real telephone survey response rates (using industry-standard methods, including dialing cell phones), has reported rates as low as 9%.

Nonresponse is an issue in mail surveys also, as letters can be returned because of inaccurate or out-of-date address information (contact rate) and people ignore surveys that they receive in the mail (cooperation rate). Nonresponse is also a growing problem in Internet surveys, as spam filters can trap e-mail messages sent to respondents (contact rate) and many people are suspicious of unfamiliar e-mails or simply disregard them (cooperation rate).

Some people care a lot about recycling, others less so.
Source: © 2009 Jupiterimages Corporation.

When Does Nonresponse Cause Bias?

The aim of probability sampling is to produce results that accurately reflect the population of interest, but incomplete coverage and nonresponse can produce sampling bias. Such bias produces results that are higher or lower than they are in the population, no matter how large the sample. Much depends, however, on what the study aims to measure and what caused incomplete coverage or nonresponse in the first place. An example will help illustrate.

A telephone survey commissioned by the City of Fort Collins, Colorado (2005) found that, perhaps somewhat surprisingly, 76% of city residents reported setting out their recycling at the curb every week. Telephone polls such as this one often have low response rates, as we have just seen. So let's consider how nonresponse bias may have influenced the result.

Consider two city residents, Joe and Kim. Joe doesn't recycle at all. He has a busy job, values convenience, and does not think recycling is all that important. Kim works freelance and recycles faithfully, even though she is not required to. She loves the outdoors, resents wasteful packaging, and is committed to doing whatever she can to help protect the environment. The polling firm calls both Joe and Kim: "Hello. We're taking a poll this evening about recycling here in Fort Collins. Your answers are confidential, and we need only about 15 minutes of your time. Can I get started?" We might predict that, given her commitment to the environment, Kim would gladly agree to cooperate. Joe, on the other hand, might want to avoid talking about his recycling habits (or lack thereof). In other words, Kim would have a much higher **propensity to respond** than Joe.

> **QUESTION**
>
> **What is the distinction between coverage bias and nonresponse bias?**

In this example, the *propensity to respond* is directly related to what the survey is trying to measure, recycling behavior. If people, like Kim, who *do* recycle cooperate more than people, like Joe, who *do not* recycle, then the survey estimate—73% of people in Fort Collins recycle weekly—will be *biased*. The bias in this case is positive—the number is larger than it would be otherwise, were there full cooperation (a 100% response rate). We depict this in Figure 5.2. Researchers refer to this as **nonresponse bias** because the nonresponders, the people (like Joe) who refuse to be interviewed, differ on average in the variable of interest (such as recycling). Since the nonresponders are underrepresented in the sample compared with the population, the proportion of recyclers reported in the population is too high.

When Propensity to Respond Produces Bias

Viewed generally, we can think of several possible causal models of the propensity to respond (see Groves, 2006), depicted in Figure 5.3. In the models, P represents the propensity to respond, Y represents what we are trying to measure in our survey, and X and Z represent other variables that we will think about shortly.

Consider, first, the *reverse cause* model, which describes the situation in the recycling poll we just discussed. In this case, Y represents recycling behavior, and P represents the likelihood that a person participates in the poll. Since Y (recycling) influences P (responding to the poll), the estimate that 73% of the people in Fort Collins faithfully recycle is biased. To determine the direction of bias in a reverse cause model, one must figure out what group is underrepresented and see how that affects the results. In the recycling poll, it is the nonrecyclers who are underrepresented, making the share who recycle too high: positive bias.

In the *common cause* model, some other variable Z drives both Y and P. Consider a university with both commuter and residential students that wants to learn about what kinds of clubs students would like. Residential students may be more involved with university life and therefore have a higher propensity of answering a survey. Residential students might also prefer different kinds of clubs. In this case, the survey will overrepresent the preferences of residential students. Again, the survey results will be subject to nonresponse bias. (Applying this

Figure 5.2 Nonresponse Bias in a Recycling Poll

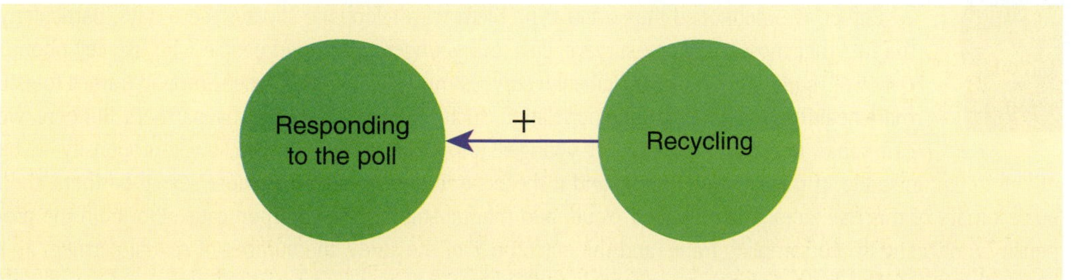

Figure 5.3 Causal Models of the Propensity to Respond

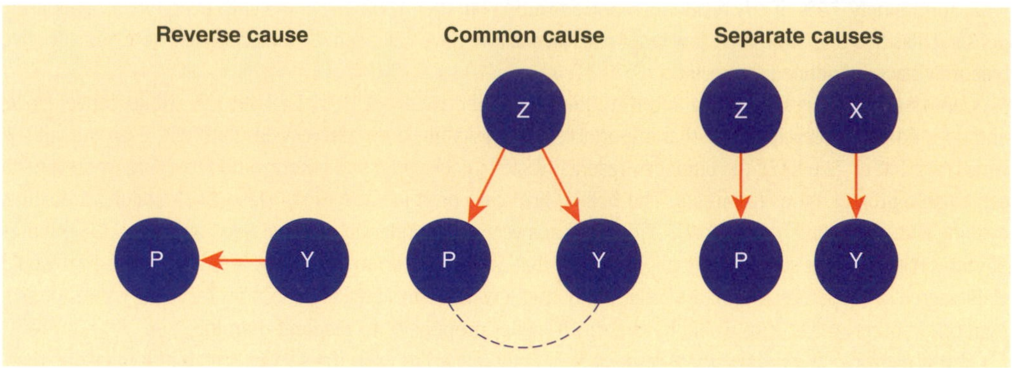

Note: In the figures, *P* stands for the propensity to respond. *Y* represents the substantive result or outcome of the study. The letters *X* and *Z* represent other variables.

Source: Groves, Robert M. (2006). "Nonresponse rates and nonresponse bias in household surveys'" *Public Opinion Quarterly* 70(5), Special Issue 2006: 646–675.

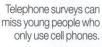

example to Figure 5.3, *Z* represents whether students are residents or commuters, and *Y* represents type of club preference.) Remember that a complete assessment of bias should include a prediction of the *direction* of bias.

When Propensity to Respond Does Not Produce Bias

But nonresponse does not always bias the outcome of a study, because the influences *Z* that affect responding may be distinct from the influences *X* that affect the outcome. This is the *separate causes* model.

A simple example of this might be an employee satisfaction survey being conducted on a day when a particularly nasty flu bug is going around the office. Having the flu is a causal factor *Z* that lowers the propensity *P* to respond to the employee satisfaction survey. But having the flu is not a cause of the outcome *Y* of job satisfaction, which of course is still caused by many other factors *X* (pay, benefits, promotion opportunities, etc.). In this case, the nonresponse is essentially random and ignorable—it does not bias the results of the study (the measured level of job satisfaction in the organization). Box 5.1 describes the steps needed to assess nonresponse bias in a particular situation.

Telephone surveys can miss young people who only use cell phones.

Source: © iStockphoto .com/Dean Mitchell.

When Do Coverage Problems Cause Bias?

We have been talking mostly about nonresponse bias, but the same ideas help us understand when *coverage bias* is a problem. So let's return to the question of how well a sampling frame covers the population of interest, how we can tell if coverage problems cause bias, and if they do how we determine the direction of bias.

Earlier, we mentioned the coverage problem with telephone surveys these days, particularly the fact that most telephone surveys leave out younger, unmarried people who use cell phones only. Still, some important public health surveys must rely on telephone sampling frames to estimate health risk behaviors of the population, such as the number of sexual partners. But here, we can sense a potential for bias: If younger, unmarried people have a lower propensity to be included in the sampling frame, and if these same people also have more sexual partners, then our estimate of this risk factor will be biased. Youth and marital status are a common cause *Z* of both the propensity *P* of being in the sampling frame and the outcome *Y* of the study, the number of sexual partners as a health risk factor. This is the *common cause* model from Figure 5.3.

Consider the case of exit polls, whose sampling frame consists of everyone exiting voting places. Those who vote through absentee ballots or use early voting options are not in the sampling frame. In the United States, military personnel often vote through absentee ballots and are more likely to vote Republican. So, exit polls have traditionally underestimated Republican votes. However, in the 2008 U.S. presidential elections, new options for early voting were heavily used by the Black community—a group that strongly supported Barack Obama. For that reason, the 2008 exit polls systematically underestimated Obama's share of the vote. This is another example of common cause: Race influenced both what the study measured (presidential vote) and the propensity to be covered (being physically at the voting place on Election Day).

But again, imperfect coverage does not necessarily produce bias. Say a summer youth program wants to survey families it served last summer about their program preferences this year but has good address information for only half the population served (because of lax and inconsistent key entry of the registration forms submitted by families). These admittedly sloppy administrative practices influence the propensity P to be included in the sampling frame but probably have no effect on the program preferences of families, which is the outcome Y of interest. *Separate causes X,* such as the socioeconomic status of the family, still may influence program preferences, but these factors are unrelated to coverage. Box 5.1 describes the steps needed to assess possible coverage bias in a study.

Sampling bias comes from several sources and goes by different names, summarized in Box 5.2.

BOX 5.1
Steps in Assessing Coverage and Nonresponse Bias

Define carefully the target population of interest.

To assess *coverage bias,*

- Identify the sampling frame—who is in the sampling frame but not the target population, and who is in the target population but not the sampling frame?
- Assess any systematic differences between those in the sampling frame and those in the target population.
- Determine whether the propensity to be covered is related in any way to what the study is measuring and, if so, how.
- Use the relationship between propensity to be covered and what the study is measuring, if any, to predict the *direction* of bias.

To assess *nonresponse bias,*

- Identify the nonresponse—who was not contacted or refused to participate?
- Assess any systematic differences between those who responded and those who did not.
- Determine whether the propensity to respond is related in any way to what the study is measuring and, if so, how.
- Use the relationship between propensity to respond and what the study is measuring, if any, to predict the *direction* of bias.

Sampling Bias Versus Generalizability (External Validity)

Sampling bias is only one aspect of the larger question of generalizability (or external validity), which as mentioned earlier depends on broader considerations, such as how the population of interest is defined and whether the

QUESTION

When does the propensity to respond cause bias?

results resonate with the findings of other studies. Sampling bias is more specific and quantitative and refers to the direction and magnitude of how the estimate from a sample differs from the truth about the population. We made a similar distinction in Chapter 4 between the broader conceptual issue of measurement validity and the narrower quantitative notion of measurement bias. And in later chapters on causation we will see something similar again when we discuss the broad issue of internal validity as well as the specific question of bias in causal estimates.

BOX 5.2
Sampling Bias

Sampling bias refers to a systematic difference between an estimate of some characteristics of a population and the truth about the population, due to the way in which the sample was designed or selected. It includes

- **Sample selection bias,** a broad term used to refer to bias from how the sample was selected.
- **Coverage bias,** distortions in the results because the sampling frame does not fully cover the population.
- **Nonresponse bias,** misleading results due to a low response rate.
- **Voluntary response bias (or volunteer bias),** results that reflect those who volunteer for a study, in contrast to a more representative sample.

Ethics of Nonresponse

When sampling widgets produced on an assembly line, say, to measure production quality, we are free to select individual widgets at will into the sample. But when we sample people for a study, we must tell them first about the study (its purpose and any potential risks) and recognize their right to voluntary participation. We introduced the principles and procedures of the ethics of human participation in research in Chapter 1 (and will return to it again in Chapter 16). But it is useful to point out here that, in an important sense, nonresponse and its potential bias are necessary costs of the need to acknowledge and respect the right of voluntary participation in research.

Although it might be possible to reduce nonresponse by deceiving people about a study or coercing them—even physically forcing them—to participate, this would not be acceptable ethically. Yet researchers still do, subtly, push these limits on occasion, for example, by saying an interview will be shorter than it really is or by implying that participation in a study is somehow required by a teacher, an employer, or another authority figure (and thus coercing participation). It is for these reasons that ethics committees (such as institutional review boards in the United States) watch over researchers and look out for the interests of the people being recruited as research participants. Although survey researchers working for businesses or other private clients are often not subject to such formal oversight, they should still be just as conscientious in considering the ethics of recruiting people to respond to surveys.

Nonprobability Sampling

Although random (or probability) sampling provides a kind of "gold standard" in terms of generalizability, we have seen that real-world random sampling can nonetheless be subject to coverage bias and/or nonresponse bias. In fact, for both practical and cost considerations, much research gets done with various forms of nonprobability sampling. These include voluntary sampling, convenience sampling, snowball sampling, and purposive sampling.

Voluntary Sampling

In an important sense, as we have just seen, all research involving human participants depends on voluntary participation—a core principle of modern research ethics. But when researchers refer to *voluntary sampling,* they mean that the participants were recruited by putting out an explicit call for volunteers. Here is an example from Craigslist.org, which is sometimes used to recruit volunteers for a study:

> Participate in a Research Study
>
> Do you have trouble falling asleep, staying asleep, or getting refreshing sleep?
>
> The Sleep Disorders Center at Rush University Medical Center is conducting a research study on adults with insomnia. If you are 18 years or older and have a sleep complaint you may qualify to participate. The study requires 8 appointments over a 3 month time period. If you qualify, you will receive a thorough sleep evaluation. For more information please call . . .

The people who end up in this study, by responding to the Craigslist ad, are a voluntary sample. Elsewhere on the same Craigslist page, we can also find calls for volunteers to take surveys of various kinds, for example, one seeking Whites to complete a survey on racial attitudes.

The concern with this kind of sampling, however, is a form of nonresponse bias—called **volunteer bias**—that refers to the fact that volunteers may differ from a more representative sample of the population in ways that influence the findings of the study. Thus, the causal models for response and coverage bias (Figure 5.3) apply when thinking about volunteer bias as well. Volunteers for an insomnia study may well suffer from more serious sleep problems, for example, than a more general population of insomniacs. Or Whites who volunteer for a survey on racial attitudes may be more open and accepting of other races than the White population overall. Thus, if the propensity to volunteer is related to the outcome of the study, as it might be in these examples, the results will be biased. Box 5.3 describes the steps to assess possible volunteer bias in a study.

BOX 5.3
Steps in Assessing Volunteer Bias

- Define carefully the target population of interest.
- To assess *volunteer bias,*
    - Identify who volunteers and how they come to volunteer. Who volunteers, and who does not volunteer?
    - Assess any systematic differences between volunteers and those in the target population.
    - Determine whether the propensity to be a volunteer is related in any way to what the study is measuring and, if so, how.
    - Use the relationship between the propensity to volunteer and what the study is measuring, if any, to predict the direction of bias.

QUESTION

What is the difference between voluntary sampling and voluntary participation in a random sample?

Convenience Sampling

Convenience sampling refers to a situation in which a researcher takes advantage of a natural gathering or easy access to people who can be recruited into a study. The study of Katrina refugees at a Red Cross shelter involved a convenience sample. Recruiting patients in a waiting room for a clinical study, or doing intercept interviews of drivers stuck in traffic, are other examples of convenience sampling. Often, undergraduate psychology majors end up in a university *subject pool,* a convenience sample for purposes of conducting psychological research.

Convenience samples suffer from a form of coverage bias, in the sense that people who happen to be available to a researcher may not cover or represent much of the target population of interest. The refugees of the Red Cross Shelter in Austin were a small slice of the hundreds of thousands of evacuees from New Orleans after Katrina struck. But as we noted, much depends on whether the propensity to be included in the sampling frame actually influences the substantive outcome of interest. If not, then results from a convenience sample can still be useful for research.

QUESTION

What is the distinction between voluntary sampling and convenience sampling?

Snowball Sampling

For some populations of interest, it may be next to impossible to identify a sampling frame to draw from. Examples of such populations include injection drug users, sex workers, gang members, followers of secret political or religious groups, or other people with hidden behaviors or rare characteristics. In such cases, researchers will often use **snowball sampling**, also called chain sampling or **respondent-driven sampling**, in which a few "seed" interviewees are asked to refer other people they know to the researcher for inclusion in the sample. This approach is facilitated by the fact that a level of rapport and trust is typically established during the interview process, opening up referrals to other members of the population who might otherwise have remained unknown to the researcher. Interestingly, some researchers have even developed ways to provide this kind of sampling with more of a statistical foundation (see www.respondentdrivensampling.org), even though it starts out as essentially a nonprobability form of sampling (see also Heckathorn, 1997).

Quota Sampling

Some nonprobability sampling approaches try to make a study's results more representative by recruiting to fill certain preestablished quotas. *Quota sampling*, as it is called, starts by dividing the population into groups or quotas, such as male and female, or ages 18–29, 30–64, and 65 or older (the quotas need to be mutually exclusive and collectively exhaustive). Quota sampling then uses convenience, voluntary, or some other nonprobability sampling approach to fill the quotas with the desired number of interviews or observations. If there is good knowledge about the population shares of each group, and if most of the important differences relevant to what the study is measuring are captured by such group characteristics, this approach can improve representativeness. However, very often bias stems from variables or characteristics that are not easily measured or anticipated (such as political ideology or personality), rather than the usual demographic or geographic variables typically used in quota sampling.

Sampling Online: Open Web Polls and Internet Access Panels

The Internet has emerged as an increasingly used method in social research, and researchers are struggling with how to sample online. Many organizations put up open web polls that invite anyone who visits their website to answer the questionnaire. Such polls suffer from a high degree of volunteer bias, because those who are most interested and motivated by the topic of the poll are the ones who respond.

How Much Should We Trust Open Web Polls?

An open web poll on a site called TheInternetParty.org and a Gallup poll based on a random telephone sample asked similar questions about the public's attitude toward the strictness of current U.S. gun laws.[2] Compare the results (The Internet Party's version of the question wording is shown in parentheses):

. . . gun laws in this country (in the United States) should be (are) . . .

	The Internet Party (Open Web Poll)	Gallup Poll (RDD Telephone Poll)
More strict (Not restrictive enough)	17%	49%
Less strict (Too restrictive)	66%	8%
Remain as they are (About right)	12%	41%
Don't know (Other)	5%	2%

There are differences in question wording, of course, but these are not likely the reason for the large discrepancy in results. Rather, gun advocates feel strongly about this issue and are motivated to search for and respond to the open web poll, while the general public is less passionate about the topic. Thus, the propensity to respond or volunteer to participate in the open web poll produced a strong bias in favor of the view held by gun advocates.

How to Create More Trustworthy Internet Surveys

Another approach to sampling in online research is the creation of **Internet access panels**, opt-in e-mail lists (or panels) of people recruited in various ways to participate in web surveys and other forms of online research. Harris Interactive, Ipsos MORI, YouGov, Toluna, and many other research firms have established and recruited online panels, some claiming to have millions of members. While these Internet access panels remain composed of volunteers, the motivation to join the panel (financial incentives form part of the recruitment pitch) are not so obviously related to the propensity to respond. Here are the results from Harris Interactive's (2008) panel on the question of whether the public favors stricter, or less strict, gun control laws:

Harris Interactive (Internet Access Panel)	
Stricter	52%
Less strict	22%
Neither	20%
Don't know	7%

[2]This Internet Party website is no longer fully functional, and the web polling results we show here, which are from 2008, are no longer available online or through web archives. For purposes of comparison, the Gallup poll results we show are from a poll also conducted in 2008 (PollingReport.com, 2013b).

These results look more like the results from the Gallup poll and seem much less biased than the open web poll by The Internet Party. It should be noted that Harris Interactive uses weighting in an attempt to remove bias. The logic is similar to quota sampling: using weights to adjust the sample so that it looks more like the population. However, Internet panels can often adjust for many more variables than typical quota sampling, including even the propensity to be online. Still, much of the result is likely attributable to the fact that the Internet access panel did not volunteer for the survey based on a passion for gun ownership. Thus, the potential for avoiding bias with an Internet panel depends critically on studying measures that are unrelated to the propensity for joining the panel.

QUESTION

Why do Internet access panels tend to produce less biased results than open web polls? In what ways are Internet access panels still likely to be biased?

While some studies suggest that Internet access panels can produce results similar to traditional random samples (Braunsberger, Wybenga, & Gates, 2007; Farrell & Petersen, 2010; Van Ryzin, 2008), other studies caution that substantial bias remains (Chang & Krosnick, 2009; Malhotra & Krosnick, 2007; Yeager et al., 2011). In the 2012 U.S. presidential election, according to an analysis in the *New York Times* by Nate Silver (2012b), several leading polls that used Internet methods were among the most accurate at predicting the final vote, while some that used traditional telephone methods and random sampling were farther off the mark (including the venerable Gallup poll). Much investigation and debate will continue about the validity of such online methods as people seek to harness the potential of the Internet for social and policy research—and as coverage and response rate problems continue to plague telephone surveys and other, more established, methods.

Purposive Sampling and Qualitative Research

Qualitative research involves sampling as well: What people should we interview in depth or observe unobtrusively in a given setting? What texts or images should we record and include in a content analysis? Sampling for qualitative research may be done randomly, using the various random sampling methods we describe later. But as we saw in Chapter 3, sampling for qualitative research often involves some form of **purposive sampling**—choosing people who have a unique perspective or occupy important roles, or selecting individuals or artifacts to represent theoretical categories or considerations (Patton, 2002). And as we also saw in Chapter 3, qualitative research often involves a small *n* or sample size.

For example, after interviewing several people in a neighborhood who oppose the construction of a new housing project, the researcher may purposively seek out supporters of the project to gain a broader perspective. In case study research, investigators typically try to pick a range of sites to visit and observe, for example, small and large schools as well as succeeding and failing schools. As we saw in Chapter 3, they may use a purposive sampling table, such as Table 5.3.

Initially, all possible schools to visit would be arrayed in this way, and then the researchers would choose one school from each category for the case study.

Qualitative researchers also need to pay attention to potential bias due to nonresponse and incomplete coverage. The propensity to participate or to be included in a study can be related to (and thus bias) the outcomes of interest, even when those outcomes are observed and recorded qualitatively. Therefore, qualitative researchers must always ask themselves: What kinds of people or cases am I missing in my research? Are there ways in which those in my study systematically differ from those left out—and if so, are the differences important to the findings of my research?

Table 5.3 Purposive Sampling Grid of Schools

	Small	Large
Succeeding	A	B
Failing	C	D

Mario Luis Small (2009), however, suggests that the primary aim of qualitative sampling should not be representativeness but rather should be a focus on causal relationships and the use of logic to determine what subjects to study, in a sequential manner. He draws analogies with how natural scientists sequentially design experiments to test different logical or causal situations, developing a generalizable causal theory out of a series of connected studies, rather than trying to represent a population.

However, if the goal is to represent a population and learn its characteristics, random sampling is the best approach.

Random (Probability) Sampling

Random sampling (also called **probability sampling**) uses chance to select people (or elements) from the population. Intuitively, it makes sense to do things this way. If we let chance do the selecting, for example, by drawing numbers from a hat, then we can expect that the people (or elements) in the sample will be fairly representative in terms of their characteristics, behaviors, or attitudes relative to the population. In other words, the sample results will be generalizable. Qualitative research can also use random sampling, for example, by selecting schools from each cell in the grid of Table 5.3 using chance so as not to unconsciously influence the findings.

But in addition to this intuitive notion of fairness and representativeness, random sampling provides a foundation for statistical inference—formal methods of assessing the precision of quantitative results from random samples.

The Contribution of Random Sampling

The theory and practice of random sampling is one of the most important inventions of modern social science. It forms the foundation for many of the economic, social, health, environmental, and demographic statistics governments around the world produce and rely on for policy and decision making. For example, major U.S. government surveys or surveillance programs based on random sampling give us statistics about the following:

- Unemployment in the U.S. labor force (the Current Population Survey, or CPS)
- Crime victimization (the NCVS)
- Air quality (ambient air quality surveillance in urban areas)
- Teen smoking and drug use (the Youth Risk Behavior Surveillance System, or YRBSS)
- Health status and health care access (the National Health Interview Survey, or NHIS)
- Capital expenditures by businesses (the Annual Capital Expenditures Survey)
- Math and language skills of schoolchildren (the National Assessment of Educational Progress, or NAEP)
- Housing costs and conditions (the American Housing Survey)
- Age, family structure, and other demographic trends (the American Community Survey)

Most governments in advanced industrial nations in the Americas, in Europe, in Asia, and elsewhere conduct similar labor force, health, and other surveys based on random sampling. And random sampling forms the basis of the major social surveys used for much academic research (such as the General Social Survey, the American National Election Studies, the European Social Survey, and the World Values Survey) as well as modern public opinion research reported every day in the media (such as the polls by Gallup, Pew, or Ipsos and the EU's Eurobarometer). Consumer confidence, presidential approval, and public opinion on a range of current policy and political issues all come from random samples.

QUESTION

What are the advantages of random (probability) sampling over nonprobability sampling?

Random Sampling Versus Randomized Experiments

It is important to note that *random sampling* is something much different from *randomized experiments,* or randomized clinical trials, as discussed in Chapter 14.

- *Random sampling* is designed to select elements from a population in order to make statistical inferences about the population. The goal is to make the sample representative of the population.
- *Randomized experiments* assign people or elements to conditions (or treatments) to test causal relationships. The goal is to make the treatment groups equivalent to each other, but not necessarily representative of any well-defined population.

Indeed, most randomized experiments rely on volunteers or convenience samples, not random samples. At the same time, most random sample surveys are purely observational studies (i.e., studies that do not manipulate independent variables to observe their effects on dependent variables) and thus provide only limited evidence of causal relationships. We will learn more about these issues in Part IV of this book. In fact, it is somewhat rare and often difficult to do a study that contains both random sampling and random assignment.

Simple Random Sampling

Various forms of random sampling are used in practice—systematic sampling, stratified sampling, cluster sampling, multistage sampling, random digit dialing (for telephone surveys), and so on. These are all forms of random sampling, and we will soon learn more about them.

But for understanding the basic theory and logic of random sampling, it is best to begin with **simple random sampling**—selecting people (or elements) from a population in such a way that each individual has an equal chance, or probability, of selection. Drawing numbers from a hat, marbles from an urn, or Ping-Pong balls from a lottery machine are examples of simple random sampling. More typically, simple random sampling involves assigning random numbers to people or units on a list (the sampling frame), and then sorting the list by the random number to select the desired number (n) to be in the sample (something easily done with an ordinary computer spreadsheet program). Although simple random sampling forms the basis of statistical theory, the other, more complex, forms of random sampling appear more often in major surveys.

Simple random sampling provides an equal chance of selection.

Source: © iStockphoto .com/Marina_Ph.

Let's consider the example of estimating unemployment, which in most countries gets done using monthly or quarterly random sample surveys of the population, such as the United States' CPS (U.S. Department of Labor, 2009). Government labor force surveys use complex forms of random sampling, and very large sample sizes, but for the purpose of learning the logic of random sampling, we will simplify things and start small.

To estimate the unemployment rate this month, let's assume that we are able to select a simple random sample of $n = 400$ individuals from the labor force. Using p to represent the sample proportion, say we get the following results:

p = 22 unemployed/400 total in the sample;

$p = .055.$

Our sample estimate of the unemployment rate is thus 5.5% based on a simple random sample of $n = 400$ people in the labor force.

Sampling Variability

Our sample unemployment rate p is unbiased, in the sense that it comes from a simple random sample that gave each individual in the population an equal chance of being selected. But this does not mean that $p = .055$ is equal to the population unemployment rate—the true unemployment rate among the millions of people in the population (the labor force), the parameter represented by uppercase P. Our sample p will probably be a bit off the mark, different from the true population parameter P.

To see why, imagine what would happen if we took another random sample of 400 people from the same population. Will we get exactly 22 who are unemployed, or in other words exactly $p = .055$ again? Probably not. Each random sample, just by the luck of the draw, can vary somewhat from the next sample—and from the population. This is referred to as **sampling variability** (or **sampling error**). When examining the results of a given random sample, therefore, we must take this sampling variability into consideration. Moreover, we would like some idea of how far off our sample estimate could be from the true unemployment rate in the population.

QUESTION

Why are the results of one random sample unlikely to match those of another random sample, even when both samples are the same size and drawn from the same population?

Sampling Distributions, Standard Errors, and Confidence Intervals

Random sampling provides a foundation for statistical inference—formal methods of assessing the precision of quantitative results from random samples. Let's see how this is done. It all begins with the idea of sampling variability, which we have just been discussing.

Because of sampling variability, a random sample is likely to differ from the population as well as from another random sample we might draw. One sample might have a few extra unemployed people while another might have a few extra employed people, purely due to the chance of who happened to be in that sample. Now imagine many, many random samples—all of the same size, from the same population. We would end up with a pile of samples, each with a somewhat different result. The long-run pattern of what we would see if we were to take many repeated samples in this way and plot the results is referred to as the *sampling distribution*. Figure 5.4 illustrates this idea of a sampling distribution. In real life, of course, we don't actually take more than one sample, but imagining what would happen if we did take many samples forms the basis of statistical inference.

Figure 5.4 Sample Result, Sampling Distribution, and Standard Error

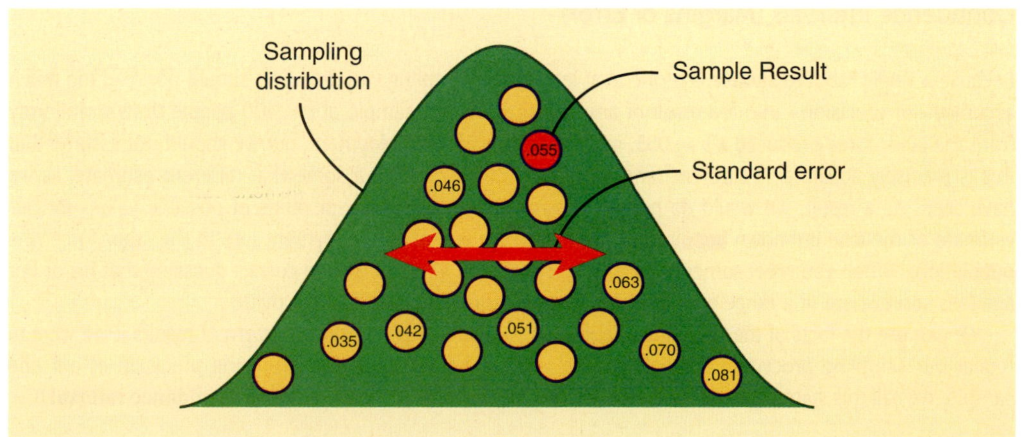

The sampling distribution has certain regularities that make it quite useful for inference. The center (or peak) of the distribution, around which many of the samples cluster, is the truth about the population (the parameter *P*). In our unemployment example, the center of the sampling distribution would be the true unemployment rate in the whole labor force. This makes intuitive sense: The average of the results of many, many samples will tend toward the result we would get from including everyone.

The sampling distribution also tends to have a predictable shape, with lots of samples clustered in the middle and fewer samples ending up at the extremes. This shape is a normal curve. In all normal curves, areas (or probabilities) under the curve can be calculated accurately by just knowing the center (mean) and spread (standard deviation) of the curve. We've already seen that the center is the truth about the population (the parameter *P*) that we are aiming to estimate. The spread, or standard deviation of the sampling distribution, is called the **standard error** (or *SE* for short). Think of the standard error as the typical difference, the average "error," you can expect to see in the results of your sample when compared with the truth about the population.

The magnitude of the standard error depends on two factors: the underlying variability of the characteristic or behavior in the population and the size of the sample. This can be seen in the basic formula for a standard error:

$$SE = \frac{\text{Variability}}{\sqrt{\text{Sample size}}}.$$

Beginning with the numerator, variability, we can see that if everyone in the labor force is employed (hence no variability in employment status in the population), then we would not need much of a sample at all to come up with a very precise estimate of the unemployment rate. Let's think about another variable—income. If everyone in a society had the exact same income (complete egalitarianism), even a small sample would be perfectly accurate. But if incomes in society differ a lot (as they in fact do), with extremes of wealth and poverty, one sample might end up with an exceptionally rich person while another might not. The sample means would vary a lot, inflating the standard error of our estimate. This can be seen in the formula, with a large numerator resulting in a bigger standard error.

QUESTION

In your own words, how would you explain the idea of a sampling distribution? And what does the standard error of a sampling distribution represent?

The sample size is even more of a factor in calculating the standard error: The more data we have to make an estimate, the smaller the standard error and thus the more precise it will be. In other words, bigger samples do not vary as much (from each other and from the truth about the population). Notice that the sample size is under the square root sign. This means that to cut the standard error in half, we would have to quadruple the sample size.

The standard error is quite useful in statistics and appears in various forms of analysis—one of which is confidence intervals.

Confidence Intervals (Margins of Error)

Because a single random sample is prone to at least some sampling variability, we should not read too much accuracy—or precision—into the result of any one sample. Our sample of $n = 400$ people drawn randomly from the labor force produced a $p = .055$, or a 5.5%, rate of unemployment, but we should not assume that this is precisely accurate. A different random sample might result in a somewhat different estimate, as we have seen. As a result, we would do better by constructing an interval or range of possible values for our estimate of the true unknown population parameter *P*—the real unemployment rate in the labor force (the population). When you meet someone for the first time, you'll be more often correct guessing that his or her age falls somewhere in a range of, say, 20 to 30 than estimating that it is exactly 26.

We can use the facts of the sampling distribution—the imaginary long-run pattern of results if we were to repeat our sampling procedure many times—to make a formal statement about the precision of our one sample. We call this statement of statistical sampling precision (really imprecision) a **confidence interval** (CI), or **margin of error** (see Box 5.4). Pollsters and public opinion researchers tend to talk about margins of error, while academic journals in health and other fields tend to use the language of confidence intervals. But they are the same thing.

Roughly speaking, two *SE*s on either side of a statistic will give us what is called a *95% confidence interval.* Here is the formula:

$$\text{Estimate} \pm 2 \times SE.$$

The reason we add and subtract two standard errors is because of the sampling distribution and its normal curve shape: 95% of all samples will fall within two standard errors of the truth about the population (the parameter *P*). So if we extend a two-standard error (2 × SE) boundary above and below our estimate, for 95% of the samples this boundary—the confidence interval—will contain the population parameter.

Returning again to our unemployment example, with a sample of $n = 400$ we estimated the unemployment rate to be 5.5%. Using a formula that is explained in Chapter 9, the standard error of this estimate turns out to be 1.1%. The confidence interval becomes

$$5.5\% \pm 2 \times 1.1\%, \text{ or}$$

$$5.5\% \pm 2.2\% = 3.3\% \text{ to } 7.7\%.$$

In words, our 5.5% estimate of the unemployment rate has a ±2.2 percentage point margin of error. Ideally, the margin of error should be referred to in units of *percentage points,* rather than as a *percent* or %. This avoids anyone thinking that the range is given as a percentage or proportionate difference relative to the base, as described further in Chapter 8. The shorter term *points* is sometimes used, which works well because it helps people avoid an incorrect interpretation.

Saying that the 95% CI of the unemployment rate is from 3.3% to 7.7% is equivalent to saying that the unemployment rate is 5.5% with a ±2.2 percentage point margin of error. Again, these are just two ways of saying the same thing.

But what does this confidence interval (margin of error) really tell us? Here is its meaning: It tells us we are 95% confident that the true unemployment rate in the population lies somewhere between 3.3% and 7.7%. The "95% confident" part is shorthand for the fact that this interval would work in capturing the truth about the population in 95% of all samples that could be selected.

BOX 5.4
Relationship Between Various Precision Measures

Smaller standard error → Smaller margin of error → Narrower CI → More precision

Larger standard error → Larger margin of error → Wider CI → Less precision

Interpreting Confidence Intervals (Margins of Error)

Interpreting confidence intervals (margins of error) takes practice, so let's try interpreting the accompanying Figure 5.5 from an MSNBC news report (November 1, 2007), specifically the subheadline "Sixty-Seven Percent of Parents Support Giving Contraceptives to Teenagers."

Figure 5.5 This news report of a poll includes margin of error.

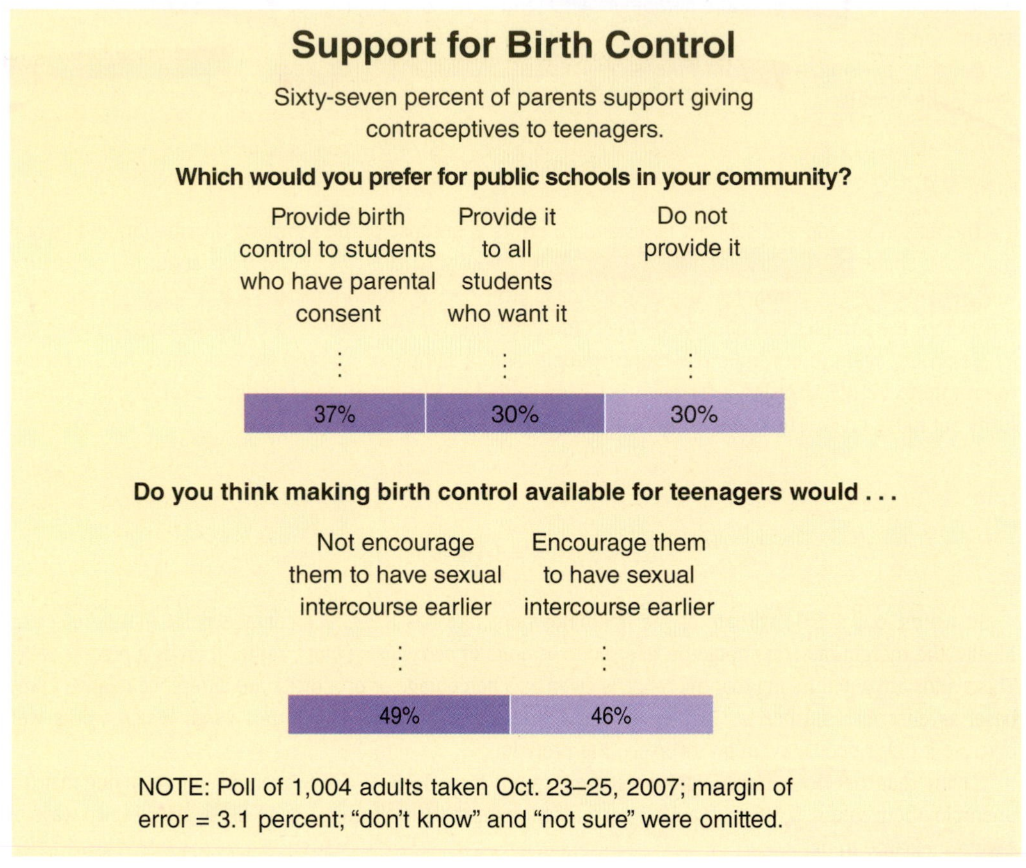

Source: MSNBC News Report (2007).

The sample proportion is $p = .67$ (or 67%), but the population P is unknown, because the pollsters interviewed only a sample of 1,004 adults (see the note in Figure 5.5), not the 200 million–plus adults in the U.S. population. Still, the margin of error of 3.1 percentage points (mentioned in the note) tells us that we are 95% confident that P (the proportion of all U.S. adults who support giving contraceptives to teenagers) is somewhere in the range of 63.9% to 70.1%. We assume this is a 95% CI estimate because that is the standard used by polling organizations.

Don't Overinterpret Margins of Error

The reported margin of error is subject to some caveats. First, the 3.1 percentage point margin of error reported here is approximate and based on the assumption of a 50/50 split ($p = .5$), which is the maximum possible variability—and thus the biggest standard error (for a given sample size). For the 67% ($p = .67$) who support giving birth control to teenagers, a result with less variability, the exact margin of error is a little less: 2.9 percentage points. But most polls report only an overall margin of error (based on $p = .5$) because it is a conservative calculation, meaning that it gives the largest possible margin of error. They also report the overall margin of error because it would be just too confusing to report separate margins of error for every percentage mentioned in a news article or report. Just looking at the sidebar here, there is technically a different margin of error for the 37%, 30% (twice), 49%, and 46% figures shown.

The second caveat is that the overall margin of error given for a poll such as this does not apply to the percentages reported for subgroups of the sample. For example, the article goes on to say this: "Minorities, older and lower-earning people were likeliest to prefer requiring parental consent, while those favoring no restriction tended to be younger and from cities or suburbs." But these are subgroups of the total $n = 1{,}004$ sample, and the number of respondents in these subgroups is certainly less—perhaps much less—than the total sample size. And as we'll see next, the smaller the sample, the larger the margin of error. So a percentage reported separately for older people or minorities, let's say, would have a much larger margin of error than 3.1 percentage points.

The third caveat is that the margin of error (or confidence interval) only expresses *sampling* or statistical error—not all of the many other kinds of error that can influence research findings. The *New York Times* uses the following standard statement for its polling results to explain this idea:

> In addition to sampling error, the practical difficulties of conducting any survey of public opinion may introduce other sources of error into the poll. Variation in the wording and order of questions, for example, may lead to somewhat different results. ("How the Poll Was Conducted," 2009)

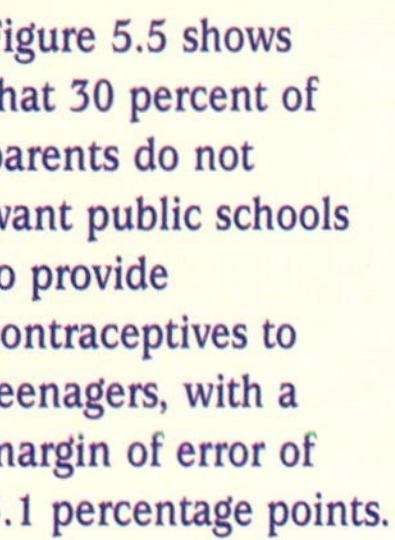

QUESTION

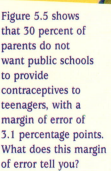

Figure 5.5 shows that 30 percent of parents do not want public schools to provide contraceptives to teenagers, with a margin of error of 3.1 percentage points. What does this margin of error tell you?

This statement highlights a form of *measurement error,* such as variations in question wording and question order that influence the results of a survey. But of additional concern with telephone surveys these days is *coverage bias,* as more young people and others switch to cell phones, and *nonresponse bias* due to the declining response rates to telephone surveys, as we saw earlier. Other kinds of error come from mistakes in processing and handling data, or from statistical programming or analytical errors. The *margin of error* does not tell us anything about how far off the mark we might be due to any of these other important sources of error, which we often must gauge only by subjective judgment.

Sample Size and the Precision of Government Statistics

Confidence intervals and margins of error express sampling precision. And as we saw, the larger the sample, the more precise the sample estimate (narrower CIs, smaller margins of error). In our labor survey of unemployment, the 95% CI based on a sample of $n = 400$ was 3.3% to 7.7%—but this is much too wide a guess for purposes of setting economic policy. A 3.3% unemployment rate would suggest that the economy is overheated and prone to inflation, while a 7.7% unemployment rate is much higher and a sign of economic weakness.

A much bigger sample, say $n = 10{,}000$, would help us increase our precision. Using the same formula as before (from Chapter 9), this much bigger sample would give us a 95% CI estimate of 5.1% to 5.9% unemployment, a better guessing range to work with for setting economic policy, although still wider than one would like. In fact, the CPS, used by the U.S. Bureau of Labor Statistics to track unemployment, employs a monthly sample of about 60,000 households.

The relationship between sample size and sampling precision explains why most government statistics are quite precise for the nation as a whole but much less precise and useful at the state (province) or especially local level. Thus, most cities in the United States don't know their monthly unemployment rate, even while the federal government releases regular, precise data on national unemployment. The same is true for many large federal surveys about health, education, crime, housing, and other policy issues.

Determining How Large a Sample You Need

If you are going to conduct a simple random sample survey, how large does your sample size need to be? We addressed this question briefly at the start of the chapter, but we are now in a better position to say more.

- First, as mentioned before, it is important to decide how much precision—how much sampling error, or alternatively how large a confidence interval (margin of error)—you need or can afford. The more precision you seek, the bigger your sample size must be. Here is a simple formula that tells you the sample size needed for a given margin of error:

$$\textit{Sample size} = \left(\frac{1}{\textit{Margin of error}}\right)^2$$

  To see how the formula works, say we decide to aim for a ±3.0 percentage point margin of error for our study, similar to the precision in the poll in the MSNBC news report. We simply plug in .03 in the formula (remember to use the decimal fraction .03—not "3.0") and get 33.33 in the parentheses, which squared becomes 1,111—a bit larger than the sample size used in the poll (1,004). This formula provides a conservative estimate of the sample size, in the sense that it gives the sample size required when the variability in the population is greatest (a 50/50 split). For very small (or very large) percentages (hence less variability), such as the unemployment rate example of 5.5%, we would not need so large a sample. However, you never know what results you're actually going to get—and you will likely calculate many things from the same survey. So using a conservative formula is not a bad idea. We should also point out that this formula only applies to percentages (or proportions) and not to means, correlations, regression slopes, or other types of statistics that you might calculate from your sample.
- Second, the sample size depends a lot on how much you plan to cut up your sample into subgroups for separate analysis. For example, do you want to compare results across race/ethnic groups? If so, the subgroup results, such as the results for Hispanics, will only be as precise as the sample size of individuals in that subgroup. Continuing with the previous formula and example, given that Hispanics make up about 17% of the U.S. population (U.S. Census Bureau, 2013b), we might guess that about 17% of our sample will be Hispanic as well. So we would need to divide our calculated sample size of 1,111 by .17 to get the total sample size needed—6,535—if we want the same level of precision, ±3.0 percentage points, for Hispanics as a subgroup (6,535 × .17 = 1,111 is another way to look at it). As you can see, cutting up the sample for subgroup analysis can have a huge effect on the required sample size. Of course, in practice researchers often must settle for less precision in their subgroup analysis.
- Third, the precision you get for a given sample size (n) does not depend on the size of the population (N). This is good news when you are interested in a large population (such as the more than 200 million adults in the United States), but bad news when your population of interest is small (say the 20,000 adult residents of Smalltown, USA). For a given level of precision, you would need the same sample size (n) to study Smalltown as you would the entire United States. Recall that the formula for the standard error, and in turn confidence intervals, only refers to the size of the sample (in the denominator) and makes no reference to the size of the population. It is the sample size alone that matters, not the share of the population included in the sample. So when it comes to choosing a population to study, you might as well think big.
- Fourth, after all these considerations, you must still guess at the response rate and adjust the initial size of your sample accordingly. If you expect only half of the people to respond, you will need to select twice as many in your initial sample to end up with the desired final number. The formulas for standard errors and confidence intervals are all based on the data you manage to collect, not the sample you start out hoping to reach.
- Fifth, when the sampling frame is easily available and contacting participants is cheap and easy, it is often best to just do a census and not sample at all. That is often the case for organizational studies, especially when using web surveys, since so many organizations have e-mail lists of members or affiliates to serve as sampling frames and the cost of web surveys is so low.

Finally, it is worth mentioning that time and resource limitations, of course, also play a critical role in determining the size of your sample. Sometimes you are only able to collect so much data—and then simply live with the level of precision it gives you. But it is important to make such trade-offs knowingly.

What Is the True Sample Size?

The *sample (n)* in statistical formulas refers to the people or elements selected randomly from a given population—and it implies that you have data on each and every one of those selected. For clarity, we will refer to this as the *true sample*. The logic of confidence intervals (margins of error) is based on the assumption that you have a true or complete random sample, without any observations missing.

But in practice, as we discussed earlier, randomly selecting people does not ensure that they will end up in your study. You may not be able to contact them, and even if you do, you can't force them to participate. This is the *response rate* problem in surveys that we discussed earlier. Yet researchers typically will call the data they have for analysis the "sample"—when they are only part of the initial, randomly selected, true sample. We prefer to call these data in hand the *observed sample*.

Is the Observed Sample a (True) Random Sample?

Let's look at an example of how the word *sample* is used in published research and how it obscures the difference between the true sample and the more limited data in hand, the observed sample. The following abstract comes from an article in *Health Services Research* titled "Understanding Employee Awareness of Health Care Quality Information: How Can Employers Benefit?" (Abraham, Feldman, & Carlin, 2004):

> *Objective.* To analyze the factors associated with employee awareness of employer disseminated quality information on [health care] providers.
>
> *Data Sources.* Primary data were collected in 2002 on a stratified, *random sample of 1,365 employees* [italics added] in 16 firms that are members of the Buyers Health Care Action Group (BHCAG) located in the Minneapolis–St. Paul region . . .
>
> *Data Collection.* Employee data were collected by phone survey . . .
>
> *Principal Findings.* Overall, the level of quality information awareness is low. However, employer communication strategies such as distributing booklets to all employees or making them available on request have a large effect on the probability of quality information awareness.

This is a useful study in a peer-reviewed journal and quite typical of how studies involving random sampling appear in print. But digging into the footnotes of the article, we find that the 1,365 employees who were interviewed represent just 60% of the true sample of 2,275 employees selected initially at random. In fact, the authors do not even mention the size of the true sample, although it can be inferred from the response rate. This is a fairly good response rate, by the way, so the authors aren't trying to hide anything. Rather, the lack of mention of the size of the true sample illustrates the tendency in published research to blur the distinction between the available observations and the true sample.

This semantic distinction matters because the response rate—the ratio of the observed sample size to the true sample size—can be surprisingly low in some kinds of research. For example, the City of Austin, Texas (Valverde & Tajalli, 2006), conducted a citizen survey by mailing questionnaires (in both English and Spanish) to 12,000 randomly selected households (the true sample), but only 1,601 households ended up returning their completed questionnaires—a response rate of only 13%. In low-cost telephone surveys, firms may dial dozens and dozens of numbers on average to complete one live interview, with response rates in the low single digits (even accounting for all the nonworking or ineligible numbers). Still, confidence intervals (margins of error) will be calculated and reported as usual. But be aware that this does nothing really to solve the problem of nonresponse bias.

Sampling in Practice

Simple random sampling provides the foundation for the basic ideas and formulas of statistical inference, but in practice, other methods of sampling must be used for logistical or substantive reasons. These methods include systematic sampling, stratified sampling, disproportionate sampling, sampling with probabilities proportional to size, multistage (cluster) sampling, and RDD sampling. But they are all variations of *random* sampling that still permit statistical inference—with certain technical modifications to the basic formulas for standard errors. We now describe each of these methods (see also Lohr, 2009).

Systematic Sampling

With simple random sampling, we typically start with some kind of list (sampling frame) and use a random number generator (like those available in an ordinary spreadsheet program) to select people or units to include in the sample. But sometimes the population of interest is fluid or mobile, and we cannot easily enumerate every individual and assign him or her a random number. Examples include commuters entering train stations, patients passing through a clinic's waiting room, museumgoers, or parents attending school meetings. In such situations, researchers often employ **systematic sampling**, which involves using intervals—say, every 20th person—beginning at a random start point.

Exit polling is one of the most common and important examples of systematic sampling. The people coming in and out of polling stations during Election Day are a fluid population to sample, yet we are keenly interested in understanding how they voted and why. To sample voters, interviewers wait outside polling stations to talk with a sample of voters. To ensure the sample is random, the interviewers use an interval—an *N*th, it is sometimes called—to select people as they are walking out. The *N*th is calculated in advance based on past turnout and a desire to end up with, say, 100 interviews by the time the polls close. If in recent elections, the turnout has averaged 4,000 at a given polling place, and assuming a response rate of 50% (being somewhat conservative), interviewers would need to approach 200 voters in order to successfully complete about 100 exit interviews. Thus, 4,000/200 is 20, so the sampling interval or *N*th would be every 20th voter. To decide whom to interview first, the field worker would pick a random number between 1 and 20, and then approach every 20th person after that. Systematic sampling is basically equivalent to simple random sampling, in terms of the calculation of standard errors, confidence intervals, and related statistics.

But real-world exit polling is more complicated than this. Exit pollsters must sample polling stations in the first place, as there are too many polling stations in most elections to send interviewers to all of them. This initial stage of sampling involves sophisticated procedures based on population and past voting patterns. As a result, the final exit poll is much more complex than a simple random sample. Sampling in practice is often like this: It can involve several stages of sampling and a mix of techniques, like systematic sampling, with other sampling approaches.

Stratified Sampling

Sometimes in sampling situations, it helps first to divide the population into groups—called **strata**. For example, the population of the United States can be divided into strata using the four major census regions (Northeast, South, Midwest, West). Then to do **stratified sampling**, a random sample is drawn separately from each group—each stratum. The strata must exhaust the entire population—everyone belongs to one group, and no one is left out. The strata must also be mutually exclusive—so that no one is in more than one group. Every state, including Hawaii and Alaska (if they are defined as being part of the population of interest), must be assigned to one region. Individuals must have only one place of residence. Someone who lives half the year in New York and half the year in Florida has to be assigned to just one of those places.

One motivation for stratified sampling is to ensure even coverage across the groups, for example, even coverage across geographic regions. Stratified sampling is often done in proportion to the size of strata. For example, most public opinion polls done of large national populations will treat the regions of the country as strata and draw proportionate random samples separately from each region (larger samples from large regions, smaller samples from small regions). Some of these national polls involve as few as 400 to 800 interviews, and thus stratified sampling helps ensure that the interviews will be evenly distributed across regions of the country.

Generally speaking, stratified sampling has advantages when there are known subgroups or clusters in the population that share characteristics of relevance to the study. The more similarity among people or elements within the strata, and the more differences between strata, the greater the need to stratify the sample. The key advantage, statistically, is that stratified sampling will produce results with more precision (less sampling variability) than the results from simple random sampling. Consider sampling doctors to learn the average number of procedures done each week. Surgeons are likely to perform many more procedures than other doctors. By stratifying the doctors into surgeons and nonsurgeons, and making the proportion of each the same as in the population, we avoid large variability due to the variation in the share of surgeons.

QUESTION

What is the distinction between systematic sampling and stratified sampling? Can you think of a way in which they could be used together?

Stratified sampling and quota sampling start out with the same approach: dividing the population into exhaustive and mutually exclusive groups. But they differ because stratified sampling uses probability sampling within the groups while quota sampling does not. But like quota sampling, stratified sampling depends critically on having accurate population counts within the groups.

Disproportionate Sampling (Oversampling)

Stratified sampling can also be used to oversample selected strata, called **oversampling** or **disproportionate sampling**. The motivation for oversampling is to be able to examine the subgroups separately and to ensure precise results for a small but oversampled subgroup. For example, Native Americans make up a small portion of the U.S. population. To get precise results for Native Americans, a survey might decide to oversample this group. Such sampling is said to be *disproportionate* because the probabilities of selection differ across strata.

In a study that examined the psychological repercussions of the terrorist attack on commuter trains in Madrid in 2004, for example, the investigators (Miguel-Tobal, Cano Vindel, Iruarrízaga, González Ordi, & Galea, 2005) took a random sample of the city's population but oversampled the neighborhoods surrounding the three train stations where the explosions occurred. A proportionate sample of Madrid's population would have resulted in too few interviews for a separate analysis of these three directly affected neighborhoods.

Sometimes when oversampling, the strata cannot be determined in advance, as they can be with geographic areas. For example, in telephone surveys, it is not possible to know in advance the race/ethnicity of the respondent, yet the study may seek to oversample, say, Black respondents (only 13% of the U.S. population), as was the case in a study of attitudes toward the death penalty (Peffley & Hurwitz, 2007). To oversample Blacks, the survey researchers must contact households, select a respondent, and identify his or her race/ethnicity, and then *screen* to get a sufficient sample of the targeted stratum. To get an equal number of Blacks and Whites, for example, every Black respondent will be interviewed, while only about 1 out of 5 randomly chosen Whites will complete a full interview on the phone (the rest will be thanked and the call ended).

Weighting the Sample

When analyzing data from a disproportionate sample, the strata can be analyzed separately with normal techniques. But to analyze the sample as a whole, that is, with all strata combined, the data must be *weighted*, or else the results will be misleading. **Weighting** (or weighting the sample) means that some of the individuals in the data count more in the analysis, while others count less, often due to disproportionate sampling or to ensure that the data from a sample better represent the population.

For example, a Eurobarometer survey investigated citizen awareness and use of 1-1-2, the European emergency telephone number, based on random samples of $n = 1{,}500$ people in each of the 27 EU countries (European Commission, 2007). This large sample allows for precise analysis of each country individually. But to combine the countries and draw conclusions about the EU as a whole, such as the reported finding that 66% of EU citizens believe that there is not enough information about 1-1-2, the sample must be weighted. This is because some EU countries, such as Germany, with more than 80 million people, are very large, while others, such as Luxembourg, with fewer than half a million people, are quite small. Thus, the Luxembourg sample needs to be given a weight of about 1/160 if the German sample gets a weight of 1. Or in other words, the 1,500 people interviewed in Luxembourg end up contributing, after weighting, fewer than 10 observations to the overall EU average.

QUESTION

What are the advantages and drawbacks of using disproportionate sampling (or oversampling)?

Loss of Precision in Oversampling

Because the 1,500 people in Luxembourg only count toward the European average 1/160th as much as the people in the German sample, the **effective sample size** for the sample as a whole (Europe) is smaller than the total number of observations from all of the European countries. With disproportionate sampling, the effective sample size is always less—and sometimes much less—than it would be had the people or elements been selected using simple random sampling. Thus, disproportionate sampling involves a trade-off: You gain more precision (smaller standard errors) for the individual strata, especially the smaller ones, but at the expense of a loss of precision (larger standard errors) for the sample as a whole, as well as more complexity in analyzing the data.

Poststratification Weighting

Some studies employ a technique called **poststratification adjustment** or **poststratification weighting**, which is different from but related to stratified sampling. Poststratification weighting involves comparing selected characteristics of the sample, for example, the regional or race/ethnic distribution, with the known distribution of the population. If the sample overrepresents one region or race/ethnic group, an adjustment (a weight < 1) is made to bring down this stratum to its proper proportion. If the sample underrepresents a region or group, then a weight > 1 is assigned to bring up its representation.

For example, in many general population surveys, women participate more readily than men, so you may end up with a *sample* percentage female $p = .60$ when the *population* percentage female $P = .50$. A poststratification weight W for females could then be constructed:

$$W = P/p = .50/.60 = .833.$$

The corresponding poststratification weight for males would be $.50/.40 = 1.25$, and thus multiplying the number of females by .833 and the number of males by 1.25 would equalize each group in the sample.

Poststratification weighting tries to accomplish the same thing, after the fact (or *post facto*), that stratified sampling does at the outset of the study. And in practice, both methods can be used together: A stratified sample can be selected at the start, and if varying response rates or other data collection issues result in disproportionate results, poststratification adjustments can be made to bring them into balance.

Sampling With Probabilities Proportional to Size

When sampling, researchers at times need to take into account not just the number of elements but their size and relative importance in the population. For example, the Census Bureau's Annual Survey of Manufactures, a major source of data on the U.S. economy, must consider in its sampling plan the fact that large manufacturers have a much greater impact on the economy than small ones. There are about 350,000 manufacturing establishments in the United States, and the Annual Survey of Manufactures samples 50,000 of them. About 9,700 of the largest manufacturers are included with certainty, while the remaining sample of medium and smaller manufacturers is created with **probability proportional to size (PPS) sampling**, in which the probability of being sampled is proportional to the size of the establishment (U.S. Census Bureau, 2009a).

Sampling with probabilities proportional to size is often used as part of a multistage sampling design, in which the first stage of sampling is done with PPS, based on the size of the geographic regions or other clusters that make up the first-stage sampling frame. The next section describes this more complex form of random sampling.

Multistage and Cluster Sampling

We have already seen how sampling in practice often involves several stages of selection. For example, in the United States there is no comprehensive national list of households to sample from, so random sampling from a single sampling frame is not possible. To select households, researchers must sample geographic areas in stages. In addition, travel costs make it prohibitively expensive to do in-person interviews of a random sample of a geographically dispersed population. As a result, researchers will seek to cluster or concentrate their interviews or observations.

Multistage sampling was developed for some of the first major government and social surveys, conducted in person by interviewers who went door to door, and is still in use today. Some surveys that use this method of sampling include the Current Population Survey, the General Social Survey, the American National Election Studies, the National Crime Victimization Survey, the American Housing Survey, the National Health Interview Survey, and the Eurobarometer. School-based surveys, such as the National Assessment of Educational Progress and the Youth Risk Behavior Surveillance System, use a form of multistage (cluster) sampling of schools.

In multistage sampling, geographic areas (typically counties in the United States) are sampled first, then census blocks (representing clusters of households) within counties, then individual housing units, and finally a randomly selected individual within the household. Figure 5.6 is from the Centers for Disease Control and Prevention (CDC; 2009b) and illustrates the multistage sampling used in the National Health and Nutrition Examination Survey, a unique survey because it includes physical examinations as well as in-person interviews.

Many of these studies also involve **cluster sampling** because the interviewer, rather than just talking with one person in the area before moving on, will typically visit several randomly selected households in the block group. This is a much better use of the interviewer's time and effort in the field. Similarly, with the school-based surveys, counties are selected, then schools, then classrooms, but at that point the survey worker visiting the school will administer questionnaires to a whole class (a cluster) rather than just one student. Again, this is a better use of the survey worker's time and effort in the school. Not all multistage samples necessarily involve clustering interviews or observations, but in practice the two approaches are often combined (and referred to as multistage cluster sampling).

Loss of Precision in Cluster Sampling

Multistage cluster samples are complex and, like disproportionate sampling, often involve some loss of sampling precision (larger standard errors) due to the clustering of observations. This is because individuals or

Figure 5.6 Multistage Sampling

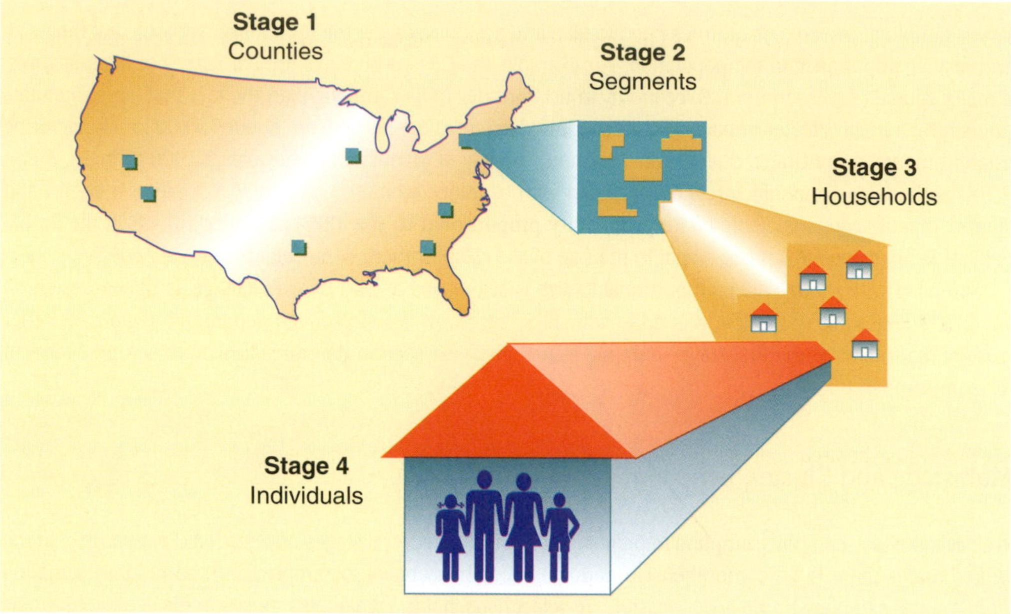

Stage 1
Counties
Stage 2
Segments
Stage 3
Households
Stage 4
Individuals

Source: Centers for Disease Control and Prevention (2009b).

Why does multistage sampling often involve clustering?

households that are clustered together may well be more alike than those sampled independently from across the total population. They share the same neighborhood, economic situation, political culture, and so on. Similarly, students in the same high school class share an educational environment and other characteristics that make them much more alike than a simple random sample of 30 students from the larger population of all high school students.

Statisticians measure this similarity within clusters using the *intraclass correlation*, which ranges from 0 (individuals in the cluster look just like a simple random sample of the population) to 1 (all individuals in the cluster look the same). The intraclass correlation is also referred to as *rho* for "rate of homogeneity." The larger the intraclass correlation, the larger the standard error.

Design Effects: Complex Survey Sampling Corrections

As we have discussed, **complex survey sampling**, such as cluster sampling and disproportionate sampling, increases standard errors relative to simple random sampling.

The **design effect** of the sample is one way sampling statisticians take into account the loss of precision due to complex survey sampling. The larger the design effect, the smaller the effective sample. For example, a design effect or *deff* = 2.0 would imply that the clustering and intraclass correlation are such that the multistage sample is only *half* as good as a simple random sample, in terms of its precision. The specific design effect depends on not only the sampling framework but also the specific variable to be corrected, since features such as intraclass correlation differ by variable. See the book by Groves, Fowler, Couper, and Lepkowski (2004) for more discussion of this issue and for more technical details.

Statistical software packages calculate standard errors using the assumption that the data are from a simple random sample, unless specific complex survey sampling commands are used. When analyzing data from complex surveys, correct your standard errors to avoid inferring more precision than is actually the case. This can be done approximately through the use of design effects provided with some complex surveys. Alternatively, it can be done more exactly with complex survey sampling commands in those statistical software packages (such as Stata or SAS) that have such commands (discussed further in Chapter 9). Such corrections are important for the large public-use government surveys described in the next chapter, since they generally use complex sampling. Only when design effects are small can such corrections be ignored.

Random Digit Dialing Sampling

In the late 1960s, as the telephone became standard equipment in most households, statisticians developed a method of sampling that gives both listed and unlisted telephone numbers an equal chance of being selected. Named *random digit dialing,* this sampling innovation ushered in a boom in telephone polls and surveys that only recently has begun to reach its limits as households increasingly screen calls, use cell phones only, and rely more on the Internet for communication.

RDD sampling in the United States works essentially by taking area codes and exchanges (the first three numbers after the area code) of known residential numbers and then generating random numbers to make up the last four digits of the phone number. These randomly created phone numbers are then dialed. Some will turn out to be nonworking numbers, fax lines, businesses, and so on. But others will turn out to be residential numbers, including both listed and unlisted numbers, and each such number will have an equal chance of being in the sample (because the numbers were generated randomly). Specialized RDD sampling firms keep up-to-date records of all working area codes and exchanges and generate high-quality RDD samples for use by survey researchers.

One of the issues to be alert to in RDD sampling is how much effort the survey organization makes in calling the RDD sample or, alternatively, how many RDD numbers it uses up to complete a study. Rigorous, reputable telephone surveyors call the RDD sample in small batches (called replicates), working each batch thoroughly by calling each number 7 to 10 times or more, on different days of the week and at different times of day, and scheduling callbacks for people who request it. Low-cost or less reputable firms call as many RDD numbers as fast as possible, looking for anyone who happens to be home and is willing to be interviewed, with little effort made to redial numbers or reschedule calls. Such practices exacerbate nonresponse bias by lowering the contact rate.

So just knowing that a survey used "RDD sampling" does not tell you how good or bad the sample really was. You need to look carefully at how much effort was made to contact the sample.

Cell Phone RDD Sampling

The large and growing shares of many populations without a landline and with only a cell (mobile) phone, and the coverage bias of telephone surveys that only call landlines, have resulted in a trend toward supplementing telephone surveys with cell phone RDD sampling. Several factors complicate such surveys and their sampling (AAPOR, 2010; Kunz & Fuchs, 2012). First, calling both cell phones and landlines complicates sampling of households with both cell phones and landlines. Second, determining both the validity of cell phones and the location of respondents is more difficult and time-consuming. Third, in the United States, laws prevent automated dialing of cell phone lines, raising the cost of calling these numbers. But the growing share of households without landlines and the resulting coverage bias, especially for certain groups (like young people), means that cell phone RDD sampling is increasingly necessary to produce accurate results from telephone surveys.

Good RDD sampling involves multiple calls to each number over several days and at various times.

Source: © iStockphoto.com/monkeybusinessimages.

Sampling and Generalizability: A Summary

This chapter has introduced you to sampling—the process of selecting people (or elements) for inclusion in a study—and how it affects generalizability. We saw how random sampling enhances representativeness because it allows the use of statistical theory to project the results of a sample to a well-defined population, within a certain margin of error. But we also saw how small, nonprobability samples can be used in experiments and qualitative research to produce generalizable knowledge, particularly about causation and when supported by strong theory. Ultimately, determining generalizability is a matter of judgment in which many aspects of a study must be taken into consideration.

Still, sampling is a critical factor in the generalizability of any study. Because sampling is such an important and at times complex task, as we saw in parts of this chapter, there are specialized sampling statisticians who are experts in the design of sampling procedures and in statistical techniques for the weighting and analysis of data from complex samples. If you need to do complex sampling, or even if you need to do secondary analysis of data from a complex sample, you may need to consult a sampling statistician for advice.

But sampling happens routinely in many kinds of formal and informal research, and consulting an expert is often not necessary. Recruiting people for a focus group, gathering feedback surveys from customers, auditing expenses, and using available data all involve sampling of a kind. Sampling all the members of an organization using an e-mail list has become quite easy. We hope that this chapter has given you ideas on how to sample—if and when the need arises.

Critically, we hope that this chapter has given you the tools to explore nonresponse bias and coverage bias—and their consequences for generalizability—in both quantitative and qualitative studies. Always ask yourself who is missing from the study, whether they are systematically different, and whether those differences could bias the results.

The ideas learned in this chapter, therefore, matter a great deal not only when doing your own research but when using the research of others. For example, knowing how sampling was done, and understanding its complexities and limitations, becomes an important part of using secondary data—the topic of Chapter 6.

BOX 5.5
Critical Questions to Ask About Sampling in Studies

- Can the study's findings be generalized and, if so, to what populations or contexts? What factors make the study more or less generalizable?
- Is the study based on a sample or a census? If a sample, is it a probability (random) sample or a nonprobability sample?
- If it is a nonprobability sample—such as a voluntary, convenience, or purposive sample—how might the type of sampling influence the obtained results?
- What kind of sampling frame was used? Does the sampling frame cover the population of interest? Is there possible coverage bias?
- Who is likely to respond, and who is not? How might nonresponse produce bias?

- How large is the sample? What is the level of statistical precision provided by the sample (confidence intervals or margins of error)?
- Did the study use simple random sampling or some form of more complex sampling? For example, did the sampling involve stratification, oversampling, multiple stages, or clustering? Why was the sampling done this way?
- Was the design effect, or the effective sample size, reported? How much precision was lost due to complex sampling?
- Were sampling or poststratification weights used? If not, should they have been used? Did the reported standard errors and related confidence intervals take account of weighting?

BOX 5.6
Tips on Doing Your Own Research: Sampling

- Define your population of interest—be precise and learn some basic facts about the population (particularly how large it is).
- Identify a sampling frame you can use, such as a list, map, or procedure that enumerates the population.
- Decide if the population is suitable for doing a census—or whether you need to sample from the population. Consider population size and ease and expense of contacting respondents.
- If you need to sample, determine what kind of sampling—probability or nonprobability. Probability (random) sampling is usually preferable because it allows for statistical inference, but sometimes circumstances permit only voluntary or convenience sampling.
- If you do probability sampling, decide what kind—systematic, stratified, multistage, clustered, disproportionate, proportional to size, or some combination. This is mostly a practical decision based on the characteristics of your population, the sampling frame, the logistics of drawing a random sample, and subgroup analyses needed.
- If you decide to do disproportionate or cluster sampling, be aware that you may need to use weights or complex survey sampling adjustments in your analysis. If you are not comfortable with this, consider a simpler sampling strategy.
- Estimate how large a sample you will need, using the basic formulas and guidelines in this chapter (see also Chapter 9). Be aware of how the need for subgroup analysis may require a larger sample.
- Anticipate strategies to reduce coverage and nonresponse bias. For example, use a good sampling frame, various modes of contact, and systematic follow-up procedures. See the tips at the end of Chapter 7 on survey research. Predict, to the extent possible, the direction and magnitude of remaining coverage and nonresponse bias.

Chapter Resources

Key Terms

- Census
- Cluster sampling
- Complex survey sampling
- Confidence interval (margin of error)
- Contact rate
- Convenience sample
- Cooperation rate
- Coverage bias
- Design effect
- Disproportionate sampling (oversampling)
- Effective sample size
- External validity
- Generalizability
- Inference
- Internet access panel
- Meta-analysis
- Multistage sampling
- Nonresponse bias
- Parameter
- Population
- Poststratification weighting (poststratification adjustment)
- Precision
- Probability proportional to size (PPS) sampling
- Probability sampling (random sampling)
- Propensity to respond
- Purposive sampling
- Random digit dialing (RDD)
- Replication
- Response rate
- Sample
- Sampling
- Sampling bias
- Sampling error
- Sampling frame
- Sampling variability
- Simple random sampling
- Snowball sampling (respondent-driven sampling)
- Standard error
- Stratified sampling (strata)
- Systematic sampling
- Voluntary sample
- Volunteer bias
- Weighting

Exercises

A Charter School's Success Story

5.1. A charter high school surveyed its alumni, from a list it maintains for fund-raising purposes, to find out how well they were doing in the job market. Nearly 50% responded, and the average (mean) salary calculated from the survey was $79,000. Do you think that this estimate is biased? How would the propensity to be covered by the list and the propensity to respond to the survey likely bias the estimate?

Communicating With Parents

5.2. Say you are a principal of a school and want to learn how well parents feel the school communicates with them. You send home a survey with students and then have each teacher follow up with a phone call to parents about how important the survey is. What kinds of nonresponse problems will you have? What bias do you think would result in your measure of school communication? Explain using a path diagram showing the propensity to respond.

Patient Satisfaction

5.3. A clinic wants to survey the satisfaction of its patients. It has few male patients and is particularly interested in determining the satisfaction of male patients and comparing it with that of female patients. What kind of sampling should the clinic use? Explain why and how it should use the data.

Parenting Styles

5.4. A city welfare services department wants to get a good description of parenting styles among parents. It feels that this will help it in assessing "problem" parents and foster parents. For a sampling frame, it gets a list of the parents or guardians of all public school students and their telephone numbers. It plans to sample randomly from that list and conduct a telephone survey.

a. To what population would this survey generalize if there were a 100% response rate? How does that compare with the population desired? Describe any coverage bias and why it occurs.
b. What real-world factors will interfere with the generalization to even the study population? Create a path diagram for the propensity to respond that you can use to predict the type and extent of nonresponse bias.

Are We Afraid of the Internet?

5.5. Internet commerce has become vital to the modern economy, yet it remains vulnerable to fear of Internet fraud and identity theft. But how afraid are we, really? A telephone survey of an RDD sample of 1,000 U.S. adults found that fully 38% did not trust online payments, banks, and other e-commerce providers. Based on what you have read in this chapter about coverage and nonresponse in telephone surveys, how might this estimate be biased?

Eating More Fruits and Vegetables

By Herman, Dena R., Gail G. Harrison, Abdelmonem A. Afifi, & Eloise Jenks. (2008, January). Effect of a targeted subsidy on intake of fruits and vegetables among low-income women in the Special Supplemental Nutrition Program for Women, Infants, and Children. *American Journal of Public Health, 98*(1), 98–105.

Objectives. Intake of fruits and vegetables protects against several common chronic diseases, and low income is associated with lower intake. We tested the effectiveness of a subsidy for fruits and vegetables to the Special Supplemental Nutrition Program for Women, Infants, and Children (WIC).

Methods. Women who enrolled for postpartum services ($n = 602$) at 3 WIC sites in Los Angeles were assigned to an intervention (farmers' market or supermarket, both with redeemable food vouchers) or control condition (a minimal nonfood incentive). Interventions were carried out for 6 months, and participants' diets were followed for an additional 6 months.

Results. Intervention participants increased their consumption of fruits and vegetables and sustained the increase 6 months after the intervention was terminated (model adjusted $R^2 = .13$, $p < .001$). Farmers' market participants showed an increase of 1.4 servings per 4186 kJ (1000 kcal) of consumed food ($p < .001$) from baseline to the end of intervention compared with controls, and supermarket participants showed an increase of 0.8 servings per 4186 kJ ($p = .02$).

Conclusions. Participants valued fresh fruits and vegetables, and adding them to the WIC food packages will result in increased fruit and vegetable consumption.

5.6. What kind of sampling do you think this study used—random (probability) sampling or nonprobability sampling—and why? How generalizable are the results?

Sampling as Used in Large Government Surveys

5.7. Identify a large government survey that is important in your field of interest or professional practice—such as NAEP, the NCVS, the CPS, the NHIS, and so on. Find the official website for the survey and read about the kind of sampling used in the survey. How large is the sample, and what type of random sampling is it (simple, systematic, multistage, etc.)? Assess the survey's coverage and response rate. Also see if the website gives information about survey weights and design effects.

Sampling as It Appears in a Published Journal Article

5.8. Find an original empirical study published in a journal in your field of interest or professional practice. Read the abstract of the article and also the section of the article that describes the sampling and data collection methods. What kind of sampling is it? Why was this type of sampling used? See if coverage and response rates are reported, and discuss the generalizability of the study's findings.

Iraqi Mortality (advanced question)

5.9. A study by Roberts, Lafta, Garfield, Khudhairi, and Burnham (2004) in the journal *Lancet* used cluster sampling techniques to estimate the death toll in Iraq after the U.S. invasion. The stunning estimate of some 100,000 excess deaths in Iraq, likely due to the U.S. invasion, made headlines and sparked controversy around the world. The study was replicated a few years later (Burnham, Lafta, Doocy, & Roberts, 2006), with similar results. Read the original study by Roberts et al. (2004) and answer the following questions:

a. Why did the researchers choose to use cluster sampling? Describe briefly how the sampling worked. Describe the effect that lack of security had on the research design.

b. Discuss the decision to exclude Fallujah. Try to use the Fallujah example to help explain intuitively why cluster sampling reduced the precision of the results.
c. What effect did using an out-of-date census have on the results? How might migration within Iraq bias the results? How might migration out of Iraq bias the results?
d. What are the pros and cons of a survey such as this compared with methods such as counting deaths at the morgues? Contrast the biases of the two methods.
e. Discuss how politics affects the decision to do (or not do) research such as this as well as decisions about how the research is conducted and how such research is interpreted.
f. What were some of the ethical concerns? How did the researchers address those?

Student Study Site

Visit the Study Site at **www.sagepub.com/remler2e** to

- test your knowledge with the self-quiz
- check your understanding of key terms with the eFlashcards
- explore helpful resources that relate directly to this chapter

Much data already exists and can be used for research.

Source: © iStockphoto.com/Tomaz Levstek.

Overview: In this chapter, you will begin learning about where quantitative data come from—with a focus on secondary or existing data available for social and policy research. You will understand the forms that secondary data can take, including micro and aggregate data, panel data, and time series. And you will become familiar with some of the main sources of secondary data, including administrative record data, published data tables, and public use microdata. With the Internet and the low cost of computing, coupled with the high cost and complexity of primary data collection, the use of secondary data has become increasingly important in many fields. And secondary data are important for practitioners who use reports based on secondary data as a basis for decisions and who can now, because of online data analysis tools, directly access the data on their own.

Objectives

Learning Objectives

After reading this chapter, you should be able to

- Identify quantitative data, including their form or structure
- Distinguish microdata from aggregate data
- Recognize the time dimension of the data (cross-sectional, longitudinal, panel, etc.)
- Identify some of the major sources of secondary quantitative data in your field (health, education, etc.)
- Find online data analysis tools that let you access and analyze major secondary data sources in your field
- Identify some major sources of secondary qualitative data
- Describe the potential and limitations of public use microdata—and determine when to consider collecting your own primary data

Secondary Data 6

Tracking the Flu

The 2012–2013 influenza season in the United States started substantially earlier and more severely than usual (Centers for Disease Control and Prevention [CDC], 2013c). Influenza (the flu) is responsible for tens of thousands of deaths in the country each year, with the elderly and young children most at risk. Certain strains of the flu (such as swine flu or bird flu) can be especially deadly. The CDC quickly found out about the early and severe flu, thanks to various sources of administrative data it tracks: hospital emergency room visits by patients with flu symptoms and purchases of over-the-counter cold and flu medications at pharmacies. The CDC even tracks Google query searches about flu and its symptoms, which are particularly valuable because they are real-time indicators (Ginsberg et al., 2009). The CDC also tracks the rate of flu vaccinations in the population through various existing surveys. In other words, the CDC has good *data* to guide its decisions—data that come from various sources and methods.

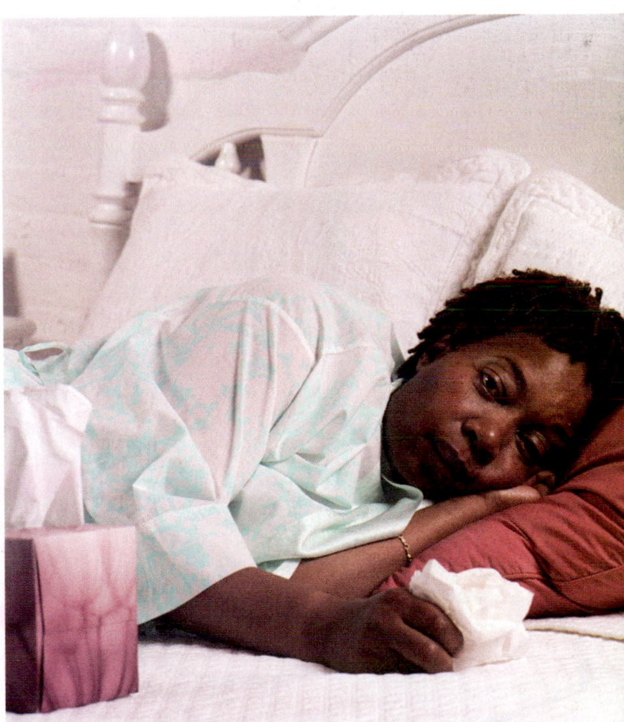

Public health officials use secondary data to monitor flu epidemics.

Source: © Thinkstock.com/ Tom Le Goff.

In this chapter, you will begin discovering sources of *quantitative* data—the most common form of data used in social and policy research. We will also learn more about existing sources of qualitative data—and how computing technology is making it easier to turn qualitative data into quantitative data. Data are the basic stuff of research—the raw material researchers work with to build an understanding of the world—so it is important to know what they are and where they come from. We begin here with *secondary data,* data that exist already because they were collected as part of a prior administrative or research activity. Low-cost computing and data storage, coupled with the Internet, have made secondary data much more widely available and useful for research. In the next chapter, we will address the topic of collecting your own *primary data* through surveys or other methods.

QUESTION

Think about your activities on computers, mobile devices, or the Internet over the last few days. How have you helped create new data online? Is it qualitative or quantitative data?

Big Data and the Virtual World

These days we live much of our lives in a virtual world. We shop, socialize, study, and collaborate with colleagues using computers and the Internet. And much of what we do in the nonvirtual world is recorded and stored electronically: from medical test results to search terms to YouTube videos of daily life.

Much of this data is qualitative: texts, images, audio, and video. Think of e-mail, blogs, tweets, YouTube videos, and the many webpages of individuals and organizations—not to mention all the pages of correspondence, testimony, and other reports and communications stored electronically by government and private organizations. Stores of numerical or quantitative data have grown explosively as well. In the public sector, there are records of taxes, spending, school attendance, fatal accidents, crimes, and economic indicators, as well regular government surveys of the population on various topics. In the private world, there are financial transactions, inventory, payroll records, commodity prices, and daily or hourly stock values for thousands of companies.

All of this accumulating data—and particularly its use for solving problems—is sometimes referred to as **Big Data** (Mayer-Schonberger & Cukier, 2013). The CDC's use of Google flu trends is an example of Big Data at work. New York City put Big Data to work to find restaurants that were illegally dumpling grease by mapping clogged sewers and matching them to restaurants without grease carters (Feuer, 2013). Learning about the sources and types of existing data is a first step toward engaging the world of Big Data.

Quantitative Data—and Their Forms

Data are facts or pieces of information, so by **quantitative data** we mean information that is recorded, coded, and stored in numerical form. (The word *data,* by the way, is plural, not singular; the word *data set,* however, is singular.) Often, this information comes from a formal process of *measurement,* as discussed in Chapter 4. Numbers provide a convenient and useful form in which to code and store data because they can be easily manipulated by computers—sorted, counted, summarized, and analyzed. The discipline of *statistics* provides a body of concepts and tools for doing this, as covered in Part III of this book.

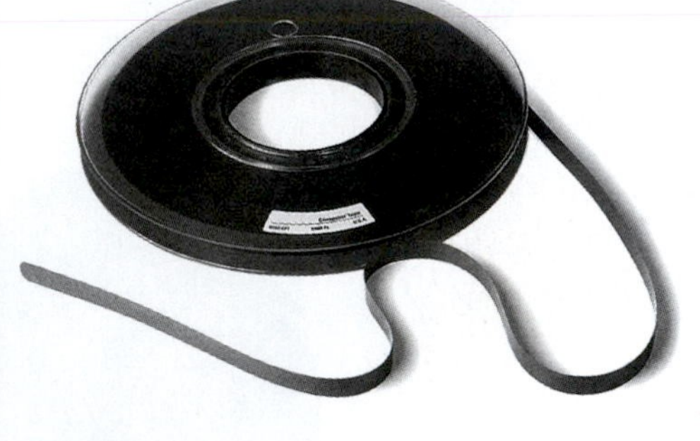

Data Management: Then and Now

Source: © iStockphoto.com/jsolie; © iStockphoto.com/Kuzma.

Quantitative Data Versus Quantitative Variables

The number of people in emergency rooms with flu symptoms, the number of Google searches with the key word *flu,* and the dollar amount of purchases of cold and flu medicine are examples of *quantitative variables.* Quantitative variables are also things such as age (in years) or income (in dollars)—any variables in which the numbers represent *quantities* of something (as we saw in Chapter 4). For example, 27 could be used to represent "27 years of age," or 31 might represent "31 thousand dollars of annual income." You can do arithmetic, such as division, on quantitative variables.

Quantitative variables, however, are not the only form of quantitative data. *Categorical variables* can also be recorded as numbers, but the numbers in this case represent *categories* (again, as we saw in Chapter 4). For example, we can record someone's gender as 1 = *male* or 2 = *female.* Or we can record someone's happiness as 1 = *very happy,* 2 = *somewhat happy,* or 3 = *not happy.* Or we can record the region of the country that someone lives in as 1 = *Northeast,* 2 = *Midwest,* 3 = *South,* or 4 = *West.* Importantly, categorical variables are also a type of quantitative data, because we can use them to sort, count, summarize, and analyze. Indeed, a large body of statistical methods and literature deals with how to analyze categorical variables (Agresti, 2007).

In addition to the data that start as quantitative (a number or a category), some qualitative data are often automatically or naturally coded into categories, turning them into quantitative data. Think of Twitter messages, which include a hashtag (#) indicating what the message is about. While the message itself is text and therefore qualitative data, by using hashtags the senders effectively code their qualitative data, allowing them to be easily counted. Indeed, Twitter tracks the number of tweets by hashtag and reports the quantitative trends over time.

Education data can be analyzed at various levels.
Source: © Thinkstock.com/ Jetta Productions.

Forms of Quantitative Data

Quantitative data come in various forms or structures. Those who produce data themselves, through surveys or experiments, tend to think of these forms or structures as *research designs*, since as researchers they *design* the form or structure of the data to suit the context and their research question. But those who use secondary data often think of these more as data *forms* or data *structures* and use the term *research design* instead to refer to what they do, analytically, with the data.

The various forms that quantitative data can take depend both on the level of aggregation (shown in Table 6.1, going across the columns) and on the time dimension (shown in Table 6.1, going down the rows). We will shortly describe both of these distinctions, and the various forms quantitative data can take, in further detail. Real-world examples of these forms of data will appear a bit later in the chapter.

Table 6.1 Forms of Data

	Level of Aggregation			
Time Dimension	**Microdata**	**Aggregated (or Ecological) Data**	**Single Measure (or Completely Aggregated) Data**	**Multilevel (or Hierarchical) Data**
Cross section	Cross-sectional microdata	Cross-sectional data on aggregate units (such as states)	A statistic on one unit (such as a country) at one point in time	Multilevel cross section
Before-after (paired samples)	Before-after microdata	Before-after data on aggregate units	Before-after comparison of one unit	Multilevel before-after data
Panel data (repeated measures or cohort studies)	Panel microdata	Panel aggregate data	Time series	Hierarchical panel data
Pooled cross sections	Pooled cross sections of microdata			Multilevel pooled cross sections

Micro, Aggregate, and Multilevel Data

The term **microdata** refers to data at their most basic level of observation—or **unit of observation**. For example, student test scores are naturally measured at the level of each individual student. A smaller unit of observation is not really possible. And if one wants to measure student test scores at the level of classrooms or schools, the scores must be aggregated (as discussed shortly). Thus, having a set of scores for individual students would constitute microdata.

BOX 6.1
Unit of Observation Versus Unit of Analysis

Unit of observation and *unit of analysis* are very close concepts. In many cases, they are one and the same, but not always. For example, when data on individual student test scores are aggregated to be analyzed at a school level, the unit of observation is the still the student—because the original microdata were collected from individual students on test day. However, if we are using aggregate test statistics on schools (such as the average test score) in a regression analysis, let's say, along with other school-level variables, the unit of analysis is the school. In other words, sometimes the unit of analysis is at a more aggregate level than the unit of observation.

But, as suggested, data are often aggregated up to a variety of higher levels, such as classrooms, schools, or districts (see Box 6.1). Data can be aggregated using a variety of statistical techniques, such as by calculating a mean score for a school, a median score, or the percentage of students in the school who pass a given threshold on the test. The term **aggregate data** refers to data that are summarized at some higher unit of analysis, whether geographic, administrative, or some other way of combining or summarizing the microdata. Aggregate data are also referred to in public health and some other fields as **ecological data**.

Data may be completely aggregated so that there is essentially only a *single* measure—such as the percentage of all students in a country meeting some national standard. Of course, we might find data that are comparable even cross-nationally, so that countries become the unit of analysis. But we may only be interested in studying trends in one country, or the data (such as scores on a national test) may be unique to that country. Alternatively, data can also be intrinsically only one number, such as the U.S. Treasury bill interest rate. There are no separate U.S. T-bill rates for different states or individuals. Figure 6.1 diagrams the distinction between microdata, aggregated data, and single-measure data.

QUESTION

Using the example of house prices, explain in your own words the differences between microdata and aggregate data.

Data may also combine different levels—so called **multilevel (or hierarchical) data**. For example, a set of data with scores for individual students could also include some school-level variables, such as whether the school is public or private. Even the average performance of the class or school, an aggregate measure, can become a contextual variable in a multilevel analysis. Looking at Figure 6.1, multilevel analysis can be thought of as drawing connections between variables across levels (such as from a classroom average to an individual test score). Multilevel data are increasingly used in many fields, including education, public health, and criminal justice (Luke, 2004).

Time Dimension of Data

The form of data also reflects the time dimension of data. Many data are **cross-sectional**—they contain measurements taken at a single point in time, such as the test scores of students in a particular year. Surveys are often cross-sectional, a snapshot of public opinion or behavior during one period of time. The Eurobarometer, for example, captures public opinion in the European Union (EU) countries based on a

Figure 6.1 Micro and Aggregate Data

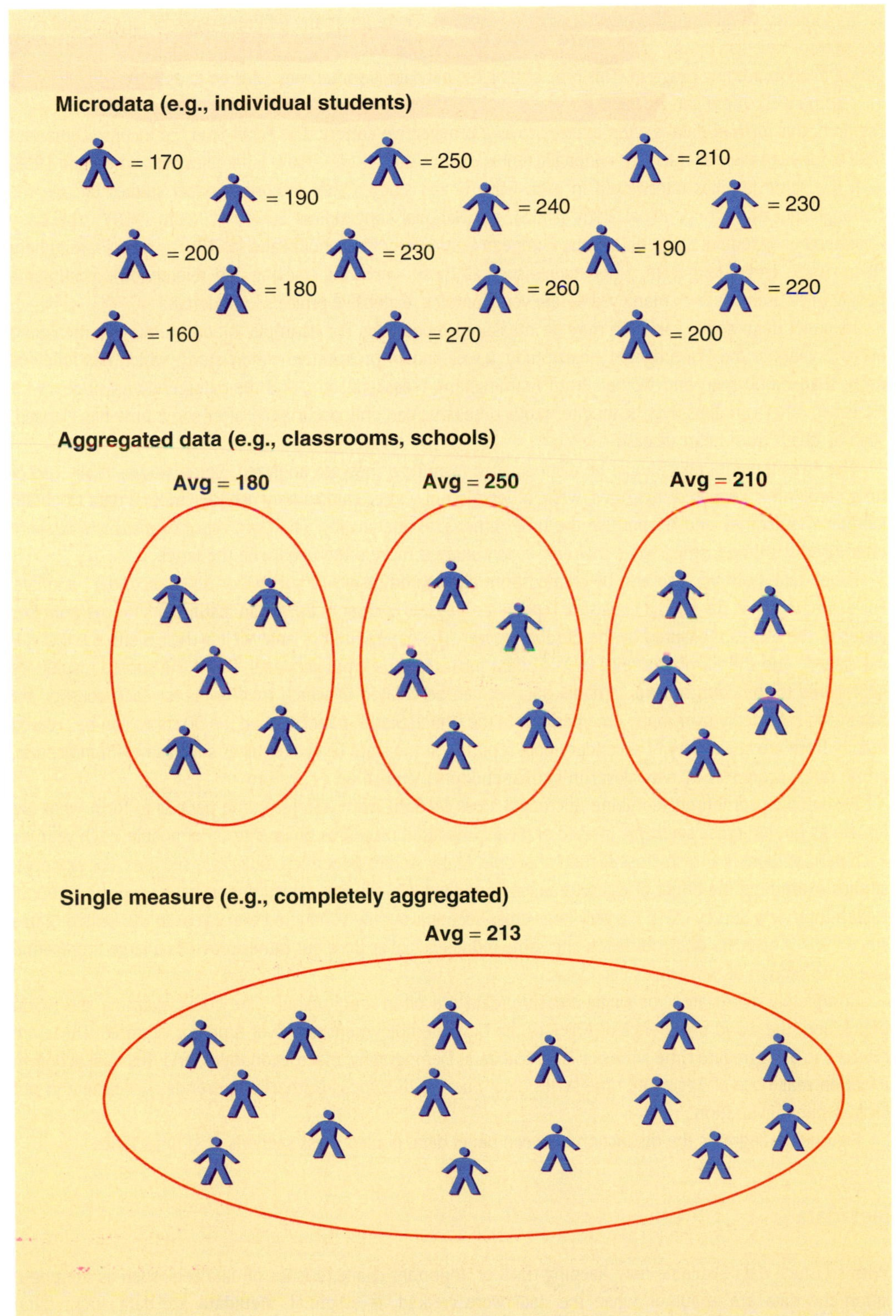

sample of about 30,000 people. Although the Standard Eurobarometer is conducted twice each year, the sample for each survey is still a new cross section of people living in the EU.

In contrast, **longitudinal data** are gathered over time. There are many different types of longitudinal data. For example, we can simply track and compare individuals at two points in time, say, before and after participating in a job training program. This type of longitudinal data is sometimes referred to as *paired-sample* data.

Alternatively, there can be *repeated measures* on the same individuals over time—or **panel data**. In health research, this form of data is often referred to as a **prospective cohort**. The Panel Study of Income Dynamics (PSID), for example, has tracked a nationally representative sample of 9,000 U.S. families over time since 1968, with the same families interviewed in each wave of the study. Other important panel studies include the National Education Longitudinal Study (NELS), the National Longitudinal Survey of Youth (NLSY), the Early Childhood Longitudinal Study (ECLS), the European Community Household Panel (ECHP), and the Framingham Heart Study. Large, long-term panel studies such as these—involving tracking and reinterviewing the same people or households over many years—are very complex, expensive projects to undertake.

In panel data, some variables may be measured repeatedly. For example, blood pressure is measured every 2 years in the Framingham Heart Study, a well-known prospective cohort study, which has followed more than 5,000 men and women from Framingham, Massachusetts, and their descendants since 1948. However, other variables may be long-term outcomes that can only occur once, after some time has elapsed, such as death from heart disease.

The form the data take should be distinguished from how they are analyzed. Some studies make use of time variation in repeated measures, while others do not. Other studies only use longitudinal data to obtain long-term outcomes and do not use the time dimension analytically. The term *repeated measures* is more often used with the former, while the term *cohort study* is more often used with the latter.

Panel data, however, can also be created from aggregated results of surveys or other secondary sources. For example, panel data could consist of repeated measures of trust in European institutions for the member states of the EU, as measured by the Eurobarometer. The natural unit of analysis for trust is still the individual citizen, and the Eurobarometer in microdata form remains cross-sectional. But if the survey results are aggregated to the country level, a panel data set can be created in which trust levels for each country are measured repeatedly over many time periods. In the United States, panel data on the 50 states can be created readily from a wide variety of secondary data reported at the state level over time, such as health indicators, crime rates, economic activity, government expenditures, and so on.

Researchers sometimes combine microdata cross sections from different time periods to form what are known as **pooled cross sections**. Instead of having repeated measures on one group of people, each year (or each period) there is a fresh cross section of people. Many studies pool microdata cross sections. For example, studies examining the effect of cigarette taxes on individuals' tobacco consumption have used the National Health Interview Survey (NHIS), a very large cross-sectional survey conducted every year in the United States since 1957. The NHIS does not follow the same individuals over time but rather provides a large representative cross section of individuals each year.

Completely aggregated, or single-measure, data are often longitudinal. One could examine the world population, the world prevalence of AIDS, or the U.S. unemployment rate over time, for example. These are referred to as aggregate **time series** or *historical* data. Demography, macroeconomics, and financial economics often make use of aggregate time-series data. Such studies focus primarily on trends over time and not cross-sectional variation.

Figure 6.2 diagrams the distinction between panel data, pooled cross sections, and time series.

QUESTION

Explain in your own words the differences between cross-sectional data, panel data, and pooled cross sections.

Metadata

With so much data available now, keeping track of important characteristics of data sets, such as the population the data are about or when the data were created, is essential. **Metadata** are data about data. Commonly collected forms of metadata include the date data were collected or obtained, the type of

Figure 6.2 Different Forms of Longitudinal Data

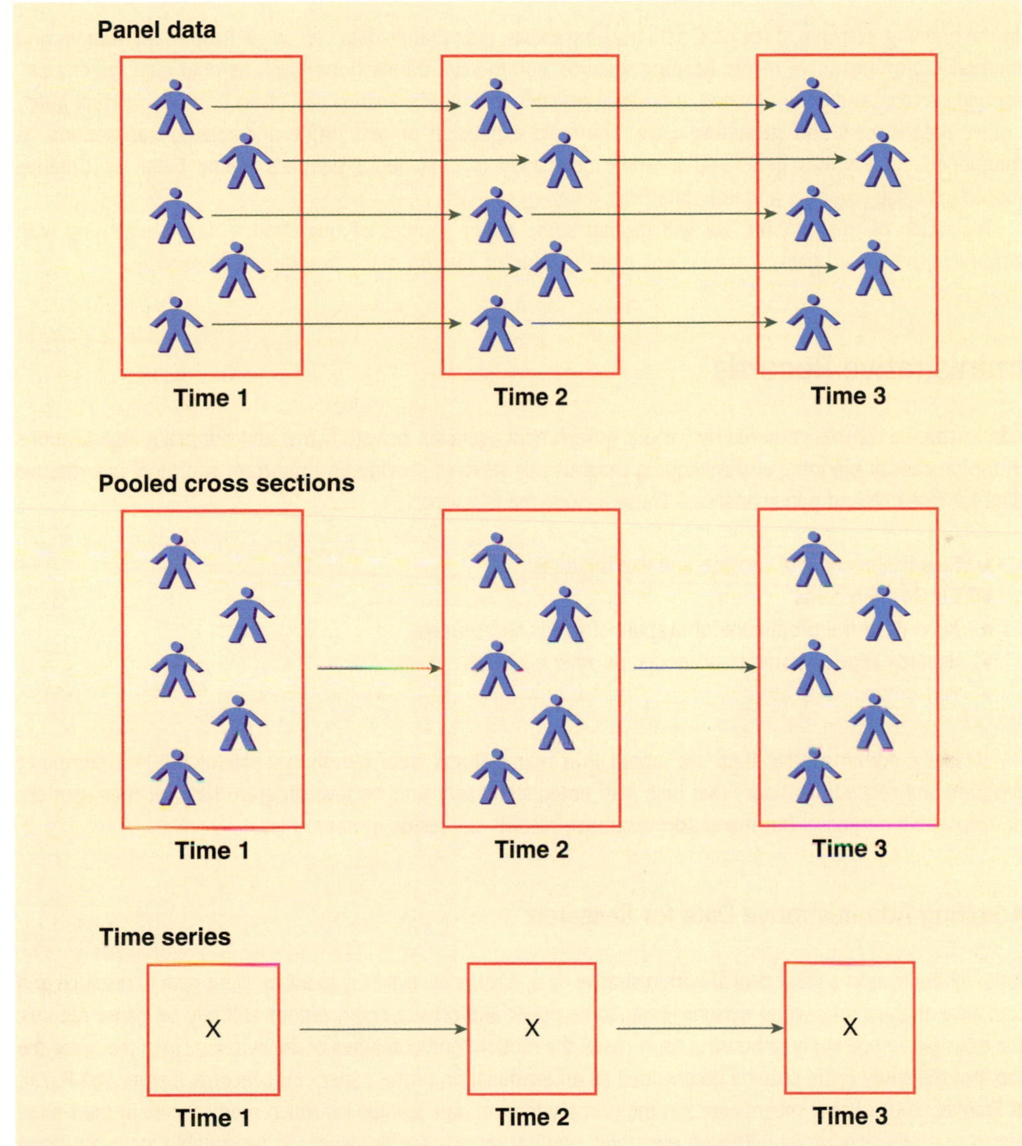

sampling used, the population the data describe, the purpose of the data, the institution or individual that collected the data, and the format of the data (Stata, SPSS, ASCI, comma delimited, etc.). Metadata are primarily used for organizing and searching archives of data, such as those of the Inter-university Consortium for Political and Social Research (ICPSR; see www.icpsr.umich.edu/icpsrweb/landing.jsp).

Qualitative data also have metadata, such as the date of the interview, the interviewer, the number of people attending a focus group, the location, and related images, text, audio, and video files. For books and other publications, metadata include information that was traditionally put in library card catalogs: author, type of publication, date of publication, and so on. Webpages on the Internet can contain set kinds of metadata, including basic text description, date of creation, and geocoded location. Metadata can itself become data for research. For example, one might track the number and dates of YouTube videos about a particular country to monitor attention to that country.

Where Do Quantitative Data Come From?

As the opening example of the CDC's flu tracking shows, quantitative data can come from many sources and methods—administrative record-keeping systems, commercial transactions (such as pharmacy purchases), sample surveys, and so on. Indeed, a creative researcher or policy analyst can often find or construct quantitative data in new and surprising ways. The rapid expansion of web traffic and related transactions, as mentioned already, has generated a whole new body of data about people's online behavior. Creative researchers also combine and link data from different sources.

For much of this chapter, we will discuss some major sources of quantitative data—beginning with administrative record data, a natural first place to look for data on many programs and services.

Administrative Records

Administrative records gathered by various government agencies, private firms, and nonprofit organizations in the process of planning and managing programs or services provide an important source of quantitative data for research and policy analysis. These include the following:

- Financial records of income and expenditures
- Employee records
- Records of the production of outputs of goods and services
- Records kept on patients, students, or other clients
- Performance indicators

Typically, administrative data are stored in a management information system (or MIS)—a computer program and related databases that help staff enter, store, sort, and retrieve program data for management or accounting purposes. But many administrative records still reside in paper files.

Adapting Administrative Data for Research

Although there exist a great deal of administrative data, it is not always easy to adapt these data to research and statistical analysis for several reasons. First, some public and private organizations still rely on paper records. For example, in one study of housing court cases, the motions and outcomes of the eviction cases that were the focus of the study could only be determined by an examination of the paper court records (Seron, Van Ryzin, & Frankel, 2001). Paper records are still the primary form of data storage for much medical care in the United States and other countries (although electronic medical records are growing). To be suitable for quantitative analysis, paper records must be retrieved, coded, and keypunched into a statistical database—a laborious task.

Do the Data Need Cleaning?

Another potential problem is that the fields, or variables, in the administrative data may need to be verified, corrected, coded, or reformatted. This process is referred to as **data cleaning**. Even if the data are stored in electronic form, some fields may be in *string* or *alphanumeric* format, and statistical software does not read or handle such nonnumeric data easily. String-formatted data often get entered inconsistently by administrative staff. For example, the type of illness may be entered as "flu," "FLU," "influenza," and so on. Spelling mistakes such as "influensa" cause further difficulties, although progress is being made with software that finds similar but not identical words. These fields may need to be cleaned and then coded into consistent numeric values, for example, "23" as a code for influenza.

Administrative data can also contain inaccurate, incomplete, or inconsistent cases. Detecting such cases and either fixing or deleting them is a time-consuming but important process, one that typically requires having or acquiring background knowledge about the populations and administrative procedures that generated the data. Examples of this kind of data cleaning that often must be done include checking that the data fall in a reasonable or possible range (for example, a date cannot be a future date); checking that the values for one variable do not make the values for other possible variables impossible; and eliminating duplicate entries. As more and more Big Data applications are found, the work of data cleaning is growing.

Does the Database Need Flattening?

Administrative records tend mostly to be organized as **relational databases**, database structures that are composed of various tables of information, such as one for suppliers and another for products, that are linked and work together—as illustrated in Figure 6.3 for a typical business organization.

Statistical software, in contrast, generally requires a **flat file**—a simple two-dimensional layout of rows and columns. In the flat-file format used for cross-sectional statistical data, the rows represent individuals—the *unit of analysis*—and the columns represent *variables.* Figure 6.4 shows a simple example, with individual respondents (the unit of analysis) represented in each row and the variables represented in the columns. Often, the trick for using administrative data in research and analysis lies in converting the data into this flat-file form.

Some more sophisticated forms of data analysis, such as panel data and multilevel data, combine various units of analysis. Relational databases often have all the information necessary for such analyses, but again, this information may not be in the form required by the software.

Cleaning and reformatting administrative data for research is time-consuming and labor-intensive, generally far more time-consuming than the actual statistical analysis itself.

Figure 6.3 A Relational Database for Administrative Data

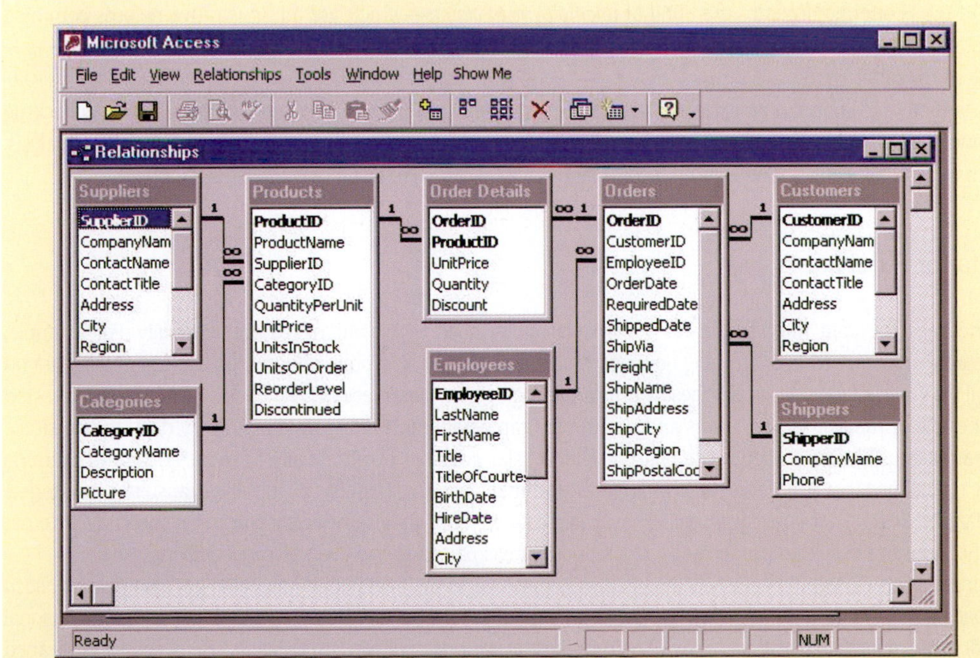

Figure 6.4 Flat-File Database for Statistical Analysis

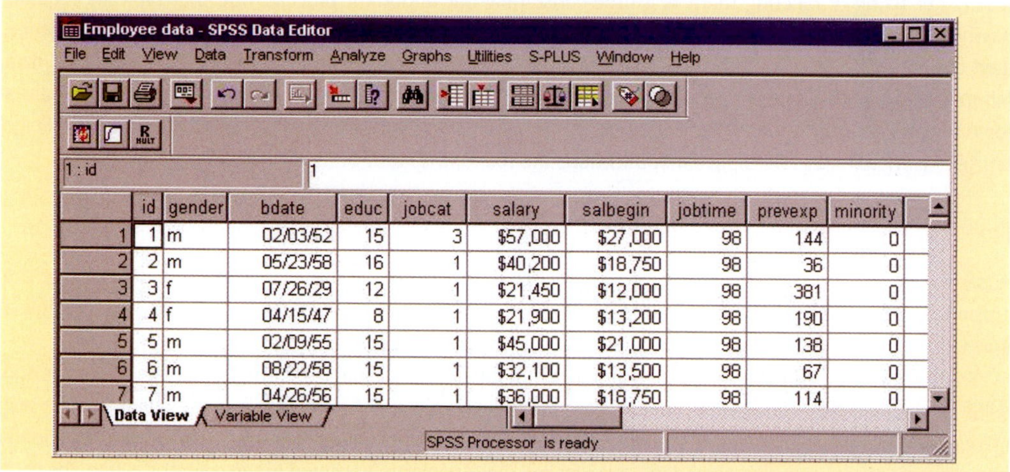

Employee data - SPSS Data Editor

File Edit View Data Transform Analyze Graphs Utilities S-PLUS Window Help

1 : id 1

	id	gender	bdate	educ	jobcat	salary	salbegin	jobtime	prevexp	minority
1	1	m	02/03/52	15	3	$57,000	$27,000	98	144	0
2	2	m	05/23/58	16	1	$40,200	$18,750	98	36	0
3	3	f	07/26/29	12	1	$21,450	$12,000	98	381	0
4	4	f	04/15/47	8	1	$21,900	$13,200	98	190	0
5	5	m	02/09/55	15	1	$45,000	$21,000	98	138	0
6	6	m	08/22/58	15	1	$32,100	$13,500	98	67	0
7	7	m	04/26/56	15	1	$36,000	$18,750	98	114	0

Data View | Variable View

SPSS Processor is ready

Vital Statistics, Crime Reports, and Unemployment Claims

Still, some administrative records—such as *vital statistics*—are widely used for demographic and policy research. Health departments require the recording of births and deaths on standardized forms, and these data are gathered and made available to help understand a great deal about the growth and survival of populations.

Another example of administrative record data often used in research are crime reports—particularly the Federal Bureau of Investigation's system of *Uniform Crime Reports.* Crimes get reported by victims and others to local law enforcement agencies, which use this information for their own administrative and strategic purposes. But since 1929, the FBI has encouraged localities to report crimes in a uniform manner to a central system so that these data can be tracked, compared, and analyzed for the United States as a whole.

In the economic domain, the filing of *unemployment claims*—which are administrative records compiled by state unemployment agencies—are closely watched by economists as a measure of the strength or weakness of the labor market.

As more and more administrative data are computerized, and both researchers and administrators become technologically and statistically savvy, administrative data will be relied on increasingly for research and analysis. Insurance claims data, Social Security records, and school records are just a few additional examples.

Data for Purchase

Sometimes the data most useful for a particular study need to be purchased commercially. For example, researchers interested in examining how pharmaceutical prices affect prescription drug use can obtain data on retail pharmaceutical sales and prices by drug and geographical identifier (e.g., zip code). Researchers interested in the role of medical expenditures and bankruptcy can obtain individual-level bankruptcy data. In one study, researchers used data on aggregate pharmaceutical sales available commercially from IMS Health to examine how regulations that support generic pharmaceutical manufacturers benefit consumers (Branstetter, Chatterjee, & Higgins, 2011). There are commercially available data on many topics, including consumer spending, Internet traffic, house prices, legal proceedings, stock prices, travel patterns, and even terrorist activity.

In some cases, the commercially sold data may come originally from publicly available government data, such as bankruptcy filings. In other cases, the data may come from proprietary businesses, seeking to make additional profit on the data that they already have. Such administrative or naturally occurring data must, of course, be cleaned and formatted for research, which is the value added by the commercial data vendor. In other cases, companies may conduct their own surveys or otherwise be the primary collectors of data, which they then sell for profit.

Ethics of Administrative Record Data

Researchers seeking to use private data from individuals that were obtained for administrative purposes unrelated to research—and sometimes provided by individuals to the government because of a legal obligation or the need to obtain benefits—face important ethical issues. Such data were not collected with informed consent and often contain private information. The government, driven by the public, carefully regulates the use of such records for research.

The Health Insurance Portability and Accountability Act (HIPAA), for example, provides strict regulation on the use and sharing of health insurance and health care records to protect people's privacy. Researchers and policy analysts seeking to obtain such records for statistical analysis must follow strict HIPAA rules and regulations. For more information, see the webpage of the Office for Civil Rights within the U.S. Department of Health and Human Services (www.hhs.gov/ocr/privacy).

A key ethical obligation in research using administrative data is that they be **nonidentifiable**—in other words, the data should not contain information that allows the researcher to figure out the identity of any particular individual. So before being received by a researcher, the data must be stripped of names, Social Security numbers, addresses, or any other information that clearly identifies who an individual is. More general information, such as someone's earnings, occupation, or the city he or she lives in, can be released while still preserving anonymity. However, that information is also limited: It must be impossible for anyone to combine all the variables (such as work history and city and education, etc.) to figure out who someone is. Small area geographic detail, such a postal zip code, is often restricted for this reason.

Researchers often want to match records across confidential data sources. For example, by combining Medicare (U.S. government health insurance for the elderly), Social Security, cancer registry, and death certificate information, researchers can learn about a variety of questions. Iezzoni (2002) describes how many different administrative data sets can be combined to learn about the effects of disability. For example, by combining all forms of health care paid for by Medicare over several years and linking them to government disability records, much can be learned about the evolution over time of a disability. Obviously, to combine such information requires Social Security numbers and names. To maintain confidentiality, the government will allow researchers to apply to have the government match the data and release them, stripped of all personal identifiers.

QUESTION

Can you think of some administrative data that you might have access to at work or school? How are the data stored, and how would you access them? What ethical issues would you face in trying to use the data for research?

With the growth in electronic data and the ease of copying and transmitting them, protecting individuals' privacy is an area of increasing concern and importance. There have been scandals in many countries about the loss, release, or theft of private data from governmental agencies and private businesses. However, the expanding availability of data also has the potential for helping us learn what lifestyles are most healthy, what educational practices help students learn, and so on. The tremendous potential value of such data suggests that we should try to find appropriate uses of administrative data, but in ways that still protect individuals' privacy.

Published Data Tables

Agencies often aggregate their microdata and make them available in published tables or downloadable spreadsheets. Table 6.2 shows an example of aggregate state-level data on poverty from the U.S. Census Bureau (2012b). The poverty figures are calculated from survey data on individual households, so the data on these households—their incomes, composition, and other characteristics captured in the survey—are the microdata. Published aggregate data tables are not as detailed as the microdata, but they are easily available, more manageable to work with, and often quite sufficient to address some research questions (such as aggregate panel studies).

Privacy and other concerns can prevent microdata from being made publicly available. But the same data aggregated to the institutional or geographic level—by averaging or reporting percentages in data tables—can be released much more freely and widely.

Table 6.2 Aggregate Data Table From the U.S. Census Bureau

[In thousands (33,311 represents 33,311,000), except as indicated. Represents number and percent below poverty in the past 12 months. Prior to 2006, the American Community Survey universe was limited to the household population and excluded the population living in institutions, college dormitories, and other group quarters. Poverty status was determined for all people except institutionalized people, people in military group quarters, people in college dormitories, and unrelated individuals under 15 years old. These groups were excluded from the numerator and denominator when calculating poverty rates. Based on a sample and subject to sampling variability].

	Number below poverty (1,000)				Percent below poverty			
	Individuals		Families		Individuals		Families	
State	2000	2009	2000	2009	2000	2009	2000	2009
United States	**33,311**	**42,868**	**6,615**	**7,956**	**12.2**	**14.3**	**9.3**	**10.5**
Alabama	672	805	146	167	15.6	17.5	12.4	13.4
Alaska	55	62	11	10	9.1	9.0	6.8	6.2
Arizona	780	1,070	150	175	15.6	16.5	11.6	11.6
Arkansas	439	527	96	113	17.0	18.8	13.0	14.8
California	4,520	5,129	832	887	13.7	14.2	10.7	10.6
Colorado	363	634	64	110	8.7	12.9	5.7	8.9
Connecticut	254	321	51	59	7.7	9.4	5.8	6.7
Delaware	70	93	14	16	9.3	10.8	6.7	7.1
District of Columbia	94	105	17	16	17.5	18.4	15.4	14.6
Florida	1,987	2,708	387	488	12.8	14.9	9.3	10.7
Georgia	999	1,575	206	301	12.6	16.5	10.0	12.7
Hawaii	103	131	19	23	8.8	10.4	6.8	7.5
Idaho	144	216	26	39	11.4	14.3	7.7	9.9
Illinois	1,335	1,667	262	309	11.1	13.3	8.6	9.9
Indiana	592	897	113	178	10.1	14.4	7.1	10.7
Iowa	281	343	53	61	10.0	11.8	7.0	7.7
Kansas	247	365	43	65	9.5	13.4	6.2	9.0
Kentucky	640	777	148	165	16.4	18.6	13.5	14.4
Louisiana	862	755	182	150	20.0	17.3	16.0	13.3
Maine	124	158	22	29	10.1	12.3	6.6	8.3
Maryland	477	505	89	85	9.3	9.1	6.6	6.1
Massachusetts	586	655	110	109	9.6	10.3	7.1	7.0
Michigan	975	1,577	196	292	10.1	16.2	7.7	11.6

State	Number below poverty (1,000)				Percent below poverty			
	Individuals		Families		Individuals		Families	
	2000	2009	2000	2009	2000	2009	2000	2009
Minnesota	328	563	66	95	6.9	11.0	5.1	7.0
Mississippi	498	624	104	131	18.2	21.9	14.2	17.3
Missouri	606	849	118	168	11.2	14.6	7.7	10.9
Montana	117	143	23	23	13.4	15.1	9.5	9.9
Nebraska	158	215	28	39	9.6	12.3	6.5	9.0
Nevada	194	322	34	57	9.9	12.4	6.9	9.0
New Hampshire	63	109	11	19	5.3	8.5	3.5	5.5
New Jersey	651	799	126	151	7.9	9.4	6.0	7.0
New Mexico	320	354	64	66	18.0	18.0	14.2	13.6
New York	2,391	2,692	491	498	13.1	16.3	9.6	11.9
North Carolina	1,018	1,478	203	289	13.1	14.2	10.7	10.8
North Dakota	71	72	14	11	11.6	11.7	8.1	6.6
Ohio	1,216	1,710	246	328	11.1	15.2	8.4	11.1
Oklahoma	459	578	100	115	13.8	16.2	11.0	12.1
Oregon	439	535	84	94	13.2	14.3	9.5	9.8
Pennsylvania	1,240	1,517	247	275	10.5	12.5	7.8	8.6
Rhode Island	108	116	23	22	10.7	11.5	8.5	8.6
South Carolina	557	754	123	150	14.4	17.1	11.7	12.9
South Dakota	83	111	16	18	11.5	14.2	8.4	9.0
Tennessee	745	1,052	158	215	13.5	17.1	10.5	13.1
Texas	3,056	4,150	639	800	15.1	17.2	12.3	13.4
Utah	192	316	40	51	8.8	11.5	7.2	7.8
Vermont	63	68	12	12	10.7	11.4	7.5	7.3
Virginia	630	803	124	148	9.2	10.5	6.8	7.5
Washington	667	804	127	133	11.6	12.3	8.6	8.1
West Virginia	327	313	72	68	18.6	17.7	14.7	13.9
Wisconsin	461	683	75	121	8.9	12.4	5.6	8.2
Wyoming	55	52	10	9	11.4	9.8	7.9	6.3

Source: U.S. Census Bureau, 2012b.

Where to Find Published Tables

Tables of aggregate data are increasingly available on the Internet from governments and other institutions. The U.S. Census Bureau provides a great deal of aggregate data on states, counties, and cities in the United States (available online from the U.S. Census Bureau), as do many other federal statistical agencies (see, e.g., data.gov). The United Nations Statistics Division, the World Bank, the European Commission's Eurostat, the Organisation of Economic Co-operation and Development (OECD), and numerous other international, governmental, and nongovernmental agencies make aggregate data available for public use.

When using aggregate data, it becomes very important to read the notes and documentation of the data carefully so that you understand the variables, the original microdata sources used to construct the variables, the years represented by the data, and any assumptions or calculations that were made in compiling the data. It is also important to carefully and fully cite where and when you downloaded or otherwise obtained your aggregate data (as published data can be updated or corrected over time).

Published Time-Series and Panel Data

Aggregate time series are frequently published online and in printed reports. Table 6.3 shows a time series of both the number and rate of homicides as recorded by the FBI's *Uniform Crime Reports* (as reported in the 2012 *Statistical Abstract* [U.S. Census Bureau, 2012a]). In the layout of longitudinal data such as these, typically, the rows—the unit of analysis—are the time periods (years, quarters, months), and the columns are the variables. Notice that for purposes of publication, the time series is condensed in the early years by presenting homicides only every 5 years (1980, 1985, 1990) instead of annually. If we were interested in homicides for the in-between years, we would need to find another published source for these FBI data. (In fact, the Bureau of Justice Statistics provides online tools for accessing more detailed time-series data on homicides and other crimes in the United States.)

QUESTION

What are the advantages and also limitations of using aggregate data from published tables?

Published data tables can report aggregate time series separately by cities, states, or other, smaller units of aggregation. This results in a form of aggregate panel data. Table 6.2, which shows poverty rates of all 50 U.S. states in 2000 and 2009, provides a basic example—and typically, aggregate panel data of this kind are available for many years. Such aggregated panel data can be analyzed with many valuable statistical techniques to answer important policy questions regarding how outcomes change over time.

Public Use Microdata

As we've said, *microdata* refers to individual-level data on people, households, or firms. **Public use microdata** refers to individual-level data collected and made available to the public. That availability is increasingly widespread. Typically, public use microdata contain information about individual respondents to large social surveys, who can number in the tens of thousands. These surveys are conducted by governmental and nongovernmental organizations. For example, the U.S. Current Population Survey (CPS)—which is publicly available from the website of the U.S. Bureau of Labor Statistics—contains data from 60,000 households each month. The CPS can be readily downloaded and used by various researchers and policy analysts (e.g., using the DataFerrett software available at TheDataWeb.org).

Secondary Analysis of Public Use Data: A New Model of Research?

Social and policy researchers are moving increasingly in the direction of relying on these public use microdata sets collected by large, sophisticated statistical agencies and research organizations (Kiecolt & Nathan, 1985). In part, this is because of the growing cost and complexity of gathering social, health, and economic

Table 6.3 Time Series Data From the FBI *Uniform Crime Reports*

[Based on the Federal Bureau of Investigation's Uniform Crime Reports Supplementary Homicide Reports. Homicide includes murder and nonnegligent manslaughter, which is the willful killing of one human being by another. Excludes deaths caused by negligence, suicide, or accident; justifiable homicides; and attempts to murder. Justifiable homicides based on the reports of law enforcement agencies are analyzed separately. Deaths from the terrorist attacks of 9/11/01 are not included. Data based soley on police investigation, as opposed to the determination of a court, medical examiner, coroner, jury, or other judicial body.]

	Number of victims						Rate[1]					
Year	Total	Male	Female	White	Black	Other	Total	Male	Female	White	Black	Other
1980	23,040	17,803	5,237	12,275	9,767	327	10.2	16.1	4.5	6.3	37.7	5.7
1985	18,980	14,095	4,885	10,590	7,891	399	7.9	12.2	4.0	5.2	27.6	5.5
1990	23,440	18,320	5,121	11,278	11,489	400	9.4	15.1	4.0	5.4	37.6	4.2
1995	21,610	16,579	5,030	10,376	10,444	581	8.2	12.7	3.7	4.8	31.6	4.9
1996	19,650	15,175	4,475	9,483	9,476	512	7.4	11.5	3.3	4.3	28.3	4.1
1997	18,210	14,079	4,132	8,620	8,842	524	6.8	10.5	3.0	3.9	26.0	4.1
1998	16,970	12,812	4,158	8,389	7,931	393	6.3	9.5	3.0	3.8	23.0	2.9
1999	15,522	11,718	3,804	7,777	7,139	458	5.7	8.6	2.7	3.5	23.5	3.3
2000	15,586	11,844	3,742	7,560	7,425	399	5.5	8.6	2.6	3.3	20.3	2.7
2001	16,037	12,256	3,782	7,884	7,552	424	5.6	8.8	2.6	3.4	20.2	2.8
2002	16,204	12,432	3,772	7,784	7,759	437	5.6	8.8	2.6	3.3	20.6	2.8
2003	16,528	12,828	3,700	7,932	7,893	468	5.7	9.0	2.5	3.4	20.7	2.9
2004	16,148	12,596	3,552	7,944	7,562	417	5.5	8.7	2.4	3.3	19.6	2.5
2005	16,740	13,169	3,571	8,045	8,015	443	5.6	9.0	2.4	3.3	20.5	2.6
2006	17,030	13,433	3,597	7,906	8,428	461	5.7	9.1	2.4	3.3	21.3	2.6
2007	16,929	13,286	3,643	7,924	8,352	402	5.6	8.9	2.4	3.3	20.9	2.2
2008	16,272	12,731	3,541	7,995	7,901	376	5.4	8.5	2.3	3.3	19.6	2.0

[1]Rate is per 100,000 inhabitants.

Source: U.S. Census Bureau (2012a, Table 301).

data from individuals and organizations. It also reflects the rapidly expanding ability to transmit and share data and results over the Internet. Even a cursory review of the contents of any major social or policy research journal will convince you of how widespread this model of doing research has become.

Know the Major Surveys in Your Field

Whether you are a practitioner, policy analyst, or researcher, you should become familiar with the major surveys in your field. These surveys often provide much of the fact base for the field and are often the primary source of information on emerging trends or policy successes and failures. Table 6.4 provides a number of very interesting and important sources of public use microdata in various fields. We encourage you to look over this table and to begin to get familiar with the surveys in your field of interest or practice.

Governments and nongovernmental organizations around the world are increasingly moving in the direction of making their microdata available for public use. Table 6.4 is far from complete, and many other useful

(Text continues on page 202)

Table 6.4 Selected Major Surveys by Policy Area

Survey Name	Purpose	Sponsor and History	Method	Data Access
		Health		
National Health Interview Survey (NHIS)	To assess health status and behaviors, including use of health care	National Center for Health Statistics (NCHS). Began in 1957	Household interview survey of about 35,000 households annually	Public use microdata are available to download from the NCHS
National Health and Nutrition Examination Survey (NHANES)	To measure health and nutritional status, based on physical examinations and laboratory tests	National Center for Health Statistics (NCHS). Began in 1959	Household interview, followed by a mobile examination center. About 9,000 individuals annually	Public use microdata are available to download from the NCHS. Limited access to some parts of the data because of confidentiality
National Health Care Surveys (NHCS)	A family of surveys to track characteristics and practices of various health care provider organizations	National Center for Health Statistics (NCHS). Began in 1973	Organization surveys using various probability sampling methods, depending on the type of organization being surveyed	Public use microdata are available to download from the NCHS
Behavioral Risk Factor Surveillance System (BRFSS)	To understand health behaviors and risks, such as diet, smoking, exercise, and many more	Conducted by state health agencies, under guidance from the Centers for Disease Control and Prevention (CDC). Began in 1984	Telephone interview survey of about 350,000 individuals annually	CDC's Web Enabled Analysis Tool (WEAT) provides online analysis. Public use microdata are available to download
Youth Risk Behavior Surveillance System (YRBSS)	To understand health behaviors and risks of the nation's youth	Conducted by the Centers for Disease Control and Prevention (CDC). State and local health agencies conduct their own YRBSSs, with guidance from the CDC. Began in 1991	Group-administered survey of a multistage random sample of schools. About 15,000 ninth through twelfth graders surveyed nationally. There are also about 40 state and 20 local YRBSSs	CDC's Youth Online provides online data access tools. Public use microdata are available to download
Medical Expenditure Panel Survey (MEPS)	To learn about U.S. health care use, costs, financing, and health insurance coverage	Conducted by the U.S. Department of Health and Human Services, Agency for Health Research and Quality (AHRQ) annually since 1996. Earlier versions started in 1977	The household component is a probability sample with 2-year panels and follow-up with health care providers. The insurance component is a probability sample of employers	The household component is available for download as public use microdata. The insurance component microdata are not available as public use data sets. All data are available in various aggregate tables. MEPSnet query tool can be used as both to generate statistics

Survey Name	Purpose	Sponsor and History	Method	Data Access
Education				
National Assessment of Educational Progress (NAEP)	To assess what students know and can do in various academic subject areas. Known as "The Nation's Report Card"	U.S. Department of Education, National Center for Education Statistics (NCES). Began in 1964 (first national assessment in 1969)	School-based, group-administered assessment of a multistage random sample of public and private school students in the United States in Grades 4, 8, and 12. About 700,000 students every 2 years	NAEP Data Explorer provides online data analysis. Public use microdata are available to download
National Education Longitudinal Study (NELS)	To study policy-relevant educational processes and outcomes by following a sample of students over time	U.S. Department of Education, National Center for Education Statistics (NCES). Began in 1988	Panel study of a random sample of eighth graders in 1988 who are followed and surveyed every 2 years	NCES Data Analysis System provides online data analysis. Public use microdata are available to download
National Household Education Survey (NHES)	To describe educational experiences in the United States, including adult education, early childhood education, and others	U.S. Department of Education, National Center for Education Statistics (NCES). Began in 1991	Some surveys are conducted repeatedly, while others are one-time surveys of topics of interest	Public use microdata are available for download
National Assessment of Adult Literacy (NAAL)	To describe English literacy of Americans 16 and older	U.S. Department of Education, National Center for Education Statistics (NCES). 2003 survey designed to be comparable with 1992 survey	Probability sample of both household and prison populations	Public use microdata are not yet available
Labor and Employment				
Current Population Survey (CPS)	To describe employment, earnings, and other labor outcomes in the United States	Joint effort of the U.S. Census Bureau and the U.S. Bureau of Labor Statistics (BLS). Began in 1948	Probability sample of households	Public use microdata and aggregate tables are available for download

(Continued)

Table 6.4 (Continued)

Survey Name	Purpose	Sponsor and History	Method	Data Access
Labor and Employment				
Panel Study of Income Dynamics (PSID)	To describe the dynamics of demographic and economic behavior in the United States	Institute for Social Research at the University of Michigan, under contract to various U.S. government agencies, currently the National Science Foundation (NSF). Began in 1968. Annual until 1997 and biennial thereafter	Panel study, following the same families. Probability sample. Oversample of low-income families	Data center tool enables creation of customized extracts. Entire public use microdata may also be downloaded
National Longitudinal Surveys, including the National Longitudinal Surveys of Youth 79 (NLSY79) and 97 (NLSY97)	To gather labor market and related information over extended periods of time and across generations. NLSY79 surveyed youth in 1979. NLSY97 surveyed youth in 1997. Both surveys continue through the present. NLSY79 Children and Young Adults surveys the biological children of women in NLSY79	U.S. Census Bureau, U.S. Bureau of Labor Statistics (BLS)	Long-term panel surveys	Public use microdata available for download
Criminal Justice, Housing, Public Programs, and Other Policy Areas				
National Crime Victimization Survey (NCVS)	To estimate the rate of victimization from various types of crime, including unreported crime	U.S. Department of Justice, Bureau of Justice Statistics. Began in 1973 (redesigned in 1992)	Household interview surveys; multistage probability sample of 76,000 households representing 135,000 individuals	National Archive of Criminal Justice Data (at University of Michigan) provides online data analysis. Public use microdata are available to download
American Housing Survey (AHS)	To assess the condition and cost of the nation's housing units and the characteristics of the occupying households	U.S. Bureau of the Census, with support from the Department of Housing and Urban Development	Household interview and observation survey. Random sample of about 55,000 housing units every 2 years	U.S. Census Bureau AHS webpage provides data tables. Public use microdata are available to download
Health and Retirement Study (HRS)	To understand employment, income, wealth, and health of Americans before and after retirement and how all of these relate to one another	Institute for Social Research at the University of Michigan, under contract to the National Institute on Aging	In-person, very in-depth panel survey conducted every 2 years	Public use microdata available for download. Sensitive data available through application procedure

Survey Name	Purpose	Sponsor and History	Method	Data Access
Criminal Justice, Housing, Public Programs, and Other Policy Areas				
Survey of Income and Program Participation (SIPP)	To understand income and public program participation in the United States to evaluate the effectiveness of government programs	U.S. Census Bureau. Began in 1984	2½-year-long panels	DataFerrett application allows the creation of customized data sets and analyses. Full public use data set may be downloaded
Fragile Families and Child Wellbeing Study	To understand the experiences of families at greater risk of breaking up and living in poverty	Shriver National Institute of Child Health and Human Development, started in 2007	Surveys of parents and in-home assessments	Public use microdata are available for download
Consumer Expenditure Survey (CES)	To provide information on the buying habits of Americans and support the price index calculations	U.S. Census Bureau, U.S. Bureau of Labor Statistics (BLS)	Probability sample of households. Both in-person interview and expenditure diary collection	Public use microdata and aggregate tables available for download
American Community Survey (ACS)	To provide frequent and geographically detailed demographic information	U.S. Census Bureau. Replaced the long form of the Decennial Census	Based on the Census. Monthly surveys combined to make representative annual survey	Public use microdata subsamples and specifically chosen data tables are available using the DataFerrett
Social and Political Attitudes (United States)				
General Social Survey (GSS)	To track a wide range of attitudes and behaviors of U.S. adults in many areas of life, such as family, work, community, religion, government, current affairs, and more	National Opinion Research Center (NORC) at the University of Chicago, with support from the National Science Foundation (NSF). Began in 1972	Household interview survey of a multistage random sample of about 4,000 U.S. adults every 2 years	GSS on Nesstar at NORC.org provides online data analysis. Public use microdata are available to download
American National Election Studies (ANES)	To measure political attitudes and voting behaviors of the population, before and after U.S. national elections	The University of Michigan and Stanford University, with support from the National Science Foundation (NSF). Began in 1948 by the University of Michigan. Received NSF support in 1977	Household interview survey of a multistage random sample of about 2,000 individuals every 2 years (during national elections). Interviews conducted with respondents both before and after the election	The ANES Guide to Public Opinion and Electoral Behavior provides data tables online. Public use microdata are available to download. University of California, Berkeley's Survey Documentation and Analysis (SDA) project provides online data analysis

(Continued)

Table 6.4 (Continued)

Survey Name	Purpose	Sponsor and History	Method	Data Access
International and Comparative Surveys				
Eurobarometer	To monitor the evolution of public opinion in the member and candidate states of the EU	European Commission (EC), Public Opinion Section. Began in 1973	Standard Eurobarometer: In-person interviews of about 1,000 individuals per country, conducted twice each year. Flash Eurobarometer: Telephone interviews of a probability sample in each country, with several surveys conducted each year	Summary data tables (PDFs) available on the EC Public Opinion website. Public use microdata are available to download from the German Social Science Infrastructure Service (GESIS)
World Values Survey (WVS)	To study changing social and political values in countries all over the world	A network of social scientists with headquarters in Stockholm, Sweden. Originated at the University of Michigan. Locally funded by participating countries	Each of the more than 50 participating countries uses its own method, but all are random samples of the general population. About 1,000 to 2,000 individuals per country	WVS provides an online data analysis tool. Public use microdata are available to download
International Social Survey Programme (ISSP)	To coordinate research goals of preexisting social surveys so that they provide a cross-national perspective	A self-funding association of member institutions, with the current secretariat in Tel Aviv, Israel. Began in 1982	Each of the 43 participating countries uses its own method, but all are random samples of the general population. About 1,000 to 2,000 individuals per country	German Social Science Infrastructure Service (GESIS) Data Archive, ZACAT online data analysis tool. Public use microdata are available to download
European Social Survey (ESS)	To study social attitudes and values across European countries	Consortium of European research institutes, currently coordinated by the City University, London, with financial support from the European Science Foundation. Began in 2002	Participating countries agree to survey a probability sample of the general population 15 years of age or older. About 1,500 individuals in each of more than 30 countries every 2 years	ESS on Nesstar provides online data analysis. Public use microdata are available to download

Survey Name	Purpose	Sponsor and History	Method	Data Access
International and Comparative Surveys				
Demographic and Health Surveys (DHS)	Provides technical assistance to more than 200 surveys in 75 countries to provide data on fertility, family planning, and maternal and child health	U.S. Agency for International Development (USAID) and other donors. Started in 1984	Representative samples. Methods vary by country	Microdata from most participating countries available for download with registration. Specialized STATcompiler and STATmapper allow creation of multicountry data tables
Living Standards Measurement Study (LSMS)	To support household surveys in many countries in order to learn and improve living standards, including employment, health, education, housing, and other areas	World Bank, Development Economics Research Group. Began in 1980	Generally probability samples of households. Methods vary by country	Some, but not all, surveys have public use microdata available for download with registration. LSMS survey finder tool available to help find appropriate surveys
German Socio-Economic Panel (GSOEP)	To understand a wide range of economic and social phenomena	German Institute for Economic Research. Same families studied since 1984. Eastern Germany included since 1990	Probability panel survey of the same families. All household members followed during family breakups	English language version available through Cornell University. Public use microdata available for download
Luxembourg Income Study (LIS)	To learn about cross-national and longitudinal income and wealth patterns, harmonizing and standardizing data across countries	Originated by Luxembourg government. Currently sponsored by social science research foundations of member countries. Began in 1983	Representative household surveys in member countries. Data harmonized by LIS	Access to microdata is through a job submission system, accepting programs in SAS, SPSS, or Stata

surveys exist. More details about many of the surveys, including their strengths and weaknesses, can be found in Kramer, Finegold, and Kuehn (2008).

Some countries collect all their major surveys under one umbrella organization, such as Statistics Canada. Other countries, such as the United States, rely on various statistical agencies representing different policy areas to manage their own surveys (see Data.gov for a directory). Large consulting firms, working under contract, are often involved in much of the actual work of gathering government survey data.

Accessing and Analyzing Public Use Data

Public use data come in various formats, with many sites providing the data already formatted for the most commonly used statistical programs—IBM® SPSS®, SAS, and Stata—or for spreadsheet programs such as Excel. In some cases, the data may come as an ASCII (or text) file, often with SPSS, SAS, or Stata routines to help the user format and label the data. Without either a preformatted data file or these formatting routines, it can be a time-consuming task to get the data into a usable format.

Importantly, the data come with a **codebook** and related documentation to help you understand how the data were collected, coded, weighted, and so on. It is very important to read this documentation carefully as you begin using the data for your own analysis.

To facilitate quick, convenient analysis and more widespread access, some government statistical agencies and other organizations have created **online data analysis tools**—allowing users to directly analyze data on the web. A good example is the National Center for Education Statistics' NAEP Data Explorer (see Figure 6.5), which provides online analysis tools for data from the National Assessment of Educational Progress (NAEP)—the "Nation's Report Card" on educational outcomes.

Data Archives

To facilitate access to public use microdata, various institutions around the world have established **data archives**. These archives store and document data from various surveys and studies, typically in a consistent

Figure 6.5 Screenshot of the NAEP Data Explorer

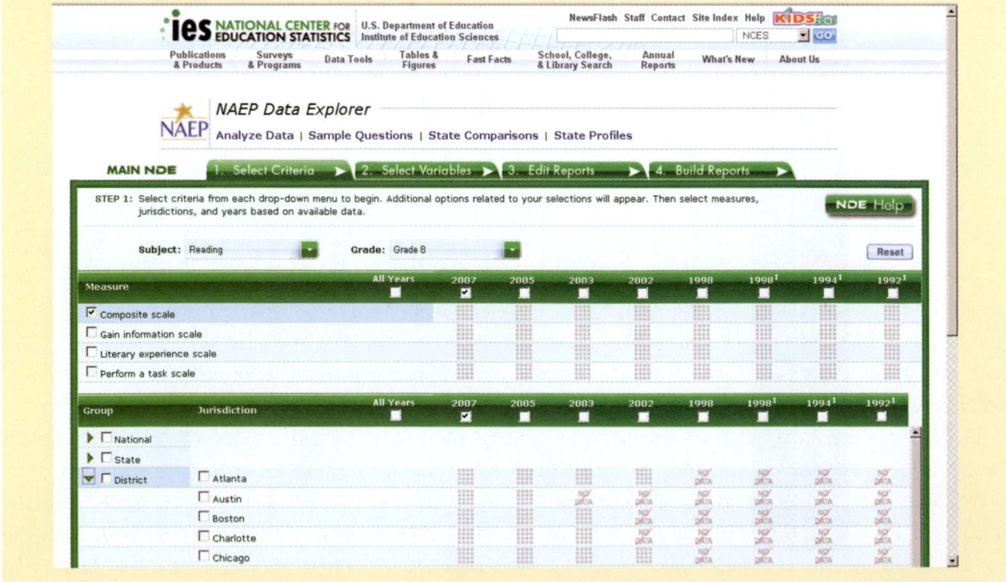

format and with technology and procedures to manage public access to the data. Here is a list of some major data archives:

- *Inter-university Consortium for Political and Social Research (ICPSR):* Housed at the University of Michigan, the ICPSR is one of the largest and most established social science data archives in the world. See www.icpsr.umich.edu.
- *German Social Science Infrastructure Service (GESIS):* A part of the Leibniz Institute for the Social Sciences with offices in major German cities, GESIS archives data and documentation from various European and international surveys. See www.gesis.org/en/za/index.htm.
- *Roper Center Public Opinion Archives:* Housed at the University of Connecticut, the Roper Center contains a huge collection of public opinion surveys covering many years (requires membership). See www.ropercenter.uconn.edu.
- *Survey Documentation and Analysis (SDA), University of California, Berkeley:* This site provides online access and analysis tools for a number of major social and political surveys. See http://sda.berkeley.edu.
- *Council of European Social Science Data Archives (CESSDA):* An umbrella organization for social science data archives across Europe. See www.nsd.uib.no/cessda/home.html.
- *UK Data Archive (UKDA):* Housed at the University of Essex, this is the largest social science data archive in the United Kingdom and, interestingly, also archives qualitative social science data. See www.data-archive.ac.uk.

Ethics of Public Use Microdata

Public use microdata reveal details about individual survey respondents, so ethical issues arise in making these data publicly available (Duncan, Jabine, & de Wolf, 1993). Most respondents to such surveys were given initial assurances of privacy and anonymity, yet the surveys capture a great deal of individual-level details that could, potentially, be used to identify individual people or households. For this reason, institutions holding public use microdata do not release much geographic detail and often top-code outlying values for variables such as income and age.

For example, to protect confidentiality, the U.S. Census Bureau releases Public Use Microdata Samples (PUMS) that contain a 1% or 5% random sample of all the forms gathered as part of the decennial U.S. Census or the American Community Survey (which is being carried out regularly and replaces the old Census Long Form as a source of more detailed household characteristics). These random samples contain limited geographic information and other identifiers to help ensure confidentiality.

For researchers who need to know the precise geographic location or other identifying information collected as part of U.S. government surveys, a system of Census Research Data Centers (RDCs) has been established that has secure facilities and strict procedures for working with confidential microdata. (See www.ces.census.gov for more information.)

QUESTION

Can you identify a source of public use microdata that is important in your work or area of interest? How could you access these data yourself?

Secondary Qualitative Data

We talked already in Chapter 3 about the use of existing qualitative data, such as stored documents or the audio recordings of 9-1-1 calls. But it is useful to return to the topic here and examine the similarities and differences with secondary quantitative data, as well as illustrate the growing value and emerging sources of secondary data for qualitative research.

Gathering primary qualitative data, for example conducting and transcribing interviews, is very time-consuming. So it is sensible, when possible, to make such data publicly available for secondary analysis and research. As mentioned already in the section on data archives, the UK Data Archive is a project that includes the archiving and public availability of qualitative data for secondary use (www.data-archive.ac.uk/create-manage/projects/qudex). Long-Sutehall, Sque, and Addington-Hall (2010) give the example of how interviews initially gathered to examine

Linking data often leads to interesting and useful research.

Source: © 2009 Jupiterimages Corporation.

organ donation were used later to study how families understand the concept of brain death. This example illustrates well the potential secondary use of qualitative data. But there are some important ethical issues raised by such secondary use, because the initial informed consents were granted for only the primary study. In general, subsequent studies must fit within the language of the original consent.

Much administrative data is qualitative, such as the audio recordings of 9-1-1 calls produced as part of the regular emergency response system. But there are many more examples: transcripts of meetings, business correspondence, court testimony, narrative personnel evaluations, clinical descriptions in electronic medical records, and audio and video recordings made as part of ordinary business or government operations. Indeed, qualitative data are increasingly gathered and stored for administrative purposes. The same ethical issues raised by the use of administrative data in general, discussed earlier, apply to qualitative administrative data as well. However, qualitative administrative data can be even more sensitive sometimes because it is difficult to disguise individual identities and thus ensure anonymity when dealing with data in the form of narratives, images, or audio recordings.

As mentioned at the start of this chapter, because more of our lives are conducted with electronic devices that connect to a virtual world, we produce increasing amounts of qualitative data online. These include publicly available postings, blogs, and images from social media as well as millions of websites of all kinds.

Linking Data

One way to shape secondary data to fit an information need—and thus to get beyond the problem of being overly driven by the available data—is to link data from various sources. Here are a few ways that this can be done:

- Survey data can be linked with administrative record data (e.g., a health survey can be linked with records of health care use).
- Survey data can be linked with aggregate data (e.g., a survey of individual households can be linked with data on surrounding community characteristics).
- Linking of data can be done through a geographic information system (GIS), which pinpoints locations of people or events, such as reported crimes and types of land use.
- Quantitative and qualitative data can be linked (e.g., a survey in which researchers followed up on their statistical findings with qualitative focus groups).

Some of the most interesting and useful research and policy analysis occur when surveys, administrative records, and other sources of data are linked together to produce a broader and more unique set of variables to work with. Linking data from different sources is one of the key features of the approach increasingly known as Big Data, which we introduced at the start of this chapter.

Some Limitations of Secondary Data

Although secondary data provide a rich and increasingly important resource for research, they have some limitations as well. And, of course, sometimes it is necessary to collect your own, primary data.

Does Data Availability Distort Research?

Some kinds of data are much more available than others. In the United States, for example, individuals older than 65 have government-provided health insurance through Medicare, while those younger than 65 get insurance from a wide variety of other sources, mostly employer-provided plans—and many lack insurance altogether. So it is much more difficult to study health care and health outcomes in the United States for those under 65 years of age. In contrast, because Medicare insurance claims are centralized and available from one source (the government), much more health care research can be—and is—done on the U.S. elderly population. In countries with universal health insurance, however, it is relatively more straightforward to study the health care of all age-groups.

This example illustrates that what data are available often determines what study gets done. Some people criticize researchers for being too "data driven"—answering only questions that can be answered with available data, even though those may not be the most important questions. These critics have a point, to be sure. But sometimes, researchers have to take what they can get, and it is arguably better to have the answers to some questions than to none at all. Still the availability of data does mean that some outcomes or topics are much more frequently studied than others.

Availability of health insurance claims data shapes health care research.

Source: © Can Stock Photo Inc./4774344sean.

When to Collect Original Data?

This chapter has stressed the availability and use of existing data—administrative records, aggregate data, and public use microdata—in large part because of the exploding growth and importance of such data in social and policy research. But still, researchers and policy analysts often find that they must collect their own quantitative data for several reasons:

- Even very large, public use microdata sources often do not provide enough data for small area studies, such as cities or neighborhoods.
- Existing data may not measure the relevant variables of interest—the measures that best meet a specific research objective.
- Existing data may not have the right *combination of variables,* making it difficult to test relationships between variables.
- Existing data may be out of date, conducted too long ago to be useful for present purposes.
- Existing data may not be fully accessible because of privacy and confidentiality concerns, as we have discussed.

The next chapter presents methods of generating your own quantitative data, such as surveys and trained observation.

Conclusion

This chapter has defined quantitative data and introduced you to various sources and methods that provide secondary data for social and policy research. Knowing where data come from or how they are produced matters, even for those who do not do research but rather read it and apply it to public policy and management. Data are the basic material of research, and each source of data has its own advantages and limitations. This chapter has given you a feel for some of the most important sources and forms of data used in contemporary social and policy research. We turn next to the challenge of collecting primary data.

BOX 6.2
Critical Questions to Ask About Secondary Data

- What was the original purpose of the data—why were they collected?
- Are they administrative data, survey data, or some other type of secondary data?
- What form or structure applies to the data? Are they microdata or aggregated? What is the time dimension of the data?
- What variables, or measures, are available in the data? What variables are not available? What kinds of questions can the data help answer?
- Is there an online analysis tool that you can use to produce customized tables or charts from the data?
- Are the microdata available to download for public use, or is their use restricted? In what formats are the data provided?
- Is there a codebook or related documentation of the data? What does the codebook provide in terms of guidelines and technical advice for using the data?

BOX 6.3
Tips on Doing Your Own Research: Secondary Data

- Learn about the various secondary data sources available in your field or policy area. Start with Table 6.4 as an initial guide and then search the Internet, talk to people, and keep your eye out for studies that might use relevant data. Decide which survey or data set is best for your research question.
- If existing public use data sets do not meet your needs well, consider administrative data in an organization you work in or know people in. But be careful because it takes a long time to learn about and clean administrative data you are not already familiar with.
- Consider whether you will be able to get the needed data by merging data sets. Pay close attention to the quality of the variables used to merge the data (for example, are ID numbers accurate and always available?).
- Determine the requirements for accessing and downloading the data file. If it is not already formatted for your statistical software, you will need to import or reformat the file. Some software (such as SPSS) will read data in many formats, while other software (such as Stata) requires a special reformatting or importing routine.

- Be sure to download the data documentation also (such as the questionnaire, the codebook, and any technical descriptions of the survey). Take time to read about and understand the purpose and design of the survey, how the data were collected, sampling and weighting issues, and other details about the data.
- Explore the data using graphs and basic descriptive statistics—see the tips at the end of Chapter 8. This will help you understand the data better.
- Learn which weighting variables are available and how they should be used in your statistical software—see the tips at the end of Chapter 5 on sampling and Chapter 9 on inference.

Chapter Resources

Key Terms

- Aggregate (ecological) data
- Big Data
- Codebook
- Cross-sectional data
- Data archive
- Data cleaning
- Flat file
- Longitudinal data
- Metadata
- Microdata
- Multilevel (hierarchical) data
- Nonidentifiable
- Online data analysis tool
- Panel data
- Pooled cross sections
- Prospective cohort
- Quantitative data
- Relational database
- Time series
- Unit of observation

Exercises

Secondary Data in the News

6.1. Find a news article about recent results of a national government survey regarding employment, health, education, or another policy area. What is the source of the data for the facts or trends reported in the article? What statistical agency produced the data?

What Form of Data?

6.2. Following are several important sources of secondary data for economic and policy research. For each, identify the form of data it provides: *panel data, repeated cross sections,* or *time series.*

a. The Survey of Income and Program Participation (SIPP)
b. The Consumer Price Index (CPI)
c. The Current Population Survey (CPS)

Find a Government Survey

6.3. Pick one of the following policy issues that most interests you:

a. Transportation/commuting patterns
b. How college students pay for their education
c. Food and nutrition habits of the population
d. Demographic characteristics of inmates of state and federal prisons
e. Drug and alcohol use among high school students
f. The victim-offender relationship in violent crimes
g. How countries compare in math and science education

Search the web, perhaps starting at a major data gateway, and find a large government survey that provides data on this issue. What is the name of the survey, and what agency sponsors it? What specific measures, or variables, does the survey provide for this issue? What kind of analysis of the issue could you do with the data?

Online Data Analysis Tools

6.4. Choose one of the major surveys for policy research from Table 6.4—one that has an online data analysis tool. Locate the online data analysis tool on the survey's website, read the relevant instructions, and run an analysis of your choosing. Interpret the results and comment on the usefulness, and limitations, of this kind of online data analysis.

Downloading Microdata

6.5. Choose one of the major surveys for policy research from Table 6.4 or another major survey that interests you and locate its website. What options are available for downloading the microdata? What formats do the data come in? Is registration or other permission required to access the data? What available documentation of the data would you also need to download to fully understand and use the microdata?

Published Aggregated Data Tables Usable for Analysis

6.6. On the Internet, find a published aggregated data table that can be used for statistical analysis. Be sure it is not a published data table of merely summary statistics and without a clear unit of analysis. Next, identify the unit of analysis and the variables in the data table. What kind of analysis might you do with these data?

Administrative Data

6.7. Think of an administrative data set with which you are familiar. How are the data stored? What reformatting, reorganization, recoding, and cleaning would be needed to make it into a flat file for research? What kinds of analysis could you do, or what kinds of questions could you answer, with these data?

Student Study Site

Visit the Study Site at **www.sagepub.com/remler2e** to

- test your knowledge with the self-quiz
- check your understanding of key terms with the eFlashcards
- explore helpful resources that relate directly to this chapter

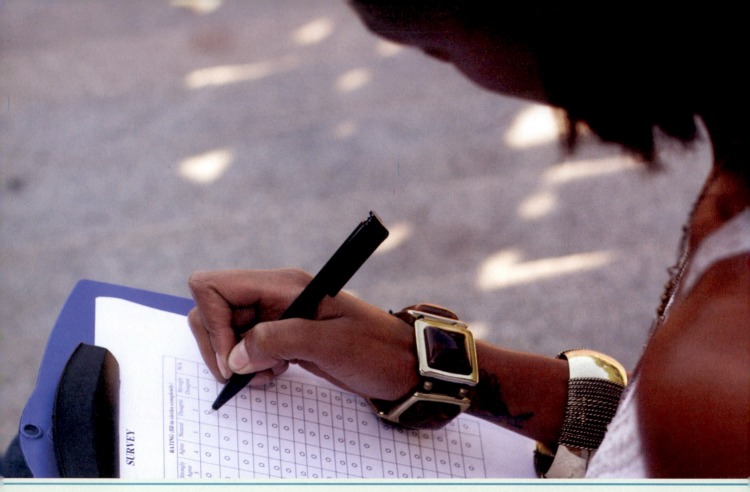

Surveys are widely used and come in various modes.
Source: © iStockphoto.com/wdstock.

Overview: In this chapter, you will learn about collecting primary data through surveys and observation. You will appreciate the strengths and weaknesses of various survey methods, the steps required in planning and implementing a survey, and the ethical issues involved. And you will be introduced to the method of trained observation, a practical form of gathering data in various public policy and management situations. Knowing about how primary data are collected is essential for doing your own research, and it will give you a better appreciation of the kinds of data that appear in research articles or reports.

Objectives

Learning Objectives

After reading this chapter, you should be able to

- Appreciate how widely used surveys have become to produce information about modern society
- Determine when it makes sense to do your own survey—and when not to
- Articulate the basic steps in the process of designing and conducting a survey
- Recognize the various modes of survey data collection (such as interviews, mail, phone, web, and more) and their advantages and limitations
- Select the best mode of survey data collection for a particular survey
- Craft a questionnaire and write good survey questions
- Understand the special ethical issues that come up in survey research
- Describe trained observation and other forms of collecting primary data

7 Surveys and Other Primary Data

Taking the Nation's Economic Pulse

There was more troubling economic news in the United States in 2010, a midterm election year. In April, the unemployment rate had climbed back up to 9.9%—verging on a 25-year high—and nonfarm payroll employment was down by some 8 million jobs from the start of the recession in 2008 (Federal Reserve Bank of St. Louis, 2013). By October, on the eve of the election, consumer sentiment had dropped again to near historic lows (Bloomberg Press, 2010), and 7 in 10 U.S. adults believed that the country was heading off on the wrong track (PollingReport.com, 2013). The battle for control of Congress became centered on which party was most to blame for the country's continuing dismal economic situation.

Our ability to understand the modern economy—and in turn the political and policy responses to its ups and downs—would not be possible without surveys. The monthly unemployment figures are from a government survey of households, and the nonfarm payroll figures come from a different government survey of business establishments. The Consumer Sentiment Index is computed from answers to a telephone survey done by the University of Michigan, and data on public opinion about the direction of the country, presidential approval, and a host of other issues derive from surveys done by various polling organizations.

Surveys form the basis for much of what we know about public health and health care, housing conditions, crime victimization, transportation use, and educational achievement across jurisdictions. And surveys are used by government and nonprofit organizations to understand and manage their employees, assess the needs of the communities they serve, and gather feedback from their clients or customers.

In this chapter, you will be introduced to the various methods and issues involved in survey research—the most important and widely used form of primary data collection in social and policy research. The chapter also introduces other forms of primary data collection, such as trained observation and primary data produced by scientific instruments.

When Should You Do a Survey?

Surveys involve the collection of information from individuals and organizations by the use of structured questionnaires or interviews. When surveys involve gathering public opinion, they are sometimes called

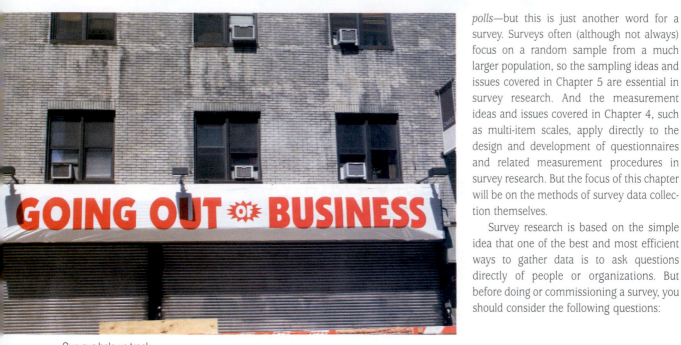

Surveys help us track economic conditions.
Source: © iStockphoto.com/vivalapenler.

polls—but this is just another word for a survey. Surveys often (although not always) focus on a random sample from a much larger population, so the sampling ideas and issues covered in Chapter 5 are essential in survey research. And the measurement ideas and issues covered in Chapter 4, such as multi-item scales, apply directly to the design and development of questionnaires and related measurement procedures in survey research. But the focus of this chapter will be on the methods of survey data collection themselves.

Survey research is based on the simple idea that one of the best and most efficient ways to gather data is to ask questions directly of people or organizations. But before doing or commissioning a survey, you should consider the following questions:

Do You Know Enough About the Topic?

To do a survey, you must understand the topic fairly well already to know what specific, structured questions to ask people. But sometimes knowledge of the topic is rudimentary, and thus a more exploratory method—such as focus groups or other qualitative interviewing—should be done first or instead of a more structured survey. Doing a survey may risk the mistake of spending precious time and resources only to ask the wrong questions.

Does the Information Exist Already in Another Source?

The information you seek from a survey may exist already in another source, so asking people or firms to provide it may be unnecessary and a waste of resources and the respondents' time. For example, we would not want to survey big-city police chiefs just to ask them about the local murder rate, the size of their annual budgets, or the number of police officers they employ. These facts are available already from the Bureau of Justice Statistics or publicly available budget documents.

Can People Tell You What You Want to Know?

People or firms may not know the information you want to gather in a survey. For example, if we're interested in how many grams of trans fat people consume in an average day, we might be tempted to ask in a health survey, "Considering all that you eat in a typical day, about how many grams of trans fat do you consume?" But people have only a vague sense of the quantity of food they eat in a day, and they know even less about how much of what they eat is trans fat (or even what trans fat is). To get this kind of detailed information on dietary intake, researchers typically ask people to keep food diaries—or even to save duplicate servings of the food they eat in bags for later laboratory analysis. Surveys are limited to topics that people can knowingly report on.

Will People Provide Truthful Answers?

People or firms may not be willing to provide information, even if they know it. In surveys of employers, we might like to know how many of the firms cheat on their taxes or employ illegal immigrants, but it is unlikely that we will get complete and truthful answers to questions such as these. Similarly, respondents to health surveys are often unwilling to report using drugs or having multiple sexual partners. In most social surveys, it is typical that a fairly large percentage of respondents refuse to provide information on their income.

But often, the situation is not so clear-cut. The information may indeed exist elsewhere, but still it can be gathered in a more timely and consistent way with a survey. People may not know exactly what they eat, but they can still report on their dietary intake in a general way and in broad food categories. If questions are worded carefully and confidentiality is ensured, respondents may even admit to some degree of illegal or socially undesirable behavior.

Because surveys involve time, effort, and expense—and because they are a burden on respondents—the decision to conduct a survey should be made carefully.

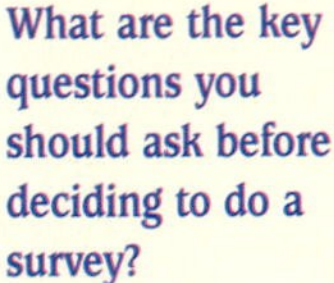

QUESTION

What are the key questions you should ask before deciding to do a survey?

Steps in the Survey Research Process

Before considering the specific methods or approaches to conducting surveys, it is helpful to get a general overview of the survey research process. Typically, a survey involves all or most of the following steps. (For a more in-depth overview of these steps, see Fowler, 2008.)

Identify the Population and Sampling Strategy

The first task is to be clear about whom to survey—the *population*. This is often not as straightforward as it might appear, as Chapter 5, on sampling, pointed out. Careful thought must be given to the geographical or organizational scope of the survey and who is, or is not, eligible to be included in the survey.

Also, thought must be given to who, within the household or organization, should be designated as the respondent. Should it be a randomly selected individual or the most knowledgeable person for the survey topic? When surveying firms or organizations, it is especially important to figure out which person within the organization to interview: the chief executive, the personnel director, a technology or other specialist, or someone else.

Finally, because the population is often large, this step in the process typically involves consideration of a statistical sampling strategy, using one or more of the sampling methods discussed in Chapter 5. Luckily, in some situations, simple sampling strategies, such as a census, work well.

Develop a Questionnaire

Developing a good questionnaire is essential, as much depends on having the right questions for analysis and asking them clearly and carefully. Frequently, it can take a fair amount of time and effort to work out the content of a questionnaire. And if multiple users of the survey data are involved, they all need some say in the process. Some exploratory qualitative research, such as *focus groups* with potential respondents, can be valuable at this stage to identify important issues to include in the survey. It is critical to start with the purpose of the survey before developing the questionnaire and to return regularly to that purpose. Later in the chapter, we provide advice and some useful guidelines for designing a questionnaire and writing good survey questions.

Pretest Questionnaire and Survey Procedures

Pretesting the questionnaire and survey procedures is a crucial, though often overlooked, step in the survey process. It gets overlooked typically because of time or cost constraints, and thus, it is important at the outset to anticipate pretesting in the schedule and budget for the survey. There are two main types of pretesting:

1. **Cognitive pretesting**, in which the wording and meaning of the questionnaire are probed carefully through a process of debriefing respondents right after completing the questionnaire or interview or by having them "talk aloud" as they complete the questionnaire. *Focus groups* (discussed in Chapter 3) can also be used to debrief a small test group of survey respondents. The point here is to uncover unclear or ambiguous wording, instructions, or formatting, as well as to suggest response categories or even questions that may be missing from the questionnaire. No matter how small or apparently simple a survey, it is crucial to have some cognitive pretesting to ensure that questions are not misunderstood.

2. **Field pretesting**, in which the complete survey procedures—the contact procedures, the finalized questionnaire or interview, the technology, and any follow-up procedures—are tested on a small sample of the population. The idea here is to implement a dress rehearsal for the full-scale survey. If any problems appear, for example, in the delivery of the questionnaire or in the technology used to gather survey responses (such as a computer-assisted script for telephone interviewing or a web-based questionnaire), they can be detected and corrected before moving ahead with the full survey.

Recruit and Train Interviewers

For those surveys that employ interviewers—to question people in person or on the telephone—the recruitment and training of these research workers is an important consideration. Interviewers need to possess certain personal qualities such as friendliness and trustworthiness and also the ability to appreciate and follow often strict survey procedures. But careful and thorough training of interviewers in proper survey interviewing techniques is also very important. Even when you have just a few interviewers—or you are the only interviewer—it is still critical to learn proper interviewing techniques and to rehearse the procedures involved in fielding your survey.

Such training typically involves at least three components. First, interviewers need training on general survey interviewing ethics and in interviewing techniques such as how to read questions consistently as written, how to avoid leading respondents or anticipating their answers, and how to probe for an answer in a neutral way. Second, interviewers must learn the specific questionnaire and the procedures for the particular survey, including any special instructions or vocabulary. And third, interviewers need to practice interviewing, both in mock interview situations and in live interviewing, ideally with oversight and feedback from supervisors. Thorough interviewer training is critical to the overall quality of the survey.

Collect Data

After pretesting and interviewer training, large-scale data collection can begin in earnest. At this step, much depends on the particular survey method, which could involve intercept interviewing, household visits, telephone calling, mailing questionnaires, or e-mailing the survey invitation—all methods we will discuss shortly. The collection of data should be monitored carefully, with frequent checking of response rates and other indicators of how the survey is working in the field. Monitoring of interviewers should be ongoing, with attention to interviewing practices that need improvement or correcting.

It is not uncommon that midcourse adjustments need to be made in the original study design, such as adding more addresses or phone numbers to the sample or even fixing mistakes in the questionnaire that were not noticed in the pretest. Follow-up efforts—such as making extra calls to nonresponders, sending additional mailings or e-mail notices, or revisiting households or firms—are an important part of good data collection, as these efforts help boost the response rate.

Enter and Prepare Data for Analysis

If the questionnaire is computerized, the responses usually get entered and written immediately to an electronic database. But surveys using any kind of paper form require either a process of manual key entry of the responses or the use of an optical scanner that recognizes the answer choices written on the paper questionnaires. Data entry often involves verification, for example, by double key entry, to reduce the chance of keypunch errors.

Regardless of how the data reach the electronic database, the format and structure of the database must be checked to make sure that there are no errors, for example, in the alignment or definition of fields or columns in the database. Typically, the database is labeled and formatted for use by statistical software. It is a good practice to prepare a memorandum describing the data, including how and when the data were collected and the layout of the data file for both current and future users of the survey data. Don't skip this last step, even if you are doing just a small survey on your own: Returning to the data after a few months, or even weeks, you may find it difficult to remember definitions, procedures, and conventions. And someone else may want or need to use your data at a later point.

Analyze Data and Present Findings

The final step in the process is the statistical analysis of the survey data and preparation of a report or other presentation of the findings. Chapters 8 through 10 describe the statistical analysis of data, and Chapter 17 discusses the presentation of research results.

Having some sense of when to consider a survey and the basic steps in the process, we turn next to the actual modes of survey data collection. We focus on the survey methods that are most widely used in social and policy research today. But know that the creativity of good survey researchers—and the ever-expanding possibilities of new technology—can result in variations on these methods and even the innovation of new ones. And sometimes, the best approach for a given situation is to combine methods—as in so-called *mixed-mode surveys*—in an effort to contact people and encourage their participation.

QUESTION

What are the key steps involved in the process of designing and conducting a survey?

Modes of Survey Data Collection

Surveys can be done through *interviews* or through the distribution of *self-administered* questionnaires, and they can be done of individuals, households, or organizations. In this section, we will describe some of the various approaches to survey research—with a focus on both the methodological and practical strengths and weaknesses of different modes of survey data collection. The term **survey mode** refers to the method or *modality* used to administer the questionnaire and collect the survey data. Understanding these modes will not only help you decide which one to use for your own survey, but will also give you a more informed perspective on the use of secondary survey data (discussed in Chapter 6) collected using different modes.

Intercept Interview Surveys

One of the simplest modes of survey research is to stop people in public places, *intercept* them, and ask questions. Market researchers often do this in shopping malls, but **intercept interview surveys** have application to social and policy research as well. For example, administrators of parks, museums, and transportation systems often use

Intercept interview surveys capture people's views on the spot.

Source: © iStockphoto.com/wdstock.

intercept interview surveys to gather information from users or customers.

Perhaps the most well-known example of an intercept interview survey is the *exit polling* done in the United States and other countries. In exit polling, and in other forms of intercept surveys, respondents are usually selected randomly using *systematic sampling*—as described in Chapter 5. This helps guard against the bias that can arise when interviewers choose respondents based on subjective factors, such as how comfortable they feel approaching the person.

The advantages of intercept interview surveys include the ability to survey people on the spot as they visit facilities, vote, or otherwise gather in public places—indeed, it is often the only practical way to survey populations in such situations. Intercept surveys can also be fairly quick to implement. But intercept interview surveys are not good for lengthy, more detailed questionnaires—because people stopped on the spot often have limited time and patience. Interviewers can be difficult to supervise, because they must work alone or in pairs in the field, so it can be hard to monitor their work.

Household Interview Surveys

Some of the earliest and most established surveys involve interviews conducted by visiting people in their homes—**household interview surveys**. For example, in the United States, the American National Election Studies, the General Social Survey, the American Housing Survey, the National Crime Victimization Survey, the National Health Interview Survey, and a number of other established government and social surveys rely on household interviews. In Europe, the standard Eurobarometer and European Social Survey, as well as the European Union Labour Force Survey, use household interviews. Most household interview surveys are based on multistage sampling, as described in Chapter 5.

QUESTION

What are the advantages and limitations of household interview surveys? Can you think of a population or setting for which this mode would be especially useful?

In the 1940s and 1950s, when some of these surveys began, it was necessary to visit households in person because the telephone was still new and did not reach all households, especially in rural areas (and many more people lived in rural areas back then). Household interview surveys are still often the only option in less developed countries. But household interviewing also is done when the questionnaire is complex (as in the case of the National Crime Victimization Survey), when visual aids are needed (as in the case of the General Social Survey), or when interviewer observations must be made (as in the case of the American Housing Survey). Some surveys, such as the National Health and Nutrition Examination Survey, even involve medical examinations, which obviously can be done only in person.

In recent years, household interviewing has been enhanced by the use of mobile computers, tablets, or other electronic devices, referred to as **computer-assisted personal interviewing** (**CAPI**). CAPI provides several advantages. First, complex questionnaires can be navigated more easily. For example, questions about children in the household can be skipped automatically for respondents who report having no children. And of course, the data get immediately entered in electronic form. In addition, the device can be used to present images, including video and sound, if needed. Also, for confidential topics, the device can be turned toward respondents so that they can read or listen to questions without being observed by the interviewer. This added confidentiality from **computer-assisted self-interviewing** (**CASI**) has been shown to be important in studies in which the survey asks about sensitive topics such as sexual behavior or drug use (Turner et al., 1998).

The household interview survey is often considered to be a gold standard of sorts, as it typically involves rigorous sampling and high response rates. It also helps that some of the most established, reputable surveys use this method. But there are some disadvantages, as well. Household interviews are time-consuming and very expensive to complete. For logistical reasons, the sampling must be clustered, which complicates the statistical analysis and leads to less precision (larger standard errors), as discussed in Chapter 5. Interviews generally cannot be monitored, and thus, there is the risk that some interviewers could make up or falsify interviews (often under pressure to produce completed interviews and achieve high response rates).

Also, the physical presence of the interviewer in the respondent's home can lead people to provide more face-saving or socially acceptable answers, known as **social desirability bias**, than they would if answering questions in private on a paper form or computer. In addition, how people answer questions can be influenced by the gender, ethnicity, age, and other characteristics of the interviewer—a problem referred to as **interviewer effects**.

QUESTION

What are the advantages and limitations of intercept interview surveys? Can you think of a population or setting for which this mode would be especially useful?

Telephone Interview Surveys

Telephone interview surveys today are much more common than in-person household interviews, in large part because they are faster and much less expensive. Most telephone surveys use random digit dialing (RDD), as described in Chapter 5, to select a random sample of households to call, although lists can be used for more specialized populations (such as members of an organization). Many telephone surveys these days use **computer-assisted telephone interviewing** (**CATI**) software that guides the interviewer in asking questions and allows for direct entry of the responses into an electronic database. The use of CATI also facilitates monitoring of interviewers and, importantly, the management of the RDD sample so that numbers can be tried carefully over various times of the day and week and so that callbacks can be scheduled. These days, a well-done telephone survey involves at least 6 to 10 attempts to call each number—some telephone surveys use as many as 15 attempts or more—spread out over a week or longer.

A great many surveys are done by telephone, including the Gallup polls, the Pew polls, the major network and newspaper polls, and most other public opinion polls that you see reported in the media. The University of Michigan's widely watched Consumer Sentiment Index is gathered from telephone interviews, as are many consumer product and marketing studies. Various important government surveys also get done by telephone, including large parts of the Current Population Survey (though initial surveys are still completed by in-person household interviews). The Behavioral Risk Factor Surveillance System (BRFSS), organized by the Centers for Disease Control and Prevention (CDC) and carried out by all 50 state health departments in the United States, is one of the world's largest systems of telephone surveys, with more than 350,000 people interviewed each year.

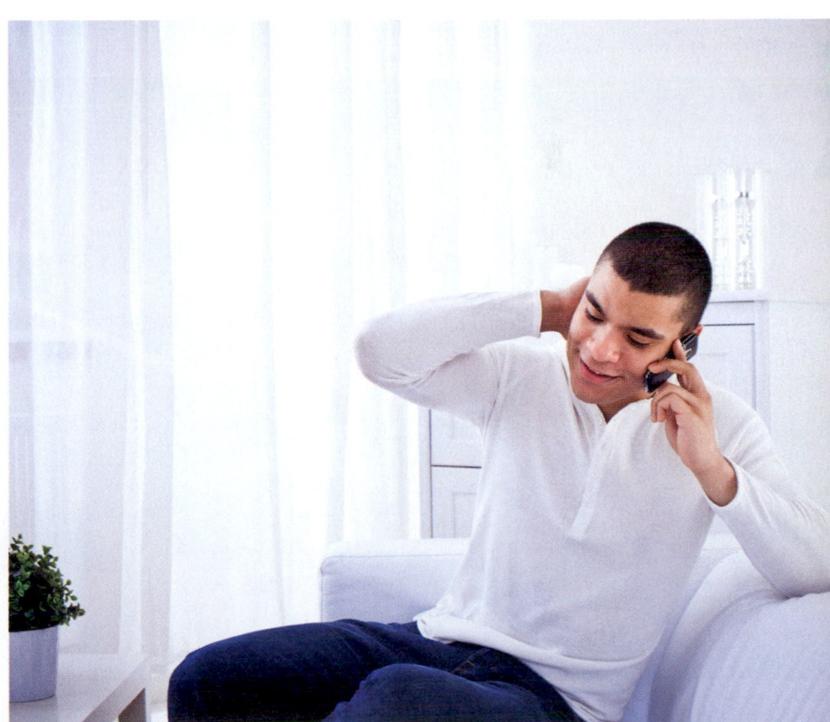

Telephone interview surveys are widely used, but response rates are declining.

Source: © iStockphoto.com/ Izabela Habur.

The advantages of telephone surveys lie in their relatively low cost (compared with household surveys) and the speed of data collection—indeed, some telephone polls can be completed in a matter of only a few days. But it has been getting much harder to reach people by telephone as more and more households screen calls or refuse to cooperate (out of fatigue from telemarketers, fund-raisers, and political calls). Moreover, increasingly, households do not even have a landline telephone anymore, relying on their cell phones or the Internet instead. Due to the growing share of households without landlines, and the coverage bias that can result, more telephone surveys are using cell phones, occasionally as the sole mode but more often as part of a dual landline–cell phone approach.

For all these reasons, the response rate to telephone surveys has been deteriorating rapidly. Results from the BRFSS—one of the most carefully conducted and rigorous systems of telephone surveying in the United States—show a decline in response rate from 63% in 1996 to 50% in 2011 (CDC, 2013a). The respected Pew Research Center for the People and the Press (2012a), which uses state-of-the-art telephone methods and is one of the few polling organizations to honestly reveal its response rates, has seen its average rate fall from 36% in 1997 to only 9% in 2012. Most other telephone surveys, often using much less rigorous methods than the BRFSS and Pew, have even lower response rates.

QUESTION

What are the advantages and limitations of telephone surveys? Can you think of a population or setting for which this mode would be especially useful?

Automated Telephone Surveys

A particularly low-cost form of telephone surveys makes use of automated interviewing, or interactive voice response (IVR) technology, which involves a recorded or automated voice instead of a live interviewer and then captures responses by touch tones or voice recognition software. This mode often suffers from very low response rates, however, as it is much easier to hang up on a machine than a live person. Also, the lack of a live interviewer makes it more difficult to guide respondents in understanding the questions or navigating skip patterns. Automated telephone interviewing, or robocalling, is also associated with so-called push polls, a kind of political advertising that pretends to collect polling data but in reality aims to change people's political views by asking leading questions. However, automated telephone surveys can be useful for short, simple questionnaires in which you need quick feedback on a timely issue.

Many surveys rely on self-administered questionnaires.
Source: © iStockphoto.com/jcamilobernal.

Mail Self-Administered Surveys

Another widely useful mode of survey research is the **mail self-administered survey**. The method is a mainstay of surveys by government statistical agencies—including the American Community Survey and the decennial U.S. Census—and involves mailing forms to respondents along with instructions to complete and return the forms. Because these forms are *self-administered,* careful attention must be paid to the clarity of the questionnaire layout and instructions. It is also very important to present a clear and compelling cover letter or other request to respondents, as much depends on the respondents' understanding of and feelings toward the survey request.

Based on his work with the U.S. Census Bureau and other survey sponsors, Don Dillman (2007) has pioneered an approach to mail surveys known as the **tailored design method** (formerly the *total design method*), or TDM. The TDM emphasizes the importance of all components of the mail survey, from the initial contacting materials, to the survey layout and design, to the timing and tone of the follow-up requests. The method emphasizes multiple contacts using different forms and modes of communication. Although Dillman stresses the need to tailor the approach to each situation, the standard TDM procedure involves the following contacts:

- A brief, prenotice letter telling the respondent to expect the survey. This is sent several days prior to the questionnaire.
- A questionnaire with a cover letter explaining the purpose and sponsorship of the survey.
- A thank-you (reminder) postcard, thanking the participant for responding (or encouraging the participant to take the time to respond, if he or she hasn't done so already). This is sent about a week after the questionnaire.
- A replacement questionnaire with a second cover letter indicating that the respondent's questionnaire has yet to be received. This is sent 2 to 4 weeks after the initial questionnaire.
- A final contact, such as a telephone call (if possible) or a special delivery mailing, emphasizing the importance of responding. This is sent about a week after the last contact.

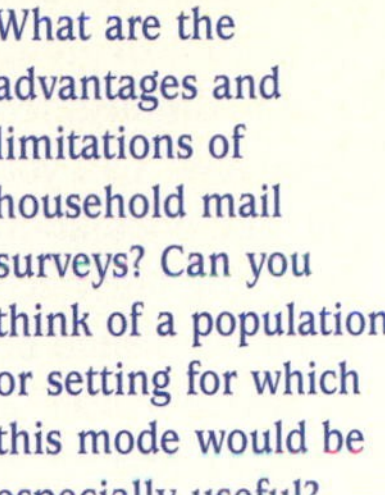

QUESTION

What are the advantages and limitations of household mail surveys? Can you think of a population or setting for which this mode would be especially useful?

As you can see, a well-done mail survey requires work and careful planning and is not a one-shot effort. The aim is to achieve an adequate response rate so that the possibility of nonresponse bias is minimized, as Chapter 5, on sampling, discusses. Follow-up mailings are particularly important.

Well-done mail surveys are not cheap, but they certainly cost much less than household interview surveys and often cost less than telephone surveys. In addition, mail surveys have the advantage of reaching households that do not have telephones or that rely only on cell phones. And mail surveys have the advantage of being more easily targeted and tied to small geographic areas such as cities or even neighborhoods. This is because in the United States and in most other countries, the postal service maintains very complete records of all residential addresses that can serve as a sampling frame for mail surveys, and these address records contain detailed postal codes that can be used to target cities or neighborhoods.

But there are limitations to mail surveys as well. They require basic literacy, so they may not be suited to countries or communities in which literacy levels are generally low. It can be difficult to control who in a household or organization gets the survey and fills it out. Also, it can be difficult to accommodate multiple languages in a mail survey, as either the questionnaire or the cover letter needs to be sent initially in multiple languages, or instructions need to be provided for how to obtain a questionnaire in another language (creating an extra hurdle for those respondents seeking to complete the questionnaire in another language). Also, self-administered mail questionnaires are not so good for complex questionnaires with lots of skipping and branching—as people tend to get confused and make mistakes or leave questions blank. Indeed, unanswered or mistakenly answered questions (such as checking multiple responses to a question when only one response is allowed) are much more common on self-administered mail surveys because there is no technological check on the logic of answers, as there is with a computer-assisted telephone

Data can be gathered by group self-administered surveys.

Source: © iStockphoto.com/skynesher.

interview or web-based questionnaire. Finally, the data from a mail survey must be entered by hand or by scanning, an imperfect process that can produce data-entry errors if people do not mark their answers clearly.

Group Self-Administered Surveys

QUESTION

What are the advantages and limitations of group self-administered surveys? Can you think of a population or setting for which this mode would be especially useful?

Self-administered questionnaires can be distributed in group settings, for example, in schools, workplaces, or community centers—a **group self-administered survey**. For such populations, this approach is more practical and cost-effective than mailing individual questionnaires, and it provides the added advantage of having a research worker on hand to provide instructions or assistance to respondents as they complete the questionnaire. Because the survey is administered to groups, the sampling involved is often some form of multistage cluster sampling. However, for some survey populations, such as organization members, a census may work well.

One of the best-known examples of a group self-administered survey is the CDC-sponsored Youth Risk Behavior Surveillance System (YRBSS), the source of U.S. national statistics on school violence, tobacco use, drug and alcohol use, sexual behaviors, diet, physical exercise, and other issues vital to the health of the nation's youth. Multistage cluster sampling is employed to pick schools and, within schools, classrooms to be surveyed (the clusters). The survey is then administered to students in their classrooms (or another meeting room) by research workers who provide instructions, distribute questionnaires, give assistance, and collect and safeguard completed questionnaires. Because the YRBSS involves minors and asks about sensitive topics, the procedures for obtaining parental permission, avoiding harm or embarrassment, and protecting confidentiality are especially important.

Group administration has clear advantages, since many completed questionnaires can be gathered by a few research workers in a relatively short period of time. And as mentioned, the live presence of these workers to guide and assist respondents is an advantage. However, it can be difficult to arrange to interrupt a school or another organization during its workday, particularly if the survey does not directly serve or benefit the organization's administrators. In group settings, care must be taken to prevent respondents from observing or influencing each other's responses. And because of the clustering often used in group-administered surveys, the precision of survey estimates is less (the standard errors are greater) than they would be if respondents were sampled individually.

Web surveys have become important and widely used.
Source: © iStockphoto.com/StockLib.

Web or Internet Surveys

In a relatively short time, **web surveys** (also referred to as **Internet surveys** or **online surveys**) have emerged as one of the most important and widely useful alternatives to the more traditional modes of survey data collection discussed thus far. With now widespread access to e-mail and the Internet for both work and home life, it has become possible to contact and solicit responses from many populations using e-mail invitations linked to a web-based questionnaire or to make more direct solicitations on websites or through social media. Indeed, a whole new industry has sprouted up around the possibilities of web-based data collection, with companies offering expert services in online research or do-it-yourself software that allows users to design and implement a web survey from any computer with Internet access.

Web surveys typically work best for situations in which there is an established e-mail list of the population, such as a membership list for a volunteer group, and the group is accustomed to getting and responding to e-mail communications. If the list is large, simple random or systematic sampling may be used—but the low cost of web surveys often means that it is feasible to attempt a complete census.

In an attempt to research a more general cross section of the population, online research companies and organizations have developed **Internet access panels**—large e-mail lists of respondents who opt in (sign up) to participate in online surveys on various topics, as discussed in Chapter 5. Government regulation of spam (unsolicited e-mail) requires that researchers obtain permission in advance, or use established lists with the permission of the list owner, before sending bulk e-mail invitations to a survey. Internet access panels can also be constructed initially from telephone or postal sampling frames so that probability sampling can be used to gather the e-mail addresses.

Typically, in a web survey, an e-mail invitation explaining the survey is sent to respondents, with an embedded link (a hyperlink) in the message that they can click on to go to the web-based questionnaire. The questionnaire itself may be hosted on the survey researcher's own server or, more likely, on the server of a company that specializes in providing web survey hosting and software (see Box 7.1). The respondents then complete the questionnaire, and the data are immediately written and stored in a database on the server. Most web-based software providers allow for real-time viewing and analysis of responses online, or the data can be downloaded for analysis using regular statistical software.

Web surveys can also work to capture feedback directly from regular visitors to a website, or increasingly through social media and Internet search engines. Surveys can be embedded into Facebook, for example, allowing researchers to recruit and collect responses from a given social network. Google has a survey tool that can recruit a general population, or target people with specific profiles or interests, while they are browsing the web (but this tool allows for asking only one question at a time).

As people increasingly access the Internet through mobile devices, such as tablet computers and smartphones, it is increasingly important that web surveys work on mobile devices as well as computers. Many software providers now offer options that allow for mobile web surveys.

BOX 7.1
Web Survey Software

There has been an explosion of web survey software programs, and they are increasingly easy to use. Companies such as SurveyMonkey, SurveyGizmo, SoGoSurvey, Qualtrics, QuestionPro, and LimeService (an open source program), as well as many others, generally host and maintain the software on their servers so that the researcher only needs access to the Internet to log in, create, send, and analyze a web survey online. The data can also be downloaded for off-line analysis using standard statistical software. This is a rapidly developing and changing market, with intense competition, so these web survey software programs keep getting better, easier, and less expensive to use. Many offer free accounts for university students.

There are many advantages to web surveys—principally, low cost and high speed. In fact, the cost of data collection (assuming access to a list of potential respondents) is often just pennies per completed questionnaire. Thousands of survey invitations can be sent at the same time, and often, respondents reply within a few days if not a few hours of receiving the e-mail or web-based solicitation. In addition, web surveys can incorporate unique elements—such as intricate skipping and branching patterns, randomization of questions, colorful graphics, photos, and multimedia elements—not possible in traditional (paper) self-administered questionnaires. Also, because the responses get written and stored directly in an online database, the cost and complication of manual or mechanical key entry of the data can be avoided entirely.

However, there are some important limitations to web surveys. The proliferation of e-mail marketing, spam, and e-mail fraud worldwide has made many people both weary and wary of bulk e-mail messages, particularly messages with embedded links asking people to "click here." Indeed, many people these days simply refuse to respond to such e-mails unless they are from a sender who is known and trusted. E-mail invitations can also appear cheap (which indeed they are), compared with a standard letter or personal phone call, so respondents feel less obligation to consider a survey request sent by e-mail. And even the Internet access panels with many thousands of potential opt-in respondents still suffer from panel fatigue or attrition and struggle with problems of false or duplicate responding (especially when financial incentives for participation are involved). Technological issues related to different operating systems, Internet connections, web browsers, or mobile devices can prevent people from completing web-based questionnaires.

Establishment (Business or Organization) Surveys

QUESTION

What are the advantages and limitations of web surveys? Can you think of a population or setting for which this mode would be especially useful?

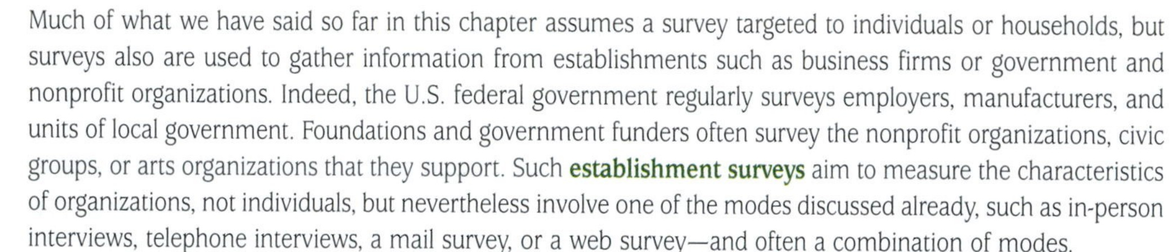

Much of what we have said so far in this chapter assumes a survey targeted to individuals or households, but surveys also are used to gather information from establishments such as business firms or government and nonprofit organizations. Indeed, the U.S. federal government regularly surveys employers, manufacturers, and units of local government. Foundations and government funders often survey the nonprofit organizations, civic groups, or arts organizations that they support. Such **establishment surveys** aim to measure the characteristics of organizations, not individuals, but nevertheless involve one of the modes discussed already, such as in-person interviews, telephone interviews, a mail survey, or a web survey—and often a combination of modes.

Surveying firms or organizations presents distinct challenges that make such surveys different from those directed at individuals or households. Perhaps the biggest difference is in the size and complexity of "the respondent," which in some cases could be an organization with thousands of employees. Key decisions must be made about whom to contact within the organization and where to direct the survey. Although most organizations have a chief executive or president, this person may not always be the appropriate or most knowledgeable respondent for the given topic of the survey. Yet it may be difficult, if not impossible, to identify the appropriate respondent from within various organizations of widely ranging sizes, structures, and job titles. Therefore, it is not uncommon for the survey still to be sent to the chief executive or president—but with instructions to designate the most knowledgeable respondent within the organization to complete the questionnaire.

But getting through to a chief executive requires communicating and dealing with various gatekeepers, which can take a great deal of time and effort. Special contact procedures, especially skillful and mature interviewers, and sustained follow-up are often needed to get through to an organization, ensure that the questionnaire reaches the right hands, and obtain a completed response. Because organizations vary so much, it is often helpful to allow for various modes of responding—by telephone interview, paper form, fax, and so on. The U.S. federal government uses this kind of mixed-mode approach for its surveys of employers and manufacturers.

Panel or Longitudinal Surveys

Another unique form of survey research is **panel surveys**, in which the same respondents are tracked and repeatedly surveyed over time, sometimes over many years. Well-known examples of panel surveys include the Panel Study of Income Dynamics (PSID), the National Education Longitudinal Study (NELS), the Medical Expenditure Panel Survey (MEPS), the Longitudinal Studies of Aging (LSOA), and the British Household Panel Survey (BHPS). The NELS, for example, started with a sample of U.S. eighth graders in 1988 and has surveyed these same individuals every 2 years since that time (the NELS panelists are now well into adulthood). Typically, panel surveys involve a combination of in-person interviews and telephone interviews or, sometimes, self-administered questionnaires.

But the real challenge in a panel survey is keeping regular track of respondents over time, particularly as they move, form or dissolve households, or suffer other disruptions in their lives. To accomplish such tracking, researchers typically ask for various point-of-contact information as part of the baseline survey (e.g., close friends or relatives), maintain communications even when survey data are not being collected, and provide financial and symbolic incentives for ongoing participation. But the problem of *panel attrition* is inevitable, as people drop out of the study for various reasons over time. For example, of the more than 18,192 individuals who completed interviews as part of the 1968 baseline to the PSID, only 5,282 were alive and available to be interviewed in 2001—despite the fact that the PSID achieved consistently high response rates, well over 90%, in any one survey year (McGonagle & Schoeni, 2006).

Choosing or Mixing Modes

For a particular survey, the advantages and limitations of one mode of survey data collection must be weighed against those of another. We have discussed many of these advantages and limitations above. For convenience, Table 7.1 attempts to summarize the various survey modes in terms of key characteristics: cost, timeliness, response rate, interviewer effects, the length and complexity of the questions that can be asked of respondents, and the potential for visuals or multimedia. But this is just a rough guide, as much depends on the particular purpose, context, and population for the survey.

> **QUESTION**
>
> **What are some of the unique challenges of establishment surveys and panel surveys?**

In some cases, the best approach can be a **mixed-mode survey** in which more than one mode of survey data collection is used. This approach is especially useful for surveying diverse populations that cannot be represented or contacted with just one mode. For example, a social services organization that serves both youth and the elderly might want to survey the youth through e-mail or social media and the elderly using a mail or telephone survey. Mixing modes brings several complications and difficulties, however. The mode influences responses, so data collected by different modes are not always equivalent, even if the questions are identical, complicating the interpretation of results. In addition, there may be no single sampling frame that works for both modes, making it difficult to sample and ensure representativeness.

Having discussed the various approaches to survey data collection, we turn next to the important task of crafting a questionnaire.

Table 7.1 Comparison of Survey Modes

Survey Mode	Cost	Timeliness	Response Rate	Interviewer Effects	Potential Survey Length	Potential Complexity of Questions	Potential for Visuals or Multimedia
Intercept interview	Medium	Medium	High	High	Short	Low	Low
Household interview	High	Slow	High	High	Long	High	High
Telephone interview	Medium	Fast	Low to medium	Medium	Medium	Medium	Low
Mail self-administered survey	Low	Medium	Low to medium	None	Medium	Low	Low
Group self-administered survey	Medium	Medium	High	Low	Medium	Low	Low
Web survey	Very low	Fast	Low	None	Medium	High	High

Crafting a Questionnaire

Researchers and also practitioners often get called on to do surveys—of community residents, clients or customers, managers, employees, students, and other populations. And although writing survey questions might seem at first glance to be a simple task, it can prove difficult to do well. This section provides some general advice on crafting your own questionnaire. For more detailed guidance, you might wish to consult specialized books by Bradburn, Sudman, and Wansink (2004), Converse and Presser (1986), Dillman (2007), or Fowler (1995).

Start With Survey Purpose and Constructs

It is best to begin not by writing questions but by focusing on the purpose of the survey. Think carefully about how the information will be used. Will different answers to various questions guide policy or practice? Thinking through the kinds of actions that follow from results can be useful in clarifying what information the survey should provide. It can help to write out a purpose statement for the survey, both to clarify your own thinking and perhaps to share with other potential users of the data.

You should also carefully define the constructs to be measured by the survey. What are you seeking to capture? What are the dimensions of the constructs? These kinds of questions should lead you to develop an outline of survey items or topics, with accompanying conceptual definitions. Such an outline is a useful way to solicit input from managers, stakeholders, or others involved in the survey.

If You Could Ask Only One or Two Questions . . .

Sometimes it helps to start by imagining that you could ask your respondents only one or two questions. What one or two questions would they be? What do you most need to know from your survey? This exercise is helpful because it is all too easy to get so immersed in the job of drafting a detailed questionnaire that you lose track of—and even forget to include—the most important questions that initially motivated your survey.

Prepare Mock Tables and Charts of Survey Results

Consider preparing some mock-ups of the final tables and charts you expect to produce or present from your survey. Although starting with the questionnaire seems like a natural first step, it is often better to work backward—to begin with the results you expect to report. In the end, your audience or users of the survey will look at the results—not the questionnaire. This way, you can then check to see if the questionnaire you design actually will produce the data you'll need to fill in your tables or charts.

Look for Prior Surveys on Your Topic

Good questionnaires are often as much the product of borrowing from other surveys as writing from scratch. It is common and considered good practice in survey research to use the exact wording of questions from prior surveys. This is referred to as *replicating* questions or using *standardized* questions. Prior surveys by government agencies and established survey research organizations typically contain questions that have been carefully developed, tested, and proven over time. (In the report about the survey and its results, citations should always be made to the original source(s) of the question wording.) In addition, replicating questions from prior surveys can allow you to compare or benchmark your results, often against national or even international norms. So you should certainly review and consider using questions on your topic that come from the major government or social surveys. For sensitive topics, such as ethnicity, income, or political affiliations, standardized questions can be especially valuable. Of course, if the question you wish to pose has not been previously developed and tested, this option is not available.

Hook Respondents With Your First Few Questions

It is worth mentioning the importance of the first few questions on your questionnaire—as they can make a critical difference to the response rate. If your respondents find the first few questions relevant, interesting, and easy to answer, chances are that they will complete the entire questionnaire. If not, they are likely to stop answering it. To illustrate, consider the two questionnaires shown in Box 7.2.

Questionnaire A in Box 7.2 opens with a detailed household income question that is not directly related to the announced topic of community safety. It is a personal question and difficult to answer so precisely (indeed, income should often be asked in broad categories to avoid this problem). Demographics, particularly personal questions like income, should typically be placed at the end of the questionnaire.

The income question in Questionnaire A is then followed by a ranking question that, although it includes community safety, is a complex cognitive task to complete (try doing it yourself, and you'll see). Ranking questions are notoriously difficult for respondents and should be avoided unless absolutely necessary. (Asking respondents instead to *rate* each item separately—say on a scale of 1 to 10—often works much better for these kinds of questions. Later, you can rank the *items* according to their means across all respondents.) With opening questions such as these, Questionnaire A is sure to turn off many would-be respondents.

In contrast, Questionnaire B begins with two relatively simple rating questions that directly relate to the announced topic of the survey. They are both easy and fairly interesting to answer, getting the respondent quickly into the task of completing the questionnaire. If more difficult or personal questions must be asked, these should be put toward the end of the questionnaire. Once respondents have committed to answering initial questions, they are much more likely to answer difficult or sensitive questions later in the questionnaire.

BOX 7.2
Comparing Opening Questions

Questionnaire A

This important survey is about *crime and safety in your community.* Your answers are confidential and will be used only for statistical purposes to better serve you and your neighbors. Thank you in advance for your participation.

1. About how much income does your household receive annually from all sources? (Please include all income earners in your household, as well as all sources of income—including wages, pensions, and investments.)

   $___ ___ ___ , ___ ___ ___ .00

2. Please rank the following priorities for local government, as you see things. (Put a 1 by your first priority, a 2 by your second priority, and so on, until you have numbered all items.)

   ___ Balance the local budget

   ___ Improve education

(Continued)

(Continued)

___ Improve community safety
___ Reduce traffic congestion
___ Promote jobs and economic development
___ Protect the natural environment
___ Other (specify): ______________________

Questionnaire B

This important survey is about *crime and safety in your community.* Your answers are confidential and will be used only for statistical purposes to better serve you and your neighbors. Thank you in advance for your participation.

1. How safe do you feel walking alone at night in the neighborhood where you live?
   a. Very safe
   b. Somewhat safe
   c. Somewhat unsafe
   d. Very unsafe
2. In the last year (12 months), would you say that the safety of your neighborhood has . . .
   a. Gotten better
   b. Gotten worse
   c. Remained about the same

Closed-Ended Versus Open-Ended Questions

Closed-ended questions provide categories for respondents to choose or check, such as those in Questionnaire B in Box 7.2. In contrast, **open-ended questions** ask respondents to answer in their own words. Novice survey designers often make the mistake of using too many—sometimes way too many—open-ended questions. Consider the questionnaire shown in Box 7.3.

The questionnaire in Box 7.3 asks legitimate questions, and it would be interesting to find out how people answer in their own words. But as respondents, we might view this questionnaire as a bit of a chore, like an essay exam, requiring three minicompositions. Imagine how daunting this questionnaire would begin to seem if it continued on with 10, 15, or 20 such questions—it would become nearly impossible to complete in a reasonable amount of time (without resorting to banal, one-word answers).

Analyzing open-ended questions—reading and summarizing perhaps hundreds or even thousands of written responses—takes a great deal of time and effort. Responses to open-ended survey questions are qualitative data, and full analysis is as time-consuming as any other analysis of qualitative data. Thus, the decision to ask open-ended questions should be made carefully and knowingly. Too often, open-ended questions get asked in surveys only to have the answers essentially discarded later because the researcher did not anticipate the time required to read and summarize them.

BOX 7.3 Questionnaire Composed of Open-Ended Questions

This important survey is about *crime and safety in your community.* Your answers are confidential and will be used only for statistical purposes to better serve you and your neighbors. Thank you in advance for your participation.

1. *What are the most important priorities for local government, as you see things?*

   ____

   ____

   ____

2. *What community safety issues or problems do you see in your neighborhood?*

   ____

   ____

   ____

3. *What steps would you like local government to take in order to help improve the safety of your neighborhood?*

   ____

   ____

Some Advice on Question Wording

Wording questions well is as much an art as a science, but experienced survey researchers have established some helpful principles. The following list of 19 principles for writing survey questions is provided by Dillman (2007), based on his substantial experience as well as careful empirical study of how people understand and respond to survey questions:

- Choose simple over specialized words (avoid social science or policy jargon).

  For example, do not ask, "Do you favor, or oppose, an increase in the excise on tobacco consumption?"

  Rather, ask, "Do you favor, or oppose, an increase in taxes on cigarettes?"

- Use as few words as possible to pose the question.

  Don't ask, "About how much did you pay last month for the electricity that you used in your household for things such as lights, appliances, and so on?"

  Rather, it is better to ask, "About how much was your electric bill last month?"

- Use complete sentences to ask questions.

  For example, don't ask simply, "Employed?" as a question.

  Instead, ask, "Are you currently employed, or not?"

- Avoid vague quantifiers when more precise estimates can be obtained.

  For example, don't ask, "Last week, did you use public transportation often, sometimes, rarely, or never?"

  Rather, it is more useful to ask, "Last week, did you use public transportation 5 or more days, 2 to 4 days, only 1 day, or not at all?"

- Avoid specificity that exceeds the respondent's potential for having an accurate, ready-made answer.

  For example, avoid asking, "Last week, exactly how many trips in total did you make using public transportation? If you used public transportation on one day to go to and from work, that would count as two trips."

  Compare this with the previous example, which asked about "days" instead of "trips" and gave ranges instead of asking for an exact count.

- Use equal numbers of positive and negative categories for scaled questions.

  For example, don't use *very satisfied/satisfied/somewhat satisfied/dissatisfied* as the categories.

  Rather, use a more symmetrical set of response categories such as *very satisfied/somewhat satisfied/somewhat dissatisfied/very dissatisfied.*

- Distinguish undecided from neutral response options by placement at the end of the scale.

  For example, in an agree–disagree question, present the response categories as *agree/disagree/unsure.*

  This is less confusing than *agree/unsure/disagree,* in which *unsure* could more easily be interpreted as a neutral response. To include an explicit neutral category, use *agree/neither agree nor disagree/disagree/unsure.*

- Avoid bias from unequal comparisons (make answer choices as neutral and as comparable as possible).

  For example, don't ask, "Are you concerned that the government will enact new antiterrorism laws that excessively restrict the average person's civil liberties, or are you not concerned about this problem?"

  Instead, make it a more equal comparison: "Which concerns you more right now: that the government will fail to enact strong antiterrorism laws, or that the government will enact new antiterrorism laws that excessively restrict the average person's civil liberties?" (Wording from a CBS News/*New York Times* poll, PollingReport.com, 2009).

- State both sides of attitude scales in the question stem.

  For example, don't write, "On a scale of 1 to 10, please indicate how satisfied you are with local public schools. (1 = *very dissatisfied* to 10 = *very satisfied*)."

  Rather, put it like this: "On a scale of 1 to 10, please indicate how satisfied, or dissatisfied, you are with local public schools. (1 = *very dissatisfied* to 10 = *very satisfied*)." It's a subtle difference, but it can matter to respondents.

- Eliminate or randomly rotate the order of "check all that apply" question formats to reduce primacy effects (the tendency to choose the first few categories listed).

  For example, a "check all that apply" question looks like this:
  Please indicate what you consider to be the top priorities for local government these days. (Check all that apply.)

  1. *Growing the local economy*
  2. *Improving public schools*
  3. *Reducing crime*

4. *Expanding public transportation options*
5. *Creating more parks and recreation opportunities*
6. *Reducing traffic congestion*
7. *Preserving the natural environment*
8. *Providing services for the elderly and disabled*
9. *Reducing racial or ethnic tensions in the community*

The first few categories will get more checks than the last few, simply because of their order in the list. This problem can be avoided, however, in web and telephone surveys that use software that allows randomization, or rotation, of categories (so that the order is not the same for each respondent).

- Develop response categories that are mutually exclusive.

  For example, when asking, "How often did you use public transportation last week?" don't use response categories such as *often, as much as possible, whenever the weather permitted,* or *just a few times.*

- Use cognitive design techniques to improve recall (such as priming respondents by asking for details about a past event or behavior).

  For example, you might ask, "During your most recent visit to your doctor, how satisfied were you with the amount of time your doctor spent with you?"

  But it might be helpful to first ask, "Was your most recent visit to your doctor for a regular checkup or for some other reason?" This reminds, or primes, the respondent to recall his or her most recent visit. Then ask, "During this visit, how satisfied were you with the amount of time your doctor spent with you?"

- Provide appropriate time referents (typically a short time period for recalling behavior—or ask for an estimation only).

  For example, you might be interested in asking, "Do you do any exercise, or not?" But it is very unclear what this means.

  Providing a time frame makes this question much more concrete: "In the last 7 days, did you do any exercise, or not?"

- Be sure that each question is technically accurate.

  For example, you might ask, "Do you own your home, are you renting, or something else?" But most home owners in the United States and other countries have a mortgage, so they do not really "own" their homes outright until they pay off their mortgage.

  It would be better to ask, "Do you own your home (with or without a mortgage), are you renting, or something else?"

- Choose question wordings that allow essential comparisons to be made with previously collected data.

  This refers to the point made earlier in this chapter about the value of using standardized questions from established government and social surveys. For example, if you are interested in measuring the amount of generalized social trust in a community, that is, how much people trust others, you could use a standard question from the General Social Survey: "Generally speaking, would you say that most people can be trusted or that you can't be too careful in dealing with people?"

- Avoid asking respondents to say "yes" to mean "no" (the problem of double negatives).

  For example, don't use this kind of awkward phrasing: "Do you support opposition to the proposed highway expansion, or not?"

  It is much clearer to ask, "Do you support, or oppose, the proposed highway expansion?"

- Avoid double-barreled questions (questions that actually contain two or more topics or elements about which respondents may have different or even contradictory opinions).

  Consider, for example, this question: "Do you agree, or disagree, that the city needs a new high school on the site where the old riverside mill now stands?" Someone may agree with the need for a new school but feel strongly that the old riverside mill should be preserved and not destroyed. For complex issues such as this, it is best to break the issue into parts and ask separate questions.

- Avoid asking respondents to make unnecessary calculations.

  For example, don't ask, "What percentage of your income each month do you spend on electricity?"

  Instead, ask the income question (annual income is usually easier for respondents), ask the electric bill question (usually a monthly bill), and then do the calculation yourself: (monthly electric bill × 12)/income.

- Ensure that response categories for ordinal categorical questions cover realistic and relevant ranges of values, and that they capture variation.

  For example, don't use an income question from a past survey with a range of incomes so outdated that almost all responses would fall into the top income category. If possible, look for current information on the range and distribution of the variable in your population.

Dillman (2007) provides a much more detailed discussion and additional examples of each of these principles.

Physical and Graphical Design

The physical and graphical design of a survey—both the overall layout and the details of formatting and presenting questions—can affect the overall propensity to respond and also the quality of individual answers. Focusing on self-administered mail and web surveys, Dillman (2007) provides extensive advice on the design elements that encourage more accurate and complete survey responses. These include the careful placement of instructions, the formatting of questions and response options, navigation aids (such as arrows), shading to visually distinguish sections, and other design considerations.

Some unique challenges come up in the graphical design of web surveys, as the questionnaire may appear differently to respondents using various devices and browsers. The web survey software you are using also imposes limitations on the look and feel of the survey. As with the wording of a questionnaire, it is also important to pretest and gather feedback on the physical and graphical design of a survey.

Put Yourself in Your Respondent's Shoes

In the design of a survey, the survey researcher's attitude vis-à-vis respondents sometimes reminds us of the driver and the pedestrian. When driving a car, we tend to view pedestrians as unaware, slow nuisances. But when we are on foot, we see drivers as reckless and arrogant. Well, the same is often true of researchers and respondents.

When asked to respond to a questionnaire, we all appreciate clear instructions, simple and straightforward questions, and short questionnaires. But when designing a survey, we frequently change our perspective—we become insensitive to respondents and unwilling to make compromises, and we demand detailed answers to overly long, often confusing questions. So when designing a survey, try to think like a respondent, *not* like a researcher. See the survey from the point of view of the real people you will be asking to complete it: Is it worth my time? Is it interesting? Is it clear and simple? Is it short?

Ethics of Survey Research

Survey research raises some unique and important ethical issues centered on contacting people, persuading them to participate, and handling potentially sensitive personal information gathered in surveys.

Informed Consent

Informed consent is a basic principle of research ethics—but it can be a challenge to implement in many survey situations. In most telephone surveys, for example, informing the respondent and obtaining his or her consent must occur in the opening minute or two of the interview. Typically, a statement is read introducing the general topic and sponsor of the survey, a statement of confidentiality is given, and the interview begins. The willingness of the respondent to begin the interview is considered then as a form of *tacit consent*. Similarly, in most online surveys, the respondent is told basic information about the survey in an e-mail, and his or her willingness to click through to the web-based questionnaire serves as tacit consent to participate. And mail surveys, as well, usually make use of tacit consent. In household interview surveys or group interview surveys, however, it is more customary to obtain a formal, written consent.

But much depends on the topic. If the questions are sensitive or involve potentially embarrassing or uncomfortable issues, then a more formal consent procedure may be required no matter what the survey mode.

Pushing for a High Response Rate

As discussed in this chapter, as well as in Chapter 5 on sampling, achieving a high response rate is critical to the quality of survey data. To obtain a high response rate, researchers make multiple contact attempts, call repeatedly, work to convince people who initially refused to participate, use multiple modes, and provide financial and other incentives. But in practice, these efforts to achieve a high response rate can turn into efforts to pressure or coerce people into responding. Respondents are sometimes even deceived by researchers regarding the length of the interview or questionnaire, out of a concern that telling them the truth up front will discourage their participation. Although high response rates are a good thing statistically, they do not justify pressuring or misleading respondents.

Overburdening Respondents

As a survey researcher, it is easy to fall into the habit of thinking that respondents should be asked to provide all the information that you might possibly need. The tendency, too often, is to add extra questions—just to be sure. But the burden should fall on the researcher to use discipline and restraint in the design of the survey, not on the respondents to make an extra effort. Moreover, overburdening respondents with excessive, redundant, or unnecessary questions not only harms them—by abusing their time and cooperation—but hurts the reputation of surveys in general and the response rate trends in society at large.

If a great deal of information is needed, or if physical measurements or lengthy tests must also be given, then the timing and format of data collection must accommodate respondents properly. For example, breaks and snacks may be used to reduce the burden on respondents, although, of course, the time burden will still be large.

Protecting Privacy and Confidentiality

In the design of surveys, identifying information or other potentially private information should be asked only if absolutely necessary. For many survey purposes, there is no need to know someone's full name and address, for example. **Anonymity** is the practice of ensuring that data acquired by the researcher do not contain information that could be used to identify respondents, such as names, addresses, telephone numbers, or e-mail or IP addresses.

If identifying information is necessary, such as to follow up with respondents or to link the survey to other data, people should be assured of **confidentiality**—meaning their identifying information is known only to the researchers and is not publicly associated with their responses. To help ensure confidentiality, the identifying information should be kept separately from the substantive answers to the questionnaire. This can be accomplished by the use of code numbers that link the contact information to the survey responses. It is often best to ask for age, income, level of education, and other personal information in broad categories rather than in detail.

When researchers ask about particularly sensitive information, such as illegal behavior, anonymity is a better choice than confidentiality (Sieber & Tolich, 2013, chap. 9). That is particularly so in cases where the law does not respect the confidentiality of data provided to researchers (Israel & Hay, 2006, chap. 7).

Some of the most interesting new uses of survey data relate to linking individual survey responses to contextual data on the surrounding neighborhood, nearby infrastructure, and the availability of amenities and public services. This is done by *geocoding,* or pinpointing the geographic location, of the surveyed households. But this creates additional privacy and confidentiality concerns, as knowing the precise street and block where a respondent lives is tantamount to knowing the respondent's identity.

Surveying Minors and Other Vulnerable Populations

Surveys of children and youth are important in social and policy research, but special procedures must be followed in conducting such surveys. For example, many institutional review boards or research ethics committees require parental consent, which must be obtained in writing in advance.

Extra safeguards apply to surveying other vulnerable populations, such as prisoners, people with cognitive impairments, the frail elderly, victims of trauma, or those in poor health.

Making Survey Data Available for Public Use

QUESTION

In what ways do survey researchers sometimes act unethically? How would you guard against such problems when doing your own survey?

Increasingly, large social and government surveys are being made available for public use over the Internet, as we have seen already in Chapter 6. This is a good thing for the advancement of research and informed public policy, as the considerable investment it takes to conduct a survey can be shared with many more researchers and policy analysts than in the past. But this widespread, public availability of individual survey responses—including details on individuals' characteristics, thoughts, and behaviors—raises ethical issues. As a result, public use survey data often contain limited geographic information on respondents and employ *top-coding* to limit the reporting of extreme values for potentially identifying variables such as income, age, or family size. Survey sponsors typically require users of public use survey data to register and to sign confidentiality statements. But the proliferation of data gathered from many sources, as described in Chapter 6, is making it harder to preserve confidentiality. Both data for purchase and publically available data sets, which on their own do not permit identification, can possibly identify individuals when linked together.

Survey data collection is a large and important topic in social and policy research. In this section, we have tried to give a useful overview of the various modes of doing surveys, the design of questionnaires, and the ethical issues involved. Although surveys are the most widely used method of collecting primary quantitative data, they are not the only one. The next section introduces other ways of gathering primary data.

Other Ways to Collect Primary Data

In addition to surveys, there are other types of primary data. Some of these we discuss separately in other chapters, particularly qualitative research (Chapter 3) and experiments (Chapters 11 and 14). Many forms of qualitative research, for example unstructured or semistructured interviews, focus groups, or ethnographic investigation, produce primary data, typically in the form of transcripts, recordings, and field notes that capture what people say and do. Similarly, experiments produce primary data too, in the form of either responses to survey instruments or the observation of behavior. But we focus here on a few additional methods of primary data collection not covered in other chapters.

Trained Observation

Quantitative data can be gathered by simply observing things—and this is the basic idea behind the method of **trained observation**. The method involves carefully *training* research workers to systematically *observe* and record conditions or behaviors, typically using an observation rating form. It has been used by researchers and policy analysts to rate neighborhoods, parks, streets, hospitals, classroom behavior, subways and buses, and public housing communities. It can be a fairly cost-effective method of data collection in that a small team of observers can cover a large number of facilities or locations in a reasonable period of time.

As we have seen in Chapter 3, observation—such as participant observation—is an important part of qualitative data collection. The distinction here is that explicit procedures are developed to quantify the observations by means of systematically coding or rating aspects of the observed situation. But it must be noted that many qualitative researchers code, count, and summarize their observations, in addition to taking notes or otherwise qualitatively recording or interpreting the situation. And quantitative trained observation can also include qualitative information, such as photographs or field notes.

Let's look at some examples of trained quantitative observation.

Observing Social Disorder

Robert Sampson, Stephen Raudenbush, and colleagues at the Project on Human Development in Chicago Neighborhoods drove an SUV slowly down the streets of 80 sampled neighborhoods in Chicago to observe, videotape, and rate neighborhood conditions, with a focus on physical and behavioral indicators of social disorder. These trained observer ratings were then analyzed along with survey data, census data, and crime reports to examine the influence of feelings of collective efficacy on levels of neighborhood crime and disorder (Sampson & Raudenbush, 1999). Here is a description of the various indicators of neighborhood disorder that were observed and recorded from the vantage point of the project's SUV:

> The researchers collected data on the following areas of interest: land use, residential housing, commercial industrial buildings, drinking establishments, recreational facilities, street conditions, the number of security persons, children, and teenagers visible, traffic, the physical condition of buildings, cigarette and cigars on the street or in the gutter, garbage, litter on the street or sidewalk, empty beer bottles visible on the street, tagging graffiti, graffiti painted over, gang graffiti, abandoned cars, condoms on the sidewalk, needles and syringes on the sidewalk, and political message graffiti. Information was also gathered on adults loitering or congregating, people drinking alcohol, peer groups, gang indicators present, intoxicated people, adults fighting or hostilely arguing, prostitution on the street, and people selling drugs. (Project on Human Development in Chicago Neighborhoods, 2008)

Going back to the "broken windows" theory from Chapter 2, you can see in this example of systematic neighborhood observation how a concept such as "disorder" might actually be measured.

Assessing Street Cleanliness

New York City's street cleanliness scorecard provides a good, applied example of the use of trained observers. Since the 1970s, the street cleanliness scorecard has produced monthly ratings of street cleanliness for each of 59 community districts in the city. The observers are trained to base their ratings on photographic standards and written definitions, as shown in Figure 7.1.

Scores in Figure 7.1 range from 1.0 (cleanest) to 3.0 (dirtiest), with a score of 1.5 or less defined as "acceptably clean." In 2012, over 95% of the city's streets were rated acceptably clean—up from less than 75% in the 1990s (City of New York, 2013).

Figure 7.1 Observers are trained to base ratings of street cleanliness on these photos and written definitions.

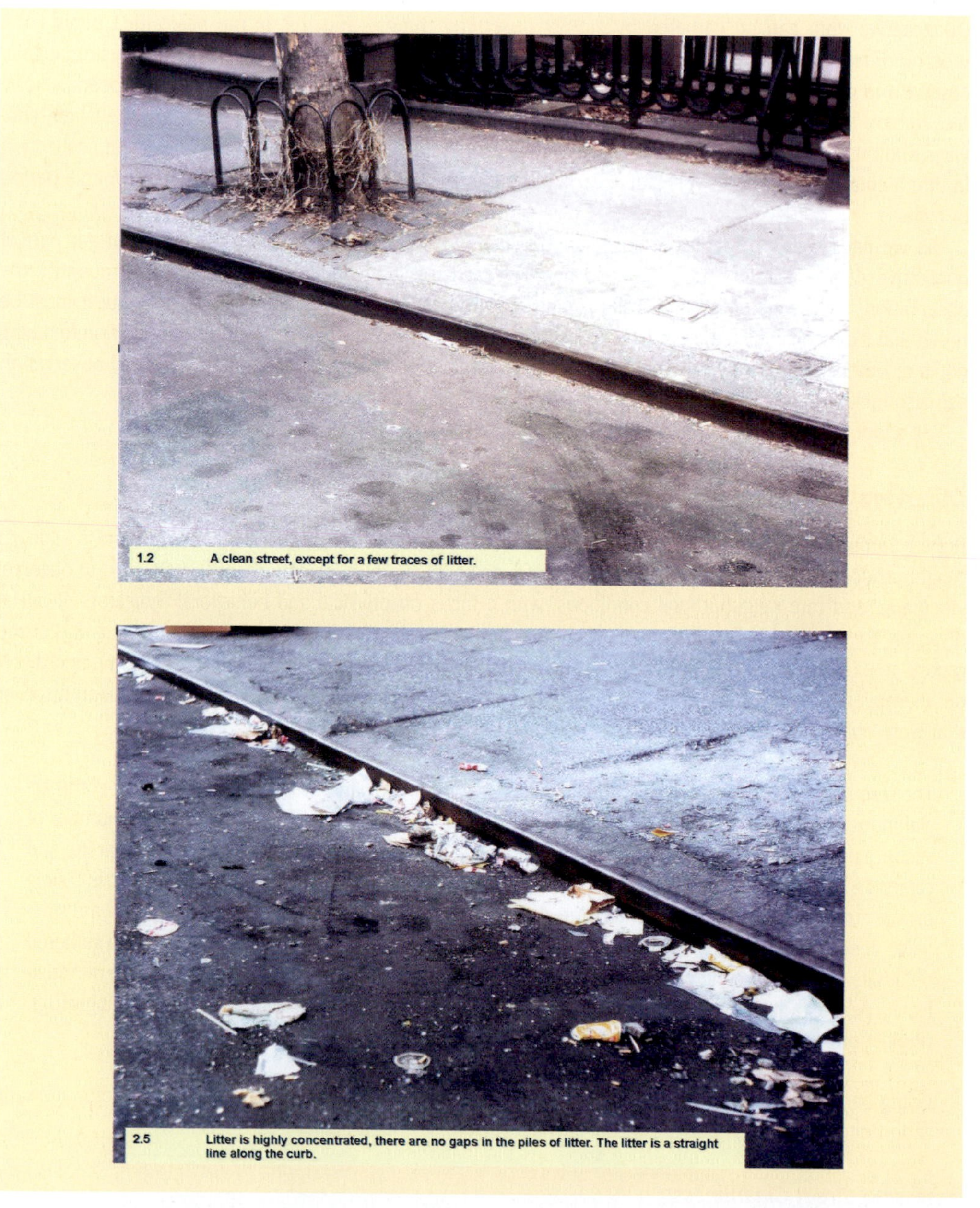

1.2
A clean street, except for a few traces of litter.
2.5
Litter is highly concentrated, there are no gaps in the piles of litter. The litter is a straight line along the curb.

Source: City of New York (2009).

Trained observers can now use handheld computers with software installed to guide their observation and ratings, as happens in the ComNET project to rate street-level neighborhood conditions (Fund for the City of New York, 2010). Importantly, the use of handheld computers can allow observers to capture qualitative data as well, such as digital photographs of conditions, which can be downloaded along with quantitative observer ratings into a centralized database.

Handheld computers are used by trained observers.

Source: © Photo courtesy of Fund for the City of New York. Center on Municipal Government Performance.

The method of trained observation typically begins with the development of a rating form along with procedures and standards, including the use of photographic standards. This development phase can involve substantial pretesting of the observation forms and procedures in the field. *Interrater reliability*—the consistency with which two or more observers rate the same object or condition, as discussed in Chapter 4—must be tested. If lacking, it should be improved through changes to the form, the rating procedures, or the training of the observers. Once the observation form and procedures are well established, actual fieldwork and data collection can begin. Still, observers must be monitored, and ongoing checks on interrater reliability must be performed.

Scientific Instruments

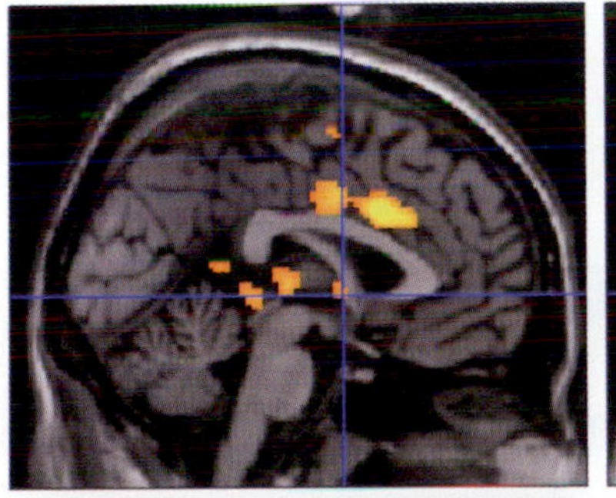

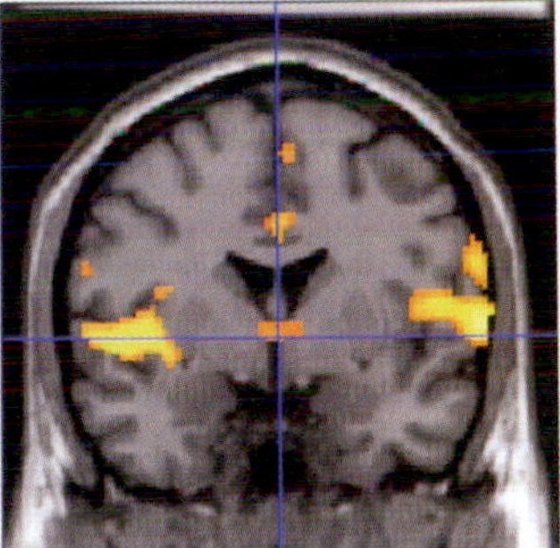

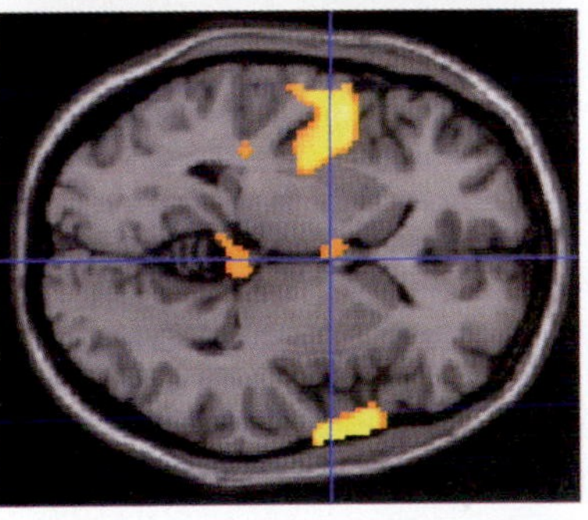

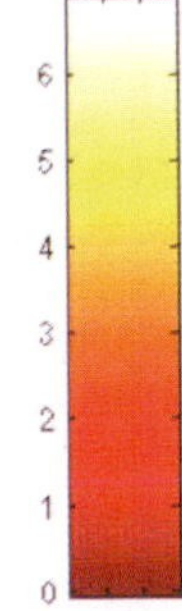

Data from scientific instruments, like this fMRI image, are increasingly used in social and policy research.

Source: © Philippe Psaila / Science Source.

One form of primary data that we have not said much about so far, and that is not covered in other chapters, is data produced by scientific instruments or laboratory equipment of various kinds. In the health sciences, examples include the readings from instruments designed to measure body weight, blood pressure, and blood sugar, as well as the various laboratory tests of blood, urine, DNA, or other body fluids or tissues. In psychology, an increasing number of studies make use of brain mapping or neuroimaging, using various technologies (such as functional magnetic resonance imaging [fMRI], positron emission tomography [PET], or electroencephalography [EEG]). Psychologists also track eye movements, reaction times, or skin conductance (also known as galvanic skin response, or GSR) using instruments and laboratory or computer equipment. In environmental science, primary data are produced by instruments measuring air quality, water quality, noise, and other environmental conditions.

Data from scientific instruments is becoming increasingly integrated into policy and social research. For example, Graff Zivin and Neidell (2012) use data on ozone levels gathered by the State of California in their investigation of the effect of pollution on worker productivity. Brain imaging studies are being increasingly used to study economic and financial decision making (Caminer, Loewenstein, & Prelec, 2005).

Computer Code and Data Extraction Algorithms

With so much life lived on computers and the Internet, we create a great deal of data in the course of our daily lives that is far from sufficiently organized and documented to constitute secondary data of the type discussed in Chapter 6. To make research use of these naturally occurring data, as it were, requires procedures not unlike the methods of observation or instrumentation used to collect primary data in the nonvirtual world. Specifically, researchers develop computer codes and other data extraction algorithms to search databases or crawl the Internet (also known as trawling)—instruments whose use and importance is growing rapidly. This is another way in which research is being influenced by the so-called Big Data revolution.

Conclusion

Despite the rapid growth of existing data use, as discussed in Chapter 6, the need for collecting original data remains. This chapter covered the many varieties of survey research that are widely used in primary data collection, including interview surveys conducted in person and by telephone and self-administered surveys conducted by mail and, increasingly, the Internet. Indeed, the use of the Internet for survey research may soon become the most widely used method, if it is not already. But primary data also come from trained observation, qualitative research, experiments, scientific instruments and laboratory equipment, and data of all kinds harvested from our expanding virtual world.

Knowing where data come from or how they are produced matters, even for those who do not do research but rather read it and apply it to public policy or management. Data are the basic material of research, and each source of data has its own advantages and limitations. This chapter has given you a feel for some of the most important sources of primary data and methods of quantitative data collection used in contemporary social and policy research.

The next step—to explore and analyze the data using the tools of statistics—is the topic of Part III.

BOX 7.4
Critical Questions to Ask About Surveys and Other Primary Data

- Did the study involve original data collection or not? Why were original data collected (as opposed to, e.g., using secondary or administrative data)?
- If data collection was done through a survey, what kind of survey was it? What modes of survey data collection were used? And what are the strengths and weaknesses of the modes?
- Who conducted the survey? Was it a professional survey firm, and if so, what kind of firm? Or was the survey conducted by the researcher and his or her assistants? How well were the interviewers or survey workers trained and monitored?
- Does the article or report provide the question wording for key variables? If not, how much does this limit your ability to judge the meaning of the results?
- Was the wording of the questions clear and unambiguous? Are any questions potentially leading or biased? Do respondents know the answers to the questions? Are they willing to answer? Were the questions pretested?
- How long was the questionnaire or interview? Were respondents burdened by the length of the questionnaire or interview, and if so, how might this influence the quality of the data?

- Did the study involve another type of original data, such as trained observation, qualitative research, experiments, or data collected from scientific instruments or laboratory equipment or extracted from the Internet or databases? If so, how valid and reliable are the measures?
- Also refer to the critical questions to ask about measurement and sampling, Chapters 4 and 5, as these are aspects of original data collection as well.

BOX 7.5
Tips on Doing Your Own Survey

- Check carefully to see if another survey has been done, or the data exist already, to answer your research question—only do your own survey or primary data collection if you really need to. See "When Should You Do a Survey?" at the beginning of the chapter.
- If you decide to do your own survey, develop a clear statement of the purpose or aims of the survey—and list the constructs (or variables) you want in your analysis. Mock up a few tables with made-up results to see if your list of variables gives you what you will need in your final research report.
- Identify the population to be surveyed and a sampling strategy—see the tips at the end of Chapter 5.
- Determine the mode, or mix of modes, that you think will work best—using what you've learned about the strengths and weaknesses of each mode (see Table 7.1 for a summary).
- Write the questionnaire using the advice on question wording given in this chapter—and ask people to review it and provide feedback. Consider using standard questions from established surveys—so search these out. Only ask questions respondents are willing and able to answer.
- Pay attention to the total design of the survey—including the graphical layout of the questionnaire, the instructions and guideposts, and your communications with respondents. The survey design is a total package, not just the questions on your questionnaire.
- Be sure to pretest your questionnaire and survey procedures in order to get feedback from potential respondents. Pay attention to particular questions or aspects of the survey that cause hesitation or confusion.
- If doing an interview survey, train your interviewers so that they ask the questions in a consistent way and follow your survey procedures. Even if you are doing all the interviews yourself, you need to be consistent and establish the procedures you will follow.
- Allow sufficient time to field your survey—especially time for multiple contacts and efforts to follow up. Consider using an alternative mode as part of your follow-up effort (such as calling people who do not respond to a mail survey, or sending a letter to people who do not respond to an e-mailed web survey).
- Have a plan for entering, cleaning, and storing your survey data—and also carefully document your survey data and procedures so that they make sense to other users and to you later (when you return to your survey data for analysis).

Chapter Resources

Key Terms

- Anonymity
- Closed-ended question
- Computer-assisted personal interviewing (CAPI)
- Computer-assisted self-interviewing (CASI)
- Computer-assisted telephone interviewing (CATI)
- Confidentiality
- Establishment survey
- Group self-administered survey
- Household interview survey
- Intercept interview survey
- Internet access panel
- Interviewer effects
- Mail self-administered survey
- Mixed-mode survey
- Open-ended question
- Panel survey
- Pretesting (cognitive pretesting, field pretesting)
- Social desirability bias
- Survey mode
- Tailored design method (TDM)
- Telephone interview survey
- Trained observation
- Web survey (Internet survey, online survey)

Exercises

Is a Survey Necessary?

7.1. Below are some variables and samples in social and policy research. For each situation, decide whether or not you think a survey is appropriate—and if not, in what other ways you might obtain the information.

a. To find out the annual budgets of a sample of nonprofit organizations
b. To find out about the job satisfaction of a sample of employees of a large public agency
c. To find out the salaries of a sample of employees of a large public agency
d. To find out how many high school students in a sample use tobacco

What Survey Mode to Use?

7.2. The City of Tampa, Florida, runs a system of senior centers where older citizens of the city can obtain services, information, and opportunities for social interaction. The city government is interested in conducting a user satisfaction survey of the centers' clients. What survey mode would you suggest that the city use? Explain why your suggested approach is better than other alternatives.

7.3. A large high-tech company is concerned about retaining employees and wants to assess their job satisfaction. What survey mode would you suggest that the company use? Explain why your suggested approach is better than other alternatives.

Design Your Own Questionnaire

7.4. You are the director of a local art museum, and you want to understand the profile and cultural habits of those attending your museum. Design a 5- to 7-item brief questionnaire to gather useful information from an intercept survey of museumgoers.

7.5. You are the director of the downtown business association, and you want to survey customers of downtown shops and restaurants. In particular, you are interested in what people like, or dislike, about shopping and dining downtown and how to encourage them to do so more often. Design a 5- to 7-item brief questionnaire to gather useful information from downtown business customers.

Conducting an Interview Survey

7.6. In this exercise, you will conduct 3 or 4 structured interviews of friends or family members. Begin by developing a brief, 5- to 7-item questionnaire, using closed-ended questions, about a familiar topic (such as musical preferences, eating habits, travel, politics, etc.). Be sure to write an introduction to your questionnaire, including a statement about the purpose of the survey and confidentiality. Conduct the interviews and mark the responses on your questionnaire. When you are finished with each interview, ask the person for his or her feedback on the survey. Write a brief summary of your experiences doing these interviews and what you learned from them.

Using Web Survey Software

7.7. Visit the websites of some of the web survey software providers mentioned in Box 7.1, or others you find out about, and decide which software you like best. Then try using the software to create a 5- to 7-item online questionnaire, using various types of closed-ended survey questions. Most software providers let you sign up for a free trial account, or they may even offer free student accounts. Be sure to pay attention to the overall visual design of your questionnaire, as well as the careful wording of questions. To pretest your web survey, send it to a few friends and ask them for their feedback (using a text box at the end of your questionnaire for their comments). See what options the software provides for analyzing and downloading the data.

Student Study Site

Visit the Study Site at **www.sagepub.com/remler2e** to

- test your knowledge with the self-quiz
- check your understanding of key terms with the eFlashcards
- explore helpful resources that relate directly to this chapter

PART III

STATISTICAL TOOLS AND THEIR INTERPRETATION

Introduction to Part III: In these chapters, you will be introduced to the tools needed to make sense of statistics used in quantitative research. It is useful to cover this material at this point in the book for a few reasons. After the steps covered in the previous chapters—measuring variables, sampling, and gathering data—the next logical step is to describe the patterns and relationships in the data. Also, certain statistical ideas and techniques are essential background to studies designed to demonstrate causation—the theme of the chapters in Part IV. In particular, the basics of regression analysis are introduced as preparation for learning how regression is used to assess causation in Part IV.

Chapter 8 provides an introduction to units and rates, variables and distributions, and basic descriptive statistics, including measures of center and spread. It also presents cross-tabs, correlation, and simple regression as the basic tools for describing relationships. Chapter 9 covers inferential statistics, including confidence intervals and hypothesis tests for proportions, means, cross-tabs, and simple regression. It also includes some simple ways of calculating sample size requirements for different statistics. And Chapter 10 focuses mostly on multiple regression but also includes an overview of other multivariate techniques, such as path analysis, factor analysis, structural equation modeling (SEM), time series analysis, and panel data analysis.

A note to instructors about Part III: The three chapters in this part contain important material but are quite different from the rest of the book and can be read or used in different ways. For a course that is essentially nonstatistical, it is possible to assign only Chapter 8, which provides just the basics, or even omit all three chapters in this part entirely. Indeed, most of the rest of the book (except Chapter 13) can be read and understood with a mostly intuitive, nonstatistical approach. For a course that aims to teach introductory statistics along with research methods, these three chapters are more essential—especially Chapters 8 and 9. Although Chapter 10 covers multiple regression in some detail and reviews other more advanced techniques, the presentation is largely intuitive and driven by examples, so it should be understandable by those who haven't had statistics before. For a course in which students have already taken one or more courses in statistics, the three chapters in Part III could be assigned for review or used as a reference. Still, we cover important issues not emphasized in more traditional statistics courses, such as the distinction between practical and statistical significance and the challenges of using regression to get at causation.

Graphing and summary statistics help you spot patterns in the data.
Source: © iStockphoto.com/Izabela Habur.

Overview: In this chapter, you will learn a variety of concepts and tools to analyze quantitative data and to interpret that analysis usefully. You will learn about the importance of units and rates, as well as basic descriptive statistics (such as mean and standard deviation) used to summarize the distribution of a variable. This chapter will also introduce you to various methods of describing relationships between variables, including cross-tabs, correlation and regression analysis (a topic continued in Chapter 9 and especially Chapter 10). You will also learn about practical significance and measures of effect size. The concepts and basic tools covered in this chapter are critical to the thoughtful and sophisticated interpretation of quantitative research.

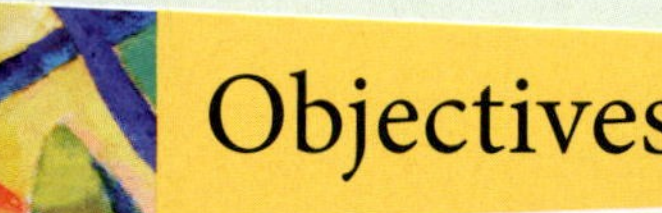

Objectives

Learning Objectives

After reading this chapter, you should be able to

- Identify the units of numbers or measurements that appear in research reports or statistical tables
- Determine when rates are more meaningful than counts and how to calculate appropriate rates
- Understand and present descriptive statistics in both graphical and numerical form
- Understand the meanings of and differences between various measures of central tendency and variability
- Understand and interpret cross-tabs, odds ratios, and simple regression analysis (slope, intercept, and *R*-squared)
- Identify the correct statistical analysis to be done for particular types of variables and relationships
- Explain what practical significance means and assess the practical significance of particular relationships

8 Making Sense of the Numbers

"Last Weekend I Walked Eight"

A good friend comes up to you with a big smile on her face and says: "I feel great—last weekend I walked eight!" You smile back at her, a bit perplexed.

What does she mean? Eight what? Did she walk eight blocks? Eight miles? Eight hours? It's hard to know how to react appropriately without more information—more context. Numbers do not speak for themselves, contrary to the popular saying, but rather require context and interpretation. That is what this chapter is about—making sense of the numbers reported as part of research, from fairly simple numbers such as "eight" to more complex statistics.

Some people are afraid or intimidated by statistics. If you are one of those people, we have some words of encouragement. First of all, it's not as bad as you probably imagine, particularly once you see in this chapter how to understand and apply statistics to interesting and important issues. And even if you consider yourself math phobic, you don't want to be silenced or cowed by colleagues or adversaries who throw numbers around. A lot of methodologically sloppy research overly impresses people because its statistical facade gives a false impression of scientific rigor. You want to be able to face the numerical results on your own, without fear, and think for yourself about what the results really mean.

I feel great—I walked eight.
Source: iStockphoto.com/unaemlag.

Units, Rates, and Ratios

Quantitative variables can appear in many units and in various forms, including counts, percentages (or proportions), rates, risks, or odds. It is important to know how to correctly interpret these numbers.

Table 8.1 Extraction of Table 1 in Gurley-Calvez et al. (2009)

Variable	NMTC Investors 2000	NMTC Investors 2004
Total income (thousands)	580.98	1020.48
Wealth (thousands)	9914.88	14163.43
Home equity (thousands)	39.88	36.09

Note: Table entries are means in dollars.

QUESTION

What is your height? Did you specify the units? Would someone from a country that measured height in different units (meters rather than feet or vice versa) understand you without the units?

What Units?

The friend in the opening example said that she "walked eight"—what made this confusing is that the statement lacked **units**. Eight *what,* we need to know. A basic but often overlooked requirement in reporting and reading research is to clearly define the **unit of measurement**. This requirement applies to tables of statistics, graphs and charts, and sentences that mention numerical results.

An example from a research paper illustrates the importance of units. Table 8.1 is an extraction of Table 1 in a paper by Tami Gurley-Calvez and colleagues (Gurley-Calvez, Gilbert, Harper, Marples, & Daly, 2009), showing summary statistics for investors in their sample data. Notice how the authors explain that each variable is in thousands. Without that explanation, it would be impossible to interpret the statistics. However, the authors do not specify that the variables are in thousands of *dollars.* While the latter fact may be obvious since the data are from the United States, it would have been even better to make the currency of dollars explicit, since researchers in other countries might read the table.

Even experienced researchers and statisticians can sometimes misinterpret or fail to clarify the unit of measurement. The importance of units cannot be overemphasized.

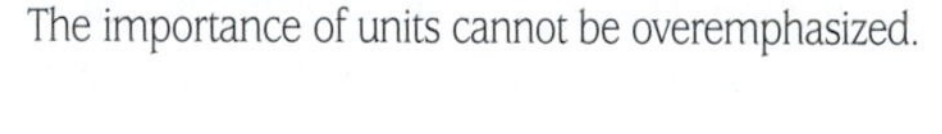

Big cities have more of everything, including pet goldfish.

Source: © Can Stock Photo Inc./ViewStock.

Rates, or Why Counts Often Mislead

Counts—such as the number of murders in a city—are useful facts to know, but as variables in statistical analysis, they often mislead. If we had data on many cities, and also measured the count of pet goldfish in each city, we might be surprised to find that—shocking news indeed—the more pet goldfish, the more murders! In fact, we would likely find quite a strong relationship. But it would be nonsense, of course—big cities have more of everything: murders, pet goldfish, park benches, and so on. Comparing or correlating counts of anything in this way is misleading.

Instead, the comparisons should be made relative to the population. Therefore, it is better to use **rates**, such as *murders per 100,000 residents.* To calculate a rate, you divide the count by the population and then multiply by the base (100,000 in the example of murders just given). Here is the basic formula:

$$\text{Rate} = (\text{Count}/\text{Population}) \times \text{Base}$$

For example, in 2011, New York City recorded 515 murders while neighboring Newark, New Jersey, recorded only 94 murders (U.S. Federal Bureau of Investigation, 2013b)—but these are counts, not rates, so we can't directly compare them. There are 8.2 million residents in New York City but only 278,000 residents in Newark. So the murder rates per 100,000 residents in the two cites are as follows:

New York: (515/8,200,000) × 100,000 = 6.3

Newark: (94/278,000) × 100,000 = 33.8

These murder rates per 100,000 residents are more comparable—and they tell a much different story than did the counts.

Percentages, such as the percentage of the population owning a pet goldfish, are also rates—goldfish owners per 100 people. (A percentage is just a rate with a base of 100.) With these new variables in hand, our shocking finding of a goldfish-murder link would surely disappear. Box 8.1 provides an example that further illustrates the importance of relevant comparisons.

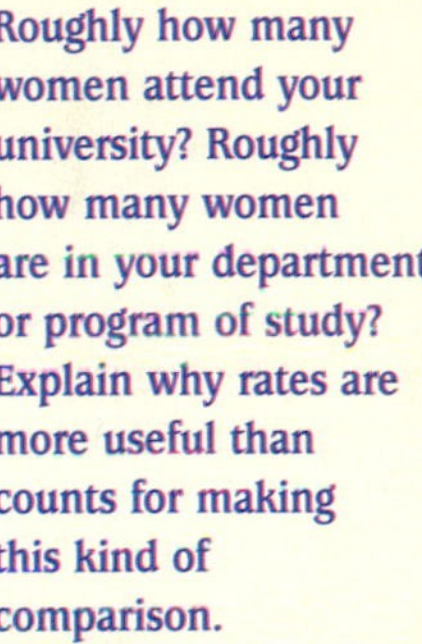

QUESTION

Roughly how many women attend your university? Roughly how many women are in your department or program of study? Explain why rates are more useful than counts for making this kind of comparison.

BOX 8.1
Relevant Comparisons

In "Going Under: A Doctor's Downfall, and a Profession's Struggle With Addiction," Jason Zengerle (2008) makes the case that anesthesiologists have a serious addiction problem. He notes that they account for 13% of physicians being treated for drug addiction.

One might not think that is serious, but Zengerle provides the relevant comparison by noting that only 5% of physicians are anesthesiologists. His evidence is even more striking when he notes that less than 5% of residents are in anesthesia, while more than 33% of residents in drug addiction treatment are in anesthesia.

By finding the right comparison, a share like a third is shown to be enormous. The easiest way to present the comparison would be to describe the rate of serious addiction among anesthesiologists compared with the rate among all doctors or other specialists.

In epidemiology and other areas of health research, rates are often referred to as **risks**—for instance, the risk of being murdered. We can say that the risk of murder in New York City is 6.3 in 100,000, while the risk of murder in Newark is 33.8 in 100,000.

Percent Change and Percentage Point Change

Say the poverty rate in a region was 10% (10 in poverty per 100 population) in 1950 but rose to 20% in 2010. How much would you say poverty had risen? You might be tempted to say, "It went up 10%," but this would be incorrect.

The key is to remember what a **percent change** means: change relative to a base. If you were lucky enough to have a salary of $100,000, and your salary rose by 10%, then your new salary would be $110,000. Here is the math:

10% Change = (($110,000 − $100,000)/$100,000) × 100

% Change = ((New − Old)/Old) × 100

Let's apply the same logic to determine the percent change of the regional poverty rate:

$$\text{Percent change in poverty rate} = ((20\% - 10\%)/10\%) \times 100 = 100\% \text{ change}$$

After all, the poverty rate doubled, right?—in other words, a 100% increase.

What is confusing is that poverty is a proportion, already measured as a percentage. Clearly, the poverty rate rises by 10 in the units it is measured in—percentage points. To make the distinction clear, we say that the poverty rate rose by 10 *percentage points*. The change in a percentage, expressed in its own units, is a **percentage point change**.

QUESTION

Suppose a particular screening test reduces the lifetime risk of dying from a particular condition from .03 (3 out of 100) to .02 (2 out of 100). What is the percentage point reduction? What is the percent reduction? Are both ways of expressing the change useful for understanding the test's effect?

Suppose you know the starting level and the percentage change, such as the $100,000 salary and 10% raise. How do you calculate the new level?

$$\text{New} = \text{Old} \times (1 + (\%\ \text{Change}/100))$$

$$\$110{,}000 = \$100{,}000 \times (1 + (10/100)) = \$100{,}000 \times 1.10$$

The Strangeness of Percent Change on the Return Trip

Suppose sometime in the future, say 2050, the poverty rate in the region mentioned earlier returns to 10%. In that case, the change in the poverty rate between 2010 and 2050 would be a 10 *percentage point* decline—the reverse of the increase between 1950 and 2010. However, measured as a *percent change,* things would look quite different. Between 2010 and 2050, the poverty rate would be cut in half or reduced by 50%:

$$\begin{aligned} \%\ \text{Change} &= ((\text{New} - \text{Old})/\text{Old}) \times 100 \\ &= ((10\% - 20\%)/20\%) \times 100 \\ &= 50\% \end{aligned}$$

Going in the reverse direction, the base was higher, so the percent change was lower. When interpreting percent change, always remember the base.

Because the percent change takes on a different value depending on the direction, this definition of percent change can be awkward in some applications. Therefore, sometimes, the midpoint between the new and the old is used as a base. For example, in economics, the *midpoint elasticity* is defined with percentages that use the midpoint as a base. Unless otherwise specified, a percent change always takes the old value as a base, but you should be aware of the option of using the midpoint.

Rates of Change and Rates of Change of Rates

How rapidly a social or economic condition, such as births, changes over time—its **rate of change**—is frequently of interest to policy makers and others. But it is important to choose an appropriate unit of time for rates of change. Should we examine change in the rate of births from month to month? Or is a year a more useful window for comparison? A year may be too long, however, for observing changes in other conditions, such as unemployment or crime.

Change over time in the number of new events may be of interest, such as the number of births per year, but as we have just seen, counts can often be deceiving. More births may simply reflect population growth, not a change in the birthrate. So it is often better to consider a percent change over time in a rate, such as a birthrate.

Odds

In some fields, such as public health, odds are commonly understood. But in many other fields, odds appear, well, a bit odd. If we think of one of two outcomes as a "success" and the other as a "failure," then the **odds** of an outcome are defined as follows:

Odds = Successes/Failures

If three out of every five high school students graduate successfully, then it follows that two of five fail to graduate. We can then say that the odds of graduating are 3/2 or 1.5.

Odds are also commonly used in the context of sports. For example, "What are the odds that the Yankees will beat the Mets?" You might say that the odds are even, or 1 to 1. Or you might say that the odds are 2 to 1 in favor of the Yankees. But these are subjective odds—guesses. In research, odds are calculated from data.

While odds can refer to the ratio of successes to failures, they can also be used to refer to any kind of dichotomous variable. For example, we could refer to the odds of getting a heart attack (vs. not getting a heart attack), the odds of committing a felony, and so on.

It's important not to confuse odds with proportion. For example, the proportion of successes would be the successes divided by the total (both successes and failures). Consider Table 8.2, showing all possible success-failure outcomes in a sample of $n = 5$ events.

Odds are familiar to many in gambling, but odds are also used in research.

Source: © 2009 Jupiterimages Corporation.

Notice that odds less than 1 indicate that a success is less likely than a failure, and odds greater than 1 indicate that a success is more likely than a failure. Both odds and proportions have a lower limit of 0. But proportions have an upper limit of 1.0 (100%), while odds have no upper limit (or infinity).

Prevalence and Incidence

In epidemiology (the study of disease), the number or share of a population that has a particular disease or condition is referred to as **prevalence**. The estimated prevalence of diabetes in U.S. adults 20 years of age or older, for example, is 23.5 million, or 10.7% of this population. This figure refers to all U.S. adults with some form of diabetes, including those who have lived with the disease for many years (National Diabetes Information Clearinghouse, n.d.).

It is also of interest to know the rate at which new cases of a disease appear in a population, which is the **incidence**. The estimated incidence of diabetes in U.S. adults 20 years of age or older in 2007 was 1.6 million new cases, or 0.7% of this population.

Table 8.2 Odds and Proportions

Successes (A)	Failures (B)	Total (C)	Odds (A/B)	Proportion (A/C)
0	5	5	0.00	.00
1	4	5	0.25	.20
2	3	5	0.67	.40
3	2	5	1.50	.60
4	1	5	4.0	.80
5	0	5	∞	1.00

The terms *prevalence* and *incidence* are sometimes used in other disciplines, for example, the prevalence and incidence of crime victimization. Regardless of the context, it is important not to confuse the two. There are many more people who have been victims of crime at some point in their lives than there are those who are victimized in a given year.

Having covered some challenges involved in making sense of units of measurement, we turn now to the basic statistical tools researchers use for describing and summarizing variables.

Statistics Starting Point: Variables in a Data Set

Chapter 2 showed how theories and models in social research are made up of variables and relationships. Statistics provides a set of tools for describing and analyzing these variables and relationships. We will begin first with the analysis of single variables.

As explained in Chapter 2, a **variable** is something that takes on different values or attributes—it is something that varies. A car can be red, blue, or green—so color is a variable. A car can also get 30 miles per gallon (mpg), 26 mpg, or 41 mpg—so miles per gallon is a variable. Color is a **categorical variable** (as explained in Chapter 4) because color is not a quantity of something but rather a characteristic that groups or categorizes cars. Miles per gallon is a **quantitative variable** because it describes quantities of an attribute—how many miles a car travels on a gallon of gas. See Chapter 4 for more about the levels of measurement of a variable. When describing or analyzing variables, the first question to ask is always "What kind of variable (categorical or quantitative) is it?" Variable type determines what kinds of analyses are—or are not—possible.

The cars in our example are the **unit of analysis**—the things, individuals, or cases that the variables describe. We introduced the idea of the unit of analysis in Chapter 2 (and again in Chapter 6). Be sure not to confuse the unit of analysis, however, with the *unit of measurement*, which we discussed earlier in the chapter. In statistics, typically, the batch of data for analysis—the *data set*—is formatted such that the rows represent the unit of analysis and the columns represent the variables. For our example of cars, the data set might look like this:

	Make	Color	MPG	Size
1	VW	Red	30	Midsize
2	Ford	Blue	26	Full
3	Fiat	Green	41	Compact
4	GM	Red	23	Full

The first variable (Make) is categorical as is the second (Color), but miles per gallon (MPG) is quantitative, as we've seen. Size is categorical as well, but it is an **ordinal categorical variable** because the size categories have an order to them: Full is larger than midsize, which is larger than compact (again see Chapter 4). Color and Make are **nominal categorical variables** because the categories can't be put in an order.

It is easy to spot the categorical variables in the example above because the data set shows the value labels (if the variable has or needs value labels, chances are it is a categorical variable). But with most statistical data sets, numerical codes are used to represent categories so that the data set really looks more like this:

	Make	Color	MPG	Size
1	4	1	30	2
2	2	2	26	3
3	1	3	41	1
4	3	1	23	3

Here we would need a *codebook* or data dictionary to tell us that for the first variable (Make), 1 = Fiat, 2 = Ford, and so on. A typical mistake for beginning analysts is to view a variable represented by numbers as quantitative when it is really categorical. The tools of statistics are often very different for categorical and quantitative variables, as you will see in this chapter (and in Chapters 9 and 10).

Data sets in statistics can be small like this one, or they can have hundreds of variables and many thousands of individuals or cases. The structure of the data set can also be more complex, for example when the data represent multiple levels or time periods (such as hierarchical, panel, or longitudinal data). We described some of the different forms or structures of data sets already in Chapter 6.

Distributions

Variables are so named because they vary—they take on different values. This variability produces a **distribution**—that is, a pattern of values spread out over the categories or numeric range of the variable. The term *distribution* by itself just refers to the values of a single variable, not how two variables are related to each other. To describe a distribution, first ask, "Is the variable categorical or quantitative?" The tools used to describe the distribution depend critically on the type of variable.

Distribution of a Categorical Variable

We examine the distribution of a categorical variable by counting the number of individuals in each category or, better, by calculating the percentage of individuals in each category. This produces a **frequency distribution** (or *frequency* for short) like that shown for the race/ethnicity of U.S. teens based on the federal government's Youth Risk Behavior Surveillance System (YRBSS) in Table 8.3. The column labeled "Valid Percent" shows the percentages disregarding the 251 individuals for whom race/ethnicity is missing.

A **bar chart** can be used to graph the distribution of a categorical variable, as shown in Figure 8.1. Bar charts show how the frequencies differ across categories more clearly than do tables. (In this bar chart, the categories are sorted from most to least frequent to provide an even clearer picture of the data.) It is always important to graph your data—this is a key first step in any analysis.

Table 8.3 Frequency Distribution of Race/Ethnicity (Youth Risk Behavior Surveillance System)

Race/Ethnicity				
		Frequency	Percent	Valid Percent
Valid	White	8321	59.3	60.3
	Black or African American	2076	14.8	15.1
	Hispanic/Latino	1184	8.4	8.6
	Multiple—Hispanic	1142	8.1	8.3
	Asian	480	3.4	3.5
	Multiple—Non-Hispanic	345	2.5	2.5
	American Indian/Alaska Native	135	1.0	1.0
	Native Hawaiian/Other Pacific Islander	108	.8	.8
Total		13790	98.2	100.0
Missing	System	251	1.8	
Total		14041	100.0	

Source: Centers for Disease Control and Prevention (n.d.).

Figure 8.1 Bar Chart of Race/Ethnicity (Youth Risk Behavior Surveillance System)

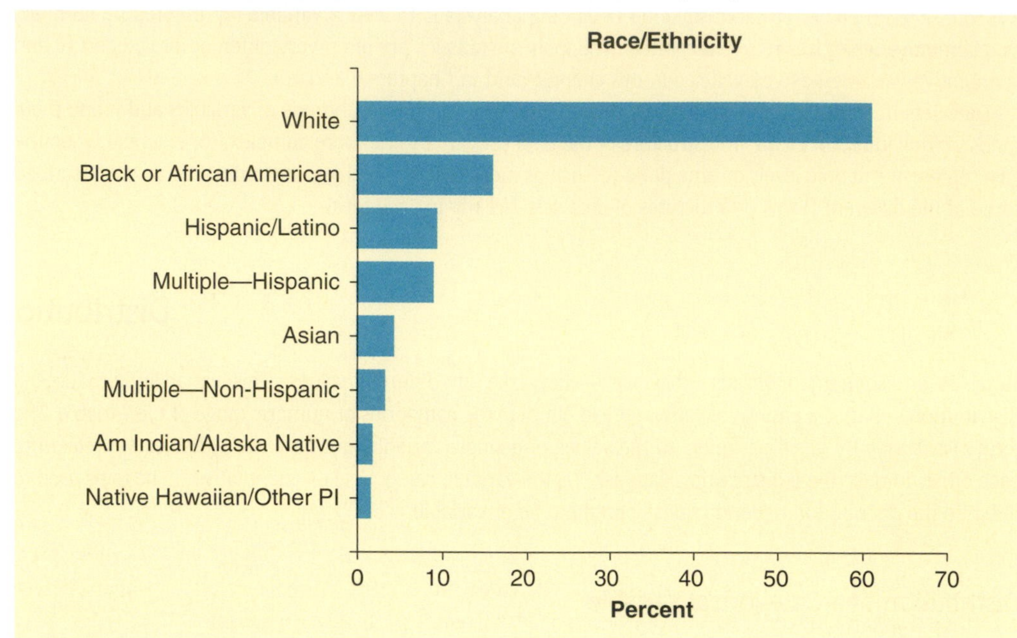

Source: Centers for Disease Control and Prevention (n.d.).

A **pie chart** can also be used to graph a categorical variable, as demonstrated in Figure 8.2. Although pie charts are popular with novice analysts, most experienced researchers prefer bar charts because they are visually simpler and work better to convey the frequencies. As can be seen from Figure 8.2, pie charts with more than a few categories can get a bit confusing.

Figure 8.2 Pie Chart of Race/ Ethnicity (Youth Risk Behavior Surveillance Survey)

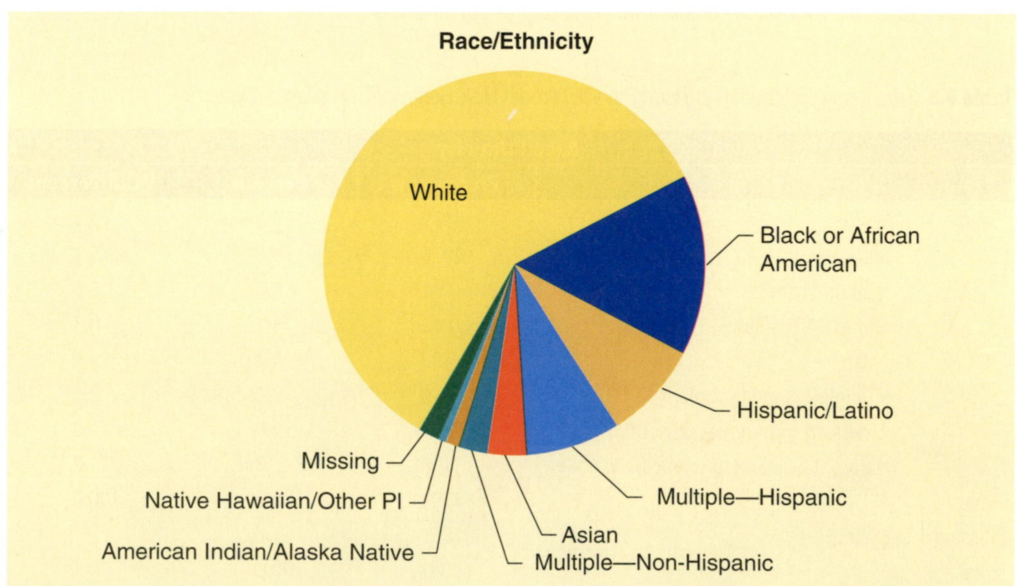

Source: Centers for Disease Control and Prevention (n.d.).

Displaying data using graphs helps you visualize your data, perceive patterns, and notice any unusual features. It is therefore an essential preliminary step in any well-done data analysis. Graphs are also very useful for presenting data.

Distribution of a Quantitative Variable

To visualize a quantitative variable, such as years of age or dollars of income, a different graph is needed: a **histogram**. Although a histogram is made up of bars, it is different from the bar chart used for a categorical variable. Figure 8.3 is a histogram showing the distribution of the weight of 14-year-olds in kilograms from the YRBSS. It shows how the individuals in the data are distributed across equal intervals of weight, in this case 5-kilogram intervals (also called *bins*).

You can see that most of the 14-year-olds weigh between 40 and about 80 kilograms, or approximately 88 to 177 pounds (a kilogram is equivalent to 2.2 pounds). The center of the distribution looks to be about 60 kilograms (132 pounds), but there is quite a spread, particularly at the upper end of the distribution (this is referred to as right skewness). We'll review more precise measures of center and spread shortly.

Explaining the variability visible in a distribution is, in an important sense, what much research is all about. We want to know why some 14-year-old kids weigh more while others weigh less. Much of this variability may be attributable to genetic factors, but a fair amount may be the result of behaviors or health habits that could be changed by public policy or some other intervention. Obesity is a growing health problem for young people, so knowing what produces variability in childhood weight can help us address this issue.

QUESTION

Would you use a bar chart or a histogram for the following variables describing employees of an organization: Job Category, Annual Salary, Sex, Age?

Figure 8.3 Histogram of Weight in Kilograms (Youth Risk Behavior Surveillance System)

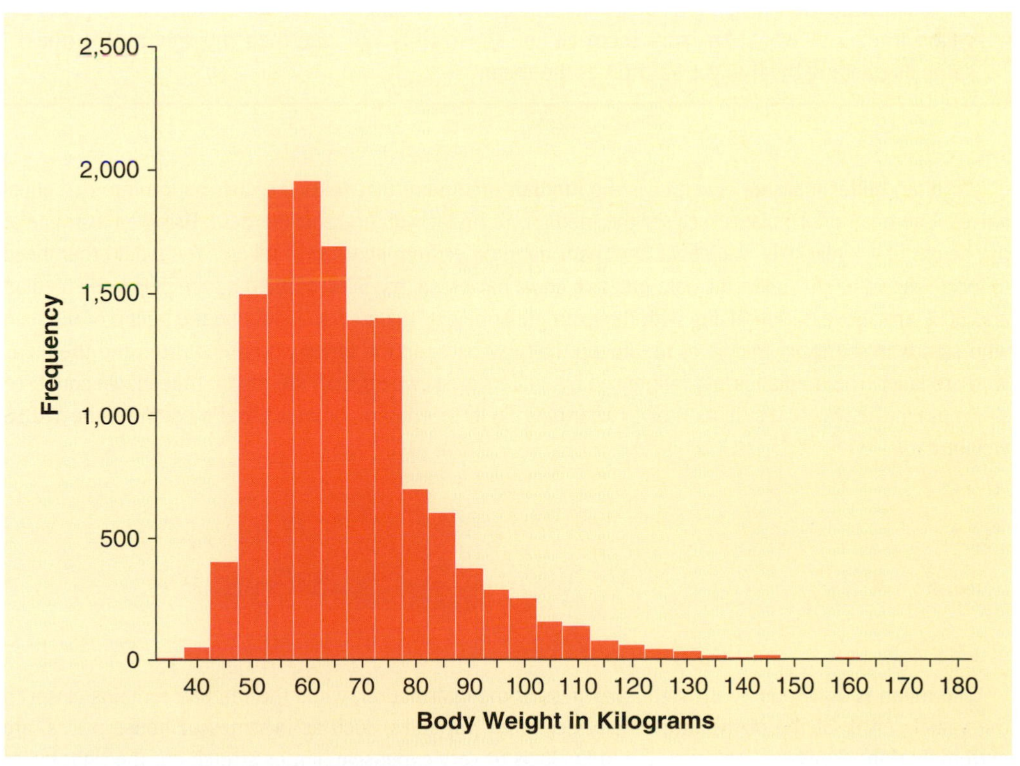

Source: Centers for Disease Control and Prevention (n.d.).

Measures of Center: Mean and Median

For quantitative variables, we can calculate summary statistics to represent the center and spread of the distribution. The center of the distribution is important because it is the middle or average—what's typical or expected.

The most common measure of the center of a distribution is the **mean**. The mean is the arithmetic average found by adding up all the values and dividing by the total number of observations (sample or population size). (See Box 8.2 for the formula.) But the mean is not always the best measure of center because it can be influenced by extreme scores (called **outliers**) or by a long tail of scores trailing out in one direction (called **skewness**). In other words, a few very high values (or very low values) have a large influence on the mean.

BOX 8.2
Mean: The Formula

The mean of a variable is simply its total divided by the number of observations. Formally,

$$\bar{x} = \frac{1}{n}\sum x_i,$$

where x_i refers to the individual observations and n refers to sample size. Σ is the summation symbol and means *add them up*.

To illustrate the use of the formula, say we have $n = 4$ cars with 30, 26, 41, and 23 miles per gallon (mpg), we would first sum them all up (Σ), which is 120, and then multiply by 1/4 (the same as dividing by 4) to get 30 mpg as the mean.

An often better measure of center is the **median**—the point that splits the distribution into two equal halves. There is no formula as such for the median. To find it, you first sort the data. Using an example of the height of 14-year-olds, you could line them up in order from shortest to tallest. You would then need to locate the value that splits the data into two equal halves, so that 50% of the data are below the median and 50% are above it. Continuing with the example of height, the median would be the height of the teen who stands in the exact middle of the lineup, halfway between the teens who are shorter and the teens who are taller. The median is less influenced by outliers or skewness than the mean. Indeed, we could see skewness in the weight distribution of 14-year-olds. So let's compare the mean and median for the YRBSS weight data:

Mean	63.1 kilograms
Median	59.9 kilograms

The mean is drawn up by the right skewness of the distribution, while the median remains closer to the visual center of the distribution. Many economic variables, such as incomes or house prices, are extremely right skewed (a few very rich individuals or very expensive homes stretch out the right tail of the distribution).

Figure 8.4 Median and Mean (Average) Net Worth of American Families

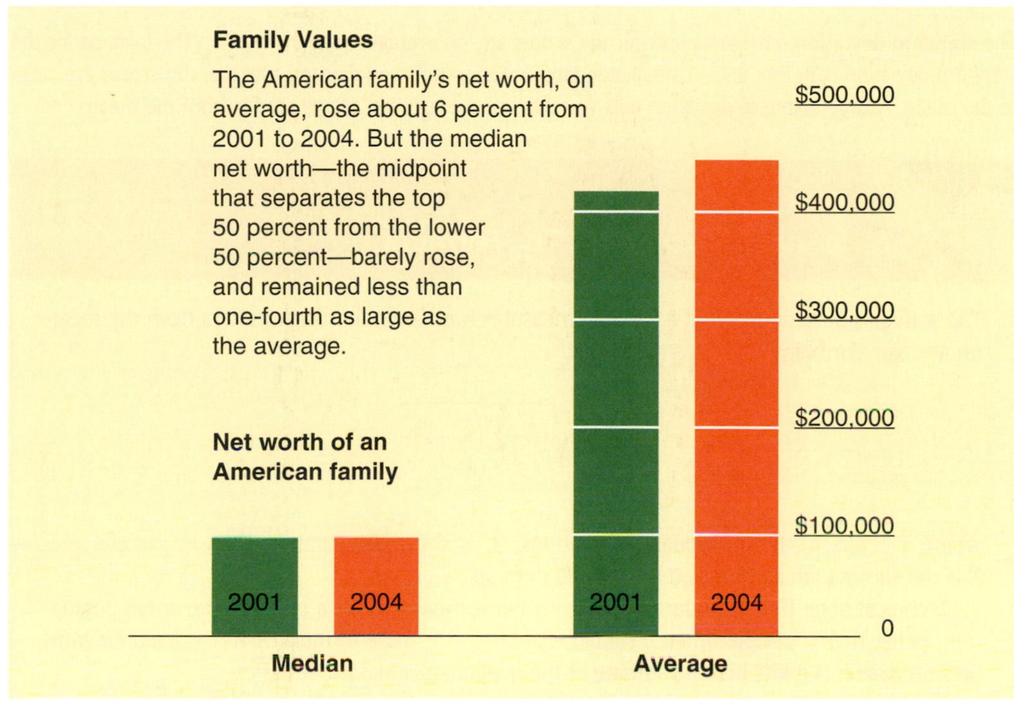

Family Values
The American family's net worth, on average, rose about 6 percent from 2001 to 2004. But the median net worth—the midpoint that separates the top 50 percent from the lower 50 percent—barely rose, and remained less than one-fourth as large as the average.
Net worth of an American family
$500,000
$400,000
$300,000
$200,000
$100,000
0
2001
2004
2001
2004
Median
Average

Source: Federal Reserve.

When to Use Median? When to Use Mean?

The *New York Times* compared the mean (which it calls "average") and median net worth of families in the United States in 2001 and 2004, as shown in Figure 8.4.[1] So how much is the typical American family actually worth? The $400,000 plus mean (average) is misleading because it reflects the large fortunes of a few very wealthy American families. The more modest median at less than $100,000 better represents how much wealth the typical American family truly possesses.

But for other purposes, the mean is quite useful, even when the distribution is skewed. Consider this example: Most people stay in the hospital only a short time, but a small number of people stay for weeks or even months on end. The median length of stay would tell us the experience of a typical patient. But from the perspective of an insurer or government agency that must pay for all hospital stays, the mean is more important. Everyone in the insurance pool (or paying taxes) needs to contribute enough to cover the total cost, including the few really long hospital stays. If people just paid to cover the median hospital stay, we would fall far short of the contributions needed to break even.

> **QUESTION**
>
> To judge if houses in a neighborhood are affordable, would you use the median or the mean house value? To figure out the tax base (total value) represented by all homes in a neighborhood, would you use the median or the mean house value?

Measures of Spread and Variation

Although usually not noticed as much, the *spread* of a distribution is just as important as, or maybe more important than, the center. Spread can be measured by the range from minimum to maximum, but the most widely used measure is the standard deviation.

[1]*New York Times.* June 4, 2006. BUSINESS/YOUR MONEY. "Economic View: When Sweet Statistics Clash With a Sour Mood," by Daniel Gross.

Standard Deviation

The **standard deviation** represents how far the scores are, on average, from the mean. (The formula for the standard deviation is in Box 8.3.) A small standard deviation tells you that, on average, the scores are close to the mean. A large standard deviation tells you that, on average, the scores are far from the mean.

BOX 8.3
Standard Deviation: The Formula

The standard deviation (*SD*) of a variable measures how far each observation is from the mean on average. Formally,

$$SD_X = \sqrt{\frac{1}{n-1}\sum\left(x_i - \bar{x}\right)^2}$$

where x_i refers to the individual observations, $\bar{x}$ is the mean, and n refers to sample size. Σ is the summation symbol and means *add them up*.

Technical note: If the standard deviation is being measured for a census—the entire population, rather than a sample—then n should replace $n - 1$ in the formula. $n - 1$ is used for samples because it is a less biased estimate of the population standard deviation.

To illustrate the use of this formula, which is a bit more complex, say again that we have $n = 4$ cars with 30, 26, 41, and 23 miles per gallon (mpg). We know already from Box 8.2 that the mean $\bar{x}$ is 30. So we start (within the parentheses first) by subtracting the mean from each observation: $30 - 30 = 0$, $26 - 30 = -4$, $41 - 30 = 11$, $23 - 30 = -7$. Notice that these are distances from the mean: The first car is at the mean (0 distance), the second car is 4 mpg below the mean, and so on. The next step is to square these differences to get rid of the negative values: $0^2 = 0$, $-4^2 = 16$, $11^2 = 121$, $-7^2 = 49$. Now we are ready to sum them up (Σ): $0 + 16 + 121 + 49 = 186$. With everything to the right of Σ having been calculated, our equation (knowing $n = 4$) boils down to this:

$$SD_X = \sqrt{\frac{1}{3}(186)}$$

The last step is then $186/3 = 62$ (this is the variance), of which we then take the square root to get 7.87—the standard deviation.

The mean height of 14-year-olds in the YRBSS is 167 centimeters (66 inches), but as expected, there is variability or spread in the heights of the children studied. How far, on average, are these individual heights from the mean? The standard deviation tells us: 9 centimeters (about 3.5 inches).

You can also use the standard deviation as a kind of yardstick to judge how typical, or extreme, a score is against the backdrop of the distribution of all scores. A 14-year-old who stands 1 standard deviation above the mean, or 176 centimeters (69 inches), is tall but not extraordinarily so. In contrast, a child who stands 2 standard deviations above the mean, or 185 centimeters (73 inches), would be highly unusual among 14-year-olds. Thus, within 1 standard deviation is not that far from the average; beyond 2 standard deviations is quite far from the mean.

Table 8.4 Literacy Score Means and Standard Deviations for Three Countries

	Mean	Standard Deviation
International average	500	100
New Zealand	529	108
South Korea	525	70
Brazil	396	86

Source: National Center for Education Statistics.

The square of the standard deviation is the **variance**. Its units are hard to understand (because they are squared units), but the variance turns out to be useful in certain statistical formulas and procedures. Statisticians often prefer the term *variance* to refer to the general idea of variability in data, and the term shows up in many statistical calculations and procedures (*R*-squared in regression is explained variance, or ANOVA—the analysis of variance).

Pay Attention to the Standard Deviation, Not Just the Mean

Let's practice interpreting standard deviations by looking at some results of an international assessment of the reading literacy of 15-year-olds, shown in Table 8.4. Which of these three countries is doing the best job at imparting reading literacy to its young people?

Most of us are drawn initially to the means and can see that New Zealand seems to be doing the best. But the scores for students in New Zealand have a relatively large standard deviation as well—meaning there is more variation, or dissimilarity, among students. Perhaps the educational system is divided, with some doing exceptionally well, while others are falling short. In contrast, Korea has a mean nearly as large but a much lower standard deviation—meaning its students score more consistently (they are more alike in reading literacy). But consistency is not always a good thing—especially if you are doing poorly, such as Brazil. The key point here is to consider more than just measures of center, like the mean, when interpreting data; think about the standard deviation as well.

Standardized (*z*) Scores

For educational tests or psychometric scales, which do not have natural units, the standard deviation is used to convert raw scores to **standardized scores** or ***z* scores**. Standardized or *z* scores are scores on a variable converted to standard deviation units. Thus, a z score = 1 means that the individual score is 1 standard deviation above the mean, and a z score = – 1.5 means that the individual score is 1.5 standard deviations below the mean. Here is the formula for a *z* score:

$$z = \frac{x - \bar{x}}{SD_x}.$$

It says, "Take a given value of *x*, subtract the mean, and divide by the standard deviation." This formula converts each individual *x* into standard deviation distances from the mean. Take, for example, a student in

New Zealand with a score of 650—what would it be in z scores? It would be $(650 - 529)/108 = 1.12$, meaning a little over one standard deviation above the mean. A student with a score of 450 would have a z score of $(450 - 529)/108 = -.73$, or about three-quarters of a standard deviation below the mean. A student with a score of 529 would have a z score of 0, a score exactly at the mean.

QUESTION

During the 2011 Occupy Wall Street demonstrations, "the 99%" became a rallying cry, referring to the bottom 99% of the income distribution. At the time, household income was roughly $506,000 at the 99th percentile, $816,000 at the 99.5th percentile, and $2,076,000 at the 99.9th percentile (Rampell, 2011). Explain in everyday language what these numbers mean.

Z scores are especially helpful when the variable is in units that do not have a natural or intuitive meaning (such as points on a test or levels on an attitude scale) or when you would like to compare scores originally measured in different units.

Quantiles: Another Way to Measure Spread

The standard deviation is a good measure of spread for symmetric distributions but not highly skewed distributions, such as wealth, income, or length of stay in a hospital, which have a few very high values. Outliers or skewness heavily influence the standard deviation, as they do the mean. In such cases, a measure based on **quantiles** is more useful.

To create quantiles of income in a sample of adults, for example, imagine first lining them up in order from the lowest to the highest income. We can then divide the lineup into equal parts, cutting it in half, which is the median or 50th percentile (a quantile). We could also define the 25th percentile, or first quartile, the income such that 25% of the people have a lower income. Similarly the 75th percentile, or third quartile, is the income at which 75% of the people have a lower income. We can measure almost any quantile, although the 25th, 50th, and 75th are most common.

For a skewed distribution, the interquartile range—the difference between the 75th and 25th percentiles—can be a better measure of spread. It would have the same units as income itself, for example, thousands of dollars in the United States. For making comparisons over time or across countries, such units can be awkward. If a unit-free measure is desired, a ratio may be used, such as the ratio of the 90th percentile to the 10th percentile in the income distribution. That measure can be used to compare inequality across countries and over long periods of time.

Coefficient of Variation: A Way to Compare Spread

The standard deviation divided by the mean is referred to as the **coefficient of variation (COV)**. The COV is useful when making comparisons across variables with different scales or units. Consider results on the height and weight of U.S. teenagers from the YRBSS, shown in Table 8.5.

Because height (in meters) and weight (in kilograms) are such different units, it's hard to compare them in terms of spread—is there more variation in height or in weight? The COV gives us the answer: There is much more spread or variation in the weight of U.S. teenagers than there is in height.

Table 8.5 Height and Weight of U.S. Teenagers (Youth Risk Behavior Surveillance System Data)

	Minimum	Maximum	Mean	Standard Deviation	Coefficient of Variation (COV)
Q6 Height (in meters)	1.27	2.11	1.69	0.10	0.06
Q7 Weight (in kilograms)	35	181	69	17	0.25

Source: Centers for Disease Control and Prevention (n.d.).

Relationships Between Categorical Variables

Having covered some of the key statistical concepts and tools for analyzing individual variables, we turn to the analysis of relationships between variables. As when describing the distribution of single variables, the analysis of relationships depends critically on the type of variables (categorical or quantitative). Different approaches work for relationships between two categorical variables, between two quantitative variables, and between one quantitative and one categorical variable.

Cross-Tabulation

Cross-tabulation (**cross-tabs** for short) is the method most often used to describe relationships between categorical variables, either ordinal or nominal. Cross-tabs (also known as *two-way tables* or *contingency tables*) are relatively straightforward and can be presented to audiences unfamiliar with statistics. They often appear in news reports of polling results, for example.

But mistakes can be made in presenting and interpreting cross-tabs. One mistake is to focus on counts and not percentages. Say we are interested in teen smoking, and we want to compare rates of teen smoking by race in the United States. Table 8.6 presents the relevant data from the YRBSS, but in the form of counts. The counts are useful for some purposes, such as inspecting the size of the sample. But it is quite difficult to compare racial groups from a table of counts alone. Although there are more than twice as many White smokers (2,888) as Hispanic smokers (1,116), there are more Whites overall than Hispanics in the sample—5,644 compared with only 1,806.

To make a more useful comparison, the *rate* of smoking within each group must be calculated and compared. As Table 8.7 shows, this can be done with *column percentages*—the cell count divided by the *column* total. (For example, the proportion of Asian teenagers who smoke, .308, is calculated from the cell count, 127, divided by the total number of Asian teenagers, 412.) Column percentages allow us to look across the racial groups and see that Hispanic teens smoke at a somewhat higher rate (56.9%) than White teens (51.2%). We can also see that the rate of smoking is highest for American Indians and Alaska Natives and lowest for Asians.

Not every kind of percentage that a cross-tab can produce, however, provides relevant comparisons. Table 8.8 shows *row percentages*—the cell count divided by the *row* total. This tells us—among smokers, for example—how many are American Indian, Asian, Black, and so on. The share of smokers who are American Indian is small, because the share of teenagers who are American Indian is small. So this is not really helpful for our purposes: What we want to do is to compare *across* racial groups, and row percentages are not helpful for this.

Table 8.6 Cross-Tab of Race/Ethnicity by Smoking (Counts Only)

	Race/Ethnicity								
Ever Smoked?	American Indian/ Alaska Native	Asian	Black or African American	Native Hawaiian/ Pacific Islander	White	Hispanic/ Latino	Multiple— Hispanic	Multiple— Non-Hispanic	Total
Yes	194	127	1,449	54	2,888	1,116	1,015	203	7,046
No	90	285	1,347	47	2,756	844	791	169	6,329
Total	284	412	2,796	101	5,644	1,960	1,806	372	13,375

Source: Data taken from: Centers for Disease Control and Prevention (n.d.).

Table 8.7 Cross-Tab of Race/Ethnicity by Smoking (Counts and Column Percentages)

	Race/Ethnicity								
Ever Smoked?	American Indian/ Alaska Native	Asian	Black or African American	Native Hawaiian/ Pacific Islander	White	Hispanic/ Latino	Multiple— Hispanic	Multiple— Non-Hispanic	Total
Yes	194	127	1,449	54	2,888	1,116	1,015	203	7,046
	68.3%	30.8%	51.8%	53.5%	51.2%	56.9%	56.2%	54.6%	52.7%
No	90	285	1,347	47	2,756	844	791	169	6,329
	31.7%	69.2%	48.2%	46.5%	48.8%	43.1%	43.8%	45.4%	47.3%
Total	284	412	2,796	101	5,644	1,960	1,806	372	13,375
	100.0%	100.0%	100.0%	100.0%	100.0%	100.0%	100.0%	100.0%	100.0%

Source: Data taken from Centers for Disease Control and Prevention (n.d.).

Table 8.8 Cross-Tab of Race/Ethnicity by Smoking (Counts and Row Percentages)

	Race/Ethnicity								
Ever Smoked?	American Indian/ Alaska Native	Asian	Black or African American	Native Hawaiian/ Pacific Islander	White	Hispanic/ Latino	Multiple— Hispanic	Multiple— Non-Hispanic	Total
Yes	194	127	1,449	54	2,888	1,116	1,015	203	7,046
	2.8%	1.8%	20.6%	0.8%	41.0%	15.8%	14.4%	2.9%	100.0%
No	90	285	1,347	47	2,756	844	791	169	6,329
	1.4%	4.5%	21.3%	0.7%	43.5%	13.3%	12.5%	2.7%	100.0%
Total	284	412	2,796	101	5,644	1,960	1,806	372	13,375
	2.1%	3.1%	20.9%	0.8%	42.2%	14.7%	13.5%	2.8%	100.0%

Source: Data taken from Centers for Disease Control and Prevention (n.d.).

QUESTION

Cross-tabs are often used with exit polls to show how people voted and why. In the 2012 U.S. presidential election, Obama won: 60% of 18- to 29-year-olds, 52% of 30- to 44-year-olds, 47% of 45- to 64-year-olds, and 44% of those over 65 (Pew Research Center, 2012b). Explain how these results come from a cross-tab. What are the independent and dependent variables?

Finally, cross-tabs can be used to produce yet a third type of percentage, *total percentages*—the cell count divided by the *overall total* (13,375 in our example). But this percentage is even less informative about the relationship between smoking and race. (The total percentages, however, can be a useful description of the overall sample.)

To help you clarify the construction of useful cross-tabs, it is sometimes good to follow these guidelines:

- Put the independent variable in the column position.
- Put the dependent variable in the row position.
- Calculate column percentages.

This way of constructing cross-tabs encourages a focus on how the dependent variable changes as you change categories of the independent variable. It is also consistent with the conventions of an x–y scatterplot for quantitative variables, in which x (the horizontal dimension) is the independent variable and y (the vertical dimension) is the dependent variable.

Relative Risks and Odds Ratios: Another Way to Show Relationships in Categorical Data

Although cross-tabs can be used to express a relationship between two *dichotomous* or *dummy* variables, health researchers and others sometimes prefer to use *relative risks* and *odds ratios.* They are not the same thing, and often people mix them up.

Relative Risks

We saw how *rates*—such as murders per 100,000 people—can be directly interpreted as *risks.* Now imagine that we want some way to describe how a rate or risk varies between two groups. Consider the data in Table 8.9 on the survival of male and female passengers on the Titanic (Simon, 2008).

The death rate for females is 154/462 = .33, or 33%. The death rate for males is 709/851 = .83, or 83%. This is what we would calculate if we were calculating column percentages in a cross-tabulation.

The *relative risk*—sometimes called the *risk ratio*—compares the probability of death in each group. The **relative risk** of death is the ratio of the risk of the two groups, which is .83/.33 = 2.5. This tells us that there was a 2.5 greater probability of death for males than for females on the Titanic. In this way, the relative risk describes the relationship between gender and dying on the Titanic, both dichotomous variables.

Odds Ratio

What were the odds that a female passenger on the Titanic died? We can calculate these odds from Table 8.9: It is the number of females who died divided by the number of females who survived, or 154/308 = 0.5. For males on the Titanic, the odds of death were 709/142 = 4.99, or very nearly 5 to 1.

The **odds ratio (OR)** compares the relative odds of death in each group. The odds ratio comparing males and females on the Titanic is 4.99/0.50 = 9.98. There are very nearly 10-fold greater odds of death for males than for females. Odds ratios like these are particularly common in medicine and epidemiology.

Notice the large difference between the odds ratio and the relative risk. There is a 2.5 times greater relative risk for a male dying on the Titanic compared with a female. However, there are 10-fold greater odds. Both show that males were much more likely to die, but the odds ratio seems to imply a larger difference.

The problem with odds ratios is that people often implicitly assume that they refer to relative risks, because it is more natural for us to think in terms of risks than odds. When possible, therefore, it is often better to avoid using odds ratios to describe relationships between two dichotomous variables. However, in certain study designs (case-control studies, discussed in Chapter 12) and certain types of analysis (logistic regression, described in Chapter 10), relative risks (and cross-tabs) cannot be calculated.

Table 8.9 Deaths of Male and Female Passengers on the Titanic

	Male	Female	Total
Survived	142	308	450
Died	709	154	863
Total	851	462	1,313
Death rate (died/total)	0.83	0.33	
Relative risk (male rate/female rate)	2.50		

Source: Simon (2008).

QUESTION

Based on the percentages of people who voted for Obama, what was the odds ratio between the 30- to 44-year-olds and those 18 to 29? Which do you think is easier to understand—odds ratios or cross-tabs?

Voting Patterns as Odds Ratios

In the 2012 U.S. presidential election, Obama won votes from 60% of 18- to 29-year-olds, 52% of 30- to 44-year-olds, 47% of 45- to 64-year-olds, and 44% of those over 65 (Pew Research Center, 2012b). The odds of voting for Obama (vs. not voting for Obama) were 60/40 = 1.5 among those 18–29 and 44/56 = .79 among those over 65. So, the odds ratio—the ratio of the odds of voting for Obama between 18- to 29-year-olds and those over 65—was 1.91.

Adjusted and Standardized Rates: When to Use Them

Many diseases or health conditions get worse with age. So if we are interested in comparing disease rates (or prevalence) across communities or demographic groups, for example, we might prefer to take this fact into account—to use age-adjusted rates.

To adjust a rate, *R*, as though it had a standard distribution among groups (such as age-groups), indexed by *g*: First determine the standard group population shares (e.g., share of the population in each age-group), s_g to be used to adjust all the rates. Second, calculate the rate within each group, R_g, for every area. Then calculate that area's adjusted rate by weighting the area's group-specific rate by the population in that age-group. By comparing age-adjusted disease rates, only differences in the rates of disease within age-groups influence the comparison; differences due to having more or fewer elderly people are removed.

$$\textit{Adjusted rate} = \sum_g R_g S_g.$$

Rates can also be adjusted using multiple regression, as discussed in Chapter 10. Adjusted rates are particularly common in epidemiology and demography (for example, see Gordis, 2000, for more information on their use in epidemiology).

Relationships Between Quantitative Variables: Scatterplots and Correlation

A relationship between two *quantitative variables*—such as education (in years) and income (in dollars)—can be graphed with a *scatterplot* and summarized numerically either by a *correlation* or by a *simple regression*.

Scatterplots

Consider Figure 8.5, which shows a **scatterplot** (sometimes called an *x–y* graph) of the relationship between gross domestic product (GDP) and years of life expectancy in 179 countries (based on data compiled by the United Nations). This relationship is evidently nonlinear (not a straight line). It is important to spot this pattern before calculating statistical summaries, because correlation, regression, and many other related techniques assume (or are most informative with) a linear relationship. Remember: Always begin your analysis by graphing the data.

For some statistical methods, such as regression, it is necessary to *transform* one or more of the variables to coax the data, as it were, into a more linear pattern. For example, if we take the *natural log* of GDP and regraph the data, we get the pattern shown in Figure 8.6, which is much closer to a linear relationship.

Influential observations and outliers are also revealed in scatterplots, and these can have a large influence on the calculation of correlations, regressions, and other numerical summaries of relationship. Again, be sure to graph your data first.

Figure 8.5 Scatterplot of GDP and Life Expectancy in 179 Countries

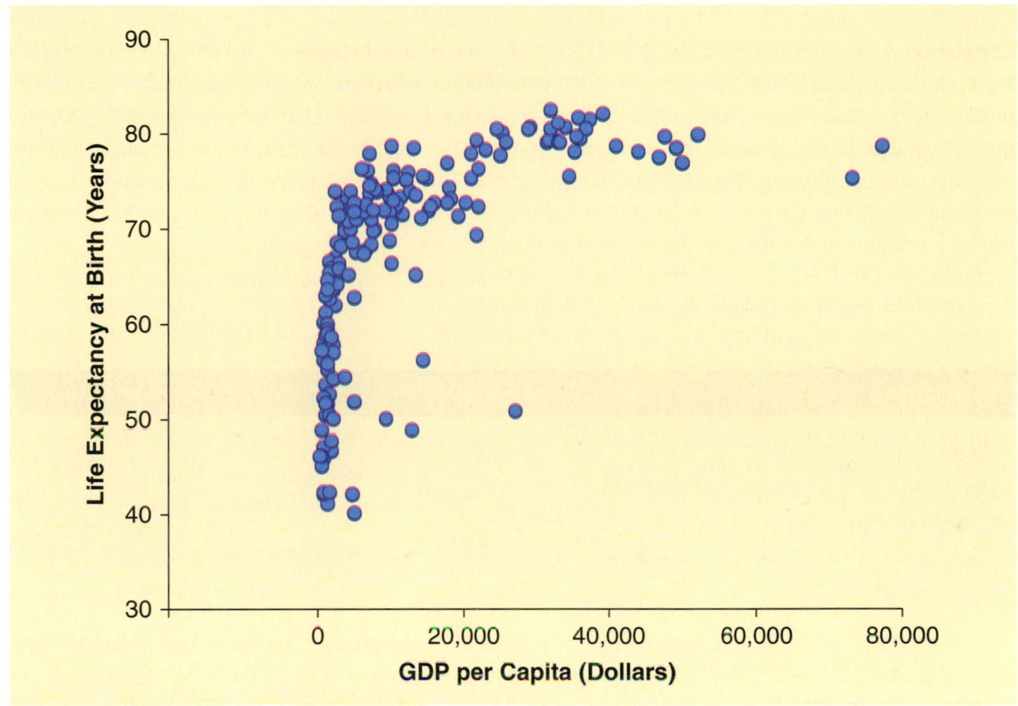

Source: United Nations.

Figure 8.6 Scatterplot of GDP Logged and Life Expectancy in 179 Countries

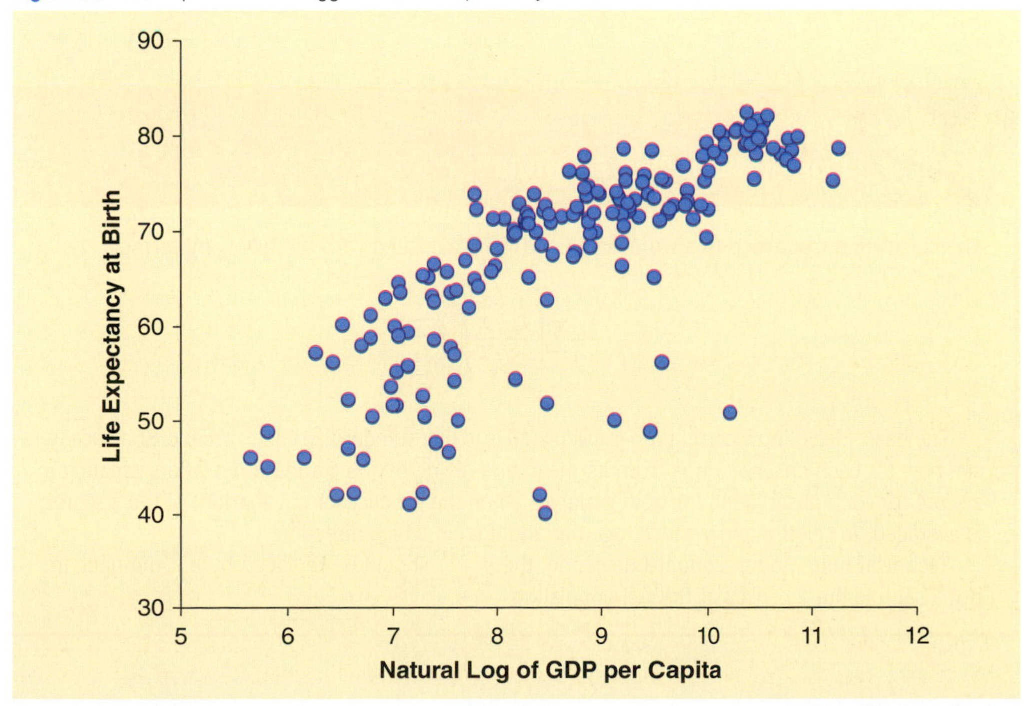

Source: United Nations.

Correlation

Correlation is a measure of the strength and direction of a relationship between two variables. It is typically represented by r, also known as Pearson r or the **correlation coefficient**, which ranges from −1 to 1, with 0 meaning no relationship. (The formula for the correlation r is in Box 8.4.) If two variables go in lockstep, then they are perfectly correlated. For example, suppose that in a particular organization, earnings are determined by number of years of education and nothing else. Then, the correlation of earnings and education would be exactly one. On the other hand, imagine that there is no relationship between how many minutes workers commute and how much they earn; then that correlation would be zero.

But beyond this, many people struggle with how to interpret the actual magnitude of a correlation. So here are some general guidelines (based on Cohen, 1992):

Correlation r	Size
.10	Small
.30	Moderate
.50	Large

It is also helpful to know this interpretation of a correlation: If a variable (x) changes by 1 standard deviation, the correlation r represents the expected standard deviation change in the other variable (y). For example, the correlation from Figure 8.6 showing GDP logged and life expectancy is $r = .8$, which is a large correlation. We can interpret this as telling us that a 1 standard deviation increase in GDP logged is associated with a .8 standard deviation change in life expectancy.

BOX 8.4
Correlation: The Formula

The correlation r between two variables (x and y) is calculated with the following formula:

$$r = \frac{1}{n-1}\sum\left(\frac{x_i - \bar{x}}{SD_x}\right)\left(\frac{y_i - \bar{y}}{SD_y}\right)$$

The basic idea of how correlation is calculated is to first standardize each variable. Specifically, see how far each observation is from its mean and divide by the standard deviation, creating a z score for each observation for both variables. Then the product (or covariation) of the z scores is averaged, to see if x and y move together and if so in which direction.

Technical note: As for standard deviation, the $n - 1$ should be replaced by n if the data are not a sample but a census of the full population.

Correlation is a unit-free measure that permits comparisons across completely different types of variables. While these features are strengths for some purposes, they are weaknesses for others. For example, we might want to know not just that education and income are positively correlated but also *how much* (on average) more highly educated individuals earn. In principle, income and education could be just as highly correlated if one more year of education was associated with earnings $10 higher on average as if one more year of education was associated with earnings $10,000 higher on average.

QUESTION

The correlation between the log of GDP and life expectancy is .79. Explain why this is consistent with the scatterplot in Figure 8.6.

Relationships Between a Categorical and a Quantitative Variable

Sometimes you are interested in describing the relationship between a categorical and a quantitative variable. Suppose, for example, that you want to compare earnings (quantitative) across different regions of the United States (categorical). Or suppose you want to know the effect of years of education (quantitative) on being employed or not (categorical). Let's look at what statistical tool you would use to answer each of these questions.

The first point is that it matters whether the categorical variable is the independent variable or the dependent variable. With respect to the first question, the independent variable—region—is categorical.

Region (categorical) → Earnings (quantitative)

In this case, you would show mean earnings by region, as in Table 8.10. As you can see, the table describes how average earnings change or vary as you move from one region of the country to another.

With respect to the second question about education and employment status, the independent variable (years of education) is quantitative, but the dependent variable (employed or not) is categorical.

Year of education (quantitative) → Employed or not (categorical)

Dependent categorical variables require more advanced techniques, such as logistic regression, some of which we describe in Chapter 10. Alternatively, you can turn any quantitative variable into a categorical ordinal one. For example, income can become income categories, in which case we could use cross-tabs. However, categorizing a quantitative variable means losing information on the variation within categories. Table 10.5 on page 334 can be used to determine what kinds of analyses can be used in which cases, including more advanced techniques.

Sometimes it can be difficult to determine which is the independent variable and which is the dependent variable. Box 8.5 gives some advice on how to decide which is which, but still it can be unclear at times and also much depends on the purpose of the analysis.

Table 8.10 Illustrating Relationship Between Categorical Independent Variable and Quantitative Dependent Variable

Mean Annual Earnings by Region in 2011			
Northeast	Midwest	South	West
$52,963	$47,314	$47,380	$49,803

Source: U.S. Census Bureau, Historical Income Tables, Table P-6 Regions.

BOX 8.5
Which One Is the Dependent Variable? Which One Is the Independent Variable?

To help answer the question, the following little model is often quite useful:

$$x \rightarrow y$$

Here x is the independent variable, and y is the dependent variable. Then ask yourself the following:

Which variable is the presumed cause (or predictor)?
Make this the independent variable—x.

Which variable is the presumed effect (or the outcome being predicted)?
Make this the dependent variable—y.
This is the variable that *depends* on the other one.
Sometimes, however, it is not clear which variable is cause and which is effect—or even whether there is any causal relationship at all between the variables. Determining causation can be tricky, as we discuss in Chapter 11.

Simple Regression: Best-Fit Straight Line

Simple regression uses a best-fit straight line to describe how one quantitative variable—the *independent variable* (often denoted as x)—predicts another quantitative variable—the *dependent variable* (often denoted as y). *Multiple regression analysis,* with more than one independent variable, will be discussed in Chapter 10. Regression analysis is perhaps the most widely used statistical method in social and policy research.

Consider the relationship between earnings and education, measured in years.[2] Figure 8.7 shows a scatterplot of the data and the regression line fitted from the data.[3] The regression line, like any straight line, is completely described by two numbers: the *slope* and the *intercept*. In regression, the slope is more commonly referred to as the **coefficient of the independent variable** (e.g., education), because it is the number the independent variable is multiplied by. The intercept is more commonly referred to as the **constant**, because its contribution to the dependent variable does not vary as the value of the independent variable changes.

In this example, the constant is −4,917, and the slope is 3,298. The regression equation, more easily interpreted if the actual variable names are used in place of x and y, is

$$\text{Earnings} = -4{,}917 + 3{,}298 \times \text{Education}.$$

Note that 3,298 is multiplied by Education *before* the constant, −4,917, is added, the conventional order of operations. The equations used to determine the coefficient and constant are given in Box 8.6. The constant term is interpreted as *the predicted value of the dependent variable when the independent variable is zero.* In this case, earnings of −\$4,917 are predicted for someone with zero years of education, which is not a realistic level of

[2]We will use simulated data because real-world data are a lot messier and thus harder to use for initial teaching.

[3]Experienced readers may be concerned that Earnings are not normally distributed and think that we should log Earnings. However, normality is only important for inference: We can calculate a least squares regression line for any variable.

Figure 8.7 Scatterplot and Regression Line Showing the Relationship Between Education and Income

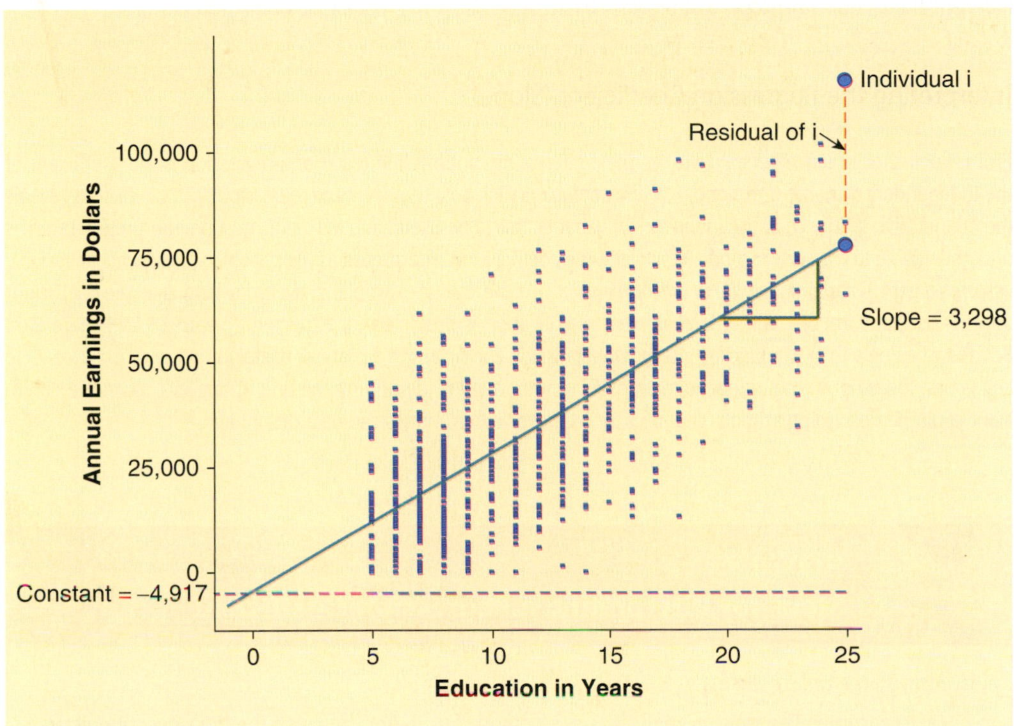

BOX 8.6
Simple Regression: The Equations

There are data points for *N* individuals, with the individuals indexed by *i*. A specific data point has independent variable value, x_i, and dependent variable value, y_i.

$$\text{Coefficient of the independent variable} = \text{Slope} = b = \frac{\sum(y_i - \bar{y})(x_i - \bar{x})}{\sum(x_i - \bar{x})^2}.$$

$$\text{constant} = a - \bar{y} - b\bar{x}.$$

$$\text{Predicted } y = \hat{y}_i = a + bx_i \qquad \text{Residual} = \hat{\varepsilon}_i = y_i - \hat{y}$$

$$SST = \sum(y_i - \bar{y})^2 \qquad SSR = \sum(\hat{y}_i - \bar{y})^2 \qquad SSE = \sum\hat{\varepsilon}_i^2 = \hat{\sigma}^2.$$

$$R^2 = \frac{SSR}{SST}.$$

Note: *SST* is the total sum of squares; *SSR* is the regression sum of squares, the explained variation; and *SSE* is the error sum of squares (sum of squared residuals).

education in modern societies but still helps define the regression equation.[4] It is, however, the coefficient of the independent variable (the slope) that provides information about the magnitude of the relationship.

Interpreting the Regression Coefficient (Slope)

From a policy or practice perspective, the most interesting, bottom-line result of a regression is the coefficient of the independent variable (the slope)—or the coefficients (slopes) in a multiple regression. The coefficient reveals the quantitative influence of the independent variable. But to be useful, a coefficient must be interpreted in terms understandable to the wider world. Technically, the coefficient is interpreted as *the change in the dependent variable associated with a one-unit increase in the independent variable.* In our example, in everyday language, the coefficient informs us that someone with one more year of education is predicted (or expected) to earn $3,298 more. Box 8.7 describes how to systematically interpret a regression coefficient in a manner useful for policy or practice. One key is first focusing on the independent variable. Another key is identifying the unit of analysis, since the coefficient could be describing schools, countries, or whatever other entities the data describe.

BOX 8.7
Steps for Interpreting a Regression Coefficient

1. *Identify the unit of analysis.*

   Our example: The unit of analysis is the person, or worker, because the data describe characteristics of people.

2. *Identify the independent variable and its units.*

   Our example: Education measured in years is the independent variable.

3. *Describe a one-unit increase in the independent variable in everyday language.*

   Our example: A person with one more year of education.

4. *Identify the dependent variable and its units.*

   Our example: Annual earnings measured in dollars is the dependent variable.

5. *The coefficient is the change in the dependent variable, which is predicted for a one-unit change in the independent variable. Describe that change in everyday language, making the units clear.*

   Our example: People with one more year of education are predicted to have earnings $3,298 higher. In other words, the coefficient predicts an additional $3,298 per year of education.

The Importance of Units in Interpreting Regression Coefficients

Just as the phrase "I walked eight" is useless without knowing the units of eight, so a regression coefficient is useless without knowing its units. In our example, the coefficient is in dollars per year of education—specifically, 3,298 dollars of additional annual income are predicted with an additional year of education.

[4]See discussion of out-of-sample extrapolation in Chapter 10 to understand why the constant is negative, and how it should be interpreted.

If earnings had been measured in *thousands of dollars* instead of *dollars,* the coefficient's numerical value would be 3.298. The numerical value of the coefficient would also change if education had been measured in *months* instead of *years*—so the units of the independent variable matter as well. The units of the coefficient are always the units of the dependent variable divided by the units of the independent variable.

We recommend writing the units of the constant and the coefficient when writing their numbers. In our example, the constant is −$4,917, and the coefficient of education is $3,298 per year. To translate this abstraction into a useful form, describe both the independent and dependent variable changes in words understandable to a larger audience. (See Box 8.7 for the systematic approach.)

$$\text{Earnings} = -\$4{,}917 + (\$3{,}298/\text{year}) \times \text{Education}.$$

Can a Regression Coefficient Be Interpreted as a Causal Effect?

When we interpreted the regression coefficient, we carefully chose the language of expectation or prediction—for example, those with one more year of education are *expected* to (or *predicted* to) earn on average $3,298 more. We took care not to say that one more year of education *causes* (or *results* in) $3,298 more in earnings (on average).

But can a regression coefficient be interpreted as the effect of the independent variable on the dependent variable?

The answer is complex. On the one hand, regression is essentially just another way of representing correlation, and correlation does not prove causation. (We will have much more to say about this in Chapter 11.) Just because education and earnings are correlated does not necessarily mean that more education causes higher earnings.[5]

On the other hand, under some circumstances described in Chapter 13 on control variables in multiple regression—and with much care and many caveats—regression *can* be used to measure a causal effect. Indeed, this is its most common application in social and policy research. The interpretation method of Box 8.7 is particularly useful when making a causal interpretation.

Changes Versus Levels

A very common error in interpreting regression results is to confuse interpretation of the regression coefficient with interpretation of the whole regression equation. The coefficient provides information about how the dependent variable *changes* when the independent variable *changes.* In our example, the coefficient says that someone with one *more* year of education is predicted to earn $3,298 *more.*

In contrast, the equation as a whole—the constant plus the coefficient multiplied by the *level* of the independent variable—provides information about the *level* of the dependent variable. To illustrate, let's predict the income for someone with 16 years of education:

$$\begin{aligned}\text{Predicted earnings} &= a + b_{educ} \times \text{Education}\\ &= -\$4{,}917 + \$3{,}298/\text{year} \times \text{Education}\\ &= -\$4{,}917 + \$3{,}298/\text{year} \times 16\text{ years}\\ &= \$47{,}851.\end{aligned}$$

[5]In fact, education does have a causal effect on earnings. In the four chapters on causation, we will illustrate how that can be proven.

Notice how we used the whole regression to predict the *level* of earnings of someone with 16 years of education to be $47,851. The distinction between the *change* represented by the coefficient and the *level* predicted by the whole equation will become important for more advanced forms of analysis covered in later chapters.

How to Interpret Regression Coefficients With Different Units of Analysis

When the data describe something other than people, such as schools, hospitals, or countries—in other words, when the unit of analysis is something other than a person—be sure to make that clear in interpreting the coefficient. Consider these examples:

- Using data on New York City neighborhoods, a regression is done with the independent variable of percent poverty and the dependent variable of asthma cases per 1,000 population. The coefficient found is 0.22. Following the steps in Box 8.7 to interpret the coefficient:
    - The unit of analysis is the neighborhood.
    - The independent variable is the neighborhood's poverty rate in percentage points.
    - A one-unit increase is a one-percentage-point higher poverty rate in a neighborhood.
    - The dependent variable is the asthma rate in cases per 1,000 population.
    - Interpretation: For every one percentage point higher a neighborhood's poverty rate, we expect the neighborhood's asthma rate to be .22 cases per 1,000 population higher.
        - We could say 2.2 cases per 10,000 population higher to make it easier to understand.

QUESTION

Suppose a regression on school-level data with an independent variable of student-to-teacher ratio and a dependent variable of reading test scores (in points) has a coefficient of −3.1. Interpret the coefficient.

- Sullivan and Dutkowsky (2012) did a regression with state-level data from the United States with cigarette tax as the independent variable and total (tax-inclusive) mean price of generic cigarettes as the dependent variable, resulting in a coefficient of 1.70. To interpret their result:
    - The unit of analysis is the state.
    - The independent variable is the state cigarette tax in dollars per pack.
    - A one-unit increase in the independent variables is a state with a one-dollar-per-pack higher tax.
    - The dependent variable is total price in dollars per pack.
    - Interpretation: For every dollar per pack a state increases its cigarette tax, we expect the mean price of generic cigarettes in the state to rise by $1.70 per pack.
    - Note that this simple analysis does not produce a good estimate of the causal effect of the state taxes, but the authors use more involved methods, covered in Chapters 13 and 15, that produce better estimates of the causal effect.

R-Squared and Residuals: How Well Does the Line Fit the Data?

***R*-squared** (defined formally in Box 8.6) expresses the proportion of the variation in the dependent variable that is explained (or predicted) by variation in the independent variables. *R*-squared is also thought of as measuring the goodness of fit of the data to the regression line. In our example, *R*-squared is .56, so we say that 56% of the variation among people in their earnings can be predicted just by variation in their education. This is a pretty strong *R*-squared—in fact, it is unrealistic in much real data to expect *R*-squared to be close to 100%. But how large an *R*-squared is needed for an acceptable fit? In simple regression, *R*-squared can be computed by (as the name suggests) squaring the correlation coefficient r. So using the rules of thumb outlined earlier for the magnitude of a correlation r, even an *R*-squared in the range of 9% to 10% would be considered at least a moderately strong relationship ($.30 \times .30 = .09$, or 9%). In other words, explaining 10% of the total variation in the dependent variable with just one independent variable is not doing all that bad.

The remaining, unexplained variation—not included in *R*-squared—is in the error terms, known as the **residuals**. Here is how to think about residuals: If the data were perfectly predicted by the regression, all the points would lie on the line. In this case, the residuals would all be zero and the *R*-squared would be one, meaning that 100% of the variation in the dependent variable was predicted using variation in the independent variable alone.

But with real data, the regression prediction (the line) does not completely coincide with the actual observed data. Consider the person, individual *i,* shown in Figure 8.7 who has 25 years of education and earns $117,375. The value of earnings predicted by *i*'s education would be $77,533, also marked on the line. The residual is this difference between the actual earnings and the predicted earnings, measured by the vertical distance from the data point to the regression line. The larger the residuals, across all data points, the poorer the fit—the smaller the residuals, the better the fit.

How Is Best Fit Defined?

The equations for the constant and the coefficient come from a criterion called *least squares,* so this form of regression is most correctly called *ordinary least squares* (OLS) regression. OLS regression chooses the constant and coefficient to minimize the sum of the square of the residuals.

While that is a reasonable method, it is clearly not the only one. Why not minimize the sum of the absolute value of residuals? That method would reduce the large influence of outliers in OLS regression analysis. Or why not minimize the horizontal distance from the data to the line? In fact, all these methods and others are both possible and reasonable, but they require a lot of numerical computation and do not have simple formulas. Historically, they were often not possible. While possible now, they are not common and should be reserved for those situations where one wants to minimize the influence of outliers.

For further reading on correlation and regression, consult an introductory statistics book (such as Friedman, Pisani, & Purves, 2007; Moore, 2009; or Salkind, 2010). For more on regression, we would recommend Lewis-Beck's (1980) *Applied Regression: An Introduction* or, for a more advanced treatment, an introductory econometrics book (such as Wooldridge, 2009).

Practical Significance

The numbers that come from analysis and research are meant to inform. Although it may seem obvious, *magnitude*—the size of the number—matters. An effect or difference may be too small to make much difference in the real world—or it may be very large and of crucial practical importance. How can we decide if an effect or relationship is large enough to matter?

The **practical significance** of a difference or relationship is the extent to which its magnitude (if true) would be important or relevant in the real world. Practical significance is also referred to as *substantive significance,* or as significance in whatever subject is being examined, such as *clinical* significance, *economic* significance, *policy* significance, and so on (J. Miller, 2004, 2005).

To determine practical significance, look directly at the magnitude of the difference or effect and see what it means when applied practically to the real world. For example, if a regression revealed that one more year of education was associated with just $1 more in annual earnings, most people would think that this effect is not economically significant. But if a year of education is associated with a boost of $10,000 per year in annual earnings, it's a much different picture. To determine the practical significance of a regression coefficient, interpret it in real-life terms, as described in Box 8.7. Knowing the units is essential for doing this.

Practical Significance Is a Matter of Judgment

Consider another example: If we learn that an antismoking campaign reduces smoking rates by 5 percentage points, that is clearly practically significant. About 20% of U.S. adults smoke, so cutting that rate to 15% would be a major accomplishment. On the other hand, if the campaign reduced smoking rates from 20.0%

to 19.5%, a cut of one half of a percentage point, many might decide that this is too small to matter in the practical world.

Still, some people might feel that a 0.5-percentage-point reduction in smoking is practically significant—especially if there are few alternatives with larger effects. There are more than 200 million adults in the United States, so even a reduction of a half of one percentage point in the rate of smoking would mean about 10 million fewer smokers (and in turn several million fewer premature deaths). Ultimately, practical significance is determined by those applying or using the results, including policy makers, advocates, and program planners, based on their values and judgment. One key question to ask when assessing the practical significance of programs is how large are the effects of plausible alternatives. That 0.5-percentage-point reduction might not be big, but what if it's a bigger effect than any of the alternative programs or interventions?

Practical Significance Is Not the Same as Practical

Often one wants to know if a program is practical, both viable and useful in the real world. Practical significance is one—but only one—part of this broader question. A program may have a practically significant effect but still be impractical for other reasons: It may be too expensive, unethical, or too culturally or politically controversial.

Effect Size

QUESTION

Think about a weight loss program for typical adults. How big an effect (in either pounds or kilos) would it need to have for you to judge it to be practically significant? If the standard deviation of adult weight in pounds is 28, and in kilos 13, what would the effect size be (using Cohen's *d*)?

One common way to examine the magnitude on an effect, and thus shed light on its practical significance, is to use various measures of **effect size**. The *correlation r,* discussed above, is one possible measure of effect size. Another commonly used measure of effect size is the ratio of the effect or difference in means to the standard deviation—sometimes called Cohen's *d* (after Jacob Cohen; see Cohen, 1992). Intuitively, an effect size provides a measure of how big a difference or effect is relative to the ordinary variation that the variable undergoes. Effect size is a way of comparing magnitudes from different variables or different studies. Cohen (1992) defined the following effect sizes for the difference between two means:

Small	Medium	Large
.20	.50	.80

To illustrate, let's consider the effects of an employment program on the time it takes for participants to find a job and on their starting wage, relative to a control group, as shown in Table 8.11. As these results show, the program has a much larger effect on reducing the days it takes to find a job than on the starting wage.

Table 8.11 An Imaginary Employment Program

	(A) Program Group	(B) Control Group	Difference (A − B)	SD	Effect Size (Difference/SD)
Days to find a job	7 days	14 days	−7 days	10 days	−.70
Starting hourly wage	$12	$11	$1	$5	.20

Statistical Software

Various software programs can be used for statistical analysis, including general-purpose spreadsheet programs, such as Excel, as well as specialized statistical software packages.

Spreadsheets

Spreadsheet software, such as Microsoft Excel, Apple Numbers, Google spreadsheets, or OpenOffice Calc, provides a number of built-in statistical analysis tools. Excel's statistical analysis tools are organized under an option called the Analysis Toolpak. If your data are quantitative and you do not have missing data, spreadsheets can do a fair amount, from basic descriptive statistics to regressions and significance testing.

But if the data include many categorical variables or missing data, spreadsheets can be somewhat limited. Using a spreadsheet is also more difficult with larger data sets containing many cases and variables. Finally, spreadsheets can be awkward to use for multiple regression with multiple independent variables. In such cases, a full statistical package may be a better choice.

Statistical Packages: SAS, SPSS, Stata, and R

SAS, IBM SPSS®, and Stata are the most widely used general-purpose statistical software packages. SAS and SPSS have both been around for decades, so many people have grown accustomed to using them. Stata is a bit newer program that has gained in popularity. All these programs do a wide range of descriptive statistics, graphing, data management, and regression, as well as various advanced methods, from specialized regression to factor analysis to multilevel modeling. For most serious data analysts or quantitative researchers, it is important to know one or more of these packages. R is an open-source (and thus free) statistical package that has a growing community of users and also developers contributing new capabilities and features.

Specialized Modeling and Matrix Language Programs

There are specialized programs for structural equation modeling, most notably LISREL, AMOS, and Mplus. And there are specialized programs for multilevel modeling, such as HLM, MLwiN, and aML.

Some prefer matrix language programs such as S, S-PLUS, GAUSS, or MATLAB. R also has matrix language capabilities. These programs allow analysts to go beyond the ready-made procedures built into the standard statistical software packages. They also allow for more control over the formulas and estimation methods used in calculating statistics.

Conclusion: Tools for Description and Causation

The tools that we have learned in this chapter are important for describing data. They are also fundamental techniques required for the next part of the book, which deals with causation. But to use these methods effectively, we must learn about statistical inference, covered in the next chapters, which involves measures of the precision of statistics and tests that help determine if differences or relationships are real or just random. And to fully tackle the question of causation, we need to learn about some additional methods that take account of many influences at once—multivariate methods. These are the topic of Chapter 10.

BOX 8.8
Tips on Doing Your Own Research: Descriptive Statistics

- Plan the analysis when you plan the design (for example, create shell tables). Consider how well the analysis result will address your research question.
- Pick a statistical package (or spreadsheet) that can do all the tests and analyses you will need. Make sure you have software documentation and a source for answering questions on the software (such as an online group of users).
- Determine the unit of analysis of your data.
- Determine the units of each variable in your data set.
- For all variables and all possible values of categorical variables, create labels (longer full names) in the software. Consult the codebook.
- Clean the data (checking for mistakes or for missing data). See Chapter 6 on cleaning data.
- Determine the types of all your variables (nominal categorical, ordinal categorical, or quantitative). Do not treat codes used for categorical variables as if they were quantitative variables.
- Decide if transformed variables would better address your research question. (For example: Would a rate be better than a count? Should you log a variable? Should you collapse categories?)
- Determine if you consider some variables independent variables and others dependent variables and, if so, identify which variables.
- Plot the distributions (using the software) of your variables and examine and describe the pattern. Make sure to use the right graph for the variable's type. Determine if there are any outliers or unusual values.
- Calculate the univariate descriptive statistics (using the software), including measures of central tendency and spread. Interpret the results. Make sure that the descriptive statistics are appropriate for a variable's type (for example, don't calculate the mean of a categorical variable). If a variable's distribution is skewed, consider using the median instead of the mean.
- Create charts and then descriptive statistics for the relationships of interest. Table 10.5 (see page 334) shows which types of analyses can be done with which types of variables. Make sure your x- and y-axes (or row and column percentages) correctly reflect your choice of independent and dependent variables.
- Interpret all your analyses in ways useful for your purpose (in policy or practice) and that address your research question(s). (For example, interpret regression coefficients using the steps in Box 8.7.)
- Assess the practical significance or magnitudes of relationships. Calculate effect sizes for relationships when possible.
- When possible, look for other analyses in the literature to which you can compare your results.

Chapter Resources

Key Terms

- Bar chart
- Categorical variable
- Coefficient of the independent variable (in regression)
- Coefficient of variation (COV)
- Constant (in regression)
- Correlation (correlation coefficient)
- Cross-tabulation (cross-tabs)
- Distribution
- Effect size
- Frequency distribution
- Histogram
- Incidence
- Mean
- Median
- Nominal categorical variable
- Odds
- Odds ratio (OR)
- Ordinal categorical variable
- Outliers
- Percent change
- Percentage point change
- Pie chart
- Practical significance
- Prevalence
- Quantiles
- Quantitative variable
- Rate of change
- Rates
- Relative risk
- Residuals
- Risk
- *R*-squared
- Scatterplot
- Simple regression
- Skewness
- Standard deviation
- Standardized scores (*z* scores)
- Units of analysis
- Units of measurement (units)
- Variable
- Variance

Exercises

8.1. Below is an excerpt from the variables page of SPSS for a data set.

Name	Label	Values
Pres92	VOTE FOR CLINTON,BUSH,PEROT	{1, BUSH} . . .
Age	AGE OF RESPONDENT	years
Agecat	Age categories	{1, less than 35} . . .
Educ	HIGHEST YEAR OF SCHOOL COMPLETED	years
Degree	RESPONDENT'S HIGHEST DEGREE	{0, lt high school} . . .
Sex	RESPONDENT'S SEX	{1, male}

a. For each variable, state whether it is quantitative, nominal categorical, or ordinal categorical.
b. What kind of graph would you use to show the distribution of Educ (highest year of school completed)?
c. What kind of graph would you use to show the distribution of Degree (highest degree)?

8.2. The following was excerpted from a data set for 1995.

Country	Population in Thousands	Literacy (% People Who Read)	Predominant Religion	Fertility (Average Number of Kids)	Predominant Climate	Daily Calorie Intake
Botswana	1,359	72	Tribal	3.13	Arid	2,375
Brazil	156,600	81	Catholic	5.19	Tropical	2,751
Bulgaria	8,900	93	Orthodox	3.95	Temperate	
Burkina Faso	10,000	15	Animist	4.00	Tropical	2,288

a. What is the unit of analysis (the individual) in this data set?
b. According to these data, in Brazil, how many people can read?
c. Give an example of two variables that could be used for a cross-tabs analysis.
d. Describe how Botswana's literacy rate is different from Burkina Faso's literacy rate as a percentage point difference and two kinds of percent differences. Discuss how such a difference should be reported to be most clear.
e. For each of the following three scatterplots based on the complete data set, state whether you think that the correlation coefficient is most likely to be close to -1, negative but close to zero, approximately zero, positive but close to zero, or close to $+1$. Briefly explain why you made the choice in each case.

i.

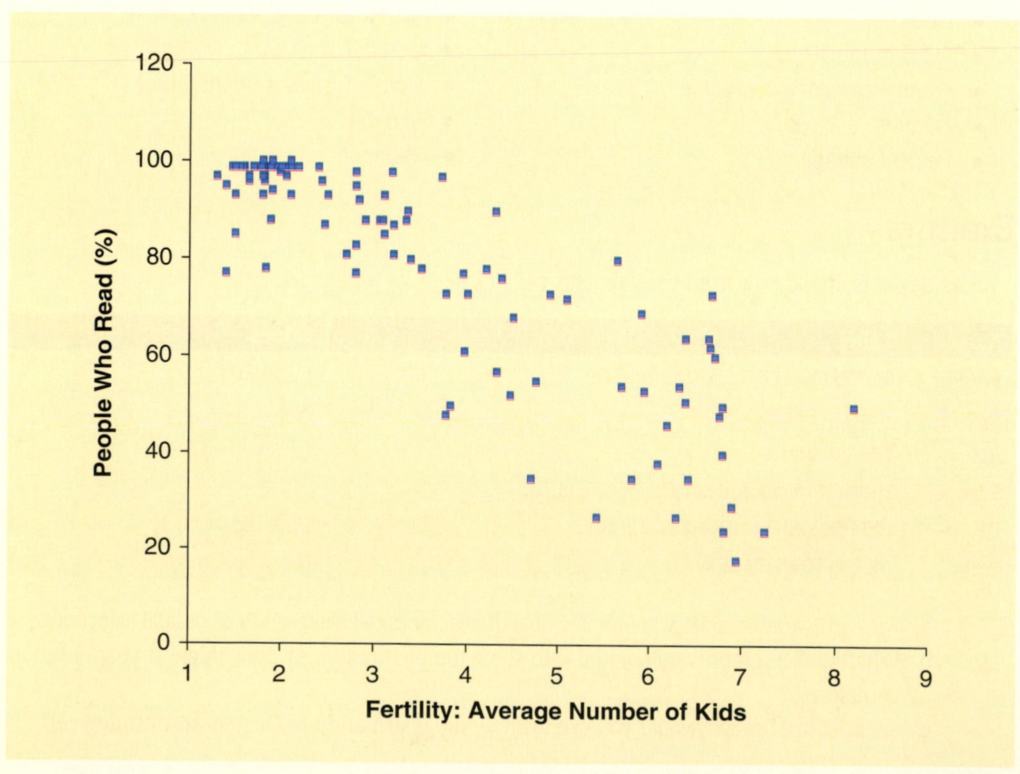

ii.

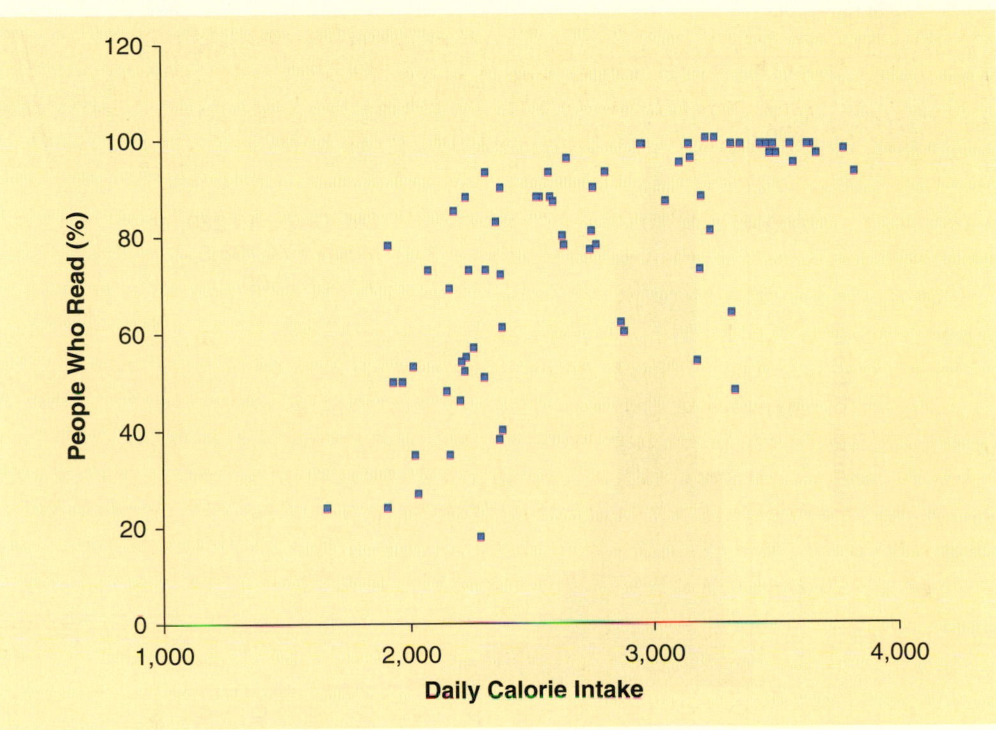
120
100
80
60
40
20
0
People Who Read (%)
1,000
2,000
3,000
4,000
Daily Calorie Intake

iii.

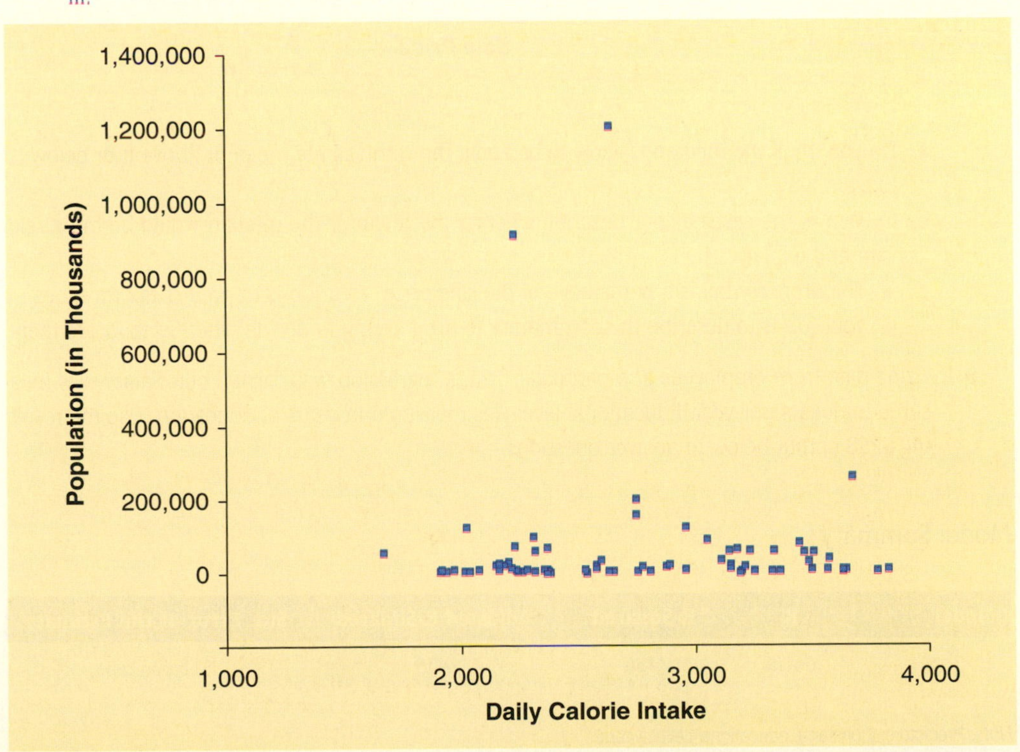
1,400,000
1,200,000
1,000,000
800,000
600,000
400,000
200,000
0
Population (in Thousands)
1,000
2,000
3,000
4,000
Daily Calorie Intake

8.3. Use the graph below on the number of homes sold at different prices in several neighborhoods:

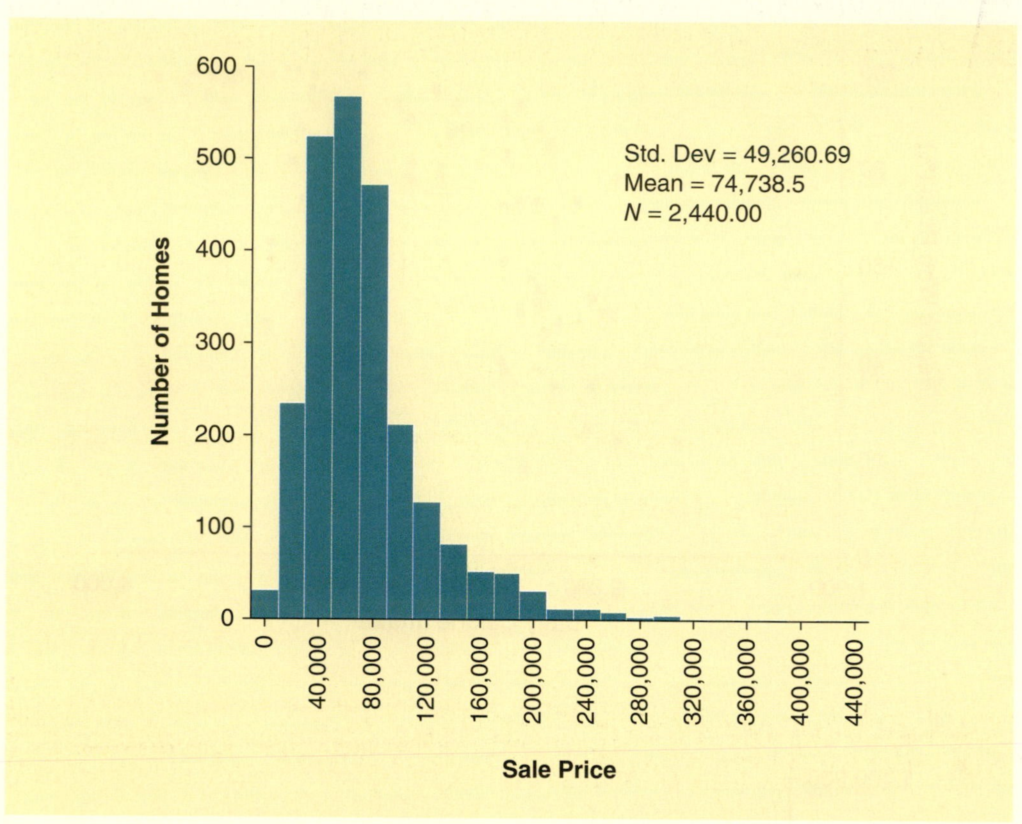

a. Do you think the median is likely to be about the same as the mean or above it or below it? Explain why.
b. In each of the cases below, describe whether the mean or the median would be more relevant and explain why:
    i. The property tax is a percentage of the sale price. Your job is to predict tax revenues.
    ii. Your job is to describe the community to firms trying to decide whether to locate there.

8.4. Using data from employees at a particular firm, a regression was carried out. Salary was measured in dollars per year. Educational level was measured in years of education. Use the resulting SPSS output below to answer questions.

Model Summary

Model	R	R-Squared	Adjusted R-Squared	Std. Error of the Estimate
1	.661 (a)	.436	.435	$12,833.540

Note: Predictors: (constant), educational Level (years)

Coefficients(a)

		Unstandardized Coefficients		Standardized Coefficients		
Model		**B**	**Std. Error**	**Beta**	**t**	**Sig.**
1	(Constant)	−18331.178	2821.912		−6.496	.000
	Educational level (years)	3909.907	204.547	.661	19.115	.000

Note: Dependent variable: current salary

a. Interpret the slope term (coefficient of the independent variable). What information does it give you? Make sure to say what units the slope term is in. Comment on and explain any striking features.

b. Interpret the constant term. What information does it give you? Make sure to say what units the constant term is in. Comment on and explain any striking features.

c. Explain the meaning of *R*-squared in general and interpret the *R*-squared result for this regression.

d. Predict the salary level of someone with 12 years of education.

8.5. In a general social survey, the following results were obtained. (RS refers to the respondent to the survey. Mother is the respondent's mother.) Interpret the results of this cross-tabulation.

RS Highest Degree × Mother a College Grad Cross-Tabulation

			Mother a College Grad		
			No	**Yes**	**Total**
RS highest degree	Less than HS	Count	211	5	216
		% within Mother a college grad	17.2%	4.0%	16.0%
	High school	Count	673	41	714
		% within Mother a college grad	54.9%	32.8%	52.9%
	Junior college	Count	72	12	84
		% within Mother a college grad	5.9%	9.6%	6.2%
	Bachelor	Count	185	44	229
		% within Mother a college grad	15.1%	35.2%	17.0%
	Graduate	Count	84	23	107
		% within Mother a college grad	6.9%	18.4%	7.9%
Total		Count	1225	125	1350
		% within Mother a college grad	100.0%	100.0%	100.0%

8.6. Incomes for a sample:

\$20,000	\$100,000	\$50,000	\$40,000	\$190,000

a. What is the mean income? Show your work and explain.
b. What is the median income? Show your work and explain.
c. Does the following sample have a higher or lower standard deviation than the one above? Explain.

\$20,000	\$100,000	\$50,000	\$40,000	\$150,000

8.7. Consider a data set of cities. z scores have been calculated for all variables. City ABC has a z score of $-.03$ for its crime rate and a z score of 2.1 for its median house prices.

Is the crime rate of ABC very low, somewhat low, about average, somewhat high, or very high? Are housing prices in ABC very low, somewhat low, about average, somewhat high, or very high? Explain briefly.

8.8. Regressions in Imaginary Worlds: A Thought Experiment

Imagine the following world with very strict laws: Those with an eighth-grade education earn \$10,000 annually. For every year of additional education, someone earns \$5,000 more. The law does not allow any variation whatsoever. Everyone goes to school until at least eighth grade.

Researchers collect data on years of education and earnings from everyone in this imaginary world. They perform a regression of earnings on education (i.e., earnings is the dependent variable, and education is the independent variable) and calculate the correlation between the two variables.

Before continuing, try to answer these questions, explaining your answers:

- What is the correlation coefficient?
- What is the *R*-squared of the regression?
- What is the regression coefficient of education? (Make sure to state its units.)

Answers:

- If we compare two individuals and one has one more year of education than the other, that person necessarily earns \$5,000 more. That is true in absolutely every single instance. So education and earnings are perfectly correlated in lockstep. The correlation is positive, because when education is higher, earnings are higher. Thus, the correlation coefficient is 1.
- If we try to predict earnings using education in a regression, we predict perfectly, because earnings are determined by education and nothing else. So *R*-squared is 1, because 100% of the variation in earnings is predicted by variation in education.
- The regression coefficient of education is \$5,000 per year: For every additional year of education, earnings are \$5,000 higher.

8.9. Examine the table below excerpted from a report about the effectiveness of the New Hope antipoverty program, which provided support to poor working families. (Also refer to the notes to the table for further information.)

Impacts of Children's Achievement for the Sample Survey
New Hope Project Five-Year Survey

	Program Group	Control Group	Difference	P-value	Effect Size[a]	
Woodcock-Johnson test[b] of achievement (Broad reading score)	98.1	96.0	2.0*	.091	.12	

Notes: Statistical significance levels are indicated as *** = 1 percent, ** = 5 percent, and * = 10 percent.

Tests were available for 816 children.

[a]The effect size is the difference between program and control group outcomes as a proportion of the standard deviation of the outcomes for both groups combined.

[b]The Woodcock-Johnson scores are age-standardized with a mean of 100 and a standard deviation of 15.

Source: Excerpt from Table 6.1 of Huston et al. (2003), "New Hope for Families and Children: Five-Year Results of a Program to Reduce Poverty and Reform Welfare."

a. Define practical significance in general and explain its importance.
b. Which number(s) would you use to assess the practical significance of the New Hope Project on reading achievement? What other information might you want to judge the practical significance of the effect?
c. Do you think that the result evaluating program effectiveness on reading achievement is practically significant? Explain.
d. Do you think that the result evaluating program effectiveness on reading achievement is statistically significant? Explain.
e. What statistical test was probably used for examining the effectiveness of the program on reading achievement? Explain very briefly.

STUDENT STUDY SITE

Visit the Study Site at **www.sagepub.com/remler2e** to

- test your knowledge with the self-quiz
- check your understanding of key terms with the eFlashcards
- explore helpful resources that relate directly to this chapter

The long-run patterns of chance events form the basis of statistical inference.

Source: © Can Stock Photo Inc./Linnea.

Overview: In this chapter, you will learn more about statistical inference: the process of generalizing from a random sample to the population from which it is drawn, including more about sampling distributions and confidence intervals. These ideas are critical for understanding the precision of statistical results obtained from samples. You will also learn about significance testing, used to probe hypotheses about the population, such as whether differences between groups or relationships between variables are more than just a fluke of who or what got sampled. You will also learn about the distinction between practical significance and statistical significance, as well as how to determine sample size and the related idea of statistical power.

Objectives

Learning Objectives

After reading this chapter, you should be able to

- Understand the idea of a sampling distribution and know its shape, center, and spread
- Understand the standard error and be able to calculate it for a proportion and a mean
- Calculate and interpret basic confidence intervals
- Understand the basic logic of statistical significance tests, including *p* values—and correctly interpret *p* values in words
- Interpret significance tests when applied to a difference in means, a regression slope, and a cross-tabulation (three basic and widely used significance tests)
- Distinguish practical from statistical significance
- Recognize the possible sources of statistical significance or insignificance in a given study
- Calculate sample size for a study and understand the issue of statistical power
- Articulate the problems and benefits of applying statistical inference to a convenience sample or census

9 Making Sense of Inferential Statistics

But Is It Significant?

"Majority now supports legalizing marijuana," announced the headline of a report on a Pew poll conducted in March 2013, based on telephone interviews with 1,501 adults selected randomly from the U.S. population (Pew Research Center for the People and the Press, 2013). Specifically, the poll found that 52% said that marijuana should be legal, the first time Pew has found a majority in favor of legalization. But is this finding statistically significant? Moreover, what does "statistically significant" really mean in this case? Looking more closely at the details of the Pew poll, we find the margin of error (or 95% confidence interval) is plus or minus 3 percentage points. This means that, based on the sample size, the true percentage of all adults in the U.S. population who favor legalization is estimated to fall between 49% and 55%. So it could be that the true percentage is really less than 50%. The Pew headline may be misleading, it turns out, because the results could reflect just a chance fluctuation in the sample when there is in fact no majority support in the U.S. population. In this sense, the results are not statistically significant (as proof that at least half of the population supports legalization of marijuana).

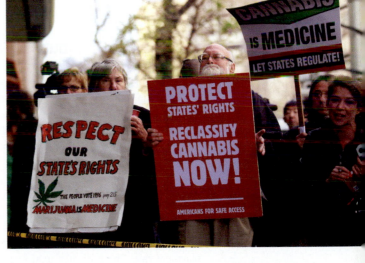

Surveys using samples seem to show that a majority support marijuana legalization: But is the majority significant?

Source: © STEPHEN LAM/ Reuters/Corbis.

The issue of whether some difference or relationship is statistically significant—real, not a fluke, and generalizable beyond those in the sample—arises frequently and is of great practical importance. To pick a few examples: Did unemployment really go up last month, or was the change only a fluke of who happened to end up in the most recent sample? Is the prevalence of diabetes greater among Hispanics than other ethnic groups, or are the group differences no larger than what you would expect by chance? Has productivity really increased after a new management initiative was introduced, or is the improvement just an ordinary fluctuation?

Statistical Inference: What's It Good For?

Like the Pew poll on marijuana legalization, the data in social and policy research often come from a random sample that aims to represent a much larger population, as we saw in Chapter 5. The monthly unemployment statistics in

QUESTION

Say a recent poll of 1,000 U.S. adults finds that 20% approve of the job Congress is doing, plus or minus 3 percentage points. Explain how this is an example of inference. What is the point estimate and precision measure from the poll? Can you think of a hypothesis these polling data could be used to test?

the United States, for example, come from the Current Population Survey (CPS), a random sample designed to enable representation of the labor force. The sample produces a statistic or *estimate* (such as the proportion unemployed last month) that aims to represent the true population **parameter** (which is unknown). The method involved in making conclusions about an unknown population parameter, based on a sample estimate, is called **statistical inference**.

There are three basic components to statistical inference: point estimates, precision, and significance tests. The **point estimate** is the statistic calculated from the sample that is our best guess as to the value of the *parameter* (the truth about the population). In the Pew poll, the point estimate is that 52% of U.S. adults support marijuana legalization. Of course, we have already learned to use point estimates. The process of analyzing a sample to get a point estimate is the same process as analyzing census data (like all the employees in an organization) or a convenience sample. The only difference is that now we interpret our sample statistic as our best guess about the unknown population parameter.

The second component of statistical inference is *precision*—determining how far off the statistic or point estimate is likely to be from the parameter—the true value in the population. Precision can be described using standard errors or confidence intervals, which were introduced in Chapter 5. We described these in terms of their most basic use for estimating population proportions or means, but standard errors and confidence intervals are used much more widely. In particular, they also apply to relationships, like regression coefficients and differences between groups.

The third component of statistical inference is *significance testing*. Significance tests, also called hypothesis tests, are used to examine the likelihood of specific hypotheses or statements about the population. For example, do a majority of U.S. adults support marijuana legalization, or not? Significance tests take many forms, but the most common and important ones are about whether differences between groups and relationships between variables are real and not just a fluke of sampling.

The logic and interpretation of statistical inference, particularly significance tests, can be confusing at times and take practice. This chapter will help you grasp these ideas and apply them with more sureness.

The Sampling Distribution: Foundation of Statistical Inference

Imagine doing a survey, using simple random sampling of 400 people, to learn the unemployment rate, as we described in Chapter 5, and finding that that 5.5% of the sample are unemployed. The figure 5.5% is the point estimate, our best guess about the population unemployment rate. But if we did the survey again, using identical methods, we would probably get a different result, say 5.1%. Nonetheless, the 5.5% estimate is still *unbiased*—in the sense that it is not systematically too high or too low. But at the same time all such estimates have *sampling error*—so it is likely to differ from the true population unemployment rate, at least by a little.

Another identical survey might find 5.6%, and so on. The reason, of course, is that due to the luck of the draw, any given sample may have a few more or a few fewer unemployed people. Real-world surveys, like the CPS, are done just once (for a particular time period) and give us just one point estimate, like the unemployment rate for last month.

To learn about statistical inference, it is useful to think about what would happen if we took many identical surveys, at the same time using the same methods, each one providing a separate estimate of the unemployment rate. The estimates from many samples (of the same size from the same population) form a **sampling distribution**, the key to understanding and interpreting inference. We introduced sampling distributions in Chapter 5, but we will now expand on that treatment, making it somewhat more technical in order to provide some more powerful inference tools.

What a Sampling Distribution Looks Like

To make our example more specific, imagine repeating a given sampling procedure many times, say, drawing up to 1,000 or more samples each of $n = 400$ people from the labor force in order to estimate unemployment. Each sample of 400 people will give us a slightly different estimate of the unemployment rate, simply due to chance fluctuations in who ends up in the sample—this again is the idea of sampling variability. The *sampling distribution* is the distribution (or plot) of the estimates from the many samples. Just as the distribution of an ordinary variable shows how often that variable takes on particular values, a sampling distribution shows how often the results from a random sample (the point estimates) take on particular values.

Remember again that this is a theoretical idea—in actual research practice, we draw only one sample of data to work with. But imagining what would happen if we took many samples rather than just one gives a background against which we can judge the results of our one real sample.

Computer simulations can be used to examine the features of sampling distributions. In Figure 9.1, we show sampling distributions made up of progressively more samples. When we have just 1 or even 10 samples, the results appear haphazard. But by the time we have taken 100 and especially 1,000 samples, a pattern emerges: The sampling distribution begins to take the shape of a *normal distribution* (shown with a line in the lower right-hand graph in Figure 9.1). This turns out to be very useful, as a normal distribution is consistent and easy to work with, especially once you know its mean and standard deviation.

As it turns out, the center or mean of any sampling distribution converges on the unknown population parameter P—which in this case we happen to know is $P = .05$ (only because this is what we, as textbook authors, set it up to be when we created the many random samples of $n = 400$ using our computer spreadsheet). Thus, the true unemployment rate in our made-up population is 5%, and the sampling distribution of 1,000 samples can be seen to center on this mark. This makes intuitive sense because the average of the many sample proportions should equal the population proportion (from which the samples were drawn). In practice, of course, the population proportion P is unknown—that is why we draw a sample p to estimate it in the first place. But it is very helpful to know that our sampling distribution is normal in shape and that its mean is the truth about the population.

Figure 9.1 Some Sampling Distributions

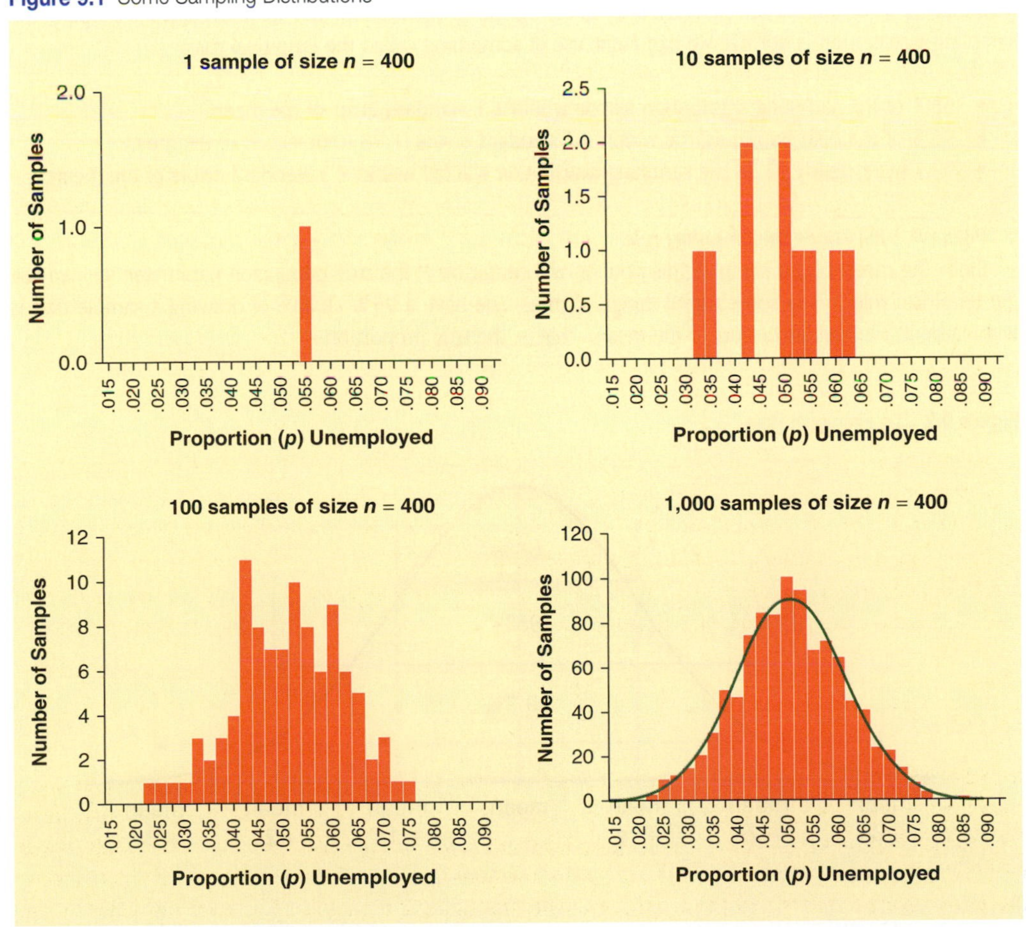

QUESTION

If we draw multiple random samples, in the same way from the same population, why do we expect to get a different result each time? Explain in your own words how the sampling distribution represents the differences we would expect to see.

The Standard Error (of a Proportion)

Recall that the **standard error** tells us the typical amount of sampling error we can expect in our point estimate. But let's look now at how to determine the standard error. Returning to the shape of the distribution, which is *normal,* we can know certain useful things about it—if we find out the spread, or standard deviation, of the sampling distribution, also called the *standard error.* As we have said before, the standard error is a measure of the precision of the estimate—how good a job we expect it to do, on average, at hitting the mark. For a percentage or sample proportion *p,* the spread or standard error (*SE*) of the sampling distribution can be found with this formula:

$$SE = \sqrt{\frac{P \times (1-P)}{n}},$$

where *P* is the population proportion (.05 in our example) and *n* is the sample size (400 in our example). Given this, the standard error *SE* would be the square root of (.05 × .95)/400, which equals 0.011 (or 1.1%). Remember that the standard error tells us roughly how precise a sample estimate is. In words, it means roughly that we can expect any one sample in this case to be about 1.1 percentage points, on average, off the true mark (the parameter, or real unemployment rate in the labor force) because of sampling variability.

Empirical Rule

Now that we've estimated the standard error of the sampling distribution, and we know that the shape of the sampling distribution is *normal,* we can make use of something called the empirical rule:

- 68% of the sampling distribution will be within ± 1 standard error of the mean.
- 95% of the distribution will be within ± 2 standard errors (1.96 to be exact) of the mean.
- 99.7%, or nearly all, of the sampling distribution will fall within ± 3 standard errors of the mean.

Figure 9.2 illustrates the empirical rule.

Since the mean of the sampling distribution will center on *P,* the true population parameter, we can use the empirical rule to say some useful things, such as "We have a 95% chance of drawing a sample that is within about ± 2 standard errors of the mean—that is, the true proportion *P.*"

Figure 9.2 The Empirical Rule

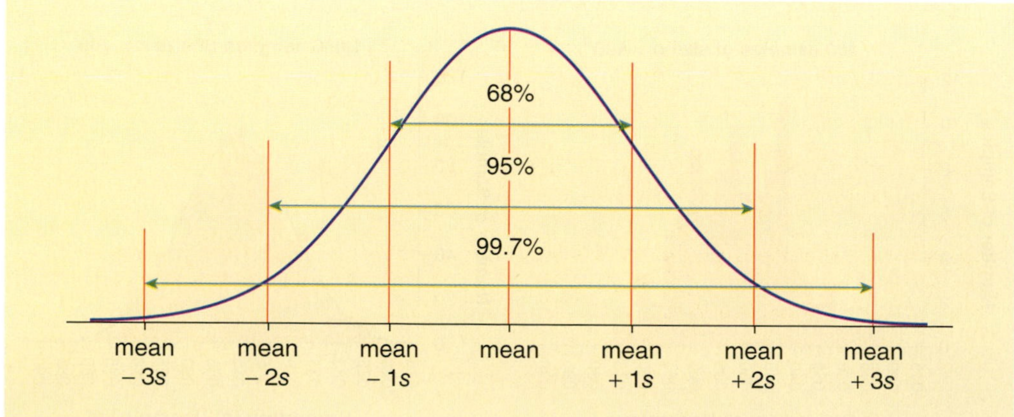

The Standard Error (of a Mean)

QUESTION

Explain in your own words why the spread of a sampling distribution provides information about the extent of sampling error.

Although we have illustrated the sampling distribution and standard error so far with a proportion, the same ideas apply to estimates of many statistics: means, variances, correlation coefficients, regression slopes, and so on. Here we will only give the additional details for the standard error of a mean. For other standard errors, you can consult a statistics textbook (such as Moore, 2009).

Whereas a proportion summarizes a categorical variable (such as being unemployed), a mean summarizes a quantitative variable (such as hours worked in the past week). And as before, we can imagine a sampling distribution of many, many means calculated from repeated samples (of the same size from the same population). The sampling distribution of a mean also turns out to be normal in shape,[1] and it also has a center that matches up with the parameter (the true mean of the population). The details of the calculation of the standard error of a mean, however, are different. Specifically, the standard error *SE* of a sample mean is

$$SE = \frac{S}{\sqrt{n}}$$

where S is the population standard deviation, which measures the spread or variability of the variable in the population, and n is the size of the sample.

Confidence Intervals

Confidence intervals tell us the range of values in which the true parameter we are trying to estimate (such as a proportion or mean) most likely falls, based on what we learned from a sample. For example, to interpret the confidence interval from our opening example in words, one would say, "We are 95% confident that the true proportion of U.S. adults who support legalizing marijuana is between 49% and 55%." Confidence intervals use the standard error and facts about the sampling distribution to provide a range, or boundary, around a sample estimate that, with a given level of confidence, contains the true population parameter. They are best known as "margins of error" from polls reported in the news.

Given what we know about the facts of the sampling distribution, it is fairly straightforward to construct a confidence interval. Roughly speaking, two standard errors on either side of a statistic give us a *95% confidence interval.* Here is the formula:

$$\text{Estimate} \pm 2 \times SE.$$

Although this formula (based on the empirical rule) is approximately correct, to get exactly 95% confidence requires exactly 1.96 standard errors. And in some situations, we might want another **level of confidence**, such as 90% or maybe 99%. If we let Z^* represent the precise number of standard errors we need to give us a desired level of confidence, the formula looks like this:[2]

$$\text{Estimate} \pm Z^* \times SE.$$

[1]The sampling distribution of a mean is close to a normal distribution when the quantitative variable in the population is not too skewed, or when the sample size is large enough. Specifically, when the sample is larger than $n = 30$, the sampling distribution of even a skewed variable tends to be close to normal in shape.

[2]The 1.96 value for Z^* depends on a sufficiently large sample size, roughly 100 or more. With smaller samples, the formula uses the T distribution instead of the Z distribution, and thus the number of standard errors needed for a 95% confidence interval is larger. See Moore (2009) for further details.

Thus, to determine the confidence interval, start at the actual statistic estimated from the sample, the point estimate, and move out in both directions a certain number (Z^*) of standard errors. To find the 95% confidence interval, as we have seen, Z^* is 1.96 *SEs*. To find the 99% confidence interval, Z^* is 2.58 *SEs*. Notice that to be more confident of capturing the true population parameter, the confidence interval must be wider. For a 90% confidence interval, Z^* is 1.65. Thus less confidence is associated with a narrower interval (for a given sample size).

Univariate Statistics and Relationships Both Have Confidence Intervals

Margins of error—confidence intervals by another name—get attached to percentages from polls. For example, we gave the example of the Pew poll that found that 52% of U.S. adults think marijuana should be legal—*plus or minus 3 percentage points*. Remember that the margin of error is twice the standard error—the similar names can be confusing.

The *plus or minus 3 percentage points* (or just *points* for short) means that we are 95% confident that the true percentage of the population that believes in legalization (the parameter) lies between 49% and 55%. But confidence intervals (and standard errors) can be attached to a wide range of other statistics, including the following statistics describing just one variable (univariate):

- A mean
- A difference in means
- An odds

Confidence intervals also can be attached to statistics describing relationships between two or more variables, including

- A regression coefficient
- An odds ratio
- A difference in means between two groups

QUESTION

Using Table 9.1, interpret in words the three different confidence intervals shown in the row labeled "Smoking some days."

To illustrate, consider Table 9.1, an extract from a study by the commissioner and others in the New York City Department of Health (Frieden et al., 2005). The table shows 95% confidence intervals for both proportions (e.g., percentage who smoke every day in 2002) and differences in proportions (e.g., percent change in smoking every day). Thus, we learn that, for 2002, we are 95% confident that the percentage of New Yorkers who smoked every day was between 13.6% and 15.4%. We are also 95% confident that the percent change (not percentage point change!) in that smoking rate was a decline of between 17.6% and 3.4%.

Indeed, you can attach a confidence interval (and a standard error) to almost any statistic calculated from sample data. Although the calculation details and difficulty vary, the meaning of all confidence intervals remains much the same: We are 95% (or 90% or 99%) confident that the true population parameter lies between the lower and upper limit of the interval.

Table 9.1 Extract of Table 1 in Frieden et al. (2005)

	Percentage in 2002 (95% CI)	Percentage in 2003 (95% CI)	Percent Change (95% CI)
Smoking every day	14.4 (13.6, 15.4)	12.9 (12.2, 13.6)	−10.5 (−17.6, −3.4)
Smoking some days	7.0 (6.4, 7.7)	6.3 (5.7, 6.8)	−13.1 (−23.7, −1.9)

Confidence Intervals Reflect Only Some Sources of Error

Confidence intervals and standard errors do not reflect all sources of error—only sampling error. But as we've seen in previous chapters, there are many other sources of error in research. Some of the sources of error *not* captured in a confidence interval (or margin of error) are as follows:

- Measurement error, from how questions are asked or understood or other errors in the measuring process
- Coverage error, from failing to include people or other units in the sampling frame
- Nonresponse error, from certain people refusing to participate
- Data processing errors, from handling or manipulating the data
- Causal inference error, from incomplete or erroneous models of the causal relationships between variables (to be discussed in Part IV)

Although confidence intervals provide useful information, these other sources of error must be considered as well in judging sample statistics.

Calculating a Confidence Interval (Margin of Error) for a Proportion

To illustrate the calculation of confidence intervals, let's consider a hypothetical example in which we seek to estimate patient satisfaction from a random sample of $n = 100$ patients who stayed last month in Metropolitan Hospital. After interviewing the people, we find that 67 reported being satisfied with their experience at the hospital (with the rest less than satisfied). Thus, the sample proportion (p) is

$$p = 67/100 = .67.$$

Now let's construct a confidence interval using the standard error *SE*—usually 2 standard errors (1.96, to be precise) on either side of our sample estimate:

$$p \pm 1.96 \times SE = .67 \pm 1.96(SE)$$

All we need now is the standard error *SE*, for which we saw a formula earlier. But recall that that formula relied on knowing the population parameter P—in our case the percentage of satisfied patients in the entire population (of all patients who visited the hospital last month). But we don't know the population parameter—indeed, that is what we are trying to estimate with our sample to begin with. So here is the trick statisticians use: They simply substitute the sample estimate (p) for the population parameter (P):

$$SE = \sqrt{\frac{p \times (1-p)}{n}}$$

The logic of this shortcut is based on the fact that the estimate (p) is a good guess (the best we have) as to what the parameter (P) might be. Moreover, especially as the sample size gets larger, the standard error (*SE*) becomes more and more influenced by the size of the sample (n) alone, and so a rough guess about p is all we really need. In addition, the larger the sample, the more accurate p is as a guess at P.

Plugging the numbers from our example into the equation, we get

$$SE = \sqrt{\frac{.67 \times (1-.67)}{100}},$$

which works out to be

$$SE = \sqrt{\frac{.2211}{100}} = \sqrt{.00211} = .047\,.$$

Thus, the *SE* is .047, which we plug into to the formula for the 95% confidence interval that we started with:

$$p \pm 1.96 \times SE$$

$$.67 \pm 1.96(.047)$$

$$.67 \pm .092$$

In words, this means we estimate that 67% of the patients who stayed at the hospital last month were satisfied with their experience, plus or minus 9 percentage points (rounding off, and assuming a 95% confidence level). Or in the language of confidence intervals, we are 95% confident that between 58% and 76% of all patients who stayed in the hospital last month were satisfied.

Variability, Sample Size, and Sampling Precision

The sample size n is in the *denominator* of the standard error, so as n increases, the standard error *SE* gets smaller. But also notice that $p \times (1 - p)$ is in the *numerator*, so as p moves farther from an even 50/50 spilt, this product gets smaller, and thus so, too, will the standard error *SE*. The closer the split is to 50/50, the more variability there is, and thus the less precise the estimate will be. Table 9.2 illustrates how the margin of error depends on *both* the sample size *and* the variability, or split, in the data.

Calculating a Confidence Interval (Margin of Error) for a Mean

We will now illustrate the calculation of a confidence interval for the mean of a quantitative variable. Continuing with the example of a survey of $n = 100$ hospital patients, say we are interested in estimating how many hours patients had to wait to be discharged from the hospital. Here are the sample results:

$$\bar{x} = 8.3 \text{ hours}, s = 5.6 \text{ hours}$$

Table 9.2 Margins of Error (95% Confidence Intervals) for Various Values of *p* and *n*

	p =				
n =	.055	.330	.500	.670	.800
100	.045	.092	.098	.092	.078
400	.022	.046	.049	.046	.039
1,000	.014	.029	.031	.029	.025
4,000	.007	.015	.015	.015	.012
10,000	.004	.009	.010	.009	.008

This means that, on average, patients in the sample waited 8.3 hours to be discharged from the hospital, with a sample standard deviation of 5.6 hours (remember that *s*, the sample standard deviation, is not the same thing as *SE*, the standard error). Now let's proceed with the calculation of the confidence interval using the following formula:

$$\text{Confidence interval} = \bar{x} \pm 1.96 \times SE = 8.3 \pm 1.96(\text{SE})$$

This is essentially the same formula that we used for a proportion, except that in place of the proportion p we now have the mean $\bar{x}$. The standard error *SE*, however, comes from the formula for the standard error of a mean that we introduced earlier:

$$SE = \frac{S}{\sqrt{n}}$$

But notice again that this formula uses the population standard deviation *S*—the spread of the variable in the population. The results of our sample of $n = 100$ give us only the sample standard deviation *s*—the spread of the variable in the sample. In practice, we don't usually know the population standard deviation *S*. The trick statisticians use, as before, is to simply substitute the known little *s* (the sample standard deviation) for the unknown big *S* (the population standard deviation):

$$SE = \frac{s}{\sqrt{n}}$$

Now we can plug in $s = 5.6$ and $n = 100$ and perform the calculations:

$$SE = \frac{s}{\sqrt{n}} = \frac{5.6}{\sqrt{100}} = \frac{5.6}{10} = .56$$

And then just substitute this result into the confidence interval formula:

$$\text{Confidence interval} = \bar{x} \pm 1.96 \times SE$$

$$\text{Confidence interval} = 8.3 \pm 1.96(.56)$$

$$\text{Confidence interval} = 8.3 \pm 1.1$$

In words, we estimate that the hospital's patients last month waited an average of 8.3 hours to be discharged, plus or minus 1.1 hours (assuming a 95% confidence level). Or in the language of confidence intervals, we are 95% confident that the average waiting time for discharge for all hospital patients last month was between 7.2 and 9.4 hours.

There is a final detail to mention: The formula we have shown for the mean uses the standard normal (*Z*) distribution, which gives the 1.96 value for 95% confidence. This is, technically speaking, not quite correct. Instead, we should use what is called the *student* t *distribution* (or just t *distribution* for short), a kind of modified (flattened-out) normal distribution that makes the probability calculations more accurate. Using the *t* distribution, the formula would be 1.98 instead of 1.96 for 95% confidence. But with rounding, the results are really not much different (unless the sample is quite small, in which case using *t* instead of *Z* results in wider confidence intervals).

In reality, we don't often have to calculate standard errors or confidence intervals in this way by hand—the statistical software does it for us. However, you need to understand enough to interpret standard errors and confidence intervals correctly.

QUESTION

Consider using surveys of the same sample size to calculate mean heights for the population of 6-year-olds in your country and the population of people of all ages there. Which will have more sampling error? Why?

How Big Does the Sample Size Need to Be? Getting the Precision You Want

When planning a study, whether a survey or another kind of study, larger samples are always valuable because they increase precision. However, larger samples usually cost more to collect. You can estimate how many subjects are needed to get the precision you require through the use of a **sample size calculation**.

Proportions: Calculating Sample Size

One rough way to calculate sample size is to use a table like Table 9.2, which we saw earlier. Say we want to estimate a characteristic like the proportion of people in an urban area who use public transportation to get to work, and we want a ± 3 percentage point margin of error with 95% confidence (the usual level). Examining the table, we can see that a sample size of $n = 1{,}000$ would give about this precision provided the actual percentage of public transit users in the population (that is, P) lies in the range of about 33% to 67% (which seems reasonable for an urban area). If the distribution is more lopsided, one way or the other, we could perhaps get away with a smaller sample size.

To be more exact, we could also use the simple formula from Chapter 5, which assumes a 50/50 split in the population and the usual 95% confidence level:

$$\text{Sample size} = n = \left(\frac{1}{\text{Margin of error}}\right)^2$$

You decide what margin of error you need, plug it into the formula, and solve for n. This formula provides a conservative estimate of the required sample size, which often makes sense because you never know what results you'll actually get—and because you'll likely calculate many statistics from the same sample.

To illustrate the calculation, let's continue with the public transit users example, in which we wanted a ± 3 percentage point margin of error. We simply plug this desired margin of error into the formula:

QUESTION

Suppose you want to survey people in your university, workplace, or other organization to learn the share who are satisfied with the organization. Explain how you would go about determining the sample size you would need to have a margin of error of 4 percentage points.

$$n = \left(\frac{1}{.03}\right)^2 = 1{,}111$$

The sample size is about the same as what we got eyeballing Table 9.2, although a bit larger because this formula uses conservative assumptions. Moreover, the calculated sample size is just a target—the actual sample size you end up with may be more or less, depending on the response rate and other unpredictable factors in data collection.

Means: Calculating Sample Size

The above calculations all involve proportions. For means, we need to make even more assumptions about the population to guess at the required sample size. Say, for example, we're interested in how long it takes people to commute to work (in minutes), so we want to estimate the mean commuting time with a margin of error of no more than ± 5 minutes with 95% confidence. Here is an approximate formula we can use:

$$\text{Sample size} = n = \left(\frac{2 * S}{\text{Margin of error}}\right)^2$$

S in this formula is the population standard deviation, in our case the standard deviation of the real distribution of commuting times for all people in our study population. We don't know this, of course—in fact, we don't even have sample data yet to estimate it. So one shortcut is to make a rough guess at the range of commuting times and divide by 6. For example, let's say the shortest commute is 0 minutes (if you work at home) and the longest commute is about 90 minutes (ballpark estimate), so the range in commuting times would be about 90 minutes, which divided by 6 is 15 minutes. Dividing by 6 is based on the empirical rule, which says that nearly all data in a normal distribution lie within ± 3 standard deviations of the center (6 standard deviations in total, from minimum to maximum). Commuting times may not be normally distributed, but we're dealing now in approximations just to get a rough cut on the sample size. Now we're ready to plug what we have into the formula:

$$n = \left(\frac{2 * 15}{5}\right)^2 = 36$$

We might round up to 40, just to be safe. But still notice how it seems to take a much smaller sample to get a moderately precise estimate of the mean, compared with the sample size required for a proportion or percentage. Although much depends on the variability in the variables you're working with, as a general rule means and other estimates from quantitative variables tend to have more precision than proportions and other estimates from categorical data.

Subgroup Analysis and Other Considerations

As pointed out in Chapter 5, one very important consideration in determining sample size is the need for subgroup analysis. Do you need to break up your sample into parts for separate analysis? And if so, how large or small are the subgroups likely to be? Essentially, you need to think of each subgroup as a separate sample from a distinct population. As a result, the precision of the statistics calculated for subgroups is only as good as the size of the subgroup sample—not the whole study sample.

Subgroup analysis can have a large impact on the required sample size. For example, if you want to analyze commuting habits for males and females separately, you would need double the sample to maintain the same precision (assuming the population of commuters is about half male and half female). To separately analyze a subgroup that was about 20% of the population with the same precision, you would need about 5 times the initial sample size. Because of the dramatically escalating scale and cost of sampling related to subgroups, researchers often must settle for less precision in their subgroup analysis, particularly for small subgroups. Another option is disproportionate sampling, as discussed in Chapter 5, which involves oversampling smaller subgroups.

Finally, the required sample size often depends on the need to detect differences between groups (as in an experiment) or to detect a relationship between variables using a statistical significance test. Statistical significance tests are the topic we turn to next.

QUESTION

Explain in your own words why the sample size needed for a particular margin of error is higher when you do subgroup analyses.

Significance Tests

If you read research articles or reports, you will certainly encounter statistical **significance tests**. They are used to determine, for example, if the effect of a job-training program is **statistically significant**, or if the reading ability of boys is "significantly" lower than it is for girls, or if the relationship between education and earnings is "significant." Academic journals, government agencies, and the courts often demand statistical significance tests as evidence. Significance tests are also widely used as part of the strategies for causation discussed in Part IV of this book.

But many people find significance testing strange—and, it turns out, for good reason. Even many academics challenge the logic and value of significance testing, with some going so far as to suggest that the procedure be abandoned altogether (Ziliak & McCloskey, 2008). Although it would be convenient to just go along with the critics and avoid the topic, it is important to first try to understand the logic and interpretation of statistical significance tests, since they are widely used.

QUESTION

You want to use polling data to test whether a candidate will get more than 50% of the vote, needed to avoid a runoff. What is your null hypothesis? What is your alternative hypothesis?

Falsification and the Logic of Significance Testing

A significance test relies on the logic of falsification—gathering evidence for the existence of something by demonstrating what it is *not*. An analogy of guessing what's inside a gift box helps demonstrate that we actually use this style of reasoning in everyday life.

Imagine that you get a nicely wrapped gift in a box from a friend. You're told not to open the box, but of course you can't help trying to guess what's inside. Say you have several guesses (hypotheses) about what's inside the box: a bicycle, a book, or a box of fancy marshmallows (your friend has funny tastes). Just by observing the size of the box, however, you rule out the bicycle hypothesis—it's just too small, even if the bike were disassembled. So it's *not* a bike. But it could still be a book or a box of marshmallows. Then you pick it up and realize it's much too lightweight to be a book. So you conclude it's *not* a book. You've now got evidence in favor of the marshmallow hypothesis by eliminating other possibilities. Of course, you still can't be sure what really *is* inside the box.

Significance testing (also called **hypothesis testing**) works in a very similar way. An explicit claim about the population, called a **null hypothesis**, is put forward. Then we look at the results from our sample data and ask, "How likely would this sample result be if the null hypothesis about the population were in fact true?" If our sample result would only rarely happen, given the null hypothesis, we reject the null. But if the result is at least somewhat likely, given the null hypothesis, we cannot reject it.

The null hypothesis is typically a statement of *no* difference or *no* relationship. There is *no* difference in the population between boys and girls in reading ability, for example. Or there is *no* relationship in the population between education and earnings. If we reject the null hypothesis, therefore, we have implicit evidence for what is called the **alternative hypothesis**—the logical complement of the null. There *is* a difference, or there *is* a relationship.

Guessing what's in a gift box resembles the logic of significance testing.

Source: © iStockphoto .com/billyfoto.

Notice that significance testing uses an implicit language of double negatives. A *statistically significant difference* between boys and girls means *not no difference,* and a *statistically significant relationship* between education and income means *not no relationship*. This is poor English, of course, but it is what significance tests tell us. This implicit double-negative language accounts for part of the struggle people have with interpreting significance tests.

Running a Significance Test

Let's practice significance testing with an example using data from the National Education Longitudinal Study (NELS), a random sample survey of middle school students in the United States (National Center for Education Statistics, 2013). Suppose we wonder if boys and girls differ in their academic achievement, as measured by a composite (reading and math) test score. As Table 9.3 shows, boys on average scored 50.4 while girls on average scored 51.5, over a point higher. That answers the question, it would seem.

But our data come from a sample of only $n = 1{,}085$ middle school students from a much larger population.[3] So perhaps we just got this difference by chance, the luck of the draw

[3]This is a random subsample of the NELS we drew for purposes of illustration; the complete NELS involved nearly 25,000 students.

as it were, when in reality there is no difference in test scores between middle school boys and girls in the United States. You should recognize this as a *null hypothesis* of *no* difference in the population between boys and girls.

But how do we tell if the difference in the means we see in our sample in Table 9.3 is large enough to rule out a null of no difference? The standard error—as a gauge of sampling variability—provides a benchmark. We can ask, "Is the observed difference large or small relative to the standard error?" If the difference is large relative to the standard error, then it is unlikely to be just a fluke of sampling, and we can probably rule out the null of no difference.

To make this idea more formal, we construct what is called a **test statistic**:

$$\text{Test statistic} = (\text{Estimate} - \text{Null})/SE$$

In our case, the sample estimate of the difference in means was −1.072 test points (meaning boys scored 1.072 points lower than girls, on average). The null hypothesis is no difference, or 0.000 points. The computer finds the standard error of the difference to be .620, so we have

$$\text{Test statistic} = (-1.072 - 0.000)/0.620 = -1.729.$$

Statistics and probability theory tell us that this test statistic takes the shape of a *t* distribution (which looks much like a normal *Z* distribution, as we mentioned earlier, although a bit flatter and more spread out). The statistical software does the *t*-test calculations for us, so we won't worry about the details here (you can find them in any introductory statistics textbook). The computer tells us that a *t* statistic of −1.729 has a probability of .084 (or 8.4%). The next thing to do is figure out what this probability—or *p* value—tells us.

p Values

The probability associated with a test statistic is called a ***p* value** for short. Here is its meaning: A *p* value represents the probability of observing the sample estimate (or an estimate even further from the null) when the null hypothesis about the population is true.[4] In our example, the *p* value tells us that with a random sample of

Table 9.3 Difference in Composite (Reading/Math) Mean Test Scores of Boy and Girls (NELS Data)

Group	Obs.	Mean	Std. Err.	Std. Dev.
Boys	542	50.408	0.438	10.202
Girls	543	51.479	0.438	10.212
Combined	1,085	50.944	0.310	10.216
Diff. (boys − girls)		−1.072	0.620	
t		−1.729		
p		0.084		

Source: NELS Data.

[4]The phrase "or . . . further from the null" makes this a two-sided hypothesis in which our alternative hypothesis includes both positive and negative differences. It is also possible to have one-sided hypotheses in which only a difference that is larger in magnitude but of the same sign is part of the alternative and used to calculate the *p* value. We do not discuss one-sided hypotheses further. See Friedman, Pisani, and Purves (2007), Moore (2009), Salkind (2010), or any introductory statistics book for more details. Statistical software packages always use two-sided hypothesis tests as their default.

$n = 1{,}085$, we have an 8.4% chance of observing a difference of 1.072 test score points (or more) when in the population there is really no difference in means between boys and girls (the null). Or to put it another way, in a world in which boys and girls have the same test scores in the population (the null), a sample of $n = 1{,}085$ would by chance show a difference in means as large as (or larger than) our results only 84 times in 1,000.

When the p value is low, we can reject the null hypothesis. In other words, a low p value means that it is very unlikely that our sample would give us a difference this large, if there is really no difference in the population. So the null must be false. Recall the gift box analogy and the language of double negatives: We demonstrate a difference in test scores by showing that there is not no difference.

Is It Significant?

To repeat: We reject the null hypothesis if the p value is low. But how low? One answer is that there are rules of thumb, as well as standards enforced by academic journals, regulatory agencies (such as the Food and Drug Administration), and the courts. The most common **significance level** is *.05,* which is 5% or 50 in 1,000. In our example, the p value is higher—it does not fall below this level of statistical significance. As a result, using the .05 level, the difference in mean test scores between boys and girls in our sample is *not* significant statistically.

Although the .05 level is widely used—indeed .05 has become almost sacrosanct in significance testing—in reality p values fall on a continuum, and we might choose to use other levels of significance. For example, we could use a significance level of .10 or 10%, in which case the difference between boys and girls in our sample would turn out to be statistically significant. Or to put it more formally, our test of the differences in means is statistically significant at the 10% level but not at the 5% level. Another possible significance level is .01 or 1%—a very strict standard for statistical significance. Clearly the boy-girl difference in our sample is not significant at this level.

If all this seems rather arbitrary, that's because in a sense it is. Deciding whether something is "statistically significant" is mostly a matter of judgment, especially when the p value is around the borderline. Much depends on the context and what decisions you will make in the real world, based on your significance test. High standards of proof might be important in some situations, such as testing the safety of new drugs. In our test score example, if we were to employ these results as the basis for investing millions in a new education initiative to help boys close the test score gap, the .10 significance level would be foolish. The p value of .084 is likely enough that we would be concerned that our results might reflect just chance, sampling error, or statistical noise. But sometimes more flexible standards of proof are appropriate. Are the results from our sample of $n = 1{,}085$ strong enough to justify looking further into the issue of the boy-girl test score gap, perhaps using other data? Of course they are—we certainly have enough evidence to at least take this next step. You might miss something important if your standards of proof are too high, especially in exploratory analysis.

Because there is no one right standard, results are often shown indicating different significance levels with asterisks or stars. For example, one star might indicate significance at the 10% level, 2 stars 5%, and 3 stars 1%. To illustrate, consider Table 9.4, an extract from Table VI in Katz, Kling, and Liebman (2001), relating to the Moving to Opportunity experiment, which we will discuss in Chapter 14. The table shows the differences in children's outcomes between families who got housing vouchers to move to a low-poverty neighborhood (treatment group) and those who did not (control group), with stars indicating the level of statistical significance of the difference. We are confident that children in the voucher group differed from children in the control group and had fewer injuries or accidents with a p value of less than .05; that they differed in asthma attacks requiring medical attention with a p value of less than .10; and that they did not differ significantly (at least at the 10% level) in going to a doctor for immunization (Katz et al., 2001).

QUESTION

For the following p values, determine if the test is statistically significant at the 10%, 5%, and 1% levels: $p = .24$, $p = .08$, $p = .003$.

Significance Tests for Simple Regression

Often researchers want to test the statistical significance of a relationship between two quantitative variables. For example, suppose we are interested in whether there is a relationship between time spent watching TV

Table 9.4 Extract From Table VI of Katz et al. (2001) on the Moving to Opportunity Experiment

	Control Mean	Experimental–Control Difference
Any injuries or accidents during the past 6 months that required medical attention	.105	−.059**
Any asthma attacks requiring medical attention	.098	−.051*
Been to doctor for regular checkup or immunization during the past 6 months	.856	−.043

Note: $^*p < .10$, $^{**}p < .05$.

Source: Katz, Lawrence F., Jeffrey R. Kling and Jeffrey B. Liebman. 2001. Moving to Opportunity in Boston: Early Results of a Randomized Mobility Experiment. *Quarterly Journal of Economics* 116: 607–54. By permission of Oxford University Press.

during weekdays and the academic performance of U.S. middle school students. We can again use the NELS, a random sample survey of U.S. middle school students, to examine this question. The most common statistical method to use in this case is regression analysis, which estimates the direction and strength of a relationship between an independent variable X and a dependent variable Y, as we saw in the last chapter.

But what does it mean to do a significance test of a relationship? Essentially, it means we are testing whether the relationship is strong enough in the sample to infer the existence of a real relationship between the two variables in the population. Or in other words, we want to rule out the possibility that the relationship is just a fluke feature of our particular sample. The null hypothesis—the starting point of all significance tests—is that there is no relationship between X and Y in the population. In a regression, no relationship means a slope of 0 (a flat line, if fitted to a scatterplot). Thus, the null hypothesis looks like this:

$$\text{Population slope} = \beta = 0$$

We then use our sample data to calculate the regression equation and to see how the slope we get compares with this null. Table 9.5 shows the results of the regression analysis of TV hours and test scores using the NELS data.

The slope in the NELS sample tells us (as we might have suspected) that TV hours are negatively associated with test scores; specifically, a student's test score drops by 1.18 points for each hour spent watching TV during weekdays (on average). But is this slope coefficient different enough from 0—the null—to be significant statistically? Could it be just a chance result in this particular sample of school kids? To answer this

Table 9.5 Regression Analysis With Significance Test (NELS Data)

Test Score Points	Coef.	Std. Err.	t	p
TV hours	−1.18	0.20	−5.87	0.0000
(constant)	56.06	0.76	73.90	0.0000

R-squared = .04; n = 964.

question, we need to compare the slope coefficient with its standard error, which represents sampling variability—or how much the slope is expected to vary from sample to sample. Specifically, we divide the slope by the standard error (which is the test statistic t):

$$t = -1.18/.20 = -5.87$$

This tells us that the sample slope of −1.18 is almost six standard errors away from 0—the null—which is highly unlikely to happen just by chance. The p value, in fact, is less than .0001 or less than 1 in 10,000. A slope like this would rarely happen by chance, so we have strong evidence to reject the null of no relationship. Or in other words, the relationship between TV hours and test scores is highly significant statistically.

In case you were wondering, the computer carries out a significance test for the constant as well, but this is not really meaningful in most regression analyses and can be ignored. But make sure not to confuse this with the statistical test of the slope.

Chi-Square Test of Cross-Tabs

Many variables are categorical, not quantitative. To test whether two categorical variables are related, a **chi-square test** can be applied to a cross-tabulation (or cross-tab for short, also called a contingency table or two-way table). The test is similar in logic to the usual test statistic but takes a somewhat different form.

The first step is to cross-tabulate the data, like the example in Table 9.6, which is again from the NELS. This table shows the relationships between type of school and whether or not the family has a daily newspaper (a proxy of the availability of learning resources at home). Looking at the column percentages, it appears that students in public schools are less likely to have a daily newspaper compared with students in religious schools and especially private schools. But is the pattern significant—does it reflect real differences in all middle school students in the United States, or is it just a fluke of this one sample?

A chi-square test helps answer this question. The first step in the test calculation is to determine what counts would be expected in the cells of the table if there were no relationship between the two variables. These are the expected cell counts shown in Table 9.6, which appear below the observed cell counts. The expected cell counts are the counts that we would find if the column percentages for public, religious, and private school students (often called *conditional distributions*) all matched the total column percentages (called the *marginal distribution*).

QUESTION

If the column percentages for "Family has newspaper" in Table 9.6 were 70%, 71%, and 72%, rather than 68%, 86%, and 90% as they really are, would you expect the p value testing for a relationship to be larger or smaller than the actual p value of .000001? Explain why.

The next step in the chi-square test is to compare the observed counts with what would be expected if there were no relationship in the population (the null hypothesis). The greater the difference, the easier it is to reject the null of no relationship.

Specifically, the chi-square formula works like this:

- *Step 1:* Find the expected count (expected if no relationship) in each cell in this way: (Row total × Column total)/Table total
- *Step 2:* Calculate the chi-square statistic = $\chi^2 = \Sigma$ (Observed − Expected)^2/Expected
- *Step 3:* Look up the associated p value using a chi-square table or software, with degrees of freedom = (Rows − 1)(Columns − 1)

Most statistical software packages will do these chi-square calculations for you, so the most important skills are to be able to interpret the p value and the patterns in the data. At the foot of Table 9.6, you can see the chi-square statistic and p value, which is extremely low (literally 1 in a million) and thus highly significant statistically. We have strong evidence from this sample that there is a relationship between school type and having a daily newspaper in the population of all U.S. middle school students.

Table 9.6 Cross-Tab and Chi-Square Test (NELS Data)

Daily Newspaper		School Type			
		Public	Religious	Private	Total
Family has	Obs	626	112	46	784
	Expect	655	92.7	36.3	784
	Col %	68.12	86.15	90.2	71.27
Family does not have	Obs	293	18	5	316
	Expect	264	37.3	14.7	316
	Col %	31.88	13.85	9.8	28.73
Total	Obs	919	130	51	1,100
	Expect	919	130	51	1,100.00
	Col %	100	100	100	100
Pearson chi2(2) = 27.4485 Pr = 0.000001					

Other Test Statistics

A *t* test for group differences, a *t* test for regression, and chi-square are just a few of many different test statistics. Others include *F* and *z* statistics. And each test statistic can be calculated in a variety of different ways depending on the analysis, for example a *t* test for one mean, a difference in means, or a regression slope. Table 9.7 shows the most common tests used for some of the most common statistical analyses.

p Values: Interpretation and Universality

The *p* value is the probability that one could have observed the result seen in the study—or a result even further from the null hypothesis—if the null hypothesis were true. The strangeness of this interpretation leads people to frequently misinterpret the *p* value. People sometimes erroneously interpret the *p* value as the probability that the null hypothesis is true, but that interpretation is wrong and can be misleading.

Table 9.7 Common Statistical Analyses and Their Test Statistics

Analysis	Usual Null Hypothesis	Test Statistic
Comparison of means	Diff = 0, No difference	*t* statistic
Comparison of proportions	Diff = 0, No difference	*z* statistic (or chi-square)
Paired sample means	Mean of differences = 0	*t* statistic
Odds ratio	*OR* = 1, No difference	Chi-square statistic
Cross-tabulation	No relationship	Chi-square statistic
Regression	Coefficient = 0, No relationship	*t* statistic
ANOVA	No difference across all means	*F* statistic

Because the details of statistical significance testing appear in many forms, depending on the data and the question, we recommend that you focus on understanding the null hypothesis and the *p* value and pay less attention to the magnitudes of *t* statistics, chi-square statistics, *F* statistics, and so on. The *p* values are universal. Once you learn their interpretation—and you know what null hypothesis is being tested—you can make sense of significance testing without knowing the technical details.

Statistical Significance, Practical Significance, and Power

Many people read too much into a significance test. Such tests help us decide if an observed difference or relationship is a fluke or not. But they do not tell us if the magnitude of the difference or relationship is big enough to matter in the real world—if it has *practical significance*. In the previous chapter we discussed practical significance and measures of effect size. Let's see now how statistical significance does not tell us the same thing.

Consider again an antismoking campaign, and let's say this time we observe a practically insignificant 0.2 percentage point reduction in smoking rate, which is nonetheless statistically significant. You might wonder how such a small difference as 0.2 percentage point could turn out to be statistically significant. It all boils down to small standard errors, most likely stemming from a very large sample size. While a smaller difference is less statistically significant, all else held equal, even a very small difference can be statistically significant if the standard errors are sufficiently smaller still. If the standard error in our smoking rate estimate is 0.05 percentage point, a difference of even just 0.2 percentage point (4 times the standard error) will be highly significant statistically.

Combinations of Statistical and Practical Significance

To illustrate the possible combinations of statistical and practical significance you may encounter in a study, Table 9.8 presents four fictional examples involving schoolchildren and their math scores. The differences in mean test scores between boys and girls and the standard errors of those differences are calculated.[5] The test statistic is then the difference divided by the standard error. Table 9.8 provides the data and calculations.

Column A shows a difference between boys and girls that is both practically and statistically significant. Boys score 50 points higher on average, and there is no possible way that this difference was a fluke of sampling (the *p* value tells us this). Policy makers should take the gender gap seriously and look for ways to address the problem.

In column B, the difference in means between boys and girls is trivial in magnitude, too small to care much about. But the difference is still statistically significant because the standard errors are so small. In other words, the means were measured with tremendous precision, due to the large sample size, so we know that the 2-point difference between boys and girls is not just a sampling fluke. But it is still just a mere 2-point difference, not of much importance in the real world of education policy and practice. Given a large enough sample, almost any difference can become statistically significant.

In column C, the difference between boys' and girls' scores is large. It would be practically significant—if it were an accurate picture of reality. But with data on only nine students and lots of variability (a high standard deviation), the standard errors are high, and the means are not estimated with much precision. Thus, the difference in means might well be just a fluke of sampling due to the very small sample size. There might be something going on here—there may be a gender gap in the scores—but we just do not know. To make a sound decision, we need more data.

In column D, the results are neither practically nor statistically significant. It might seem like these results are of little use for policy or practice, but in fact, they provide valuable information. Practically important differences between boys' and girls' test scores have been ruled out. Policy makers would know that they do not need to worry about a gender gap.

[5]To make things simpler, we will assume that the standard deviation is the same for boys and girls.

Table 9.8 Scenarios for All Possible Combinations of Statistical and Practical Significance

All Possible Combinations of Statistical and Practical Significance: Four Made-Up Examples Comparing Boys' and Girls' Mean Test Scores				
	A	**B**	**C**	**D**
Sample size	10,000	10,000	9	1,000
Overall mean test score	200	200	200	200
Standard deviation	25	25	100	25
Girls' mean test score	175	199	175	199
Boys' mean test score	225	201	225	201
Δ = Difference in Test Score (Boys' − Girls')	50	2	50	2
Effect size	$= \Delta/SD$ = 50/25 = 2	$= \Delta/SD$ = 2/25 = .08	$= \Delta/SD$ = 50/100 = .5	$= \Delta/SD$ = 2/25 = .08
Practically significant?	Yes	No	Yes (If difference true)	No
Standard error of the difference in test score mean*	$= 2 \times SD/\sqrt{N}$ $= 2 \times 25/\sqrt{10{,}000}$ = .5	$= 2 \times SD/\sqrt{N}$ $= 2 \times 25/\sqrt{10{,}000}$ = .5	$= 2 \times SD/\sqrt{N}$ $= 2 \times 100/\sqrt{9}$ = 66.6	$= 2 \times SD/\sqrt{N}$ $= 2 \times 25/\sqrt{1{,}000}$ = 1.58
t statistic for test of difference	$= \Delta/SE$ = 50/.5 = 100	$= \Delta/SE$ = 2/.5 = 4	$= \Delta/SE$ = 50/66.6 = 0.75	$= \Delta/SE$ = 2/1.58 = 1.26
p value	$p < .0001$	$p < .001$	$p > .40$	$p > .20$
Statistically significant?	Yes	Yes	No	No
Qualitative description	An important difference that's really there.	Lots of data make small, unimportant difference statistically significant.	Could be large, important difference, but we can't be sure. Not enough data to tell.	We're sure that there is no difference of a magnitude large enough to matter.

Note: *The standard error of the difference between two groups with equal standard deviations and equal sample sizes (as in this case) is $2 \times SD/\sqrt{N}$, where N/2 is the sample size of each group.

The easiest way to see that a practically significant difference has been ruled out is to calculate the confidence intervals. A 95% confidence interval for the 2-point difference in means is roughly $2 \pm 2 \times 1.58 = 2 \pm 3.2 = -1.2$ to 5.2. So we are 95% confident that the true result lies somewhere between boys scoring 1.2 points below and 5.2 points above girls. Provided we don't consider the magnitude of either the upper or lower bounds of the confidence interval to be of a practically important magnitude, we have ruled out practically important results.

QUESTION

Consider a study to determine if participation in a new job training program leads to higher hourly wage earnings. Describe a situation in which a gain of only $0.05 in hourly earnings could still be statistically significant. Describe a situation in which, despite a statistically *in*significant result, the new program is associated with a gain of $10.00 in hourly earnings.

Statistically Insignificant Results Can Be Useful

Statistically insignificant results are interesting and informative, provided they come with narrow confidence intervals. If a finding of a difference or an effect would be interesting, the finding of no difference or no effect is also interesting, provided you're *sure* that there really is no difference or no effect.

Unfortunately, it is often hard to publish statistically insignificant results. But it can be done by emphasizing the narrow confidence intervals and how striking and interesting the lack of effect is. In fact, a major problem in the scientific literature is the publication bias toward statistically significant results, which can make it seem like something is effective when it is not. In fact, that tendency undermines the usefulness and accuracy of meta-analysis studies that combine the results from many different articles to produce a more precise result. (Meta-analysis was discussed in Chapter 5.)

Although our example used a comparison of means (independent samples t test), the same ideas apply to all kinds of significance tests, including regression and cross-tabs. For any kind of significance test, pay attention to the magnitude of the effect or effects—not just the p value. Just because something is statistically significant does not mean that it is practically significant—its magnitude could be tiny. In these days of explosive quantities of data, this situation is increasingly common.

Box 9.1 summarizes the various possible causes of statistical significance and insignificance and the different kinds of practical conclusions that should be drawn.

BOX 9.1
Sources of Statistical Significance and of Statistical Insignificance

Sources of Statistical Significance

1. Large, practically important differences or relationships
    - Large differences swamp standard errors → statistical significance
    - You can conclude that a practically significant difference exists.
2. Very small standard errors
    - Usually due to very large sample size
    - Very precise measures
    - Very small, practically insignificant differences can still be large relative to smaller standard errors → statistical significance
    - Be wary of statistically significant results that have no practical significance.

Sources of Statistical Insignificance

1. Large standard errors
    - Usually due to small sample size
    - Even large magnitude differences could be a fluke of who was sampled.
    - Be aware that the lack of statistical significance does not necessarily mean that there is no practically significant difference. It can mean that there is not enough data to know.
2. Differences of a very small magnitude
    - With sufficiently narrow confidence intervals, you know that no practically significant difference exists.

Failing to Recognize a Difference: Type II Errors

Another set of ideas can help sort out the same kind of issues. Think about the example of a new drug being compared with an existing treatment. Two possibilities exist: (1) The new drug is better, and (2) the new drug is not better. Suppose standard policy is to accept the evidence that the drug is better if you can reject the hypothesis of no difference with a *p* value of .05 or less. In other words, we are willing to accept a 5% risk that we will conclude that the new drug is better when in fact it is not.

This is an example of **Type I error**—the null hypothesis of no difference is in fact true, but we erroneously reject it. Conventional standards for statistical significance limit the probability of a Type I error to 1% or 5% (sometimes even 10% is considered OK, for exploratory studies). The idea is that to accept a new treatment or program as effective, we want to be sure that it really is better.

Unfortunately, the less likely we are to make Type I errors, the more likely we will make another type of error, called a **Type II error**—accepting the null of no difference when in fact it is false and should be rejected (see Table 9.9). In the drug testing example, a Type II error would happen if we concluded that the new drug is not effective (we accepted the null) when the new drug is in fact better.

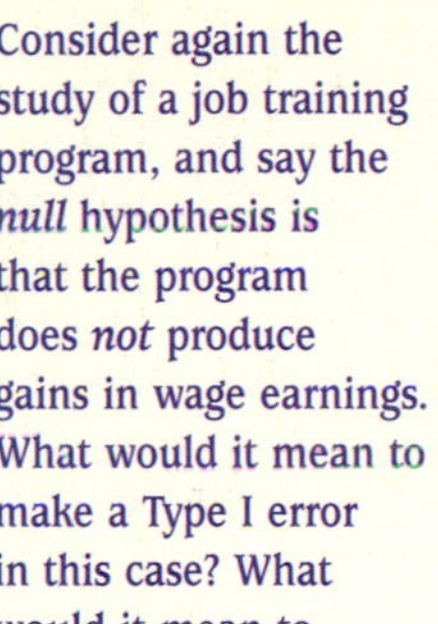

Consider again the study of a job training program, and say the *null* hypothesis is that the program does *not* produce gains in wage earnings. What would it mean to make a Type I error in this case? What would it mean to make a Type II error?

Mathematically, the smaller the likelihood of a Type I error, the larger the likelihood of a Type II error. The only way to reduce the probability of both kinds of errors is to get more data (a larger sample size). But in many situations, gathering more data is expensive. And in others, it is not even possible. For example, think about a series of annual test score results for a given school system or changes in the world population over time. There are only a certain number of years' worth of data; we just can't get any more. In such cases, it may be worth accepting a greater risk of Type I error probability to reduce Type II error.

Power

Another way of looking at this issue is to ask, "How well will the researchers be able to tell if the null is false?" This is referred to as statistical **power**—the ability to recognize that the null is false. Formally, power is defined as follows:

$$\text{Power} = 1 - \text{Probability of a Type II error}$$

Power is very important, yet it is too often overlooked. That is largely because it is hard to calculate and does not pop out automatically from a statistical software package. To calculate it, one needs to know the true differences and distributions in the population, and, of course, we do not (that is why we are doing inference in the first place). Bloom (1995), however, provides useful guidance on how to calculate and report a **minimal detectable effect**, the smallest difference or effect that a particular study has the power to detect (to reject the null hypothesis) at a given level of significance.

You should know a few key points about statistical power. First, the larger the sample size, the more power you will have to detect differences or effects. Second, the stricter the standard of proof—in other words, the lower you set your significance level and thus your probability of Type I error—the less power you will have.

Table 9.9 Type I and Type II Errors

	Null Hypothesis Is True	Alternative Hypothesis Is True (Null Hypothesis Is False)
Accept null hypothesis	Correct decision	Type II error
Reject null hypothesis	Type I error	Correct decision

In certain circumstances, particularly when you have no control over the sample size, it may be worth accepting a higher p value to get more power. At the very least, power is something to ask about and calculate.

Multiple Comparison Corrections

Sometimes researchers use many dependent variables to test group differences. And sometimes when analyzing many groups, they will test all possible group-to-group matchups to see how each group differs from the others. When so many statistical tests are performed, some differences may be statistically significant just by chance. When data are mined in this kind of fashion, without prior hypotheses, a higher bar is needed for statistical significance. In such cases, the p value should be corrected using a **multiple comparison correction**.

There are a number of different approaches to such corrections, including the Bonferroni, Scheffé, and more recent methods. There is an extensive technical literature on multiple comparison corrections and the specifics of the corrections (see Howell, 2007, for an introduction to the issue). Moreover, when and even whether specific multiple comparison corrections are desired is disputed (Rothman, 1990) with some researchers concluding that they are not usually required (Gelman, Hill, & Yajima, 2012). However, understand that if you perform many, many significance tests, without any specific theory, some of them will turn out significant by chance and not due to any real differences. The best approach is to start with substantive hypotheses. After that, exploring data is fine and even valuable, but be aware that the results are only suggestive until tested with new data. This is another version of the point made in Chapter 1 about requiring new data for theories found inductively.

Sample Size Calculations for Significance Tests

We saw earlier in this chapter how you can determine what sample size is needed based on the precision desired for single proportions or means, although assumptions are required. Similarly, when a study is designed to produce a statistical significance test comparing two groups, sample size can be calculated in advance, but with even more assumptions required. As before, having more subjects (a larger sample size) increases precision, meaning you are more likely to be able to detect statistically significant differences between groups.

But how many in each group is enough? One way to figure this out is to use something called Lehr's equation (Belle, 2008), which looks like this:

$$\text{Sample size per group} = n = 16/\Delta^2,$$

where Δ is the standardized difference in means, or effect size. According to Cohen (1992), effect sizes for the difference in means correspond approximately to these magnitudes: .20 is small, .50 is medium, and .80 is large. Admittedly, this is a bit vague and rather rough, but the point is to make a first cut at sample size. If we put Lehr's formula together with Cohen's effect size guidelines, we get this:

	Small	Medium	Large
Effect size (Δ)	.20	.50	.80
Lehr's equation	$16/.20^2$	$16/.50^2$	$16/.80^2$
Sample size per group (n)	400	64	25

The effect size Δ is the difference in group means divided by the standard deviation (in the population, or sometimes just the control group). So you can calculate this value more precisely if you make an educated guess about the difference you will see in the means (usually the smallest difference that would be meaningful to detect) and the standard deviation (which sometimes can be approximated with the range divided by 6, because in most approximately normal distributions the range lies within 3 standard deviations of the mean).

All of this is fine for basic back-of-the-envelope calculations, but you should know that Lehr's equation assumes that the probability of Type I error is .05 and that the probability of Type II error is .20 (a power of .80). You may want to test out other probability and power levels, as well as avoid the hassles of hand calculation. Fortunately, nowadays most statistical software packages (such as Stata) provide basic tools for the calculation of sample size and statistical power. There are several specialized programs as well that can be downloaded for free, including PS: Power and Sample Size Calculation from Vanderbilt University and G*Power from the University of Dusseldorf.

Adjusting Inference for Clustering and Other Complex Sampling

The basic textbook and software formulas and methods for statistical inference, including standard errors, confidence intervals, and significance tests of regression, are usually based on simple random sampling. But when using complex sampling methods such as clustering, stratification, oversampling, and multistage sampling (discussed in Chapter 5), the usual formulas for confidence intervals, standard errors, and significance tests are not correct. These formulas must be adjusted to take into account the complex nature of the sampling.

The intuition behind the need for adjustment can be made clear with an example. Consider a clustering study in which first schools are sampled and then students are sampled within each school. If there are 1,000 students in the sample, the usual formula for the standard error will be based on having 1,000 independent students. But the students in the same schools are likely to be more similar to one another than to students in another randomly selected school—certainly the same region, perhaps similar socioeconomic background or ethnicity, many of the same teachers, and so on. So all these variables are clustered, and in effect, there are essentially fewer than 1,000 fresh data points. For this reason, standard errors (and thus confidence intervals and significance tests) should be corrected for clustering. Similar intuitions apply for oversampling and stratification.

Unless instructed otherwise, statistical packages assume that data are a simple random sample and use the usual formulas. Some statistical software packages (such as SAS and Stata) contain commands that make these adjustments to the reported standard errors, if the sampling method is entered correctly. An alternative approach is to use resampling methods of calculating standard errors, such as the jackknife or bootstrap method (Mooney & Duval, 1993).

Issues and Extensions of Statistical Inference

We will now consider some issues and extensions of statistical inference that are important to consider whenever you read about or use confidence intervals and significance tests. The issues are related to the interpretation of statistical inference and the extensions to alternative methodologies for deriving estimates of sampling variability and uncertainty.

Inference With a Nonprobability Sample: What Does It Mean?

The entire foundation of statistical inference is based on random sampling. Often, however, we do not have a pure random sample—far from it. As we saw in Chapter 5 on sampling, there are many problems of

QUESTION

Explain in your own words the problems of interpreting statistical significance tests on data from a census and on data from a convenience sample. How does the idea of a superpopulation help?

inadequate coverage and nonresponse when attempting to do random sampling in the real world. So we typically end up with an imperfect random sample at best, one that can be biased in complex and unknown ways. The confidence intervals and significance tests based on imperfect random samples are likewise imperfect.

Moreover, much research gets done using nonprobability samples, such as convenience samples, voluntary samples, or even censuses of a whole population. A study of organizational behavior, for example, may rely on a survey of employees in one nearby organization (a convenience sample). A health study may recruit volunteers for an experiment (a voluntary sample). And there are many studies that rely on aggregate data on the 50 U.S. states, or all the countries in the world, in order to test relationships between variables such as poverty, education, and health status. Statistical significance tests, standard errors, and confidence intervals are widely used in contexts like these. But are they valid? And what do they mean?

In some cases, researchers who apply the tools of statistical inference to nonprobability samples are acting "as if" the data come from a random sample of some vaguely defined or even imaginary population, sometimes thought of as a *superpopulation* (Berk & Freedman, 2003). Consider, for example, a study of all the employees in one organization to determine whether productivity has really increased after a new management initiative. The use of a statistical significance test could be based (implicitly) on the idea that the employees are a random sample from a superpopulation of employees in similar organizations. Or a study of all of India's states (a census) could be treated as if drawn from a much larger superpopulation of potential Indian states. But often the analogy is a stretch, and the meaning of the inference is uncertain.

Another approach to the foundations of inference is common when examining relationships, particularly regression models, and is the basis of econometrics. The confidence intervals and statistical significance tests for both ordinary regression and more advanced forms of regression are based on the idea that the dependent variable, and sometimes the independent variables, is driven by some sort of stochastic (random) process. For example, researchers might *assume* that earnings are driven by education, experience, occupation, and other variables plus a *normally distributed random error term*. Such assumptions are used to derive standard error formulas, eliminating the need to assume that the data are from a random sample of a well-defined population. With these assumptions, inference is well defined for censuses or convenience samples. However, these are assumptions, which researchers do not always test. Moreover, the available tests of violations are often weak.[6]

Finally, some convenience sample studies are randomized experiments, the focus of Chapter 14, in which a treatment group and a control group are randomly assigned—essentially each is a random sample of the study population. In this case, hypothesis tests of differences between treatment and control groups are quite rigorous, although inferences beyond the study population are more uncertain.

Bootstrapping: Inference for Statistics With No Standard Error Formulas

While all statistics have standard errors, we only gave the formulas for the standard errors of means and proportions. Statistics, like regression coefficients, have slightly more complicated standard error formulas, and some statistics have much more complicated formulas, not always available in software packages. And for still other statistics, there are no standard error formulas at all: Even highly capable statisticians have found them too hard to figure out.

Luckily, in this age of powerful computing, there is an alternative called **bootstrapping**. This refers to various computer-intensive procedures for simulating a sampling distribution by repeatedly resampling—with replacement—from the original sample itself. Because each observation is returned to the pool after being selected (sampling with replacement), a computer can generate hundreds or even thousands of

[6]The tests are weak because they are based on a null hypothesis of the assumption being true. An example is the test for heteroskedasticity, which means the errors are normally distributed but the variance of the error differs with values of the independent variable. The null in this case is homoskedasticity—the required assumption for inference.

resamples from the original sample. Each time, the estimate of interest is calculated (a mean, a difference in means, a regression coefficient, or whatever), and thus the standard error can be estimated from the distribution of the estimates from the many resamples. Bootstrapping is sometimes preferred even when formulas for standard errors exist because it requires fewer assumptions than the classical approach to standard errors (Mooney & Duval, 1993).

Bayesian Inference

By now it should be clear that working with data creates lots of uncertainty, particularly uncertainty in how to make generalizations or predictions from the findings of just one study. The approach we have relied on views each study as one realization of a sampling process from a great many possible samples that could have been drawn (the sampling distribution). This approach is referred to as **frequentist inference** because it views probability in terms of the frequency of events. Think of a p value of, say, .02: it means that our sample would occur by chance in 2 of 100 sampling events (assuming the null hypothesis is true). A feature of frequentist inference is that the statistical analysis does not incorporate prior knowledge of the population or behavior of interest.

An alternative view of statistics and data analysis is Bayesian. In **Bayesian inference**, the researcher starts with some guess or **prior probability** about the cause of an event or the truth about a population. (See Kruschke, 2010, for a relatively accessible introduction to doing Bayesian analysis.) Observations are then made and sample data collected and analyzed to update the probability, which is referred to as a **posterior probability**. In this manner, Bayesian inference zeros in on the parameter of interest. Bayesian methods are sometimes criticized because they involve "subjective probabilities," rather than basing probability calculations on the actual long-run pattern of real events. They are also often much more computationally complicated. But Bayesian inference has certain advantages over the frequentist approach, especially when observations are dynamic or sparse.

The overwhelming majority of studies and analyses use frequentist statistics. However, in how people actually think and talk about statistical results, almost everyone is an unofficial or intuitive Bayesian. A study that estimates the sensitivity of immigration to wage differences would be interpreted in light of prior studies estimating the same or similar sensitivities. In almost every case, people come to a new study with a prior expectation—at least some expectations of likely magnitudes—of what the study estimates, if only from theory or common sense. And the results of any new study are added to the prior expectations to give what is essentially a posterior view that integrates both.

Conclusion

The tools of statistical inference are widely used in almost all forms of quantitative research and analysis. They are important for determining the precision of statistics calculated from samples, including univariate statistics, such as election poll results, and also relationships, such as differences between voting patterns of men and women. These tools are also important for figuring out if differences and relationships are "really there"—are generalizable—through statistical significance tests. However, one must also treat statistical significance tests cautiously: Rigid p-value cutoffs for statistical significance are often arbitrary, much depends on sample size and statistical power, and statistically significant results may not indicate substantive significance in the real world.

Statistical significance tests are required for the next part of the book, which deals with causation. But to fully tackle the question of causation, we need to learn about some additional methods that take account of many influences at once—multivariate methods. These are the topic of the next chapter.

BOX 9.2
Tips on Doing Your Own Research: Inferential Statistics

- Perform sample size and power calculations *before* collecting data to determine the needed sample size. Many statistical software packages have sample size and power commands. Since these calculations require assumptions, examine the implications using a range of assumed values.
- Plan the inferential statistics analysis when you plan the design.
- Graph your data and examine descriptive statistics *before* doing inferential statistics—see the tips on descriptive statistics at the end of Chapter 8.
- If your data come from a census or convenience sample, decide whether inferential statistics are appropriate (they may not be). Think carefully about the interpretation you will give to inferential statistics in your study.
- Determine the types (quantitative, ordinal categorical, or nominal categorical) and roles (independent variable, dependent variable) of all variables to be used in significance tests. Determine the appropriate statistical significance test to use—see Table 9.7 in this chapter and Table 10.5 in the next chapter.
- Check that assumptions needed for particular significance tests (such as large enough sample sizes) are satisfied.
- Calculate confidence intervals for all estimates of interest, even when also implementing significance testing. Interpret the practical significance of the boundaries of the confidence intervals.
- For all statistical significance tests, interpret the *p* values in words and determine whether the results are statistically significant at the 10%, 5%, and 1% levels. Consider what should be the appropriate significance level for your data, research questions, and context.
- For each significance test result, determine the reasons for statistical significance or lack of significance (such as a small or large sample size), paying attention to practical significance. See Box 9.1.
- If complex survey sampling was used, make sure that your software can adjust inferential statistics properly. Determine the weights and sampling method and enter them into the software. Alternatively, learn the design effect. See tips on complex survey sampling at the end of Chapter 5.

Chapter Resources

Key Terms

- Alternative hypothesis
- Bayesian inference
- Bootstrapping
- Chi-square test
- Confidence intervals
- Frequentist inference
- Level of confidence
- Minimal detectable effect
- Multiple comparison correction
- Null hypothesis
- *p* value
- Parameter

- Point estimate
- Posterior probability
- Power
- Prior probability
- Sample size calculation
- Sampling distribution
- Significance level
- Significance (hypothesis) tests
- Standard error
- Statistical inference
- Statistical significance
- Test statistic
- Type I error
- Type II error

Exercises

9.1. From a random sample of births in three states, the data on birth weight were analyzed. Birth weight is measured in grams.

Descriptives

			Statistic	Std. Error
Birth weight (grams)	Mean		3330.99	1.705
	95% confidence interval for mean	Lower bound	3327.65	
		Upper bound	3334.33	
	Standard deviation		555.899	

a. Explain how to interpret the 95% confidence interval of the birth weight mean. What does it tell us about births in the three states sampled?
b. Explain what information the standard deviation provides.
c. Explain what information the standard error of the mean provides. Explain how it is related to the confidence interval.
d. Explain how and why the standard error of the mean and the standard deviation are related.
e. What other factor affects the standard error of the mean? Explain as intuitively as possible why it does so.
f. What would the 90% confidence interval look like relative to the 95% confidence interval? Explain why.

9.2. A survey of n = 100 employees in a large organization in Ohio finds that 70% are satisfied with their job.

a. Construct a 95% confidence interval around the 70% estimate. Explain in words what this confidence interval tells you. How generalizable is this estimate?
b. An industry report suggests that, nationwide, 75% of employees in similar firms are satisfied with their jobs. Does the 70% estimate for the Ohio organization indicate a statistically significant difference from the national norm? Use the confidence interval you just calculated to answer this question and draw a conclusion.

9.3. Calculate the sample size you would need for each of the following situations (using the basic formulas provided in this chapter):

a. A sample survey that provides a margin of error of $\pm$ 2 percentage points.

b. A sample of cars on a stretch of highway that results in a mean estimate of the speed of the traffic that has a margin of error ± 2 miles per hour. (Hint: Assume the range of speeds is between 40 and 80 miles per hour.)
c. A comparison of hourly wages between men and women in which you would have enough power to detect even a small difference (defined by Cohen as an effect size of 0.20).

9.4. A regression of income on years of experience is performed using a sample of people who work in not-for-profits. Income is measured in thousands of dollars, and experience is measured in years of experience.

a. What units is the slope coefficient (the coefficient of years of experience) in?
b. If the slope coefficient had the value 0.85, what would that tell you?
c. If the *p* value associated with the slope coefficient were .03, what would that tell you? Make sure to include the null and alternative hypotheses being tested as part of your explanation. Make sure that you explain what the number .03 actually tells you.

9.5. Data are gathered on 16 students. Half of the students are randomly assigned to a new tutoring program, and half have their usual school experience. A study finds that test scores for the tutoring program students are on average 10 points higher than those for the other students. The *p* value for a test of improvement from the program is 0.3, not significant at even the 10% level.

a. If mean test scores are 200 and the standard deviation is 40, are these results practically significant, in your opinion? Explain what practical significance means.
b. Explain what causes this result to be not statistically significant.
c. Do you conclude that the tutoring program is ineffective because the results are not statistically significant?

9.6. A recent poll found that 60% of Americans support raising taxes on incomes above $250,000. The details for the poll results stated that the "margin of sampling error is plus or minus 3.5 percentage points."

a. Calculate the 95% confidence interval for support for that policy.
b. Interpret the 95% confidence interval in words.
c. A prior poll had shown 55% of Americans supporting the policy. Are the results of the two polls statistically significantly different?
d. Express the change in the results between the prior poll and the current poll in two different ways.
e. The poll also broke down the policy support results by region of the country (e.g., Northeast). Explain how the margin of error would differ for the regional results and why.

9.7. A regression was run using a data set of U.S. colleges from years gone by. In-state tuition is in dollars ($).

Regression output:

Model Summary

Model	R	R-Squared	Adjusted R-Squared	Std. Error of the Estimate
1	.613[a]	.375	.371	55.5495

a. Predictors: (Constant), Percentage of faculty with PhD degrees

Coefficients[a]

Model		Unstandardized Coefficients		Standardized Coefficients	t	Sig.
		B	Std. Error	Beta		
1	(Constant)	316.700	18.764		16.878	.000
	Percentage of faculty with PhD degrees	2.419	.244	.613	9.893	.000

a. Dependent Variable: Average Verbal SAT Score

a. Interpret the coefficient of "Percentage of faculty with PhD degrees."
b. Interpret the statistical significance tests associated with "Percentage of faculty with PhD degrees." State the null and alternative hypotheses, whether the relationship is statistically significant, and the interpretation of the p value.
c. Discuss the practical significance of the coefficient of "Percentage of faculty with PhD degrees."

9.8. A survey was conducted of younger people in the United States. The data were used for the cross-tab analysis and chi-square below.

Cigarettes—Past Year Use * Age Category Cross-tabulation

			Age Category				Total
			12–17	18–25	26–34	35 or over	
Cigarettes—Past Year Use	Did not use within past year	Count	614	581	575	578	2348
		% within Cigarettes—Past Year Use	26.1%	24.7%	24.5%	24.6%	100.0%
		% within Age Category	81.6%	54.2%	41.7%	40.8%	50.8%
	Used within past year	Count	138	491	805	838	2272
		% within Cigarettes—Past Year Use	6.1%	21.6%	35.4%	36.9%	100.0%
		% within Age Category	18.4%	45.8%	58.3%	59.2%	49.2%
Total		Count	752	1072	1380	1416	4620
		% within Cigarettes—Past Year Use	16.3%	23.2%	29.9%	30.6%	100.0%
		% within Age Category	100.0%	100.0%	100.0%	100.0%	100.0%

Chi-Square Tests

	Value	df	Asymp. Sig. (2-sided)
Pearson Chi-Square	393.784[a]	3	.000
Likelihood Ratio	418.413	3	.000
Linear-by-Linear Association	316.244	1	.000
N of Valid Cases	4620		

a. 0 cells (0.0%) have expected count less than 5. The minimum expected count is 369.81.

a. For the values 24.7% and 41.7% in the top few rows, interpret each in words and explain how they were calculated.
b. Which variable would you choose as the independent variable in this relationship? Explain why in one sentence.
c. Interpret the results of this cross-tab, both giving an overall qualitative summary and backing up your summary with some specific numbers.
d. For the chi-square test results, state the null and alternative hypotheses, whether the result is statistically significant, and the interpretation of the *p* value.

9.9. Analysts of the 2012 U.S. presidential election noted that gays were among the groups who went strongly for Obama. You want to explore the relationship between voting for Obama and sexual orientation. You have two data sets:

a. Data set A: Exit poll data. The variables include the candidate voted for in the presidential election, sexual orientation, and other demographic and political variables.
b. Data set B: County-level data on the percentage of presidential votes cast for Obama; the percentage of the adult population who consider themselves gay, lesbian, or bisexual; and the percentage of the population in racial, ethnic, religious, and income categories.
c. For each data set (A and B separately), describe how you would analyze the relationship between support for Obama and sexual orientation. Specifically, state

- The unit of analysis
- The variable definition and type of variable (quantitative, ordinal categorical, or nominal categorical) for each variable to be used
- The statistical analysis to be performed (e.g., comparison of means) and a brief explanation of what is to be done
- If any graph could show the relationship, the type of graph and variables to be used
- The statistical significance tests to be performed

Student Study Site

Visit the Study Site at **www.sagepub.com/remler2e** to

- test your knowledge with the self-quiz
- check your understanding of key terms with the eFlashcards
- explore helpful resources that relate directly to this chapter

Multivariate analysis considers relationships among many variables at the same time.

Source: © istockphoto/wellglad.

Overview: In this chapter, you will learn statistical tools for analyzing multiple variables at the same time—multivariate statistics. In particular, this chapter will help you understand multiple regression—the most widely used statistical method in social and policy research. You will learn about confidence intervals and significance tests for regression, interaction terms, how categorical variables can be included as independent or dependent variables, and how to transform variables when necessary. And you will learn many other practical tips for doing and interpreting multiple regression. (These skills will be put to work again in Chapter 13, where you will learn more about how to use multiple regression to estimate the causal effect of one variable on another.) In this chapter, you will also get an overview of other advanced multivariate methods—their basic purposes as well as some of their strengths and weaknesses. Statistical methods have become increasingly sophisticated, but this chapter will help you understand the aims, assumptions, and interpretation of the most widely used multivariate statistics in an intuitive, largely nonmathematical way.

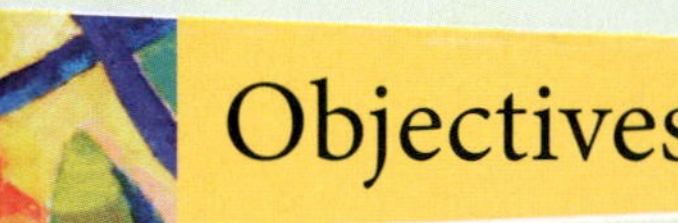

Objectives

Learning Objectives

After reading this chapter, you should be able to

- Interpret regression coefficients in a manner meaningful for policy or practice, with emphasis on *prediction*
- Understand why multicollinearity limits what regression models can be estimated
- Interpret confidence intervals and hypothesis tests in regression
- Interpret coefficients of dummy variables
- Interpret coefficients of interaction variables
- Recognize the wide variety of multivariate methods and identify the situations when each is appropriate

Making Sense of Multivariate Statistics

10

The real world is more than two dimensional—many factors exert their influence at the same time and in complex ways. Your health, for example, is a result of your age, diet, lifestyle, and family history, as well as the interactions of these influences. In addition, we often observe the real world only indirectly, through multiple indicators. What you call your "health" is really a composite of many things, such as functional ability, blood pressure, cholesterol levels, body weight, disease, even mood, and so on.

This chapter is about statistical methods for dealing with multiple variables at the same time—**multivariate statistics**. It focuses primarily on multiple regression, the most widely used statistical tool for social and policy research. But an overview of other multivariate techniques will appear at the end of the chapter.

This chapter, like the previous chapters, is about tools, rather than about a particular area of research. The tools by themselves cannot answer important policy and practice questions, but answering such questions often requires these tools.

Multiple Regression: The Basics

Most outcomes have many causes—that is the basic idea behind multiple regression. **Multiple regression** predicts a dependent variable (y) using several independent variables (x_1, x_2, etc.). It is a direct extension of simple regression, introduced in Chapter 8, but with two or more (sometimes many more) independent variables:

$$y = a + b_1x_1 + b_2x_2 + \dots b_kx_k.$$

In this equation, y is the dependent variable or outcome and the xs are the independent variables (1 through k)—also referred to as explanatory variables. The bs represent the coefficients of each independent variable and are of particular interest because they express how the independent variables are related to the dependent variable. (Note that b_1x_1, for example, really means "b_1 times x_1" and is written this way to simplify reading the equation.) The term **regression**, without any modifier, refers to any method for predicting a dependent variable with one or more independent variables, including simple and multiple regression, as well as more advanced models.

To illustrate, consider the following multiple regression to predict earnings (y) using years of education (x_1) and years of work experience (x_2):

$$\text{Predicted earnings} = a + b_{\text{Ed}} \times \text{Education} + b_{\text{Exp}} \times \text{Experience}$$

$$= -\$6{,}739 + \$3{,}292/\text{year} \times \text{Education} + \$415/\text{year} \times \text{Experience}$$

This multiple regression was calculated using statistical software and the same (simulated) data used to illustrate simple regression in Chapter 8 (Figure 8.7), but again now we are using more than one independent variable. The *R-squared* turns out to be .57, or 57%.

Let's now consider the interpretation of multiple regression, which in most respects remains analogous to simple regression as discussed in Chapter 8. Thus, in this example we have the following:

- The constant (*a*) of – $6,739 is the predicted value of the dependent variable when all the independent variables (both education and experience) are 0. Notice that 0 years of education (not even first grade) is not a very meaningful value in a modern society. The constant is mathematically necessary, even if it may lack a social or practical meaning.
- Each slope or coefficient (*b*) describes how much the dependent variable is predicted to change when the corresponding independent variable increases by one unit—*holding all other independent variables constant*. This last part is what makes multiple regression different from simple regression. Thus, $3,292 is the amount of additional earnings predicted for someone with one more year of education but no difference in experience—in other words, holding work experience constant. And $415 is the amount of additional earnings predicted for someone with one more year of experience—holding education constant. Notice that holding constant works both ways (and more, if other variables are included as well).
- *R-squared* is the proportion of variation in the dependent variable explained by variation in *all* the independent variables. Thus, education *and* work experience together explain 57% of the variation in earnings.

QUESTION

Using the regression equation above, calculate how much more you would expect someone with four more years of education to earn, holding constant years of experience.

We will skip the equations for multiple regression. But if you're interested in the underlying details and formulas, we suggest that you consult the brief book by Lewis-Beck (1980) or the more extended treatment in Wooldridge (2009). Box 10.1 describes how to implement multiple regression with statistical software.

BOX 10.1
How to Run a Multiple Regression Using Software

You can run multiple regressions using statistical software packages, such as SAS, SPSS, and Stata, described also in Chapter 8. It is fairly easy to do. First, the data must be read or entered into the software (see Chapter 6 for more about the layout and structure of quantitative data). Then, using a point-and-click menu or a command line in a program, you specify the dependent variable and your selection of independent variables. The software treats the independent variables equally and does not distinguish between the independent variable of interest and the control variables—that is your job as part of the interpretation.

The software then performs the calculations and produces output in the form of a regression table. The regression table typically includes the constant term, the coefficients for each of the independent variables, the associated standard errors and significance tests on the coefficients, the *R*-squared fit statistic, and various other results. (Examples were shown in Chapter 9 with the National Education Longitudinal Study data.)

Multiple regression can also be done with spreadsheet software, such as Excel, although it is somewhat more limited and cumbersome. For example, some spreadsheets will not handle missing values, and the columns representing the independent variables typically must be contiguous in the spreadsheet (requiring cutting and pasting if you want to try out different combinations of independent variables).

If you are doing many different calculations, it is best to type out scripts or create programs for a statistical software package, rather than using just the point-and-click menu. Otherwise, it may be hard to reproduce your results and know for sure how the calculations were done.

Multiple regression is used for two main purposes:

- First, it can be used to predict a dependent variable using a combination of independent variables. For example, it can be used to predict tax revenues for a region from a combination of economic and demographic variables. As a *best linear predictor,* multiple regression also has value as a description of the data—what variables are jointly related to or associated with tax revenues.
- Second, multiple regression can sometimes be used to estimate whether one variable affects another, causally—and the magnitude of the effect. For example, it is used to estimate the causal effect tobacco taxes have on the rate of smoking, holding other variables constant. This is also referred to as *statistical control.*

Using multiple regression for estimating causal effects can be tricky and involves important logical and conceptual issues, which we cover fully in Chapters 12 and 13. So we begin here with multiple regression for prediction as an introduction to the basic statistical issues.[1]

Multiple Regression for Prediction

To predict the earnings of someone with 12 years of education and 10 years of experience, from the equation presented above, simply plug these values into the equation like this:

Predicted earnings = – \$6,739 + (\$3,292/year × 12 years) + (\$415/year × 10 years) = \$36,915

The result says that we predict, based on our data, that someone with 12 years of education and 10 years of work experience would earn \$36,915. Box 10.2 outlines the steps involved in doing prediction with regression. Of course, as with simple regression, this does not mean that a given person with 12 years of education and 10 years of work experience will earn exactly \$36,915; it just means that this is our best guess, our expected value on average.

[1]However, occasionally, when discussing some other aspect of multiple regression, we will use the term *effect* of an independent variable, even though we have not done the work to justify a causal interpretation. We do this purely when it helps create a much more readable sentence. Again, a true causal effect requires more justification, as discussed in Chapters 12 and 13.

BOX 10.2
Steps for Predicting With Regression

1. Using data and software, find the constant (a) and coefficients of the independent variables (b_1, b_2, . . . b_k) for the regression equation:

$$y = a + b_1x_1 + b_2x_2 + \ldots + b_kx_k.$$

2. Plug in desired values of x_1, x_2, . . . x_k into the equation. (Remember that b_1x_1 means b_1 times x_1.)
3. Calculate the predicted value of y.

QUESTION

Using the regression equation above, predict earnings for someone with 12 years of education and 4 years of experience.

The Danger (and Necessity) of Out-of-Sample Extrapolation

Using regression to make a prediction far from the data used to fit the regression is referred to as **out-of-sample extrapolation**. From our example, we know that one more year of education predicts \$3,292 more in earnings, holding experience constant. So would completing as much as 40 years of formal education lead to a *much larger* paycheck (an additional 40 × \$3,292 or \$131,680)?

We need to be careful: The regression equation is fitted using data we have on people who mostly have between at least 8 and not more than about 20 years of education, with no one above 25 years of education. Predicting the income of someone with 40 years of education assumes that the line would fit the same way well beyond the range of the actual data—but we have no evidence that it does. Because the constant is the predicted value of the dependent variable when all the independent variables are 0—which may have little real-world meaning—it is frequently an out-of-sample extrapolation as well.

Unfortunately, the real-world demands of policy and practice frequently require out-of-sample predictions, for example, predicting a decrease in smoking rates from a large increase in tobacco taxes. In such cases, we often want to predict what would happen when variables (such as tobacco taxes) take on values that they have never taken on before. In such cases, there is no alternative to out-of-sample extrapolation. Such extrapolations are more trustworthy to the extent that the following conditions hold: The plugged-in values are not too different from the range of values in the data, the model fits the data well (a high *R*-squared), and multiple models and varying assumptions give a similar answer. This last point refers to what are known as **robustness** checks, and they are essential to good prediction.

R-Squared and Adjusted *R*-Squared

In multiple regression, *R*-squared expresses the variation in the dependent variable predicted or explained (in a statistical sense) by *all* the independent variables combined. And as we have just seen, a higher *R*-squared is generally better for prediction because it means a tighter fit to the data and less error around the line. *R*-squared, however, does not need to be near perfect to do good prediction—it all depends on the situation and on available data.

Adding a variable to a multiple regression always increases *R*-squared—at least a little. Even adding a variable that consists entirely of random noise will increase the *R*-squared, although it does not really contribute any meaningful predictive power. To tell whether a variable really adds predictive power, researchers often use an **adjusted *R*-squared** instead. It adjusts for the number of independent variables in the multiple regression equation, and it tends to give somewhat smaller R-squared values. Technically, adjusted *R*-squared is an unbiased estimator of the population *R*-squared—the proportion of variation in the dependent variable predicted or explained by all the independent variables *in the population*.

A word of caution about interpreting *R*-squared: The standard definition of *R*-squared (or adjusted *R*-squared) as the proportion of variation *explained* by the independent variables can be misleading. It really means "explained" in a statistical sense only, not necessarily a causal sense. The body weight of people in kilos perfectly explains their body weight in pounds, in a statistical sense, but this tells us very little. Explaining what causes variation in *y* is more complicated and difficult than just running a regression and getting a high *R*-squared, as the chapters in Part IV will help make clearer.

All Else Held Constant: A Bit More Mathematics

The equations and proofs behind multiple regression are not our focus here. (There are many excellent treatments, for example Lewis-Beck, 1980, or Wooldridge, 2009.) However, useful insight can be gained by looking intuitively at what all the mathematics behind multiple regression actually accomplishes.

In a simple regression, the variation in the independent variable that is shared with the dependent variable determines the regression coefficient. In our simple regression example, the effect of education on earnings is identified by their shared variation.

In multiple regression, the variation in a given independent variable that it shares with the other independent variables in the equation is removed: It does not count. Only the remaining, unique variation in the independent variable that it shares with the dependent variable produces the regression coefficient. In our example, only variation in education that is uncorrelated with variation in experience contributes to the estimate of the effect of education on earnings.

QUESTION

In regression of predicting earnings based on education and experience, the *R*-squared was .57. In words, what does this *R*-squared tell you? How would the adjusted *R*-squared be different?

Venn Diagrams Illustrate the Multiple Regression Method

Kennedy (2003) developed the use of Venn diagrams to illustrate how multiple regression works. Venn diagrams illustrating our current earnings and education example are illustrated in Figure 10.1. Each circle represents the total variation of that variable. The shaded part illustrates the covariation used to calculate the coefficient of education—effectively the information used for the estimation.

For the simple regression of Education on Earnings, shown in the left panel, the shaded area is simply the overlap of those two variables. All of the covariation between both variables contributes to the simple regression coefficient of education estimate. For the multiple regression shown in the right panel, the shaded area is only the covariation of Earnings and Education that does not also overlap with Experience. The regression coefficient of Education, b_{Ed}, in this multiple regression is determined by the variation shared by Earnings and Education that is not also shared by Experience.

Figure 10.1 Venn Diagram Illustration of Simple and Multiple Regression

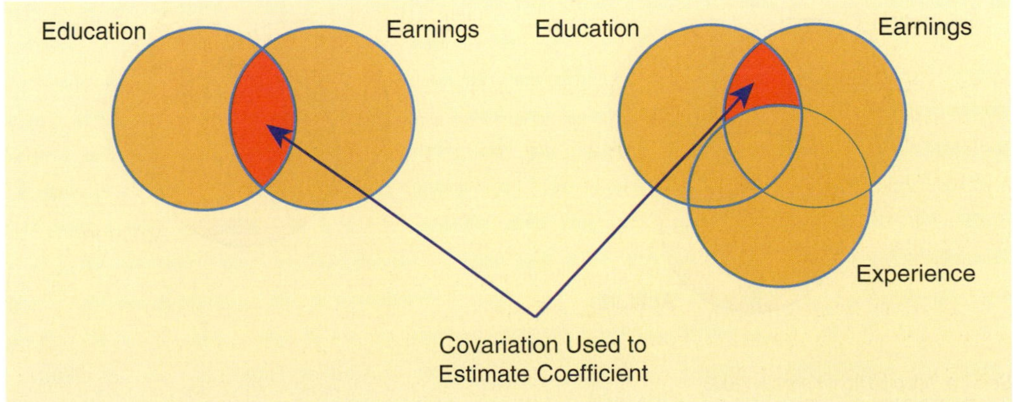

Source: Adapted from Kennedy (2003).

Multicollinearity

When two variables are perfectly correlated—when they move in perfect lockstep—we cannot tell them (or more precisely their variation) apart. For the statistical purposes of regression, they are essentially the same variable. This is called *perfect collinearity.* In such a case, both variables cannot be used as independent variables in the same multiple regression—we can only use one of them.

Perfect **multicollinearity** occurs when an independent variable is a perfect linear combination of two or more of the other independent variables. (Perfect collinearity is just a special case, a perfect linear relationship with just one other independent variable.) In such cases, the variable provides no unique information that cannot be obtained from the other variables. Again, we cannot use all these variables together in the same multiple regression.

When the independent variables are highly correlated, but not perfectly correlated, they may be included in the same equation—but it can make it difficult to estimate the coefficients with precision. This is also known as multicollinearity, and although it is not perfect multicollinearity, it can still cause problems.

When You Can't Disentangle the Independent Variables

An imaginary example might help illustrate multicollinearity. Say we live in a world where aptitude at a young age exactly determines how much education a person receives—the variables aptitude and education, in other words, are perfectly collinear (correlated). And say that both variables influence earnings. Now imagine that we want to do a multiple regression to determine the separate effects of both education and aptitude on earnings. How can we disentangle one from the other? We cannot. All that we can know is that education or aptitude, or some combination of the two, increases earnings, but we have no way to assign credit to one variable or the other.

In a Venn diagram, if Education and Aptitude were perfectly correlated, their circles would sit right on top of one another, leaving no area of unique overlap between just Education and Earnings. So it would be impossible to estimate coefficients for both. This is an example of perfect collinearity. If statistical software were given such data and a command to regress Earnings on both Aptitude and Education, the package would simply drop one of the two independent variables from the equation.

But in most cases the variables are only partially collinear, as shown in Figure 10.2. In the left panel is the case in which there is some overlap among the variables, but still there remains plenty of unique covariation between Education and Earnings, separate from Aptitude, for the computer to calculate the coefficient.

Figure 10.2 Venn Diagrams of Collinearity

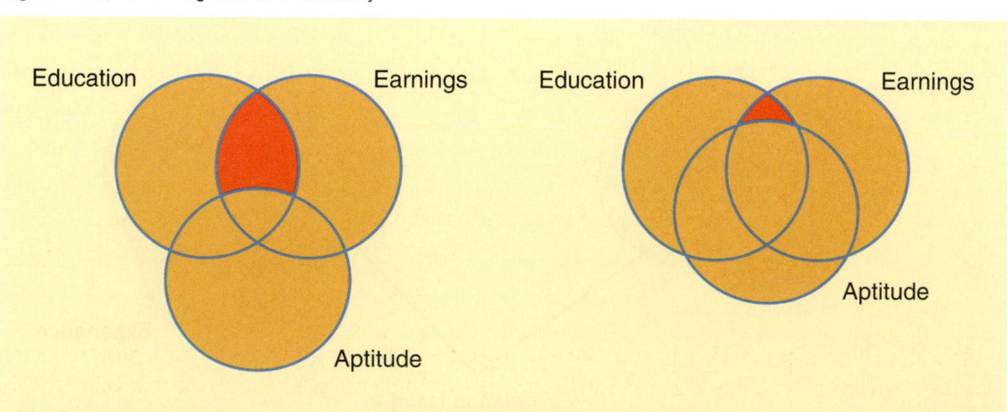

Source: Adapted from Kennedy (2003).

The more collinear Education and Aptitude are, however, the smaller the unique overlap area between Earnings and Education, as shown in the right panel of Figure 10.2. The more multicollinear the independent variables become, the less information there is available to estimate the regression coefficients. This greater multicollinearity means the regression coefficients will have larger standard errors and thus less precision (larger confidence intervals and weaker significance tests). This problem tends to get worse when more independent variables are added, especially when they overlap with each other, as each new variable will tend to chip away at the shaded area (the unique covariation) needed to estimate the coefficient.

How Many Independent Variables Can One Regression Have?

How many independent variables can one regression have? It depends on many factors, but the most important is how much data you have: More data allow for more observations, more information, and thus more coefficients that can be estimated. A common rule of thumb is that one independent variable can be added for every 10 observations.

However, it also depends on the extent of multicollinearity, as just discussed, because you can't include many variables if their variation overlaps a lot. It also depends on how much variation there is in the independent variable to begin with (because if it does not vary much, it cannot covary with the dependent variable much). Most critically, it also depends on how precisely you want to estimate the coefficients. Indeed, the question of how many independent variables are possible is best understood as a problem of precision, which will be clearer after inference for regression, which we cover shortly.

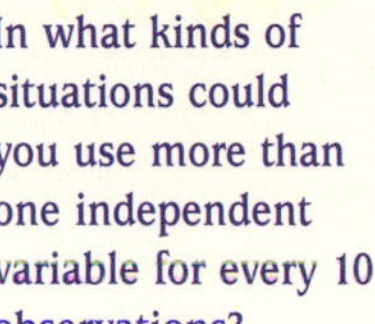

In what kinds of situations could you use more than one independent variable for every 10 observations?

Standardized Coefficients: The Relative Importance of Independent Variables

It can be useful to express the coefficients of a regression in terms of the standard deviations—called standardized coefficients (or beta weights). The interpretation is similar to a correlation: The *predicted number of standard deviations* y *changes, given a 1-standard-deviation increase in* x. In simple regression (with only one independent variable), the standardized coefficient is in fact equivalent to the correlation *r*.

In multiple regression, however, the interpretation is a bit different: The *predicted number of standard deviations* y *changes, given a 1-standard-deviation increase in* x*—holding all the other independent variables constant.*

Standardized coefficients are useful because, in the context of multiple regression, they are directly comparable and tell us how important the independent variables are relative to each other. The largest beta weight is thus the most important predictor, the second largest beta the next most important, and so on. Although it depends on many considerations, we might suggest these rough guidelines for judging the magnitude of a standardized coefficient in a multiple regression analysis:

beta = .10	Small
beta = .20	Medium
beta = .30	Large

Standardized coefficients are particularly useful when the units of the independent variable(s) and/or dependent variable have no obvious real-world meaning, as when a variable is an index or a scale. For this reason, standardized coefficients are commonly used in disciplines such as psychology that often use multi-item scales.

Inference for Regression

The multiple regression coefficients or slopes (*bs*) are estimates calculated from data, often data from a random sample. And just as a basic mean or proportion from a random sample is an estimate of the *true* mean or proportion in the population—the *parameter*—so too are the regression coefficients (or sample slopes) estimates of the true slopes in the population.

Standard Error of the Coefficient

As estimates of population parameters, multiple regression coefficients can be off the mark because of *sampling variability.* To express this sampling variability, we use *standard errors of the coefficients.* Consider Table 10.1, which shows the influence of homework and TV watching on standardized test scores. These results are from a random subsample of $n = 100$ students in the National Education Longitudinal Study (NELS).[2]

The results tell us that we predict 1.54 test points more for a student who spends one more hour on homework, holding constant hours spent watching TV. In contrast, for a student who spends one more hour watching TV, holding constant time on homework, we predict a test score .083 lower (a negative slope). These are the estimates or coefficients—the *bs*. The standard errors of these coefficients are also shown: .629 and .044, respectively. These tell us how much sampling error there is in the coefficients.

The bigger the sample size (the more data), the more precise the regression coefficient and thus the smaller the standard errors of the coefficients. This sample size effect is true for any statistic: The more data, the more precision.

Table 10.2 shows a much larger random subsample of $n = 10{,}000$ students in the NELS. The coefficients change somewhat: They are now 1.457 for homework hours and −.097 for TV-watching hours. But the really big difference is in the standard errors, .062 and .004, respectively. They are now one-tenth as large as they were in the previous table, when the sample was only 100. So these coefficient estimates are much more precise than before.

Table 10.1 Regression Results, NELS Subsample of $n = 100$

	b	Std. Error
(Constant)	46.636	2.882
Number of hours spent on homework per week	1.540	.629
Number of hours spent watching TV on weekdays	−.083	.044

Note: Dependent variable is the standardized test score (reading, math) on a 0 to 100 scale.

Source: NELS Data.

Table 10.2 Regression Results, NELS Subsample of $n = 10{,}000$

	b	Std. Error
(Constant)	46.184	.278
Number of hours spent on homework per week	1.457	.062
Number of hours spent watching TV on weekdays	−.097	.004

Note: Dependent variable is the standardized test score (reading, math) on a 0 to 100 scale.

Source: NELS Data.

[2]The NELS is a longitudinal survey that began in 1988 with a cohort of eighth graders, who were resurveyed in 1990, 1992, 1994, and 2000. It is a project of the U.S. Department of Education, National Center for Education Statistics. See its entry in Table 6.4.

Table 10.3 Regression Results, NELS Subsample of n = 100, Showing Confidence Intervals

			95% Confidence Interval for b	
	b	Std. Error	Lower Bound	Upper Bound
(Constant)	46.636	2.884	40.919	52.352
Number of hours spent on homework per week	1.540	.629	.295	2.786
Number of hours spent watching TV on weekdays	−.083	.044	−.170	.004

Note: Dependent variable is the standardized test score (reading, math) on a 0 to 100 scale.

Source: NELS Data.

Confidence Intervals in Regression

Confidence intervals (CIs) are calculated from standard errors for regression coefficients in the same way as for any other statistics. A 95% CI of the regression coefficient is usually about ±2 standard errors.[3] Table 10.3 shows the results again for a small subsample of 100 students in the NELS, this time with the confidence intervals. We can interpret these confidence intervals as telling us that, with 95% confidence, the true constant and coefficients (the parameters) lie somewhere between the lower and upper bounds shown in the table.

Confidence Interval of a Predicted Value

When regression is used for prediction, it is often desirable to have an estimate of the confidence interval of the prediction, also referred to as the prediction error. The prediction has error not only because of the standard errors of the coefficients but also because of the residuals, which are the individual errors in fit around the regression line. In fact, the further away from the means of the independent variables, the greater the prediction error, because the fit is not as good. Most statistical packages can calculate prediction errors and confidence intervals for predicted values.

QUESTION

Interpret in words the confidence interval for the coefficient of number of hours spent on homework per week.

Significance Testing in Regression

With multiple regression, there are many coefficients and thus many different hypotheses to test. However, the most basic test is whether there is a relationship between the dependent variable and the independent variable of interest, holding the other independent variables constant.

In this case, the null hypothesis is that the parameter (the slope of the population) is 0—meaning no relationship. The formal statistical test is a t test, as explained in Chapter 9 for the case of simple regression. Most statistical packages produce output that automatically contains t statistics and p values associated with each coefficient in the regression. Table 10.4 shows the significance test results for the same NELS regression: The t statistic to test the hypothesis that hours spent on homework (holding constant hours spent on TV) have no effect (denoted t) is 2.45, and the associated p value is .016. This is a low probability, less than the standard .05 cutoff, so we can conclude that the coefficient is statistically significant—it is a strong enough relationship that it seems unlikely to have come from a population in which the slope was 0.

[3]Two standard errors is an approximation of 1.96, which is based on the normal or Z distribution and works when the sample size is large. Computer software uses the t distribution, which is also 1.96 when the sample is large but becomes more than 1.96 (thus producing wider confidence intervals) as the sample gets smaller.

Table 10.4 Regression Results, NELS Subsample of n = 100, Showing Significance (t) Tests

	b	Std. Error	*t*	*p* Value
(Constant)	46.636	2.884	16.168	.000
Number of hours spent on homework per week	1.540	.629	2.451	.016
Number of hours spent watching TV on weekdays	−.083	.044	−1.897	.060

Note: Dependent variable is the standardized test score (reading, math) on a 0 to 100 scale.

Source: NELS Data.

It may be useful to test null hypotheses other than the idea that the slope is 0. For example, you might wish to test whether the coefficient is significantly larger than some standard of effectiveness. You may wish to test whether two coefficients have the same value or not. Or you may wish to see if a coefficient has changed meaningfully from its previous value when adding another independent variable. Remember that the *p* value given by software corresponds to a test of a null hypothesis of 0 (no relationship in the population); this may—or may not—correspond to the substantive hypothesis you have in mind.

Influences on Inference in Multiple Regression

We saw earlier how a larger sample reduces the standard error and, in turn, narrows the confidence interval and strengthens the significance tests (bigger *t* statistics). But sample size is not the only factor influencing the standard errors in a regression.

QUESTION

State the null hypothesis for the *p* values associated with TV watching in Table 10.4. Would you reject or accept the null—and in turn what would your conclusion be?

Another important factor is how spread out the data are from the best-fit regression line, which is determined by the size of the residuals and denoted by σ. If the data fit very tightly around the regression line, it is easy to accurately fit the straight line, even without many data points. Thus a poor fit, described by a low *R*-squared and a high σ, results in higher standard errors. In contrast, a good fit, described by high *R*-squared and low σ, will result in smaller standard errors.

Another influence on the standard error of the regression coefficient is the amount of variation in the independent variable. If there is little variation, then it is difficult to tell how changing the independent variable changes the dependent variable. In the extreme, imagine trying to determine the effect of TV watching using a sample of students who all spend the exact same number of hours in front of the TV—it's impossible. The more variation there is in the independent variable, the more easily the slope (regression coefficient) can be measured—and thus the smaller the standard errors.

Multicollinearity also has an important influence on the standard errors. If the independent variables are highly correlated with one another, if their variation overlaps substantially, you have little unique information left over to precisely estimate the regression coefficients (recall Figure 10.2). As a result, the more multicollinearity among the independent variables, the larger the standard errors.

The Effect of Adding Independent Variables on Precision

When researchers use multiple regression for prediction, they sometimes think that more predictors—more independent variables—can only help. But this is not always the case. On the one hand, to the extent that an added variable raises explanatory power, raising the *R*-squared and reducing the residuals (σ), the standard errors are reduced. So adding variables that do a good job at explaining *y* generally helps things. On the other hand, if the newly added independent variable is highly multicollinear with the other independent variables, the standard errors increase (as we just saw), thus making things worse.

Categorical Independent Variables

Regression is an intrinsically quantitative method, yet many plausible independent variables are categorical—such as occupation, race, and gender. So we might like to include them, for example, in a regression analysis of earnings. Fortunately, categorical variables can be turned into *dummy variables,* which can be used as if they were quantitative. Even more fortunately, interpreting the regression coefficient of a dummy variable is easier than interpreting the coefficient of a quantitative variable. Dummy variables were described in Chapter 4, but we will review the idea here.

Dummy Variables in Regression

A **dummy** (or indicator) **variable** is a variable that is 1 if true and 0 if false. For example, a *Female* dummy variable takes on the value of 1 if the individual is a woman and takes on the value of 0 if the individual is a man. A dummy variable can be used in regression as if it were a quantitative variable because order means something: Higher values of the Female dummy variable mean more femaleness, as it were. Scale also means something: A one-unit increase means changing from a male to a female.

Any variable that has only two possible values, any dichotomous variable, can be made into a dummy variable. It is arbitrary which of the two possible values defines the dummy variable. For example, a *Male* dummy variable could have been chosen instead of the Female dummy variable. Whichever category is 0 becomes the *reference category.* For a *Female* dummy variable, the reference category is male, and for a *Male* dummy variable, the reference category is female.

What happens when we use a dummy variable as an independent variable in regression? Returning to the simulated-data example of earnings, a regression of earnings on a Female dummy variable results in the following equation:

$$\text{Earnings} = a + b_{\text{Fem}} \times \text{Female}$$

$$= \$37{,}314 + -\$5{,}272 \times \text{Female}$$

The coefficient of a dummy variable is easy to interpret: In this case, it tells us that females earn \$5,272 less, on average, than males (the reference category). To examine this more formally and fully: Using the regression equation to make predictions, we find that men earn, on average, \$37,314. For a man, the Female variable takes on the value of 0, so Earnings are predicted to be $\$37{,}314 + (-\$5{,}272 \times 0) = \$37{,}314$, which is the constant. And we find that women are predicted to earn (on average) $\$37{,}314 + (-\$5{,}272 \times 1) = \$32{,}042$. You can also see from these calculations that, on average, women earn \$5,272 less than men. Again, that is in fact the interpretation of the coefficient of the Female dummy variable: On average women earn \$5,272 less per year than men.

More technically, one interprets the coefficient as the difference between the average of earnings (the dependent variable) for women (Female = 1) and the average for men (Female = 0). The coefficient of a dummy variable shows how the dependent variable differs, on average, between the two groups.

If a Male dummy variable had been used instead, its coefficient would have been (positive) \$5,272, just the negative of the coefficient of the Female dummy variable.

Dummy variables are widely used to represent programs or treatments in experimental and quasi experimental studies (covered in Chapters 14 and 15). Some individuals participate in a program or receive a treatment (coded 1), while others—those in the control group—do not (coded 0).

Isn't There a Simpler Way to Estimate Differences in Means?

You might wonder why anyone would bother to do a regression to learn the difference in average earnings between men and women. Why not just calculate the mean of earnings for females and earnings for males and examine the difference? In fact, if that is all you are interested in, then forget the regression and just look at the difference in means.

But dummy variables are useful in multiple regressions because most often we want additional independent variables as well. This allows us to learn about how being female predicts earnings, holding constant other variables such as education, experience, occupation, and so on. Such a regression might help us find out how much of the earnings difference between men and women could be attributed to discrimination rather than to differences in background or qualifications. We will learn much more about these ideas in Chapter 13, on observational studies with control variables.

QUESTION

Write out the same regression equation for Earnings but with a Male (in place of a Female) dummy variable. Interpret the constant and the coefficient of this new equation.

Categorical Variables With More Than Two Possible Values

Of course, many categorical variables that would make good predictors—such as occupation and race—have more than two possible values. Luckily, such categorical variables can still be used as independent variables in regression by creating a set of dummy variables. This is best illustrated with an example.

Consider a race variable with five categories: *White, Black, Hispanic, Asian,* and *Other.* It is possible to create five dummy variables, one for each race category. If an individual is Asian, for example, then the dummy variables White, Black, Hispanic, and Other all have the value of 0, while the dummy variable Asian has the value of 1. (See also Box 10.3.)

BOX 10.3
Representing a Categorical Variable With More Than Two Categories: Diabetes Example

Diabetes status can be broken into three categories:

- No diabetes
- Type 1 diabetes
- Type 2 diabetes

So it is possible to create three diabetes dummy variables:

NoDiabetes =	0	if person has diabetes (either type 1 or type 2)
	1	if person does not have diabetes (neither type 1 nor type 2)
Type1Diabetes =	0	if person does not have type 1 diabetes (person may have type 2 or no diabetes)
	1	if person has type 1 diabetes (person must not have type 2)
Type2Diabetes =	0	if person does not have type 2 diabetes (person may have type 1 or no diabetes)
	1	if person has type 2 diabetes (person must not have type 1)

Any two of the three dummy variables could be used in a regression. For example, just Type1Diabetes and Type2Diabetes could be used. The coefficient of each would then describe the effect of that kind of diabetes compared with not having diabetes (the reference category).

Once we convert our categorical variables of interest into sets of dummy variables, it is possible to include any combination of categorical and quantitative variables we want as independent variables in our regression analysis. The interpretation of the coefficient is then supplemented with the usual modifier, "holding all other independent variables constant."

To figure out someone's race, however, you would need to know only four of the five possible variables. For example, suppose dummy variables for each status other than White are provided. If the others are all 0, we know that the person must be White. If one of the others is 1, then we know that the value of White must be 0. Therefore, all five variables are perfectly multicollinear.

To include a categorical variable as an independent variable in a regression, simply include all possible dummy variables but one. The omitted category is referred to as the *reference category*, since all effects are measured relative to that omitted, or reference, category:

$$\text{Number of dummy variables needed for regression} = \text{Number of categories} - 1$$

What If Someone Belongs in More Than One Category?

Using our race variable, everyone had to be in one and only one of the five categories. However, in reality, people can fall into more than one race category. Hispanics can be Black or White, for example, and some people are of mixed race. In fact, to deal (partially) with this very problem, the U.S. Census Bureau changed its race question, eliminating Hispanic as a race and creating a separate Hispanic variable (Grieco & Cassidy, 2001). Unfortunately, to use a categorical variable in statistical analysis, we must have an *exhaustive and mutually exclusive* list of categories, even if that doesn't fit so well with reality.

What to Do With Missing Values?

If an observation has a missing value for one of the variables, most statistical software will drop it from the regression analysis. Since this both reduces the amount of data (and thus precision) and may reduce generalizability, if those missing data are not a random subset, researchers try to avoid missing data. For categorical variables, it is possible to avoid dropping the observations by creating another category: missing data. For example, race would be included through dummy variables for Black, Hispanic, Asian, Other, and Missing Race, with White being the reference (omitted) category. This strategy is only good if a reasonable share of the sample has a missing value for race.

Interpreting the Coefficient of a Dummy Variable

Box 10.4 lays out the systematic steps for interpreting the coefficient of a dummy variable. The units of the coefficient of any dummy variable are those of the dependent variable. The reference category, however, must be made clear, since it is arbitrary. If we estimate the effect of gender on earnings, we can describe the effect of being female relative to being male, or the effect of being male relative to being female, depending on how we have coded the gender variable.

BOX 10.4
Interpreting the Coefficient of a Dummy Variable

Steps	Example A	Example B
1. Identify the unit of analysis (who or what the data describe).	Person (worker) is the unit of analysis.	Patient is the unit of analysis.
2. Identify the dummy variable whose coefficient is to be interpreted. (It is the indicator category [coded 1].)	*Female* is the dummy variable, so the indicator category is Female = 1.	*Type1Diabetes* is the dummy variable, so the indicator category is Type1Diabetes = 1.
3. Identify the reference category (the omitted category).	*Male* is the reference category (Female = 0).	*No diabetes* is the reference category (Type1Diabetes = 0). (Another category, *Type2Diabetes,* is also measured relative to not having diabetes.)
4. Describe the change from reference category to indicator category.[4]	Switching from *male* to *female.*	Switching from *no diabetes* to *type 1 diabetes.*
5. Identify the dependent variable and its units.	Earnings in dollars.	Medical expenditures in dollars.
6. The coefficient is the difference, on average, between the indicator and the reference category of the dependent variable.	The earnings difference (in dollars) between female workers and male workers (on average).	The medical expenditures difference (in dollars) between patients with type 1 diabetes and patients with no diabetes (on average).

More categories bring more choices of a reference category, so it is important to choose a reference category that makes interpretation easy and relevant. To illustrate, consider a regression to determine the effect of different levels of education (different degrees) on earnings. One option is to make the reference category high school dropout. In that case, the coefficient of the variable, CollegeGraduate would reveal the differences in earnings between college graduates and high school dropouts, not the most meaningful contrast. But if we make high school graduate the reference category, the coefficient would reveal the difference in earnings between college graduates and high school graduates—the premium for completing college. And the coefficient of Dropout would reveal the penalty for dropping out. It makes more sense to set things up in this way.

Another option is to use what is called **effect coding**, which is a way of coding a set of dummy variables representing multiple categories so that the regression coefficients turn out to be contrasts with a grand mean (the mean of the means of each category). It is accomplished by coding the reference group −1 instead of 0 across the other categories (see Hardy, 1993, for details). Effect coding is useful when you want to see how the group mean differs from an overall average, rather than from a specific reference group.

[4]Technically, this is true because switching from the reference category to the indicator category is equivalent to a one-unit increase in the independent variable.

Analysis of Variance (ANOVA)

ANOVA is a statistical method that comes from experimental research (discussed in Chapter 14) and that compares the means of a dependent variable across treatment categories. It is equivalent to a regression with a set of dummy variables representing a single categorical variable, but ANOVA results are presented and interpreted somewhat differently.

First, the statistical significance test that appears in ANOVA (an F test) applies to all the differences between means combined (what statisticians call an *omnibus test*), rather than testing each category against a reference group as in regression. However, regression output from statistical software also provides an equivalent F test for the whole regression model. Second, the ANOVA results focus on a comparison of how much of the dependent variable's variation occurs *between* the independent variable categories (and thus is predicted by them) versus how much of the dependent variable's variation occurs *within* the independent variable categories (and thus is not predicted by them). This is related to R-squared in regression, which is the percentage of variation explained or predicted by the model.

ANOVA can be extended to include more than one categorical variable (factor) as well as quantitative variables (covariates). It is then referred to as factorial ANOVA, or two-way ANOVA, or as *analysis of covariance* (ANCOVA) if there are covariates. Because multiple regression can accomplish many of the same aims and is now more familiar to many researchers, you do not see ANOVA or ANCOVA used as much as in the past. But it remains common in much experimental research in fields such as psychology and medicine.

QUESTION

Create a set of dummy variables for regression that specify region of the United States (the Census categories are Northeast, South, Midwest, and West). Which would you make the reference category, and why?

Interactions in Regression

Sometimes the effect of one variable depends on the value of another. For example, the effect of having diabetes on medical expenditures may depend on whether or not the person also has hypertension. In that case, hypertension is a *moderator* of diabetes, as we defined this type of variable in Chapter 2. This phenomenon is different from the effect of hypertension itself and can be modeled in regression with an interaction term.

An **interaction variable** is a variable defined as the product of two other variables. For example, we could define an interaction as the product of a dummy variable for diabetes and a dummy variable for hypertension. In this case,

$$\text{Inter} = \text{Hyper} \times \text{Diabetes}.$$

The variable Inter takes on the value 1 for someone who has *both* hypertension and diabetes and takes on the value 0 for everyone else.

Interaction variables are particularly useful for some kinds of program evaluation analyses, such as difference-in-differences, as described in Chapter 15.

How to Use and Interpret Interaction Variables

Consider predicting an individual's medical expenditures using data on his or her diabetes and hypertension status. A regression without an interaction would be

$$\text{Exp} = a + b_{\text{diab}}\text{Diabetes} + b_{\text{hyper}}\text{Hyper}.$$

The coefficient b_{diab} predicts the difference in medical expenditures, for a patient with diabetes relative to a patient without diabetes, holding constant hypertension status. And the coefficient b_{hyper} predicts the difference in medical expenditures, for a hypertensive relative to a nonhypertensive, holding constant diabetes status.

With no interaction, however, we cannot detect if the effect of one variable influences the magnitude of the effect of the other. To do that, we include an interaction term:

$$\text{Exp} = a + b_{\text{diab}}\text{Diabetes} + b_{\text{hyper}}\text{Hyper} + b_{\text{int}}\text{Inter}$$

Now, we need to interpret the coefficient of the interaction. Moreover, once an interaction term is used, the interpretation of the coefficients of the diabetes and hypertension variables (referred to as *simple main effects*) becomes somewhat more complicated. We describe both below.

Interpreting the Simple Main Effects With Dummy Variable Interactions

Interpretation is most easily explained using a numerical example. Suppose

- a = \$1,200
- b_{diab} = \$1,000
- b_{hyper} = \$700
- b_{int} = \$1,500

Using the regression equation, we can see the average expenditures for someone:

without diabetes or hypertension	$= a + b_{\text{diab}} \times 0 + b_{\text{hyper}} \times 0 + b_{\text{int}} \times 0$ $= a$ = \$1,200
with diabetes, without hypertension	$= a + b_{\text{diab}} \times 1 + b_{\text{hyper}} \times 0 + b_{\text{int}} \times 0$ $= a + b_{\text{diab}}$ = \$1,200 + \$1,000 = \$2,200
without diabetes, with hypertension	$= a + b_{\text{diab}} \times 0 + b_{\text{hyper}} \times 1 + b_{\text{int}} \times 0$ $= a + b_{\text{hyper}}$ = \$1,200 + \$700 = \$1,900
with diabetes, with hypertension	$= a + b_{\text{diab}} \times 1 + b_{\text{hyper}} \times 1 + b_{\text{int}} \times 1$ $= a + b_{\text{diab}} + b_{\text{hyper}} + b_{\text{int}}$ = \$1,200 + \$1,000 + \$700 + \$1,500 = \$4,400

Thus, it can be seen that the coefficient b_{diab} predicts the difference in expenditures for a diabetic relative to a nondiabetic, for someone who is *not* hypertensive (simple main effect of diabetes). The coefficient b_{hyper} predicts the difference in expenditures for a hypertensive relative to a nonhypertensive, for someone who is *not* diabetic (simple main effect of hypertension). Thus, to interpret the simple main effect when there is an interaction of two dummy variables, the reference category of both dummy variables must be known.

Interpreting the Coefficient of the Interaction: The Effect on the Effect

Among those who have hypertension, those with diabetes have mean expenditures \$2,500 higher than those without diabetes. This difference is composed of the \$1,000 effect of diabetes among those without hypertension and the additional $1,500 that having hypertension raises the effect of diabetes. The *interaction* is how much the second disease changes the effect of the first, above its simple main effect.

It can be interpreted symmetrically. The $1,500 is also the amount that having diabetes raises the simple main effect of hypertension, from $700 to $700 + $1,500 = $2,200. Among those with hypertension, those with diabetes have average expenditures $2,200 higher. So the coefficient b_{int} predicts the difference in the hypertensive effect between diabetics and nondiabetics; it also predicts the difference in the diabetic effect between hypertensives and nonhypertensives.

Interactions With Quantitative Variables

Thus far, we have illustrated and discussed interactions with dummy variables only. But interactions can also involve quantitative variables. For example, imagine that the effect of age (in years) on medical expenditures depends on whether one has diabetes or not. In that case, we could define an interaction variable, Inter = Diabetes × Age. The interaction variable takes on the value of 0 for everyone who is not diabetic and takes on the value of their age for everyone who is diabetic. The regression equation is as follows:

$$\text{Expenditures} = a + b_{age}\text{Age} + b_{diab}\text{Diabetes} + b_{int}\text{Inter}$$

In this example, the coefficient b_{age} tells us how much each additional year of age raises medical expenses on average for nondiabetics. The coefficient b_{int} tells us how much *more* an additional year of age raises medical expenses for a diabetic, *above* what an additional year raises expenditures for a nondiabetic. And the coefficient b_{diab} predicts the difference in expenditures for a diabetic relative to a nondiabetic, for someone who is 0 years old. (This can be more intuitively thought of as the constant term in a regression of expenditures on age among those with diabetes.)

QUESTION

Suppose two variables in a regression each have a large effect on the dependent variable, but the coefficient for the interaction of the two variables is zero. What does this tell you?

Always Include Both Main Effects

When using an interaction variable, it is important always to include both main effects as independent variables in the regression. Even if you think the variable does not have its own main effect on the outcome, leaving it out of the equation risks producing bias. If, for example, age does have its own main effect on expenditures, despite our assumption to the contrary, leaving age out of the equation would then assign the main effect of age to the interaction term. A word of caution about interaction variables: Multicollinearity often arises when you attempt to include an interaction variable, especially when the two variables you are interacting are correlated with each other.

Functional Form and Transformations in Regression

Simple regression is a best-fit *straight* line. Multiple regression is a multivariate version of the same thing, with every independent variable having a *linear* effect. However, not all relationships are linear. For example, average health expenditures are higher for both low-income and higher-income people but lower for middle-income people—a U-shaped relationship. For another example, the effect of experience on earnings is first very high but then diminishes and eventually flattens out.

Fitting such relationships with an ordinary linear regression is hazardous for several reasons. First, we will often fail to find a relationship if the true relationship is nonlinear (such as a U-shaped relationship) and if we rely solely on linear regression. Second, even if a relationship is found, a linear regression will be a poor fit for a nonlinear pattern, and our predictions will be off the mark. Third, the formulas for statistical inference in regression are based on having normally distributed errors. Fitting the wrong relationship—often called misspecification—will result in nonnormal errors and thus inaccurate inference formulas.

How to Fit a Curved Relationship

Regression can be used to fit nonlinear relationships by adding a quadratic (squared) or a higher-order polynomial version (such as a cubic) of the independent variable, along with the usual linear term of the variable. For example, it is common to use experience and experience-squared as independent variables in a regression to predict earnings, like this:

$$\text{Earnings} = a + b_{\text{exp}}\text{Experience} + b_{\text{sqr}}\text{Experience}^2$$

Say, hypothetically, that a = \$12,000, b_{exp} = \$6,000/year, and b_{sqr} = –\$150/year^2. In this case, the negative coefficient of experience-squared captures the diminishing marginal effect of experience. Figure 10.3 shows the same equation graphically. Quadratics like this can also capture an increasing marginal effect, in which case the coefficient of the squared term would be positive and the line would instead bend upward.

When a quadratic or other polynomial term is included in a regression, the two coefficients must be interpreted together. For example, the effect of an additional year of work experience depends on the level of experience the person starts with. An additional year of experience counts for more early in one's career and less later on.

In addition to polynomials, independent variables may be transformed in a variety of ways, for example, into exponentials. The dependent variable may also be transformed. The transformations chosen can be determined by theory, or they can be determined by examining the data to determine what fits. Always graph the data, even though multivariate patterns can be hard to discern.

How to Interpret Regression Coefficients When a Variable Is Logged

One particular transformation, the *log,* is extremely common. Variables such as earnings, medical expenditures, and housing prices are often highly skewed, because they can't go below 0, but they have a small number of very high values. To be used in regression, whether as independent or dependent variables, such variables are almost always transformed by taking their natural log.[5]

For example, Figure 8.5 from Chapter 8 showed how the relationship between the gross domestic product (GDP) of nations, which is right-skewed, and life expectancy is nonlinear. Figure 8.6 (again see Chapter 8) then showed how this relationship can be coaxed into a linear pattern by taking the natural log of GDP.

Interpreting regression coefficients when the variables have been logged turns out to be fairly simple. The change in a logged variable is just the proportional change in the unlogged variable. Consider a regression with log earnings as the dependent variable and years of education as the independent variable, whose coefficient is .03. That would mean that someone with one more year of education would be predicted to have .03 more earnings proportionally—or 3% more. In other words, take the coefficient, multiply it by 100, and the predicted percent change is given.

Things are even easier when both dependent and independent variables are logged. Consider a regression of log medical expenditures on log length of stay. The coefficient reveals the percent change in medical expenditures due to a 1% change in length of stay. The percent change in one variable due to a 1% change in another is referred to as the *elasticity* and is common in economics.

QUESTION

Describe a situation in which you might want to log a variable before using it in a regression.

[5]In fact, earnings would essentially never be used in a real regression study. We chose to illustrate regression using earnings, instead of log earnings, because it made it easier to explain how to interpret the coefficient. This decision further forced us to use simulated (made-up) data, because no real earnings data would have behaved well unlogged.

Figure 10.3 Nonlinear (Quadratic) Relationship Between Experience and Earnings (Simulated Data)

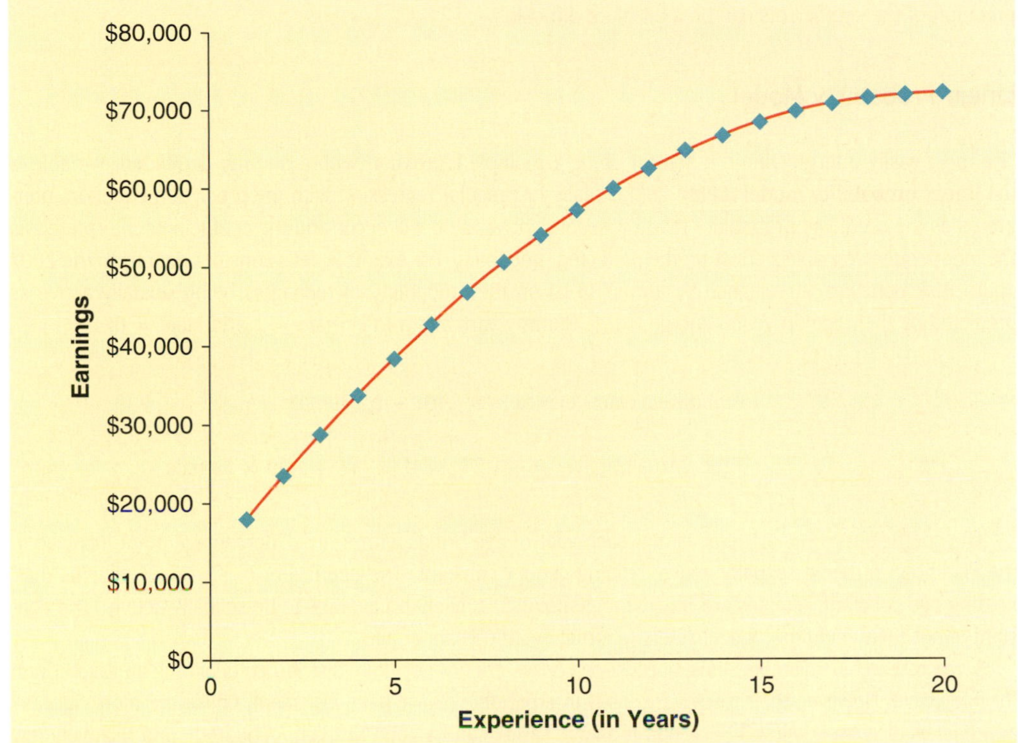

The Value of Robustness and Transparency

As discussed earlier, out-of-sample extrapolation can be hazardous, although it is often necessary to make such predictions for policy purposes. To further exacerbate the problem, different functional forms can result in quite different out-of-sample extrapolations. If the line is straight, we expect one thing; if it curves down, we might expect something quite different.

Policy-relevant relationships, such as how subsidizing health insurance influences people's decision to obtain coverage, can be modeled in a variety of different but reasonable ways. Such models are often used to predict the effects of a policy, such as a particular health care reform, that represents a large change from the way things are—in other words, out-of-sample extrapolations. As illustrated by Remler, Graff Zivin, and Glied (2004), out-of-sample extrapolations exacerbate the functional form differences, causing predictions from different models to diverge a great deal. In related work, Glied, Remler, and Graff Zivin (2002) propose guidelines for such extrapolations and encourage transparency of methods so that others may duplicate the calculation. Most of all, the robustness of different functional forms and models should be assessed. If the results are robust, they gain credibility. If they are not, then we at least realize our ignorance.

Categorical Variables as Dependent Variables in Regression

Many outcomes or dependent variables of interest in policy and practice are categorical—for example, graduating from high school or not, having a felony conviction or not, and having a disease or not. There are several forms of regression for dummy dependent variables such as these, including the linear probability model, logistic regression, and probit regression. They are similar to ordinary regression, although the interpretation of the coefficients can be a bit more difficult.

Linear Probability Model

The most easily interpretable method for doing a multiple regression with a dummy dependent variable is the **linear probability model (LPM)**. LPM is really just regular regression with the prediction equation interpreted as the predicted probability that the dependent variable will occur and the coefficients interpreted as the independent variable's effect on the predicted probability. For example, let's consider data from the 2007 Youth Risk Behavior Surveillance System (YRBSS) on the probability of teenagers being sexually active as predicted by their age (in years) and gender (a dummy variable, with Female = 1 and Male = 0).

$$\text{Prob(Sexuallyactive)} = a + b_{age}\text{Age} + b_{fem}\text{Female}$$

$$\text{Prob(Sexuallyactive)} = -1.27 + .11 \times \text{Age} - .05 \times \text{Female}$$

The coefficient $b_{age} = .11$ tells us that each year of age brings with it an 11 percentage point increase in the likelihood of being sexually active, holding gender constant. The coefficient $b_{fem} = -.05$ tells us that, holding age constant, females are 5 percentage points *less* likely on average to be sexually active. (The constant is not meaningful because it refers to a male with 0 years of age.)

Some researchers dismiss LPMs, because the errors are not normally distributed (violating an assumption for inference). However, their results are easily interpretable (as we have just seen), unlike the more rigorous approaches discussed below. LPM requires a large sample and a good fit (high R-squared), and relatively few of the predictions should fall outside the 0 to 1 range. To test whether it is appropriate to use an LPM, its predictions should be examined and also compared with one of the more rigorous methods below.

Logistic and Probit Regression

Two more rigorous regression models for predicting dummy dependent variables are **logistic regression** (**logit**, for short) and *probit regression*, of which logistic is more common. For the logit equation, the log odds of an event are predicted. For the probit, as for the LPM, the probability is predicted. We will not go into any technical details about these methods (for a good introduction, see Pampel, 2000). However, it is possible to read, even read critically, studies using these methods without understanding their technical complexities.

QUESTION

Suppose that a logistic regression analysis of graduating high school (yes or no) has an odds ratio for Male equal to .85. What does that say about whether males or females are more likely to graduate?

Unlike regular ordinary least squares (OLS) or LPM coefficients, the coefficients of logit and probit regressions cannot be interpreted meaningfully without doing some calculations. For logit regressions, the most common calculation converts the coefficients into odds ratios—the kind discussed in Chapter 8.

Consider some logistic regression results from the same YRBSS data and variables as before used to predict whether teenagers are likely to be sexually active, based on their age and gender. Logistic regression output provides the odds ratio for Age, which turns out to be 1.62, meaning that the odds of being sexually active, holding gender constant, increase by this amount with each year of age. The odds ratio for Female is .81, meaning that the odds of being sexually active for females, holding age constant, are .81 to 1 (teenage girls are less likely to be sexually active on average than teenage boys). These results parallel those from the LPM.

It is also important to consider how good a fit a logit or probit model is, using one of its goodness-of-fit measures, such as the pseudo R-squared (which is similar to R-squared in ordinary regression).

Marginal Effects

The effects of independent variables in logit or probit regressions can be described using a **marginal effect** (or incremental effect)—the predicted difference in the probability due to a specified change in the relevant independent variable. Marginal effects may be calculated for probit and logistic regressions using means of the independent variables, but it is better to calculate them for each data point and then average.

What If the Dependent Variable Has More Than Two Categories?

Any categorical variable with more than two categories can be collapsed into a dummy variable. For example, self-reported health status (excellent, good, fair, poor) can be converted into two categories, Poor Health and Not-Poor Health (better than poor health). Therefore, the techniques above, such as the LPM or logistic regression, can be used for such categorical variables. However, collapsing categories often results in the loss of important information, such as differences within the various better-than-poor health categories.

Fortunately, some more advanced regression techniques allow for categorical dependent variables with multiple categories. *Ordered logit* and *ordered probit* allow ordinal categorical variables to be used as dependent variables. *Multinomial logit* (also called *conditional logit*) and *multinomial probit* allow nominal categorical variables to be used as dependent variables.

Beware of Unrealistic Underlying Assumptions

The complexity of the regression methods with dependent categorical variables raises issues beyond just those of interpretation. The underlying equations are based on a variety of assumptions, and those assumptions may not be realistic.

For example, multinomial logit assumes the *independence of irrelevant alternatives* (*IIA*). IIA means that adding another alternative or changing the characteristics of another alternative does not affect the relative odds between the two alternatives considered in a specific multinomial logit equation. This is not true in many cases. A famous illustration shows that the choice between commuting on a blue bus or on a train is unchanged by the addition of a red bus, even though a red bus and a blue bus are obviously close substitutes (McFadden, 1974). Careful nesting of logits can alleviate the IIA problem.

Which Statistical Methods Can I Use?

As you have seen, the appropriate statistical method depends on the type and quantity of variables. We have introduced some, although certainly not all, of the most important methods. To help you determine which statistical methods are available in a particular situation, we provide Table 10.5. The columns describe different possible types of dependent variables, while the rows describe different possible types of independent variables. The corresponding cell then provides possible statistical methods. For example, when both the independent and dependent variables are quantitative, ordinary regression (ordinary least squares regression, abbreviated OLS) may be used.

While this table is a useful guide, the methods above may not always apply. For example, OLS regression is intended for continuous variables—quantitative variables that can take on any value. A count variable (such as the number of jobs someone has held) must be a positive integer (or 0). In many circumstances, OLS regression cannot be used for count data. In the limited dependent variables section below, we discuss some of the circumstances in which another method is required.

Table 10.5 Which Statistical Methods Can I Use?

Independent Variable Type	Dependent Variable Type			
	Quantitative	**Dichotomous (Dummy)**	**Ordinal Categorical**	**Nominal Categorical**
Quantitative	OLS regression	Logit or probit Less rigorous: Linear probability model (LPM)	Ordered logit or probit	Multinomial logit or probit
Dichotomous (Dummy)	(1) *t* test (comparison of means) (2) OLS regression with single dummy as independent variable	(1) Cross-tabs and χ^2 test if only a single independent variable (no controls) (2) *z* test (comparison of proportions) (no controls) (3) Logit or probit with single dummy as independent variable (4) Less rigorous: LPM with single dummy as independent variable	(1) Cross-tabs and χ^2 test if only a single independent variable (no controls) This "wastes" information contained in ordering. (2) Ordered logit or probit with single dummy as independent variable	(1) Cross-tabs and χ^2 test if only a single independent variable (no controls) (2) Multinomial logit or probit with dummy as independent variable
Ordinal Categorical	(1) OLS regression with dummies as independent variables (2) ANOVA	(1) Cross-tabs and χ^2 test if only a single independent variable (no controls) (2) Logit or probit with dummies as independent variables (3) Less rigorous: LPM with dummies as independent variables	(1) Cross-tabs and χ^2 test if only a single independent variable (no controls) This "wastes" information contained in ordering. (2) Ordered logit or probit with dummies as independent variables	(1) Cross-tabs and χ^2 test if only a single independent variable (no controls) (2) Multinomial logit or probit with dummies as independent variables
Nominal Categorical	(1) OLS regression with dummies as independent variables (2) ANOVA	(1) Cross-tabs and χ^2 test if only a single independent variable (no controls) (2) Logit or probit with dummies as independent variables (3) Less rigorous: LPM with dummies as independent variables	(1) Cross-tabs and χ^2 test if only a single independent variable (no controls) This "wastes" information contained in ordering. (2) Ordered logit or probit with dummies as independent variables	(1) Cross-tabs and χ^2 test if only a single independent variable (no controls) (2) Multinomial logit or probit with dummies as independent variables

Note: It is possible to create a dichotomous variable from any ordinal or nominal variable by combining categories. However, this throws out information. It may nonetheless be desirable if cell sizes are small.

Other Multivariate Methods

Many research studies use multiple regression in one of the forms we have discussed. However, some studies use other multivariate methods. It is beyond the scope of this book to even introduce all the quantitative analysis methods used in applied social research. However, we can provide a brief lay of the land—a sort of road map to some of the most common multivariate methods, along with their basic purposes and a few strengths and weaknesses.

Path Analysis

Often, researchers want to explore a complex set of relationships between many variables, making use of theory that describes and restricts the relationships. **Path analysis** does this by estimating the pattern of relationships between variables in a presumed causal structure.

Path analysis typically begins with a path diagram such as the ones introduced in Chapter 2. The results are presented as path coefficients next to the arrows linking the variables in the path diagram. The numerical estimates typically come from a set of ordinary regressions.

The main strength of path analysis is that it encourages researchers to specify and examine the presumed causal order of variables, in the form of a path diagram, and to empirically estimate both direct and indirect effects. This is illustrated in the path diagram of Figure 10.4.

The coefficients on the direct paths of education → earnings, age → earnings, and experience → earnings come from the following standardized regression:

$$\text{Earnings} = .40 \times \text{Education} + .10 \times \text{Age} + .30 \times \text{Experience}$$

The remaining two paths, age → education and age → experience, come from the following simple regressions:

$$\text{Education} = -.20 \times \text{Age}$$

$$\text{Experience} = .50 \times \text{Age}$$

Figure 10.4 Example of Results of Path Analysis

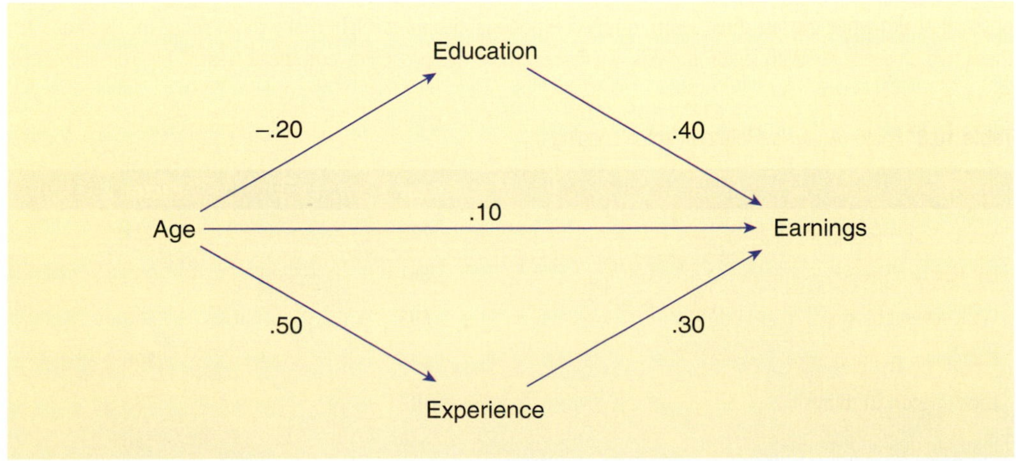

As these last two equations are simple regressions, these standardized coefficients are equivalent to the correlation r between the variables.

The results of the path analysis help us interpret how age influences earnings. According to these data, age has only a modest *direct* effect on earnings—which would be our conclusion had we used the regression analysis alone. But age has a larger *indirect* effect on earnings through experience, which can be calculated by multiplying the coefficients along the path: $.50 \times .30 = .15$ (older people have more experience, and experience leads to more earnings). The indirect effect of age through education, however, is negative: $-.20 \times .40 = -.08$ (older people tend to be less educated, and education boosts earnings). The *total* effect of age on earnings is composed of the direct effect plus the indirect effects: $.10 + .15 - .08 = .17$. In this way, path analysis helps illuminate indirect effects, in addition to direct effects, and provides a fuller picture of the pattern of relationships among variables.

While path analysis's greatest strength is its ability to explore and explain a particular theory, described by a path diagram, its dependence on that theory is also the method's greatest weakness. Path analysis is a structural method: What it can find is dictated by the structure, the path diagram that is assumed to be true.

Factor Analysis

In Chapter 4, on measurement, we saw how many indicators can be combined to create a scale. **Factor analysis** is a multivariate method that helps with this task by empirically grouping many variables (indicators) into a smaller set of underlying *factors*. For this reason, it is sometimes referred to as a *data reduction* method. Because it reduces many overlapping variables into fewer, less overlapping (less correlated) factors, it can help with the multicollinearity problem in regression discussed earlier.

To give an example of factor analysis, say we ask people in a health survey how often they do the following:

1. Walk up several flights of stairs
2. Lift heavy objects
3. Walk several blocks
4. Feel down in the dumps
5. Lack interest in things
6. Find life dull and routine

Although these are six separate variables that we could analyze individually, the first three seem to indicate physical health while the last three seem to reflect emotional health. It might make more sense for us to use just these two dimensions. With factor analysis, we can examine this possibility empirically—as Table 10.6 illustrates.

Table 10.6 Factor Analysis (Rotated Factor Loadings)

	Factor 1	Factor 2
Walk up several flights of stairs	**.722**	.122
Lift heavy objects	**.661**	.083
Walk several blocks	**.698**	.100
Feel down in the dumps	.043	**.806**
Lack interest in things	.102	**.786**
Find life dull and routine	.097	**.749**

The numbers shown are **factor loadings**, essentially correlations between the variables and the underlying factors (two in this case). These results show a coherent pattern: The first three variables load highly on factor 1 (see the bolded factor loadings) while the second three variables load highly on factor 2 (again, see the bolded factor loadings). Thus, the results support our idea of combining the first three variables to represent one factor, and combining the next three to represent a second factor. The first factor seems to relate to physical health, while the second factor seems to relate to mental health. In this case, physical health and mental health are *latent constructs,* variables that are not directly observable (as discussed in Chapter 4).

There are many options in factor analysis for extracting initial factors, selecting how many factors to retain, and rotating the factor solution so that the factor loadings can be interpreted (for an introduction to these issues see Kim & Mueller, 1978). Much depends also on the features available in the statistical software you are using.

So far we have been talking about the traditional method of **exploratory factor analysis** in which the researcher does not use theory to impose a structure on the factor analysis. Specifically, the researcher lets the data and software choose the number of factors and estimate how the items correlate with each factor.

Confirmatory Factor Analysis: Making Use of Theory

Alternatively, researchers can use measurement theory to specify both the number of latent variables (factors) and which variables are related to each latent variable (which variables load onto each factor). This is referred to as **confirmatory factor analysis,** because it uses factor analysis to confirm a particular measurement model. In the above example, the researcher could have specified that two factors, one for physical health and one for mental health, existed and that the first three variables related to the physical health factor and the second three variables related to the mental health factor. The factor analysis would be performed under those restrictions. The data would then serve two purposes: (1) to create the best representation of physical and mental health through the factor loadings, and (2) to test or confirm the measurement model through goodness-of-fit measures. Confirmatory factor analysis is actually a form of structural equation modeling, which we cover next.

QUESTION

In what situations do researchers use factor analysis?

Structural Equation Modeling

Structural equation modeling (SEM) essentially combines both factor and path analysis into one estimation method. In fact, SEM is the method most often used for confirmatory factor analysis, and some prefer to use SEM in place of regression to estimate ordinary path models. But in its full form, SEM includes both a structural model, as in path analysis, and factors represented by multiple indicators.

SEM has several strengths. First, causal models of latent variables can be explored in a manner that allows the data to be optimized simultaneously for both purposes: causal structure and measurement. Second, by explicitly removing the measurement error from the latent variables, the causal model can be more reliably estimated. Third, as with path models, SEM results show more explicitly how variables are related to each other.

Figure 10.5 shows an example from an SEM study of influences on trust of the civil service across 33 nations (Van Ryzin, 2009). The main outcome, Trust of the civil service, is an observed variable. However, the main hypothesized causes, Government process and Government outcomes, are factors, or latent variables, observed in the real world through their indicators.

In the diagram, observed variables are shown in rectangles with latent variables shown in ovals. The estimates (standardized coefficients in this case) are next to each of the arrows. The structural coefficients are interpreted the same way as path coefficients, and the factor coefficients are equivalent to factor loadings. (The small circles connected to each observed variable represent unique components, and the coefficients next to these small circles are the explained variances.)

As with path analysis and all structural methods, SEM's main weakness is its sensitivity to the theory. This weakness can be somewhat alleviated by testing competing theories, but all the results are driven by strong assumptions about the causal relationships among the variables.

Figure 10.5 Example of Structural Equation Modeling Results

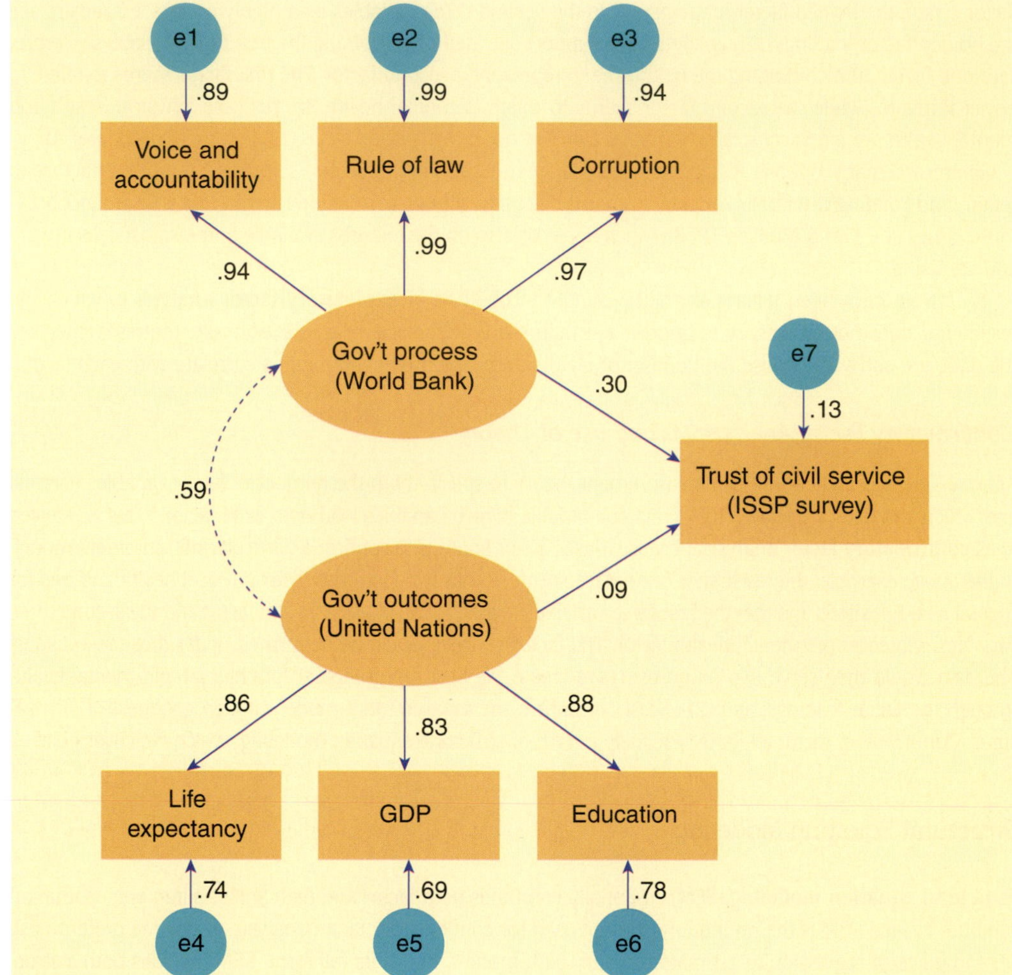

Note: ISSP, International Social Survey Program.

Source: Adapted from Van Ryzin (2009).

Multilevel Models

Theories and models used to estimate the theories must specify the unit of analysis. Using the example of the determinants of crime, do we model crime on an individual level? A neighborhood level? A city level? A country level? One can imagine influences that work at each of these levels. An individual's family background matters, but so does the degree of order in his or her neighborhood and the job opportunities in his or her city. Moreover, some variables are determined at the higher level by higher-level processes and influenced by what happens at the lower levels.

Multilevel models (also known as **hierarchical models**) allow researchers to jointly consider variables measured at different units of analysis, such as how crime at the individual level, order at the neighborhood level, and job opportunities at the city level are jointly determined. Because it allows researchers to consider the influence of context on individuals, multilevel modeling has become especially important in fields such as education, public health, and criminal justice.

Figure 10.6 Example of Multilevel Model

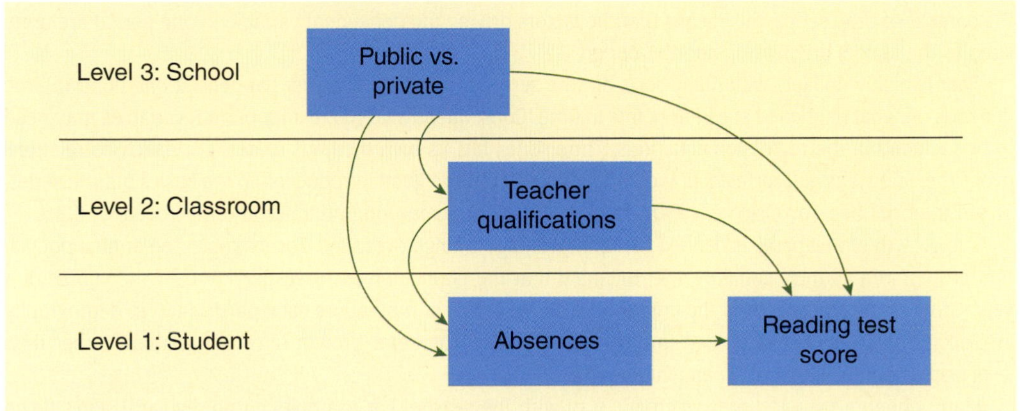

Source: Leonard, Bourke, and Schofield (2002).

Figure 10.6 illustrates a multilevel model using education variables that are measured at the school, classroom, and individual levels. To estimate the model, we might have data, say, on 10 schools, 100 classrooms (10 in each school), and 2,000 students (20 in each classroom). Thus, each variable in the model describes a different unit of analysis, yet we would estimate it all as one model.

There are variations on multilevel modeling, some of which fall short of full multilevel modeling. For example, we could create a dummy variable for the public-private school status of each student and also assign dummy variables to the qualification levels of their teachers, and then run the model as an individual-level regression. But this approach is not as good because it multiplies the observations at a higher level (we have just 100 teachers, not 2,000), distorting the standard errors (although this can be corrected by using clustered standard errors), and it does not give information on cross-level effects and interactions. See Luke (2004) for more information on the motivations for and detailed methods of multilevel modeling.

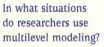

QUESTION

In what situations do researchers use multilevel modeling?

Time Series and Forecasting

In time-series data, the variation is over time, rather than being cross-sectional variation. For example, a time series might consist of world population in each year over 20 years. Using regression is more difficult with time-series data than with cross-sectional data—treacherous, even, in some cases.

Time Trends and Correlation Over Time

Over time, the number of computers per capita is rising, and the population is growing. If a regression of computers per capita on population were performed using time-series data, it would show a strong relationship. In fact, any time series generally going up (or down) over time would seem strongly related to any series going up (or down) over time. But that could just be the general trend of both. With time-series data that have a trend over time, care must be taken with regressions.

The simplest approach is to include a linear time trend in the regression equation. In this way, the coefficient describes how the deviations from trend of the variables are related. For example, by estimating the regression

$$\text{ComputersPerCap} = a + b_{pop}\text{Population} + b_{trend}\text{Year},$$

the coefficient b_{pop} reveals the extent that variations from trend in the two series are correlated.

But time series is more complicated than most regressions for other reasons. A basic assumption of inference for regression is that the error terms (other factors driving the dependent variable) are independent. In the context of time series, this means that the factors driving the dependent variable in one period are unrelated to the factors driving it in another period.

That is highly unlikely with many sorts of time series. In general, whatever happens at one point in time depends on what happened at earlier points in time. Consequently, lagged (earlier period) variables may need to be included in the regression equations. Time series has its own methods to deal with such correlations over time, known as *autocorrelation*. Wooldridge (2009) offers a good introduction to the basics of time series, or see the brief book by Ostrom (1990). These methods are common in finance and macroeconomics.

The growth of a variable is defined as the percentage change over time. For example, the annual population growth in a country could be 1%, meaning that the population increases by 1% over the course of a year. Growth rates must specify the unit of time. Some forms of time-series data, particularly in demography and economics, are best described through growth rates. Therefore, growth rates of variables, rather than levels, are often used as the dependent variables.

Many phenomena vary in a systematic way with the season. For example, hiring regularly slows down around Christmas. To focus on variation driven by other factors or changes that represent "real" changes, such data are often seasonally adjusted. Specifically, the effects of the seasons are estimated using a long time series. The seasonal variation is then predicted and subtracted from the actual data.

Forecasting means using data from time series in the past to predict future values of the dependent variable(s). Forecasting is particularly common in demography and economics. Forecasting is, in some sense, an out-of-sample extrapolation. The further into the future a forecast must go, the more out of sample it must go—and therefore the less confidence we can have in it.

Panel Data Methods

Panel data, described in Chapter 6, often consist of repeated measures of the same variables for the same individuals over time. These data thus combine both cross-sectional and time-series variation. A number of special methods exist to make use of these multiple dimensions. One method is known as *fixed effects*.[6] The idea is that there is some particular characteristic (related to the dependent variable) that varies across individuals and is unknown but does not vary over time. In this case, an individual-specific dummy variable is included in the regression. Essentially, the regression is estimated from the relationships between changes over time in individuals' dependent variable and changes in their independent variables. This is discussed further in Chapter 15 on natural and quasi experiments.

Spatial Analysis

Spatial data of many kinds are becoming increasingly available due to geographic information systems (GIS). GIS generally refers to a broad set of techniques that range from creating spatial data (e.g., identifying the geographic coordinates for events or calculating distances between features of interest) to creating maps. Spatial analysis builds on GIS, in that spatial data are used with spatial methods.

Spatial methods are typically used to conduct analysis of spatial properties such as identifying spatial patterns in data, for example, clustering of mortality or poverty (Center for Spatially Integrated Social Science, 2009). As for time series that have to be concerned with temporal autocorrelation, care must often be taken with spatial data, because each location is similar to and not independent of nearby locations; this is called spatial autocorrelation. A simple form of spatial analysis uses cross-sectional data where the unit

[6]This refers to the fixed-effects method of econometrics, not the fixed-effects method of experimental analysis and design.

of analysis is a location, perhaps a very finely defined location, with variables, such as mortality, describing the location. One variation is a "hot" or "cold" spot analysis in which one looks for clusters of especially high or low mortality. The Center for Spatially Integrated Social Science provides many references and resources (www.csiss.org).[7]

Limited Dependent Variables

A regular regression implicitly assumes that the dependent variable is a quantitative variable that can take on any value. It can be positive or negative. It is continuous and not restricted to integers or any particular region. A dependent variable that cannot take on all possible values is known as a *limited dependent variable*. We have already examined categorical variables, which are one special kind of limited dependent variable. However, there are other kinds.

Many variables cannot possibly take on values below 0. For example, it is not possible to have a negative weight. These can result in what is called truncated variables. Regression models exist to treat such situations, such as the Tobit model. The Poisson model can be used for dependent variables that are counts—nonnegative integers. In other circumstances, the variable can take on a full range of values, but we cannot observe them, because they are censored. For example, many surveys top-code income; that is, they do not provide measures of income over a certain amount, but simply describe those incomes as top-coded. A closely related case is referred to as *truncated data,* which is essentially sample selection bias, because the sample is truncated in a way that is related to what is being estimated.

There are more advanced methods for dealing with all these problems. They are beyond the scope of this book. (See Wooldridge, 2009, for further treatment.) However, there are two things that you do need to know. First, ignoring such problems, unless their magnitude is small, can be a mistake that leads to wrong conclusions. Second, the methods that do exist frequently depend on quite a few assumptions. They work by substituting functional form assumptions to predict data or relationships that are not known. In some cases, the assumptions used are good, but in other cases, they are not.

Survival Analysis

Frequently, researchers want to predict the length of time until some event, such as the length of an unemployment spell (time until a job is found) or how long someone lives (time until death) following treatment of a particular disease. Such analysis is often referred to as *survival analysis*, due to its use in medical research. It is a particularly important form of limited dependent variable. In addition to the natural restrictions to the form the variable can take, data are often censored, because the data collection ends before all individuals reach the event (e.g., death, employment).

More Multivariate Methods Not Covered

We have only been able to give an overview of some of the multivariate methods most commonly used in social and policy research. There are many more, with each field or discipline having its own preferred tool kit of techniques. To understand any of these methods, it helps to focus on the big picture of why the method is needed and what it provides. What questions does the method help answer? What insight does it provide? How does it differ from methods you already know? How is it the same?

---

[7]We thank Deborah Balk for providing us with information on spatial analysis.

Conclusion

Social and policy phenomena are complex and involve many variables. Each variable is related to many other variables like threads in an intricate web. For this reason, analysis of such phenomena frequently requires multivariate techniques. Moreover, many of the multivariate techniques of this chapter become essential tools for getting at causation, discovering what causes what and properly estimating the size of causal effects. But by themselves, these tools and techniques are not sufficient. Theory, careful thought, and additional evidence are required. The next part of the book discusses what else you need to know to investigate and demonstrate causation.

BOX 10.5
Tips on Doing Your Own Research: Multivariate Statistics

- Calculate and interpret univariate and bivariate descriptive statistics—and the associated inferential statistics, particularly confidence intervals—*before* calculating multivariate statistics. See tips on doing your own research on descriptive and inferential statistics at the ends of Chapters 8 and 9.
- Plan the multivariate analysis when you plan the design (including shell tables). Consider how well the analysis will address your research question.
- Determine the independent and dependent variables.
- Determine the type of variable (quantitative, ordinal categorical, or nominal categorical) for all independent and dependent variables.
- Using variable type and role (as independent or dependent variable), determine what forms of multivariate analysis are possible. See Table 10.5.
- For all categorical independent variables, decide which category should be the reference (omitted category) based on ease and relevance of interpretation—or decide if effect coding would provide the easiest and most relevant interpretation.
- First carry out and interpret the *planned* multivariate analyses and only *afterwards* try alternative specifications and analyses.
- When more than a few calculations are being done, it is good practice to use a script or command program in a statistical software package, rather than the point-and-click menu. You will need to be able to reproduce your analyses.
- When doing multiple regression, examine the extent of multicollinearity in your data, using both a correlation matrix for all independent variables and the full multiple regressions. Determine if you need to drop one or more independent variables from the analysis due to multicollinearity. When deciding which of two collinear variables to drop, estimate the regression both ways.
- Determine if any of the (quantitative) independent variables or dependent variables should be transformed (such as taking the natural log).
- Determine if the relationship with any (quantitative) independent variables is nonlinear and if so consider adding polynomials or breaking the variable into different ordinal categorical variables.

Chapter Resources

Key Terms

- Adjusted *R*-squared
- ANOVA
- Confirmatory factor analysis
- Dummy variable
- Effect coding
- Exploratory factor analysis
- Factor analysis
- Factor loadings
- Forecasting
- Interaction variable
- Linear probability model (LPM)
- Logistic (logit) regression
- Marginal effect
- Multicollinearity
- Multilevel (hierarchical) models
- Multiple regression
- Multivariate statistics
- Out-of-sample extrapolation
- Path analysis
- Regression
- Robustness
- Structural equation modeling (SEM)

Exercises

10.1. Consider the following simulated results from a multiple regression using state-level data in the United States. The dependent variable is the state's smoking rate (measured as a percentage). The independent variables are the tax on cigarettes, measured in cents per pack, and a dummy variable indicating whether or not the state has a tobacco industry. The results are as follows:

$$\text{SmokeRate} = 15 - .5 \times \text{CigTax} + 20 \times \text{TobaccoIndustry}$$

Interpret the constant term, the coefficient of CigTax, and the coefficient of TobaccoIndustry. Make sure to state the units of each.

10.2. Consider a regression of medical costs on the independent variables Type1Diabetes and Type2Diabetes, described in Box 10.3. The unit of analysis is the patient.

a. What information does the coefficient of Type1Diabetes provide? What information does the coefficient of Type2Diabetes provide?
b. Suppose that, using data from many patients at many hospitals, the coefficient of Type1Diabetes is $300 and the coefficient of Type2Diabetes is $150. What is the expenditure difference between Type 1 and Type 2 diabetes predicted to be?

These next two questions refer to an *Imaginary World B* (from Chapter 8). Imagine the following world with very strict laws: Everyone goes to school until at least eighth grade. Earnings are $10,000 for someone with an eighth-grade education and no experience. Each additional year of education increases earnings by $2,000, and each additional year of experience increases earnings by $1,000.

10.3. First study done in Imaginary World B

Researchers collect data on years of education and earnings from everyone in this imaginary world. They perform a regression of earnings on education (i.e., earnings is the dependent variable and education is the independent variable). Note that the only independent variable is education. They also calculate the correlation between the two variables.

a. What is the correlation coefficient (very roughly)? Explain why it has that value.
b. What is the *R*-squared of the regression (very roughly)?[8]

10.4. Second study done in Imaginary World B

Now, suppose researchers do a multiple regression of earnings on education and experience.

a. What is the *R*-squared of the regression?
b. What is the regression coefficient of education? (Make sure to state its units.)
c. What is the regression coefficient of experience?

10.5. A regression was run using a data set of U.S. colleges from years gone by. The variable "Public" is a dummy (indicator) variable for whether the college is public. In-state tuition is in dollars ($). Use the output of those regressions (below) to answer the questions that follow.

Model Summary

Model	R	*R*-Squared	Adjusted *R*-Squared	Std. Error of the Estimate
1	.890[a]	.792	.788	$1,731.909

a. Predictors: (Constant), Average verbal SAT score, Public, Percentage of faculty with PhD degrees

Coefficients[a]

Model		Unstandardized Coefficients		Standardized Coefficients	*t*	Sig.
		B	Std. Error	Beta		
1	(Constant)	–5147.936	1040.970		–4.945	.000
	Percentage of faculty with PhD degrees	22.988	10.377	.109	2.215	.028
	Public	–5339.047	324.613	–.659	–16.447	.000
	Average verbal SAT score	22.183	2.692	.415	8.241	.000

a. Dependent Variable: In-state Tuition

a. Interpret the *R*-squared and adjusted *R*-squared.
b. Interpret the constant. Do you think that it has an out-of-sample prediction issue?
c. Interpret the coefficient of "Percentage of faculty with PhD degrees." Is it statistically significant? State the null and alternative hypotheses. Is it practically significant?
d. Interpret the coefficient of "Public." Is it statistically significant? State the null and alternative hypotheses. Is it practically significant?

[8]You may wonder why we don't ask what the coefficient of education is. In fact, more information is required to know that—it depends on whether there is any correlation between education and experience. This issue will be covered in Chapter 11.

10.6. In a particular hospital, you run a regression of admission cost on a male dummy variable, age, and an interaction of age and the male dummy variable. You get the following results:

$$\text{Cost} = \$1{,}000 + \$300(\text{male}) + \$50(\text{age}) - \$5(\text{male} \times \text{age})$$

a. What would you predict for the cost of a 50-year-old woman?
b. What is the difference between what you would predict for the cost of a 41-year-old man and what you would predict for the cost of a 40-year-old man?
c. Interpret in words the coefficients of male, age, and their interaction.

10.7. A logistic regression is run among heart attack victims with the dependent variable being whether or not the patient had a bypass operation performed. Suppose it is found that the odds ratio for an indicator variable for non-White is a (statistically significant) 0.7, after controlling for age and other medical conditions. How do you interpret this result?

10.8. What multivariate method is suitable for the following research purposes?

a. Reducing a set of attitude questions in a survey to a smaller number of attitude dimensions.
b. Estimating the links between variables in a causal structure with several independent variables and several intervening variables.
c. Examining how school-level characteristics and classroom-level characteristics influence individual test scores of elementary school students.
d. Testing the relationship between increasing tobacco taxes and decreasing rates of smoking in the United States from 1960 to 2010.
e. Tracking a sample of 100 small start-up businesses regularly each year to see how differences in access to financing impacts their survival over time.

Student Study Site

Visit the Study Site at **www.sagepub.com/remler2e** to

- test your knowledge with the self-quiz
- check your understanding of key terms with the eFlashcards
- explore helpful resources that relate directly to this chapter

PART IV

STRATEGIES FOR CAUSATION

Research aims not only to describe the world as it is but to explain how it works—to uncover the causes of important outcomes such as safety, health, education, or economic security—and thus to give us clues about how to change the world and (hopefully) make it better. In fact, causal research often focuses on testing whether a specific program affects the outcome—and by how much. But it turns out to be somewhat tricky to uncover a true cause-and-effect relationship in the real world—and to gauge its true magnitude. This part of the book will help you think critically about causation and how to use various research strategies to uncover it. These strategies include statistical techniques that try to isolate a causal relationship, experiments that intervene in order to test causation, and natural and quasi experiments that probe causation in real-world settings. A thoughtful appreciation of the complexities of causation, together with an ability to carefully judge various kinds of evidence of cause and effect, is one of the most important skills for any researcher or consumer of research.

Watering causes a garden to grow.
Source: © iStockphoto/Cristian Baitg.

Overview: In this chapter, you will learn that correlation does not imply causation. You will discover other possible causal explanations for a correlation—such as reverse causation and common causes—and see how they can make correlation a biased indicator of the magnitude of a causal effect. Much of the problem arises because real-world programs or treatments—the independent variables of interest—are self-selected and therefore endogenous. Because causation is so difficult to pin down, you will see how it helps to think about it in terms of a counterfactual definition—or what would happen, with and without the cause. Experimentation provides an idealized approach to estimating the counterfactual by intervening from outside—making an exogenous change—and by controlling other variables. But experimentation is not always possible or ethical. This chapter thus provides both the motivation and the conceptual tools needed to understand and apply various empirical strategies—covered fully in the chapters that follow—for establishing causation and measuring causal effects.

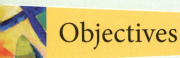

Objectives

Learning Objectives

After reading this chapter, you should be able to

- Identify various possible causal explanations for a correlation between two variables
- Spot unjustified claims of causation, both implicit and explicit, in studies, media stories, professional settings, and even everyday conversations
- Understand and articulate the concept of bias when estimating a causal effect
- Predict the direction of bias in a correlation used to estimate a causal effect, in a particular application
- Recognize how self-selection often makes the independent variable of interest endogenous, with respect to the dependent variable, and know how to recognize the problem of endogeneity in a given situation
- Understand the idea of a counterfactual and how it can be used to interpret a causal effect
- Identify an intervention or experiment that could help uncover causation, and recognize how an experiment produces exogeneity

Causation 11

Family Dinners and Teenage Substance Abuse

According to a national survey, teens who have dinner frequently with their families use drugs and alcohol less than teens who do so only infrequently. Teen drug and alcohol abuse is a major public health issue, so the survey got a lot of attention. The results inspired a public health movement titled *Family Day—A Day to Eat Dinner With Your Children*. Clearly, those behind this movement believe that if they could get parents to spend more time with their teens, by having family dinners, for example, teen drinking and drug usage would decline (see Box 11.1).

Will eating dinner regularly as a family make teens less likely to use drugs?

Source: © Can Stock Photo Inc./AndreyPopov.

Correlation Is Not Causation

This national survey shows that time spent at the family dinner table is negatively *correlated* with—or negatively associated with—use of drugs and alcohol. (The relationship is *negative,* because the *more* teens eat dinner with their families, the *less* they use drugs and alcohol—as we learned in Chapter 2.) The study treats family dinners as the *independent variable* and drug and alcohol use as the *dependent variable.* After reading these results, we are tempted to conclude that family time around the dinner table *causes* teens to use less alcohol and drugs. We tend to want to jump from correlation to causation.

Regular family dinners might in fact produce less teen drinking and drug use—the relationship could be causal. But there are plausible alternative explanations—which we will look at shortly—for why teens who

BOX 11.1
Children Who Have Frequent Family Dinners Less Likely to Use Marijuana, Tobacco, and Drink Alcohol

NEW YORK, Sept. 15, PRNewswire. From 2003 to 2008 research by the National Center on Addiction and Substance Abuse (CASA) at Columbia University has consistently found that children who have frequent family dinners are less likely to use marijuana, tobacco and drink alcohol. CASA research reveals that compared to children who have frequent family dinners (five or more per week), children who have infrequent family dinners (less than three per week) are two and a half times likelier to have used marijuana and tobacco, and one and a half times likelier to have drunk alcohol.

Teens Who Have Used Substances by Frequency of Family Dinners (Average Over 6 Years: 2003–2008)

Ever Used	0–2 Dinners/Week	5–7 Dinners/Week
Alcohol	48%	30%
Tobacco	29%	13%
Marijuana	27%	11%

Monday, September 22nd will mark CASA's eighth annual 'Family Day—A Day to Eat Dinner with Your Children(™)' celebration. Family Day is a national movement to inform parents that the parental engagement fostered during frequent family dinners is an effective tool to help keep America's children substance free and reminds parents that "Dinner Makes A Difference!" "If you asked me based on CASA's 16 years of intensive examination of substance abuse and addiction in our nation what's the most effective thing we can do to curb this scourge and protect our children, I would say parental engagement. And there is no more effective example of this than frequent family dinners," said Joseph A. Califano, Jr., CASA's chairman and president and former U.S. Secretary of Health, Education, and Welfare. "Years of surveying teens have consistently shown that the more often they have dinner with their parents, the less likely they are to smoke, drink and use drugs."

Source: www.reuters.com/article/pressRelease/idUS183576 + 15-Sep-2008 + PRN20080915.

frequently eat dinner with their families are less likely to use drugs and alcohol. Not all these reasons imply that if you could persuade parents to have more family dinners, teen drug and alcohol usage would decline.

More people carry umbrellas to work in the morning on days when it rains in the afternoon. However, we don't believe that carrying umbrellas causes rain. "Correlation is not causation" is an easy enough caveat to appreciate in nonsense examples such as umbrellas and rain. However, it is much harder to resist jumping to a causal conclusion when the correlation corresponds to what we already believe is true and good. After all, family dinners must produce good things—right? Remaining critical takes work.

To remain critical, we will spell out some possible causal models of the observed correlation, using the method of path diagrams from Chapter 2. We will then begin to learn strategies for empirically identifying causation. Thus, this chapter lays both the conceptual groundwork and the initial empirical framework for causal, as opposed to purely descriptive, research. Subsequent chapters will go deeper into the various research designs and statistical strategies used to get at causation in actual social and policy research.

Possible Explanations of a Correlation

Let's consider some possible explanations, or models, for the correlation between frequency of family dinners and drug use by teens.

Causation and Reverse Causation

To begin with, there is the initial possibility that family time (the independent variable) does, indeed, cause less substance abuse (the dependent variable)—as the press release (Box 11.1) implies. This causal model appears in the upper part of Figure 11.1. Path model diagrams—and theory development in general—are a key tool in causal research.

But the causal relationship implied by the press release is only one of several plausible explanations. What if teens who drink, smoke, and use drugs simply want to avoid being detected, so they stay away from home—and avoid the dinner table at night? Surely this is a plausible explanation as well. This possibility—**reverse causation**—is shown in the lower part of Figure 11.1.

When contemplating a correlation that seems to imply causation, ask yourself: Could it work the other way around? Could it be reverse causation?

Common Causes

Another possibility is that psychologically more mature teens—that is, teens who act more grown up and identify more with adults—prefer to spend more time with their parents, and their parents probably prefer to spend more time with them. Such teens also may have more self-control and perhaps a greater awareness of the negative life consequences of drinking and drugs, factors likely to lead to less use. In other words, a maturity factor might underlie both family dinners and drug use, making them correlated but not causally connected.

We refer to this situation as a **common cause,** and it is depicted in Figure 11.2. Family dinners and drug use are only correlated (represented by the dotted curved line with no arrows) because they both reflect the same common cause, the maturity level of teenagers. Note again that this correlation between family dinners and drug use remains true empirically—however, it is not causation, not a result of family dinners causally driving (reducing) drug use. Researchers sometimes call this a **spurious relationship** or *spurious correlation*.

Figure 11.1 Causation and Reverse Causation

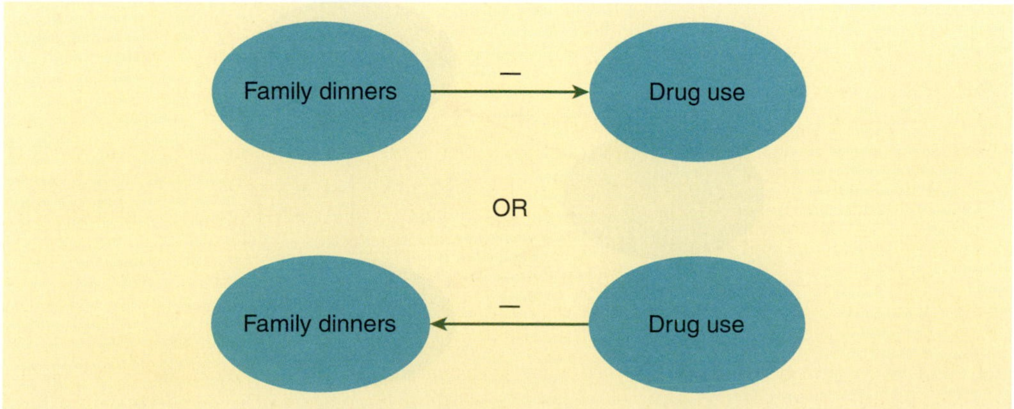

QUESTION

A survey of college students found that Facebook use was associated with lower grades (Hamilton, 2009). What are three causal interpretations of this correlation?

When trying to determine if a variable is a common cause, it is important to determine whether or not it is an *antecedent*, meaning that it causally comes *before* both the independent and dependent variables.

Bias From a Common Cause

Now, let's suppose again that family time does have a causal effect on drug use after all—but its influence is mixed up with a common cause. Figure 11.3 shows an example of this, where the psychological maturity of the teen influences both frequency of family dinners and drug use, as before (Figure 11.2), but now frequency of family dinners does indeed exert some causal influence of its own on drug use.

This pattern of causation is quite common yet tricky, because if we don't take account of the maturity factor, the connection between frequency of family dinners and drug use will appear exaggerated—it will be *biased*. That's because the influence of maturity flows through and gets mixed up with effect of family dinners. **Confounding** is another common term for this phenomenon—maturity confounds family time and drug use. (We will learn several commonly used terms for the same phenomenon in Chapter 12; see especially Box 12.1.)

Figure 11.2 Common Cause

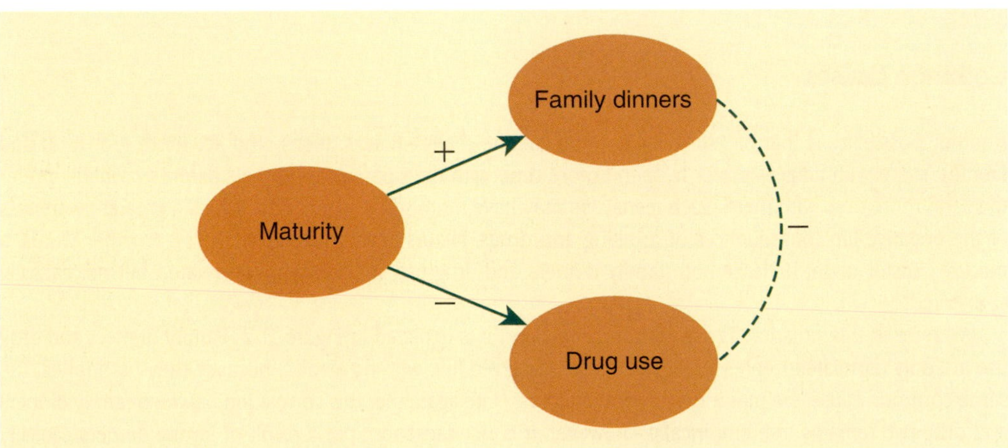

Figure 11.3 Bias From a Common Cause

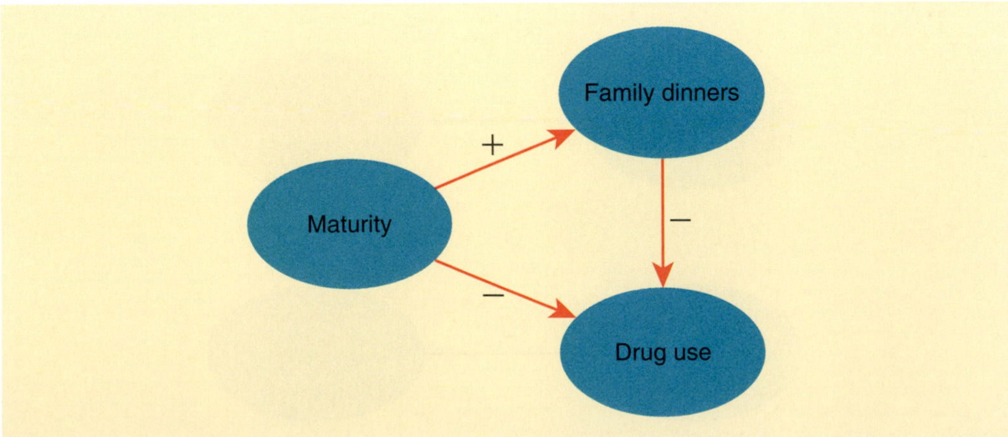

The national survey suggests, for example, that marijuana use would drop from 27% to just 11% (a decline of 16 percentage points) if families that failed to eat dinner together frequently just changed their ways—a big effect. We can illustrate the magnitude of the difference: If 1 million families in the United States made this change, we would expect about 160,000 fewer teens to use marijuana.

But is the size of this estimated effect biased? The estimate was based on the assumption that *all* of the difference in marijuana use was due to differences in family dinner time. It does not take account of possible common causes, such as the level of maturity of the teenagers (or whether the parents are working long hours, divorced, etc.). We don't want to make the mistake of thinking that some cause will produce a big change in the world when, in fact, it will produce only a small one. Again, knowing the correct *magnitude* of a causal effect is important.

Bias, as described in Part II of the book, refers to a systematic error (distortion) in the strength or even sign of an estimate of something of interest. In Chapter 4, we saw how measurements can be biased, for example, by people underreporting socially undesirable behavior (like drug use). And in Chapter 5, we saw how samples can be biased, for example, by overrepresenting people who are interested in a particular topic (like recycling). But these examples are all about bias in *describing* something, like the percentage of people who use illegal drugs or who recycle. But now in this part of the book, the bias we are concerned with is bias in the estimate of a causal effect. Bias in this sense refers to a distortion in the strength or even direction of an estimated causal relationship. Such bias is often due to the influence of common causes (especially when they are not accounted for).

Bias From an Unknown or Complex Common Cause

Bias (confounding) can come from an unknown or complex common cause as well. This situation can be represented by a curved line with arrows connecting the variables, as in Figure 11.4. Say drug dealing is more prevalent in urban areas and, thus, teenagers living in urban areas are more likely to be exposed to drugs. And suppose also that families that live in urban areas, as a result of a variety of cultural and lifestyle factors, have less frequent family dinners. Living in urban areas, however, does not *cause* less frequent family dinners, per se. Rather, both urban living and family dinners themselves have some unknown, complex common causes that lead them to be correlated with each other. We will have more to say about this issue in Chapter 12, but it is important here to note the similarity with Figure 11.3 and to recognize that common causes can still exert bias even when they are not entirely clear or fully understood.

Figure 11.4 Bias From an Unknown Common Cause

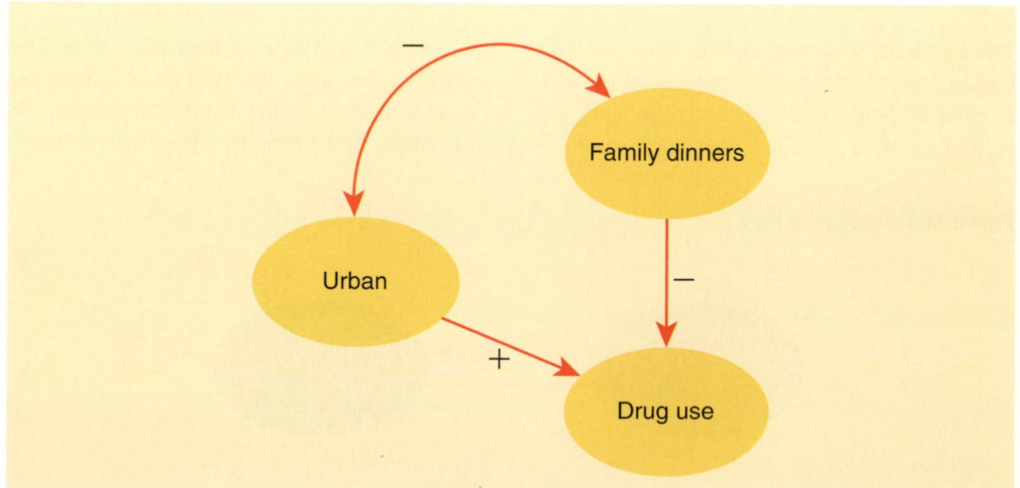

QUESTION

The study of Facebook use and grades (Hamilton, 2009) found that Facebook users had an average GPA that was about 1 point lower than that of nonusers. How might this 1-point difference be biased by a common cause or reverse causation?

Bias From Reverse Causation: Simultaneity Bias

It is also possible that both causation and reverse causation are true at the same time—simultaneously. Suppose, for example, that family dinners really do cause a reduction in teen drug abuse but that, at the same time, teens who use drugs still seek to avoid family dinners. This possibility is shown in Figure 11.5. Once again, the magnitude of the causal effect of family dinners implied by the press release—a 16-percentage-point decline in drug use—would be biased because some share of these 16 points would be the result of drug-using kids skipping out on family dinners. In econometrics, this is known as **simultaneity bias** because it stems from causal relationships that simultaneously go in both directions.

Some More Correlations That Imply Causation

As you can see, trying to decide if a correlation is due to causation—and if so, how much of it is causation—turns out to be more difficult than it at first appears to be. So let's practice these ideas by looking at a few other policy-related examples of correlations that seem to imply causation.

Are Busy Hospitals Better?

Practice, practice, practice if you want to get better at something, so the saying goes—but does this advice apply to hospitals too? Evidence indicates that hospitals performing a higher volume of a given procedure, such as heart valve replacement, do have better outcomes (fewer complications and deaths). As a result, some heart patients decide only to consider high-volume hospitals, and some state governments set volume standards in an effort to reduce risk.

But could this be a case of reverse causation? After all, if a restaurant serves good food, it's more likely to be crowded with happy diners. Perhaps hospitals that do a successful job at replacing heart valves simply attract more heart patients. Or could the higher-volume, better-outcome relationship reflect a common cause? One possible common cause might be the level of health insurance coverage in the populations served by different hospitals. Hospitals that serve affluent populations, covered by first-rate health insurance, might be more likely to receive referrals for valve replacements than hospitals serving populations with only limited health insurance coverage. Health insurance coverage also helps ensure earlier diagnosis and better postoperative care, potentially resulting in fewer complications and deaths.

The Power of a Library Card

Various studies show that students who own library cards read more and perform better on standardized language arts tests (e.g., Whitehead, 2004). So it is not surprising to find some education leaders attempting to boost academic performance by distributing library cards to all students, as the minister of education did in New Brunswick, Canada (Communications New Brunswick, 2004). We are tempted to hope that ownership

Figure 11.5 Simultaneity Bias

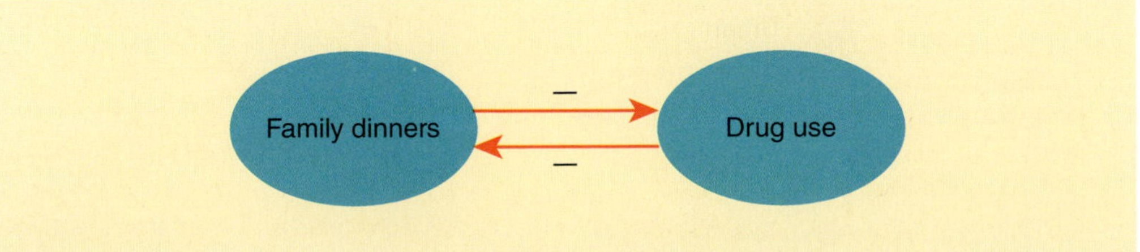

of a library card itself *causes* kids to read more. But reverse causation is quite likely in this case—the kids who already read a lot are the ones who have the library cards. There could well be common causes at work too, such as parents who value and encourage their children to read *and* own a library card.

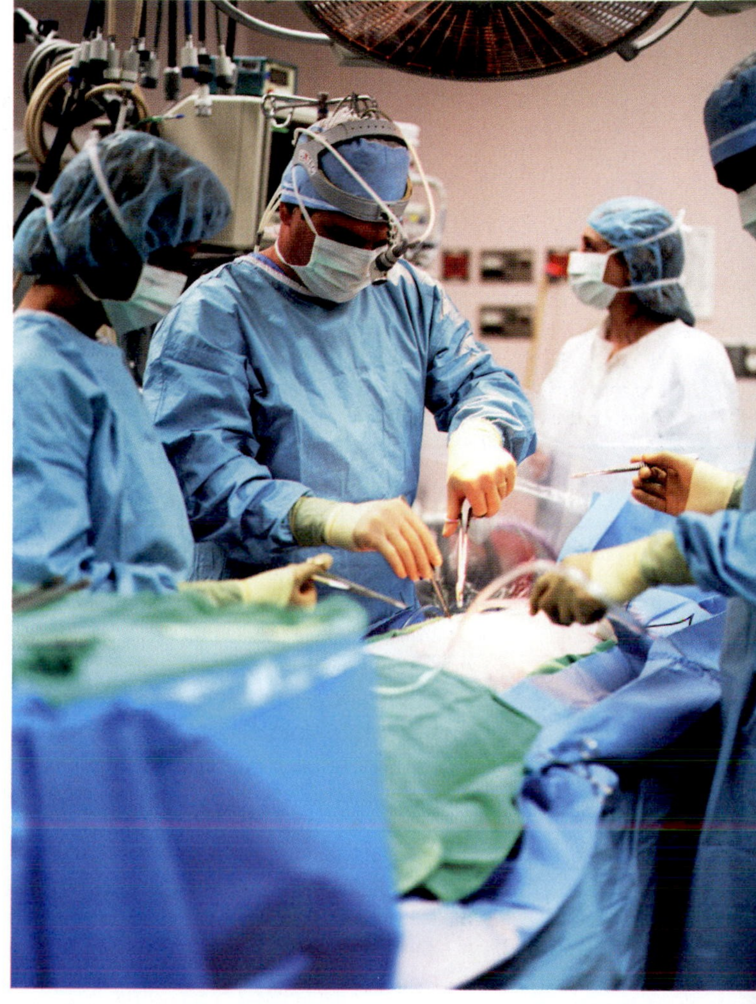

Patients at high-volume hospitals experience better outcomes. Does high volume *cause* better outcomes?

Source: © 2009 Jupiterimages Corporation.

Are Organizations With Happy Workers More Successful?

A number of studies of businesses and other organizations find that those with high levels of employee satisfaction are also more successful (as measured by such things as profits or market value) (e.g., Best, 2008). So management gurus urge organizations to do what's needed to make their workers happier. But it could well be that success itself breeds happiness—because of more pay and benefits, fewer layoffs, and less stressed-out bosses. Everybody is in a better mood when the organization is doing well. Common causes are also likely, for example, when a particular industry is in a downturn because of larger-scale changes in the economy, society, or technology. Imagine working at the once dominant photographic film company Kodak during the years when consumers switched to using digital cameras. Such a trend both hurts the firm and discourages the workers.

There are many correlations in the world, and often they suggest causal relationships that would be useful for policy or practice—but only if they are indeed causal. We want to find ways to reduce drug use, improve patient outcomes, get kids to read, and make organizations more productive. But it is important to understand that causation might flow in the opposite direction. And common causes may be at work behind the scenes, making the correlation a biased if not a false indication of causation.

Causal Mechanisms

In Chapter 2, we noted that a key element of a theory is a **causal mechanism**—some notion of *how* the independent and dependent variables are related. The causal mechanism can be thought of also as the process, or chain of cause-effect linkages, that transmits (mediates) the causal effect. Furthermore, we modeled this situation by specifying *intervening variables,* or *mediators,* that lie along the causal pathway between the independent and dependent variables.

Returning to our opening example, let's consider a causal mechanism through which family dinners could result in less drinking and drug use. One possibility is that regular family dinners facilitate *communication* between parents and teenagers. As a result, parents better understand the social pressures and day-to-day exposure to drugs faced by their teenagers and will take steps to help them cope. And the teenagers learn from their parents during family dinners too, both about the dangers of drug use and about their parents'

Figure 11.6 Causal Mechanism Shown as an Intervening Variable

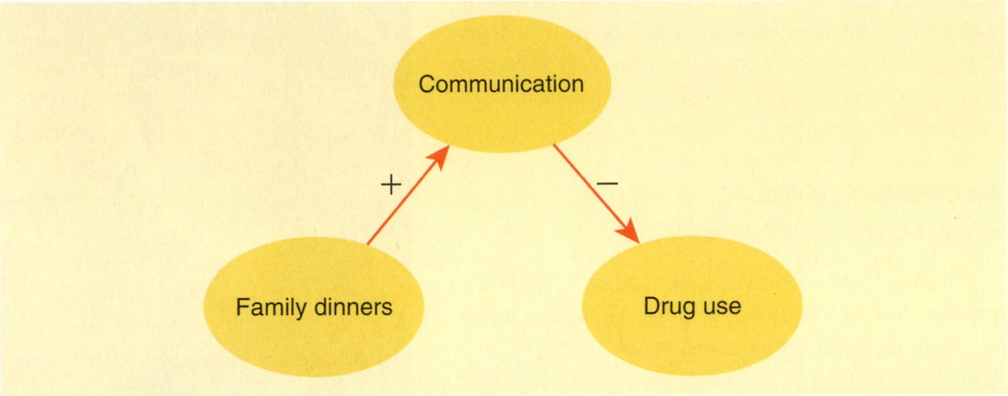

concern for them. Figure 11.6 shows this mechanism of *communication* in path diagram form as an intervening variable between family dinners and drug use.

Note that the causal mechanism is not an alternative explanation for a correlation, as in the case of a common cause or reverse causation, but rather a more detailed version of a causal interpretation of the relationship between x and y.

We could add additional intervening variables to elaborate the causal mechanism, for example, putting a variable representing, say, *coping strategies* between communication and drug use. Whether to specify an intervening variable, and how many intervening variables are needed to elaborate the causal mechanism, depends on the context. Would this information change the substantive implications of the research? Would it change the way a program is designed? If so, then the intervening variables should be spelled out.

Indirect and Direct Causal Effects

This discussion of mechanisms suggests that there can be an **indirect effect**, in the sense that the independent variable influences the dependent variable only through its causal effect on one or more intervening variables. Smaller classes (as we theorized in Chapter 2) may cause kids to learn more because small classes allow teachers to more effectively manage class time and to provide more one-on-one assistance to struggling students. In a way, all causal relationships can be said to be indirect—there must be some mechanism linking cause and effect.

Still, researchers speak about a **direct effect** when the intervening causal process or mechanism is nearly immediate, fairly mechanical, or so obvious that it does not need spelling out. For example, higher gasoline prices cause people to drive less—but articulating the causal process seems unnecessary:

Gas price → Awareness of price → Sensitivity to price → Drive less

We can probably take for granted that drivers are aware of gas prices, since they are posted in big numbers at nearly all gas stations (and also you notice what it costs to fill your tank). And it also makes sense to assume that most people are price sensitive, meaning they will want to reduce consumption when prices go up. So for most research purposes, we can ignore these intervening variables and instead just assume a direct effect of gas prices on driving habits.

However, what matters for a mechanism always depends on context: Price has a greater effect when it is salient—when people are well aware of price. But this is not always the case, as for example with the price people pay for the electricity they consume at home each day (in which case awareness of price might indeed be an important intervening variable to consider).

Chance Correlations and Statistical Significance

Correlation between two variables, such as family time and drug use, could occur by chance. In such a case, there may be no causal explanation at all for the correlation—not even a common cause. The two variables just happen to be correlated because of some fluke or coincidence.

For example, in a particular metropolitan area, during a given period of time, more auto accidents may occur on odd-numbered days of the month than on even-numbered days. This pattern can happen just by chance, and if we were to collect data over the long run (a larger sample size), we might well see that accidents eventually balance out across even and odd days. But in the short run, we might be tempted to jump to an erroneous causal conclusion: Watch out—avoid the roadways on odd-numbered days!

Statistical significance tests, discussed in Chapter 9, can check to see if a difference or correlation is unlikely to be the result of mere chance coincidence. Statistical significance tests can rule out chance as the explanation for a correlation. The size of the correlation and the amount of the available data (sample size) are key factors in gauging statistical significance.

But importantly, just eliminating chance does not prove causation: Alternative explanations—reverse causation or a common cause—could still be responsible for a genuine nonchance correlation. *No statistical significance test on its own can ever prove causation.* It does not matter how fancy or clever the test is. Proving causation requires further reasoning strategies and ways to gather and analyze evidence, which is what this chapter and the others in Part IV provide.

QUESTION

Assuming Facebook use does lead to lower grades, what might be the causal mechanism? What intervening variables would represent this mechanism?

Arrows, Arrows Everywhere

Real-world correlations can be due to all the causal pathways discussed so far—causation, reverse causation, common causes (including complex common causes), mechanisms, and even chance—operating at once. Figure 11.7 shows this kind of complex causal model.

Figure 11.7 Complexity: Many Causal Relationships

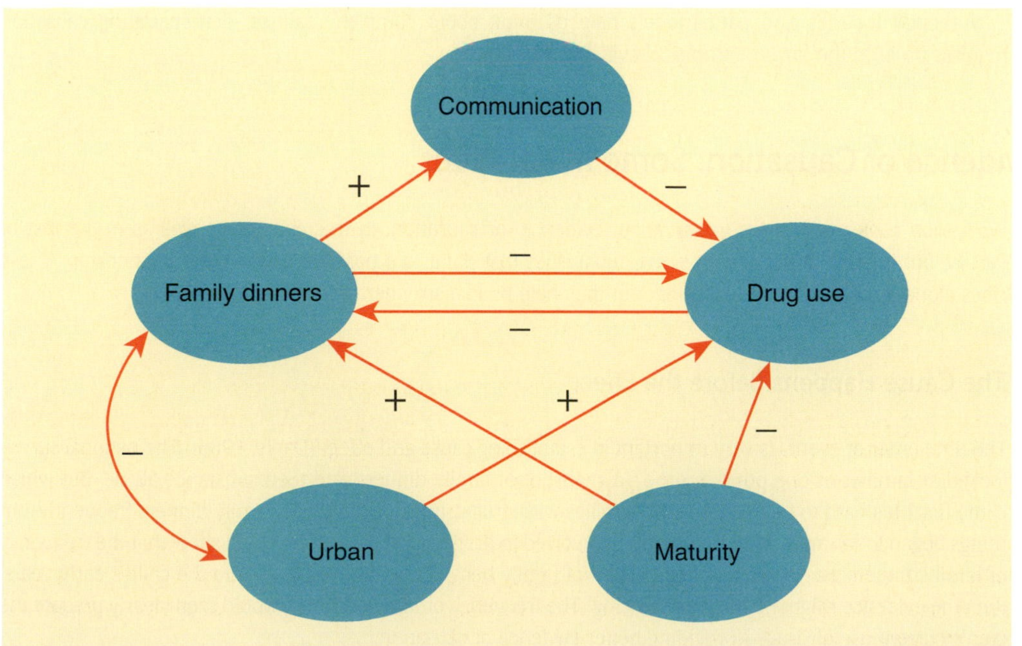

Reviews of previous research on the topic of drinking and drug use among teens would undoubtedly add more common causes and more mechanisms. Prior research would also likely give us some sense of the relative importance of different factors. All this reflects the fact that a behavior such as teen substance abuse has complex origins and is mixed up with other things going on in the lives and personalities of teens and their parents. After all, if it were a simple picture, teen drinking and drug use would be an easy social problem to fix.

Why Worry About the Correct Causal Model?

We worry about a correct causal model because it guides the actions we take. If regular family dinners simply and directly influence drug and alcohol use, then encouraging families to spend more time around the dinner table with their kids holds promise as a national prevention strategy. With the help of some clever social marketing consultants, we can fill the airwaves and put up billboards with convincing appeals to families to devote more time and attention to the traditional mealtime (as the program's sponsors indeed have done). As a result, teen drinking and drug use should decrease.

But if it turns out to be a case of reverse causation, then all our time and money spent on boosting the popularity of family dinners would be wasted (at least in terms of doing something about drug and alcohol abuse). This would be like trying to make it rain by handing out umbrellas on the street. Clearly, we need to know in which direction the causal arrow really flows.

Situations of common causes have important practical consequences, too. If family time and drug use are both the effects of some common cause, such as maturity, then we might want to turn our attention to that common cause and ignore family dinner time as the key factor. Or if family time's effect on drug use is real but appears larger than it really is—if it is biased—because of a common cause (even an unknown or complex common cause), we will be misled in our judgments about the importance of promoting family time as a policy lever.

And if family time's influence on drug use works indirectly through some mechanism, such as better communication between parents and teens, then perhaps we can more directly influence drug use by focusing more specifically on the intervening variable(s). Maybe it is not family dinners per se that we should target but any type of activity that encourages communication—going on family outings, sharing hobbies, and so on.

Although theories and path models help us think about complex realities, demonstrating causation requires proof in the form of empirical evidence.

Evidence of Causation: Some Initial Clues

We'll soon have much more to say about evidence for causation, in this chapter as well as in the rest of Part IV, but it helps to begin with some initial clues that point to a possible cause-effect relationship. These clues alone are not proof of causation, but they help build a stronger case.

The Cause Happens Before the Effect

The time order of events is very important in establishing cause and effect (Davis, 1985). The national survey looked at families at one point in time—a snapshot of family dinners and teen substance abuse. But which came first? It's hard to tell. Perhaps the families with drug-using kids once had family dinners frequently, but things began to fall apart after the teens got involved in drugs. But if the survey could show that the frequency of family dinners was an established pattern of family behavior, going well back into the child's early years, then the evidence might be more convincing. The frequency of family dinners would then clearly predate the teen's current use of drugs—providing better evidence of causation.

When Is Time Order Misleading? Expectations

Because human beings are intelligent and often try to predict the future, determining the time order of events is not as easy at it might first appear. Consider again the example of umbrellas and rain. If you think about it, often, people start carrying umbrellas before the rain arrives. So if we rely just on the naive time order of our everyday observations, we may jump to the conclusion that umbrellas are the cause and rain the effect.

But of course, people carry umbrellas when they *expect* rain, perhaps because it was forecast by meteorologists or perhaps because they saw dark clouds in the morning sky. Meteorological conditions cause rain. These conditions also give us signs in advance that we perceive (such as dark clouds), causing us to expect rain and therefore to carry umbrellas. The meteorological conditions precede and cause rain. They also cause expectations of rain in people, which cause (and precede) umbrella carrying. Thus, meteorological conditions are a common cause of both rain and umbrella carrying and do indeed precede both of them.

Expectations of what will happen in the future play a particularly important role in finance and economics. So before taking time precedence as evidence supporting causation, consider whether human expectations may be at work. And think about possible prior common causes.

The Correlation Appears in Many Different Contexts

Rarely does a correlation from one study, in one particular time and place, provide definitive evidence of cause and effect. But a correlation that turns up repeatedly, across different contexts, becomes more convincing. Does a volume-outcome relationship appear in studies of different types of surgery? Does it appear in studies in different regions of the country, or even different countries of the world? The more often the correlation appears, in different contexts, the more we begin to suspect causation. This is why *replication*—the repeating of studies in different places—is so important in research.

However, biased studies can also be reliably replicated (see Box 11.2). So replication is a necessary—but not sufficient—condition for causation.

BOX 11.2
Prominent Epidemiologists Discuss Clues of Causation

When trying to decide if some factor, such as traffic density, secondhand smoke, hormone replacement therapy, or oatmeal consumption, contributes to getting a disease, epidemiologists must often rely on the kinds of evidence we discuss, including replication, time precedence, plausible mechanism, magnitude of effect, and the control variables strategy we will look at in Chapters 12 and 13.

The highly regarded journal *Science* interviewed many prominent epidemiologists about what constitutes sufficient evidence to infer causation (Taubes & Mann, 1995). While some epidemiologists considered replication a compelling element, David Sackett of Oxford University said, “If there’s an inherent bias, it wouldn’t make any difference how many times it’s replicated. Bias times 12 is still bias” (Taubes & Mann, 1995, p. 169).

A Plausible Mechanism and Qualitative Evidence

A *plausible* mechanism for a causal relationship strengthens the case for causation. If a causal relationship has no plausible mechanism, then other forms of evidence, such as replication, tend to be viewed skeptically.

For example, without a plausible causal mechanism through which even or odd days of the month influence traffic fatalities, most people would view that causal hypothesis skeptically.

Evidence for a plausible mechanism further strengthens the case for causation. Sometimes such evidence comes from prior studies or experiments that specifically investigated the mechanism in other contexts. For example, perhaps other studies have found that frequent communication with parents is a protective factor against drug use. Another kind of evidence is provided by intervening variables that, in a statistical analysis, account for (or mediate) the relationship between the independent and dependent variables. If the survey of teens measured quality of parental communication, would this account for the association between family dinners and drug use?

Qualitative research can also provide evidence of a causal mechanism (as discussed in Chapter 3). In a focus group or in-depth interview, will teens say that having family dinners regularly is meaningful to them? Do they report that this plays a role in their decision to use, or not use, drugs and alcohol? Do they talk about what happens during family dinners that influences their thinking? If unbiased qualitative research clearly supports the presumed causal mechanism, we can more easily believe that the statistical correlation reflects a true cause-effect relationship.

There Are No Plausible Alternative Explanations

Determining causation can be viewed as a competition among alternative explanations—which is a lot of what we have been talking about so far in this chapter. But these alternative explanations, too, must be plausible. If we (or our critics) can't come up with any plausible alternative explanations, then the case for a cause-effect relationship gains credibility.

Take the example of presidential approval in the United States following the September 11, 2001, terrorist attacks (see Figure 11.8). President Bush's popularity jumped nearly 30 points just after the attacks occurred. Did the attacks cause U.S. citizens to rally around the president and view him favorably, driving the large and sudden change in public opinion? Or is there a plausible alternative explanation for this large and sudden jump?

Figure 11.8 U.S. Presidential Approval Before and After 9/11

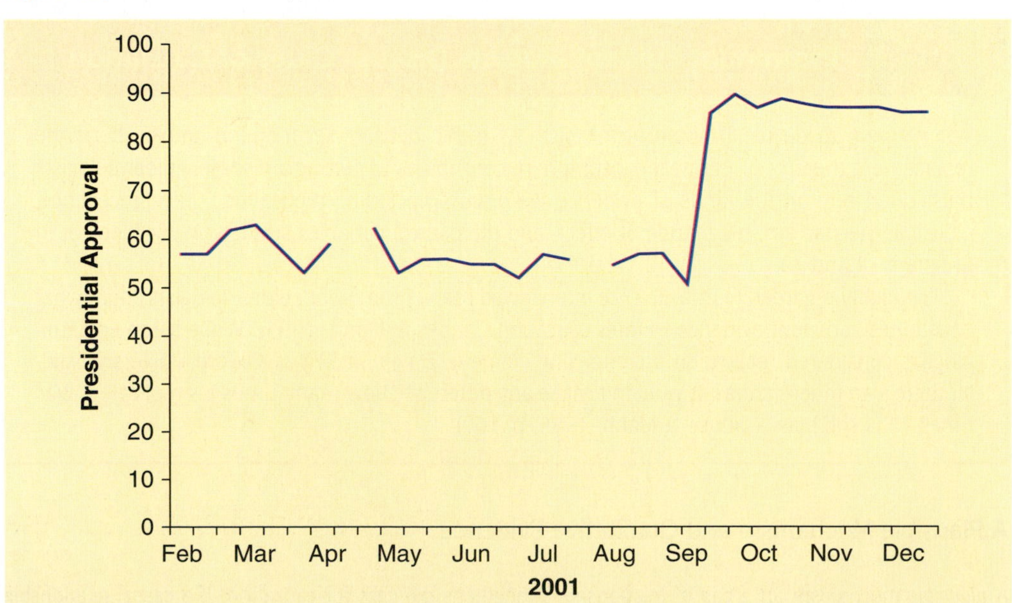

Source: Gallup poll. POLLING REPORT, INC. http://www.pollingreport.com/BushJob1.htm.

On the day of the 9/11 terrorist attacks, President Bush was visiting an elementary school in Florida to promote his new education bill. Perhaps this televised demonstration of his commitment to education, or the popularity of the bill itself, captured the public's imagination at the same moment as the attacks. But this appears highly implausible. Presidential approval does not skyrocket because of a proposed education bill. In fact, it is hard to come up with any plausible event—other than the horrific attacks of 9/11—that could produce such a sudden and big change in the nation's mood. In this way, the lack of plausible alternative explanations builds the case for causation.

More typically, however, many plausible alternative explanations can be found. And we are often unsure which one represents the truth.

Common Causes Are Accounted For in the Analysis

Evidence for causation gains strength when plausible common causes are taken into account in the analysis (researchers say *controlled for*). Suppose girls read more than boys, and suppose also that more girls own library cards. Then the correlation between owning a library card and reading ability reflects an underlying gender difference, a common cause. But in the analysis of the data, we can address this by looking at the library card → reading relationship separately for boys and for girls. Do *boys* with library cards read more than *boys* without library cards? Do *girls* with library cards read more than *girls* without library cards? If the relationship still holds, separately for girls and boys, then gender is not a common cause—so we eliminate this alternative explanation.

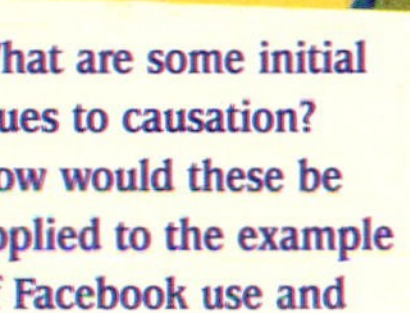

QUESTION

What are some initial clues to causation? How would these be applied to the example of Facebook use and grades?

Of course, eliminating one alternative explanation—one possible common cause—still leaves others. What if the parents encourage both reading and owning a library card? We could continue with the same strategy, splitting the kids into a group whose parents encourage reading and a group whose parents don't. The problem now, however, is that this characteristic of parents is more difficult to measure than a fact such as the sex of the child. Accounting for a common cause in the analysis only works if we have a measure of that common cause.

We will have much more to say about statistically taking account of common causes—the control variables strategy—in Chapters 12 and 13.

Detective Work and Shoe Leather

Finding clues to causation is a lot like detective work: It takes patience, lots of questioning of various suspects, and the piecing together of many bits of evidence. We will cover statistical strategies for probing causation later in Part IV, but as the statistician David Freedman (1991) reminds us, it is important to be aware of the limitations to demonstrating causation with statistical analysis techniques alone. He argues that good causal research requires work, or shoe leather—such as doing in-depth case studies, engaging in qualitative investigation on the ground, making shrewd observations, and importantly intervening in the real world in order to probe causation by trying to make things happen (more on this shortly). As Freedman summarizes, "statistical technique can seldom be an adequate substitute for good [research] design, relevant data, and testing predictions against reality in a variety of settings" (Freedman, 1991, p. 291).

Self-Selection and Endogeneity

Why is it so difficult to know which explanations of a correlation are true? One answer is that often our independent variables of interest—such as family time, health care procedure volume, or owning a library card—reflect *choices*. Frequency of family dinners is driven by choices, both the choices of teens and the choices of parents. Factors such as personality, occupation, family history, and so on influence these choices. Similarly, patients (and doctors acting on their behalf) choose hospitals, and the patients who choose high-volume hospitals may be different (more educated, more urban, better insured, healthier, etc.) than the patients who choose low-volume hospitals.

Much of what we do and value in life focuses on choices: our favorite pastimes, our career choices, deciding where to live, whom to marry, how to spend our free time. We value choice and free will. But human choice and free will complicate our understanding of causal relationships in social and policy research.

Self-Selection

The influence of choices is referred to in research as the **self-selection** problem, and it is ubiquitous. Self-selection happens when the individuals studied, or someone acting on their behalf, choose their category or level of the independent variable of interest.

As a consequence of self-selection, teens who eat dinner often with their families may be different from teens who don't—and the parents may be different, as well. Also, patients in low- and high-volume hospitals may differ in a variety of characteristics—characteristics that influence their health outcomes. In this way, self-selection introduces many possible common causes into the picture. This makes it quite difficult to attribute any observed difference in the dependent variable—such as substance abuse or health outcomes—solely to the independent variable of interest (family time or health care procedure volume).

To conclude, for example, that the difference in health outcomes between patients in high- and low-volume hospitals truly stems from the hospital volume, and not something else, we would need the patients, doctors, and all other relevant features of the hospitals to be comparable. But, because of self-selection, they are not.

Endogeneity

As it turns out, self-selection is one common source of a more general problem referred to as the **endogeneity** of the independent variable. An **endogenous** independent variable is one whose value is caused by variables or processes that also affect the dependent variable—or by the dependent variable itself. In other words, if there is a common cause—or if there is reverse causation—the independent variable of interest is said to be endogenous.

What does self-selection mean—and how does it often lead to an endogenous independent variable?

Endogeneity is often due to self-selection, but it may also be due to other processes. For example, some hospitals may obstruct or even deny care to patients with certain risky conditions or characteristics, giving preference to those patients with the best chance for success. This is a form of *treatment selection*. This positively biased selection is also called *cream skimming*, selecting only those patients who are most likely to thrive after treatment. Thus, various forms of treatment selection, such as cream skimming, are another source of endogeneity in the independent variable—it is a process that introduces common causes, and thus bias, into the picture.

Various other political, administrative, or cultural processes can likewise bring in common causes. We will have more to say about endogeneity later on in this chapter when we introduce its converse, exogeneity, in detail.

The Counterfactual Definition of Causation

We've seen that many things may cause teen drug use, and family dinners may be part of the explanation, all of it, or perhaps none of it. We've learned some concepts that help us think about various alternative explanations, but how do we get to the truth? How can we know the unique, causal effect of family time on drinking and drug use—or whether such effects exist at all? To answer this question, we need to back up a little and think about what it means to say that one thing causes another—that is, what we really mean by **causation** (also known as *causality*, as described in Box 11.3).

BOX 11.3
Causation and Causality—Two Words for the Same Thing

We use the term *causation* to refer to the idea of a cause-effect relationship. Others use the term *causality* (Bunge, 2011; Pearl, 2009)—but the two terms mean the same thing. Causation/causality is notoriously difficult to define without sounding circular (for example, it can be defined as *the act of causing something to happen*). Moreover, the idea of causation/causality has been understood somewhat differently across disciplines, historical periods, and cultures.

Philosophers of science have written volumes on the question of causation, but for practical purposes, we can simply state that a *cause* is something that produces some change—an *effect*—in the world (Blalock, 1961; Pearl, 2009; Woodward, 2003). Our interest in causation (even our natural tendency to think causally) is motivated by our deep-seated desire to manipulate or control the world we live in and depend on for survival (Sloman, 2009; Woodward, 2003). For example, we learn that watering our garden regularly will help make it grow and that if we don't water the garden it will probably not thrive. We conclude that watering our garden *causes* it to thrive and thus produce food.

With a time machine, we could observe the counterfactual.

Source: © Moviestore collection Ltd/Alamy.

Our interest in a particular cause, such as watering the garden, does not mean other causes are not at work also (as we said before in Chapter 2). The garden may thrive or not because of other causes at work at the same time, such as the weather or the threat of plant-eating insects or animals. But as a practical matter we often need to focus on one cause at a time in order to isolate a causal effect in the real world. Causes do not have to work every time to be useful—they do not have to be *deterministic*. If watering usually helps the garden thrive, even if sometimes it does not (because of the many other causes also at work), we still have useful knowledge. Merely *probabilistic* causes are often all we have to work with.

With these qualifications in mind, let's return to defining what we mean by a cause. In an important sense, we often identify a cause by observing its effect in the world. More specifically, we compare things as they are with the cause present to things as they are (or would be) absent the cause. The world as it would be without the cause present is referred to as the **counterfactual** (Morgan & Winship, 2007; Pearl, 2009).

The garden without watering it—yet with everything else exactly the same (soil, sunlight, temperature, etc.)—is the counterfactual. How would the garden thrive if we did not water it? (Probably not so well.) How would it thrive if we did water it? (Much better, most likely.) Comparing the counterfactual with observed reality gives us a measure of the *effect* of watering the garden—what this action has *caused* to happen. Again, we often know a cause by its effect. (See Box 11.4 for how to think about counterfactuals in advance of observation, using the idea of potential outcomes.)

BOX 11.4
Counterfactuals and Potential Outcomes

In the real world, one thing actually happens in a particular case, and the other does not. So we can refer to what might have happened but did not as the *counterfactual*. But that language can sometimes be confusing when we are referring to what *might* happen in a future or hypothetical situation. For example, if we are thinking about family dinners in a particular family next year or family dinners in the abstract, which one, family dinners or no family dinners, is the counterfactual, and which one is the "factual"?

To avoid such confusion, Rubin (2005), one of the innovators in this field, uses the term *potential outcomes*. With this term, all possible potential outcomes are treated equivalently. Other important innovators, including Manski (1995) and Heckman (2000), also sometimes use the *potential outcomes* term. However, we use the increasingly common term *counterfactual*, using it to mean simply another potential outcome. See Morgan and Winship (2007) for further discussion of the history and technicalities of the counterfactual.

If We Only Had a Time Machine

Strictly speaking, a counterfactual can never be observed. Reality cannot be two things at one time. The same garden, at the same moment in time, cannot be both well watered and not watered at all. Returning to our example of family dinners and drug use, the counterfactual is also not directly observable. A teenager during a given period of time cannot have both frequent and infrequent family dinners. Yet to really measure the effect of frequent family dinners on a teenager's life, we need to know what his or her life would be like if we took those family dinners away.

QUESTION

How would you describe the idea of a counterfactual in your own words?

A time machine of the kind found in science fiction (such as the one in the picture) would be the ideal instrument for gauging the counterfactual. We could climb into the machine, send ourselves back in time, and then change just one thing or action of interest (the cause), such as watering our garden or not. Then we could return to the present to see what had changed (the effect), such as whether our garden had thrived or not. By comparing two versions of the same period of time, we could directly observe the counterfactual as well as the factual, and thus understand with certainty the relationship between cause and effect.

Alas, we have no time machines, so we need other devices or strategies to estimate counterfactuals and therefore assess causation. The most effective device researchers rely on is experimentation.

Experimentation and Exogeneity: Making Things Happen

Experimentation refers to the act of manipulating a cause to observe an effect—or, as one philosopher of science puts it, *making things happen* (Woodward, 2003). Experimentation contrasts with passive observation—or just *watching things happen*. Let's consider a new example that helps illustrate the contrast between these two approaches to figuring out causation.

Can Exercise Cure Depression?

A counselor at an assisted living community in Arizona is worried: She notices that a resident, Emily, is feeling tired often, staying in bed much of the day, and taking little interest in the people and activities around her. Emily's husband died recently, and her children and grandchildren live far away. The counselor worries that Emily may be depressed (a common mental health problem facing the world's growing elderly population).

Then one spring day, the counselor notices that Emily has signed herself up for the Morning Birds, an exercise club that meets each day for a walk around the grounds. Emily starts getting up in the morning to join the group, and she soon appears much more interested and engaged in her surroundings. The counselor clearly observes a big improvement in Emily's mood. Regular exercise, it seems, has cured Emily of her depression. The counselor wonders if it would be a good idea to encourage other depressed residents to exercise.

In a laboratory in China, some rats in a cage were feeling a bit down as well. They had been subjected to weeks of unpredictable stresses: having their tails held down for 5 minutes, a series of intermittent foot shocks, a swim in cold water, and so on. All these stresses were short in duration, spaced carefully over many hours, and not physically harmful, but they added up to a distinct pattern of what psychologists call learned helplessness—a psychological state very similar to depression in humans. The scientists confirmed the onset of depression in these rats by observing a decrease in their exploratory behavior and a reduction in their consumption of sucrose solution (Zheng et al., 2006).

People choose to exercise.
Source: © iStockphoto.com/nycshooter.

Observing that the rats had indeed become depressed, the scientists then introduced an exercise wheel into the rats' cage. After a few days with the exercise wheel, the rats began to exhibit increased exploratory behavior and began to consume more sucrose solution, signs that their depression had abated. The scientists concluded that exercise caused a reduction in the depressive symptoms of these rats.

Why Experimentation Beats Passive Observation

Emily's elevated mood after joining the club should not convince us that exercise relieves depression. She made the choice to begin exercising—so her exposure to exercise was *self-selected* and thus quite likely *endogenous*. Perhaps Emily started exercising *because* she began feeling better, a case of *reverse causation*. Or perhaps something else—a *common cause*, such as the arrival of the longer, warmer days of spring—influenced both her decision to begin exercising and her rosier outlook.

The rat experiment, however, does provide convincing evidence that exercise alleviates depression. This is because the researchers *made it happen*—they imposed exercise on the rats to observe whether or not it influenced depression (which itself was imposed on the rats at the start of the experiment). We might find the experiment distasteful, even cruel. And we might complain that it is much too artificial to guide policy and practice for the elderly or anyone else suffering from depression (rats are not like people, after all). But the experiment does do a good job of demonstrating cause and effect.

Experimenters give rats an exercise wheel—or take it away.

Source: © 2009 Jupiterimages Corporation.

We'll return to the important question of the ethics of experimentation as well as to the issue of limited generalizability. But before that, let's try to understand and appreciate the key features of experimentation that provide good evidence of causation.

Exogeneity: Intervening in the World

Experiments involve some kind of **intervention** or **treatment**, a focused attempt to manipulate specific features of the environment or context in a way that is deliberately independent of and apart from the choices, preferences, or other characteristics of the subjects in the experiment. Interventions or treatments take many forms, such as administering a drug or therapy (hence the term *treatment*) but also giving out information, starting a program, providing counseling, making a change in rules or law, restructuring an organization, and so on. We will be giving many real-world examples in later chapters of Part IV.

Such interventions or treatments aim to make the independent variable **exogenous** instead of endogenous. *Exogenous* means "from outside," which in the context of research means outside the setting or system being investigated. More specifically, **exogeneity** refers to situations in which variation in the independent variable happens separately from other factors, such as when scientists manipulate the independent variable in a planned way. In the rat experiment, the researchers initially deprived the rats of exercise by not providing a wheel in their cage; then, later, they introduced it exogenously—from outside. Although the rats chose, in a sense, to run on the wheel (something rats like to do), the rats did not choose to have the wheel placed in their cage in the first place. The scientists did that. Furthermore, the scientists did not give the exercise wheel only to the lively-looking rats or to rats that were especially down in the dumps. In an experiment, the treatment is not self-selected, and there is no other type of favoritism or bias shown in assigning the treatment. In this way, an experimental treatment is designed to be truly *exogenous*—it comes completely from outside the complex of factors influencing the outcome.

In Emily's case, as we already noted, the exercising was self-selected and thus endogenous. So a plausible alternative explanation is reverse causation, that the better mood came before the exercise. But what if, somehow, we could intervene in the situation—such as shown in Figure 11.9—in order to manipulate Emily's exercising separately and apart from her mood or anything else happening in her life? If the causal influence really runs in reverse, then such an intervention, an exogenous push to exercise, will do nothing—the arrow is flowing in the wrong direction for this to cause an improvement in mood. If, however, the causal arrow flows from exercise to mood, then an intervention that encourages exercise will in turn affect her mood. Finding a way to intervene and make exercise exogenous—perhaps by actively convincing Emily to join the club, rather than waiting for her to voluntarily join—would help *identify* which way the causal arrow truly flows.

Let's consider the same picture in the context of a common cause, such as the arrival of spring weather, as shown in Figure 11.10. Again, if we could find a way to intervene and exogenously push Emily to exercise—actively counsel her to join the exercise club, rather than wait for her to voluntarily do it (or not) on her own—we could learn a lot. If Emily's exercising and her mood only reflect the common cause *weather,* and not a causal effect, then an intervention to encourage her to exercise does nothing. But if the causal arrow flows from exercising to mood, then the exercise intervention will change her mood.

QUESTION

How would you describe the idea of exogeneity in your own words?

However, we need to worry here about the timing of our intervention—suppose it coincides still with the arrival of spring. How can we eliminate the change of seasons as a factor, or any other change, for that matter, that may also be influencing Emily's mood? Ideally, we would like to control all such factors—fix them, hold them constant.

Figure 11.9 An Intervention Helps Disentangle Reverse Causation From Causation

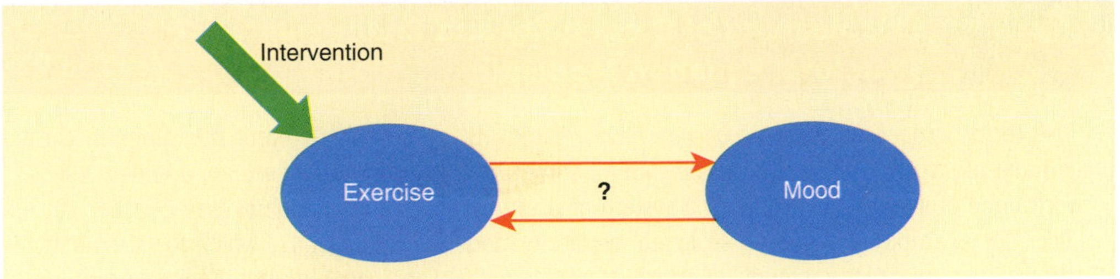

Figure 11.10 An Intervention Helps Disentangle a Common Cause From Causation

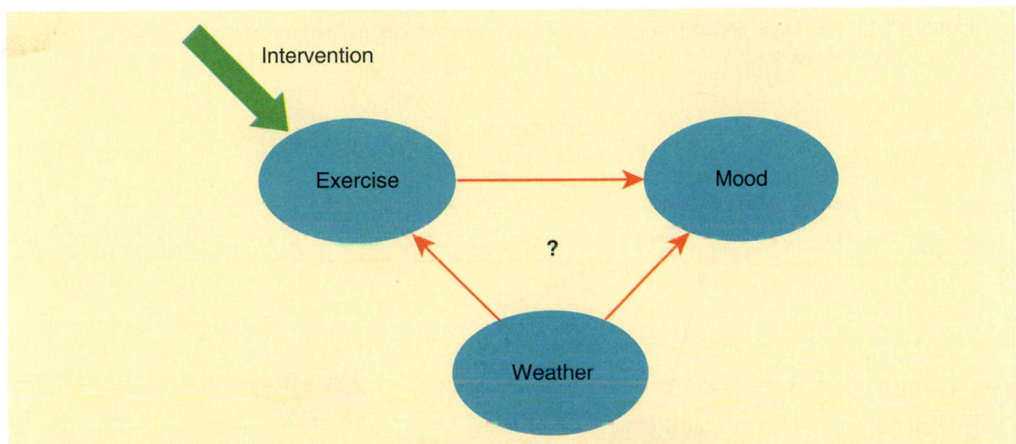

BOX 11.5
Exogenous or Endogenous? It Depends on the Dependent Variable

It makes sense to think of an independent variable as being *exogenous* or *endogenous* only in relation to a particular dependent variable. The same independent variable, in other words, may be exogenous with respect to one dependent variable but endogenous with respect to a different dependent variable.

Consider a study that looked at the effect of no-fault divorce laws on long-term outcomes of children, such as marriage and education level (Gruber, 2004). For children in a given family, whether or not the state in which they live has a no-fault divorce law is largely exogenous: It does not depend on self-selection by the family or on family characteristics that also affect the children's future education or marriage. But at the state level, state legislatures choose to pass no-fault divorce laws—they self-select such a policy—based on various factors, including most likely the aggregate rate of divorce in the state.

Therefore, no-fault divorce laws can be considered largely *exogenous* to individual children's long-term prospects for marriage and education. But which states have no-fault divorce laws, and when they pass such laws, is likely *endogenous* to state-level divorce rates. Thus the same independent variable could be either exogenous or endogenous:

Exogenous: No-fault divorce law → Children's prospects for marriage/education

Endogenous: No-fault divorce law → State's divorce rate

BOX 11.6
The Meaning of Exogeneity and Endogeneity in Structural Equation Modeling

The terms *exogeneity* and *endogeneity* have related but somewhat different meanings in the context of *structural equation modeling* (SEM; sometimes called *causal modeling*), a widely used technique of statistically analyzing a system of presumed causal relationships (see Chapter 10). Take, for example, the stylized structural equation model in Figure 11.11, which for simplicity shows only the structural model of causal relationships between variables, not the measurement model of observable indicators for each latent variable.

Figure 11.11 Path Model Showing Endogenous and Exogenous Variables as Defined in Structural Equation Modeling

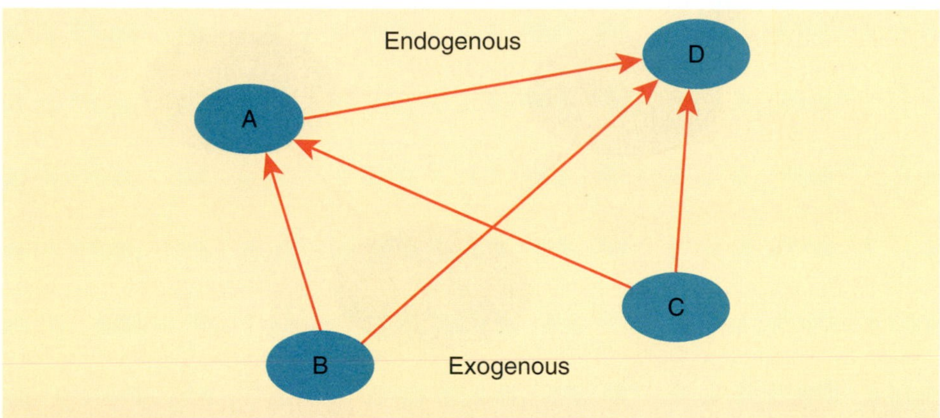

In this model, variables *A* and *D* are labeled "Endogenous" because they have arrows leading into them; that is, they are "caused" by other variables in the system (the model). In contrast, variables *B* and *C* are labeled "Exogenous" because they have only arrows coming out of them, no arrows pointing into them, so they are not "caused" by any other variables in the system (the model). SEM definitions are somewhat different because the focus is on a system of many cause-effect relationships, rather than just one independent variable and one dependent variable.

A key question, however, in SEM is whether just labeling variables as endogenous or exogenous corresponds to the causal relationships as they exist in the real world. Could there perhaps be another variable, *E* (not shown), that is a common cause of both *B* and *C*? If so, then *B* and *C* would be endogenous too—regardless of how they are labeled in the structural equation model.

Control: Holding Things Constant

Returning to the rat experiment, the impact of exercise on depression was measured by comparing the rats' exploratory behavior and consumption of sucrose solution before and after the introduction of an exercise wheel. For this comparison to lead to a valid causal conclusion, the experimenters had to carefully *control* (or *hold constant*) other possible causes of the change in the rats' behavior. The feeding schedule, the presence of people in the room, the cleaning of cages, the temperature and lighting in the laboratory—all these aspects of the rats' environment had to be exactly the same both before and after the introduction of the exercise wheel. This is referred to as **experimental control**. Only by carefully controlling, or holding constant, other possible causes could the experimenters attribute the outcome to the treatment and only the treatment.

Contrast this situation with Emily in her retirement community in Arizona. The season was changing, the days growing longer and the weather warmer. Perhaps Emily had some new neighbors who befriended her. Or maybe she changed her medication or diet. In short, the features of Emily's environment before and after joining the exercise group were not in any way controlled; they were natural and variable. So it is quite difficult to separate out the influence of exercising from everything else that was going on in Emily herself and in her surroundings.

Statistical Control: Holding Things Constant in the Analysis

Researchers who cannot physically hold things constant often attempt to accomplish the next best thing in their analysis—*statistically controlling* other variables. We noted this idea earlier, and it will form the central theme of Chapters 12 and 13. Here, it is important simply to distinguish experimental control—physically or materially holding conditions constant—from attempts to hold variables constant in the analysis. There are additional ways researchers attempt to control, or hold constant, extraneous influences—such as by matching or using case controls, topics covered in Chapter 12.

Experimentation: The Basic Steps

Figure 11.12 summarizes the basic steps in experimentation. First, we measure the dependent variable; then we intervene to try to make something happen; and then we observe the dependent variable again. Importantly, the intervention must be exogenous—imposed from outside the situation being studied—not self-selected or otherwise endogenous. In addition, other possible causes of the outcome need to be controlled, held constant, so that the intervention is the only change. The outcome at the start provides an estimate of the *counterfactual*—what the outcome would be like at the end of the experiment had the intervention not happened. Of course, we do intervene, so we don't really know what would have happened had we not. But we hope that our controls are strong enough that the outcome would, apart from the intervention, remain the same as it was before.

Figure 11.12 The Basic Process of Experimentation

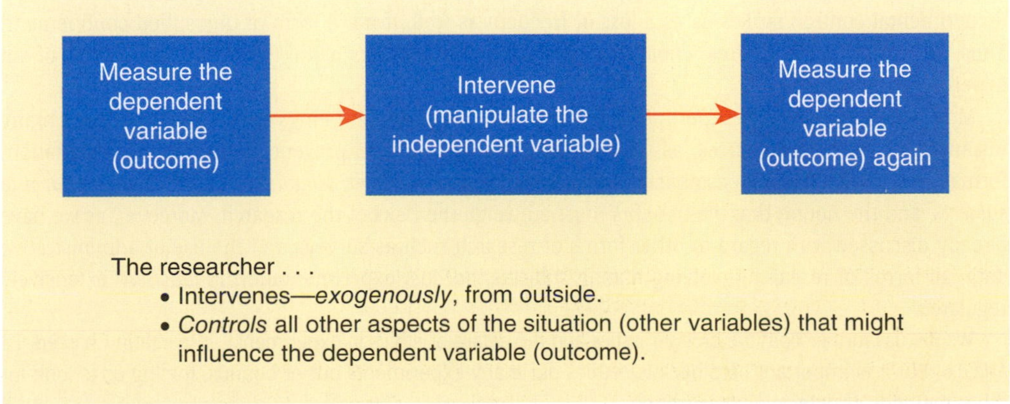
Measure the dependent variable (outcome)
Intervene (manipulate the independent variable)
Measure the dependent variable (outcome) again
The researcher . . .
• Intervenes—*exogenously*, from outside.
• *Controls* all other aspects of the situation (other variables) that might influence the dependent variable (outcome).

Comparative Experiments

Because it is often difficult to physically hold constant everything that might make a difference, real-world experiments typically compare a so-called treatment group that is exposed to the intervention with a control group that is not. The control group gives information on what would have happened to the treatment group had it not been exposed to the intervention—in other words, it gives us an estimate of the counterfactual. We will have much more to say about this comparative design in Chapter 14, on randomized field experiments.

Although experimentation provides good evidence of causation, it is often not practical in the real world of policy and practice for a variety of reasons.

Limited Generalizability of Experiments

Experiments are, almost by definition, artificial. Laboratory scientists create settings, produce interventions, and confine and manipulate their subjects. This artificiality raises important questions about the results of any experiment: Is the experimental setting a good representation of reality? Do things work the same way in the outside world? Can the results be generalized to real people going about their daily lives? Often it's a stretch. Indeed, one of the reasons experiments do not appear more often in applied research—even assuming they were practical and ethical—is that we often want to know how things will work in the real world, not in some artificial laboratory.

So there is a trade-off: good evidence of causation versus realism and the ability to generalize to practical situations. Still, as we will see in the chapters that follow, there are ways to bring experiments into the real world, such as *randomized field experiments* and various types of *quasi experiments.*

Ethical Limitations of Experiments

For most of us, images of experimentation are not very happy ones. Indeed, there seems to be something almost sinister about the typical experiment—the cold-hearted scientist inflicting painful treatments on innocent beings so as to manipulate some aspect of their health or behavior. The very features of experimentation that (as we have been arguing) provide good evidence of causation—exogenous interventions and control—also raise serious ethical issues.

As scientists, we may prefer to intervene and impose treatments that cannot be self-selected, but as human beings, we find this notion objectionable. Indeed, we generally value and seek as much freedom (self-selection) as possible in our daily lives. Similarly, strict constraint on a person's environment (experimental control) strikes us as a loss of freedom as well, if not a form of unjustified confinement. Thus, the importance of free choice in ethics directly conflicts with the basic framework of an experiment.

Moreover, the history of experimentation involving both human beings and animals includes many instances of unethical practices, as we discussed in Chapter 1. To prevent unethical experimentation, formal principles have been established, including *informed consent, voluntary participation, no harm to subjects,* and the notion that the benefits must outweigh the risks of the research. Moreover, as we have already discussed with regard to other forms of research such as surveys and the use of administrative data, all forms of research involving human subjects, not just experimentation in labs, are extensively regulated.

We discuss further both the broader issues and the details of ethics in experimental research in Chapters 14 and 16. But it is important here because ethics put many experiments out of bounds, forcing us to look for other methods of determining causation.

Experimentation, Policy, and Practice

QUESTION

What are the key features of experimentation for uncovering causation?

By focusing on the logic and advantages of experimentation, we are not suggesting that this is the only or even the best approach to uncovering causation in applied social and policy research. Indeed, much of the rest of the book is about techniques that can be used in place of traditional experimentation to answer important policy and practice questions. However, a clear understanding of experimentation—particularly the ideas of exogeneity and control—will enable you to develop and evaluate real-world research strategies that address causal questions with other methods.

Conclusion: End of Innocence

This chapter should mark the end of your innocence about correlation implying causation—even (or especially) when the correlation confirms some theory that you believe in. We hope that you will always remain skeptical and alert to alternative theories that might explain the correlation. But you may feel a bit overwhelmed, even discouraged, by now. After all, you probably want to do something about problems such as teen drinking and drug use, or seek to improve health outcomes, or pursue some other important policy or practice goal. But given the fact that it seems that the causal arrows could go in many possible directions, how are you ever supposed to figure out how to make a real difference?

We have provided some initial ideas in this chapter—ideas that will be developed more fully in the chapters that follow. For example, randomized field experiments (Chapter 14) and natural and quasi experiments (Chapter 15) incorporate the key ideas of exogeneity and control to investigate causal relationships. Another idea is to take account of common causes by measuring them and incorporating them into the analysis. This is the strategy of control variables—the topic of the next chapter—perhaps one of the most common types of research applied to public policy and practice.

BOX 11.7
Critical Questions to Ask About Causation

- What is the implied causal relationship in a given study, report, or news story? Which variable is assumed to be the independent variable (cause), and which the dependent variable (effect)?
- Could the implied causal relationship work the other way around—could it be reverse causation? How plausible is this?
- What common causes might be at work behind the scenes? How plausible are these common causes as an alternative explanation of the correlation? How might they bias the reported results?
- Was the independent variable—the assumed cause—self-selected? If so, how might this bias the reported results?
- Did the study acknowledge the possibility of reverse causation or common causes? Were alternative explanations considered?
- Did the study rule out plausible alternative explanations, either by the use of logical argument or by reference to empirical evidence? How convincing are the arguments or evidence?
- Did the study try to make something happen using an intervention or treatment (experimentation), or did it just passively watch things happen?

BOX 11.8
Tips on Doing Your Own Research: Causation

- Determine the cause (independent variable, intervention, treatment, program) and effect (dependent variable, outcome) you wish to study.
- Before starting a causal research study, check for the initial clues described in this chapter. If several of these are not met, the relationship may not be causal. But remember that while these indicators of causation are important, they are not proof of causation.
- Do not jump to conclusions—avoid thinking of correlation alone as evidence for causation.
- Try to determine not only whether a causal relationship exists, but also its magnitude, when possible.
- Consider all possible causal explanations of a correlation, including reverse causation and common causes, including complex common causes. Predict the direction of bias, if any, that may come from these influences.
- Determine if it is possible to do an experiment—to intervene, creating an exogenous push on the independent variable. But be aware of the ethical implications.
- Determine if it is possible to control, or hold constant, other possible influences.
- After you have developed a research design, evaluate it for possible weaknesses in the evidence of causation or possible bias in the estimated causal effect.

Chapter Resources

Key Terms

- Bias (in a causal estimate)
- Causal mechanism (mechanism)
- Causation
- Common cause
- Confounding
- Counterfactual
- Direct effect
- Endogeneity (endogenous)
- Exogeneity (exogenous)
- Experimental control
- Experimentation
- Indirect effect
- Intervention
- Reverse causation
- Self-selection
- Simultaneity bias
- Spurious relationship
- Treatment

Exercises

Do Private Schools Prepare Kids Better Than Public Schools?

11.1. Education studies suggest that kids who attend private schools are much more likely to graduate and go on to college than kids who attend public schools. Does this correlation between private schooling and going to college imply causation? What are some alternative causal explanations?

Can Computer Skills Help Welfare Recipients Find Work?

11.2. Agency records show that welfare recipients in an economically distressed county who volunteer for a computer skills class are more likely to get off welfare and find a job than other welfare recipients in the county. Did the new computer skills cause this better outcome? What are some alternative causal explanations?

"Study finds a link . . ."

11.3. Do a web search using the phrase "study finds a link" and look for a news article, webpage, or blog post that interests you. Then answer these questions:

a. What are the presumed cause (x) and effect (y) in the study?
b. Did the researchers intervene in order to manipulate x (make things happen), or did they just observe or make measurements (watch things happen)?
c. Is x exogenous or endogenous with respect to y in the study? And why do you think so?
d. Does the study seem to provide good evidence of causation? Why or why not?

Exogenous or Endogenous?

11.4. See if you can decide:

a. Is a person's level of education endogenous or exogenous to his or her income? Explain why.
b. Is a person's Zodiac sign endogenous or exogenous to his or her income? Explain why.
c. Is the choice of whether or not to put a child in day care endogenous or exogenous to a child's behavior? Explain why.
d. Is a city's spending (per capita) on police protection endogenous or exogenous to the city's crime rate? Explain why.
e. Are a state's medical malpractice laws endogenous or exogenous to a gynecologist's choice of whether to do a C-section for a particular woman giving birth? Explain why.

Make It Exogenous

11.5. First, consider how x might be endogenous with respect to y in each example below. Next, think of a way to intervene to make x exogenous to y.

a. x = time spent on Facebook; y = grades in school
b. x = use of a nicotine patch; y = smoking
c. x = frequency of police patrols; y = crime rate
d. x = class size; y = reading test scores
e. x = high health insurance deductible; y = health
f. x = employee participation in decision making; y = profitability of the company

Your Counterfactual Life

11.6. For each of the following common events or occurrences in your life (your factuals), imagine the counterfactuals. What does the resulting contrast tell you about the causal effect of the event on your life?

Example: Graduating high school. (The counterfactual would be your life having not graduated from high school. Imagining this counterfactual would give you some sense of the causal effect that graduating high school has had on your life.)

Imagine the counterfactual for . . .

a. An important job or internship that you had
b. A recent major purchase that you made
c. A friendship or romance you had with someone
d. Your choice of a college or degree program

Alternative Causal Explanations of Correlations

11.7. In several observational studies, alcohol abuse is correlated with suicide attempts among adolescents. Some propose that teen suicide can be prevented through alcohol prevention programs.

a. In these *studies*, what would you guess is the unit of analysis? What is the independent variable? What is the dependent variable?
b. In the proposed policy *intervention* (*not* the studies), what is the independent variable? What is the dependent variable?
c. Create a path model showing a mechanism consistent with the proposed *intervention* above.
d. Create a path model showing an alternative theory that *both* is consistent with the correlation described in the studies and contradicts the causation implicit in the proposal. Briefly explain your path model in words.

11.8. According to a newspaper article, a study shows that "among men in their 50s, having a wife who earns more money is associated with poorer health. Among the highest earning couples in [the] study, a husband who earns less than his wife is 60 percent less likely to be in good health compared with men who earn more than their wives" (Parker-Pope, 2010).

a. Your uncle reads about this study and says, "See! A woman who earns more than her husband hurts his pride so much, it hurts his health." Draw a path diagram to illustrate the theory in your uncle's head. Draw as many mechanisms as your uncle provided, no more and no less.
b. Create a theory that *both* explains (predicts) the results of the study *and* contradicts your uncle's causal theory. Draw a path diagram to illustrate this theory. Explain the theory in a few words, preferably ones your uncle would understand.

Student Study Site

Visit the Study Site at **www.sagepub.com/remler2e** to

- test your knowledge with the self-quiz
- check your understanding of key terms with the eFlashcards
- explore helpful resources that relate directly to this chapter

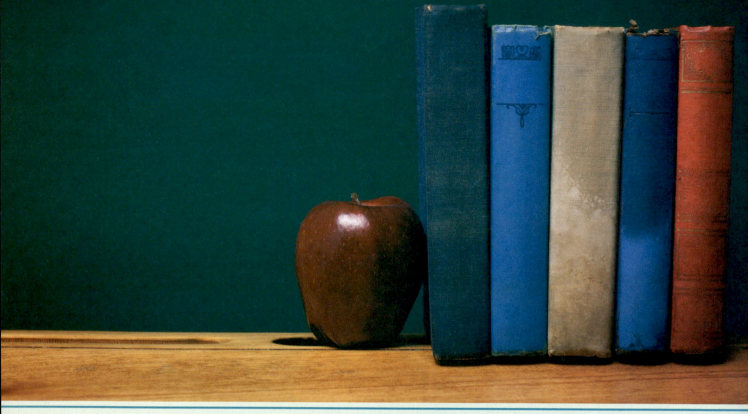

Do private schools really educate children better than public schools?

Source: © iStockphoto.com/ideabug.

Overview: In this chapter, you will learn how researchers use observational studies not only to describe the world but also to estimate causal effects by controlling for the influence of other variables. You will learn how to identify appropriate and inappropriate control variables. And you will learn to evaluate when the use of control variables is not adequate to determine causal effects. You will learn about matching, case-control studies, and a straightforward way to implement statistical control—stratification. Observational studies are widely used for estimating causal effects in applied research, so learning about the logic and limitations of such studies is particularly useful.

Objectives

Learning Objectives

After reading this chapter, you should be able to

- Explain the bias that often results from using observational studies to estimate causal effects
- Recognize the similarities and differences between matching, case controls, and statistical controls as strategies to reduce or eliminate bias in causal estimates using observational studies
- Identify important control variables that a given observational study should take into account
- Spot omitted variables, as well as variables that should not have been used as controls, in a given study
- Understand and explain the limitations of the control variables strategy for making causal conclusions, particularly the role of unmeasured variables
- Predict the direction of bias in a particular study, with the help of a path diagram

Observational Studies 12

Private Versus Public Schools

Do private schools educate children better than public (government) schools? Many people think so, at least as judged by their willingness to pay out of pocket for private education while forgoing free public schools. And we hear increasing calls for the privatization of education, in the form of school vouchers or charter schools, as a solution to educational reform. Much of this enthusiasm for private schools rests on the observation that kids in private schools perform better, at least as measured by the National Assessment of Educational Progress (NAEP). Known as "The Nation's Report Card," the NAEP is a rigorous sample survey of more than 300,000 public and private school children in Grades 4 and 8 in more than 13,000 schools across the United States.

Many people believe private schools offer a better education than public schools, but what does the evidence suggest?"

Source: © iStockphoto.com/MichaelDeLeon.

According to the NAEP, public school fourth graders scored only 218 on a scale of reading ability—but their private school counterparts scored 237 (National Center for Education Statistics, 2009). And this 19-point difference is *practically* significant relative to other differences: Since the 1970s, the overall progress in reading scores nationwide has been only about 12 points. But the public school–private school difference could be due to a variety of common causes of private schooling and test scores. What would a study that accounted for such common causes show?

What Is an Observational Study?

The NAEP data are considered an **observational study**. Of course, all research involves observation of some kind, but in an *observational* study, researchers do not attempt to change or manipulate variables to test their effects; they simply observe or measure things as they are in the "natural," unaltered world (Rosenbaum, 2002). In contrast, experiments manipulate or change variables, as we just saw in Chapter 11. We will return to the topic of experiments in more detail in Chapter 14. But to fully appreciate the advantages of experiments, it is important to consider how researchers try to estimate causal relationships using observational studies, often in the form of existing government surveys or administrative data. Moreover, the great majority of social and policy research you will see in journals, reports, or the news media comes from observational studies, so it is essential to learn about the logic and limitations of this type of research.

Chapter 6 described many of the sources of data typically used in observational studies. Some examples include the following:

- Social surveys that ask about the characteristics, behaviors, or attitudes of a population (such as the Gallup and Pew polls)
- Administrative record data on crimes, hospital admissions, or auto accidents (such as the FBI's *Uniform Crime Reports* or birth and death certificates collected by most governments across the globe)
- Secondary data from large government surveys, such as the NAEP, the Current Population Survey (CPS), the Eurobarometer, and many others
- Digital data gathered from consumer transactions, communications, web searches, and so on

The Gold Standard for Description—but Not for Causal Estimation

For *describing* the world, observational studies are exactly what we need, although subject to all the potential limitations of measurement and sampling we described in earlier chapters. The NAEP is often referred to as the "gold standard" for measuring educational performance, and it does an excellent job at *describing* the differences between public and private school students: The 19-point test score gap between public and private schools is a valid description of things as they are in American education. Moreover, describing the world accurately is important: We need an accurate description of a problem before we can even begin to think about how to change it.

However, the policy question here that motivates politicians and parents is a different one: "If students currently in public schools went to private schools, what would happen to *their* test scores?" This is an example of a causal question with a presumed *counterfactual*—what would happen if something were done differently? Unfortunately, as we saw in the previous chapter, answering such a question with an observational study is not so easy. Still, most applied research must rely on observational studies such as analysis of the NAEP to answer causal questions. So it becomes essential for you to understand the limitations of such studies—as well as their potential to inform policy and practice.

Limitations of an Observational Study

What are the limitations of observational studies such as analysis of the NAEP for answering causal questions? Reflect for a moment on why some students go to public schools and other students go to private schools. The income and wealth of the students' families, the quality of schools where they live, the parents' interest in education, the students' interest in education, the extent of students' behavioral problems, and the families' religious traditions—along with a host of other motivations and preferences of the students and their families—will influence that choice.

Why are most studies that rely on surveys or administrative data considered observational studies?

This is the problem of *self-selection* we learned about in the previous chapter. And schools often select students as well—a form of treatment selection. Together, such mechanisms make the kind of school a child attends *endogenous*—determined by variables or processes that also influence the dependent variable.

In observational studies, as it turns out, the independent variables we are interested in are very often self-selected or otherwise endogenous. Using observational data to answer causal questions requires us to deal with this endogeneity.

Control Variables

To address the problem of endogeneity in observational data, researchers try to make fairer comparisons—apples-to-apples comparisons, as it were. For example, they compare the test scores of private and public school children, adjusting for the effect of other variables such as family income that might influence test scores. Such adjusting variables are called **control variables**.

Controlling for variables can be done with various statistical and matching methods that will be explained later in this chapter. But first, it's important to understand the logic of control variables, without the statistical details, and to see how control variables can change our understanding of a relationship.

How Control Variables Help Disentangle a Causal Effect

The U.S. Department of Education commissioned a study to compare public and private schools, and to do so, the researchers used data from the NAEP (National Center for Education Statistics, 2006). To make a fair, apples-to-apples comparison, the researchers did not simply compare public and private schools on reading and math scores. Such a comparison would not be fair, because the scores of private school kids do not make a good *counterfactual* for what would happen to the scores of public school kids if they switched to private schools. Instead, the researchers used control variables to make the comparison fairer—and thus create a better estimate of this counterfactual.

For example, it would not be fair to compare students in private schools whose families have a computer in the home with students in public schools whose families do not have a computer in the home. We wouldn't know if the difference in their reading scores was due to the different schools—or due to the computers at home. Thus, one control variable that the researchers used was the presence of a computer in the home.

When added to the analysis of observational data, control variables work by *holding constant*—or *statistically equalizing*—the individuals in terms of the characteristics measured by the control variables. In effect, they allow us to see how test scores differ between public and private school students whose families are identical in terms of having a computer in the home.

Of course, public and private school students differ in a variety of ways likely to influence student test scores, beyond just the presence of a computer. The control variables used in the government's study were these:

- Computer in the home
- Number of books in the home
- Eligibility for free lunch (based on family income)
- Participation in Title I (for economically disadvantaged students)
- Gender
- Race/ethnicity
- Student has a disability
- English language learner
- Number of absences

How to Choose Control Variables

Why were these control variables chosen? They represent characteristics of students that differ between public and private schools—differences that the researchers believe may influence reading scores. In other words, these variables represent likely *common causes* of both school type and reading ability.

For example, private schools might have more girls (because they have more same-sex schools that appeal especially to girls), and girls may read better in fourth grade than boys. If we control for gender, we avoid this problem of comparing public schools with more boys to private schools with more girls. The race/ethnicity variable works the same way. If we control statistically for race/ethnicity, then we make public and private schools equal in terms of their representation of race/ethnic groups. Public schools may serve more students with disabilities (including learning disabilities) and also more English language learners (recent immigrants), both characteristics that might well lead kids to score lower on reading tests. The number of books in the home and the presence of a computer represent resources for learning and also serve as a proxy for the educational level of the parents. Eligibility for free lunch and participation in Title I (a federal program for economically disadvantaged students) are both indicators of the income or economic status of the students. Number of absences reflects the health of the child but also perhaps the amount of discipline and supervision the child receives at home.[1] The U.S. Department of Education controlled for, or held constant, all these potential common causes in its study.

How Did Control Variables Change the Estimate of a Causal Effect?

What happened to the public school–private school test gap in reading when these common cause variables were controlled for or held constant? The difference in average test scores fell to only one tenth of one point, practically zero, and not significant statistically. The control variables wiped out nearly all the original 19-point difference between public and private schools in fourth-grade reading performance.

To put it another way, the government study suggests that the public school–private school test gap in reading appears to be due to differences in student characteristics (the control variables)—not something that private schools per se do, such as requiring uniforms, using traditional curricula, teaching values, and so on. The study implies that if you sent the public school students to private schools—the counterfactual—their reading test scores would not improve. The use of control variables gives us a better estimate of this counterfactual, although still not a perfect one. So the message that the pundits took away from the simple observational NAEP data—send the public school kids to private schools and they will read better—was contradicted by this study.

QUESTION

When comparing the health status of people living in two different communities, why does it make sense to control (or adjust) for age?

Control variables can be implemented with a variety of methods, ranging from the simple to the statistically complex. One intuitive approach is matching—holding variables constant by finding cases that match on the relevant control variables.

Matching and Case-Control Studies

When using observational studies to get at causation, researchers use two basic strategies to achieve control or comparability. The most widely used approach is statistical control, which we mentioned above and will illustrate in detail a bit later. The other approach is matching cases in order to neutralize the influence of common causes. Case-control studies are a variation on the strategy of matching.

Matching

The idea of **matching** is to find individuals or cases who are as similar as possible on relevant characteristics, usually potential common causes, in order to get at an unbiased estimate of a causal effect. Matching can be done at a group or individual level.

Let's continue with the example of public versus private schools and first consider **group-level matching** (also called *aggregate matching*), say at the level of the school. There are many more public than private schools in the United States, so what might make the most sense is to start with a sample of private schools and search for public schools that are close matches in terms of relevant characteris-

[1]Later, we discuss why including the number of absences as a control variable could be problematic.

tics. But what are the relevant characteristics? This is always the key question when matching, because the success of the strategy—and the resulting comparability of the selected public and private schools—depends a great deal on our matching criteria. One factor might be the difference between affluent suburban communities and lower-income urban areas, since the socioeconomic status and education level of families influence the school performance of their kids. School size might be another factor, as some evidence suggests that small schools often do better (e.g., Bloom, Thompson, & Unterman, 2010). Table 12.1 illustrates the basic idea.

As the table indicates, the 25 private schools in the sample tend to be small and to be found in affluent suburban communities. Thus, we need to find a set of 25 public schools that match this pattern. There are probably many large public schools to choose from, in which case we could select them randomly or use additional matching criteria (such as distance, perhaps). Finding small public schools might be more difficult, so we may have to use all that we can find. Notice that the matched sample of public schools will turn out to be rather unrepresentative of all public schools (in terms of location and size, at least). This can limit the generalizability of matching studies.

The very fact that small public schools are rare suggests that they may be unusual, perhaps with a specialized curriculum, and thus not so comparable to their matched private schools in ways that matter to the outcome. If we started with a larger sample of private schools, it would be possible to match on more variables. But even with a very large sample, researchers cannot come close to matching on everything they might want to or at the level of precision they might hope for. This is another limitation of matching studies.

Group-level matching is also often imprecise in part because of all the unique characteristics that often crop up *within* groups. Therefore, many studies attempt to match at an individual level, which is more precise but also more complicated to carry out.

Individual-level matching involves sorting individuals into various categories and then selecting or recruiting matching individuals. For example, if private school kids are more likely to be non-Hispanic Whites, to have a computer and books at home, and to be native English speakers, then we would search for public school kids that match these characteristics. In a large database of students, for example, we could use these search criteria to select a sample that matches the profile of the private school kids. Sophisticated matching techniques, which make use of various multivariate methods, allow for the best possible matches; we cover these techniques in the next chapter.

Matching on Prior Outcome Measures

Researchers will sometimes match using an earlier measure of the outcome (or dependent variable), such as test scores from an earlier school year. (Such measures are often referred to as **pretests**, even when they are not in fact test scores.) This is usually a very good strategy, as the pretest captures or represents many of the causes that also affect the outcome (because it is the same variable, only a different point in time).

However, when groups differ significantly at the outset, individual matching using pretests can sometimes be problematic. All variables tend to move up and down just due to random events—measurement error. For example, a child who had an unusually low test score (for that child) in one year is likely to move back toward his or her average the next time, while a student with an unusually high score in one year is

Table 12.1 Table to Illustrate Matching Public and Private Schools

	Private Schools		Public Schools	
	Urban	Suburban	Urban	Suburban
Large school	2	8	??	??
Small school	3	12	??	??

likely to score lower next time. This effect is known as *regression to the mean*. So if we match higher-scoring kids from a public school, say, to lower-scoring kids from a private school (because this produces what seem to be more comparable groups at the start), the chosen public school kids are likely to score lower the next year, and the chosen private school kids will score higher the next year—only because of regression to the mean.

Case-Control Studies

A **case-control study** is a type of matching but one in which individuals who experience an outcome, such as having a disease or dropping out of school, are compared with similar individuals who did not experience this same outcome (Gordis, 2000). Those who have the disease or drop out of school are referred to as **cases**, while those who do not are referred to as **controls**. The cases and controls are then examined to see if they differ in selected independent variable(s) of interest. If so, then the differing independent variables are taken to be risk factors—perhaps causes—of the outcome. It helps to consider a real example.

What Kind of Intersections Increase Pedestrian Fatalities?

Thousands of older pedestrians are killed by cars each year, so it is important to know how to design intersections better to reduce the risk of injury and death to a growing elderly population. With this aim in mind, Thomas Koepsell and colleagues (2002) conducted a case-control study involving 282 intersections in six cities at which older pedestrians had been hit by a car. They compared these 282 *cases* with a matched set of *controls*—nearby intersections with similar physical and traffic characteristics. They then compared the intersections in terms of the presence of crosswalk markings, traffic signals, and stop signs—in other words, they searched for various causes. "Almost all of the excess risk," they found, "was . . . associated with marked crosswalks at sites with no traffic signal or stop sign" (Koepsell et al., 2002, p. 2136). The marked crosswalks apparently encouraged older pedestrians to enter the street, but without the protection of a stop sign or traffic light to restrain oncoming cars. This may seem like an obvious finding, but not obvious enough apparently to prevent the construction of dozens of such intersections in the first place.

Can intersections be designed better to protect pedestrians?
Source: © 2009 Jupiterimages Corporation.

Notice that the outcome—an older person being struck by a car—is known in advance, and it defines the cases. The cause (or treatment) is unknown; it is what the researchers look for in their analysis. This is much different from matching studies in which the presence of the presumed cause (such as attending a private school) defines one group (the treatment group), the absence of the presumed cause (not attending private school, or in other words, attending public school) defines the comparison group (the control group), and then the researcher looks to see if there is a difference in outcomes. Thus, in case-control studies different dependent variable groups are made equivalent on matching variables, whereas in matching studies different independent variable groups are made equivalent on matching variables. Note also that in case-control studies the dependent variables must be categorical and in matching studies the main independent variable of interest must be categorical.

Strengths of Case-Control Studies

Case-control studies provide one of the only ways—frequently *the* only way—to study outcomes that occur only rarely in a population. Other methods, such as experiments or regression analysis of survey data, both covered later, will often result in too few if any cases of a rare outcome to include in the analysis. For this reason, case-control studies are common in epidemiology for studying the causes of various diseases, traumas, and other relatively rare health outcomes. Case-control studies are also useful in criminal justice, such as studying the risk factors associated with employees who commit embezzlement, and in any other area of policy or management research where outcomes are rare. Case-control studies are also useful for outcomes that occur a long time after their causes.

Weaknesses of Case-Control Studies

Because the outcome of interest is often rare, case-control studies typically start with an available set of cases, such as the set of street intersections at which older pedestrians had been killed. While cases and controls may be from a clearly defined population, such as all intersections in the six cities, often they are not. For example, cases might be all patients with a rare disease at a hospital that has expertise in treating that disease, so the population from which the cases are drawn becomes hard to define, making the generalizability unclear.

Moreover, in such situations, controls may simply be a convenience sample. A convenience sample of controls has two problems. First, generalizability is further reduced. Second, the comparability of the controls is unclear, making selection of the appropriate controls difficult and potentially biasing the estimated causal effects. The quality of a case-control study rests critically on how the controls are chosen.

When controls are selected through matching, the matching variables must be chosen carefully. The goal is to make cases and controls comparable in variables that might affect the outcome—except the independent variables of interest to be explored. Unfortunately, researchers may not always know what should be a matching variable and what should be allowed as a possible independent variable of interest—a risk factor. Researchers use theory and prior evidence to guide those choices, but they cannot know for sure that the right matching variables have been used. Matching on exogenous variables, however, is generally safe.

Case-control studies cannot provide the actual prevalence (or means) of any outcomes or the size of a treatment effect; they provide only odds ratios (and measures calculated from them). For example, the study of pedestrian accidents revealed a roughly 2:1 ratio of the odds of injury at a marked crosswalk to the odds of injury without a marked crosswalk (Koepsell et al., 2002, p. 2141). (See Chapter 8 for a review of odds ratios.) That is extremely valuable information, but it does not provide information on how common such injuries are in general. Nor does it provide information on how many injuries will be avoided by redesigning crosswalks.

Both matching and case-control studies hold variables constant by selecting cases that are similar on relevant variables, often discarding or ignoring the rest of the cases. Another approach is to use a wide range of cases but to hold variables constant statistically—that is, statistical control.

Statistical Control: An Empirical Example

Education is widely seen as the key to a better job with higher earnings and as a source of national prosperity. As a result, students and their families make real sacrifices to get more education—and governments provide education grants and loans. Many believe that if people can just change one thing about themselves—the amount of education they have—they will produce and earn more. Note again that this implies a counterfactual—how people would be different if they had more education. In other words, education is thought to have a substantial *causal* effect on earnings.

QUESTION

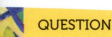

How are matching and case-control studies similar, and how are they different?

Let's look at the relationship between education and earnings to see how **statistical control**—holding variables constant in the analysis—works, using some real data. The belief that more education will increase earnings is grounded in the observation that generally people with more education do indeed earn more. Data from the National Longitudinal Survey of Youth (NLSY) show that those with a college degree or more education earned an average of $61,500 annually, while those with less education earned an average of $29,500, a difference in annual earnings of $32,000 (Table 12.2).[2]

But these results do not mean that we can tell a room full of people without college degrees that if they graduated from college, their annual earnings would rise by $32,000, on average. Once again, our observational study is only observing reality as it is now—it is not observing the counterfactual, what would happen if those with less education got more (or those with more got less). The amount of education that someone gets is self-selected and therefore endogenous—affected by variables that might also affect earnings. We'll see this fact illustrated soon, using actual data from the NLSY. But we can use control variables to help us sort things out—to get as close as possible to observing the counterfactual, and thus to make better causal conclusions.

Step 1: Speculate on Common Causes

The first step is to reflect on how people with and without college degrees may differ—and why. We suspect that they differ on average in many ways other than their educational level: their parents' educational levels, their parents' incomes, their interest in and aptitude for learning, and so on. If these same variables also affect the dependent variable—if they are *common causes* of both going to college and earnings—then we should include them in our analysis as control variables.

Let's think about how some of these differences might be common causes of both going to college and earnings. To begin with, college-educated mothers and fathers might be able to help their children more with their studies, encourage their children to take college-preparatory classes, and insist that their children apply to college. So whether or not someone gets a college degree is likely to be partially caused by his or her parents' having a college degree—an example of the independent variable being driven by parents' education. It is also possible that parents with more education can use their professional connections as well as their knowledge of professional careers to help their children get higher-paying jobs, whether or not their children attend college. Thus, parental education is a likely *common cause,* a variable that influences both the independent and the dependent variables.

Similarly, people with more interest in and aptitude for learning will not only be more likely to go to college, on average, but probably would also do more on-the-job learning that helps them advance faster, whether or not they attend college. Thus, aptitude would be a common cause, too. If we thought about it some more, we could probably come up with a variety of other common cause variables. And we should remember that some common causes are complex, not simple one-step relationships. We can use existing theory, common sense, qualitative research, and prior empirical studies to identify these potential common causes. This is the first, and probably most important, step in using control variables.

Table 12.2 Average Annual Earnings (NLSY, 2002)

No College Degree (A)	College Degree (B)	Difference (B – A) "Effect of College"
$29,500	$61,500	$32,000

[2]All calculations for this chapter use the 2002 NLSY and were done with the publicly available data, extracted by Jingyun Jiang, whom we thank for her excellent work. The data are described further at www.bls.gov/nls/nlsy79.htm. All calculations are weighted with the cross-sectional weights for 2002 and were performed on a consistent sample with no missing data for any of the variables used in the analysis. Note that the sample with no missing data may not be fully representative if data are not missing at random.

Step 2: Look for Differences

QUESTION

What is another possible common cause of both education and earnings?

The second step is to look at the data to see how groups with different values of the independent variable compare in terms of potential common causes, complex common causes, and proxies for both. In our example, we can examine how individuals with and without a college degree differ in ways that might also affect their earnings. The NLSY contains information on the education of the parents, scores on an aptitude test of the person surveyed when he or she was young, and a large variety of variables going back to youth.[3]

Table 12.3 shows this comparison. We see from the table that those with a college degree are less likely to have lived in poverty as children. And they are much more likely to have had mothers with a college degree and also with professional, technical, or managerial work experience. Those with a college degree also had fathers who completed more education. The two groups also differ in terms of race, with more Blacks among the group without a college degree. Notably, those with a college degree had an average aptitude score of 74 points (on a standardized test) at age 14, while those without a college degree had an average score of only 40, a substantial difference. Overall, we see that going well back into their youth, those with college degrees and those without college degrees differed in many ways. When comparing their earnings, we are comparing "apples to oranges," not "apples to apples."

How much does education raise earnings?

Source: © Can Stock Photo Inc./rpernell.

Step 3: Stratify by Control Variables

One of the most striking differences between those with a college degree and those without can be found in their average aptitude scores at age 14. Those with greater academic aptitude would certainly be likely to obtain more education, perhaps because they enjoyed it more or found it easier. Academic aptitude might also make individuals more productive and better paid later in life, regardless of the benefits of schooling.[4] So ideally, we would like to give both groups the same aptitude score.

One way we can do this is to **stratify** the data, also known as *conditioning* (Morgan & Winship, 2007, chap. 3). Specifically, we break up our data into groups—called *strata*—based on aptitude scores. The variable used to divide up our observations into groups, aptitude score, becomes the control variable. College degree is the independent variable of interest, and earnings is the dependent variable. The **stratification** of the data

[3]In fact, this is why we use the NLSY data for this chapter. Many other data sets have the education and earnings results, and they are more commonly and easily used to provide results such as those in Table 12.2. However, such data sets, for example, the CPS, do not contain information such as parents' education and therefore do not supply the control variables that we want.

[4]There is a long and controversial literature on the extent to which aptitude tests such as the one used in the NLSY do in fact measure academic aptitude or instead measure other things, such as family socioeconomic background. We do not want to enter into that debate here. For the moment, just assume that the scores measure something, perhaps quality education in early childhood—anything that would also *independently affect earnings*. It does not matter for our purposes here if that something is innate ability, socioeconomic status, the quality of education at earlier ages, or something else altogether.

into groups based on the control variable allows us to compare the mean earnings of those with different amounts of education, but similar aptitude scores. (As a result, this specific control variable technique is known as *stratified comparison of means.*) It should be noted that here we are talking about stratification and strata as a way to implement statistical control, which is different from (but related to) stratification and strata used in sampling (see Chapter 5).

To implement statistical control using stratification, we can begin by identifying a "high aptitude" stratum, defined as those scoring in the top third of all scores. We did this already in Table 12.3, and we see there that among those with college degrees, 72% had high aptitude scores, while among those without college degrees, only 20% did. This is a big difference, as we noted before when looking at the means. Now, we want to control for this difference—hold it constant or condition on it—in other words, equalize people in terms of this key variable.

How Does Controlling for Aptitude Change the Estimated Effect of College?

Table 12.4 shows the mean earnings of those with and without college degrees, but now stratified by higher and lower aptitude. Among those with high aptitude scores, average earnings are $67,600 for college degree holders, compared with $39,800 for non-college degree holders—a difference of $27,800. Among those with lower aptitude scores, average earnings are $45,600 for college degree holders, compared with $26,900 for non-college degree holders—a difference of $18,700.

Compare these college degree "effects" with the effect of $32,000 based on the unstratified data, the same result we had in Table 12.2. Among both high and lower aptitude groups, the gap between college and non-college degree holders is smaller than the $32,000 gap we observed initially in our comparison of earnings. So we see that by controlling for aptitude, the magnitude of the effect of getting a college degree has been reduced appreciably.

You probably noticed in Table 12.4 that the effect of more education seems to *differ* between the high aptitude score group and the lower aptitude score group. The boost in income from education appears larger among the higher scorers—$27,800—than among the lower scorers—$18,700. This is an example of an *interaction*, as described in Chapter 2. Specifically, the effect of the independent variable, education, on income depends on the level of another variable, aptitude.[5]

Table 12.3 People With and Without College Degrees (NLSY, 2002)

	No College Degree	College Degree
Family in poverty during childhood	15%	8%
Mother has a college degree or higher	5%	25%
Mother is a professional or technical worker	8%	27%
Mother is a manager	4%	8%
Highest grade completed by father	11	14
White	82%	91%
Black	15%	7%
Hispanic	3%	2%
Aptitude score at age 14	40	74
High aptitude score	20%	72%

[5]There is a substantial technical literature on different forms that interactions can take, "multiplicative," "additive," and so on. This distinction is not so important for consumers of research. However, whether or not there are interactions *is* important. Always remember that the magnitude of the effect of one variable, such as education, could differ depending on the level of some other variable, such as aptitude test score.

Table 12.4 Mean Earnings by Education, Controlling for Aptitude (NLSY, 2002)

	Less Than a College Degree	College Degree or Higher	"Effect" of College Degree
High aptitude scores	\$39,800	\$67,600	\$27,800
Lower aptitude scores	\$26,900	\$45,600	\$18,700
Both groups combined	\$29,500	\$61,500	\$32,000

Omitted Variable Bias

Our initial \$32,000 estimate of the causal effect suffered from what researchers call **omitted variable bias**—bias that results when we fail to control for a common cause. Naive interpretation of the unstratified difference in earnings between those with and those without a college degree led us to incorrectly attribute to educational differences some of the earnings differences that were due to differences in *aptitude score*. The naive interpretation got the magnitude of the effect of education wrong.

In Chapter 11, we saw several similar examples of how such naive interpretation of a correlation might get the magnitude of a causal effect wrong, such as the effect of family dinners. But in that chapter we did not learn ways for determining the actual *amount* of such bias. Now, with control variables, we have begun to discover how to figure this out.

Omitted variables go by a variety of names, including **confounder** and *lurking variable*. Also going by a variety of names is the bias in estimated causal effects that stems from failing to control for such variables. The different terms are described in Box 12.1.

BOX 12.1
Omitted Variables—and the Bias They Cause—by Any Other Name

Omitted variables—and the bias that results from failing to control for them—go by many other names, depending on discipline, context, and intellectual tradition. Below are many of these other labels for an omitted variable, followed by a few of the other labels for omitted variable bias. Since nuances and aspects of the definitions vary, we also include brief descriptions of their meanings, using x to describe the independent variable and y to describe the dependent variable.

Antecedent—A variable that causally comes *before* both x and y, and thus is viewed as a potential common cause.

Common cause—A variable that drives both x and y and therefore should be used as a control.

Confounder—A variable that confounds or distorts the estimate of a causal relationship between x and y (usually because it is a common cause of both). This is the most common term in epidemiology, medicine, public health, psychology, sociology, and other such disciplines.

(Continued)

(Continued)

Control variable—A common cause, complex common cause, or proxy that is measured and included in the analysis of the relationship between x and y in order to remove bias.

Covariate—A variable that is correlated (covaries) with both x and y and is included in the analysis.

Extraneous variable—A variable that is extraneous (not of substantive interest) to the investigation of the relationship between x and y, but nevertheless needs to be taken into account in order to reduce bias.

Lurking variable—A variable that lurks (unseen) in the background and thus potentially biases the estimated causal relationship between x and y. This term is common in statistics.

Omitted variable—A common cause that, because it is omitted from the analysis of the relationship between x and y, results in a biased estimate of a causal effect. This is the most common term in economics.

The type of bias discussed in this chapter refers to an estimate of a causal effect—correlation, difference in means, regression coefficient, and so on—being systematically distorted from the true casual effect, due to failing to control for a common cause. It includes the following:

Confounding—A distortion in a correlation or other measure of association between two variables due to a third variable (common cause) that is unmeasured or unaccounted for. This is the most common term in epidemiology, medicine, public health, psychology, sociology, and other such disciplines.

Omitted variable bias—Bias in a regression or other analysis due to failure to include or adjust for important common causes.

Spurious relationship—The estimated causal relationship when it consists entirely of bias, because the true causal effect is zero.

Treatment selection bias—A misleading comparison between treatment and control groups because of how people were selected into groups, usually when not based on random assignment (see Chapters 14 and 15).[6]

While controlling for aptitude lowers the estimated effect of a college degree, the effect is still substantial. In fact, more sophisticated methods to be covered in later chapters (including multiple regression and a variety of natural experiments) provide much more compelling evidence that education really does have a substantial causal effect on earnings.[7] Nonetheless, it is important to use the control variables to get the *magnitude* of the effect right.

A control variable can eliminate a relationship, reduce it in magnitude, increase it in magnitude, even reverse the direction of the relationship, or have no effect whatsoever. Any of these is possible when control variables are added into the analysis.

[6]Some researchers often just say "selection bias" when referring to treatment selection bias—bias in the estimated causal effect due to self-selection into treatment groups. This abbreviated term can be confusing because (other) researchers often say "selection bias" when referring to sample selection bias, bias in description, as discussed in Chapter 5. To be safe, always specify whether you are talking about treatment selection bias or sample selection bias.

[7]See Card (1999).

A Different Choice of Control Variable

Let's see what happens to the education and earnings relationship when we stratify with a different control variable—whether the mother has a college degree or not. The results are shown in Table 12.5. In this case, we see that the apparent "effect" of a college degree, $32,000, was actually slightly strengthened among those with a college graduate mother, to $36,100, although it was weakened among those whose mother lacks a college degree, to $29,300. Once again, there appears to be an interaction: The effects of a college degree differ by mother's education.

Multiple Control Variables

So far, we have shown how to control for one variable at a time. We had to choose between aptitude and mother's education. However, based on our theories and our initial examination of how those with and without college degrees differ, we should control for both these variables and perhaps many others, and we should control for them all at once. After all, we want our groups to be comparable in every way that matters.

Unfortunately, it is difficult to use stratification to control for many variables at once. Suppose that we try to control for both aptitude and mother's education at the same time. We get a table such as Table 12.6, which has two deep layers and in effect involves looking at four different comparisons.

Although this table is hard enough to keep in one's head, imagine if we had more than two categories for each of the control variables. Suppose, for example, we had separate categories for high school dropouts and those with graduate degrees, resulting in four education categories. We certainly could (and probably should) break up the aptitude variable into more than two categories as well. Next, imagine trying to control for three or four variables at once, rather than just two variables. Suppose, for example, that we wanted to add in childhood poverty status, resulting in even more layering of the cross-tab. You can see how complex and confusing the table would get. And there is another problem with such layering: The amount of data in the cells of the table (cell sizes) would become very small, making it difficult to estimate the many comparisons with any kind of precision.

Table 12.5 Mean Earnings by Education, Controlling for Mother's Education (NLSY, 2002)

	Less Than a College Degree	College Degree or Higher	"Effect" of College Degree
Mother college graduate	$34,200	$70,300	$36,100
Mother not college graduate	$29,300	$58,600	$29,300
Both groups combined	$29,500	$61,500	$32,000

Table 12.6 Mean Earnings by Education, Controlling for Aptitude and Mother's Education (NLSY, 2002)

		Less Than a College Degree	College Degree or Higher	"Effect" of College Degree
High aptitude score	Mother college graduate	$40,803	$74,284	$33,481
	Mother not college graduate	$39,753	$64,809	$25,056
Lower aptitude score	Mother college graduate	$29,951	$48,093	$18,142
	Mother not college graduate	$26,761	$45,219	$18,458

QUESTION

To compare the rate (prevalence) of heart disease in two communities (A and B), what would it look like to stratify the results by age (using three age categories)? What age categories would you use?

Fortunately, there is an alternative to stratification that can overcome many of these limitations—the technique of *multiple regression,* which will be covered in the next chapter. Although multiple regression comes with a bit more technical baggage, the important conceptual issues are the same for stratification and for regression. So before ending this chapter and turning to multiple regression, let's consider the important conceptual issue of how to choose control variables.

What If the Dependent Variable Is Categorical? Layered Cross-tabs

In the example of education and earning, the dependent variable—earnings—is quantitative, so we have focused on comparing means. How can stratification be implemented if the dependent variable is categorical? We can illustrate how using data from a New York City survey that looked at people's perceptions of the fairness of the police (Muzzio & Van Ryzin, 2001).

Table 12.7a shows a cross-tabulation of the survey data, and you can see that 56% of higher-income people (those earning more than $35,000 annually) consider the police generally fair, compared with only 48% of lower-income people (those earning $35,000 or less)—an 8-point difference, which is highly significant statistically. But does that mean that having a lower income causes people to view the police as less fair? Or could there be an omitted variable, correlated with income, a common cause of both income and fairness perceptions? One likely candidate is race: Non-Whites are more often the victims of police profiling, and mistreatment of minority communities by police has long been an issue. Also, non-Whites on average have lower incomes than Whites. What would happen to the relationship between income and fairness perceptions if we were to control for race? What method could we use?

It turns out we can still use the stratification approach, breaking out two separate cross-tabs by race, as shown in Table12.7b. This stratified cross-tab is sometimes also referred to as a **layered cross-tab**. As the table shows, the income-fairness relationship we saw initially essentially disappears when we stratify the cross-tab by race—in other words, when we control for race. This suggests that income was not a cause of fairness perceptions, but rather the relationship was biased because of the omitted variable, race.

Table 12.7a Relationship Between Income and Perception of Police Fairness: Is There Omitted Variable Bias?

Are the NYC police generally fair in the way they handle people?	Income last year		Total
	< $35,000	$35,000 +	
Yes	48.4	56.4	52.7
No	41.8	34.8	38.1
Don't know	9.8	8.8	9.2
Total percent	100.0	100.0	100.0
	Sample size n = 1,796		
	Chi-sqr(2) = 11.78, p = 0.003		

Source: Muzzio and Van Ryzin (2001).

Table 12.7b Relationship Between Income and Perception of Police Fairness, Controlling for Race: Omitted Variable Bias Revealed Through Layered Cross-tabs

Are the NYC police generally fair in the way they handle people?	White			Non-White		
	Income last year		Total	Income last year		Total
	< $35,000	$35,000 +		< $35,000	$35,000 +	
Yes	69.1	69.4	69.3	41.6	44.2	42.8
No	21.3	21.6	21.5	48.6	47.3	48.0
Don't Know	9.7	9.1	9.2	9.8	8.5	9.2
Total percent	100.0	100.0	100.0	100.0	100.0	100.0
	Sample size n = 671			Sample size n = 1,125		
	Chi-sqr(2) = 1.04, p = 0.60			Chi-sqr(2) = 0.07, p = 0.97		

Source: Muzzio and Van Ryzin (2001).

How to Choose Control Variables

How do you know if your study, or a study you are reading, includes the right control variables? To answer this question, ask yourself first, "Are there any common causes that are not included in the analysis?" If an important common cause is omitted, then we will erroneously attribute its influence to the independent variable of interest: The study will suffer from *omitted variable bias*. If family wealth drives both educational level and getting a high-paying job—and we fail to *control* for family wealth—we will think that simply getting more education will raise income by more than it actually does.

But identifying the right control variables is not an easy task—even for experienced researchers. Perhaps it is best to begin with a few basic precautions:

- Simply "using control variables" of any kind in a study does not mean that the results are correct and unbiased. The study may have used the wrong control variables, or something important may still be missing. Beware of people who assure you that they have "controlled for all the usual variables": There is no such thing as a standard set of control variables (e.g., sex, race, and income) that works for every (or even most) studies.
- Beware at the same time of the "kitchen sink" approach: throwing everything into the analysis as a control variable. As you will see shortly, you can overdo the use of control variables and be just as wrong (biased) in doing so as you would be by omitting an important control variable.

The choice of control variables involves careful thought and, importantly, an understanding of the theory or model of relationships among important variables. As a practical matter, much depends as well on the availability of data—you must have an empirical measure of the common cause variable, or at least a proxy (about which we will have more to say shortly), before you can employ it as a control variable.

What's Driving the Independent Variable?

The key to finding the right control variables is figuring out what drives the independent variable—what drives selection (such as selecting to go to private school instead of public school). Cook, Shadish, and Wong (2008) show that in many cases an observational study using control variables can get a good unbiased estimate of a causal effect, but only if the controls include measures of all important variables driving the independent variable. But how does one figure out what those variables are?

Think about a situation in which college students get to select either math training or vocabulary training, and then the researcher tries to estimate the causal effect of math training on later math achievement. What do you think might drive some students to pick math training while others pick vocabulary training? Might those who pick math be better at math? In fact, Steiner, Cook, Shadish, and Clark (2010) found that whether students liked—or disliked—math strongly drove the training they chose: 30% of those who chose math training did so because they liked it, while 21% of those who chose vocabulary training did so to avoid math (pp. 259–260). Steiner et al. also found that, as a consequence, two variables measuring a student's preference for math were crucial to reducing bias in estimates of the effectiveness of math training on math achievement. Prior math skill, it turned out, was not nearly as crucial.[8]

How did these researchers know that the preference for math would be an important driver of selection that they should control for? In fact, they collected data on a vast array of potential control variables: 23 constructs, based on 156 items, covering five dimensions, including pretests of ability, prior academic achievement, topic preference, and psychological predisposition (including traits like conscientiousness). They say that they got their long list from "theory and a common-sense appraisal."

Indeed, theory is the best place to begin when selecting control variables. Theory can be used to help figure out what is and is not a common cause variable. Drawing a path diagram, such as that shown in Figure 12.1, helps us make our theory explicit and find common causes. Specifically, it calls our attention to variables that have arrows leading to *both* x (the independent variable of interest) *and* y (the dependent variable). And be skeptical: You may not have thought of all the potential factors driving selection. You need to aggressively seek all possible explanations. In the study of college students, the researchers might easily have decided that preexisting math skill was the key driver and overlooked interest in math.

Figure 12.1 Path Diagram Used to Find Common Causes

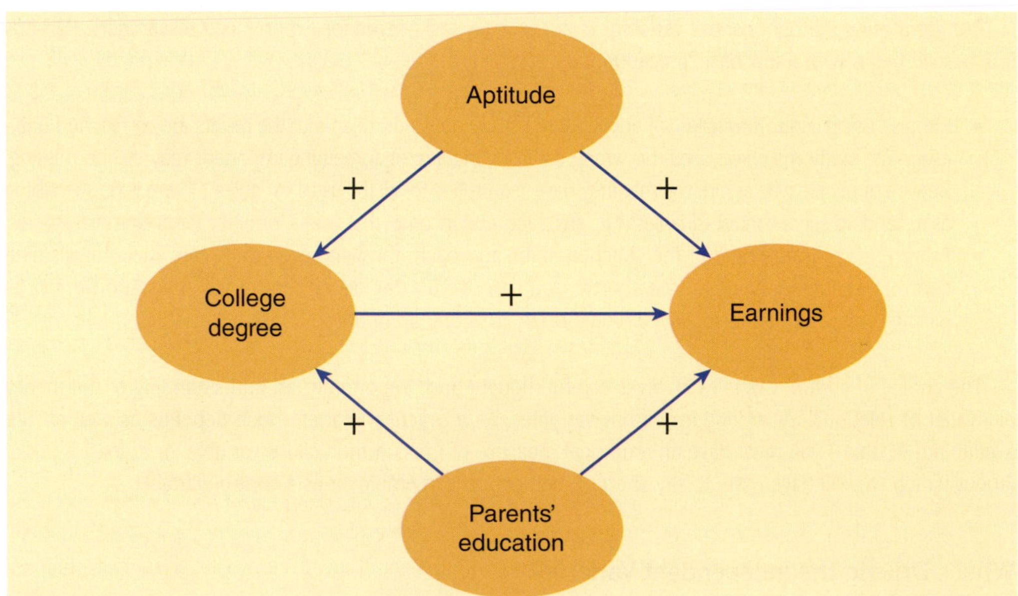

[8]The researchers were able to determine the amount of bias because they had unbiased estimates of the true causal effects thanks to an interesting study design: Study participants were randomly assigned into either the observational study or a randomized experiment, in which subjects were in turn randomized into math or vocabulary training (Shadish, Clark, & Steiner, 2008). We discuss such randomized experiments, and why they provide unbiased estimates of causal effects, in Chapter 14.

For many studies, however, theory, common sense, and skeptical thinking won't be enough. After all, a bunch of professors might have a good understanding about which factors drive college students to select or avoid particular courses, but they might not know as much about what really drives working-class families in urban areas to select private schools over public ones.

Here are some other ways to develop your theory of what drives the independent variable: read a lot about the topic, including newspaper reports, advocacy publications, popular books, and so on. And, of course, read scholarly studies, especially those in which your independent variable of interest is the study's dependent variable: You want to know what drives your independent variable. Another source of ideas is to talk informally with experts, advocates, or practitioners who have hands-on knowledge of the problem or program. Beyond informal talking, formal *qualitative research*—involving case studies, in-depth interviews, or focus groups—is another very important way to generate many useful ideas about what factors drive selection of the independent variable.

Two common approaches to picking control variables can be used to generate ideas, but they should be used with care. First, other researchers who tried to estimate the same causal effect also had to pick control variables, and their choices can give you ideas—but prior studies may have missed things or done something wrong. Second, you can search for patterns of correlation in the data—specifically, variables that empirically correlate with both the independent and the dependent variables of interest. But be careful here: The fact that a variable is empirically related to both the dependent and independent variables does not, in itself, necessarily make it a good candidate for a control variable. It could instead be an *intervening variable,* something along the causal pathway of how the independent variable works, and thus should *not* be controlled for, as we explain shortly. Again, a well-thought-out theory will help you avoid this mistake.

Encouragingly, when all relevant common causes are used as control variables, observational studies with control variables can produce fairly unbiased causal estimates (Cook et al., 2008; Cook & Steiner, 2010). But getting all relevant common causes requires extensive theorizing and searching through existing knowledge and evidence to determine what control variables are truly needed—and when possible, launching other forms of investigation. Perhaps the best approach is to anticipate the need for the full range of control variables and incorporate them ahead of time in the design of surveys or other procedures used to collect data for the study—a kind of prospective observational study (Rubin, 2007; Steiner et al., 2010). Such work is the real job of statistical analysis using control variables, and the importance of this task cannot be emphasized enough.

Do Not Use Intervening Variables as Controls

Path diagrams and theory can also help prevent the use of controls that worsen bias. Suppose, for example, that people with a college degree learn to write better and that writing skills are a key factor in getting a higher-paying job. This theory is depicted in Figure 12.2. In that case, writing ability is an *intervening variable,* a *mechanism* through which a college degree raises income. Empirically, writing ability would be correlated with both educational level and income, and thus seem like a potential common cause and therefore a potential control variable.

Using an intervening variable such as writing ability as a control variable, however, would be a serious mistake. It could bias the estimate of the effect of having a college degree by taking writing ability completely out of the picture. Rather, we should allow our comparison to include differences in writing ability—because it is precisely such skill gains that result from a college education and that employers reward.

In general, adding an intervening variable as a control variable is a mistake that can lead to misleading causal conclusions. It is sometimes referred to as *overcontrolling,* and it can result in just as much bias as omitting an important common cause.

What If a Variable Is Both a Common Cause and an Intervening Variable?

Recall that in the study of public and private schools *daily attendance* was used as a control variable. On the one hand, daily attendance could reflect differences in a student's health or family life, factors that we would

Figure 12.2 Path Diagram of an Intervening Variable

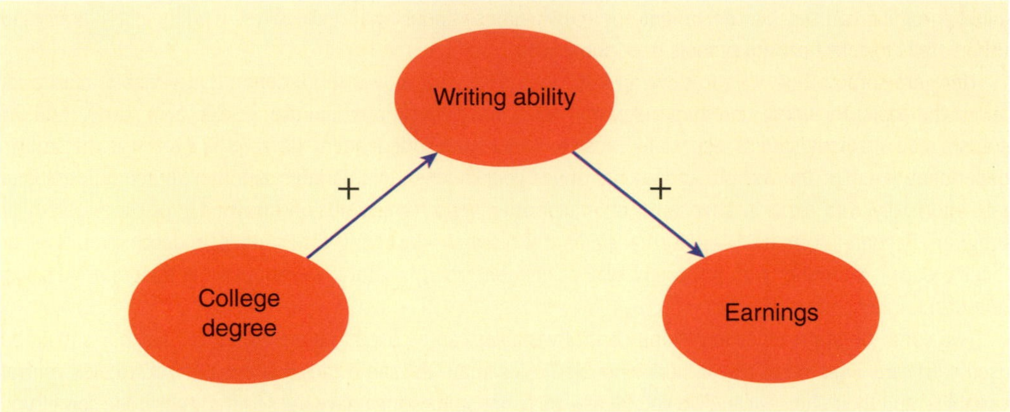

want to control for when comparing public and private school students—especially if no direct measures of health or family life are available. On the other hand, daily attendance could be due to school leadership and policies—part of what schools do to provide a good education. If so, attendance would be an intervening variable—something along the causal pathway between type of school and reading ability—part of the causal *mechanism*. In that case, we would not want to control for it. What should we do?

There is no right answer in such situations—much depends on judgment. Whenever a variable could be both a common cause and an intervening variable, a good practice is to show the results both with and without it as a control. Then observe how sensitive the results are to this alternation, and consider what possible reasons might explain any difference in results. Which theories (and effect magnitudes) are consistent with the difference?

Empirically Assessing Mediation

The reason not to use an intervening variable as a control is that it will remove or take away part of the causal effect—whatever occurs through the intervening variable (mediator). But sometimes you want to know how much of a causal effect is due to the mediator, if any. For example, you might want to know how much of the effect of education is due to improved writing ability. In this case, you would want to compare the estimated causal effect with and without the mediator, writing ability, as a control. This is referred to as mediation analysis (Baron & Kenny, 1986). David A. Kenny, an originator of this kind of analysis, has a useful website that explains the logic and statistical techniques of assessing mediation effects (see www.davidakenny.net).

Complex Common Causes and Unexplained Correlations

Sometimes a variable can be correlated with both the independent variable and the dependent variable—but you have no theory or explanation of why this is so. Because of the complexity of many social phenomena, two variables may be related through a chain of causation that runs too deep to be clearly understood. In other words, the correlation may be due to a complex or unknown common cause, as described in the previous chapter.

Consider the variable years of age as a possible control variable in an analysis of the effect of education on earnings. Age could influence both education and earnings directly, due to historical and life experiences, and thus be a common cause. But even if age is not a direct common cause and even if no explicit theories of its effect on education and earnings can be found, age remains a likely complex common cause that should be included as a control variable. Why? Because age is clearly exogenous, it could not possibly be affected by education and thus could not be an intervening variable.[9]

This gives us a clue as to how to proceed: If there is a variable correlated with both the independent and dependent variables—*and* it could not possibly be an intervening variable—then it may be a complex common cause and should be considered as a control variable. Unfortunately, the situation is often ambiguous and the decision not so clear-cut. When there is no simple answer, it is often best to do the analysis both with and without the variable as a control and see how sensitive the results are with this alternation.

Causes That Can Be Ignored

Variables that are causes of the dependent variable (*y*) but not the independent variable of interest (*x*) are not *common* causes and can be omitted without causing bias. Take the example of musical ability and earnings. Say that musical ability in a young person predicts fairly well an individual's chances of having a career as a musician, which probably does not pay very well on average (even including the very few who hit it really big in pop music or entertainment). Thus, musical ability may influence earnings, albeit in a downward direction. Yet musically talented kids may get just as much education, on average, as their less musically talented peers. In this situation, it would do little good to control for musical ability in our analysis of the effect of education on earnings, despite the fact that musical ability predicts earnings.[10]

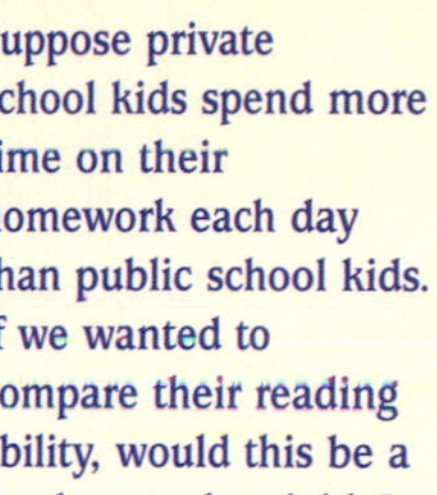

Suppose private school kids spend more time on their homework each day than public school kids. If we wanted to compare their reading ability, would this be a good control variable? Why, or why not?

What about causes that influence *only* the independent variable of interest (*x*) but not the dependent variable (*y*)? To continue with our education and earnings example, if states differ in financial aid laws, then those laws would drive part of the variation in how much education people get while not driving earnings (except through education). Such variables should not be included as control variables. However, as we will see in Chapter 15, these variables will prove valuable for estimating causal effects, through their use as *instrumental variables.*

Choosing Good Control Variables Depends on Your Question

The right choice of control variables depends a great deal on the question you're asking. Consider the case of the effect of race on income. One analysis might aim to determine if there is presently racial discrimination in hiring and salaries. To answer this question, one wants to compare people of different races but with similar jobs, qualifications, and work experience. Clearly, these should all be considered as control variables.

However, one might also want to ask whether people of different races enjoy different standards of living for a variety of structural reasons that promote, or discourage, their life chances. These could include the effects of historical discrimination, de facto school segregation, family wealth and connections, cultural norms and expectations, and other structural factors that thereby reduce the level and quality of education someone receives, the jobs he or she seeks, and so on. In that case, education and prior work experiences are probably not valid controls because they are intervening variables—variables that represent the

[9]As a practical matter, both age and experience cannot be included because of multicollinearity, discussed in Chapter 10. In fact, in many data sets, experience is not known and is estimated from age and education.

[10]However, when using multiple regression, under some circumstances including these variables as "controls" (i.e., additional independent variables) can increase the precision of our estimates. Our point here is that omitting them will not cause any *bias.* A researcher might also include them in a multiple regression due to an interest in the effects of these variables themselves or a wish to learn about all of the determinants of earnings. We return to this point in Chapter 13.

mechanism or process through which disadvantage occurs in society. A different question is being asked here, requiring a different set of control variables.

Unmeasured Variables and Omitted Variable Bias

In most real-world quantitative observational studies, measures of all the desired common causes are simply not going to be available. For example, in studies of the effect of education on income, one might want to have a measure of *ambition,* which would presumably affect both educational attainment and earnings. Measures of ambition are not generally found in most surveys or administrative data. When such important common causes are not available in the data, we refer to them as **unmeasured variables**, sometimes known as unobservables (see Box 12.2). The inability to include such unmeasured variables means that the results of the study are, at least to some extent, biased—they suffer from omitted variable bias.

BOX 12.2
Jargon: Unmeasured Variables and Unobservables

Researchers frequently refer to variables that they believe to be important but that they do not have in their data as *unobservables,* because the variables are unobservable to the researcher. However, that term implies that the variables are intrinsically unobservable, which may not be the case. By using the term *unmeasured variable,* we hope to suggest that at some point, perhaps in some future study, the potentially important variable could be measured and thus both observed and used as a control variable.

Researchers should try, if only in future studies, to get measures of the unmeasured common causes and, if possible, do a prospective observational study. Nonetheless, in any given study, it is almost inevitable that some common cause is missing and thus that some omitted variable bias exists. Still, we argue that this bias does not totally undermine observational studies. Rather, studies should acknowledge such biases and assess their direction and potential magnitudes. Identifying influential unmeasured variables also highlights what data should be collected in future studies.

Proxies

One possible way around the problem of unmeasured variables and the resulting omitted variable bias is to find *proxies,* measured variables that stand in for or substitute for the unmeasured variables. Moreover, in working with real data, we often are required to move from our theories about relevant common cause variables—aptitude, family connections, and so on—to variables that we can find in the data.

There are a number of issues to think about here. First, we often cannot get the variable we would really like, so we have to use a *proxy,* just as we did in Chapter 4, when our focus was on description. Second, we often have to work hard to try to get the variables we want. In our education and earnings example, there are many other—and much better—sources of data, such as the CPS, on education and earnings. However, those data don't contain much information on common cause variables of both education and earnings or even very good proxies for those common cause variables. In contrast, because the NLSY has data going back to respondents' youth, it does have good proxies for common cause variables. Therefore, we used the NLSY, and indeed, such data needs are one reason why the government funds a longitudinal survey—a difficult and expensive task.

Conclusion: Observational Studies in Perspective

All of the difficulties and limitations of using observational studies to estimate casual effects may seem discouraging. Indeed, there are some researchers who insist that only experiments can ever provide good evidence about causation. But remember that the perfect study does not exist: All studies have their weaknesses, even experiments. Moreover, much can be learned from observational studies with control variables, despite the fact that there will likely remain some unmeasured variables—and therefore omitted variable bias of some kind. Thus there will always be caveats attached to the causal evidence from an observational study.

The next chapter gets into more of the details of implementing statistical control using multiple regression and its extensions. But the really hard work of the control variable approach lies not in the technicalities of the different statistical methods. Rather, it lies in figuring out what variables drive the independent variable and determining potential common causes—and in getting measures of those variables, or at least good proxies. It lies in determining whether a potential control variable is an intervening variable and, when in doubt, estimating the effects in several ways. And it lies in predicting the bias from remaining unmeasured omitted variables and making careful interpretations. The control variable method is not a simple recipe with every step spelled out.

BOX 12.3
Critical Questions to Ask About Observational Studies With Control Variables

- Does the study use control variables, or does it rely just on simple differences or correlations to infer causation?
- Does the study implement control variables using matching, stratification, or some form of multiple regression?
- What control or matching variables does the study employ—and why were they selected? Is there an explicit theory, or rationale, given for picking the control variables? Does the choice of control variables match the research question?
- How much effort did the researchers put into finding good control variables? Did they identify and include measures of important control variables as part of data collection? Or was the choice of control variables just an afterthought?
- What important common cause variables are omitted? What bias (sign and magnitude) might result from omitting these common cause variables?
- Are variables included as controls that should not be, in particular plausible intervening variables?
- Do the researchers demonstrate an awareness of the limitations and caveats involved in drawing causal conclusions?

BOX 12.4
Tips on Doing Your Own Research: Observational Studies With Control Variables

- Identify your independent variable of interest and your dependent variable. When estimating causal effects, it is usually best to focus on one independent variable of interest and one dependent variable, although you may have more (such as several dependent variables that are closely related).
- Identify your desired control (or matching) variables. Use theory, qualitative research, prior empirical studies, wide reading, and so on to identify the key variables driving your independent variable. Assess which ones might also drive your dependent variable and thus be potential common causes, including complex common causes. Use path diagrams and think widely and skeptically.
- Using theory, prior studies, and so on, identify all plausible mechanisms (intervening variables) through which the independent variable could affect the dependent variable. Do not use intervening variables as controls. If a variable is both a common cause and an intervening variable, do the analysis with and without that variable as a control.
- Identify data for the analysis and assess the extent to which it has valid and reliable measures of the desired independent, dependent, and control (or matching) variables. Does a suitable data set already exist? If so, see also tips at the end of Chapter 6 on doing your own research with secondary data. If not, can you collect primary data? If so, see also tips at the end of Chapter 7 on doing your own survey.
- Recognize the type of variable (quantitative or categorical) for your independent, dependent, and control variables. Using the variable types and the number of important control variables, determine if stratified comparison of means or layered cross-tabs are possible. If not, you will need to implement the control variable study using multiple regression, as described in Chapter 13.
- After stratifying by control variables, calculate appropriate confidence intervals and hypothesis tests. See also tips at the ends of Chapters 8 and 9.
- Always calculate the (presumably biased) estimates without controls and compare them with the (presumably less biased) estimates with controls. Assess the differences between the two estimates and compare them with what you expected to find. Adjust your theory, based on the evidence.
- Implement the planned analysis first and then try variations in order to examine the robustness of results. For example, try different combinations of control variables, especially when control variables could also be potential intervening variables.

Chapter Resources

Key Terms

- Case (in a case-control study)
- Case-control study
- Confounder
- Confounding
- Control (in a case-control study)
- Control variable
- Group-level (aggregate) matching
- Individual-level matching

- Layered cross-tabs
- Matching
- Observational study
- Omitted variable
- Omitted variable bias
- Pretest
- Statistical control
- Stratification
- Stratify
- Treatment selection bias
- Unmeasured variables

EXERCISES

Education and Earnings Continued

11.1. Think of some other common causes of education and earnings in the real world—other than those mentioned in this chapter. When estimating the causal effect of education on earnings, what bias might result from their omission?

Thinking About Important Control Variables to Include

11.2. Following are some possible relationships that we might find in observational data that come, say, from a sample survey of U.S. adults:

a. Computer skills → Earnings
b. Exercise → Diabetes
c. Marital status → Happiness

Given that these simple relationships come from observational data, and that we are interested in getting at the true causal effects suggested by the arrows, what control variables would we need? Think about likely common causes of both variables, and be careful not to pick intervening variables.

Country Matchmaking

11.3. Freedom House, an advocacy organization, classifies countries as "free" versus "partly free" or "not free." Say you are interested in whether freedom causes countries to be more prosperous (lower poverty). Below are five "free" countries in 2013, according to Freedom House:

a. Costa Rica, Uruguay, Ghana, India, South Korea
b. First, find the Map of Freedom on the organization's website: www.freedomhouse.org.
c. For each of the five "free" countries above, find a matching "partly free" or "not free" country.
d. What criteria (variables) did you use to make your matches? Why do these make good control variables?
e. Would a comparison of poverty in the five "free" countries with the five matching countries you chose demonstrate that freedom is the cause? Why, or why not?

Planning for Control Variables

11.4. Think of a cause (x) and an outcome (y) in your field of interest that you might measure in a survey. Then do the following:

a. Draw the basic $x \rightarrow y$ causal diagram, substituting in the names of your chosen variables. Would you expect a positive or negative relationship, and how strong would it be?

b. Write survey questions to measure x and measure y.
c. Now, think of all the relevant common causes. Use path diagrams to picture the possibilities, and look up information on the topic to give you more ideas. Make a comprehensive list of the common causes.
d. What additional survey questions would you include in your questionnaire to measure these common causes? Would proxies help you measure some of them?

Part-Time Faculty and Graduation Rates

11.5. Some studies find that colleges that make greater use of part-time faculty have lower graduation rates.

a. Describe a common cause theory that *both* explains the correlation described above *and* does *not* imply that part-time faculty cause lower graduation rates. Use a path diagram as well as a brief description in words.
b. Does your theory reveal a control variable that could be used to create more convincing evidence of a causal effect—an estimate with less bias? If so, explain why and how you could do such a control variable study. If not, explain why not and what kind of theory you would need to help you find a control variable.
c. Describe a reverse causation theory that *both* explains the correlation described above *and* does *not* imply that part-time faculty cause lower graduation rates. Use a path diagram as well as a brief description in words. Can you find a control variable to eliminate the bias of the reverse causation theory?

Why Did They Do That?

11.6. Find an article in your field or on a topic of interest to you—an article that involves observational data and control variables. (A great many studies in social and policy research are of this type, so you should be able to find one readily in research journals in your field.) Find the main table in the article that shows the stratification or multiple regression results.

Which variable is the independent variable of interest? Or is the analysis focused on multiple causes? Which variables are the control variables? Why did the researchers choose the control variables that they did? Are there any important variables missing—in other words, is there possible omitted variables bias? If so, try to predict the direction of the bias.

Student Study Site

Visit the Study Site at **www.sagepub.com/remler2e** to

- test your knowledge with the self-quiz
- check your understanding of key terms with the eFlashcards
- explore helpful resources that relate directly to this chapter

How much does taxing cigarettes reduce smoking?

Source: © iStockphoto.com/ozgurdonmaz.

Objectives: Building on the understanding of observational studies developed in the previous chapter, this chapter explains the use of regression analysis to estimate causal effects. Regression analysis allows researchers great flexibility to include a variety of control variables that, if chosen thoughtfully, can reduce common cause bias in observational studies. Despite important limitations, it is perhaps the most common approach to causation found in nearly all areas of social and policy research. The aim of the chapter is to provide a largely intuitive, nontechnical introduction to this important topic—while at the same time giving sufficient statistical details to help guide the practice of regression analysis in your own research. Importantly, the chapter also aims to help you understand and evaluate regression-based evidence of causation in published studies. In addition, we provide an introduction to more advanced, multivariate matching techniques, which are becoming an increasingly important extension of and alternative to regression analysis.

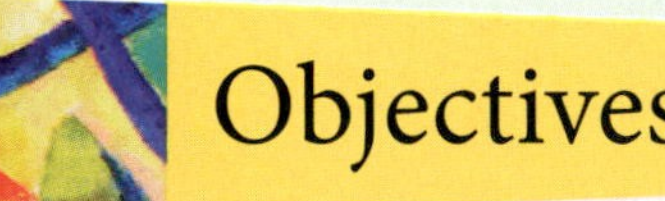

Objectives

Learning Objectives

After reading this chapter, you should be able to

- Explain how regression can be used for both description (prediction) and causal estimation, and recognize the difference
- Explain how regression can be used to control for many variables at once, and to control for quantitative as well as categorical variables
- Interpret regression coefficients as causal effects in terms useful for policy and practice—while recognizing and articulating caveats and weaknesses as causal effect estimates
- Recognize multivariate matching methods and the situations in which they are valuable

13 Using Regression to Estimate Causal Effects

Cigarette Taxes and Smoking

Many people—especially young people—will quit or reduce smoking when the government imposes high taxes on cigarettes, raising prices. Reduced rates of smoking, in turn, can improve health, save lives, and even decrease some medical costs. As a result, state governments in the United States have increased cigarette taxes dramatically, from just a few cents a pack in the 1970s to well over $2 a pack in 2011 (Centers for Disease Control and Prevention, 2013b). The initial causal evidence linking taxes and smoking came from observational studies like the one published by Lewit and Coate (1982) in the *Journal of Health Economics,* which eventually had a large influence on tax and health policy in the United States and Canada (Kennedy School of Government, 1993). Using data from a national health survey—observational data—together with information on local cigarette taxes, Lewit and Coate did a series of regression analyses to estimate the causal effect of cigarette prices on smoking behavior. In their analyses, they controlled statistically for individual characteristics that might influence smoking and be correlated with local cigarette prices, such as family income, family size, education, age, sex, race, marital status, and health status, and they controlled for different regions of the country and for the size of the local community. Having adjusted for these variables, they estimated that a 10% increase in the price of cigarettes would lead to a 4% decline in smoking—a large causal effect.

In this chapter, you will learn how regression analyses like these can be used to estimate causal effects with only observational (nonexperimental) data. But you will also learn about the limitations of this strategy and about the need to remain cautious in making causal conclusions. Still, thoughtful regression analyses can and do often provide important insights about the origins of and solutions to many of our most pressing social problems and policy issues.

From Stratification to Multiple Regression

In the previous chapter, we illustrated the control variable strategy using stratification because it is a familiar method and relatively straightforward to explain and interpret. But in most social and policy studies, researchers use *multiple regression* (of one kind or another) to control statistically for potential common causes that may produce bias. Multiple regression handles several of the important limitations we encountered in the last chapter with stratification, such as needing to use more than one or two control variables at a time and handling quantitative (noncategorical) variables. In the cigarette tax study by Lewit and Coate (1982), for example, they controlled for at least 10 variables, and their main independent variable (Price) and several of their control variables (Family Income, Family Size, and Age) were quantitative variables with many values.

Using More Than One (or Two) Control Variables

Smoking behavior is influenced by many things—a person's age, education, income, gender, and marital status, as well as by the characteristics of the community he or she lives in. When trying to isolate the causal effect of just one factor, such as attitudes toward smoking, all of these other variables must be controlled for—*at the same time.* Stratifying the data by more than two or three of these control variables would soon make the results nearly impossible to interpret. Stratification by many variables can also be imprecise because each of the many resulting subgroups yields so little data.

Multiple regression can incorporate many control variables at the same time. In effect, the impact of one independent variable is measured, holding all the control variables constant. Mathematically, multiple regression treats the independent variable of interest and the control variables in exactly the same way—they are all just "independent variables" in the regression equation. It is the researcher's choice to focus on just one of these variables as an estimate of a causal effect—an independent variable in the causal (or experimental) sense. This contrasts with the use of multiple regression purely for prediction or description, as described in Chapter 10.

Control Variables That Are Quantitative

Is there another control variable you think should be added to learn the effect of cigarette prices on smoking?

Age (in years) and Income (in dollars) are quantitative variables. If Lewit and Coate (1982) had used stratification to control for these variables, they would have needed to break their data into age and income groups—in other words, collapse the many values into categorical variables. Let's say they created two age-groups, "Over 40" and "40 and Under," and perhaps also two income groups, "Above Average Income" and "Below Average Income." But within these groups, age and income would still vary quite a bit. The supposedly comparable groups created by stratification into two groups are not, in fact, completely comparable in age or income. To really control for these variables, the researchers would need to consider the full range of variation in age and income.

The same point applies to their independent variable of interest: cigarette prices. If Lewit and Coate had to rely on stratification, they would need to categorize cigarette prices also, perhaps into just two (High, Low) or three (High, Medium, Low) price categories. But again there is interesting variation within these price categories, and ultimately the study aimed to estimate how changes in price as a quantitative variable related to changes in smoking behavior. Multiple regression is not limited to categorical independent variables only and thus accommodates the full range of quantitative variables in an analysis.

From Description to Causation: The Education-Earnings Link Reconsidered

When using multiple regression to implement a control variable strategy, there is a tendency to get wrapped up in the technicalities even though the conceptual issues and context, as described in the previous chapter, matter most. For this reason, we have thus far separated the statistical aspects of regression (in Part III, especially Chapter 10) from the conceptual aspects of using control variables for causal research (in Chapter 12), so that each could have its due and not cloud the other. We are now in a position to put the two more closely together.

To do so, we continue with the education and annual earnings example with National Longitudinal Survey of Youth (NLSY) data from the previous chapter. We first examine that relationship with simple regression, a best-fit straight line: An *independent variable* (x) predicts a *dependent variable* (y). Figure 13.1 shows a scatterplot of the data and the regression line fitted from the data,[1] which is described by the coefficient of education (or slope) and the constant (or intercept). In this example, the constant is −$47,113, and the coefficient of education is $6,268/year (i.e., $6,268 per year), or, in equation form,

$$\text{Earnings} = -\$47{,}113 + \$6{,}268/\text{year} \times \text{Education}.$$

The formulas used to determine the coefficient and constant were given in Chapter 8.

(You probably noticed that the data in Figure 13.1 look a bit strange: so many data points at exactly $236,000 of earnings but none above $130,000. The reason is *top-coding:* To protect the privacy of participants in the NLSY, any earnings greater than $130,000 are top-coded at the average of all earnings above that value, $236,000.)

We were careful in Part III (Chapters 8–10) to use regression results such as this only for *prediction* (or description) and not as evidence of *causation*. Simple regression—regression with one independent variable (as in this example)—is, after all, essentially another form of correlation. Thus, we were careful not to say, for example, that if someone got one more year of education, we would expect that person to earn $6,268 more *as a result*.

Figure 13.1 Simple Regression of Earnings on Education (NLSY, 2002)

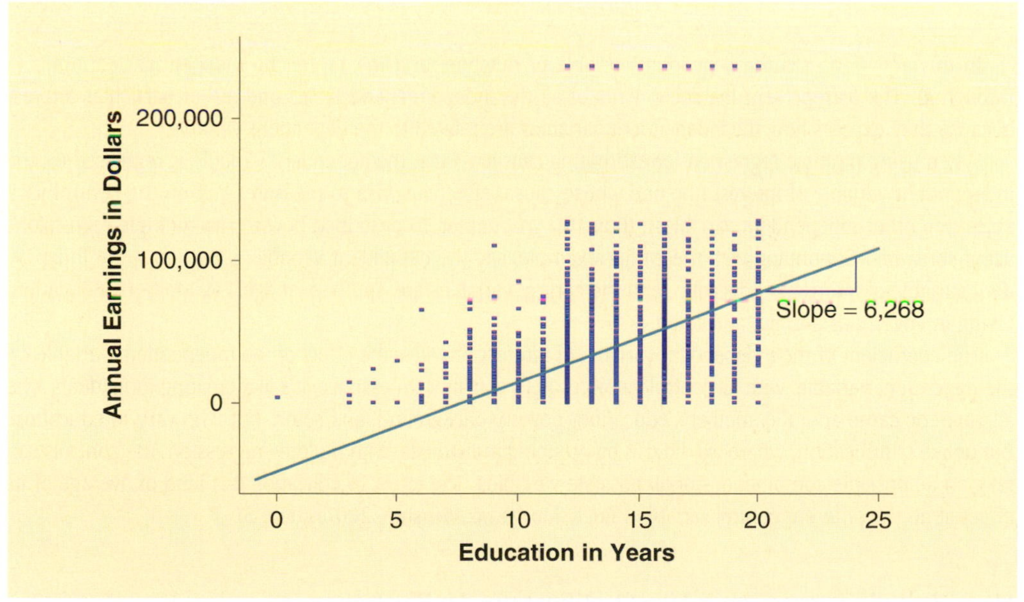

[1]Experienced readers may be concerned that Earnings are not normally distributed and that we should therefore log Earnings. By using unlogged earnings, we will not fit the data as well, and our inference results, such as p values and standard errors, are not accurate. Almost any published study would use log earnings, but unlogged earnings are easier for explaining concepts, and therefore we use them here. See Chapter 10 for the interpretation of coefficients with logged variables.

When x Is Exogenous, Regressions Estimate Causal Effects

QUESTION

Why does a lottery for private school vouchers make Private School exogenous? Why would exogenous Private School allow us to estimate the causal effect of Private School in a regression?

In many situations, like the question of cigarette taxes and smoking or education and earnings, we would very much like to use regression to make such counterfactual claims. And we can—when the independent variable is exogenous. If education were exogenously determined, assigned through the toss of a coin and without any self-selection, we could interpret the slope causally. This would be an exogenous push or intervention, as we described in Chapter 11, and therefore, it would enable us to trace out the causal consequences. Therefore, we could honestly tell a large group of people that if they all got one more year of education, their earnings would rise by an average of \$6,268.

Although it is a rare occurrence, every now and then such variables do turn out to be exogenous in the real world. Governments run lotteries to award limited school vouchers or health insurance coverage, for example. We will learn how to identify and use such situations, referred to as *natural experiments,* in Chapter 15. But in most cases, unfortunately, it is extremely unlikely that our independent variable of interest, for example, Education, is in fact exogenous. To interpret regression coefficients causally—to tell people how much more they can expect to earn with more education (the counterfactual)—we need to add all the right control variables. And to do that, we need to go beyond simple regression to multiple regression.

Multiple Regression: Brief Overview and Interpretation

Multiple regression predicts or explains a dependent variable (y) using several independent variables (x_1, x_2, and so on), as explained also in Chapter 10. It is a direct extension of simple regression, but with two or more (sometimes many more) independent variables:

$$y = a + b_1x_1 + b_2x_2 + \dots b_kx_k$$

In this equation, y is the dependent variable or outcome and the xs are the independent variables (1 through k). The bs represent the coefficients of all the independent variables and are of particular interest because they express how the independent variables are related to the dependent variable.[2]

When using multiple regression for estimating causal effects, the dependent variable is regressed on the independent variable of interest (the one whose causal effect we wish to measure) and on the control variables (the other independent variables). (Box 10.1 in Chapter 10 described how to run multiple regressions using software.) Continuing with the earlier example, say the dependent variable is Earnings, the independent variable of interest is Education, and the control variables are Aptitude (at age 14), Mother's Education, Living in Poverty as a Child, and so on.

The coefficient of the independent variable of interest provides the effect of the independent variable on the dependent variable, with all control variables held constant. In essence, it's like creating individuals who all have the same aptitude, mother's education, poverty background, and so on, but who vary in education. But unlike stratification, where we did this by grouping individuals, with multiple regression, the controls can take on all possible combinations of all possible variables. The effect of education is a kind of average of its effect at all the different control variable values (Morgan & Winship, 2007, chap. 5).

How Multiple Regression Is Like Stratification: An Illustration

Figure 13.1 illustrates a simple regression of Earnings on Education with no controls, Earnings = a + b_{Ed} Education. Because Education is not exogenous, however, we cannot interpret b_{Ed} as the causal effect of one more year of education, as we would like to. This is the same problem that we had in the naive

[2]Recall from Chapter 10 that the coefficients, such as b_1, multiply the independent variables, such as x_1. Placing them right next to one another implies multiplication.

comparison in the last chapter, in Table 12.1, but now we are not just comparing two educational categories—we are looking across all the possible values that the quantitative variable Years of Education can take on.

Now, we will control for Aptitude by stratifying the regression, just as we stratified the comparison of means earlier, using a categorical high aptitude variable indicating the top third of aptitude scores. We will run one regression with the high aptitude portion of the data and another regression with the lower aptitude portion of the data. The two resulting regressions, one for high aptitude and one for lower aptitude, are illustrated in Figure 13.2.

The slopes of the stratified regressions, shown in Figure 13.2, are now \$6,876/year for High Aptitude and \$3,561/year for Not High Aptitude. The Not High Aptitude slope is notably less than the slope of the original unstratified regression, \$6,268/year, shown in Figure 13.1. We can see that much of the original apparent effect of education was due to the individuals in the High Aptitude group.

This result is similar to what we saw in the last chapter, in Table 12.3, in which controlling for aptitude reduced the initial \$32,000 effect to \$27,800 for the High Aptitude group and to \$18,700 for the Not High Aptitude group. In both cases, stratifying by the aptitude indictor variable dramatically reduced the magnitude of the apparent effect of education on earnings for the Not High Aptitude group.

Multiple regression is basically the same idea, but it is not mathematically equivalent.[3] Consider the multiple regression equation Earnings = $a + b_{Ed}$Education + b_{apt}Aptitude. The variable Aptitude is now a quantitative score, not just two groups defined by having high and low aptitude. The multiple regression works by essentially estimating the effect of education on earnings for many different aptitude levels represented by the quantitative score. So unlike when we stratified, we can now take advantage of the full range of variation in aptitude scores. (We described what multiple regression estimates somewhat more fully in Chapter 10.)

How do the stratified regressions compare with the multiple regression? The effect of Education in the multiple regression, b_{Ed}, depends on the effect of Education at many different levels of Aptitude. Very roughly,

Figure 13.2 Regressions Stratified by High Aptitude Variable (NLSY, 2002)

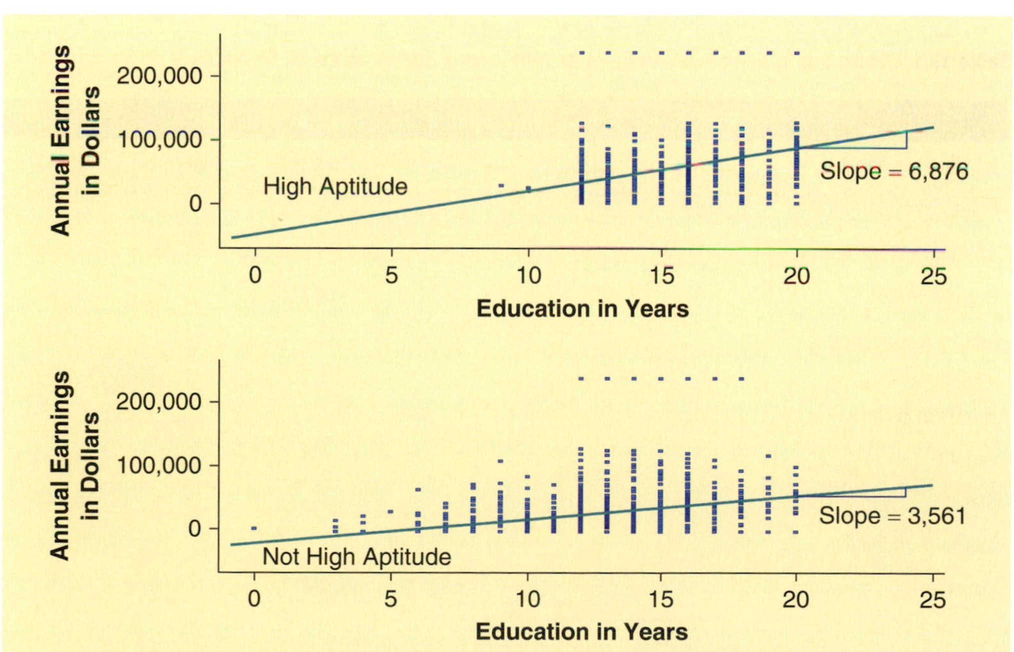

[3]It would be literally equivalent if the test score variable was simply a categorical variable with the two categories of *high test score* and *lower test score* and if the multiple regression was estimated with the additional independent variable of an interaction between the high test score variable and Education.

QUESTION

Explain how both stratification and multiple regression can be used to "hold other variables constant."

the effect of Education estimated in a multiple regression is some kind of combination of the two b_{Ed}s from the stratified regressions. In fact, putting the quantitative variable Aptitude in as a control variable results in an Education coefficient of $4,135/year (see Table 13.1).

Specification: How the Choice of Control Variables Influences Regression Results

In multiple regression, the estimated effect of an independent variable of interest depends a great deal on which control variables are used. We illustrate this in Table 13.1, which shows the results with different combinations of control variables, or different **specifications**, in adjacent columns—a common method of presenting such results.

Let's begin by considering how these regression results compare with our initial results using stratification. Specification 1 shows the regression estimate of the effect of having a college education on earnings, which is $32,000—the same difference we obtained from simple comparison of means. Notice also that the constant is $29,515, which is the average earnings of those without a college degree. The average earnings of those with a college degree is $29,500 + $32,000 = $61,500. Again, this is the same initial result we obtained in the last chapter (see Table 12.1). But with regression, we can now look at the effect of Education (in years)—a variable with more range, more variation. Specification 2 shows this effect, which is $6,268 ($p$ value $< .001$)[4] more in earnings for each year of education completed. This is the same slope as in Figure 13.1.

Now, we can begin to add control variables. In Specification 3, we include an aptitude score from the person's youth as a control variable. As a result, the coefficient of Education becomes $4,135/year, while the coefficient of Aptitude itself is $297/point. Thus, Aptitude was an omitted variable in Specification 1, and

Table 13.1 Coefficients in Regressions of Earnings With Various Specifications (NLSY, 2002)

	Spec 1	Spec 2	Spec 3	Spec 4	Spec 5	Spec 6
Education (years)		6,268**	4,135**	4,962**	4,042**	4,847**
College graduate or not	32,000**					
Aptitude (AFQT score)			297**		286**	208**
High aptitude				13,027**		
Mother's education (years)					363*	323
Family in poverty						969
Female						−25,735**
Black						−3,447
Mother a manager						2,714
Constant	29,500**	−47,113**	−32,686**	−33,833**	−35,108**	−28,163**

Notes: $^{**}p < .01$; $^{*}p < .05$; dependent variable is Earnings (in dollars) in 2002; AFQT, Armed Forces Qualification Test.

[4]Recall again, as explained in Footnote 1, that because Earnings are skewed and we did not use the log of Earnings as the dependent variable, the assumptions needed for inference are not well met and so p values may not be accurate.

the coefficient in the simple regression suffered from omitted variable bias. The bias from omitting Aptitude is large—controlling for it reduces the Education coefficient from $6,268/year to $4,135/year.

These multiple regression results are analogous to Table 12.3 (the stratification results) in the last chapter, but they make use of the full range of variation of both Education and Aptitude. To give some sense of what is lost with just stratification, consider what happens when instead of using Aptitude itself as a control variable in multiple regression, we use the dummy variable indicating high aptitude scores. In that case, the coefficient of Education only drops to $4,962/year, rather than to $4,135/year (Specification 4 of Table 13.1).

Adding More Control Variables

A major advantage of multiple regression over stratification is that many control variables can be used at the same time. What happens if we include both Aptitude and Mother's Education as control variables? Now, the coefficient of Education drops a bit more, to $4,042/year (Specification 5). As we saw in stratification, Mother's Education creates some omitted variable bias, but not nearly as much as Aptitude.

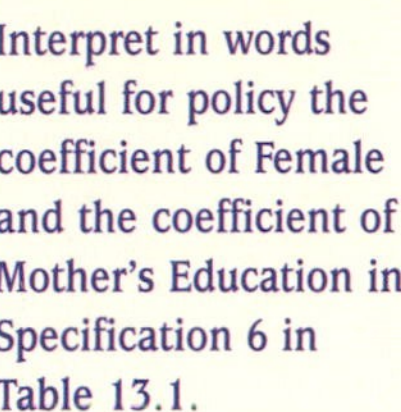

QUESTION

Interpret in words useful for policy the coefficient of Female and the coefficient of Mother's Education in Specification 6 in Table 13.1.

With multiple regression, as we have just seen, it is possible to add lots of control variables at the same time. Suppose we add controls for Mother's Education, Poverty Status of Family in Youth, Gender, Race, and Mother Having a Managerial Career, arguably all common causes or proxies for complex common causes. The coefficient of Education actually climbs back somewhat, to $4,874/year (Specification 6). This illustrates how our estimate of the effect of education on earnings depends, crucially, on the availability and choice of control variables.

What About Unmeasured Variables?

QUESTION

Is there an additional variable you would like to add as a control to the regression of Education on Earnings? How hard would it be to find a measure of that variable in existing data sets?

Even if researchers control for every relevant variable they can lay their hands on, and even if the full range of variation of the variables is used, multiple regression does *not* solve the problem of *unmeasured variables* and the omitted variable bias it can cause. A multiple regression study is not unbiased just because it has controls—it must have all the relevant common causes as controls and no others. The best solution is to investigate what drives the independent variable and go out and obtain measures for all candidate control variables. However, even with more limited variables, multiple regression does provide some tools for investigating the effects of control variables, as we have just seen in the section on adding and removing controls.

To practice these ideas—and to get a better feel for interpreting multiple regression results—we turn next to an example of a pair of published studies in which multiple regression is used to answer a causal question.

The Effect of Breast-Feeding on Intelligence: Is There a Causal Connection?

The effects of breast-feeding are of substantial medical, public health, and public policy interest. There are highly plausible mechanisms through which breast-feeding could influence an infant's healthy development, and studies support this idea. Interest has grown in demonstrating the long-term effects of breast-feeding on many outcomes, including intelligence. Many of the early studies that related breast-feeding to intelligence were based on naive interpretations of simple associations. Those studies were criticized for not controlling for potential common causes, such as the mother's education. Mothers with more education are more likely to breast-feed, so the studies could potentially be biased due to the common cause of mother's education.[5]

To address such concerns, Mortensen, Michaelsen, Sanders, and Reinsch (2002) examined the relationship between the duration of breast-feeding and adult intelligence (of the breast-fed child), with Duration of Breast-Feeding as the independent variable. The control variables were Education and Social Status of

[5]In medicine and public health, *confounding* is the most common term for omitted variable bias. See Box 12.1.

Parents; Single-Mother Status; Mother Height, Age, and Weight Gain During Pregnancy; Cigarette Consumption; Number of Pregnancies; Estimated Gestational Age; Birth Weight; Birth Length; and indexes of pregnancy and delivery complications.

Mortensen et al. found that, even after adding all these controls, the relationship between breast-feeding duration and adult intelligence was both statistically significant and of reasonable practical magnitude. Consistent with the earlier studies, this was evidence that breast-feeding boosts (causes) intelligence.

Other researchers, however, challenged that result as still suffering from omitted variable bias. To illustrate such bias as well as how to read and interpret a control variable study implemented through multiple regression, we trace in detail a later study by Der, Batty, and Deary (2006) that challenged studies such as those of Mortensen et al. (2002).

Step 1: Speculate on Common Causes

Remember that Step 1 of a control variable study involves using theory, common sense, and other evidence to think of any and all possible common causes. It is important to be aggressive in speculating about potential bias due to unmeasured variables. Der et al. (2006) thought that the controls used by Mortensen et al. (2002) and others still missed important common causes. In particular, they were familiar with the large literature on the heritability (genetic correlation) of intelligence. Mother's education was probably related but not a sufficient proxy and a different variable.

So Der et al. (2006) decided to do a study that would include the mother's score on an aptitude test (the Armed Forces Qualification Test [AFQT]) as a control. They used the NLSY, the same data that we have used to illustrate the relationship between education and earnings. Their dependent variables were several different aptitude tests taken by the children at various ages. The main independent variable of interest was whether or not the mother breast-fed the child.

QUESTION

Is there another variable you would like to add to Table 13.2, to see if it differs among breast-feeding and not breast-feeding mothers and their babies? Explain why. What difference do you predict?

Step 2: Examine the Relationship Between the Independent Variable of Interest and Potential Common Causes

Step 2 of a control variable study is to examine the relationship between the independent variable of interest and the potential common causes. Der et al. (2006) do this in Table 1 of their paper, reproduced as Table 13.2. Notice, for example, that the mean AFQT score was about 26 for mothers who did not breast-feed as compared with about 46 for mothers who did. The difference is statistically significant at $p < .001$. (The difference is also presented as an odds ratio, which is common in medical research.) The practical magnitude of the 20-point difference is quite large—it is close to 1 standard deviation. To look at another difference, the poverty rates differ dramatically, with about 36% of families in poverty among mothers who do not breast-feed as compared with a poverty rate of about 16% among those who do. Again, the difference is strongly statistically significant. Indeed, all the differences in Table 13.2 are statistically significant, except for male infant and gestation in weeks. Many of these differences, such as the poverty rate difference, also appear practically significant.

Step 3: Implement Control Variables Through Multiple Regression

The third step of a control variable study is to implement the control variable and observe the effect of the independent variable on the dependent variable, holding constant all the controls.

Whether or not the child was breast-fed is a dummy variable. As discussed in Chapter 10, the coefficient of a dummy variable is the difference in the average value of the dependent variable between those with and those without the characteristic. In this case, the coefficient of Breast-Feeding reveals the difference in average test score between children who were breast-fed and those who were not, holding constant all the control variables. Ideally, the coefficient of Breast-Feeding will reveal the difference between breast-feeding and its counterfactual—and thus the causal effect of breast-feeding.

Der et al. (2006) performed a multiple regression using all the control variables that had statistically significant differences in Table 13.2 but not those with statistically insignificant differences. In contrast to that practice, some researchers believe that all variables theorized to have an effect should be included in the regression, not just those with statistically significant differences or effects. They worry about data mining and its potential to find chance correlations that happen to be in the data.

The multiple regression results are shown in Table 13.3. The four columns, marked PIAT, Maths, and so on, refer to four dependent variables—the total (composite) test taken by the children and its individual

Table 13.2 Association of Potential Confounders With Breast-Feeding

Confounder	Not Breast-Fed		Breast-Fed		Odds Ratio* (95% Confidence Interval)	*p* Value
	Mean *(SD)* or %	No	Mean *(SD)* or %	No		
Mother's AFQT score	26.24 (22.33)	3,001	46.44 (27.76)	2,701	2.30 (2.16 to 2.44)	< 0.001
Mother's education	11.50 (2.14)	3,119	12.79 (2.48)	2,819	1.83 (1.73 to 1.95)	< 0.001
Mother's age	23.83 (4.50)	3,125	25.79 (4.64)	2,823	1.55 (1.47 to 1.64)	< 0.001
HOME cognitive stimulation	94.09 (16.62)	2,844	101.00 (14.26)	2,620	1.59 (1.50 to 1.69)	< 0.001
HOME emotional support	95.18 (16.54)	2,791	100.67 (14.45)	2,601	1.44 (1.36 to 1.52)	< 0.001
Gestation (weeks)	39.05 (1.58)	3,125	39.01 (1.55)	2,823	0.97 (0.93 to 1.03)	0.315
Birth weight (g)	3,390 (47)	3,125	3,470 (47)	2,823	1.21 (1.15 to 1.27)	< 0.001
Birth order	1.97 (1.07)	3,125	1.85 (1.02)	2,823	0.90 (0.85 to 0.94)	< 0.001
Family in poverty†	36.4%	3,108	15.8%	2,817	0.33 (0.29 to 0.37)	< 0.001
Mother smoked in pregnancy†	35.7%	3,120	25.6%	2,816	0.62 (0.55 to 0.69)	< 0.001
Male infant†	51.7%	3,125	50.6%	2,823	0.96 (0.87 to 1.06	0.413
Hispanic††	49.4%	615	50.6%	630	0.72 (0.63 to 0.82)	< 0.001
Black††	74.9%	1,264	25.1%	423	0.24 (0.21 to 0.27)	< 0.001
Not Black/ Hispanic††	41.3%	1,246	58.7%	1,770	1.00	

AFQT = Armed Forces Qualification Test; HOME = home observation of the environment.

†Odds ratios for breast-feeding are per 1 *SD* of mother's AFQT score, education, age, HOME scores, gestation, and birth weight.

††Reference groups are family not in poverty, mother did not smoke in pregnancy, female.

*Row percentage.

Source: Reproduced from "Effect of breast feeding on intelligence in children: prospective study, sibling pairs analysis, and meta-analysis." Der, Geoff, G David Batty, and Ian J Deary. 2006. With permission from BMJ Publishing Group Ltd.

Table 13.3 Mutually Adjusted Effects of Breast-Feeding and Confounders on Cognitive Outcomes in 3,161 Mothers, 5,475 Children, and 16,744 Assessments

	PIAT-Total		Maths*		Reading*		-	
Confounder	**B (*SE*)**	***p***	**B (*SE*)**	***p***	**B (*SE*)**	***p***	**B (*SE*)**	***p***
Breast-feeding	0.52 (0.36)	0.149	0.52 (0.34)	0.130	0.36 (0.37)	0.332	0.52 (0.35)	0.134
Mother's AFQT score	4.43 (0.26)	< 0.001	3.87 (0.25)	< 0.001	3.77 (0.27)	<0.001	3.97 (0.25)	< 0.001
Mother's education	1.03 (0.24)	< 0.001	1.10 (0.23)	< 0.001	0.96 (0.25)	< 0.001	0.62 (0.23)	0.007
Family in poverty	– 1.72 (0.41)	< 0.001	– 0.98 (0.39)	0.012	– 1.70 (0.42)	< 0.001	– 1.82 (0.39)	< 0.001
Mother's age	0.98 (0.20)	< 0.001	0.72 (0.19)	< 0.001	1.05 (0.20)	< 0.001	0.69 (0.19)	< 0.001
Mother smoked in pregnancy	0.08 (0.38)	0.839	0.37 (0.36)	0.305	– 0.11 (0.39)	0.771	0.14 (0.36	0.694
HOME cognitive stimulation	0.83 (0.10)	< 0.001	0.78 (0.12)	< 0.001	0.79 (0.11)	< 0.001	1.13 (0.12)	< 0.001
HOME emotional support	0.17 (0.09)	0.072	0.25 (0.11)	0.020	0.15 (0.10)	0.120	0.14 (0.11)	0.200
Birth weight	0.32 (0.16)	0.047	0.40 (0.15)	0.010	0.20 (0.17)	0.234	0.25 (0.16)	0.113
Birth order	– 1.54 (0.18)	< 0.001	– 0.79 (0.17)	< 0.001	– 1.47 (0.19)	< 0.001	– 1.69 (0.18)	< 0.001
Hispanic	– 0.36 (0.52)	0.494	– 1.85 (0.49)	< 0.001	0.33 (0.53)	0.534	0.48 (0.49)	0.329
Black	– 0.90 (0.50)	0.074	– 2.79 (0.47)	< 0.001	0.54 (0.52)	0.299	– 0.03 (0.48)	0.950

PIAT= Peabody Individual Achievement Test; AFQT = Armed Forces Qualification Test; HOME = home observation for measurement of the environment.

*Individual components of PIAT.

Source: Reproduced from "Effect of breast feeding on intelligence in children: prospective study, sibling pairs analysis, and meta-analysis." Der, Geoff, G David Batty, and Ian J Deary. 2006. With permission from BMJ Publishing Group Ltd.

components. We will focus on the PIAT total for our detailed exploration. The coefficient column (marked *B*) refers to the coefficient of the variable listed. For example, the coefficient of Breast-Feeding is 0.52, the coefficient of Mother's AFQT Score is 4.43, and the coefficient of Mother Smoked in Pregnancy is 0.08.

Next to the coefficients, their standard errors are given in parentheses. For example, the standard error of the Breast-Feeding coefficient is 0.36, and the standard error of the Mother's AFQT Score coefficient is 0.26. The standard error provides information about the sampling error in the coefficient—information about the lack of precision due to sampling. Next to the coefficients and standard errors are *p* values associated with a test of whether or not the coefficient is 0—no relationship between that variable and the child's intelligence test score.

How to Interpret Multiple Regression Coefficients: Effects of Controls

Next, we practice interpreting multiple regression results by first focusing on the effects of the control variables—effects that are not our main interest. The coefficient of Family in Poverty is −1.72 points. Remember to pay attention to the units of any coefficient. The coefficient of a dummy variable has the units of the dependent variable—the points of the PIAT, in this case. The Family in Poverty coefficient shows that being in poverty lowers a child's score on the PIAT by 1.72 points, holding constant all the other variables, including Breast-Feeding. The coefficient of Poverty is statistically significant, with a *p* value of < .001, ruling out chance as an explanation of the magnitude of the effect. Finally, we should examine the practical significance of the effect of Poverty—a 1.72-point decline is not that big relative to a standard deviation of 15 points, but it is not nothing, either. In any multiple regression study, the coefficients of all the control variables should be examined to make sure that their sign and magnitude are plausible.

What of the effect of Mother's AFQT Score, the variable omitted from prior studies? It was strongly statistically significant ($p < .001$). To interpret its magnitude practically, we need to know that AFQT was measured in terms of its standard deviation.[6] So the coefficient shows that a 1 standard deviation increase in a mother's AFQT score results in a 4.43-point increase in her child's PIAT score—almost a third of a standard deviation increase, quite a large effect.

How to Interpret Multiple Regression Coefficients: Effect of Interest

Now, we turn to the coefficient of interest, the coefficient of Breast-Feeding. Its coefficient is 0.52 points. First, note that it is not statistically significant—the *p* value is .149, well above the conventional threshold of .05 and even well above .10. Recalling from Chapter 9 how to interpret a *p* value, we see that there is about a 15% chance that we could have gotten the .52-point effect or something of greater magnitude even if, in fact, there was no effect of Breast-Feeding on Intelligence. So the estimated Breast-Feeding effect could be due to just chance in who got sampled.

Even if a result is not statistically significant, it is important to examine the practical significance of the upper and lower bounds of the confidence intervals. Recall from Chapter 9 that a statistically insignificant result with a small standard error (i.e., a narrow confidence interval) could be quite informative and reveal that the study definitively ruled out a practically significant effect.

A 95% confidence interval is roughly 2 standard errors in either direction from the estimated effect. In this case, we are 95% confident that the effect of Breast-Feeding on PIAT Score is somewhere between $.52 - 2 \times .36 = -0.20$ points and $.52 + 2 \times .36 = 1.24$ points. Compared with the effect of Mother's AFQT Score or Education, the effect of Breast-Feeding is small in a practical sense. We can conclude that, controlling for Mother's AFQT Score and the other controls, Breast-Feeding does not have any effect on Intelligence.

[6]In Der et al. (2006), the effects of all quantitative (nondummy) variables were measured in terms of standard deviations. This is similar to having a partially standardized coefficient; standardized coefficients were discussed in Chapter 10.

QUESTION

Explain in ordinary language why the coefficient of Breast-Feeding was biased without controls.

Adding and Removing Controls: What Can Be Learned?

Since prior studies that did not have mother's aptitude test score as a control found substantial effects of breast-feeding on intelligence, it is important to understand the relationship between those results and this one. More generally, understanding the mechanism of an effect is valuable. Examining how coefficients change as controls are added and removed can help shed light on this issue.

Table 13.4 shows the coefficient of Breast-Feeding (and its standard error) from several separate regressions. The top row, marked *Unadjusted,* shows the effect of Breast-Feeding on PIAT Score, without any control

Table 13.4 Effect of Breast-Feeding on Cognitive Outcomes, Unadjusted and Adjusted Singly for Each Confounder, in 3,161 Mothers, 5,475 Children, and 16,744 Assessments

	PIAT—Total		Maths*		Reading*		Comprehension*	
	B (SE)	%†	B (SE)	%†	B (SE)	%†	B (SE)	%†
Unadjusted	4.69 (0.38)		4.65 (0.36)		4.09 (0.38)		4.22 (0.36)	
Adjusted for:								
Mother's AFQT score	1.30 (0.36)	72	1.30 (0.34)	72	1.02 (0.37)††	75	1.21 (0.35)	71
Mother's education	2.95 (0.37)	37	3.06 (0.35)	34	2.38 (0.37)	42	2.69 (0.35)	36
Family in poverty	3.94 (0.38)	16	3.96 (0.36)	15	3.30 (0.37)	19	3.46 (0.35)	18
Mother's age	4.29 (0.38)	9	4.18 (0.36)	10	3.64 (0.38)	11	3.96 (0.36)	6
Mother smoked in pregnancy	4.60 (0.38)	2	4.60 (0.36)	1	3.98 (0.38)	3	4.14 (0.36)	2
HOME cognitive stimulation	4.29 (0.37)	8	4.20 (0.35)	10	3.66 (0.37)	10	3.64 (0.35)	14
HOME emotional support	4.57 (0.38)	3	4.47 (0.36)	4	3.96 (0.38)	3	4.06 (0.36)	4
Birth weight	4.60 (0.38)	2	4.52 (0.36)	3	4.02 (0.38)	2	4.15 (0.36)	2
Birth order	4.55 (0.38)	3	4.57 (0.36)	2	3.94 (0.37)	4	4.01 (0.35)	5
Race	3.65 (0.38)	22	3.30 (0.36)	29	3.32 (0.39)	19	3.34 (0.37)	21

Note: All significant at $p < .001$ except where marked.

PIAT = Peabody Individual Achievement Test; AFQT = Armed Forces Qualification Test; HOME = home observation for measurement of the environment.

*Individual components of PIAT.

†Percentage of unadjusted figure.

††p = 0.006.

Source: Reproduced from "Effect of breast feeding on intelligence in children: prospective study, sibling pairs analysis, and meta-analysis." Der, Geoff, G David Batty, and Ian J Deary. 2006. With permission from BMJ Publishing Group Ltd.

variables. The biased naive estimate of the effect of Breast-Feeding on PIAT Score is about 4.7 points. The rows beneath the unadjusted effect all show the coefficient of Breast-Feeding with a different *single* control variable. For example, for the PIAT, the coefficient of Breast-Feeding when Mother's AFQT Score is a control is reduced to 1.30 points. This represents a reduction of 72% relative to the unadjusted coefficient of about 4.7 points. That percent reduction is also shown next to each coefficient and its standard error. The percent effect of Mother's AFQT Score is greater than that of any other control variable used individually.

The findings of prior studies can be understood by examining the effect of Mother's Education used as a single control. In that case, the effect of Mother's Education on PIAT Score is estimated to be 2.96 points per year, almost three times its estimated effect when Mother's AFQT Score is also used as a control. That contrast reveals that Mother's AFQT Score apparently drives both Mother's Education and Child's Aptitude Test Score.

Notice that in this study, the authors first presented the results with only one control (Der et al., 2006, Table 2) at a time *before* the full results with all the controls. We might wonder why they did that, since a great advantage of multiple regression as a means of implementing control variables is precisely its ability to implement many controls at once, and they had reason to believe that all were important. We can speculate that they probably did this for several reasons. First, they were addressing a literature that had found substantial effects, and they wanted to illustrate that Mother's AFQT Score was an important variable and that, without it, Mother's Education seemed very important. Second, in the medical and public health literatures, stratification is a common form of control variable analysis, particularly layered cross-tabs, and so they wanted to present evidence in a form familiar and understandable to their audience. In Chapter 17, we discuss such choices in presenting research results.

More generally, the point is that much can be learned by seeing results with and without certain controls. This can show us how much each variable's omission biased the original correlation, and in what direction. In addition, each specification sheds light on a somewhat different question. For example, the last chapter discussed a mediation analysis in which you specifically seek to probe the share of a causal effect due to a particular intervening variable. Suppose that we believed that breast-feeding boosts intelligence because it increases emotional attachment. If so, we might try specifications with, and without, a variable measuring emotional attachment and interpret the difference in results as a gauge of how much of the breast-feeding effect it explained (or mediated) by emotional attachment.

Technical Complexities

The actual Der et al. (2006) study differed from the usual straightforward multiple regression study in one respect. The NLSY has multiple observations of the children's test scores, and the researchers wanted to take advantage of the statistical power these observations provided. However, clearly, multiple observations of the same child are not unrelated; they are correlated. Moreover, mothers often had more than one child, and presumably, siblings are correlated. Therefore, the researchers had to use a more advanced technique that adjusted the standard errors for these various correlations. (This issue was discussed in Chapter 9.)

Notice, however, that it was possible to understand and interpret many of the main results of the paper without knowing anything about this technical complexity. Provided you, as a reader, are able to trust that the authors got their technical details right, you can focus on the part that interests you and make real use of the results. In Chapter 17, we discuss issues such as peer review and journal prestige that can provide some assurance that technical matters were probably handled correctly.

QUESTION

Can you think of a reason why controlling for whether the mother smoked did not have a large effect on the Breast-Feeding coefficient (it changed from 4.69 to 4.60 in Table 13.4)?

Further Topics in Regression for Estimating Causal Effects

Now that you've become more familiar with the control variables strategy using multiple regression, there are a few further topics to consider in both interpreting and implementing this approach.

Possible Effects of Adding Control Variables

In the breast-feeding study, adding Mother's AFQT Score as a control variable *eliminated* the effect of breast-feeding on the child's cognitive outcomes. In the earlier example of earnings and education, controlling for aptitude score *reduced* the magnitude of the effect of education—but did not eliminate it.

Adding control variables can have two other types of effects, although they are less frequent. A control variable could *increase* the magnitude of the effect of the independent variable of interest. Or a control variable could *reverse* the sign or direction of the effect of the independent variable of interest. It all depends on the magnitude and sign of the effect of the control on the independent variable and the magnitude and sign of the effect of the independent variable of interest on the dependent variable. In other words, different patterns of correlation among the key variables can alter the effect control variables have on the estimate of the causal effect.

Interactions, Functional Forms, and Categorical Dependent Variables

All the technical extensions to multiple regression, introduced in Chapter 10 when using multiple regression for prediction, apply when the method is used to determine causal effects with control variables. For example, moderation—when the effect of one variable depends on the magnitude of the other variable—is implemented using interaction terms. More flexible functional forms, such as logs and polynomials, can be used. And categorical dependent variables can be accommodated with probit, logistic, linear probability, ordered logit, conditional logit, and other models. Valid causal interpretations depend on the issues described in this chapter, of course, but otherwise, everything carries over from the use of multiple regression purely for description or prediction.

The Decision to Focus on One Causal Effect—and the Confusion It Can Cause

Because estimating causal effects is so difficult, often researchers (particularly in economics and program evaluation) choose to focus their efforts on estimating the effect of just one independent variable. We have already seen several examples of this: the effect of education on earnings, the effect of breast-feeding on cognitive development, and the effect of cigarette prices on smoking. In these studies, the focus is on the independent variable of interest, with the other independent variables selected primarily as control variables that serve to improve the one causal estimate.

Other researchers (in sociology and other fields) tend to focus on multiple causes of the dependent variable in the same analysis. For example, they might be interested in the various factors in a person's life that influence earnings, not just education. Or they might want to develop a causal model of the many influences on the cognitive development of children, not just the effect of breast-feeding. In such studies, most of the independent variables are viewed as causes of interest in their own right, not as control variables. (See Box 13.1 about the use of the term *control variable*.) These studies also tend to be interested in comparing the effects of multiple causes, such as how much of an effect breast-feeding has on cognitive development compared with nutrition, early childhood education, parental influences, and so on.

Researchers probing single causes and those probing multiple causes both use multiple regression (or related techniques), and their statistical tables often look similar. But they view what they are trying to do with multiple regression very differently, and this sometimes leads to confusion and contention. So it is important to make clear the difference in research questions and purposes for using multiple regression. It is also important to understand that both kinds of research can be useful and informative.

BOX 13.1
When to Call Something a Control Variable

In our main focus on the effect of one independent variable of interest, we referred to the other independent variables as **control variables**. As we use the term, the purpose of a *control variable* is to statistically equalize comparisons across the independent variable of interest. Some researchers often use the term *control variable* to refer to all the independent variables, but we suggest reserving the term *control variable* for a variable used to disentangle the causal effect of the independent variable of interest. In a multicause model, use the term *independent variable* for all the causes.

When Is Low *R*-Squared a Problem?

As explained in Chapters 8 and 10, the *R*-squared of a regression is the proportion of the variation in the dependent variable that can be predicted by (or "explained by") the independent variables. A low *R*-squared means that many of the important causes of the dependent variable are not in the equation. In doing prediction, the *R*-squared is obviously very important—we want the most accurate prediction possible (although useful predictions can still be made without a high *R*-squared). As the example in Box 13.2 illustrates, actuaries care a lot about whether someone's occupation predicts his or her use of health care—regardless of whether it is causal. As a result, many people pay a lot of attention to *R*-squared.

But when using multiple regression to get at causation, *R*-squared itself is not as important. The focus is instead on the coefficient of the independent variable of interest, including both its statistical and its practical significance. Even in a regression with a low *R*-squared, such statistical significance and practical significance are still quite possible. Many dependent variables in social and policy research—variables such as Earnings, Smoking, Cognitive Development, and Consumption of Health Care—have multiple and varied causes. Most of these causes are out of the reach of policy and practice. If a variable that can be influenced by policy or practice has a statistical and practical effect, it is important to know that—even if that variable does not explain all that much total variation in the outcome.

Of course, if the goal is to understand and demonstrate as many causes of the dependent variable as possible, *R*-squared matters. Once again, much depends on the aims of the study and the reasons for using multiple regression.

QUESTION

When would a researcher want to focus on how going to a private school compared with a public school affects test scores? When would a researcher want to focus on all the variables driving test scores?

Software Doesn't Know the Difference, but You Should

Whether multiple regression is being used for prediction, description, disentangling a single causal effect, or estimating many causal effects together, the multiple regression commands in the statistical software are the same. The software just asks for the dependent variable and the independent variables. The calculations the software performs do not depend on the purpose. However, how a researcher should choose those independent variables and how multiple regression results should be interpreted depend very much on what the purpose is.

The proliferation, advanced capabilities, and ease of use of both computers and software today make it easy to run regressions. However, just as one needs to be very careful about the quality and meaning of the data, one needs to be just as careful about the choice of control variables and the interpretation of the results.

BOX 13.2
The Health of Taxi Drivers: Prediction Versus Causation

Actuaries for health insurance companies try to predict individuals' likelihood of being hospitalized, having doctors' visits, and so on, to determine what premiums they should be charged. They use regression models with independent variables such as age, gender, medical history (if available), occupation, and so on.

Some occupations are associated with greater risk . . . but do they *cause* greater risk?

Source: © 2009 Jupiterimages Corporation.

An actuary might find, for example, that taxi drivers are more likely than those in many other occupations to have heart attacks. This effect could be causal, with a mechanism of taxi driving raising stress and stress causing heart attacks. Alternatively, people could end up driving taxis because they have fewer options and harder past lives, and those fewer options and harder past lives would have made them more prone to heart attacks no matter what their occupation. That alternative would be an example of common cause.

Would the actuary and the health insurance plan employing the actuary need to know *why* being a taxi driver predicts having a heart attack? No. Their task is to determine health insurance premiums, so they only need to predict health care usage in the most accurate and precise way possible. They do not need to know whether a predictor variable is itself causal or really a proxy for some common cause.

Public health officials, in contrast, might care *why* taxi drivers are more prone to heart attacks. Their job is to develop and implement policies to improve the health of the public. If driving a taxi is truly responsible for making someone more likely to have a heart attack, a public health official might want to change aspects of taxi drivers' working conditions, such as the length of shifts. On the other hand, if driving a taxi is just a proxy for what drives heart attacks, then public health officials might want to focus on those other causes to see if they could perhaps change them.

Both public health policy and insurance premiums are determined, in part, by multiple regression models such as the ones we have described. But the very different purposes mean that they should be interpreted and applied in different ways.

Multivariate Matching: Using Propensity Scores

Multiple linear regression (ordinary least squares) is the most widely used technique for trying to estimate a causal effect using observational data—much more common than matching. But in today's world of large data sets and cheap computational power, other techniques are increasingly practical and widely used. That includes not only other regression methods like logistic regression but also more sophisticated matching techniques, which build on more advanced regression approaches.

Propensity Score Matching

Recall from the last chapter how hard it is to match along many variables at the same time and with finely grained categories. When matching public and private school students, we wanted to match on race, ethnicity, school size, parents' income, parent's education, books at home, computers at home, and so on. The task was almost impossible even with very large data sets.

But a technique called **propensity score matching** can be used to match along many variables, including noncategorical variables, at the same time (Rosenbaum & Rubin, 1985). For example, we might have administrative data on many school-age kids in a jurisdiction—including their exact age, gender, race, language ability, family income, and so on. We could then use these data to estimate a statistical equation that predicts attending a private school. (That equation is most commonly a logistic regression.) The resulting equation produces a predicted probability (propensity) of being a private school student. Those who have high propensity scores but do *not* attend private school are used to create the comparison group.

Not One Method but Four

Although people often refer to "the" propensity score method, in fact propensity scores can be used in multiple ways, sometimes confusing study readers. Williamson, Morley, Lucas, and Carpenter (2012) provide a clear introduction to the four main propensity score methods, while Guo and Fraser (2010) provide details needed for implementation.

The first approach is stratification on the propensity scores. For example, all students with a propensity to attend private school between 0 and 0.1 would be in one stratum and would be treated as matched—as close enough to be considered an apples-to-apples comparison. The effect of private school for the students in that stratum is estimated as the difference in achievement between those who actually attend private school and those who actually attend public school. This is repeated for each stratum in turn, and then the effect for the whole sample is estimated by combining all the strata estimates, weighted by the sample share in each stratum.

The second approach looks at every single private school student and finds the public school student who is the closest match—the one with the nearest propensity score. For each such pair, the effect of private school relative to public school is calculated, and the effect for the sample is just the sum. With this approach, many public school students may not be used while others may be used many times over. In some cases, a poor match—larger than desired difference in propensity scores—may be accepted. In other cases, the researcher may decide that there is no matching public school student—a lack of *overlap*—and must drop the private school student from the study. Thus, the lack of similarity between private and public schools results in loss of data and reduced generalizability.

The third and fourth approaches to propensity scores are really variants of regression. For the third approach, an ordinary regression is run, but the propensity scores are used as weights. For the fourth, the propensity score is simply used as a covariate.

Propensity Scores Cannot Fix Bias Due to Unmeasured Variables

Despite its ability to match on many variables at once, and its other advantages, even the propensity score technique cannot make up for important unmeasured variables. Indeed, propensity score matching might exacerbate the problem in some circumstances. For example, if a few students seem exactly like the type who would attend private school—they have a very high propensity score, in other words—but they go to public school, we might worry that they may be different in some important, unmeasured way that affects the outcome.

No statistical approach to analyzing observational data can ever make up for not having reliable measures of all the common cause variables. This is part of the broader limitation of statistical analysis alone to truly get at causation.

Conclusion: A Widely Used Strategy, With Drawbacks

Observational studies with control variables are the most widely used method for estimating causal effects in applied social research. However, as we have seen, the method has drawbacks. Control variables cannot solve the problem of reverse causation. And often, important common causes are unmeasured, leading to omitted variable bias. Data with measures of every relevant common cause are often not available. Sometimes observational data, even if used in the best possible control variables study, cannot provide convincing causal effect estimates. To really get at causation, we often need to intervene in the world and try to make things happen—by using experiments. The next chapter describes randomized experiments, which often do provide convincing causal effect estimates, although they have their own limitations and weaknesses as well.

BOX 13.3
Critical Questions to Ask About Studies That Use Regression to Estimate Causal Effects

- Is the independent variable of interest (the cause) clearly defined and distinguished from the control variables?
- To what extent was the independent variable self-selected? How exogenous or endogenous is the independent variable? Is reverse causation a possibility?
- How were the control variables selected? Was an explanation given for why they were included in the analysis? How convincing was the explanation?
- Are any important possible common causes not captured by the control variables? Do the researchers discuss these?
- Do the researchers present and discuss alternative specifications or combinations of control variables to show how robust their findings are?

BOX 13.4
Tips on Doing Your Own Research: Multiple Regression to Estimate Causal Effects

- Begin with the tips at the end of the last chapter on observational studies—the most important issues are covered there.
- Determine if the dependent variable is categorical, and if so, use an appropriate advanced regression technique, such as logistic or ordered logistic regression (see Table 10.5).
- Interpret the coefficients of the independent variable of interest in language useful for policy or practice—and interpret it as a causal effect, but with appropriate caveats.
- Determine theoretically if interactions are appropriate for some independent variables. Examine empirically the effect of such interactions.
- If two independent variables are highly collinear, estimate specifications that drop each of them and compare the results.

- Estimate various specifications but make sure that each new specification is driven by theory and/or empirical evidence. For example, if an independent variable has a skewed distribution, use it logged in one specification and unlogged in another.
- Always interpret the coefficients of the control variables in terms relevant to policy and practice.
- Estimate all the planned analyses first, and only *afterward* explore unplanned specifications, being aware of the pitfalls of such data mining.
- Implement multiple regression correctly, as one would for prediction. For example, make sure to calculate appropriate inferential statistics. See tips at the end of Chapters 9 and 10.

Chapter Resources

Key Terms

- Control variables
- Propensity score matching
- Specifications

Exercises

13.1. A great many studies in most areas of applied social or policy research are based on regression analysis of observational studies. Look up three published studies in your field or area of interest. Are they observational studies or experimental studies? If observational, do they use some form of regression analysis to estimate causal effects? What are the main independent variables (in the causal sense)? What are the control variables?

13.2. Using the Excel file "UN-HDR-2011" on the resources/supplementary materials webpage, identify a potential cause–effect relationship ($x \rightarrow y$) between two variables in the data that are of interest to you. Then, using statistical software, do the following:

a. Produce a scatterplot of the relationship to examine the correlation visually. Be sure to add the linear regression (trend) line to your scatterplot.
b. Run a simple (bivariate) regression analysis of the relationship. Interpret the slope, statistical significance (t test, p value), and R-squared.
c. Finally, identify a third variable that may be a potential common cause of both your x and y variables and include this variable in a multiple regression analysis. Interpret the difference between these results and your simple (bivariate) results.
d. Summarize all of your analysis and results in the form of a memo to a policy maker or an organization with an interest in the topic. Be sure to discuss the strengths, and limitations, of this kind of analysis for demonstrating a cause-effect relationship.

13.3. A researcher heard about a company that was considered very friendly to women 40 years ago, when it was not so common. He wanted to determine whether this company had discriminated on the basis of gender. He examined the salaries of employees when hired and ran a regression in which StartingAnnualSalary (in dollars) was the dependent variable and the independent variables were Education (in years) and a Female dummy variable. (Note that for this organization in this period, mean starting salary was $6,806, median was $6,000, and standard deviation was $3,148.) Results are below:

	Coefficient	Standard error of coefficient	*t* statistic	*p* value
Education (in years)	588.128	39.462	14.904	.000
Female	−1,672.307	228.341	−7.324	.000
Constant	−366.273	587.382	−.624	.533
R-squared = .462				

a. Interpret in words the coefficient of the Female variable. Is it statistically significant? Is it practically significant?
b. Imagine you wanted to evaluate whether gender discrimination was occurring at this business at the same time. Describe another control variable you would want, briefly justifying your choice and the problems from omitting it.

How Much Is a Garden Worth in Manhattan?

13.4. Say you are asked to study how much outdoor space (a balcony, garden, or patio) raises the price of an apartment in an expensive New York City neighborhood, the West Village.[7] To answer this question, you have obtained a random sample of 32 out of the 290 current listings for residential apartments in the West Village area listed through the *New York Times* (as of August 2009). The data include the following variables:

Price—listed price of the apartment, in dollars
Bedrooms—number of bedrooms
Bathrooms—number of bathrooms
Rooms—number of total rooms in the apartment
SqFt—number of square feet in the apartment
Age—age of the apartment building, in years
Garage—1 if garage is available in the building, otherwise 0
Pets—1 if pets allowed, otherwise 0
Doorman—1 if building has a doorman, otherwise 0
Fireplace—1 if apartment has a fireplace, otherwise 0
Elevator—1 if building has an elevator, otherwise 0
Outdoor—1 if apartment has a balcony, garden, or patio, otherwise 0

[7]We thank Thaddeus Hackworth for creating the initial version of this question.

Your first analysis is a regression with Price as the dependent variable and Outdoor as the only independent variable. Your results are:

	Coefficient	Standard error of coefficient	*t* statistic	*p* value
Outdoor	597,148.1	171,711.8	3.48	.002
Constant	691,851.9	67,875.0	10.19	.000
R-squared	.287			

a. What is the regression equation, including the coefficients from your regression analysis and their units?
b. Using just this output, what is your estimate (so far) of the effect of outdoor space on the listing price of an apartment?
c. Are there any potential sources of bias? Predict the direction of bias.
d. For your next analysis, you run a regression with Price as the dependent variable and Outdoor and SqFt as the independent variables. Using the results below, what is the new regression equation, including the coefficients from the regression analysis and units?

	Coefficient	Standard error of coefficient	*t* statistic	*p* value
Outdoor	237,493.8	102,555.9	2.316	.028
SqFt	951.7	111.9	8.505	.000
Constant	28,078.5	86,344.7	.325	.747
R-squared	.796			

e. Based on just the analysis so far, what is the estimated effect of outdoor space on the listing price of an apartment?
f. Why is it different than in the earlier regression?
g. Are there any other potential sources of bias? If so, how would you control for them ideally? How would you control for them with the data available?
h. How do you interpret the coefficient for SqFt?
i. How would having more than 32 observations change your results?

Teenage Pregnancy and Earnings (Advanced Question)

13.5. Imagine trying to do a control variable study with observational data to determine the effect of teenage pregnancy on earnings in middle age. Consider the issue of whether education is an appropriate control variable.[8]

a. Could education be an intervening variable? Describe a theory consistent with that.
b. Could education be a common cause? Describe a theory consistent with that.

[8]We thank Sanders Korenman for this example.

c. Consider how having longitudinal data on education at different points in time might help decide how to use education as a control variable.
d. Could education be a complex common cause, perhaps a proxy for interest in or aptitude for education? Describe a theory consistent with that. What would that theory imply about using education as a control variable?
e. If you could have any variables you liked in a long-term longitudinal data set, such as the National Longitudinal Survey of Youth, what variables would you want to deal with the complex common cause problem just suggested?

Student Study Site

Visit the Study Site at **www.sagepub.com/remler2e** to

- test your knowledge with the self-quiz
- check your understanding of key terms with the eFlashcards
- explore helpful resources that relate directly to this chapter

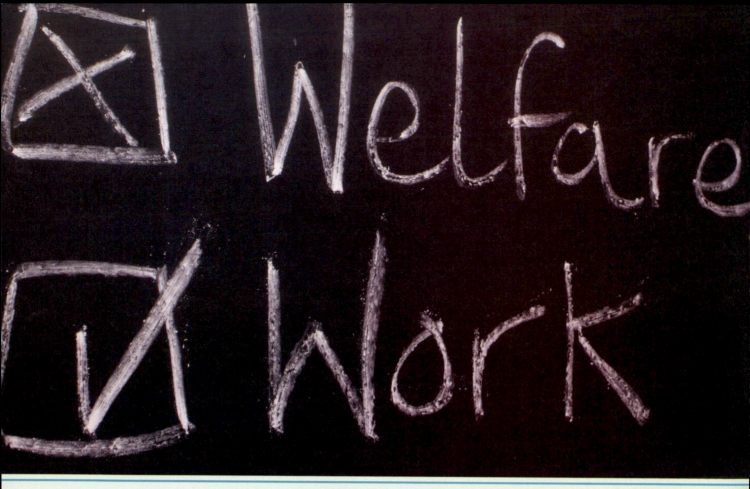

A randomized experiment looked at the effect of welfare time limits on employment.

Source: © iStockphoto.com/Thinglass.

Overview: This chapter introduces you to the randomized experiment—the "gold standard" in social and policy research for demonstrating causation. You will learn the logic and structure of a randomized experiment—in particular, how it creates statistically equivalent groups and eliminates bias from common causes and reverse causation. And you will understand how random assignment—the key feature of such experiments—differs from random sampling (covered in Chapter 5). You will also become aware of the limited generalizability of many randomized experiments as well as appreciate the practical, ethical, and other limitations of such studies. And you will learn variations in the design of randomized experiments and become aware of issues that arise in the analysis of experimental data. Despite important advantages, the randomized experiment is not always the best design for research.

Objectives

Learning Objectives

After reading this chapter, you should be able to

- Recognize randomized experiments, as distinguished from observational studies (and natural or quasi experiments)
- Distinguish random assignment from random sampling, and understand how random assignment produces statistical equivalence
- Explain why randomized experiments are considered the "gold standard" for estimating causal effects
- Understand the reasons for limited generalizability in many randomized experiments
- Assess the generalizability of particular randomized experiments
- Identify implementation issues and human artifacts that may undermine a given randomized experiment
- Recognize multiarm, factorial, cluster randomization, and within-subjects designs and the information they provide

14 Randomized Experiments

Time Limits on Welfare

Aid to Families with Dependent Children (AFDC) began in the 1930s under the New Deal as the United States' welfare program for poor widows. But it came under increasing criticism in the postwar decades for creating disincentives to work and, according to some, discouraging marriage (only single-parent families were eligible for AFDC). By the 1990s, many advocated time limits on the receipt of welfare to prevent it from being seen as a way of life and to encourage recipients to find and keep a job. But advocates for the poor and others warned that time limits would remove a vital safety net for struggling families and punish them unfairly for employment problems beyond their control. Time limits on welfare have been very controversial.

How could this debate be informed by research? Evidence from government surveys suggests that families who stay on welfare for a short time are more likely to find jobs and earn better wages, compared with long-term welfare families. But this could be a case of reverse causation: Finding a good job causes families to leave welfare, not the other way around. Or it could reflect a common cause, such as motivation, which might make people both less likely to stay on welfare and more successful in the job market. And even the clever use of control variables—the strategy discussed in the previous chapters—does not deal with reverse causation and unmeasured common causes, such as motivation.

What we would prefer is more solid evidence of causation—the kind of evidence that comes not just from watching things happen but from intervening in the world to try to make things happen, by doing an experiment (such as the ones we saw in Chapter 11). But how can you get such evidence outside of a controlled laboratory—in the real world of public policy and programs? One important strategy is the randomized experiment, often described as the "gold standard" for rigorous evidence of causation and increasingly preferred these days for purposes of policy making and program evaluation. However, even randomized experiments have some drawbacks and are far from the last word on a controversial topic such as time-limited welfare.

Florida's Family Transition Program: A Randomized Experiment

The State of Florida's Family Transition Program (FTP) is a randomized experiment to evaluate time limits on welfare (Bloom et al., 2000). The program was implemented in Escambia County, in the panhandle section of the state, around Pensacola. Let's use this example to examine the various components of a randomized experiment, as diagrammed in Figure 14.1.

Figure 14.1 Components of a Randomized Experiment

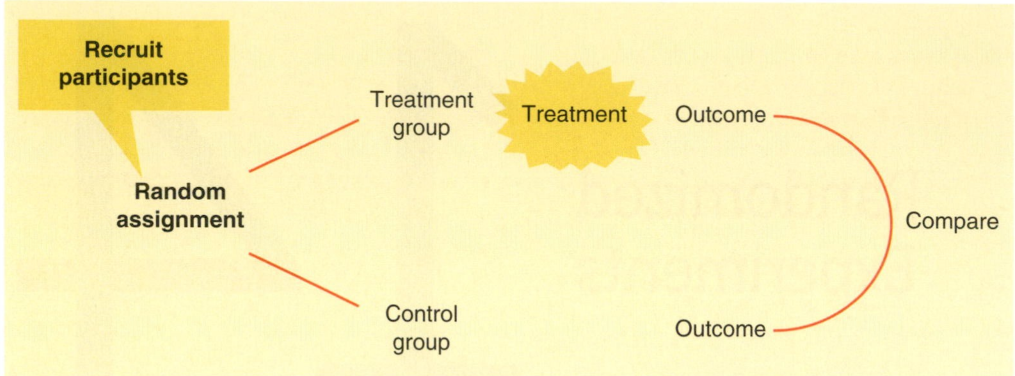

Beginning in 1994, welfare recipients who lived in the county were assigned to either the treatment group or the control group—randomly, by the flip of the coin, as it were (more on this later). This method of assigning treatment is the defining feature of a **randomized experiment**. Randomized experiments are also known as **randomized controlled trials** (RCTs), and in medicine as **randomized clinical trials**.

The **control group** was enrolled in the usual AFDC program, while the **treatment group** was enrolled in the new FTP. In general, the treatment group receives the intervention the study is designed to investigate—time-limited welfare in this case. The control group, also known as the *control condition*, typically receives either no treatment or the usual treatment. In clinical trials, the control group often receives a **placebo**—an inert or ineffective treatment, such as a pill with no active ingredients. The control group always serves to estimate the counterfactual—what would happen to members of the treatment group if they did not get the treatment.

The FTP program—the **treatment**—imposed a time limit on welfare payments of 24 months (in any 60-month period). But it also included an array of incentives (such as an earned income disregard) and services (such as child care) to encourage recipients to find and keep jobs. Therefore, the treatment is really a package that comprises *all* these features—everything that differs from the usual AFDC available to the control group.

QUESTION

What are the key components of a randomized experiment?

Since welfare benefits apply not only to mothers but to their children as well, it is *families* that were randomized. Therefore, families were the **experimental subjects *or* units**, the units randomized to the treatment and control conditions. Thus, both mother and child *outcomes* could be (and were) measured and assessed.

The outcomes of particular interest in the evaluation of FTP were mothers' employment, mothers' earnings, and children's school performance. These outcomes were then compared across treatment and control groups. How much did the mothers in the treatment group earn relative to the control group? How did children of FTP families perform in school, relative to children of families getting the usual AFDC? We will look at what the data have to say shortly. But first, let's examine more closely why the comparisons set up by a randomized experiment such as the FTP evaluation provide such convincing evidence of causation.

Random Assignment: Creating Statistical Equivalence

Recall from Chapter 11 that in a controlled laboratory setting, we establish two key conditions that allow us to answer causal questions—exogeneity and control. In a randomized experiment, **random assignment** (also known as *randomization*) is used to provide, or withhold, an intervention or treatment following a procedure similar to flipping a coin. The intervention or treatment is not self-selected, targeted to the needy, or based on any individual characteristics that could influence the outcome later on. In this way, random assignment ensures that the treatment is exogenous.

In a laboratory setting, other variables that might affect the outcome are experimentally controlled—physically held constant. But in most real-world social, medical, and policy settings, it is impossible to hold constant all the various factors that might influence a complex outcome such as the earnings of mothers or the performance of children in school. Indeed, that is why we used control variables in the previous chapter. Randomization addresses this problem too, not by physically holding things constant or by employing control variables, but by producing **statistical equivalence**. Statistical equivalence balances the treatment and control groups in terms of both measured and unmeasured variables, with the bounds of chance differences.

Think of statistical equivalence this way: Ideally, we want to compare apples with apples. But if we cannot find identical fruits for both baskets, we can at least ensure that we have essentially the same *mix* of fruits in each basket. Provided there are enough pieces of fruit (sample size)—and that they were all well mixed together ahead of time (random assignment)—the two baskets of fruit will be statistically equivalent. Because the control group is statistically equivalent to the treatment group, it can be used to estimate the counterfactual.

Random Assignment in Practice

Let's look more closely at how random assignment is used to make the FTP treatment group and AFDC control group statistically equivalent. After completing some initial paperwork on families, but before placing them in a program, welfare caseworkers in Pensacola contacted the Manpower Demonstration Research Corporation (MDRC), the research organization managing the evaluation (see Box 14.1). MDRC used a computer to randomly assign the families to either FTP (the treatment group) or AFDC (the control group). The caseworkers then completed the enrollment process into the appropriate program. MDRC could have used the flip of an ordinary coin to do the random assignment, but a computer routine makes the process more structured, more easily traceable, and less susceptible to conscious or unconscious tampering. Table 14.1 demonstrates random assignment using a computerized random number generator.

BOX 14.1
Manpower Demonstration Research Corporation (MDRC)

MDRC is an influential policy research organization known for its use of randomized field experiments to evaluate public programs, including Florida's Family Transition Program. Here is what the organization says about itself on its website, www.mdrc.org:

> *Created in 1974 by the Ford Foundation and a group of federal agencies, MDRC is a nonprofit, nonpartisan education and social policy research organization dedicated to learning what works to improve programs and policies that affect the poor. MDRC is best known for mounting large-scale demonstrations and evaluations of real-world policies and programs targeted to low-income people. We helped pioneer the use of random assignment—the same highly reliable methodology used to test new medicines—in our evaluations. From welfare policy to high school reform, MDRC's work has helped to shape legislation, program design, and operational practices across the country. Working in fields where emotion and ideology often dominate public debates, MDRC is a source of objective, unbiased evidence about cost-effective solutions that can be replicated and expanded to scale.*

Source: MRDC, http://www.mdrc.org/about/about-mdrc-history

Table 14.1 shows the name of the applicant and the date and time the caseworker contacted MDRC.[1] At the time of the call, the random number was picked by the computer from all possible numbers between 0 and 100, with each number having an equal probability of selection. The preestablished rule for assignment was that random numbers less than 50 were assigned to AFDC, while random numbers equal to or greater than 50 were assigned to FTP. Thus, the first two applicants were assigned to AFDC, the next four applicants were assigned to FTP, and the last applicant shown was assigned to AFDC.

Although there may be short-run imbalances in the assignment of treatment and control group members, over the long run, as this process of random assignment continues and the sample size becomes large enough, the number of applicants in each group will be approximately the same. In Pensacola, a total of 2,817 families were randomly assigned in this way, and 1,405 ended up in FTP and 1,412 in AFDC.

Haphazard Randomization

Notice that it takes deliberation and discipline to do proper random assignment; *random* in the context of a randomized experiment does not mean haphazard or lackadaisical. Indeed, it takes a good deal of control of the situation to assign people or other units to treatment groups based strictly on a random number.

There are, however, occasions when researchers do rely on **haphazard randomization**, meaning a less formal procedure that mimics true random assignment. This can happen especially when doing random assignment would be unnatural or disruptive to ordinary social behavior. For example, an influential experiment about decision overload (Iyengar & Lepper, 2000) set up two tasting booths in an upscale grocery store on consecutive Saturdays to test whether offering 24 varieties of jam at one booth, versus only 6 varieties of jam at the other booth, would influence interest in the product and subsequent purchasing behavior. The results showed that people actually purchased jam much more often when exposed to only 6 choices, suggesting that 24 choices may have overloaded their ability to make a decision. The location of the two booths in the store was switched every hour, and this pattern was reversed on the second Saturday. Still, shoppers were not randomly assigned to pass by one booth or the other—attempting to do so would clearly make them aware of the study and perhaps self-conscious about their shopping behavior, thus altering it. The researchers instead relied on the haphazard randomization from the natural conflux of shoppers as they roamed the aisles of the grocery store. Such studies can provide strong evidence of causation, but they are not genuine randomized experiments because they lack true random assignment.

QUESTION

How is true random assignment different from haphazard random assignment?

Table 14.1 Random Assignment

Applicant Name	Date/Time	Random Number	Assignment
P. Jones	3/21/94 9:10 AM	38.2	AFDC
J. Aristide	3/21/94 11:45 AM	10.1	AFDC
K. Smith	3/21/94 2:20 PM	59.6	FTP
B. Thomas	3/22/94 10:05 AM	89.9	FTP
L. Sanchez	3/22/94 12:00 PM	88.5	FTP
N. Allen	3/23/94 9:55 AM	95.8	FTP
C. Fernandez	3/23/94 1:15 PM	1.4	AFDC

[1]These are artificial data but based generally on the procedures used in the FTP evaluation, as described in Bloom et al. (2000).

Statistical Equivalence: A Look at the Data

What does true random assignment, as implemented in the FTP evaluation using computer-generated random numbers, actually achieve? Notice that the values of the random numbers were the sole basis for assigning a family to the FTP treatment or to the AFDC control condition, and the values were generated entirely by chance selection. The values selected, therefore, were not related in any way to the characteristics of the applicant families. Compared with those assigned low random numbers, families assigned high random numbers were not any younger or older, more or less educated, smaller or larger, and so on.

One way to look at what random assignment achieves is to compare the means of the treatment and control groups formed by use of the random variable, before the start of the program. Table 14.2 does this for three relevant variables: Education, Age, and Work Experience.[2]

The differences in means between the treatment and control groups are trivial. In fact, they are only random differences, as confirmed by statistical significance tests (indicated by the lack of stars in Table 14.2). So we say that the two groups are *statistically equivalent,* that is, equivalent within the bounds of what differences might arise just by chance.

Table 14.3 is a matrix of correlation coefficients that illustrates this same point another way. Recall from Chapter 8 that correlation coefficients range from −1 to +1 and indicate the direction and strength of a statistical relationship. A correlation coefficient of zero indicates no relationship. The correlations between the random number and the other variables are all very close to zero, indicating no relationship. Thus, the random number is only very weakly (due to random chance) correlated with the variables Education, Age, and Work Experience. In contrast, Education is negatively related to Age (older people did not get as much education as younger people generally do these days) and positively related to Work Experience. Indeed, all the variables other than the random number have statistically significant (starred) relationships with each other. Provided the number of subjects is large enough so that any chance differences average out, randomized assignment ensures statistical equivalence.

QUESTION

How do you know that statistical equivalence applies even to variables that you cannot observe or measure?

Table 14.2 Comparing Means

	Treatment	Control
Education (years)	11.6	11.5
Age (years)	34.5	34.7
Work Experience (years)	7.7	8.0

Table 14.3 Correlations Among Variables

	Random Number	Education	Age	Work Experience
Random Number	1.00	0.01	−0.01	−0.02
Education	0.01	1.00	−0.11*	0.34*
Age	−0.01	−0.11*	1.00	0.25*
Work Experience	−0.02	0.34*	0.25*	1.00

Note: * $p < .05$.

[2]These results are not from the actual FTP evaluation but rather are based on real data from another survey. For purposes of this numerical example, the survey respondents were assigned to a treatment group and a control group using a random number.

Why Random Assignment Is Better Than Matching or Control Variables

We want this kind of statistical equivalence not only for variables that we have measured, such as Education, Age, and Work Experience, but also for important characteristics that are not measured, such as having neighbors with good job connections or being highly motivated. Fortunately, because the FTP evaluation used random assignment, the near-zero correlations and the trivial differences in means happen not just with these three variables (Education, Age, and Work Experience) but also with any other variables or characteristics we might think of. It applies to characteristics that are easy to record, such as the number of children in the family, as well as those that are more elusive or difficult to measure, such as personality or motivation. Whatever it is, the random number will be uncorrelated with it (or nearly so), and the means for the treatment and control groups created by use of the random number will be the same, except for chance differences.

This fact, statistical equivalence on *all* variables, is what makes random assignment better than matching and better than using control variables. No matter how careful or detailed the matching—or how sophisticated the control variables—there is always the possibility that some unmeasured difference or common cause lurks beneath the surface and may bias the results later on. Random assignment statistically equalizes the groups across all possible variables—measured, unmeasured, and even unimagined alike.

Matching, Then Random Assignment

Matching, however, can often be used together with random assignment, especially when dealing with small samples. For example, we could first match welfare recipients in terms of work experience and education, and then use random assignment to decide which individual in a matched pair is assigned to the treatment group and which is assigned to the control group. This helps ensure balance across treatment and control groups on at least a few relevant variables (the matching variables, plus other variables correlated with the matching variables). Again, this is especially useful when the sample size is small because, with small samples assigned to each treatment group, fairly large imbalances could possibly result from just chance alone.

Findings: What Happened in Pensacola

We've seen how random assignment makes families in the FTP treatment and AFDC control groups statistically equivalent. If we left well enough alone, yet followed the families over time, we would logically expect much the same outcome from both groups—jobs, births, divorces, whatever it is we're interested in. But of course, we don't leave things alone: We intervene and expose one group to the new FTP program and the other to the old AFDC program. Since this difference in treatments is the only variable that systematically distinguishes the two groups, any difference in outcomes can be attributed to the treatment and the treatment alone.

So let's look now at what actually happened to the 2,817 families in the Pensacola area that were randomly assigned to the FTP treatment (the new time-limited welfare program) or the AFDC control condition. Were the outcomes the same or not? After 4 years, only 6% of families in the FTP treatment ended up receiving welfare on a long-term basis, compared with 17% in the AFDC control group. Families in the FTP treatment group had more earnings earlier on in the study period, although by the end of the 4 years, the two groups had about the same earnings. There was little difference between the groups in material hardship, with both groups reporting frequent difficulties paying bills and buying food and other necessities. As for the children, there were no real differences between the treatment and control group in the children's educational performance at the elementary levels. At the upper grade levels, however, the children in the FTP treatment group actually performed somewhat worse in school than did those in the AFDC control group. The researchers speculated that the increased maternal employment associated with FTP might have had negative consequences for some of the older children. (Speculation such as this can be addressed with qualitative research, as we discuss later.)

Evidence-Based Public Policies?

Many in the United States, including organizations such as the Coalition for Evidence-Based Policy (described in the organization's own words in Box 14.2), advocate wider use of randomized experiments because of their superior evidence of causation. In the United Kingdom, the government has begun funding a network of "What Works" centers that provide rigorous evidence for making social policy, modeled after the randomized experiments traditionally used to evaluate health programs and treatments (Cabinet Office, 2013). In the area of antipoverty programs in developing countries, the Abdul Latif Jameel Poverty Action Lab at the Massachusetts Institute of Technology (MIT) provides another example of the drive to use rigorous evidence based on randomized experiments to tackle difficult social and economic problems around the world (see www.povertyactionlab.org).

QUESTION

Why are randomized experiments often mentioned in arguments that public policy should be more evidence based?

BOX 14.2
The Coalition for Evidence-Based Policy

The Coalition for Evidence-Based Policy is a nonprofit organization that promotes the use of randomized experiments to evaluate social programs. Here is what the coalition says about itself on its website, www.coalition4evidence.org:

> *A nonprofit, nonpartisan organization, the Coalition seeks to increase government effectiveness through the use of rigorous evidence about what works. In the field of medicine, public policies based on scientifically-rigorous evidence have produced extraordinary advances in health over the past 50 years. By contrast, in most areas of social policy—such as education, poverty reduction, and crime prevention—government programs often are implemented with little regard to evidence, costing billions of dollars yet failing to address critical social problems. However, rigorous studies have identified a few highly-effective program models and strategies ("interventions"), suggesting that a concerted government effort to build the number of these proven interventions, and spur their widespread use, could bring rapid progress to social policy similar to that which transformed medicine.*
>
> *The Coalition advocates many types of research to identify the most promising social interventions. However, a central theme of our advocacy, consistent with the recommendation of a recent National Academy of Sciences report, is that evidence of effectiveness generally cannot be considered definitive without ultimate confirmation in well-conducted randomized controlled trials.*

Source: Coalition for Evidence-Based Policy (2009).

The Logic of Randomized Experiments: Exogeneity Revisited

A randomized experiment seeks to isolate the causal relationship between one explanatory variable, the treatment (x), or intervention, and one or more response variables, or outcomes (y). If we were to draw a model of just this relationship, it would look like this:

$$\text{Treatment} \rightarrow \text{Outcome}$$

or

$$x \rightarrow y$$

But what about all the other multifarious, real-world chains of cause and effect that produce a complex outcome such as employment? Indeed, all the intricate personal and situational causes of employment do still come into play—one's education, age, work experience, motivation, local job market, and so on. But because of random assignment, as we have just seen, the treatment itself is not related to any of these other factors. The treatment cuts through this tangle of nonexperimental influences as a light beam cuts through a driving rain. Figure 14.2 provides a visual image, a path model, of what a randomized experiment achieves.

All the other variables and influences are still there in Figure 14.2, and they still have their relationships with employment (the outcome) and each other. The experiment doesn't change any of this. But the treatment variable, as the dotted lines and 0 correlations indicate, is not related to any of these other variables or influences. It operates alone and apart.

As a result, the link between the treatment and the outcome emerges as an unbiased—in the sense of unconfounded with any other variable or influence—estimate of the effect of the treatment, and the treatment alone, on the outcome.

So variable x, the treatment, is known to be independent from and uncorrelated with all other variables causing y—in other words, it is *exogenous.*

Take another brief example: A student's performance on a test is produced by a process or system (which we could represent by a model) that includes the influence of parents, siblings, teachers, peers, innate ability, sleep and eating habits, school curriculum, and all the other factors that go into how well a student performs on a given day when he or she takes a test. If we want to know the true effect, for example, of class size as a factor, we want

Figure 14.2 Path Model of the FTP Experiment

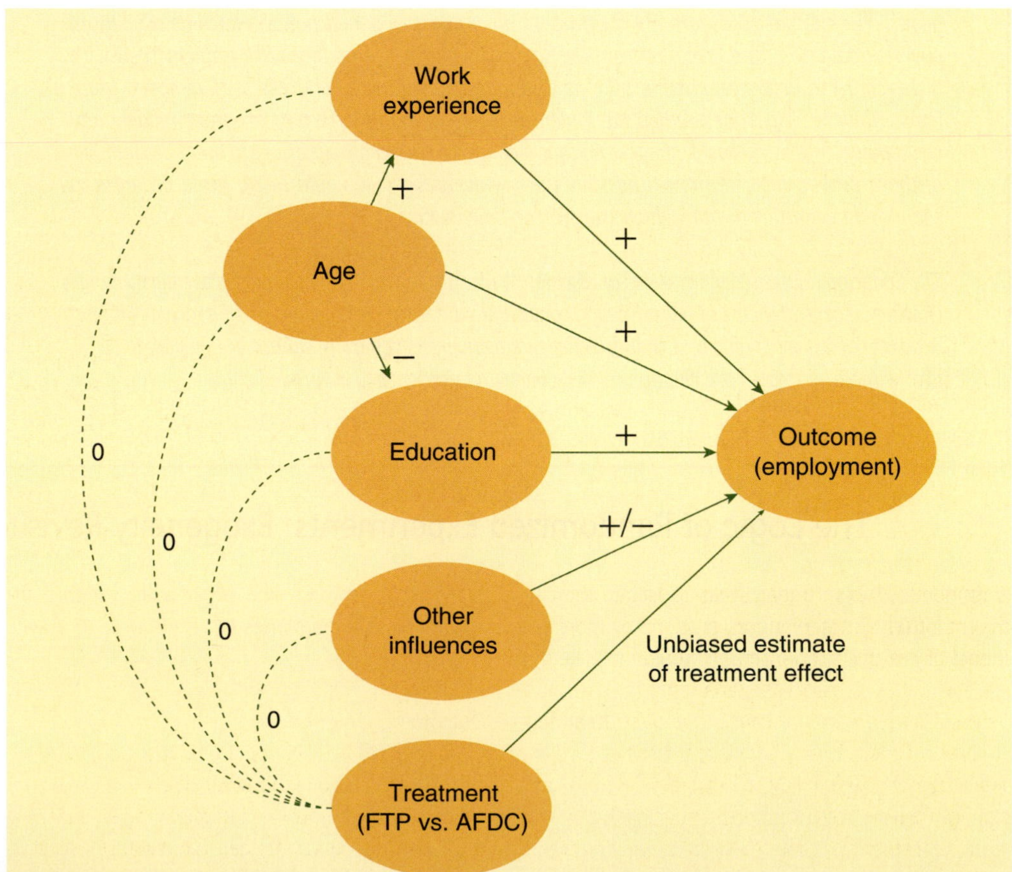

class size to be exogenous—to come from outside this messy tangle of other variables and relationships that influence the student's reading performance. Assigning class size randomly to students ensures this: It imposes a given class size on students from outside—from above as it were—regardless of the other characteristics or influences exerting themselves on the student. Thus, class size randomly assigned is exogenous.

Statistical Significance of an Experimental Result

Statistical significance tests—such as a *t* test for the difference between two means (discussed in Chapter 9)—has a special meaning in the context of a randomized experiment. Let's say we observe that a result, average reading test score, appears higher in the treatment group than in the control group—like this:

$$\text{Treatment group mean} = 223$$

$$\text{Control group mean} = 216$$

There are four possible explanations—and only four—for this correlation between the treatment (x) and the outcome (y):

1. x caused y.
2. y caused x (reverse causation).
3. Something else (a common cause) produced the correlation between x and y.
4. The correlation between x and y just happened by chance.

Many causes influence how well a student does on a test.

Source: © iStockphoto.com/LeventKonuk.

In a randomized experiment, the researcher's ability to intervene and impose a treatment, exogenously, eliminates Number 2 as an explanation. And the statistical equivalence produced by random assignment, as we have just seen, eliminates Number 3 as a possible explanation.

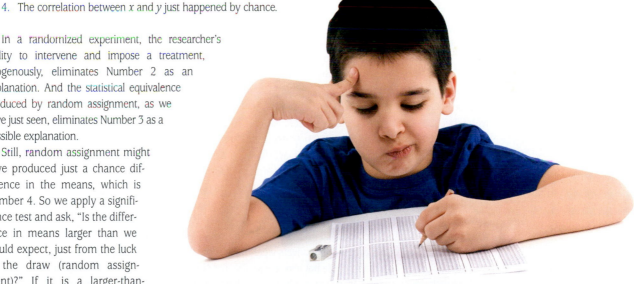

Still, random assignment might have produced just a chance difference in the means, which is Number 4. So we apply a significance test and ask, "Is the difference in means larger than we would expect, just from the luck of the draw (random assignment)?" If it is a larger-than-chance difference—if the result is statistically significant—then we can reject Number 4 as an explanation. And so the winner is . . . Number 1, the treatment caused the difference.

One important lesson here is that statistical significance tests cannot prove causation on their own; to do so, they must be considered together with the overall design of the study, such as a randomized experiment. Statistical significance tests used in nonexperimental studies to estimate causal effects must be interpreted with caution.

In Chapter 9, we cautioned about applying statistical significance tests (and other inferential statistics) to samples not based on probability sampling, such as convenience samples. Happily, these cautions do *not* apply when testing for differences between arms in a randomized experiment. Because both the treatment and control groups are randomly assigned, such statistical significance tests are completely correct, no matter how the study subjects were sampled.

QUESTION

Why does a statistical significance test tell us less in an observational study than it does in a randomized experiment?

Do the Results Have Practical or Policy Significance?

Beware of statistically significant *yet practically trivial* treatment effects. With a large enough treatment and control group, even minor differences in means can turn out to be statistically significant. And because the result comes from a randomized experiment, we know the treatment caused the difference. So it can happen that a randomized experiment gives us strong evidence that the treatment caused a tiny effect. Always look carefully at the size, or magnitude, of the reported treatment effect—not just its statistical significance.

The Settings of Randomized Experiments

Randomized experiments can be implemented in various settings, including in specialized locations or laboratories, in natural social settings (the field), or in the pages of a survey. Combinations are possible as well, for example when a mobile laboratory is taken out into the field, or when a survey experiment is conducted in a laboratory setting.

Lab Experiments

We talked a bit about some **lab experiments,** experiments that take place in a laboratory or other specialized location, in Chapter 11 because they illustrate well the logic of experimentation: intervening to create exogenous change in one variable, while holding other variables constant. Laboratory experiments have a long history in psychology and are increasingly popular in other social sciences, such as economics and political science, as well as some areas of applied social and policy research. Important examples can be found in the related fields of behavioral economics, decision theory, and game theory, which have produced a flurry of fascinating studies in recent years using subjects recruited to laboratory settings at universities and other locations. Typically, the subjects are asked to make decisions, or play strategic games, in controlled settings with other subjects in small groups or seated alone in front of a computer terminal. Ariely's (2010) *Predictably Irrational,* Thaler and Sunstein's (2008) *Nudge,* and Kahneman's (2011) *Thinking Fast and Slow* are all best-selling books by important authors that are full of interesting examples of experiments about human behavior and decision making, often with important public policy implications.

A study by a team of researchers at the University of Utah (Drews, Yazdani, Godfrey, Cooper, & Strayer, 2009) provides a good example of another kind of lab experiment with direct policy applications. Concerned about the dangers of texting while driving, these researchers recruited 40 young adults to a laboratory in which there was a driving simulator and compared their driving performance while being engaged, or not engaged, in text messaging. They found that text-messaging drivers were much more likely to be involved in crashes (as recorded by the simulator) than drivers who were not text messaging. For obvious ethical reasons, this experiment could not be done with drivers in real cars on real roadways, which would put the participants and others at risk for serious injury and even death. Conducting the experiment in a laboratory with a driving simulator makes sense—and it provided useful findings that have informed the policy debate about laws restricting texting while driving.

Field Experiments

The FTP evaluation in Florida is a **field experiment** because it took place in the real-world setting of Pensacola, with real welfare recipients and their families. This is the defining characteristic of field experiments: They take place in the real social world, not in some artificial laboratory or simulator. Field experiments get their name from the early days of experimental research in which scientists (such as the originator of randomized experiments, the statistician Ronald A. Fisher) studied agricultural interventions in a real cornfield or wheat field, as opposed to the laboratory or greenhouse. In the context of social research, the term *field* refers to a real neighborhood or community, a real business or other organization, or any other naturally existing social setting (Gerber & Green, 2012).

Randomized field experiments typically take substantial time, organization, and management, particularly if they involve multiple sites, complex programs, and long-term outcomes. Indeed, implementing randomization in the field often runs into many practical barriers (see Box 14.3). Consequently, randomized field experiments are often performed by relatively large contract research organizations with experience in randomized field experiments. In the United States, in addition to MDRC (see Box 14.1), a pioneer in the field, Mathematica Policy Research (www.mathematica-mpr.com) and Abt Associates (www.abtassociates.com) are major firms with such capabilities (Greenberg, Shroder, & Onstott, 1999). However, other organizations—academic, nonprofit, and for-profit—also implement various kinds of randomized field experiments. For example, MIT's Poverty Action Lab conducts experimental studies in poorer countries aimed at evaluating interventions to reduce global poverty and advocating for randomized experiments in economic development research (see Box 14.4). Randomized field experiments have probed the causal effects of a wide range of programs and have influenced policy, including the RAND Health Insurance Experiment (see Box 14.5), the Perry Preschool Study (see Box 14.7), the Moving to Opportunity demonstration (see Box 14.8), and numerous others. To get a sense of the variety of studies being conducted these days in various policy areas and in different locations around the world, visit the websites of MDRC (www.mdrc.org) and the Poverty Action Lab (www.povertyactionlab.org).

Some field experiments happen without people even knowing that they are part of an experiment. For example, political scientists Gerber, Karlan, and Bergan (2009) studied the impact of newspapers on political attitudes and voter turnout by randomly assigning free newspaper subscriptions to a sample of households in Prince William County, Virginia, that did not previously subscribe to a newspaper. There were two treatment groups, one that received the *Washington Post* (a more liberal paper) and one the *Washington Times* (a more conservative paper), and also a control group that did not receive any newspaper. The newspaper subscriptions (which were announced by a postcard as if the household won a free sweepstakes) began delivery several months prior to Virginia's 2005 gubernatorial election. Results suggested little impact of either newspaper on political knowledge or attitude measures, a slight positive effect on voter turnout, and a larger effect in terms of favoring the Democratic candidate (regardless of which newspaper the person received). People were aware that they had received a free newspaper subscription, of course, but they did not know that this was part of a political science experiment and were not told the newspaper subscription was connected in any way to the postelection telephone survey used to measure their attitudes and voting behavior several months later.

BOX 14.3
Practical Difficulties in a Field Experiment About Online Education

Bowen, Chingos, Lack, and Nygren (2012) performed a randomized field experiment to evaluate a hybrid, largely interactive online introductory statistics course (compared with traditional methods of teaching statistics) at six public university colleges. The practical difficulties they confronted are common for randomized field experiments. For example, they were able to randomize students but not instructors, and the hybrid-online classes ended up with less experienced instructors than the traditional classes. Other practical problems included administrative leadership changes and difficulties integrating the randomization into scheduling and registration logistics in ways that would not disadvantage students.

(Continued)

(Continued)

The researchers provide practical suggestions to those who wish to run a randomized field experiment to evaluate online and hybrid courses in higher education (Bowen et al., 2012, Appendix C, pp. 43–52), but their suggestions are useful for many kinds of randomized field experiments, particularly multisite studies. Specifically, such studies are "complicated and involve coordination of many different people and administrative groups" (Bowen et al., 2012, p. 43). They recommend that each site have an engaged coordinator who has a long history of involvement in the relevant administrative functions, such as scheduling, and that the person be senior enough to be influential but not too senior. They also note that planning must take place far in advance and that fielding a pilot student at *each* site is important, since administrative and other practices can vary.

BOX 14.4
Abduf Latif Jameel Poverty Action Lab at MIT

Although only founded in 2003, the Poverty Action Lab has rapidly become influential in development economics. Two of its founders, Abhijit Banerjee and Esther Duflo, have described many of the studies and what they have learned about poverty in a very readable book, *Poor Economics: A Radical Rethinking of the Way to Fight Global Poverty* (2011). Here is how the organization describes itself on its website:

> *The Abdul Latif Jameel Poverty Action Lab (J-PAL) was established in 2003 as a research center at the Economics Department at the Massachusetts Institute of Technology. Since then, it has grown into a global network of researchers who use randomized evaluations to answer critical policy questions in the fight against poverty.*

J-PAL's mission is to reduce poverty by ensuring that policy is based on scientific evidence, and research is translated into action. We do this through three main activities:

- ***Conducting Rigorous Impact Evaluations**:* J-PAL researchers conduct randomized evaluations to test and improve the effectiveness of programs and policies aimed at reducing poverty.
- ***Policy Outreach**:* J-PAL's policy group analyzes and disseminates research results and builds partnerships with policymakers to ensure that policy is driven by evidence, and effective programs are scaled up.
- ***Capacity Building**:* J-PAL equips practitioners with the expertise to carry out their own rigorous evaluations through training courses and joint research projects.

Source: www.povertyactionlab.org/about-j-pal

Survey Experiments

Surveys (as discussed in Chapter 7) are widely used in observational studies (see Chapter 12) and also to measure outcomes in experiments, such as the newspaper and voting behavior study just discussed. But the term **survey experiment** refers to a method of incorporating an experiment in the design and structure of the survey instrument itself. Often, researchers employ survey experiments to test the effects of variations in questionnaire design or wording, sometimes referred to as a **split-ballot survey**. Survey experiments have become much easier to conduct these days because most web survey software programs have built-in capabilities to randomly assign respondents to different questions or branches of an online questionnaire.

Because voting is a socially desirable behavior, survey researchers worry that people overreport their voting behavior in surveys. To address this problem, Belli, Moore, and VanHoewyk (2006) designed a survey experiment to compare a standard way of asking people if they voted with a longer, face-saving version of the voting question. The 1,464 respondents to the telephone survey were randomly assigned to different versions of the voting question (using a randomization feature in the computer-assisted telephone interviewing, or CATI, system [see Chapter 7] used to conduct the survey). The findings showed that people substantially overreport voting when asked the standard question, compared with the new question that gives them a face-saving way to confess that they did not vote. Studies like these can help reduce bias in survey measurements of many important behaviors, like substance abuse or crime victimization.

But survey experiments are useful for more than just improving survey questions. For example, Krueger and Kuziemko (2013) examined the willingness of uninsured Americans to buy health insurance by embedding an experiment in the Gallup-Healthways daily poll of a random sample of U.S. adults. Here is the question they added to the poll to be asked of all respondents without health insurance:

> *If you could get a health insurance policy for yourself that is as good as the one that members of Congress have, given your current financial situation, would you buy it for $[X] a year, which works out to $[X/12] per month?*

They then randomly varied the value of *X*, the cost of the insurance, to test people's willingness to acquire health coverage at various price points. Their results suggest that uninsured Americans appear quite willing to buy health insurance—if the price is right. Using their experimental findings, Krueger and Kuziemko estimate that more than 60% of uninsured Americans would buy coverage if the price were $2,000 a year. Given the reduced cost of insurance provided by the Affordable Care Act (ACA), the study suggests that the ACA would provide 39 million previously uninsured Americans with health insurance coverage.

QUESTION

What are the key differences between lab, field, and survey experiments?

Notice that this survey experiment has an important advantage over other kinds of experiments: It starts with a random sample of all U.S. adults, so the results not only provide good causal evidence but generalize to the population of all uninsured adults in the United States. It is this feature that allows the researchers to project their findings to 39 million people (even though the survey experiment asked only 1,332 people the health insurance question). Most laboratory experiments and even field experiments have much more limited generalizability, which is the topic of the next section.

Generalizability of Randomized Experiments

Although randomized experiments provide convincing evidence of cause and effect, this often comes at a price: limited generalizability. We will look at some of the reasons for this trade-off, which is particularly relevant for laboratory and field experiments. At the outset, however, it is important to understand the basic difference between random assignment and random sampling.

Random Assignment Versus Random Sampling

Randomized experiments demonstrate causation primarily through the device of *random assignment,* as we have seen. However, random assignment to a treatment or control group is not at all the same thing as *random sampling*—and it is critical to distinguish the two.

Random sampling, discussed in Chapter 5, uses chance to select a sample of units from a larger population, as when telephone numbers are dialed at random to conduct an opinion poll. Using relatively small samples of large populations, random sampling enables accurate *descriptions* of the population, including accurate descriptions of the correlations within those populations. As we have seen, random *sampling* by itself, however, does nothing to help establish a cause-effect relationship between variables.

Limits of Random Sampling Revisited: The Current Population Survey

The Current Population Survey (CPS), which involves a scientifically conducted random sample of about 60,000 households in all 50 states in the United States, shows convincingly that owning a computer is strongly associated with greater employment and earnings. Does this prove that computer ownership *causes* greater earnings? Not really. It could be that having a job gives people the extra income to afford a computer (reverse causation), not the other way around. Maybe those who own computers are more comfortable with and good at technology, and it is this talent that causes their higher employment and earnings along with their ownership of a computer (common cause). Maybe those who don't own computers simply tend to be older people who did not grow up with computer technology, and older people are less likely to be working and earning high incomes (another common cause).

The CPS is one of the most important and most rigorous random sample surveys of the U.S. population, but it still provides us only with evidence of correlation—not causation. To try to disentangle the causal effect of computer ownership on earnings, we could use the control variables approach from Chapters 12 and 13, first speculating on and looking for evidence of common causes and then including relevant control variables in a multiple regression. However, the effect we estimate from control variables could still be biased due to reverse causation and unmeasured common causes. To get really convincing evidence of whether and how much computer ownership causally influences people's ability to work and earn money, we would need to set up an experiment that uses random *assignment*. We could randomly assign people to a treatment group that gets a free computer, let's say, and a control group that does not. We could then follow up after some time and compare their earnings.

QUESTION

How would you use *random sampling* to study the relationship between exercise and mood? How would you use *random assignment* to study this same relationship? Explain the differences between the two studies in terms of what we might learn.

Random Sampling for Generalizability Versus Random Assignment for Causal Evidence

Figure 14.3 shows another way to understand the differences between random sampling and random assignment, and the effects of shortcomings in each. Consider the population that one would like to know something about (at the top of the diagram). If the population is sampled randomly, the study's results will generalize back to the population. So random sampling provides good generalizability. Next consider how study subjects end up in the treatment and control groups. If some endogenous process (such as self-selection) determines allocation to treatment, then estimates of causal effects will be biased and the evidence weak. If subjects are assigned randomly, however, we will have an unbiased estimate of the causal effect of the treatment. So random assignment provides good evidence of causation. But notice how you could have one without the other: random sampling, but not random assignment (as in many surveys)—and thus good generalizability but poor causal evidence; or alternatively, a voluntary or convenience sample, but true random assignment (as in many experiments)—and thus good causal evidence but poor generalizability.

The Limited Settings: What Would Happen If Time or Place Were Different?

Because they take place in the real world of policy and programs, randomized field experiments are more realistic than small-scale, highly artificial laboratory experiments. Clearly, the recruitment of nearby volunteers to come to a lab at a university (or other location) and participate in an experiment represents just one small corner of the world. But because of the challenges and constraints of experimenting in the real world, even field experiments can still have limited generalizability.

Geographic Limitations

The Pensacola time-limited welfare experiment provided rigorous evidence of cause and effect—but only for welfare applicants in Escambia County, Florida. The researchers make a case that Escambia County is fairly typical of Florida counties. But how would such a policy work in a different part of the country, say, in a

Figure 14.3 Random Assignment Versus Random Sampling

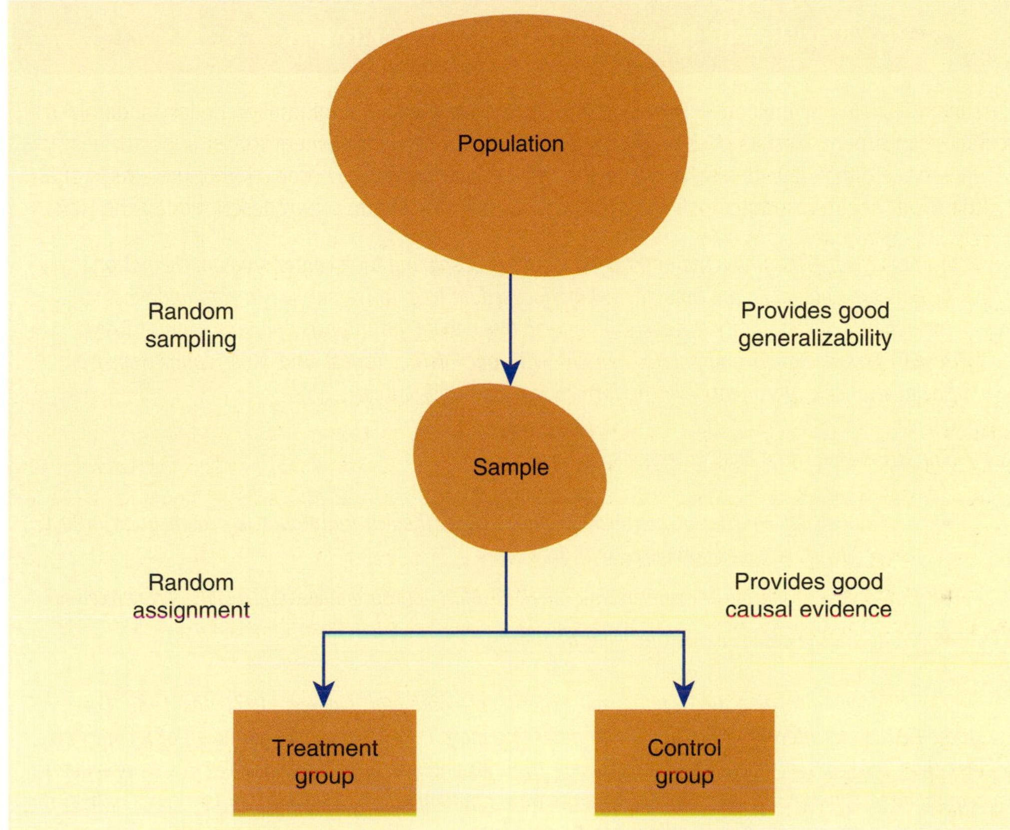

northern big city or a western rural area? The Pensacola experiment cannot directly answer these questions because its findings are limited in space.

The fact that experiments require a great deal of planning and close control often means that they must be confined to one small area or location. Only the most expensive social experiments—such as the RAND Health Insurance Experiment (see Box 14.5) or the Moving to Opportunity (see Box 14.8) housing voucher experiment—can afford to operate in multiple locations. But even these experiments include only a handful of locations. In contrast, many (though certainly not all) observational studies involve large probability samples representing large national or even international populations.

Limitations in Time

The period of the FTP experiment, the mid-1990s, had a fairly strong labor market. Indeed, the majority of families in the AFDC control group left welfare and found jobs during the study period. What would the effects of time limits look like in a weaker labor market, say, during a severe recession? The Pensacola experiment cannot directly answer this question because its findings are limited in time. For programs and outcomes of social relevance, effects may vary over time in important ways.

Randomized field experiments can sometimes take quite a long time to plan and implement, with final results arriving many years after the study was initially commissioned to answer a policy or practice issue. In this way, randomized field experiments can have limited generalizability to more immediate policy or practice debates. In contrast, the use of observational data from existing government and other surveys typically provides much faster results (although with less certainty about causation).

BOX 14.5
The RAND Health Insurance Experiment

The RAND Health Insurance Experiment (HIE) was a 15-year, multimillion-dollar randomized field experiment. Results of the study helped make the cash copayment to visit a doctor nearly universal. To this day, its results are used as inputs for virtually any projection of the effects of a change in health insurance policy. Here is the RAND Corporation's own description of the HIE:

> *In the early 1970s, financing and the impact of cost sharing took center stage in the national health care debate. At the time, the debate focused on free, universal health care and whether the benefits would justify the costs. To inform this debate, an interdisciplinary team of RAND researchers designed and carried out the HIE, one of the largest and most comprehensive social science experiments ever performed in the United States.*
>
> *The HIE posed three basic questions:*
>
> - *How does cost sharing or membership in an HMO [health maintenance organization] affect use of health services compared with free care?*
> - *How does cost sharing or membership in an HMO affect appropriateness and quality of care received?*
> - *What are the consequences for health?*
>
> *The HIE was a large-scale, randomized experiment conducted between 1971 and 1982. For the study, RAND recruited 2,750 families encompassing more than 7,700 individuals, all of whom were less than 65 years of age. They were chosen from six sites across the United States to provide a regional and urban/rural balance. Participants were randomly assigned to one of five types of health insurance plans created specifically for the experiment.*

Source: RAND Corporation (n.d.). See Newhouse & Insurance Experiment Group (1993) for further information.

Volunteers and Generalizability

Most laboratory experiments and many randomized field experiments rely on volunteers. For example, because of ethical and practical reasons, most clinical trials in medicine obtain their subjects by recruiting informed volunteers from a hospital or its surrounding community. (See the Johns Hopkins advertisement below.) Volunteers may be quite different from those who do not volunteer. They may suffer more from the ailment being treated; they may have stronger financial or other motivations to join the experiment; and they may trust more in doctors and modern medicine. The effectiveness of the treatment in a group of volunteers, therefore, may be quite different from its effectiveness in a group of nonvolunteers.

Volunteering makes the participants in a randomized experiment different from what random sampling would provide. Volunteers could differ in systematic ways that influence the effect of the treatment and hence the generalizability of the experimental results to a broader population. Even if those who volunteer look like the population on observable characteristics, such as age or education, they might be different in unobservable ways relevant to the outcome of the study. The results of an experiment thus generalize only to the people or other units like those that volunteered.

For example, think about a randomized field experiment to evaluate the effect of a substance abuse treatment program. Individuals who are utterly unmotivated to kick the habit might refuse to participate, while those who genuinely want to stop using drugs are likely to volunteer. In this case, the experiment would

Advertisement to recruit volunteers for an experiment.

Do you sometimes use narcotic drugs to get high?

(Heroin, Percocet, Oxycontin, Vicodin, Codeine or similar medications)

Johns Hopkins researchers are testing an investigational new medication for similarity to narcotics and to learn what doses are tolerated.

Volunteers must NOT be: addicted, in recovery, or seeking or in need of treatment.

Requires a 36-day stay in our residential research unit at the Hopkins Bayview Campus

Compensation of up to $2,420

Call

555-555-5555

for phone screening

Source: Craigslist.org

estimate the effect of the program on *drug users already motivated to quit*. Results would not generalize to the population of drug users at large.[3]

If we only want to know about the effectiveness on strongly motivated volunteers, these estimates work well. But what if we need to judge the effects on those under court-ordered treatment? Or to give advice to those who are reluctant to participate in the treatment? Always think about who will volunteer and therefore what population the randomized experiment will generalize to.

The Ideal Study: Random Sampling, Then Random Assignment

In an ideal world, researchers would first randomly *sample* subjects from a population of interest (say, all welfare-eligible families in the United States). They would then randomly *assign* the individuals in the sample to a treatment group and control group, apply (or withhold) the treatment, and observe the outcome. The estimated cause-effect relationship would then be generalizable to the whole population from which the sample came, and we would have the best of all possible studies: solid causal evidence (thanks to random *assignment*) and wide generalizability (thanks to random *sampling*).

But imagine how difficult it would be to keep track of several hundred or more treatment and control group members scattered across nearly as many cities and towns, not to mention how difficult it would be to provide each one with a uniform program or other treatment, especially if this involves a package of services that requires administrative support. Unless the treatment is very simple to implement, such as providing different versions of a questionnaire to survey respondents in a survey experiment, as discussed earlier, doing random sampling and then random assignment is not feasible for most policies or programs of interest.

However, a National Science Foundation–funded program called Time-sharing Experiments for the Social Sciences (TESS) has tried to increase the use of such random assignment experiments implemented on random samples of broad populations (see Box 14.6). One of the goals of the program is to increase the

[3]Thanks to Katherine M. Harris for suggesting this example.

generalizability of randomized experiments, particularly for topics in which a convenience sample (most often, undergraduate students at university campuses) may be inadequate or misleading. Most of the studies using TESS are in fact survey experiments and not treatments that require more complex or involved interventions. In her comprehensive book about survey experiments, Diana Mutz (2011) documents the many types of studies conducted using the TESS project and discusses its advantages, as well as its limitations, for doing more broadly generalizable causal research in the social sciences.

BOX 14.6
Time-sharing Experiments for the Social Sciences (TESS)

Time-sharing Experiments for the Social Sciences (TESS) offers researchers the opportunity to capture the internal validity of experiments while also realizing the benefits of working with a large, diverse population of research participants.

Investigators submit proposals for experiments, and TESS fields successful proposals for free on a representative sample of adults in the United States using GfK (formerly Knowledge Networks), a highly-respected Internet survey platform.

Source: http://www.tessexperiments.org/

Generalizability of the Treatment

One of the limitations of laboratory and survey experiments is that the treatments or interventions can be highly artificial. In a lab experiment about texting and driving, for example, we might wonder whether someone's driving performance in a simulator in a lab would be the same as his or her driving performance in a real car on the roadways. Perhaps the participants try harder in the lab or relax less than they would in their own cars, resulting in more attention to the road than when driving as part of their everyday lives. Alternatively, perhaps the simulator is somehow more difficult for them to use and recognize, resulting in more mistakes (accidents) than would happen when driving a real car. Generalizing the results of this particular lab experiment depends a great deal on how well the simulator represents driving in the real world.

The generalizability of survey experiments also suffers typically from artificial or hypothetical treatments, even when the surveys reflect random samples of a large population. The survey experiment about buying health insurance, for example, asked just one hypothetical yes/no question—but does this capture how people make such a major purchase decision in their real lives? Buying health insurance involves studying the details of various plans, which can be difficult and often frustrating to comprehend. Moreover, purchasing the insurance requires filling out lengthy forms and then—importantly—using your credit card or writing out a check. How many times have you intended to buy something, only to back out when the time came to put your money on the table? For these reasons, it can be difficult to generalize from an artificial or hypothetical survey question to people's real behavior in the world. This illustrates the idea that there is more to the generalizability of research than just representative sampling.

Even field experiments can have treatments that may not generalize. Field experiments often involve model programs that are carefully administered by motivated staff and funders. But when the program gets taken to scale, moving out of the "hothouse," as it were, subtle yet important changes can occur that may alter the effectiveness of the program. The staff administering the program may care less about clients than during the experimental period. The procedures of the program may become more confusing and bureaucratic. Even important features of the program—such as the amount of funding for services—may change. Because of the possibility of such changes, the treatment itself in a randomized field experiment may not generalize to how it would operate as a full-scale program.

Generalizability in the Long Run: Will the Effect Always Be the Same?

Often, randomized field experiments test a pilot program or treatment in a limited location and period of time. And because they do not involve permanent, guaranteed, or full-scale programs, they often miss the kind of long-run effects that may reflect people's strategic behavior or the reactions of other interested parties. Such effects are known in economics as *general equilibrium effects*, and they are particularly difficult to measure in randomized experiments. As a result, the effect of a full-scale program or treatment may turn out to be quite different from what was observed in the initial experiment.

Consider the important example of domestic violence and whether mandatory arrest, even when the victim opposes it, could reduce such violence, particularly homicides. In the early 1980s, the city of Minneapolis implemented an experiment in which police responding to domestic violence incidents were randomly assigned to follow three different policies: make an arrest, impose a short-term separation of aggressor and victim, or do what was then the more traditional course of action and simply give advisement (Sherman & Berk, 1984). They found that violence over the next 6 months was lower in cases where arrest was mandatory. The results of this randomized experiment, along with changing social norms about domestic violence and legal decisions, were influential in changing laws: By 2003, 15 (out of 50) U.S. states had mandatory arrest laws, and another 8 had recommended arrest rules.

After such laws were in place, Iyengar (2009) investigated the long-run, full-scale effect of mandatory arrest laws on domestic violence homicides. Because such laws were implemented at different times in different states, she was able to make use of a fairly rigorous type of natural experiment (described in the next chapter). Her study showed that some domestic violence victims, knowing an arrest of the aggressor was mandatory, became less willing to report domestic violence, which in turn increased the probability that violence would escalate to homicide—an unintended outcome of the mandatory arrest policy, and an outcome directly opposite to the findings of the initial Minneapolis experiment.

Part of the problem is that randomized experiments typically affect only a small share of those who would be in a full-scale intervention. For example, with the RAND Health Insurance Experiment, people assigned to a high cost-sharing (high-deductible) policy were only a very small share of any one local doctor's pool of patients. A local doctor might be aware of one patient's cost-sharing burden and consciously try to help save the patient money, but that doctor would not feel his income threatened by cost sharing in general. If the doctor's entire pool of patients had high deductibles, however, the doctor might react quite differently. In general, a policy can have spillovers—positive and negative—that affect both those who receive treatment and others.

QUESTION

What are some of the factors that often limit the generalizability of results from a randomized experiment?

In sum, most randomized experiments rely on volunteers, occur in limited locations and times, and involve treatments that may be artificial, hypothetical, or unlike full-scale programs or interventions. Therefore, randomized experiments may not generalize as desired to the real world of policy and programs.

Variations on the Design of Experiments

So far, we have considered randomized experiments that have tended to look a certain way—one treatment group and one control group, with individuals randomized to each condition and a comparison of outcomes. But there are variations on the design of such experiments, so that randomized experiments can appear different and more complex than Figure 14.1 suggests.

Cluster Randomization

Some experiments involve **cluster randomization**, meaning groups or clusters, rather than individuals, are randomized. This is illustrated in Figure 14.4. As the figure shows, clustering results in randomizing fewer, larger aggregate units to the treatment and control conditions. In some settings, cluster randomization is much more practical. For example, when testing a new curriculum, we might randomize the treatment to classrooms rather than to individual students. This makes sense because a new curriculum must be implemented by a teacher who cannot deliver two different types of content to randomly chosen students in the same classroom.

Cluster randomization is also valuable, because it helps prevent leakage of the treatment to the control group. If students in each condition are not at least somewhat isolated, they can learn from each other in ways that influence the results. A related issue is that cluster randomization helps in the assessment of spillover effects—both positive and negative. For example, health treatments of contagious diseases help prevent the spread of those diseases, which can be observed only in clusters of people who are in contact with each other. Miguel and Kremer (2004) illustrate how randomizing whole schools to deworming treatment can capture positive spillovers of the intervention on health and education outcomes.

How does cluster randomization help incorporate spillover effects?

Because cluster randomization involves randomizing fewer aggregate units, a drawback is less statistical power—less statistical equivalence from randomization. Ideally one would randomize many clusters, but that is often impractical and expensive. If there are only a few aggregate units to randomly assign (as the four clusters shown in the simplified Figure 14.4), cluster randomization turns into more of a quasi experiment (discussed in Chapter 15).

Figure 14.4 Individual-Level and Cluster Randomization (Random Assignment)

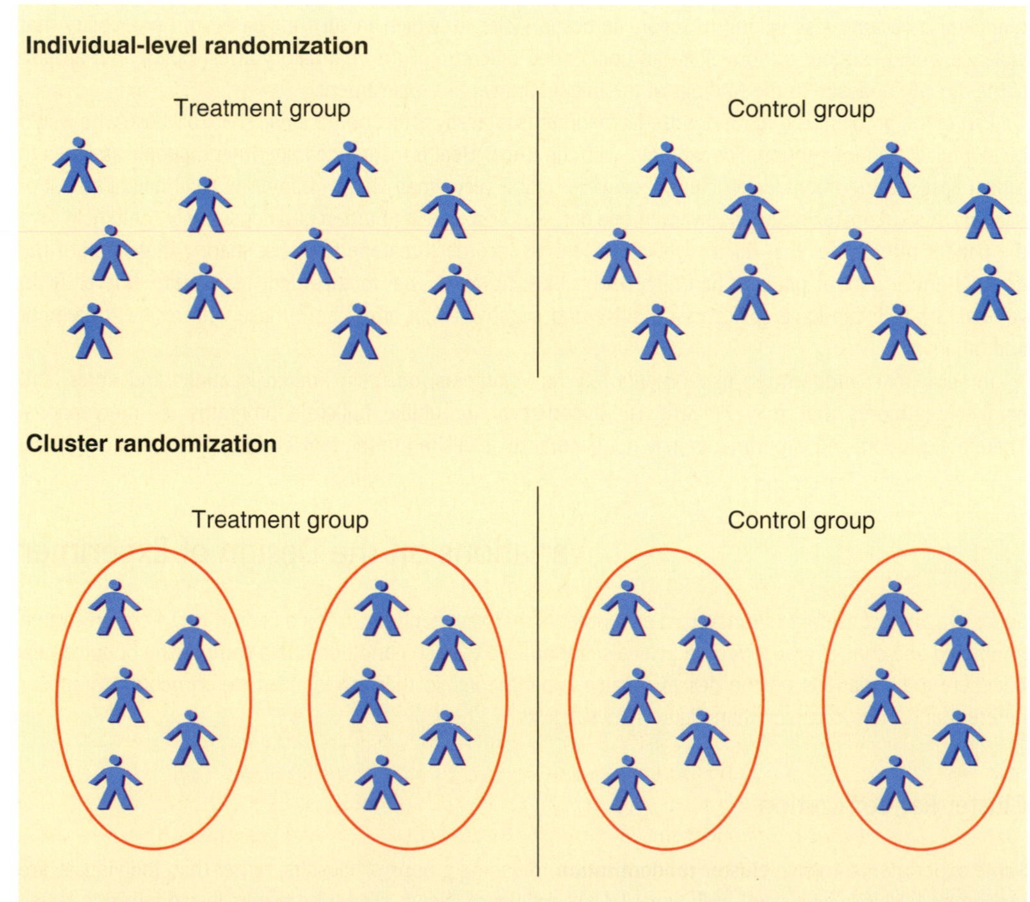

Arms in an Experiment

In the classic randomized experiment we described (Figure 14.1), one treatment condition is compared with one control condition. But often we wish to investigate and compare several possible treatments and even contrast them with more than one control (such as usual and nothing). In fact, a randomized study can compare multiple possible treatment or control conditions, often referred to as **arms of an experiment**. The RAND Health Insurance Experiment (see Box 14.5), one of the largest policy experiments ever, had 5 main arms, including 4 cost-sharing health insurance plans and one free plan, although minor variations in the 4 cost-sharing plans actually resulted in a total of up to 14 arms (13 cost-sharing plans and one free plan). The Moving to Opportunity housing voucher experiment (see Box 14.8) had 3 arms: housing vouchers with a low-poverty-neighborhood requirement (that families move to low-poverty census tracts), ordinary housing vouchers (without a low-poverty-neighborhood requirement), and a control group.

With three or more arms in an experiment, the analysis of results involves more than one comparison. For example, an experiment with three arms (two treatment groups, say, and one control group—like the Moving to Opportunity demonstration) would require the following comparisons:

- Treatment 1 vs. Control
- Treatment 2 vs. Control
- Treatment 1 vs. Treatment 2

In other words, we could analyze how effective each treatment is, relative to the control condition. In addition, we could compare the two treatments with each other to see which is more effective. With 4 arms, we could make 6 comparisons—and with five arms we could make 11 comparisons. With so many comparisons, however, interpreting the results can be a challenge. In addition, there is a statistical problem of making multiple comparisons, as discussed in Chapter 9. Essentially, the more pairs of treatments we compare, the more likely at least one pair will have a statistically significant difference due to chance. Although this problem tends to be ignored in practice, it can be addressed through formal multiple comparison corrections, such as the Bonferroni correction.

Levels of a Treatment: Probing a Dose-Response Relationship

An experiment can reflect differences in the dosage or degree of a treatment, not just comparisons between categorically different kinds of treatment. For example, the survey experiment about willingness to buy health insurance tested annual premiums of $4,000, $3,000, and $2,000. In a study of the purchase and use of mosquito nets to combat malaria, Pascaline Dupas (2009) simultaneously randomly assigned households to several different amounts of subsidy for the nets as well as different ways of framing the advantages.

Such experiments offer the benefit of allowing tests for a possible **dose-response relationship**—or how the effect of the experiment varies, as the dosage increases. The resulting trend may be linear (the larger the dose, the larger the response), curvilinear (as when an increasing dose reaches a point of diminishing response), or abrupt (as when the effect kicks in all at once only when the dosage reaches a particular level). However, to detect such subtle trends requires more like five or more dosage levels.

Notice that this kind of dose-response information cannot be obtained from the usual experiment with just one treatment group and one control group. Indeed, one of the key limitations of many experiments is that the independent variable of interest is only categorical—for example, large class size versus small class size—while in many observational studies the independent variables are quantitative, such as the actual number of students per class (which in a large data set might range, say, from 18 to 37 students, with a distribution across every class size in between).

Factors in an Experiment: Probing Interactions

So far, we have focused on experiments examining the effect of a single independent variable. Some experiments try to examine the effect of more than one independent variable, called **factors**, and how they interact with one another. These are referred to as **factorial experiments**. The simplest and most common is a two-factor design in which two independent variables each take on two possible values, in all possible combinations, resulting in four arms. For example, a public health experiment in Indonesia (Lind et al., 2004) examined the effects of iron and zinc supplements on the development of infants, randomizing subjects to one of four conditions:

Arm 1: 10 mg iron

Arm 2: 10 mg zinc

Arm 3: 10 mg iron and 10 mg zinc

Arm 4: Placebo (no iron, no zinc)

The iron supplement constitutes the first factor, the zinc supplement is the second factor, and the combined supplement tests the *interaction* of the two factors, all of which are compared with a control condition (placebo).

This particular study found that both iron and zinc were individually beneficial—in experimental language, they had **main effects** that were positive and significant.[4] A main effect is the average effect of one factor across levels of the other factors in the experiment. But a factorial experiment also provides information about a possible **interaction effect**—meaning an effect of both factors together that is more (or less) than the sum of the two main effects. In this particular study, it turned out, there was no evidence that the two supplements together provided any additional boost to the physical or cognitive development of young children in Indonesia, beyond the beneficial effect that each supplement provided on its own. So there was no evidence of an interaction effect.

QUESTION

What is the difference between arms and factors in an experiment?

Sometimes experiments test more than two factors, and even more than two levels per factor, although the sample size must be quite large to do this. Even a 2 × 2 × 2 factorial experiment would have eight conditions or groups to populate with subjects. Moreover, the interpretation of main and interaction effects can become quite complex and difficult. In a 2 × 2 × 2 factorial experiment, you would need to interpret three main effects, three two-way interactions, and one three-way interaction. Still, it can be useful to learn how causes of an outcome work in combination, or in conflict—information that cannot be had from only a series of single-factor experiments.

Within-Subjects (Crossover) Experiments

In the FTP evaluation, researchers assigned families randomly to either the usual AFDC program or the new FTP program. Families could end up in either one group or the other—but not both. This is referred to as a **between-subjects experiment** because the comparison is *between* subjects or units in the treatment group and the control group. Even if we assign people to three or more treatment groups, as long as they stay in those groups, we still have a between-subjects experiment.

But an experiment can also apply two or more treatments to the *same* people, at different times (and in varied order). This is known as a **within-subjects experiment** because the experimental conditions are

[4]Sometimes, particularly when analyzing data using regression models, researchers will use the term *main effect* to refer to the effect of one variable (such as Zinc) when there is none of the other variable (such as Iron), rather than the average of No Iron and 10 mg of Iron. But that is not the correct usage for experiments.

varied *within* each person or unit so that each gets exposed to both the treatment and control conditions. As it turns out, the texting and driving experiment (Drews et al., 2009) used a within-subjects design: It first randomized people to driving only or to texting while driving—and then had people switch to the other condition. The 20 young drivers in the experiment, therefore, each drove in the simulator twice, once while texting and once while not texting. Such studies are also known as a **crossover experiment** because subjects start in one condition and then *cross over* to the other condition. Yet another term used to describe this kind of study is a **repeated-measures experiment**, because repeated outcome measures are taken on each subject after exposure to each condition, although repeated-measures studies can also be observational, not experimental, and simply observe (measure) people repeatedly over time.

The main advantage of a within-subjects experiment is the efficiency of using the same subjects twice (or more), doubling (or more) the number of observations. This is especially important when it takes effort to recruit people to a lab or another location, brief them, set them up on an apparatus (like the driving simulator), and then make observations. After doing all this work, why not test people under several different conditions? Moreover, testing the same people in both conditions has the advantage of removing the wide variability that often comes from having entirely different people in the treatment and control groups. But within-subjects experiments have drawbacks as well. The main problems are that the effect of the first treatment can *carry over* to the second condition, and also individuals can learn from the first condition in ways that influence their response to the second condition. In the texting and driving experiment, for example, the young adults undoubtedly learned how to use the simulator after the first attempt, so they were better at it on the second try.

Artifacts in Experiments

People will be people—and this adds another layer of complexity to randomized experiments when applied to social and policy research. People can figure out what the experiment is about, and what the researcher expects of them. They can imagine what the effects of the treatment will do to them—and even convince themselves that it is happening. Researchers themselves can let their expectations cloud their observations, measurements, and data analysis. Rosnow and Rosenthal (1997) label these *artifacts* and define them as "unintended or uncontrolled human aspects of the research situation that confound the investigator's conclusions about what went on in the study" (p. 3).

The Hawthorne Effect and the Advantage of Unobtrusive Measures

Randomized experiments confront the problem that the situation under study must be disturbed to be observed. Thus, not even the control group, strictly speaking, represents a purely natural condition. Still, we use the control group as a *counterfactual* estimate—what would happen in the absence of treatment. But, in actual fact, we are unable to measure what would happen without recruitment, informed consent, measurement, and all the rest of the experiences the treatment and control groups go through to be part of the study.

In fact, people often react simply to being studied—many research subjects will change their behavior in response to the attention paid to them by the researchers. This phenomenon is known as the **Hawthorne effect** (Draper, 2008).

Because of the Hawthorne effect, researchers often prefer **unobtrusive** or **nonreactive measures**—measures that occur naturally or routinely, or otherwise do not disturb the subjects in an experiment (Webb, Campbell, Schwartz, & Sechrest, 1999). In a school-based experiment, for example, the usual tests given each year to all students would be a kind of unobtrusive measure, since they are not imposed by the experimenters.

The need for unobtrusive or nonreactive measures arises in nonexperimental research as well, however, including purely descriptive studies of people's attitudes or behaviors. For example, say we are trying to measure the food intake of a sample of adults and ask them to save duplicate servings of what they eat in bags for laboratory analysis (a method sometimes used to study food intake). The act of saving duplicate servings in bags, however, is quite likely to alter what people eat—it is an obtrusive, reactive method that makes people much more self-conscious of the type and quantity of food they consume.

Placebo Effect and Blinding

Perhaps the most famous human artifact is the so-called **placebo effect**—the fact that people often respond to any kind of treatment, even a completely phony or useless one. Although related to the Hawthorne effect, the placebo effect refers to people's specific beliefs in the treatment rather than to their more general reactions to being studied or observed (Draper, 2008). The placebo effect takes its name from placebo treatments in medical studies—inert treatments masked as real ones. For example, if we were to give you an inert pill (without mentioning that it was only an inert pill) and tell you that the pill was designed to make people mentally more alert while learning complex material such as research methods, it might actually work. You might feel more alert, read more carefully, and get more out of this book. But this effect would be entirely due to your belief in the power of the pill—not anything in the pill itself.

Blind experiments help correct this problem by keeping subjects ignorant of which group they are in. For a placebo to work, subjects must be ignorant of whether they are in the treatment or control arm—ignorant about whether they have received the real treatment or the placebo. Because both treatment and control groups are subject to the same placebo effect, the control group makes a valid counterfactual to the treatment group.

Researchers themselves can distort the results of an experiment, either consciously or unconsciously, when they know who is getting the real treatment and not just the placebo. For example, researchers who want a new treatment to succeed might make observations or record measurements so that the treatment group has better outcomes, even quite unconsciously. This weakness can be addressed through **double-blind experiments**, in which the research workers who interact with the subjects, or make measurements, are also ignorant about which group the subjects are in.

The Difficulty of Placebos in Social Policy Experiments

Giving the control group a placebo is practical for drug studies but more difficult for many social programs. After all, people know whether or not they went through a job training program, received a housing voucher, or obtained free health insurance. Thus, the placebo effect is a real issue in many randomized social or policy experiments.

For example, consider the results of the famous Perry Preschool Study (see Box 14.7), which is widely cited as evidence for the long-term benefits of early childhood education. The experiment evaluated a model preschool program in Ypsilanti, Michigan, and the research team followed up with 58 kids in the treatment group and 65 in the control group for an unusually long time, well into their adulthood. Interestingly, although the initial effects on IQ and achievement tests had mostly leveled off by second grade, the researchers began to discover large differences by adolescence and into adulthood. The treatment group was more likely to graduate from high school, go to college, earn more income, own a house, and stay out of prison.

But why this delayed reaction? As the treatment group members matured into adulthood, they were regularly contacted and interviewed by the research team and even the media, heightening their awareness of their special status as Perry Preschool graduates. They might have come to view themselves as special and to be aware that the researchers and others in society had high expectations of them. Perhaps these expectations encouraged them to finish school, go to college, buy a house, and so on. Or perhaps the effects of high-quality preschool are indeed latent for a time, only to emerge with force later on in life. But the placebo effect possibility at least deserves careful consideration in such social policy experiments.

BOX 14.7
The Perry Preschool Study

The HighScope Perry Preschool Project is one of the longest-running randomized field experiments to test a public policy or program. It involved 123 African American children from Ypsilanti, Michigan, identified in the 1960s as being at high risk for school failure and related problems. Here is how the HighScope Educational Research Foundation, the organization that ran the experiment, describes it:

> *From 1962–1967, at ages 3 and 4, the subjects were randomly divided into a program group that received a high-quality preschool program based on HighScope's participatory learning approach and a comparison group who received no preschool program. In the study's most recent phase, 97% of the study participants still living were interviewed at age 40. Additional data were gathered from the subjects' school, social services, and arrest records.*
>
> *The study found that adults at age 40 who had the preschool program had higher earnings, were more likely to hold a job, had committed fewer crimes, and were more likely to have graduated from high school than adults who did not have preschool.*

Source: HighScope Educational Research Foundation (2005).

Contamination

In a randomized experiment, the researcher controls what treatment the subjects are exposed to—at least, in theory. In practice, however, the control group may gain access or exposure to the treatment, either intentionally or unintentionally. For example, in an experimental evaluation of a new curriculum, the teachers in the control group might find out about the new curriculum, from casual conversation or observation, and decide to try some of the methods or materials themselves. This is one example of **contamination**—when something happens in the course of implementing the study that compromises the integrity and logic of the experiment. One of the reasons to use cluster randomization, as discussed earlier, is to isolate people in a given treatment group from contact with other treatment or control groups so as to minimize the risk of contamination.

Demoralization and Rivalry

The members of the control group may feel neglected and left out because they are not getting the promising new treatment. They could become *demoralized* and take a turn for the worse (worse than they would have been had they not been involved in the experiment to begin with). If so, the treatment would seem more effective than it really is.

Alternatively, the control group may engage in *competitive rivalry*, as when the teachers of classes designated as the control group try extra hard to teach their kids to read so that they don't fall behind those classes that received the special, model reading curriculum.

Cluster randomization can help reduce both demoralization and rivalry by reducing people's contact with and even awareness of those who are in the other arms of the experiment. Nonetheless, both phenomena make the experience of the control group different in the experimental setting than it would be in the real, unmanipulated world.

Noncompliance

Another problem can occur when the treatment group fails to fully follow the treatment, a problem referred to as **noncompliance**. For example, people may grow weary of the side effects of a medication and stop taking it, or they may fail to complete a training program. In this case, the treatment whose effect is being measured is not the one intended or advertised.

Often with real-world programs or treatments, the best we can do is to offer it or make it available—we can't force people to comply. As a result, what we may want to estimate after all is the effect of simply providing treatment, not necessarily having it taken up fully. We will have more to say about this issue shortly when we discuss the analysis of data from randomized experiments. In fact, the term *noncompliance* comes from medicine and may be inappropriately derogatory in the context of social experiments.

Attrition

Another problem with randomized experiments in the real world is **attrition**—participants dropping out from the experiment. For example, members of the control group may lose interest in the experiment (after all, they are not getting the fancy new treatment, so why continue?). If those who drop out are systematically different from those who do not drop out, the study results may be biased. Researchers can examine empirically whether those who drop out differ in measured variables from those who do not. If they do differ, methods exist to lessen the bias. Of course, those who drop out could also differ in unmeasured ways.

How is doing experiments with people more difficult than, say, experimenting with plants?

If there is no final outcome data for those who drop out, attrition bias due to unmeasured differences is extremely difficult to avoid. However, if some outcome or proxy outcome can be found, then the bias can be reduced by simply comparing everyone in the treatment group, dropout or not, with everyone in the control group. We will cover this approach in more detail shortly.

Both noncompliance and attrition are, in an important sense, an inevitable consequence of voluntary participation—the ethical principle that says people can refuse to participate or withdraw from a study whenever they choose. Ethical limitations on research with human subjects often mean that experiments do not go as planned.

Analysis of Randomized Experiments

The analysis of data from a randomized experiment is usually more straightforward than the analysis of observational data to estimate a causal effect. Analyzing randomized experiments does not typically require theorizing about and modeling common causes (as we did in the previous chapter), because a well-done randomized experiment statistically equalizes groups on all variables (measured and unmeasured). Therefore, the analysis of randomized experiments generally does not require control variables or multiple regression.

With just one treatment group and one control group, an experiment can be analyzed simply by comparing means (with a two-sample t test of significance) or proportions (with a two-sample z test for proportions or a chi-square test). ANOVA (analysis of variance, discussed in Chapter 10) can be used to compare three or more group means across all arms of an experiment as well as to examine interactions (Brown & Melamed, 1990). With some simple modifications, ordinary regression analysis with dummy variables representing the treatments or factors can also be used to analyze experimental data. But because experiments can have complex effects, and sometimes they do not always turn out as planned, complexities can crop up in the analysis of randomized experiments (Bloom, 2005).

Balancing and the Occasional Need for Control Variables

One possible wrinkle is that an important influence on the outcome cannot be *balanced* in the arms because the sample size is too small. Balancing refers to equalization of common causes in the arms of an experiment so that the treatment and control groups are equivalent in all relevant ways. In medicine, for example, randomized experiments generally have the sample size chosen to ensure precision for medical outcomes, but researchers sometimes want to analyze financial outcomes, such as cost, also. Because costs and their causes (such as length of stay in the hospital) are often very skewed (a small number of extremely large values), the treatment and control arms may not be statistically equalized for those variables; thus, the use of certain control variables may be appropriate.

When control variables are used in the analysis of an experiment, researchers often refer to them as **covariates**. The statistical technique employed in such situations is typically ANCOVA (analysis of covariance) or multiple regression to incorporate control variables (or covariates) in the analysis of an experiment. But in most cases, randomized experiments do not require control variables.

Sample Size and Minimal Detectable Effects

When conducting a randomized experiment, the analysis should be planned in advance to ensure an adequate sample size. Sample size refers to the number of units or subjects in the treatment and control groups. Clustering reduces the effective sample size because the clusters (e.g., classrooms), not the individuals within clusters (e.g., students), are randomized. Additional arms in an experiment also reduce the effective sample size because the units or subjects must be divided across multiple treatment groups. Sample size matters: You do not want to waste the time, effort, and money required to conduct a randomized experiment only to end up with insufficient precision to draw useful conclusions.

Sample size calculations, such as the ones described in Chapter 9, always require assumptions, such as assumptions about the variances of key variables. However, for experiments, one must also specify the desired **minimal detectable effect**—the smallest effect that would still have practical significance. The smaller this desired minimal detectable effect, the more precision and therefore the larger the sample size needed to detect it. Bloom (1995) provides a useful approach to these issues.

Heterogeneous Treatment Effects

We have been referring to *the* treatment effect, using the singular. However, it is reasonable to expect that different people respond differently to time limits on welfare, housing vouchers, texting while driving, or any other treatment—something researchers call **heterogeneous treatment effects**. For example, time limits may have different effects for mothers with young children than for mothers with teenagers. Time limits might differently affect someone with a self-reliant personality than they might affect someone who prefers structure and authority. In a randomized experiment, what we really estimate is an **average treatment effect**, which is as the term suggests the average of the various individual effects that the treatment has on each person who participates in the study.

For observable characteristics, such as gender, it is possible to use the data to see how treatment effects differ between groups that vary in that characteristic. For example, the Moving to Opportunity study looked at the effects on boys and girls separately. The researchers found that moving to a higher-income neighborhood improved educational outcomes for girls but worsened them for boys. Of course, subgroups have smaller sample sizes and therefore less statistical precision.

The effects of treatment also probably differ among some subgroups that we are unable to identify. For example, the effects of job training or welfare time limits might be different depending on the motivation of the participants. But if we lack a measure of motivation, we are unable to see how treatment effectiveness varies with motivation and are forced to average over subjects with different motivation levels.

Intent to Treat Analysis

As we have seen, units or subjects in a randomized experiment sometimes drop out of the study (attrition) or fail to comply or take up the treatment. What if these people started with systematically different outcomes or would respond differently from those who remain in the study and comply fully with the treatment? If we simply remove the dropouts or noncompliers from our analysis, we could bias the estimated treatment effects.

The safest method for dealing with either attrition or noncompliance is referred to as **intent to treat** (**ITT**). Specifically, everyone is kept in his or her original randomized group—treatment or control. The ITT effect is the difference in outcome between the originally assigned treatment and control groups, regardless of whether those in the treatment group actually got the treatment or not. ITT avoids all self-selection problems—whether due to noncompliance or due to attrition.

ITT works well for noncompliance. However, for attrition, final outcomes may not be collected for those who leave, and it may be impossible to calculate an ITT estimate. To the extent that ITT can be calculated, however, it is often the most relevant effect to estimate because, as we noted earlier in this chapter, often in the real world we can only offer treatments—not force people to use them.

Nonetheless, policy makers and researchers sometimes would like to know the actual effect of treatment itself. An example will make this clearer.

Treatment of the Treated in Moving to Opportunity

Moving to Opportunity (MTO) is a randomized experiment in which low-income families in the treatment group were given vouchers usable only in low-poverty neighborhoods and counseling to help them find housing in those neighborhoods (De Souza Briggs, Popkin, & Goering, 2010; Ludwig et al., 2008; Sanbonmatsu et al., 2011). MTO is described further in Box 14.8. Still, slightly less than half of those in the treatment group in fact moved to low-poverty neighborhoods. In the jargon of medical randomized clinical trials, slightly less than half "complied," although their lack of compliance may have been due to factors beyond their control.

Although the ITT estimate is useful, the researchers (Ludwig et al., 2008, pp. 152–153) decided that

> for both scientific reasons (to understand the direct causal effect of location on outcomes) and policy reasons (to allow extrapolation to other mobility programs and settings where compliance rates may be different), it would be desirable to have an estimate of the impact of moving per se.

Therefore, the researchers also estimated what is referred to as the **treatment of the treated** (**TOT**)—an estimate of the effect of the treatment on those who were actually exposed to it.

To understand TOT, we must first consider several categories of subjects, as illustrated in Table 14.4. Within those families in the treatment group (those given vouchers for low-poverty neighborhoods) in the first column, some moved (the compliers), and some did not (the noncompliers). And evidence shows that compliers and noncompliers differ in ways that may influence the outcome.

Because the control group was created through randomization, it also contains two subgroups that are statistically equivalent to the treatment subgroups: would-be compliers and would-be noncompliers. They are equivalent on average to the corresponding treatment subgroups, subject only to small statistical fluctuations. In a randomized experiment, the control group implements the counterfactual—what would happen to the treatment group if it did not have the treatment. The same is true of these subgroups.

For the TOT estimator, we would like to know the difference in outcomes between the treatment group compliers (Subgroup A) and the control group would-be compliers (Subgroup B). Our only problem is that we cannot observe the control group would-be compliers (Subgroup B) because we don't know which of the families not offered vouchers would in fact use them, if they were given the chance.

To calculate the TOT estimator, therefore, we must make some assumptions: First, being placed in the treatment group has no effect on noncompliers. Second, being in the control group has no effect on anyone,

Table 14.4 Subgroups in Moving to Opportunity for TOT Calculation

	Treatment Group	Control Group
Compliers	A Moved to low-poverty neighborhood using voucher Only group affected by experiment	B Would have moved to low-poverty neighborhood if given voucher but not given voucher No effect of experiment assumed
Noncompliers	C Did not move to low-poverty neighborhood despite having voucher No effect of experiment assumed	D Would not have moved to low-poverty neighborhood if given voucher; and in fact not given voucher No effect of experiment assumed

either would-be compliers or would-be noncompliers. In other words, we assume no human artifacts of being in an experiment, for example, no Hawthorne effect. With these assumptions, *among those who would not comply,* the effect of being in the treatment group relative to the control group is zero, because neither subgroup is affected in any way.

Consequently, the entire ITT effect is driven by the difference between the treatment and control groups *among those who would comply.* From that we know that

$$\text{ITT} = \text{Share compliers} \times \text{TOT}.$$

The share of compliers (a proportion) is known from the experimental group, and it must be the same in the control group, due to randomization. Thus, the TOT effect is simply the ITT effect divided by the share of compliers:

$$\text{TOT} = \text{ITT/Share compliers}.$$

The TOT is larger than the ITT because, though all the ITT effect was due only to the compliers, the effect was attributed to the larger group of both compliers and noncompliers. (See Ludwig et al., 2008, pp. 152–154, and Orr et al., 2003, Appendix B, for further discussion.)

Because slightly less than half of those offered vouchers in fact moved to low-poverty neighborhoods, the difference between the ITT and TOT estimates was large in the MTO evaluation. For example, using the ITT estimator, parents given vouchers to move to a low-poverty neighborhood had a psychological distress measure of 0.1 standard deviations lower than those not given vouchers. But using the TOT estimator, those who moved had a psychological distress measure of 0.2 standard deviations lower than those who did not move, among those who would move if given vouchers (Ludwig et al., 2008, p. 163). The TOT estimate is twice the ITT estimate because only about half of those given vouchers "complied"—moved to a low-poverty neighborhood.

See Sanbonmatsu et al. (2011) for a complete description of the experiment and final results. See Ludwig et al. (2008) for a valuable discussion of what can and cannot be learned from randomized experiments using the MTO example.

Ethics of Randomized Experiments

Randomized experiments must meet all the usual ethical requirements of any human subjects research: beneficence, no harm to subjects, justice, informed consent, and voluntary participation. But randomized experiments in social and policy research often take place in everyday settings, like schools, doctor's offices,

BOX 14.8 The Moving to Opportunity Demonstration

In the 1990s, the U.S. Department of Housing and Urban Development (HUD) conducted a large-scale randomized field experiment called Moving to Opportunity for Fair Housing (MTO) (De Souza Briggs, Popkin, & Goering, 2010; Sanbonmatsu et al., 2011). MTO examined the issue of how poor families living in housing projects run by the local public housing authority (PHA) could benefit from housing vouchers and counseling that allowed them to move to low-poverty neighborhoods with better schools, safety, and public services. Here is HUD's description of the experimental design of MTO:

> *Five public housing authorities (Baltimore, Boston, Chicago, Los Angeles, and New York City) administer HUD contracts under this 10-year demonstration. Within the PHAs, randomly selected experimental groups of households with children receive housing counseling and vouchers that must be used in areas with less than 10 percent poverty. Families chosen for the experimental group receive tenant-based Section 8 rental assistance that helps pay their rent, as well as housing counseling to help them find and successfully use housing in low-poverty areas. Two control groups are included to test the effects of the program: one group already receiving Section 8 assistance and another just coming into the Section 8 program.*

Source: U.S. Department of Housing and Urban Development (n.d.).

QUESTION

Which analysis, ITT or TOT, do you think would provide a more useful estimate for policy makers and prospective dieters of the real effect of a 10-week highly restrictive weight-loss diet?

and workplaces, and can affect people's health, education, job search, and earnings. Such high stakes raise particular ethical issues for many randomized experiments applied to policy and practice.

Something for Everyone: The Principle of Beneficence

One such ethical issue is that no arm of a randomized experiment should harm people; moreover, each arm should provide at least some benefit (even if just a small benefit). But often, randomized experiments are done because the researchers believe that some new intervention is better than the usual one. So it may not seem ethical to randomize some to receive what the researchers believe is an inferior intervention (or lack of intervention). We need to ask what would happen to people without any study. If people would receive nothing or the usual program, then it can be argued that being in the control arm would not harm them. Yet it still would not benefit them either. One option is to make sure that both arms get the intervention, but perhaps one gets it at a later time. For example, Miguel and Kremer (2004) randomly allocated primary schools in Kenya to receive deworming (treatment to reduce worms that invade intestines, causing illness and lower nutrition) in the first year, but then extended the intervention to control schools in the following year.

One approach to ensuring that all study participants benefit is to pay expenses or even provide financial incentives to participate. This is an ethically complicated area where people disagree. Participation in a randomized experiment is supposed to be a free choice, uncoerced. Some believe that offering financial benefits to those who are poor is essentially coercion. Meanwhile, others believe that it is unfair to use the time of poor people without compensating them.

Another consequence of beneficence is that it may not be possible to have a control arm, in the strict sense that the control receives nothing or just the standard treatment. Many randomized field experiments compare a variety of alternative treatments, such as math training or vocabulary training, but with no group receiving no training, even though this may represent the real counterfactual of interest.

The principles of beneficence and no harm to subjects may be easier to satisfy when the benefits of the intervention or treatment are truly uncertain. Of course, why would one do a randomized experiment if the benefits were known? But it is complicated: A particular study's researchers—or some other group of people—might all *believe* or *suspect* that one approach is better, even if there is no real evidence and others have doubts. Whose beliefs matter? Many education researchers and policy makers want to investigate the effects of online education, but some instructors believe it is not as effective as traditional forms of education. Those instructors might believe that a randomized experiment would be unethical. But would it? Remember that beliefs can be wrong and one should always look at the existing evidence.

In some experiments, evidence of negative side effects or even especially effective treatments will lead researchers to decide to stop the experiment early. If early results show a treatment is causing harm to people, obviously this implies that the experiment must end as it clearly violates the principle of no harm to subjects. For example, several large clinical trials testing the potential benefits of vitamin E were stopped because those taking the supplements turned out to be at increased risk of mortality (Offit, 2013). But even evidence of treatment effectiveness can prompt researchers to stop an experiment early in order to give the treatment to the control group. Although it may limit the scientific findings, it is not ethical to withhold a clearly effective treatment from those in the control group who could benefit from it.

Informed Consent When the Stakes Are High

Providing informed consent in randomized field experiments (including randomized clinical trials) can be especially critical because the potential outcomes can be important ones, such as having an illness cured, graduating from high school, or getting a job. People's lives can be permanently impacted, unlike in most survey experiments and many lab experiments.

All randomized experiments have the further complication that they must at least implicitly explain the idea of potential outcomes and describe at least three potential outcomes (counterfactuals): what happens with participation in the treatment arm, what happens with participation in the control arm, and what happens with no participation at all. Since presumably there is uncertainty about expected outcomes (why else do the experiment?), the information provided must inevitably grapple with probabilities—a notoriously difficult concept for humans to grasp.

Cluster randomized experiments, such as when schools, hospitals, or neighborhoods are randomized, raise some difficult issues about informed consent (Macklin, 2013). Who, if anyone, must consent? In a hospital where the intervention is, say, educating nurses, nurses presumably must consent. But what about the nurses' patients? Generally, if patients' information is used anonymously, their consent is not considered necessary. If a neighborhood is randomized to some completely public and free kind of action, then typically individual consent is not needed. For example, Duflo, Banerjee, Glennerster, and Kinnan (2013) worked with a microfinance company in India and randomized some neighborhoods to earlier entry by the company and not others. Since, with or without an experiment, companies get to decide which neighborhoods they market in and when residents are free to ignore them, consent is not needed for the randomization.

Is Randomization Itself Unethical?

Some people find randomization distasteful or even an ethically wrong way to allocate things. This can be true even when what is being given out is "extra" and not something people would otherwise expect to receive. For example, New York City's housing agency had a small program to provide rent assistance to families at risk of becoming homeless. In the initial version, families had to seek out the program (Buckley, 2010). This led to fears of self-selection and worries that the program was not, in fact, effective, if the savvy families who self-selected into the program might have managed well enough on their own in other ways (through help from relatives, other programs, finding cheaper housing alternatives, and so on).

To settle this question and learn the value of the program, the agency decided to do a randomized experiment (Rolston, Geyer, & Locke, 2013). But there was significant controversy and backlash, with one local politician stating, "I don't think homeless people in our time, or in any time, should be treated like lab rats" (Buckley, 2010). Supporters of the study note that there was no clear entitlement and that the city government did not have funds to extend rent assistance to everyone.

Others, however, see randomization as a very fair way to allocate often scarce resources. Rachel Glennerster (2012) of the Poverty Action Lab explains, "In all the work I have done on randomized evaluations in developing countries, I have never heard people in the communities in which I work express the view that randomization is unethical. To them, randomization is a very fair way to distribute limited resources, much fairer than the usual allocation systems—which see more projects go to communities with better political connections or closer to a nice hotel that aid workers can stay in" (p. R12).

Qualitative Methods and Randomized Experiments

Randomized experiments generally fall into the category of quantitative research, but there are important ways in which qualitative research can help inform both the design and the interpretation of a randomized experiment.

Before an experiment is implemented, exploratory qualitative research can inform the study's design, including the choice of variables for which quantitative data are gathered and identification of appropriate sites or locations for the experiment. As an experiment is implemented, qualitative methods can help discover contamination or human artifacts of the experiment. And both during and after implementation, qualitative methods can help reveal the possible mechanisms or processes that produced the observed outcome, particularly if the experiment results in a somewhat unexpected outcome.

For example, as part of the MTO evaluation, the U.S. Department of Housing and Urban Development (HUD) commissioned a series of exploratory studies, many of which used qualitative methods. These explorations suggested that the vouchers provided to the treatment group might be influencing family health, safety, delinquency patterns, and educational outcomes but perhaps not employment or economic status.

Qualitative research also helped later on, when preliminary statistical analysis showed few if any of the expected educational benefits of residential relocation of the treatment group. In the MTO experiment, qualitative researchers interviewed families in their homes and communities after relocation and observed that, although the families had relocated to lower-poverty neighborhoods, many continued to send their children to the same schools that they attended when they lived in public housing (Ferryman, Briggs, Popkin, & Rendón, 2008). This was due in part to friendship patterns and social connections that tied families to their old neighborhood. It was also due to the simple fact that the families with vouchers did not move all that far away to begin with. (There were lower-poverty neighborhoods near the old public housing neighborhoods, and most families preferred this option to relocating to a more distant suburban area outside the city.) Other qualitative research revealed the mechanism behind why relocated families did not find better jobs than control families (Turney, Clampet-Lundquist, Edin, Kling, & Duncan, 2006). These sorts of insights, visible to qualitative researchers on the ground, helped HUD to interpret what turned out to be complex and somewhat unexpected statistical findings from this large randomized field experiment.

Conclusion: A Gold Standard, With Limitations

Randomized experiments, including lab, field, and survey experiments, are considered the "gold standard" for demonstrating cause-effect relationships. They work by using random assignment to create statistically equivalent treatment and control groups, removing any potential bias from common cause variables—both measured and unmeasured. In this way, randomized experiments offer a major advantage over observational studies with control variables, which can only take into account measured common causes. Randomized experiments generally provide more convincing evidence of causation than any other method.

But randomized experiments have important limitations as well. Randomized experiments typically look at only one—or only a few—independent variables at a time, and variables that have just a few values (doses). Randomized experiments often have limited generalizability because of their reliance on volunteers, their focus on small areas or populations, their use of specialized or artificial treatments that do not resemble full-scale programs or interventions, and their inability to capture long-run effects that incorporate reactions of those outside the experiment. And randomized experiments can break down due to contamination, attrition, human artifacts, and other problems that occur in the field. Finally, it is not always possible to implement full random assignment for various ethical, political, or practical reasons.

Perhaps a more fundamental weakness is that randomized experiments do not reveal why or how an intervention works—or doesn't work. Several critiques attribute this problem to a focus on impact assessment rather than theory investigation (Deaton, 2010; Heckman & Smith, 1995). For example, Deaton (2010) notes that learning the average effect of railroads on poverty in China does little to explain how, why, or under what circumstances railroads influence poverty. Thus, it will not tell us where and when to expand railroads or what other types of programs might work. Deaton also emphasizes the problem discussed earlier that when programs become full-scale and permanent, other actors adjust their behavior, as when domestic violence victims became less likely to report abuse knowing that it would lead to mandatory arrest. He again notes that theory is needed to predict such reactions and finds randomized experiments ill suited to such learning. But it is possible to construct randomized experiments that inform theory. Many of Banerjee and Duflo's (2011) experiments on global poverty alleviation, for example, show theoretical insights, although incremental and contingent ones.

Because randomized experiments are often expensive and take a long time, Besharov (2009) worries that policy makers will not be able to wait for the results. By focusing too much effort on randomized experiments, therefore, researchers may be making themselves less useful to policy makers. In addition, it is not feasible to investigate every potential intervention—or even come remotely close. There are simply too many interventions to test all of them; for many interventions and situations, theory (or sometimes just common sense) can provide information about their effectiveness.

For all these reasons, the next chapter looks at studies that attempt to preserve some of the strengths of randomized experiments in the face of real-world constraints—hybrid studies known as natural experiments or quasi experiments.

BOX 14.9
Critical Questions to Ask About a Randomized Experiment

- Was it a true randomized experiment—in other words, were the treatment and control groups formed by random assignment? Look closely: Often things don't quite turn out as planned. How might shortcomings in random assignment bias the results?
- Did people (or other units in the experiment, such as families, classrooms, or organizations) remain in the experiment, or did some drop out or leave? If so, how might this affect the results of the experiment?
- Was the treatment implemented as planned? And did all of those in the treatment group actually receive the treatment? How might problems in administering the treatment, or failure of participants to take up the treatment, bias the results?
- Was there anything unusual about the treatment? Were the staff members especially motivated? Were the services especially well funded? How similar, or different, was the treatment, in comparison with other programs like it?

(Continued)

(Continued)

- Is the placebo effect a possible explanation for the results? Was the treatment group aware of the researchers' expectations, and if so, could this have influenced the treatment group's behavior?
- Where was the experiment conducted, when, and who participated? How generalizable are the study's findings to other places, programs, or people?
- How large were the reported treatment effects, in substantive or policy terms? Beware of "statistically significant" treatment effects that turn out, on closer inspection, to be only trivial differences in policy terms or in the lives of participants.

BOX 14.10
Tips on Doing Your Own Research: Randomized Experiments

- Identify the intervention (treatment, independent variable) and outcome(s) of interest.
- Identify the number of treatment arms and the values they will take on (dosage levels). Also determine whether there will be a control group and, if so, identify whether it will receive a placebo, the usual treatment (standard of care), or nothing at all.
- Determine how the outcomes will be measured. See also tips at the end of Chapter 4 on measurement.
- Determine if interactions among treatments are important and, if so, whether to have a factorial design. Be aware that more factors mean more arms and thus more subjects to recruit.
- Consider whether you will expose subjects to only one treatment (a between-subjects design) or give each subject two or more treatments in a random sequence (a within-subjects design). Often this depends on the nature of the treatment, and on the difficulty of recruiting and setting up subjects to participate in the experiment.
- Plan the types of analysis to be done *in advance,* including statistical significance tests. Given your planned analysis, perform *sample size* and *power* calculations to determine the number of subjects. See Chapter 9 on statistical inference.
- Determine the study setting of your experiment—field, lab, or survey. Be aware of the advantages and limitations of each setting. For example, see Box 14.3 about some of the practical challenges of field experiments.
- Determine how subjects will be recruited. Consider both practicalities and the population to which the study will generalize. Create a subject recruitment plan.
- Think about what human artifacts are likely (attrition, contamination, etc.) by anticipating how the research subjects will experience the experiment. Consider design modifications (e.g., blinding) to reduce artifacts.
- Ensure that the experiment is ethical, for example, that all subjects are fully informed and will benefit at least somewhat. See Chapter 16 for help with informed consent documents.
- Compare baseline descriptive statistics between treatment and control arms to make sure that randomization was carried out properly.
- If there is attrition or noncompliance, consider doing an analysis of both the intent to treat (ITT) and the effect of the treatment of the treated (TOT).

Chapter Resources

Key Terms

- Arms of an experiment
- Attrition
- Average treatment effect
- Between-subjects experiment
- Blind experiment
- Cluster randomization
- Contamination
- Control group
- Covariate
- Crossover experiment
- Dose-response relationship
- Double-blind experiment
- Experimental subjects (units)
- Factorial experiments
- Factors (in an experiment)
- Field experiment
- Haphazard randomization
- Hawthorne effect
- Heterogeneous treatment effect
- Intent to treat (ITT)
- Interaction effect
- Lab experiment
- Main effect
- Minimal detectable effect
- Noncompliance
- Placebo
- Placebo effect
- Random assignment
- Randomized experiment (randomized controlled trial [RCT])
- Repeated-measures experiment
- Statistical equivalence
- Survey experiment (split-ballot survey)
- Treatment
- Treatment group
- Treatment of the treated (TOT)
- Unobtrusive (nonreactive) measures
- Within-subjects experiment

Exercises

Statistical Equivalence: Seeing Is Believing

14.1. Take an ordinary deck of 52 playing cards, shuffle the cards well, and deal them into two piles of 26. Notice that you have *randomly assigned* the cards to two groups. Now, count the number of red cards in each group. Is it exactly 13, or a little less or more? Reshuffle the deck and repeat (or have different groups or individuals in class doing this at the same time). Average the results together.

a. How does this card game illustrate the idea of *statistical equivalence*?
b. Why isn't the result exactly 13 red cards after each shuffle? How does this shed light on the use of a significance test in a randomized experiment?

Random Assignment Versus Random Sampling

14.2. Below are several examples of research. For each one, decide if it involves random assignment or random sampling.

a. A law center selects 900 civil court records at random from the archive to investigate the effect of having, versus not having, legal representation (a lawyer) on the outcome of the case.

b. A clinic recruits drug users and divides them, randomly, into two groups to test the effectiveness of a new prevention therapy.
c. A government statistical agency takes a probability sample of the nation's public school students and then randomly administers two different versions of a reading test to compare their difficulty.

Treatment for Alcoholism

14.3. A large randomized field experiment of treatment for alcoholics was conducted with 10,000 subjects. They were randomized to either an intensive short-term inpatient treatment program or a less intensive long-term outpatient treatment program with equal total costs. The main outcome measure is long-term (5-year) sobriety. Results showed that 35% of those in the inpatient program remained sober for 5 years, while 55% of those in the outpatient program remained sober for 5 years.

a. The *p* value associated with a test of the difference between the programs was less than .001. What is the statistical significance of these results?
b. What is the practical significance of these results?
c. The study was performed according to standard ethical principles of informed consent: Subjects were fully informed about what the study would entail and voluntarily chose to participate. What kinds of alcoholics would agree to participate in the experiment? What kinds would not?
d. Someone reading this impressive study concludes that long-term sobriety rates of *all* alcoholics would be 20 percentage points higher if *all* alcoholics received long-term outpatient treatment than if all alcoholics received short-term inpatient treatment. Do you think this conclusion is valid? Explain.
e. The study as described does not shed light on why the outpatient program had better results—the mechanism. Describe how the use of one qualitative method (e.g., open-ended interviews, structured interviews, focus groups, observation) during the experiment could have shed light on this issue. Briefly describe which method you think would have been best and why.

Randomized Experiment in Your Field

14.4. Search one of the major journals in your field of interest for an example of a published study that is a randomized experiment. Read the abstract carefully, as well as other sections of the article as required. Then answer the following questions:

a. How did you know that it was a randomized experiment? What term was used to describe the study—*clinical trial, randomized controlled trial,* or another term?
b. How many arms were there in the experiment? How many factors?
c. How were subjects recruited into the experiment? How might this have affected the generalizability of the results?
d. Was there any contamination or attrition? How might this bias the results?

Design Your Own Experiment

14.5. For each of the research questions below, design an experiment to answer the causal question. Be sure to specify a setting (lab, field, survey), as well as the number of arms, treatment levels, or factors (if appropriate) in your experiment. Also consider how many subjects you would use, how you would recruit them, and whether your experiment would be a between-subjects or within-subjects design.

a. Does exercising make people happier?
b. Does knowing that a political candidate is gay make people less likely to vote for him?
c. Does having an e-reader make people read more?
d. Does knowing that a job seeker spent time in prison make employers less likely to hire the person?
e. Does the amount of an award for each correct word influence how well people do at solving a crossword puzzle?

Ethics of Randomized Experiments on Craigslist

14.6. Look on the Internet for a notice recruiting people to be part of a randomized experiment, often called a randomized control trial. Craigslist, for example, contains such notices.

a. What ethical issues are raised by this trial? Is the randomization itself a concern? The main treatment(s) of interest? The control group? What ethical issues are raised by the types of people recruited to be in the trial—or excluded from participation?
b. Do you have concerns about how the recruitment was done?
c. Do you see any ways in which the study might be improved from the perspective of what is learned but be made worse ethically?

Who Matters More, Parents or Teachers?

14.7. Here is an edited excerpt from an article on Bloomberg.com (Staley, 2011):

Professor List will track the results of more than 600 students in Chicago—including 150 at this school. His goal is to find out whether investing in teachers[,] or, alternatively, in parents, leads to more gains in kids' educational performance . . .

List sketches out the design of the experiment . . . Local families with kids 3 to 5 years old were encouraged to enter a lottery and were randomly sorted into three groups.

Students selected to attend the Griffin school are enrolled in the free, all-day preschool.

Children in another group aren't enrolled in the school, while their guardians take courses at a "parenting academy" and receive cash or scholarships valued at up to $7,000 annually as a reward.

The more than 300 kids in the third contingent receive no benefits—nor do their parents—and serve as a control group.

List and his collaborators . . . will monitor the students through annual tests, attendance records and graduation rates. As the students move into adulthood, their employment, pay and criminal records, if any, will also be tracked. While early results from the experiment may be published as soon as this year, the project has money to follow the students "until they die," List says.

a. What is the research question of this study?
b. Name one long-term outcome of interest to the researchers.
c. What is the name of this kind of study?

d. Show the shell of a table that would demonstrate that the randomization was effective. (Just use two variables to illustrate.) What statistical significance test(s) would the researchers use?
e. For the long-term outcome you named, describe briefly how the researchers would determine the results of the study for that outcome.
f. Suppose another researcher says that she already knows that parents matter much more than schools from her observational studies done using control variables. For example, she finds that children whose parents read to them regularly earn more on average (when they become adults) than those whose parents don't, even after controlling for parents' education and earnings and many other factors. She says that this expensive randomized experiment is a waste of money. What kind of statistical analysis would she have performed?
g. What is the counterfactual question associated with her causal effect of parents' reading?
h. Give one theory that would predict that her estimate of the causal effect of parents' reading on their children's future earnings would be upwardly biased. (A path diagram may help.)

Student Study Site

Visit the Study Site at **www.sagepub.com/remler2e** to

- test your knowledge with the self-quiz
- check your understanding of key terms with the eFlashcards
- explore helpful resources that relate directly to this chapter

Welfar
Work

Revenues from a casino lifted Cherokee families out of poverty: a natural experiment.

Source: © iStockphoto.com/mbbirdy.

Overview: In this chapter, you will learn about natural and quasi experiments—studies that occur in real-world settings yet approximate some of the advantageous features of a randomized experiment. Much applied policy research and program evaluation relies on natural or quasi experiments, in large part because randomized experiments are often impractical or unethical. It is therefore important to know how to identify or create the key features of natural or quasi experiments—exogeneity and comparability—and to assess the causal evidence provided by the most commonly seen designs for such studies (such as difference-in-differences or interrupted time series). This chapter will also help you be alert to opportunities to plan or administer programs in ways that help create strong quasi experiments to better inform policy and management.

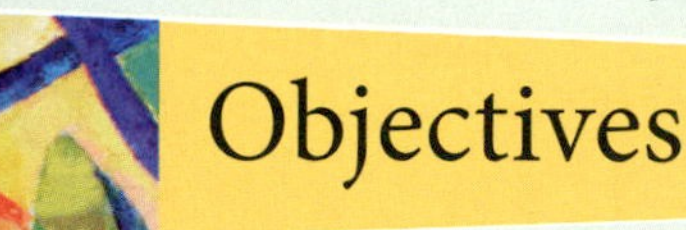

Objectives

Learning Objectives

After reading this chapter, you should be able to

- Identify natural and quasi experiments, as distinct from observational studies or randomized experiments
- Explain how natural and quasi experiments can be used to estimate a causal effect
- Identify exogenous events that can be used as natural experiments
- Suggest ways to design programs to create a quasi experiment
- Identify different types of natural and quasi experiments
- For a given natural or quasi experiment, describe the strengths and weaknesses of the causal evidence
- Determine the population, treatment, and context that a given natural or quasi-experimental study generalizes to

Natural and Quasi Experiments 15

A Casino Benefits the Mental Health of Cherokee Children

Jane Costello, a mental health researcher, was at work on a long-term study of psychiatric symptoms of children in rural North Carolina, about a quarter of them from a Cherokee reservation. Midway through the study, the Cherokees opened a casino on the reservation, providing profit-sharing payments to reservation families—suddenly lifting them out of poverty. Unexpectedly, Costello and her fellow researchers found themselves with a unique opportunity to observe the causal effect of ending poverty on the mental health of children (Costello, Compton, Keeler, & Angold, 2003).[1]

Costello's results showed that among the children lifted out of poverty by the casino payments, conduct and oppositional disorders improved substantially, yet anxiety and depression did not. Poverty causes (at least in part) conduct and oppositional disorders, Costello and her colleagues could conclude, but not anxiety or depression. This was an interesting finding with important public health and social policy implications.

Researchers had long observed the correlation between poverty and poor mental health, among both children and adults, but they didn't know if poverty caused psychiatric problems (and which ones), if psychiatric problems caused low income, or if other factors caused both. But in Costello's study, the change in income came from a completely outside (exogenous) source, the new casino. This created a *natural experiment* in which additional income was suddenly added to a poor community, independent of the efforts and characteristics of the families, allowing a clearer look at the pure effect of poverty on the mental health of the children.

What Are Natural and Quasi Experiments?

Natural experiment and *quasi experiment* are terms applied to a wide variety of studies that resemble the randomized experiments we discussed in the previous chapter but that lack the researcher control or random assignment characteristic of a true randomized experiment. They come in many forms, including before-after comparisons, cross-sectional comparisons of treated and untreated groups, and a combination of before-after and group-to-group comparisons (known as difference-in-differences), as will be explained later in this chapter.

---

[1]Accounts of this work have also appeared in the general media, including O'Connor (2003).

Natural and quasi experiments are important for several reasons. First, because of practical or ethical constraints, randomized experiments are often not possible in social and policy research. Second, because of these constraints, a great many policy studies or program evaluations end up being natural or quasi experiments—so you will likely encounter these types of studies frequently in practice and in the literature. Third, even many studies designed as randomized experiments suffer from attrition or noncompliance, becoming essentially quasi experiments. Fourth, natural or quasi experiments can be carried out on a larger scale or in more realistic settings more often than randomized experiments, enhancing their generalizability and relevance for policy or management decisions. And finally, practitioners can carry out these kinds of studies more easily in their own programs or organizations.

But it is important to point out that these advantages come at a price: Natural and quasi experiments typically exhibit more weaknesses than randomized experiments in terms of demonstrating causation and estimating causal effects. Understanding these weaknesses, as well as what makes for a strong natural or quasi experiment, is an important theme of this chapter.

Natural Experiments: Finding Exogeneity in the World

In a **natural experiment**, a researcher looks for and finds a naturally occurring situation in which the independent variable of interest just happens to be exogenous to the outcome (the dependent variable of interest). In short, the researcher discovers something quite close to a randomized experiment that occurs on its own in the natural or social world. The Cherokee casino is a natural experiment: The sudden extra income provided to reservation families, but not to nearby poor families, just happened. The opening of the casino provided an exogenous boost to family incomes on the reservation, an increase that was independent of the habits, motivations, dispositions, and other factors that could also have influenced the mental health of children. In other words, the families on the reservation did not *self-select* into behavior (such as getting a college degree) that resulted in their higher income—the boost in income just happened, like winning the lottery.

Another key to a natural experiment is the ability to make comparisons—either over time or to a group that did not get the treatment. In the casino study, the researchers began collecting data before the casino opened (they happened to be tracking mental health problems for other purposes). Therefore, they had a *before* measure (or *pretest*) of mental health to compare with mental health *after* the casino opened (a *posttest*). This before or pretest measure provides an estimate of the *counterfactual:* what would have been the mental health status of the children had the casino not opened. By comparing the change, the researchers were able to infer the causal effect of income on mental health.

Moreover, the researchers also gathered data on families not living on the Cherokee reservation and thus not eligible for the sudden additional income from the casino. This unexposed *comparison group* also provides an estimate of the counterfactual. The researchers compared the mental health of reservation children whose families got the income boost with similar poor children whose families did not. The difference revealed the effect of the income on mental health.

Combining the before-after comparison with a comparison group, unexposed to the treatment, adds extra strength to a study—as we'll see later on in this chapter.

What's "Natural" About a Natural Experiment?

The "natural" part of the term *natural experiment* requires some explanation. Sometimes a natural experiment involves a truly natural event—such as a hurricane or a heat wave. But often the event is "natural" in the sense that it was not a planned intervention intended to influence the outcome of interest—nor was it designed to estimate causal effects. The Cherokee casino was certainly not a natural event like a flood, and it involved a good amount of financial and architectural planning. But the casino was *not* planned or intended as an intervention or treatment aimed at improving the mental health of children—the outcome of interest (dependent variable) in Costello's study. Moreover, Costello and colleagues had no control over assignment of the casino payments; they were just lucky that the payments were distributed in a largely exogenous way, affecting only one group of poor families and not the other. Thus the casino and its associated boost in income can be considered a "natural" experiment *with respect to* children's mental health.

Some elevated trains pass close by schools: a natural experiment.

Source: © iStockphoto.com/Terraxplorer.

Most Observational Studies Are Not Natural Experiments

Researchers do not create natural experiments—they find them, as Costello and her colleagues did. In this way, natural experiments resemble observational studies—studies in which the world is observed as is, without any attempt to manipulate or intervene. However, most observational studies are *not* natural experiments. Finding a good natural experiment is a bit like finding a nugget of gold in a creek bed. It happens sometimes, but there are a lot more ordinary pebbles in the creek than gold nuggets.

How does a natural experiment differ, then, from an observational study? As we saw in Chapters 11 and 12, the independent variables of interest in most observational studies suffer from endogeneity. In observational studies, people self-select values of the independent variable (treatments) for themselves based on their own motivations or interests, such as choosing to get a college degree. Or others select treatments for them based on merit or need, such as determining that a family is needy enough to qualify for a government benefit.

In a natural experiment, some chance event helps ensure that treatment selection is *not* related to relevant individual characteristics or needs. For example, *all* Cherokee families on the reservation received higher income because of the casino, not just those in which the parents worked harder, got more education, or had a special need for income support. Thus, in a natural experiment, instead of the usual self-selection or other treatment selection bias that generally occurs, something happens that mimics the exogeneity of a randomized experiment. Exogeneity—but exogeneity not created by the researcher—is the defining characteristic of a natural experiment.

Examples of Natural Experiments

To get a better feel for how to recognize a natural experiment, it helps to briefly look at a few more examples.

> **QUESTION**
>
> **How is the elevated subway study similar to and different from a randomized experiment? How is the study similar to and different from an observational study?**

Does noise inhibit learning? Psychologists Arline Bronzaft and Dennis McCarthy were able to investigate the impact of noise on learning by finding a New York City elementary school built close to an elevated subway line. The train, which passed at regular intervals throughout the day, ran close by one side of the school building but not the other. Teachers were assigned to classrooms and children to teachers in a fairly random way at the start of each school year. This resulted in a strong natural experiment involving a treatment group of students on the noisy side of the school and a comparison group on the quiet side. Bronzaft and McCarthy (1975) found that "the mean reading scores of classes on the noisy side tended to lag three to four months (based on a 10-month school

The Olympics stopped traffic in Atlanta: a natural experiment.
Source: © Can Stock Photo Inc./aberenyi.

year) behind their quiet side matches" (p. 517). This study led to efforts by transportation officials to implement noise abatement programs on elevated train tracks near schools.

Does car traffic cause childhood asthma? Public health researcher Michael Friedman and colleagues took advantage of the 1996 Summer Olympics in Atlanta to study the impact of traffic patterns on asthma. During the 17 days of the Olympic Games, the City of Atlanta implemented an alternative transportation plan that greatly restricted cars in favor of buses and other forms of mass transit. Using pediatric medical records for the periods before, during, and after the Olympics, the study found a 40% decline in the rate of childhood asthma emergencies and hospitalizations during the Olympics. This natural experiment provides fairly good evidence of the causal impact of traffic on asthma because of the abrupt, exogenous nature of this one-time alteration in Atlanta's transportation patterns. According to Friedman, Powell, Hutwagner, Graham, and Teague (2001): "These data provide support for efforts to reduce air pollution and improve health via reductions in motor vehicle traffic" (p. 897). Clearly, it would be hard to imagine how the same hypotheses could be tested using a traditional randomized experiment on something so massive as the traffic patterns of a major metropolitan area.

We will look shortly at what specific features make some natural experiments stronger or weaker, with respect to their causal evidence. But because these features are also relevant to quasi experiments, we turn now to defining quasi experiments and considering some examples.

Quasi Experiments: Evaluating Interventions Without Random Assignment

Very often, treatments that influence outcomes don't just happen naturally—they are interventions or programs implemented precisely to influence outcomes. Often researchers would like to evaluate the effects of such interventions on the intended outcomes. But they cannot fully randomize people or other units to treatment and control groups. That could be because the treatment must be allocated based on technical or political considerations, or because evaluation of the program occurs after important funding and targeting decisions have been made, or because entirely withholding a treatment is unethical, or for a host of other possible reasons. Here is where we find **quasi experiments**—studies of interventions or planned treatments that resemble randomized field experiments but lack full random assignment.

To understand the features of a quasi experiment, it is helpful to consider a real example.

Letting Residents Run Public Housing

In the 1990s, the U.S. Department of Housing and Urban Development (HUD) implemented a grant program to encourage resident management of low-income public housing projects (see Van Ryzin, 1996). Inspired by earlier, spontaneous efforts by residents who organized to improve life in troubled public housing projects, HUD implemented a program of grants and technical assistance to selected housing projects in 11 cities nationwide to establish resident management corporations (RMCs). These nonprofit RMCs, controlled and staffed by residents, managed the housing projects and initiated activities aimed at long-standing community issues such as crime, vandalism, and unemployment. Although the researchers did not determine which projects were selected for the program, they were able to determine which projects composed the comparison group.

A federal program encouraged resident management in selected public housing developments: a quasi experiment.

Source: © iStockphoto.com/ginga71.

Selected is the critical word—the HUD-funded projects were not just any housing projects but ones that thought themselves, or were judged by HUD, to be good candidates for the program. Technical and political considerations also played a role in project selection. Thus the treatment (the award of HUD funding) was not randomly assigned, although it was only given to some projects in an area and not others.

To evaluate the effectiveness of the program, a set of similar housing projects in the same cities but that did not receive the HUD grants was identified as a comparison group.

The term **comparison group** is often used in the context of quasi experiments rather than *control group,* the term used in randomized experiments, to highlight the lack of random assignment. (However, researchers do not always obey this distinction, so still look closely at how the assignment was done.) Surveys and other data were collected on the families living in the treatment and comparison groups to measure the possible effects of resident management on maintenance conditions, security, economic well-being, and residential quality of life.

The housing projects were not randomly assigned to receive the HUD grants, and families were not randomly relocated to different public housing projects. That would not be practical—or ethical. However, by finding matching housing projects in the same cities that were similar in their population and architectural characteristics to the ones that received the HUD grants, the hope was that they could provide a reasonably valid comparison. But because treatment assignment depended in part on the history and motivation of the resident leaders who applied to participate in the program, and on HUD's administrative selection criteria for awarding grants, HUD's evaluation is best described as a weak quasi experiment.

Programs aim to get more kids to walk to school.

Source: © 2009 Jupiterimages Corporation.

Some Other Examples of Quasi Experiments

Again, it helps to get a feel for quasi experiments by considering a few more examples. Notice how the treatments are intentional, with respect to the outcome of interest, and that these studies have comparison groups—although these are not randomly formed control groups.

Encouraging Kids to Walk to School. Rosie McKee and colleagues evaluated a physical fitness program that encouraged kids in Scotland to walk to school (McKee, Mutrie, Crawford, & Green, 2007). The program involved

QUESTION

How is the residential management study similar to and different from a randomized experiment? How is the study similar to and different from an observational study?

active travel as part of the curriculum, and it provided interactive travel-planning resources for children and their families to use at home. The school that received the program was compared with another nearby school that did not. Both schools had similar socioeconomic and demographic profiles—but of course children were not randomly assigned to their school. Surveys and the mapping of travel routes were used to measure walking to school, both before and after the intervention. The treatment school students increased their average distance walking to school by more than 8 times and experienced a correspondingly large reduction in their average daily distance driving to school. The comparison school had only a very minor change during the year in average walking and driving distances.

Cracking Down on Gun Dealers. Daniel Webster and colleagues evaluated efforts by three cities—Chicago, Detroit, and Gary—to use undercover sting operations along with lawsuits to shut down gun dealers suspected of selling illegal firearms to criminals (Webster, Bulzacchelli, Zeoli, & Vernick, 2006). Comparison cities were identified that were similar in size and demographics but were not at the time engaged in an aggressive crackdown on gun dealers. Webster and colleagues found an abrupt reduction of new guns in the hands of arrested criminals in Chicago, some reduction of new guns in Detroit, and not much of a change in Gary. The percentage of new guns changed little over the same period in the comparison cities. The authors concluded,

> The announcement of police stings and lawsuits against suspect gun dealers appeared to have reduced the supply of new guns to criminals in Chicago significantly, and may have contributed to beneficial effects in Detroit. Given the important role that gun stores play in supplying guns to criminals in the US, further efforts of this type are warranted and should be evaluated. (Webster et al., 2006, p. 225)

Why Distinguish Natural Experiments From Quasi Experiments?

Not everyone defines the terms *natural experiment* and *quasi experiment* as we do here. (See Box 15.1 for the origins of both terms.) For example, some refer to natural experiments as a form of quasi experiment or even call their study a "naturally occurring quasi experiment." Others consider the terms *natural* and *quasi experiment* interchangeable—with both referring to any study that falls short of a true randomized experiment.

But we believe that it is important to distinguish quasi experiments from natural experiments because in a quasi experiment, the independent variable (or treatment) is a planned intervention (such as a policy or program) specifically aimed at influencing an outcome. Moreover, the intervention is implemented in way that sets up a comparison or otherwise makes the treatment at least somewhat exogenous. This fact alerts us to opportunities to exert policy or administrative control over the assignment of treatments (programs, benefits, or services) in a way that generates more valid causal evaluations. (In Box 15.2, we provide a decision tree to help distinguish natural and quasi experiments, as we define them, and also to situate these studies relative to observational studies and randomized experiments.)

Cracking down on illegal gun sales.
Source: © iStockphoto.com/shapecharge.

BOX 15.1
Origins of the Terms *Natural Experiment* and *Quasi Experiment*

Campbell and Stanley (1963) coined the term *quasi experiment* in an influential chapter on education evaluation. The term quickly caught on and now appears widely not only in education but in criminal justice, public administration, social work, public health, and other fields. In a successor book, the authors Shadish, Cook, and Campbell (2002) define a quasi experiment as an experiment that "lack[s] random assignment . . . but that otherwise [has] similar purposes and structural attributes to randomized experiments" (p. 104).

The term *natural experiment* evolved later than the term *quasi experiment* and is more popular among economists, who often do not do any kind of experimentation, even a weak quasi experiment (Meyer, 1995; Rosenzweig & Wolpin, 2000). However, economists have long paid attention to the idea of exogeneity and thus are alert to situations in which it naturally occurs.

BOX 15.2
A Decision Tree for Categorizing Studies

In previous chapters, we've looked at observational studies (Chapters 12 and 13) and contrasted these with randomized experiments (Chapter 14). In this chapter, we've added natural and quasi experiments to the picture—making the landscape of studies a bit more complex. So to review and clarify these various types of studies, Figure 15.1 provides a decision tree that can be used to help sort out these distinctions.

Beginning at the top of the tree in Figure 15.1, we ask if the independent variable (or treatment) happens naturally, or is it an intervention designed to change *Y*? Recall that, although most social, political, or economic activities are planned in one sense, we are talking here about interventions or treatments that are planned or intended to influence the outcome that the study looks at. Casinos are planned—but they are not planned or intended to improve children's mental health and not controlled by researchers.

Consider the left branch—when the independent variable *X* occurs naturally or is unplanned. Here we need to ask if the independent variable is self-selected, as it usually is, or is it exogenous? Most things in the world are not randomly assigned (exogenous)—how much education someone gets, exercising, having dinner with your family, and so on. All these things are driven by characteristics that in turn drive other things too. Thus, in most studies under this branch, *X* is endogenous, and thus they are *observational studies.*

But as we've just seen, sometimes researchers get lucky, and a naturally occurring event turns out to be exogenous. A new casino suddenly raises family income in a community in ways unrelated to family motivations or characteristics, or the Olympics arrives and suddenly puts a halt to all car traffic in the city. These kinds of "naturally" occurring, exogenous events produce *natural experiments.* To the extent that *X* is less exogenous, natural experiments dissolve into observational studies.

Moving over to the right branch, we have an independent variable (*X*) that is an intervention (treatment) specifically designed to influence an outcome of interest (*Y*). There are three options here, depending on how much control there is over assignment of the intervention. The best

(Continued)

(Continued)

Figure 15.1 Decision Tree for Categorizing Studies

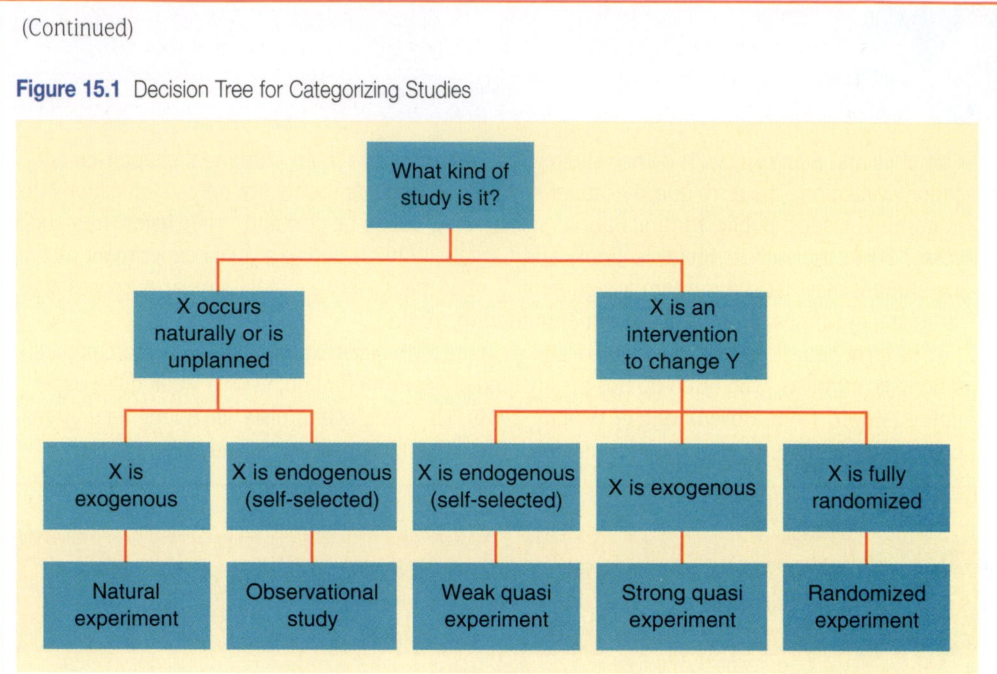

causal evidence comes, of course, from a *randomized experiment* in which the independent variable (*X*) is assigned randomly to individuals.

Close, but not as good, is when *X* is an intervention that is manipulated or implemented in some way that makes it fairly exogenous—perhaps by being assigned randomly at a larger group level (cluster randomization), or implemented in some other way that is largely unrelated to relevant characteristics. This situation makes for a *strong quasi experiment*.

Finally, there may be an intervention (*X*), such as a program or treatment designed to produce an outcome, but still the program is largely self-selected or administered in ways that create bias. For example, people may volunteer for the treatment, or ethical considerations based on need may dictate who gets into the program. This situation is best described as a *weak quasi experiment*. However, a very weak quasi experiment of this kind often borders on becoming an observational study.

How to Create Good Quasi Experiments When Planning and Implementing Programs

Below are some ways to create good causal evidence as part of program planning and implementation:

- Provide the treatment to some, but not all, eligible recipients to have a comparison group. Although this raises important ethical issues, often a program must operate with limited resources anyway and cannot serve everyone in all places at all times.
- If program resources are scarce and must be rationed, assign the treatment randomly if at all possible—or at least in some way that is fairly exogenous to the outcome. Again, this may not be possible ethically or politically, but it is important to point out that random assignment is in many situations a fair way to ration limited resources.
- If you can't randomly assign *individuals,* at least look for opportunities to randomly or otherwise exogenously assign the treatment to *groups* (such as schools) or geographic areas (such as neighborhoods).

Randomly assigning the program at the level of a group or geographic area—even if the program involves relatively few groups or areas—still makes the treatment at least somewhat exogenous.

- If the treatment is a full-coverage or universal program, try to control the timing of program implementation, so that the treatment begins earlier with some participants or in some settings, and later in others. If such variation in the timing of implementation is exogenous to the outcome, then it can be used to estimate a causal effect.
- Finally, it is very important to think ahead and gather outcome measures *before,* as well as after, the start of the program. This is often straightforward with administrative record data or existing performance measures, which tend to get collected on an ongoing basis anyway but should be considered also with surveys and other forms of original data collection designed to evaluate specific outcomes.

Some time ago, Campbell (1969) introduced the notion of the "experimenting society" in which policies and programs are designed to provide more solid knowledge of causation—of what works. And increasingly today, we see pressure in many fields for "evidence-based" programs and management practices—reflecting a demand for greater rigor in assessing what works. While the limitations of randomized experiments (as discussed in Chapter 14) often prevent experimentation in the traditional sense, we should remain aware of the potential to design and implement programs in ways that allow for at least the best possible quasi experiments.

The recent tradition of natural experiments in economics also suggests that researchers need to be on the lookout for strong natural experiments that provide opportunities for good causal evidence by mimicking true random assignment. A good example is Oregon's health insurance lottery (see Box 15.3), which rationed free health insurance using a random lottery system because of state budget constraints.

BOX 15.3
Oregon's Health Insurance Lottery

When health economist Katherine Baicker heard about the planned lottery for health insurance coverage, she realized that she had found a great natural experiment that was "the chance of a lifetime" (Lacy, 2009). Here is a newspaper account of the lottery:

> *March 7, 2008—This week Oregon state will begin conducting a lottery with the prize being free health care, reports the Associated Press. Over 80,000 people have signed up to participate since January, although only 3,000 will make the cut and receive coverage under the Oregon Health Plan's standard benefit program.*
>
> *At its peak in 1995 the Oregon Health Plan covered 132,000 Oregonians, but due to a recession and the budget cuts that followed, the program was closed to newcomers in 2004. Only recently has the state managed to find the money to enroll 3,000 new members. According to the Oregon Department of Human Services, there are an estimated 600,000 people in the state who are uninsured.*

What were the eventual results of this natural experiment? The study showed that the health insurance expansion reduced out-of-pocket expenditures and debt, but it did not improve health status (except for depression), despite increasing health care usage (Baicker et al., 2013; Finkelstein et al., 2012). The extensive media reaction that followed release of these findings showed just how influential a natural experiment can be.

Source: National Academy of Sciences (2008).

Internal Validity of Natural and Quasi Experiments

QUESTION

What kinds of actions should those involved in implementing new programs and interventions take to ensure good quasi-experimental evaluations?

Internal validity is a term researchers use to talk about the strength of causal evidence provided by various types of natural and quasi experiments, as well as traditional randomized experiments. A study that provides convincing, unambiguous evidence of cause and effect is said to have "good internal validity." The greater a study's internal validity, the less biased the causal effect it estimates. Randomized experiments, for example, generally have very good internal validity. We will now look more closely at how to judge the internal validity of a given natural or quasi experiment—a somewhat more complex matter.

Exogeneity and Comparability

For a natural or quasi experiment to be able to reveal genuine causal effects—for it to have good internal validity—two basic conditions are needed. First, the treatment or independent variable of interest must be *exogenous.* In other words, the variation in the independent variable can't be driven by anything related to the outcome. This might happen naturally, as in the case of the Cherokee casino (a natural experiment), or by design, as in a randomized experiment or a strong quasi experiment.

Second, the treatment and comparison groups must be truly *comparable*—or homogeneous—the same in all relevant ways. For *measured* characteristics, the researcher can simply look at the available data to see how equivalent the treatment and comparison groups appear to be. For *unmeasured* characteristics, we cannot tell so easily and so must try to reason or guess if important unseen differences might lie beneath the surface.

How Did People Get the Treatment?

To judge the internal validity of a natural or quasi experiment—to assess the likely degree to which the treatment is exogenous and the groups are comparable—it is important to have a theory of how individuals got to be in the treatment versus the comparison group. In short, we need a theory of what drives the *independent variable.* In a true randomized experiment, the theory is a simple one: Units were randomly assigned to treatment and control groups by a flip of the coin, a randomly generated number, or similar means. In a natural or quasi experiment, the theory is often more complex.

For example, did energetic, engaged, or politically connected tenant leaders in a housing project help secure the HUD grant? Such leaders might also help keep crime down anyway, with or without the help of the program. By learning what drove the independent variable, or treatment selection, we understand how our groups might not be comparable in relevant ways. Notice that this task is very similar to the efforts required to find good control variables for observational studies (as discussed in Chapters 12 and 13). The difference is that in this case, the goal (or hope) is that learning what drives the independent variable will help demonstrate exogeneity and comparability, perhaps eliminating the need to rely only on control variables.

QUESTION

What are the key elements of both natural and quasi experiments?

Nothing's Perfect

The goal here is not necessarily perfection—much can be learned from studies that have some weaknesses, as indeed all studies have. Few real-world natural or quasi experiments will have perfect exogeneity and comparability (homogeneity). There is a continuum along both these dimensions. The validity of the causal conclusions drawn must be assessed on a case-by-case basis.

Generalizability of Natural and Quasi Experiments

The generalizability—or *external validity*—of quasi experiments and natural experiments often turns out to be better than in randomized field experiments, despite the fact that quasi experiments typically provide weaker evidence of causation (*internal validity*). This is because quasi and natural experiments often involve real-world programs or interventions operating at scale, as it were, in contrast to many randomized experiments that involve somewhat artificial treatments on a relatively small group of volunteers. Recall from Chapter 14 how a randomized experiment found that a pilot mandatory arrest program in Minneapolis reduced domestic violence; but when a later natural experiment examined full and permanent implementation of mandatory arrest laws in different states, at different times, it showed an increase in homicides due to lower reporting of domestic violence by victims.

But it all depends, of course, on the details of the particular study. A few large-scale randomized experiments, such as the RAND Health Insurance Experiment or the Moving to Opportunity demonstration (discussed in Chapter 14), involved multiple cities, and lasted for years, enhancing their generalizability. And there have been many small-scale natural or quasi experiments with only limited generalizability, such as the natural experiment in one New York City public school that studied the effects of elevated train noise on learning (Bronzaft & McCarthy, 1975). Still, natural and quasi experiments typically occur in real-world settings that more closely resemble the actual contexts and constraints faced by policy makers and practitioners.

A key issue is how well the study's setting and participants reflect a broader population of interest. For example, in the Cherokee casino study, the participants in the study came from one Native American community in a rural area. Would the effect of income on mental health be the same in a population of poor Whites in Appalachia, or low-income African American populations living in the inner city of Chicago or Los Angeles? In the HUD study, the resident management program in fact targeted mostly big-city public housing authorities, often with a history of severe management problems. We might wonder: Are the results of this HUD evaluation generalizable to all types of housing authorities, particularly the smaller authorities that do not share the characteristics and management problems of the large, urban housing authorities?

Generalizability of the Treatment Effect

In a randomized experiment, each and every individual is randomly assigned to treatment and control groups. Thus, the effect of the treatment applies to the entire study group, at least on average (because of heterogeneous treatment effects), and in turn applies to whatever larger population the study subjects represent.

But in some natural and quasi experiments, the treatment applies only to some—not all—of those in the treatment group. In the Cherokee casino study, for example, the researchers were especially interested in how being lifted out of poverty—crossing the official poverty line from poor to not poor—influenced mental health. Indeed, much of their data analysis focused on this exogenous change in poverty status. But this change did not happen for those Cherokee families with incomes already above the poverty line before the casino opened. Thus, the treatment effect of a natural or quasi experiment only generalizes to those who were exogenously affected. We will have more to say about this issue in the context of discussing the strategies of instrumental variables and regression discontinuity later on in this chapter.

Having defined natural and quasi experiments and considered some of the issues they raise regarding evidence of causation (internal validity) and generalizability (external validity), we turn next to a more detailed look at the various *types* of natural and quasi experimental studies.

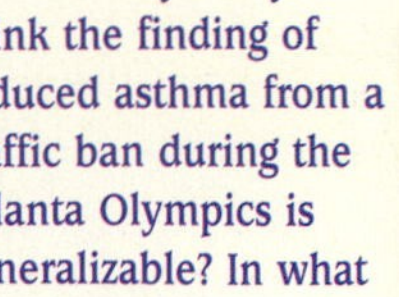

QUESTION

In what ways do you think the finding of reduced asthma from a traffic ban during the Atlanta Olympics is generalizable? In what ways is this finding not generalizable?

Types of Natural and Quasi Experimental Studies

You can find many varieties of natural and quasi experiments—indeed, clever researchers keep coming up with new variations. Shadish et al. (2002), for example, identify at least 18 different quasi-experimental designs. In this section, we will look in more detail at those natural and quasi experiments most frequently employed in social and policy research.

Before-After Studies

In the natural experiment from Atlanta described earlier, researchers measured childhood asthma rates *before* the Olympics and compared them with the asthma rates *after* the opening ceremony, when car traffic was drastically curtailed throughout the metropolitan area. There was no comparison group, just a single group (the population of Atlanta) compared at two points in time. Figure 15.2 shows the outlines of this **before-after study**, which is also called a *one-group pretest-posttest* design (or just a *pre-post comparison*).

In the Atlanta study, for example, asthma events (acute care cases) declined from a mean of 4.2 daily cases before the Olympics to only 2.5 daily cases during the Olympics (a practically and statistically quite significant difference), based on administrative data from the Georgia Medicaid claims file.

Weaknesses of Before-After Studies

Although before-after studies are intuitive, they have several inherent weaknesses. Because natural and quasi experiments are not conducted in a lab, researchers do not have the ability to hold all relevant surroundings constant—the world goes on. Campbell and Stanley (1963) referred to this as *history*. The economy, the weather, social trends, political crises—all sorts of events can happen around the time of the treatment, and some of these events could also influence the outcome. This greatly complicates efforts to attribute observed outcome change to the treatment alone.

Figure 15.2 Before-After Study

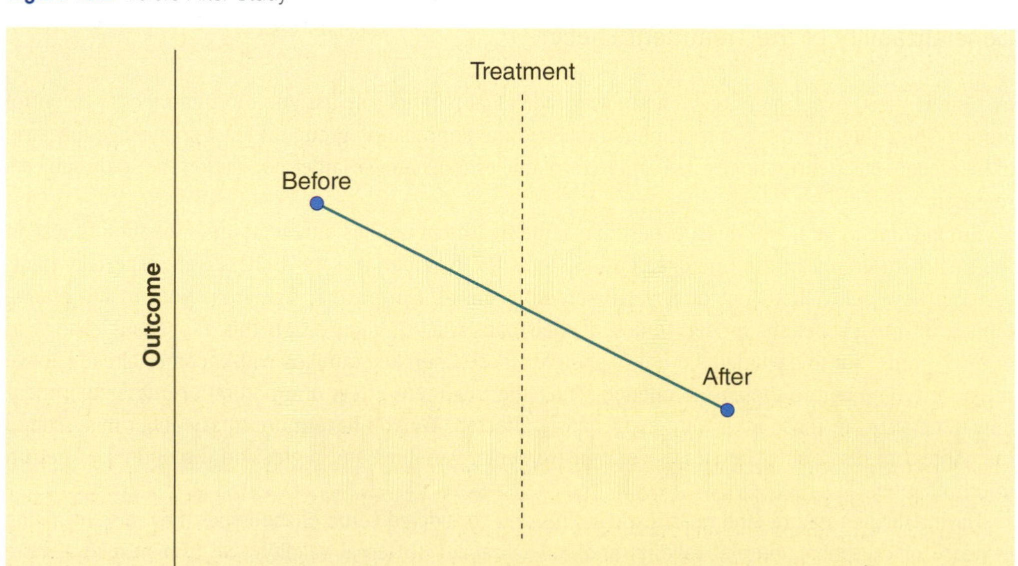

In the Atlanta study, for example, changes in the weather and other asthma triggers might have coincided with the Olympics, raising doubts about whether the alteration in traffic patterns alone caused the entire observed drop in asthma. For this reason, the researchers measured temperature, humidity, barometric pressure, and mold counts during the study period. As it turned out, none of these potential alternative explanations changed in a significant way over the study period.

This suggests a strategy to strengthen the internal validity of a before-after study: Think carefully about what might both influence the outcome *and* coincide with the timing of the treatment—and then find a way to measure it. To the extent plausible alternative explanations can be eliminated in this way, the causal evidence in favor of the treatment gains credibility.

In addition to coinciding external events, people or groups often experience internal changes over time. Second graders, for example, learn to read better by the end of the school year—in part just because they have matured socially and cognitively. New employees in an organization gradually learn how to do their jobs better, so their productivity grows over time. Campbell and Stanley (1963) refer to this as *maturation*. Internal, maturational changes can also bias a before-after study. But they are often difficult to observe and distinguish from the treatment itself.

Thus, many things can drive change over time. A simple before-after comparison largely *assumes* that the change in the dependent variable is due to change in the independent variable, the change in treatment. But this may not be the case.

Statistical Analysis of Before-After Studies

The statistical analysis of a before-after study is usually straightforward: a basic comparison of means or proportions and an appropriate significance test of the difference (a t test or z test, respectively). If repeated measurements are made on the same individuals, a *gain-score* or *paired-sample* approach can be used to increase statistical precision (the ability to detect a statistically significant effect).

QUESTION

Think of a new program that was implemented at your university, at your workplace, or in another familiar setting and an outcome it was designed to affect. How good would the internal validity of a before-after study be?

Be Careful Interpreting Significance Tests for Quasi and Natural Experiments

Remember, however, that tests of statistical significance and confidence intervals (inference) are based on having either random sampling or random assignment, but that many quasi and natural experiments have neither, such as in the walking-to-school study described earlier that used just a few convenient schools for both treatment and comparison groups (McKee et al., 2007). In such cases, as we described in Chapter 9, care must be taken in interpreting statistical significance tests. This caution applies to all quasi and natural experiments with neither random sampling nor random assignment, not just before-after studies.

Interrupted Time Series

A before-after comparison is much improved when multiple measurements, or a *time series,* of the outcome can be gathered both before and after the treatment. This design is referred to as an **interrupted time series**—a series of periodic measurements interrupted in the middle by the treatment.

For example, Andreas Muller (2004) studied the repeal of Florida's motorcycle helmet law by tracking monthly motorcycle fatalities for several years before and after the law's repeal. Because of Florida's steady population growth and other factors, such as motorcycle registrations and traffic volume, motor vehicle fatalities had been gradually increasing before the helmet law was revoked, although at a very modest rate. But the number of motorcycle fatalities jumped suddenly and quite visibly in the period after the repeal of the helmet law in July 2000.

Such time-series studies are often done with a single aggregate measure repeated over time, as is the case with the Florida study of motorcycle fatalities. However, time-series studies can also be done with panel data—repeated measurements of many individuals over time. We discuss panel data later on in this chapter.

Advantages of Interrupted Time Series

The big advantage of an interrupted time-series study is that it helps answer the question of what the trend in the outcome variable looked like before the intervention. Was there a directional trend (up or down) anyway, or was the trend fairly flat?

Figure 15.3 illustrates the point: Situation A is one in which the higher scores on the outcome after the treatment are clearly part of a more general upward trend over time. In contrast, Situation B is one in which the higher outcome scores after the treatment indicate a marked change from the previous trend. Situation A indicates no causal effect, while Situation B suggests causation. And the evidence from Situation B provides much better evidence of causation than a basic before-after comparison of only two point estimates. Of course, it is still possible in Situation B that something else affecting the outcome happened at the very same time as the treatment. But because this is less plausible than Situation A (an existing trend), the evidence of causation in Situation B is much stronger.

Statistical Analysis of Interrupted Time Series

Statistically, an interrupted time series can be analyzed in various ways. For example, ordinary regression analysis can be used with an equation like the following:

$$\text{Outcome} = a + b_{\text{Treat}}\text{Treatment} + b_{\text{Time}}\text{Time} + b_{\text{Inter}}(\text{Treatment} \times \text{Time})$$

- The treatment dummy variable (Treatment) is coded 0 for the time periods before the interruption and 1 for the periods after. Its coefficient, b_{Treat}, describes the change in the dependent variable (presumably) due to the treatment.
- The time trend variable (Time) is coded 0, 1, 2, 3, and so on for each time period in the series. Its coefficient, b_{Time}, captures the general linear trend over time.
- The final variable is an interaction of the time trend and treatment variables (Treatment × Time). Its coefficient, b_{Inter}, captures any change in the slope of the line due to the treatment or that might be concurrent with the interruption.

Figure 15.3 Interrupted Time Series

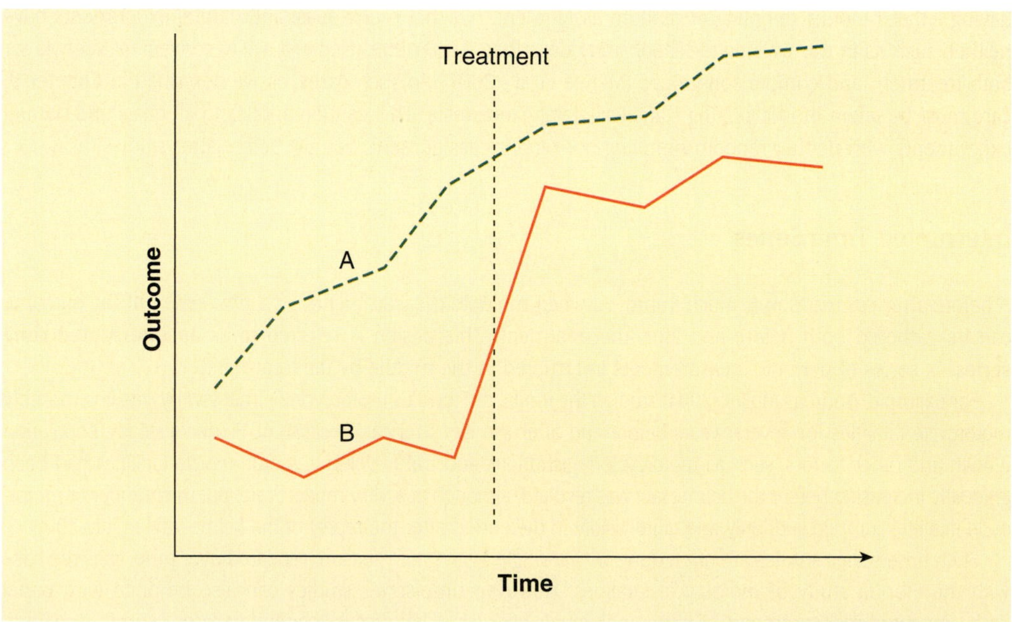

For more details on this kind of regression analysis, see McDowall, McCleary, Meidinger, and Hay (1980) or Mohr (1995). However, time-series analysis can be complicated because what happens in one period may be driven by what happened earlier (autocorrelation, discussed in Chapter 10). Consequently, more specialized versions of regression and other time-series methods are often used (Ostrom, 1990). But a picture of the data can tell us a great deal: In most cases, a treatment effect that is large enough to have practical significance (as opposed to just statistical significance) is clearly visible from simply the plotted time series.

QUESTION

Why is an interrupted time series better than a before-after study?

Cross-Sectional Comparisons

Before-after studies and interrupted time series make use of variation over time—*longitudinal* variation. But many natural and quasi experiments make use of *cross-sectional* comparisons—comparing two groups, only one of which received the treatment. Such a study is also referred to as a *static group comparison* or a *posttest-only design with nonequivalent groups.*

HUD's evaluation of resident management of public housing is an example of a cross-sectional comparison. The survey that measured the quality of life in the treatment and comparison buildings was conducted only after HUD awarded the grants and the program took effect. Figure 15.4 shows this design schematically.

The key to the internal validity of such a quasi experiment is the comparability of the groups. Were they really the same, in terms of the outcome variable, before the treatment was introduced? Could there be some difference between the groups—other than exposure to the treatment—that explains the observed treatment effect?

Was the HUD Program Effective?

Table 15.1 illustrates the difference between the treatment and comparison groups in the HUD evaluation on three outcomes: building maintenance, security, and tenants' satisfaction with their housing. All these outcomes come from the survey, so they are based on residents' judgments of conditions *after* the program's implementation, and each is measured from 0 (*lowest possible score*) to 100 (*highest possible score*).

Figure 15.4 Cross-Sectional Comparison

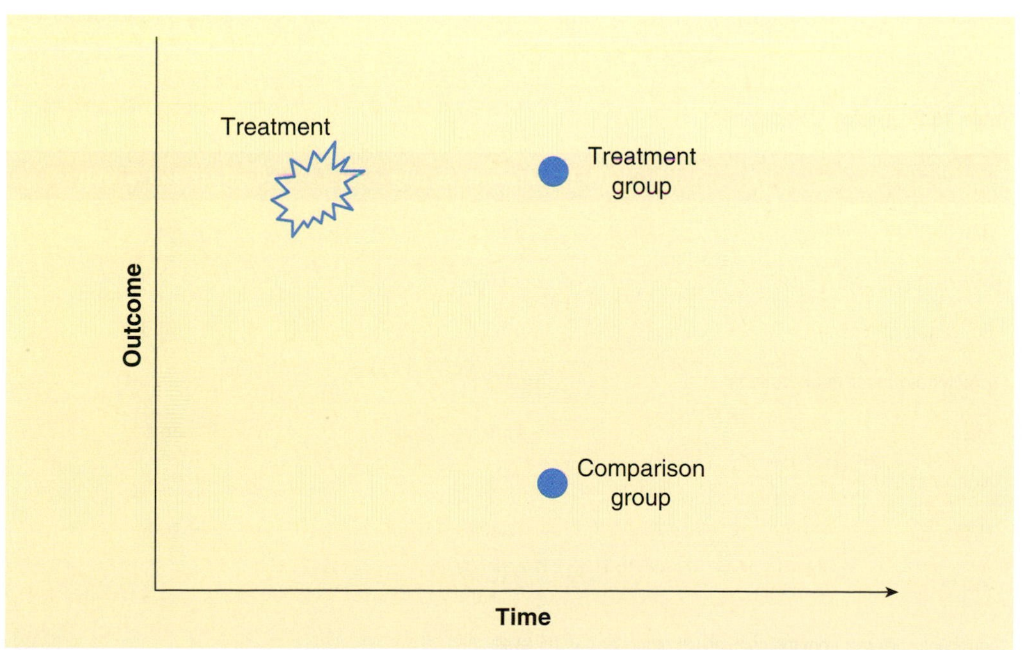

Table 15.1 Judging Outcomes (All Scores Are 0 to 100 Indexes)

	RMC (Treatment) Group	Comparison Group
Building maintenance index	63.3*	50.2
Security index	49.5	46.2
Housing satisfaction index	47.0*	38.8

*Significantly different from the comparison group (at $p < .05$ level).

The results show that residents in the treatment group judge building maintenance and security as better on average than do residents in the comparison group, and the RMC (treatment) group also appears more satisfied with its housing. The difference in security, however, is relatively small in substantive terms and not statistically significant. Still, it does seem from these outcome measures that conditions overall are better for residents in the RMC (treatment) group.

If the two groups were truly identical in all ways other than the RMC program, then these differences would give us an unbiased estimate of the treatment effect. This is a big "if," however. Recall that the buildings applied to HUD to participate in the program, and HUD selected worthy applicants for funding—so both self-selection and administrative selection processes could make the treatment group different from the comparison group.

One way to address this question is to compare measured characteristics of the groups using available data, as Table 15.2 illustrates. We can see that the two groups appear roughly similar, although the RMC group is slightly better educated and older; has higher household income; has fewer males and Hispanics; and is more likely to have married members. The differences in age, income, gender, Hispanic ethnicity, and marital status are statistically significant.

Moreover, unmeasured characteristics—not captured by the survey or other available data sources—could be relevant to outcomes such as building maintenance, security, or housing satisfaction. For example, the resident-managed buildings might have dynamic resident leaders, or a tight-knit group of neighbors who

Table 15.2 Judging Comparability

	RMC (Treatment) Group	Comparison Group
Age of householder	49.2*	43.6
Size of household (persons)	3.0	2.9
Education (in years)	10.5	10.3
Household income (in dollars)	$6,223*	$5,021
Male	15%*	26%
Non-White	98%	95%
Hispanic	6%*	20%
Married	10%*	4%

*Significantly different from the comparison group (at $p < .05$ level).

already got along well and helped each other. Because these kinds of characteristics were not measured in the survey, we cannot check if the two sets of housing projects are truly comparable in these ways.

Randomized experiments are so convincing precisely because the treatment and control groups are comparable in terms of both measured *and* unmeasured characteristics. If it turns out that the treatment and comparison groups are not comparable in some way relevant to the outcomes, which remains a possibility in a natural or quasi experiment, our conclusions about the effect of the treatment will be less certain.

We should emphasize here that it is *not* important that the treatment and comparison groups be equivalent in ways that have nothing to do with the outcome. For example, if one public housing project has blue trim on its windows and doors and another has red trim, provided trim color does not affect security or other outcomes of interest (as we assume it does not), the variable trim color will not matter.

Statistical Analysis of a Cross-Sectional Comparison

The basic statistical analysis for this type of study starts with a comparison of means or proportions, as we saw in Table 15.1. But because group differences on other variables may well exist, as we saw in Table 15.2, the analysis should include *control variables* that attempt to capture the relevant group differences that may influence the outcome. In an important sense, the analysis closely resembles the control variable strategy discussed in Chapters 12 and 13 for observational studies.

QUESTION

What could have made the HUD study a stronger quasi experiment?

Prospective and Retrospective Studies

For quasi experiments, natural experiments, and even observational studies, the quality of the study often depends on whether it is *prospective* or *retrospective*. In a **prospective study**, researchers look ahead—they decide to do the study in advance and take steps to track and measure subjects over time in order to observe what happens to them. For example, a study published in the *New England Journal of Medicine* (Yanovski et al., 2000) investigated weight gain from holiday eating by following a convenience sample of 195 adults and weighing them regularly before, during, and after the U.S. holiday season (which runs from Thanksgiving through New Year's Day). They found no weight gain during the months leading up to the holidays, a weight gain during the holidays, and yet no significant weight loss during the months after the holidays—suggesting that holiday eating may have longer-term effects on weight gain. Such studies in epidemiology and medicine are often called *cohort studies* because they follow a cohort—a group meeting some criteria at a particular point in time—forward in time.

Prospective studies can be observational—with no intervention or other kind of manipulation of the independent variable. But importantly, quasi experiments can also be prospective, which makes for a much stronger study. In particular, prospective quasi experiments provide the opportunity to collect pretest data, as well as other variables related to the outcomes. And they provide the opportunity to create more comparable treatment and comparison groups. Cook, Shadish, and Wong (2008) advocate prospectively matching whole groups of geographically and otherwise similar entities.

In contrast, a **retrospective study** looks backward, with researchers deciding to do the study only after events have happened. They either use administrative data that was already collected—or must ask subjects to recall outcomes. For example, the Atlanta Olympics study, discussed earlier, on the effect of automobile traffic on asthma was retrospective (Friedman et al., 2001). It reconstructed past trends in childhood asthma events using administrative record data. The logic of the analysis, however, was much the same as the holiday weight gain study; the asthma study was a comparison of the period before, during, and after the treatment (independent variable of interest).

Many natural and quasi experiments turn out to be retrospective because researchers only discover them after the fact. Some epidemiologists and others argue that prospective studies are better at accounting for confounding and alternative explanations, in part because the time order of events can be more clearly determined. But much depends on the available data, on the logic and thoroughness of the analysis, and, of course, on the exogeneity of the treatment and the comparability of the groups. There can be quite convincing retrospective natural and quasi experiments, as well as prospective studies with dubious findings because of self-selection, attrition, or other sources of bias.

Longitudinal Data Collection and Longitudinal Analysis

QUESTION

What is the difference between a retrospective study and a prospective study? What advantages do prospective studies have?

As we have seen, some natural and quasi experiments use *longitudinal* comparisons (such as before-after studies or interrupted time series), while others rely on *cross-sectional* comparisons. But the term *longitudinal study* can be confusing, because sometimes it only refers to the data collection and other times it also refers to the analysis. All longitudinal studies have measurements that occur over time, whereas cross-sectional studies gather data at one point in time.

The confusion comes because some studies involve a cross-sectional *analysis* of longitudinal data. For example, we may analyze the cross-sectional difference in fifth-grade test scores for students who did, or did not, have intensive preschooling many years earlier—in other words, a study of a long-term effect. Box 15.4 explains this issue, which is often a source of confusion when researchers from different disciplines use the term *longitudinal*.

BOX 15.4
Cross-Sectional Analysis of Longitudinal Data

A *cross-sectional analysis* can be done on longitudinal data, although this idea may seem counterintuitive at first glance. For example, say we have standardized test scores (Y) from a group of fifth graders tested this year. And say we also have records of whether they did, or did not, participate in an intensive preschool program (X) offered by the school 6 years ago on a voluntary basis. Thus, X (the preschool program) predates Y (the fifth-grade test) by 6 years, so the *data* are longitudinal in a sense. The data could even have come from a truly longitudinal study that followed the children since preschool. But in our analysis, we still basically compare the mean scores of those who did, and those who did not, participate in intensive preschool at one point in time (with appropriate control variables, of course)—a cross-sectional analysis.

In a truly longitudinal *analysis,* in contrast, the statistical analysis makes explicit use of changes over time in the measured variables. An example of this kind of analysis is a difference-in-differences study, including *panel data* analysis, discussed a bit later on in this chapter.

Difference-in-Differences Strategy

As we have seen, both before-after and cross-sectional comparisons have weaknesses in terms of internal validity—that is, providing a convincing demonstration of causation. By putting them together—having two before-after comparisons, one for the treatment and another for the comparison group—we create a much stronger study: a **difference-in-differences study** (often called *diff-in-diff* for short). The study gets its name from the fact that it compares the *difference* between two before-after *differences.* Some refer to this study as a **pre-post study with a comparison group.**

We highlight the difference-in-differences strategy here because it is quite feasible in real-world policy or practice settings, it can be understood by a wide audience, and it provides fairly good evidence of causation. Of course, certain conditions must be met in order to get good causal evidence. These conditions, as well as an understanding of the difference-in-differences in general, are best understood through a real example.

Do Parental Notification Laws Reduce Teenage Abortions and Births?

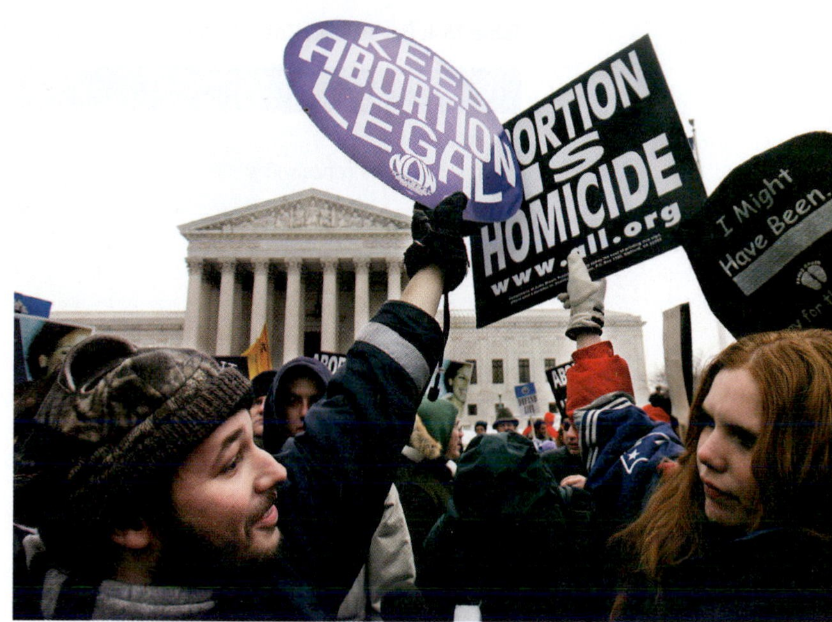

A difference-in-differences study revealed the effect of parental notification of abortion.

Source: Alex Wong/Getty Images News.

Researchers Colman, Joyce, and Kaestner (2008) used a difference-in-differences strategy to investigate the effect of a Texas parental notification law on abortion and birthrates. The 1999 law required that parents of a pregnant girl younger than 18 years be notified before an abortion. Before the law, no parental notification was required.

We could just consider what happened before and after the law was implemented (a before-after study). But both abortion rates and birthrates for teenagers have been steadily declining, due to broader social changes. It would be helpful to have a comparison group, unexposed to the law, to capture this trend (and thus better estimate a counterfactual). So Colman et al. compared Texas teenagers who conceived at age 17 with Texas teenagers who conceived at age 18. The 18-year-olds were only slightly older, yet not legally subject to the state's parental notification laws.

Table 15.3, adapted from the study, shows the number of abortions per 1,000 female population in the two age-groups, before and after the notification law change. We see that among 18-year-olds, abortion rates fell by 1.5 abortions per 1,000, while among 17-year-olds, abortion rates dropped by 3.4 abortions per 1,000. The difference in the differences is −1.9. The conclusion is that, compared with what abortion rates would have been (the counterfactual), parental notification laws reduced abortions among teenage girls by 1.91 per 1,000.

Table 15.4[2] shows a similar analysis of birthrates. Among the 17-year-olds, birthrates per 1,000 fell much less (−0.2) than they did among 18-year-olds (−2.9). The conclusion here is that, compared with what they would have been (the counterfactual), the parental notification law caused a 2.7 per 1,000 rise in teenage births. Thus, these two tables show that the law reduced abortions at the same time that it increased births to 17-year-olds in Texas.

Table 15.3 Abortion Rates for Texas Residents Aged 17 and 18 Who Conceived

	1999[a]	2000	Difference
Treatment group Texas teens who conceived at 17	18.7	15.3	−3.4
Comparison group Texas teens who conceived at 18	28.3	26.9	−1.5
Difference in differences	−3.4 − (−1.5) = −1.9**		

Note: Abortion rates are defined as the number of abortions per 1,000 age-specific female population.

[a]1999 refers to the period August 1, 1998, to July 31, 1999—before the parental notification law came into effect.

**Significant at 5%.

Source: Adapted from Colman et al. (2008).

[2]Table 15.4 and the birthrate numbers we quote differ slightly from Colman et al. for pedagogical reasons. Their rounding of the correct results obscured the analysis.

Table 15.4 Birthrates for Texas Residents Aged 17 and 18 Who Conceived

	1999[a]	2000	Difference
Treatment group Texas teens who conceived at 17	86.0	85.8	−0.2
Comparison group Texas teens who conceived at 18	116.8	113.9	−2.9
Difference in differences	−0.2 − (−2.9) = 2.7*		

Note: Birthrates are defined as the number of births per 1,000 age-specific female population.

[a]1999 refers to the period August 1, 1998, to July 31, 1999—before the parental notification law came into effect.

*Significant at 10%.

Source: Adapted from Colman et al. (2008).

What Does a Difference-in-Differences Study Assume?

Ideally, in a difference-in-differences study, the treatment and comparison groups are as similar as possible, except for being exposed to the treatment. But the strategy can work well even when the two groups are not a perfect match. Girls who conceive at age 17 and those who conceive at age 18 differ in many ways other than being subject to the parental notification law. One obvious difference, shown in the table, is that abortion rates and birthrates are higher for the older girls. So 18-year-olds are not the perfect comparison group. But such dissimilarities, even in the outcomes of interest such as abortion rates and birthrates, do not necessarily undermine a difference-in-differences study. What really matters is whether the underlying *change* or *trend* would be the same in the absence of the treatment.

This crucial assumption of equal change or parallel trends in a difference-in-differences study is illustrated in Figure 15.5. The usual, cross-sectional estimate of the difference between the groups is A − B. The difference-in-differences strategy uses the A − C comparison, which is an improvement. But notice that we assume that the initial difference in levels (equal to the vertical distance D − E) would have remained constant over time (becoming B − C) if the treatment group had not received the treatment. In other words, a difference-in-differences study assumes that the change over time in the comparison group is the same change that would happen to the treatment group if it did not get the treatment (the counterfactual).[3]

Abortion rates and birthrates were trending down anyway in Texas. But did they trend down faster for one age-group than another? If so, this would undermine the study's conclusions. If not, then the comparison between 17-year-olds and 18-year-olds remains valid.

Researchers sometimes find that although the time trends are not similar across the groups, the proportional changes in the trends are comparable. This often happens in cases when the initial levels of the two groups are quite different. In such situations, researchers will take log transformations of the variables and do a difference-in-differences study on the log-transformed dependent variables. (In fact, Colman and colleagues [2008] also did that analysis, just to be sure.) Moreover, when the treatment and comparison groups differ a great deal in initial level, assuming that their logs have the same trend can be as problematic as assuming that their levels have the same trend.

In real-world applied social policy research, the perfect comparison group is rarely available. The authors of the abortion study might have compared Texas with another similar state that did not pass a parental notification law, focusing on just 17-year-olds in the two states. But the detailed data necessary for such a

[3]Technically, a difference-in-differences estimate is (A − E) − (B − D) = A − C, since C = E + (B − D).

Figure 15.5 Difference-in-Differences Assumptions

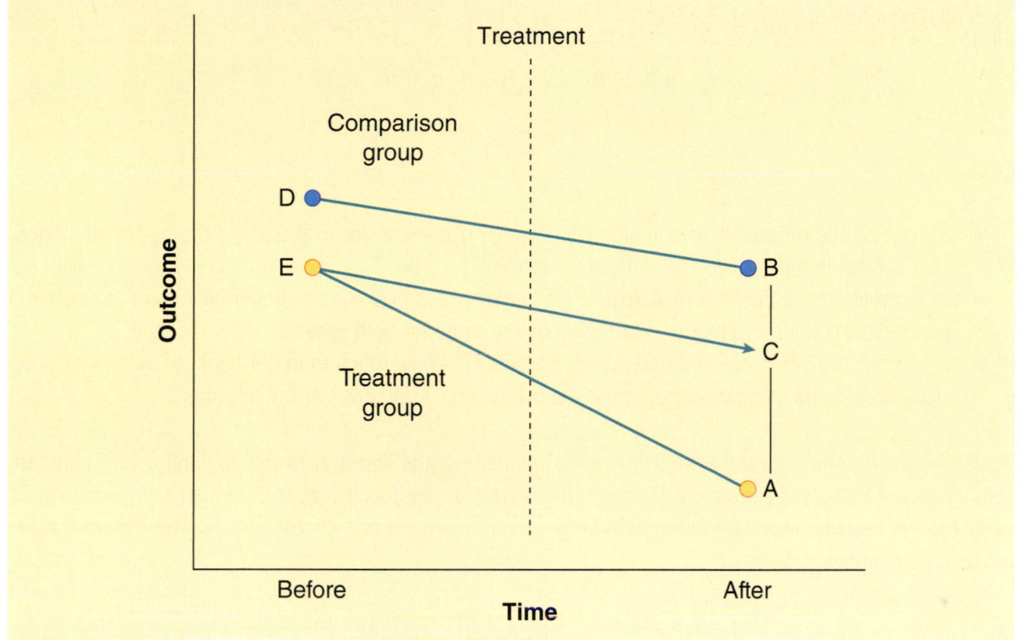

study are not gathered in most states.[4] Moreover, such a comparison group would not be perfect either: States have different demographic characteristics, birthrates and abortion rates, and trends. The choice of 18-year-olds in the same state, although not perfect, was still a good one for this study.

Retrospective Pretests and Other Retrospective Variables

A difference-in-differences study is usually longitudinal, requiring a before-after measurement of some kind. But it is possible to take advantage of the strengths of the difference-in-differences approach in a purely cross-sectional study by using a *retrospective pretest*. A retrospective pretest is typically a question in a survey that asks about an outcome in the past. For example, in an evaluation of a drug abuse prevention program—in which we are using a cross-sectional survey to compare participants in the program with a comparison group—we can ask both groups to recall their level of drug use several years ago. Then we can calculate the change in drug use, from then until now, in both groups and use a difference-in-differences analysis. In this way, the retrospective pretest provides cross-sectional data that can be analyzed with a difference-in-differences approach.

Difference-in-Differences in a Regression Framework

The analysis of a difference-in-differences study can also be performed in a regression framework, which offers some advantages. Here is how it works: A dummy variable is constructed for whether or not the individual is in the treatment group, denoted below as *Rx*. Another dummy variable is constructed for whether

[4]In fact, these researchers and others did studies using other states for the comparison group, but other states did not have detailed data on birth dates and conception dates. So those other studies had to look at age at delivery, resulting in somewhat misleading results. See Colman et al. (2008). Since ages of conception are very private data, they were, of course, subject to intense confidentiality restrictions and human subjects oversight. The researchers got the data stripped on all personal identification but nonetheless had to keep them very secure.

or not it is the postperiod, denoted as Post. Finally, an interaction variable is constructed as the product of those two variables, denoted as Post × *Rx*.

A regression is run with the model:

$$Y = a + b_{Rx}Rx + b_{post}\text{Post} + b_{int}(\text{Post} \times Rx),$$

where

- b_{Rx} reveals the difference in outcome (Y) between treatment and comparison during the preperiod. This is what is assumed to stay constant over time.
- b_{post} reveals the difference in outcome (Y) between postperiod and preperiod for the comparison group. This is the trend that is assumed to be the same for both groups.
- b_{int} reveals the difference in difference in outcome (Y)—how much more (or less) the treatment group *changes* than the comparison group, or the presumed causal effect of the treatment.

This regression-based approach to difference-in-differences is identical to the straightforward comparisons of means discussed previously. However, the regression approach can be extended to include control variables that capture important differences between the treatment and control groups. These control variables can be denoted as Cont:

$$Y = a + b_{Rx}Rx + b_{post}\text{Post} + b_{int}(\text{Post} \times Rx) + b_{cont}\text{Cont}$$

QUESTION

Explain the basic logic of a difference-in-differences study.

Control variables allow the researcher to account for relevant factors that are changing differently in the two groups, allowing the assumption that the treatment group would have had the same change or trend, absent the treatment, to be somewhat relaxed (only unmeasured differences between the two groups need to be assumed to be constant).

Panel Data for Difference-in-Differences

The difference-in-differences studies that we have considered so far made use of just one change over time and at a group level. However, with *panel data*—that is, repeated measurements on the same individuals over several time periods—it is possible to consider many individual changes and pool their effects. In essence, panel data allow for many difference-in-differences over time for each individual in the study. The individuals may be people or households, but panel data can also represent schools, organizations, neighborhoods, cities, states, or even nations over time.

Consider the example of marriage and the earnings of men. Studies have shown that married men earn more on average than unmarried men. Is the effect causal? Does marriage cause men to take work more seriously and thus earn more? Or are men who earn more just more likely to get married?

Korenman and Neumark (1991) examined this question in an article titled "Does Marriage Make Men More Productive?" They employed panel data that followed men for several years and observed their marital status, wages, and other variables. Their analysis looked at how much men's wages changed when they married (or divorced) and compared those changes with what occurred when their marital status did not change. Thus, changes in wages associated with changes in marital status were employed to *identify* the effect of marital status on wages.

Panel data provide the following advantages in a difference-in-differences study:

- Repeated observations over time of the same individuals
- More periods of time

- More possible independent variable values
- More individuals
- Other control variables

More generally, a panel difference-in-differences study measures the correlation of changes in the independent variable for specific individuals with changes in the dependent variable for the same individual. It makes use of within-subjects variation, as distinct from between-subjects variation. Each subject acts as his or her own control, in some sense.

Does marriage lead men to earn more?

Source: © iStockphoto.com/TriggerPhoto.

What Do Panel Difference-in-Differences Studies Assume?

A study such as the one by Korenman and Neumark (1991) uses *fixed effects*—specifically, a method in which each individual has a dummy variable—to capture individual differences. But this assumes that any differences between men relevant to both their wages and their marital status remain constant over time. For example, if emotional stability is an unmeasured common cause that affects both wages and marriage, the method implicitly assumes that emotional stability remains constant over the study. But of course this may not be true—emotional stability may also change over time, potentially resulting in bias.

In this fixed-effects panel study, only those who change their marital status provide information about the effect of marriage on wages. These "changers," in other words, are used to identify the effect of marriage on wages. To illustrate, Table 15.5 shows how the marital status of five men, labeled A through E, changes over time. We see that Men A and C provide no information whatsoever, because their marital status doesn't change in the study period. Man B provides information only in the transition from Year 2 to Year 3. Man D provides information in the transitions between Years 1 and 2 and Years 4 and 5. Man E provides information from the transition between Years 4 and 5. The estimate of the marriage effect is based only on the changes in wages that are associated with these individuals' changes in marriage status.

Weaknesses of Panel Difference-in-Differences Studies

Panel difference-in-differences studies offer many advantages, but they also have limitations. One relates to generalizability: It is difficult to determine what population the study's findings apply to. As we have seen,

Table 15.5 Panel Data on Men Marrying Over Time

Man	Year 1	Year 2	Year 3	Year 4	Year 5
A	Married	Married	Married	Married	Married
B	Single	Single	Married	Married	Married
C	Single	Single	Single	Single	Single
D	Single	Married	Married	Married	Single
E	Single	Single	Single	Single	Married

Source: Korenman and Neumark (1991).

the identification strategy relies on "changers," such as men who marry or divorce, to calculate a treatment effect. Men who stay single and men who stay married do not come into the picture. Also, men who change marital status more often contribute more to the effect. But such men may not be typical, and therefore, the estimated treatment effect may not generalize to all or even most men.

The fact that only changers contribute to the estimation also reduces the share of the sample that contributes to the analysis, sometimes dramatically. So what seems like a large sample over many years becomes effectively only a small sample when the focus is on only those individuals who change their status. This makes it much harder to obtain statistically significant results. The reliance on changers also means that coding errors can have a large influence. An error in marital status for 1 year will add a lot of error.

QUESTION

How does having panel data provide for many differences over time and across individuals?

Another weakness with such panel studies is that the time scale might not be sufficient for all the independent variables to affect the dependent variable. Using longer time lags can deal with this, but that brings its own problems.

Finally, the biggest issue is the potential endogeneity of the changes, making whatever idiosyncratic factors drive men's earnings not constant over time and related to both the independent and dependent variables. Is the *change* in marital status endogenous? Are changes in independent variables caused by changes in some other factor that also affects the dependent variable—a common cause? For example, do women choose to marry men whose wages appear likely to rise? Are changes in the independent variable caused by changes in the dependent variable—reverse causation? For example, do men wait to propose until their earnings start to increase? To provide strong causal evidence, the changes in the independent variable need to be exogenous, from something like a natural experiment. But in fact many panel difference-in-differences studies are really observational studies.

Instrumental Variables and Regression Discontinuity

Estimating the quantitative magnitude of a causal effect is an important goal, especially in research for policy or practice. When the treatment group represents a program—a complete package, as it were—natural and quasi experiments directly estimate the magnitude of the causal effect. In the HUD study, for example, the treatment group represents buildings run by resident-controlled nonprofit corporations, a novel approach to public housing management. In other studies, however, the treatment-control distinction serves as a device (an *instrument*) for manipulating an underlying variable of interest. (Note that this kind of instrument is not the same as an instrument of measurement, such as a survey.)

Instrumental Variables

When the treatment group–control group distinction works as a device to manipulate an underlying variable—and when that underlying variable can also be measured directly—researchers sometimes use an extension of the natural experiment method known as the **instrumental variables (IV) study** (Angrist & Krueger, 2001). An **instrument** is a variable that causes the independent variable to change but does not affect the outcome in any way, other than through the independent variable.

In the elevated train noise study (Bronzaft & McCarthy, 1975), the researchers compared student outcomes between the different sides of the school and did not estimate the effect of noise itself. However, Side of School could have served as an instrument for noise, because the side of the school caused noise to vary but was itself unrelated to student learning. But researchers would have needed measures of noise exposure over the school year to estimate the effect of noise by using Side of School as an instrument. Technically, if we want to learn the causal effect of X on Y, but X is endogenous to Y, we look for an instrument Z. For Z to be a valid instrument, it must be related to X and exogenous to Y.

The method of instrumental variables is best illustrated with an example.

Maternal Smoking, Cigarette Taxes, and Birth Weight

Mothers who smoke while pregnant reduce the birth weight of their babies. Of course, mothers who smoke while pregnant may differ from mothers who don't smoke in ways likely to affect their babies. In other words, smoking is likely endogenous to birth weight. Evans and Ringel (1999) estimate the effect of maternal smoking on birth weight, using cigarette taxes as an instrument.

Whether or not people smoke is affected by cigarette taxes. Cigarette taxes vary across states and have varied over time. Therefore, some of the variation in maternal smoking is driven by variation in cigarette taxes. That variation, and only that variation, in maternal smoking is used to estimate the effect of maternal smoking on birth weight. In this way, common causes of both maternal smoking and birth weight are excluded from the estimate. Box 15.5 provides a helpful way to identify a valid instrumental variable.

BOX 15.5
How to Determine If an Instrument Is Valid

One of the best ways to determine a valid instrumental variable is to say aloud that "*X* only affects *Y* through its effect on *Z*"—but substitute the variable names for *X*, *Y*, and *Z*. For example, "Cigarette taxes only affect birth weight through their effect on maternal smoking." Sounds reasonable, right?[5] If it does not, then *Z* is not likely to be a valid instrumental variable. Here are the steps:

- State the outcome or dependent variable of interest, *Y*.
- State the independent variable of interest, *X*.
- Find the candidate instrument *Z*.
- Does *Z* affect *X* in a fairly substantial manner?
- If not, it cannot be a good instrument.
- Does *Z* affect *Y* in any way other than through *X*?
- If so, it is not a valid instrument.

Generalizability of IV Studies

IV estimates may not generalize to the entire study population. Consider the maternal smoking study. Perhaps some mothers are determined to smoke and will smoke no matter how high cigarette taxes go. Other mothers would never smoke, and the level of cigarette taxes is irrelevant to them. Only mothers whose smoking status is affected by cigarette taxes, the instrument, will contribute to the estimate of the effect of smoking on birth weight. Thus, the generalizability of the estimate is reduced and often unclear. An IV estimate is referred to, in the technical literature, as a *local average treatment effect* because it is an average among only the "local" group affected by the instrument (Imbens & Angrist, 1994). This term is contrasted with the *average treatment effect* estimated by randomized experiments. (See Harris and Remler [1998] for a relatively accessible treatment of the generalizability of instrumental variable estimates.)

Deaton (2010) and others are particularly critical of IV studies, arguing that there is no reason to believe that the group randomized by an instrument is a group of particular policy interest. Others contend, however, that those randomized by real-world instruments, such as those mothers who are deterred by higher taxes, are often the marginal people likely to be of policy relevance.

[5]One of us (DKR) thanks Joshua Angrist for teaching her this "trick."

QUESTION

Why does an instrumental variable study provide strong causal evidence? What group does it generalize to?

This reduced and ambiguous generalizability was also a feature of the panel difference-in-differences study and, it turns out, many natural experiments. IV studies are simply a specific way to use natural experiments.

Regression Discontinuity

Suppose that students are accepted into a compensatory program only if they score below a certain threshold on a standardized test. Students just above the threshold are presumably very similar but not exposed to the program. Intuitively, the effect of the program on an outcome could be determined by comparing the two groups on either side of the cut point. If they experience very different outcomes, this would suggest a large treatment effect; a small difference would suggest little effect.

This is the essential logic of a **regression discontinuity** study—a study that applies when assignment to the treatment is based on a cut point for a single quantitative assignment variable.

Regression discontinuity studies are analyzed, as the name suggests, in a regression framework:

$$\text{Outcome} = b_0 + b_{\text{Assign}}\text{Assignment} + b_{\text{Treat}}\text{Treatment} + b_{\text{Inter}}(\text{Treatment} \times \text{Assignment})$$

Assignment is the quantitative variable whose scores alone determine assignment to the treatment group. Its coefficient, b_{Assign}, captures the effect of the variable that is used to determine assignment. For example, it could be the ordinary effect of the standardized test used for admission. *Treatment* is a dummy variable coded 1 if the individual is in the treatment group and 0 if the individual is in the comparison group. If the treatment itself has an effect, we expect to see it in its coefficient, b_{Treat}. The interaction term (Treatment × Assignment) can be included if the analyst expects the treatment to change the effect of the assigning variable, not just cause a change in the level. For example, if a program not only improves student performance but also increases the effect of standardized test scores, there would be an interaction. It is also possible to add further controls or use a more flexible functional form for the effect of the assignment variable.

Napoli and Hiltner (1993) used a regression discontinuity design to evaluate a developmental reading program for community college students. Students were assigned to the program based strictly on having a score below 80 on a reading comprehension test. The researchers then examined the effect of the program on the students' later grade-point averages (GPAs). The results, presented in Figure 15.6, suggest that the program was effective. Notice how the regression line for those in the developmental reading program appears higher, shifted up, at the cut point (the slope also appears to be a bit flatter). This finding provides evidence that GPAs of students in the program were higher than they would have otherwise been (if we projected the line for the nondevelopmental comparison group back across the cut point).

QUESTION

Why does a regression discontinuity provide strong causal evidence? What group does it generalize to?

A regression discontinuity is an especially strong quasi experiment, although it applies only in rather specific circumstances. It too suffers from limited generalizability: Because estimates are based on those just above and below the cutoff, the estimated effects are also local average treatment effects that may not generalize to those who are either well above or well below the cutoff.

Ethics of Quasi and Natural Experiments

Among the attractions of natural and quasi experiments is that they tend to raise fewer ethical problems than randomized experiments, because they tend to occur in more natural settings. Still, they are not without ethical issues.

In a natural experiment, researchers do not manipulate the treatment that people receive—they just observe a treatment that happens to be randomized by some natural or unintentional process. Therefore, natural experiments avoid some of the ethical dilemmas that characterize many true experiments. Still, data

Figure 15.6 Regression Discontinuity Evaluation of a Developmental Reading Program

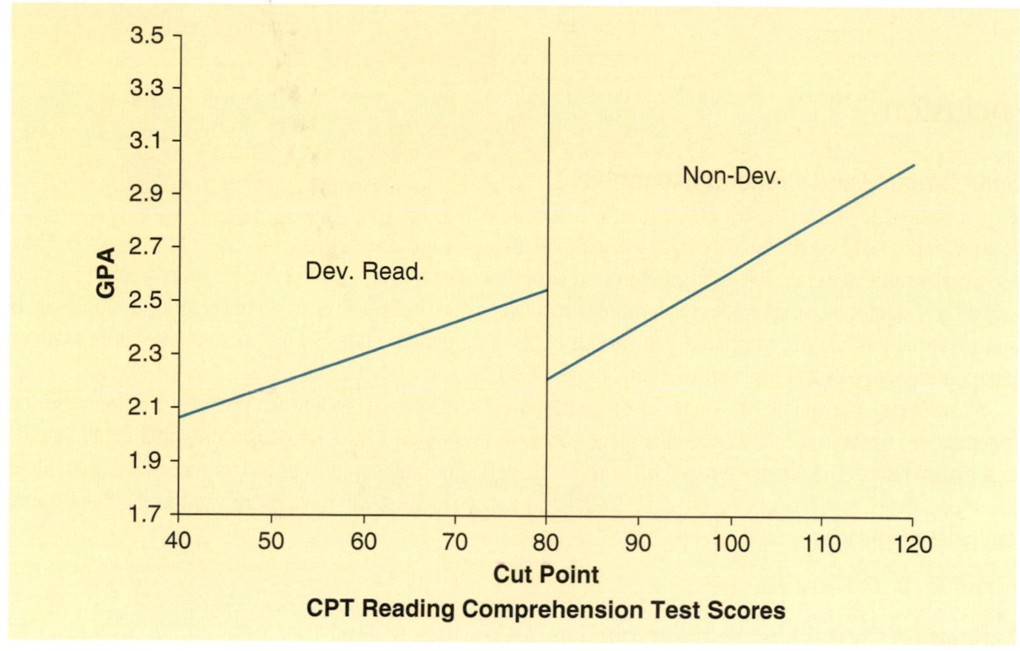

Source: Napoli and Hiltner (1993).

collection for natural experiments must be carried out ethically, just as for descriptive research. For example, the study of parental notification laws for abortion used extremely sensitive data that had to be stripped of identifiers and treated as highly confidential.

Quasi experiments may raise larger ethical issues, depending on the extent to which researchers manipulate the intervention and the importance of its outcomes in the lives of participants. In many weak quasi experiments, researchers have little influence on who receives the treatment of interest and are much more involved with selection of comparison groups and data collection. In such circumstances, ethical issues are, again, more like those of descriptive studies.

In stronger quasi experiments, however, researchers do manipulate the treatment—altering what happens in subjects' lives. For example, researchers may determine who gets a new program first and who gets it later—or not at all. Consider, for example, a study of the effect of an instruction program for children with severe learning disabilities that was rolled out for different children at different times to enable estimation of its causal effect (Kellett & Nind, 2001). The teachers implementing the program became increasingly convinced of its effectiveness and saw the delays in implementing it for children in the comparison group as "lost opportunities for progress" (p. 53).

The ethical issues in such strong quasi experiments depend significantly on the nature of the intervention or treatment and the stakes involved in the outcomes. If the study involves haphazard randomization that provides some store shoppers 6 choices of jam and other shoppers 24 choices of jam, as in the Iyengar and Lepper (2000) study described in the previous chapter, the stakes are low, and the study is without any ethical difficulties. But many quasi experiments take place in real-world settings that affect people's educational, labor market, health, and other important outcomes—that is one of their great advantages. In such cases, manipulation of the treatment can have the same high stakes as some randomized field experiments. When the researchers are working with the organization that controls programs in these areas, such as the school administration and teachers in the learning disabilities study, care must be taken not to exploit such power.

Conclusion

Searching for and Creating Exogeneity

Natural and quasi experiments are widely used to estimate causal effects in social and policy research. They are usually more generalizable than randomized experiments, often less costly, and frequently more feasible and ethical. And they can provide much more convincing causal estimates than do observational studies with control variables. It is not surprising that various types of natural and quasi experiments have come to dominate cutting-edge causal research in many applied fields.

In assessing the validity of a natural or quasi experiment, understanding what drove the treatment or independent variable is critical. We encourage you to always be on the lookout for events that could be natural experiments. And we encourage you to try to shape the implementation of programs in ways that allow for strong quasi experiments. In this way, social and policy research will have more valid and generalizable estimates of important causal effects.

Estimating Causal Effects in Perspective: A Wrap-up to Part IV

Research in the aid of policy and practice must often focus on causal effects. Yet resources are limited. To choose the most cost-effective programs, we need to know how truly effective a program really will be. As we showed in the first chapter of Part IV on causation (Chapter 11), estimating causal effects in applied social areas is difficult. In the real world, most variables whose effects we would like to know are endogenous. (For further reading and more advanced treatments, see Angrist & Pischke, 2009; Langbein & Felbinger, 2006; Morgan & Winship, 2007.)

There are three basic approaches. The first is to use observational data with control variables (using stratification, regression, or propensity score matching), as we demonstrated in Chapters 12 and 13. To the extent that common causes of both outcome and independent variables are measured, their effect can be removed and the true causal effect isolated. However, the bias of any unmeasured common causes persists—and it is very difficult to get all the relevant common causes, almost impossible with most observational data sets. Moreover, the problem of reverse causation cannot be addressed simply with control variables.

The second approach is randomized experiments, which we covered in Chapter 14. Randomized experiments use random assignment to make the treatment or independent variable exogenous and, therefore, do a great job of estimating causal effects. However, they are expensive, sometimes unethical or impractical, and often so artificial or dependent on volunteers that generalizability is poor.

The third method is natural and quasi experiments, the topic of this chapter. These are not one method but rather a large collection of methods in which exogeneity is found or created in a form that often falls short of a true randomized experiment. These methods may be a researcher's best shot at getting a fairly good estimate of a causal effect. Therefore, as we have urged, researchers should always be on the lookout for natural experiments or opportunities to create strong quasi experiments.

When searching for research that is useful for policy and practice, we hope that you will be cognizant of the weaknesses of the various types of studies used to estimate causal effects. Yet, at the same time, we would caution you not to be too dismissive—most studies have their strengths too. Through a variety of studies, each with different strengths and weaknesses, it is possible to learn a great deal about what causes what—and how large the effect is. We hope that the various research examples we provided illustrate how much we can learn with the limited tools we have.

BOX 15.6
Critical Questions to Ask About Natural and Quasi Experiments

- Is the study a natural experiment, a quasi experiment, or neither (such as an observational study)? Is the treatment intentional or planned (with respect to the outcome) or not?
- What kind of natural or quasi experiment is it? Think about the possibilities: a before-after study, an interrupted time series, a cross-sectional comparison, a difference-in-differences study, and so on.
- What kind of variation in the treatment (independent variable of interest) is being used to estimate its effect on the dependent variable? Can you describe in everyday language how the treatment effect is being "identified" or traced out?
- What drove the treatment variation used in the estimation? Was it exogenous to the outcome?
- How comparable is the comparison group (or whatever constitutes the counterfactual, such as the before period)?
- Who was affected by the variation used in the estimation? What population does that generalize to?

BOX 15.7
Tips on Doing Your Own Research: Natural and Quasi Experiments

- Identify the independent variable (treatment) and outcome(s) of interest.
- Search for real-world situations in which the independent variable of interest is exogenous to the outcome(s) of interest. If you find such a situation, you have a natural experiment.
- Search for opportunities in which you can make the treatment exogenous to the outcome(s) of interest. For example, can you give the treatment to one subset first and the rest later? If you find such a situation, you have the opportunity to create a quasi experiment. See the list of strategies in the section "How to Create Good Quasi Experiments When Planning and Implementing Programs."
- Examine what is driving the independent variable through theory, skeptical thinking, informal investigation, and (if possible) qualitative research.
- Using the analysis of what is driving the independent variable and the practicalities of data collection, determine the specific design (before-after comparison, interrupted time series, difference-in-differences, regression discontinuity, etc.). If possible, use more than one design (more than one method of estimating the causal effect). Choose designs to maximize exogeneity and comparability, and thus minimize the bias in estimated causal effects.
- To obtain the data needed, search for existing data—or data that would be collected anyway. If these do not exist or will not be sufficiently valid and reliable, plan necessary data collection (and see tips at the end of Chapter 7). If possible, collect data prospectively, starting before treatments are implemented.
- If implementing a strong quasi experiment, determine how the treatment will be implemented and develop a plan to recruit subjects, if necessary. Plan analyses in advance and carry out sample size and power calculations to determine the number of subjects. See also tips at the end of Chapter 14.

Chapter Resources

Key Terms

- Before-after study (one-group pretest-posttest, pre-post comparison)
- Comparison group
- Difference-in-differences study
- Instrument
- Instrumental variables (IV) study
- Internal validity
- Interrupted time series
- Natural experiment
- Pre-post study with a comparison group
- Prospective study
- Quasi experiment
- Regression discontinuity
- Retrospective study

Exercises

Family Income and Child Mental Health

15.1. Think of a variety of different causal pathways that could explain the correlation between the family income of a child and the child's mental health. Include examples of mechanisms (intervening variables) for causation, common causes, and reverse causation.

a. Draw path diagrams to illustrate.
b. What counterfactual question would you like to answer to address the causal question of the effect of poverty on mental health?
c. Describe a randomized experiment that could be used to answer this question and that meets ethical standards.
d. Compare the validity of the causal conclusions of the casino natural experiment with that of the randomized experiment.
e. Compare the generalizability of the casino natural experiment with that of the randomized experiment.

Noise, Student Learning, and Diligent Teachers

15.2. Recall the Bronzaft and McCarthy (1975) study of how train noise affected student learning. How might a conscientious teacher respond to the noise? Might such a teacher aggressively pursue a classroom on the less noisy side of the building? If so, how might that affect your conclusions from this study? Explain.

HMOs and Medical Care Usage

15.3. Suppose two manufacturing companies merge and one company switches to the more restrictive health insurance options (only closed-panel health maintenance organizations, or HMOs) of the other company.

a. Explain why this provides a natural experiment that could be used to evaluate the effects of closed-panel HMOs on medical care usage.

b. Describe the data that you would want to collect for such a study.
c. Describe how you would analyze the data.
d. Discuss the validity of the causal conclusions. What weaknesses are there?
e. Discuss the generalizability of the study.

Evaluating Transit System Changes

15.4. Here are some excerpts from an Op-Ed contribution from the *New York Times* Sunday City section, by E. S. Savas (2007):

> Transit officials are decentralizing the subway system to improve service, cleanliness and on-time performance by appointing individual managers for each of the 24 lines. . . .
>
> The authority plans to start with the No. 7 and L lines and evaluate the pilot program by surveying riders after about three months. This implies only modest goals, as that time is too short for major improvements.
>
> Moreover, more money and manpower are to be allocated to those lines, making it impossible to figure out whether any improvements result from better management or more spending. The plan seems loaded to elicit favorable comments in the short term from riders on those particular lines, which unlike the other 22 lines are isolated: they have separate tracks.

Evaluators of the present plan could use a difference-in-differences framework to evaluate the impact of their decentralization program. Savas notes three problems that undermine the ability of such an evaluation to allow generalizations to the long-term effects of creating individual managers for each of the 24 lines.

a. Briefly describe the difference-in-differences framework that could be used to do an evaluation of the decentralization program.
b. Explain the three problems Savas describes. Explain how they would undermine the desired generalization from your difference-in-differences study.

Design Your Own Diff-in-Diff Study

15.5. Think of a program (intervention) and the outcome it is designed to affect in your field of interest.

a. Design a difference-in-differences quasi experiment to estimate the effect of the intervention on the outcome.
b. Describe what you would measure and how you would analyze the data.
c. How convincing will the evidence of causation be (the interval validity)? Will the estimated causal effect be biased? If there will be bias in the causal effect estimated, can you predict its direction?
d. How generalizable will the results be? Would generalizability to a larger group be useful?
e. Think about the organizational, political, and managerial factors involved in implementing the quasi experiment. How far in advance should you start collecting data—or are needed data already collected for other purposes? Will the allocation of interventions require a lot of information? Will the allocation be controversial?

Does Posting Calories Reduce Calories Consumed? When Studies Conflict . . .

15.6. A law requiring the posting of calories in all chain restaurants went into effect in 2008 in New York City (NYC). Two studies (Bollinger, Leslie, & Sorensen, 2011; Elbel, Gyamfi, & Kersh, 2011) attempted to determine the causal effect of calorie posting on calories consumed in restaurants. The table below illustrates their main features.

	Starbucks Study (Bollinger, Leslie, & Sorensen, 2011)	**Fast-Food Restaurants Study (Elbel, Gyamfi, & Kersh, 2011)**
Type of study	Difference-in-differences Pre-2008 vs. post-2008 Treatment city: NYC Comparison cities: Boston and Philadelphia	Difference-in-differences Pre-2008 vs. post-2008 Treatment city: NYC Comparison city: Newark, NJ
Restaurants	Starbucks	McDonald's, KFC, Wendy's, and Burger King
Data sources	Individual transaction-level data from company	Individual receipt data and survey data (only from those who participated in the survey)
Study subjects (type of customer)	All Starbucks customers in NYC, Boston, and Philadelphia	Children and adolescents in randomly sampled restaurants in low-income sections of NYC and Newark
Finding	6% reduction in calories consumed per transaction, due entirely to changes in food consumption, and no changes in calories consumed in drinks	No decline in calories (< 0.2% increase, not statistically significant)

a. Both studies use the NYC law change as a "natural experiment." Explain why these are natural experiments, particularly how the intervention is exogenous. Discuss the quality of the evidence of causation that these studies provide.
b. Both studies are difference-in-differences studies. Show the table that would be used to create the estimated effect for the Starbucks study. Explain what would be calculated.
c. Describe the populations studied in each study. How do they compare? To what population does each study generalize?
d. Why might the two studies have had different findings?
e. How might the effect of total calories consumed differ from what these studies estimated?
f. Suppose that your city was planning to require calorie posting in chain restaurants next year and you hoped to do a study to learn the effect on calories consumed. What comparison city would you choose for your study? Explain the advantages and disadvantages of your choice of comparison city.

Preventing Falls by Nursing Home Residents

15.7. Below are an edited extract of the abstract and a table from Teresi et al. (2013):

Objectives: The aim was to conduct a . . . study to estimate the effects of implementing evidence-based education and best practice programs in nursing homes (NHs) on falls, negative affect and behavior, and the associated societal costs.

Design: A quasi-experimental design, a variant of a cluster randomized trial of implementation research examining transfer of research findings into practice, was used to compare outcomes among three groups of residents in 15 nursing homes per group.

Methods: Forty-five NHs participated in one of three conditions: (1) standard training, (2) training and implementation modules provided to facility staff, or (3) staff training and implementation modules augmented by surveyor training. After application of exclusion and matching criteria, nursing homes were selected at random within three regions of New York State. Outcomes were assessed using medical records and the Minimum Data Set.

Results: The main finding was a significant reduction of between 5 and 12 annual falls in a typical nursing home. While both intervention groups resulted in fall reduction, the larger and significant reduction occurred in the group without surveyor training. A significant reduction in negative affect associated with training staff and surveyors was observed. Net cost savings from fall prevention was estimated.

Conclusions: A low cost intervention targeting dissemination of evidence-based best practices in nursing homes can result in the potential for fall reduction, and cost savings.

Baseline Characteristics of the Study Sample %s or Means (SD in Parentheses)

	Exp. Group 1 Staff Trained	Exp. Group 2 Staff and Surveyors Trained	Control Standard Training	Total
Age	81.60 (11.31)	82.71 (10.44)	81.88 (10.94)	82.12 (10.87)
Female	72.42%	74.07%	72.42%	73.07%
Race Ethnicity				
American Indian or Alaska Native	0.31%	0.17%	0.32%	0.26%
Asian or Pacific Islander	1.42%	0.14%	0.14%	0.53%
African American/Black, Not of Hispanic Origin	13.10%	1.20%	5.19%	6.02%
Hispanic	7.33%	0.31%	0.51%	2.52%
White, Not of Hispanic Origin	77.84%	98.19%	93.84%	90.67%
Marital Status				
Never Married	17.83%	11.15%	14.53%	14.19%
Married	16.62%	23.29%	21.63%	20.76%
Widowed	56.02%	58.63%	55.77%	59.98%
Separated	2.63%	1.34%	1.11%	1.67%
Divorced	6.91%	5.59%	6.96%	6.40%

** Significant at the 0.01 level.

Source: Teresi et al (2013).

a. Discuss how well this study does (or does not) provide good causal evidence (internal validity) of the effects of best practice training. Support your statement with a description of the methods used and data in the table, and explain your logic.
b. Discuss the generalizability (external validity) of this study of the effects of best practice training. Support your statement with a description of the methods used and data in the table, and explain your logic.
c. How should the results be presented in a table? (Create a shell table containing made-up numbers or symbols.) Present results for two outcomes: (1) whether there was any fall in the last 180 days and (2) the number of falls over the last 180 days. How would you calculate the effect (causal impact) of best practice training for staff only? How would you calculate the effect (causal impact) of best practice training for staff and surveyors? Explain in words and show the calculation using your made-up numbers or symbols.

Student Study Site

Visit the Study Site at **www.sagepub.com/remler2e** to

- test your knowledge with the self-quiz
- check your understanding of key terms with the eFlashcards
- explore helpful resources that relate directly to this chapter

PART V

CONTEXT AND COMMUNICATION

Thus far, we have focused mostly on the methods of research itself—how to conduct it and how to usefully interpret the resulting evidence. But research, particularly applied research, does not exist in a vacuum. It influences and is influenced by the broader political, social, and economic context. In this final part of the book, we first address the politics and production of research, including how research influences policy and who conducts and pays for research. We also cover some additional ethical issues and procedures established to protect people who participate in research. We then address the practical topics of how to find published studies, how to review the research literature, and how to communicate research you have done so others can understand and make use of it.

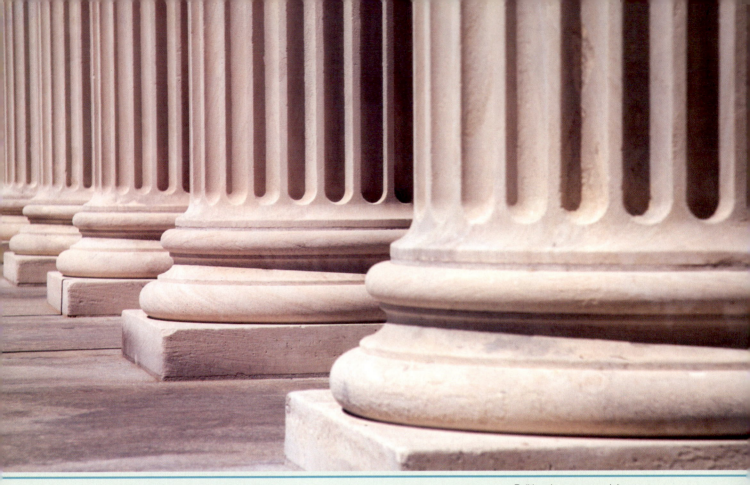

Politics shapes research in many ways.
Source: © iStockphoto.com/Marje.

Overview: In this chapter, you will learn about how research fits into the broader political context and the policy-making process, including the pathways through which research influences policy and practice as well as the barriers to its effective use and influence. You will also find out about how research is produced, including the different sources of research funding and the types of institutions that conduct research. And—although you have been exposed to research ethics throughout this book—you will learn more in this chapter about the history of research ethics and the formal rules and procedures that have been established to protect participants in research. Finally, you will be introduced to other ethical issues involved in applying research to policy and practice.

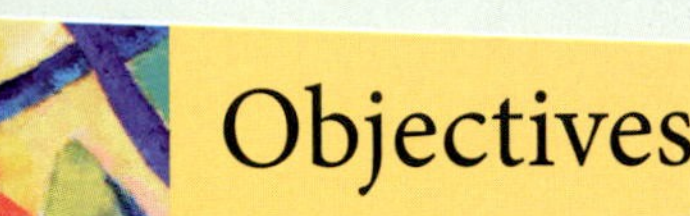

Objectives

Learning Objectives

After reading this chapter, you should be able to

- Describe political and ethical issues involved in applying research to policy and practice
- Extract useful results from research and apply them to policy and practice
- Predict barriers to research influencing policy and practice
- Recognize who conducts research, various kinds of research institutions, and how research is funded
- Determine if a research project is ethical and identify ethical ambiguities where they exist
- Determine the ethical review procedures and documents necessary for obtaining approval for your research, particularly informed consent forms
- Analyze the broader ethical issues of how a research project is chosen and how its results are communicated

16 The Politics, Production, and Ethics of Research

Risking Your Baby's Health

A television advertisement by the National Breastfeeding Campaign, sponsored by the U.S. Department of Health and Human Services and a group called the Ad Council, shows images of two pregnant women in a logrolling competition. "You'd never take risks before your baby is born," the ad says. "Why start after?" (U.S. Department of Health and Human Services, 2009). The message clearly suggests that bottle-feeding your baby, instead of breast-feeding, represents a serious risk to your baby's health and well-being. But how good is the research evidence about the benefits of breast-feeding? Is the evidence strong enough to justify a government-funded national campaign using this kind of scare tactic? And what would be the potential health risks if we waited for more or better evidence and did nothing to promote breast-feeding?

There is a large literature on the relationship between breast-feeding and a variety of health and other early childhood outcomes, including stomach and respiratory infections, asthma, obesity, diabetes, and cognitive development. Many (although certainly not all) of the associations between breast-feeding and these outcomes were shown to be statistically significant, and some were large enough to be practically significant as well. But nearly all the studies were observational, and the independent variable of interest, breast-feeding, is likely to be endogenous with respect to many of these outcomes. For example, better-educated and higher-income mothers tend to breast-feed more, and of course they also have more financial and other resources to devote to the care and upbringing of their young children. Even accounting for income and education, mothers who breast-feed may devote more time and effort in other ways to improving their children's nutrition, health care, and early education. So the causal evidence from observational studies alone remains weak—but there was little else available when the campaign was launched.

What kind of evidence do we need for making public policy? Should the threshold of evidence be higher to employ scare tactics like those in the National Breastfeeding Campaign ad? Does the public need to be made aware of the caveats and limitations of the research used to set this kind of policy or make these kinds of recommendations? And if so, how should this be done? How does the difficulty of doing randomized experiments with complex, personal behaviors such as breast-feeding affect the standard of evidence required to take action? These are the difficult questions that arise when using research to make policy or inform practice.

The National Breastfeeding Campaign also highlights how culture and values interact with research. Wolf (2007) contends that the weakness of the causal evidence about the true effects of breast-feeding was ignored because the findings fit well with a culture of "total motherhood" in our society, particularly among the well educated. Culture and politics shape research at all levels and stages: what research is done and what research is not done; which research results are ignored; and which results are believed and promoted.

In this chapter, we will look at the complex role of research in the political and policy-making process. We will also learn about the institutions that support and conduct research. And we will examine more closely the ethics of conducting—and communicating—research.

From Research to Policy

As a way to begin thinking about how research influences policy and practice, let's initially consider a kind of idealized rational model of analyzing and making public policy.

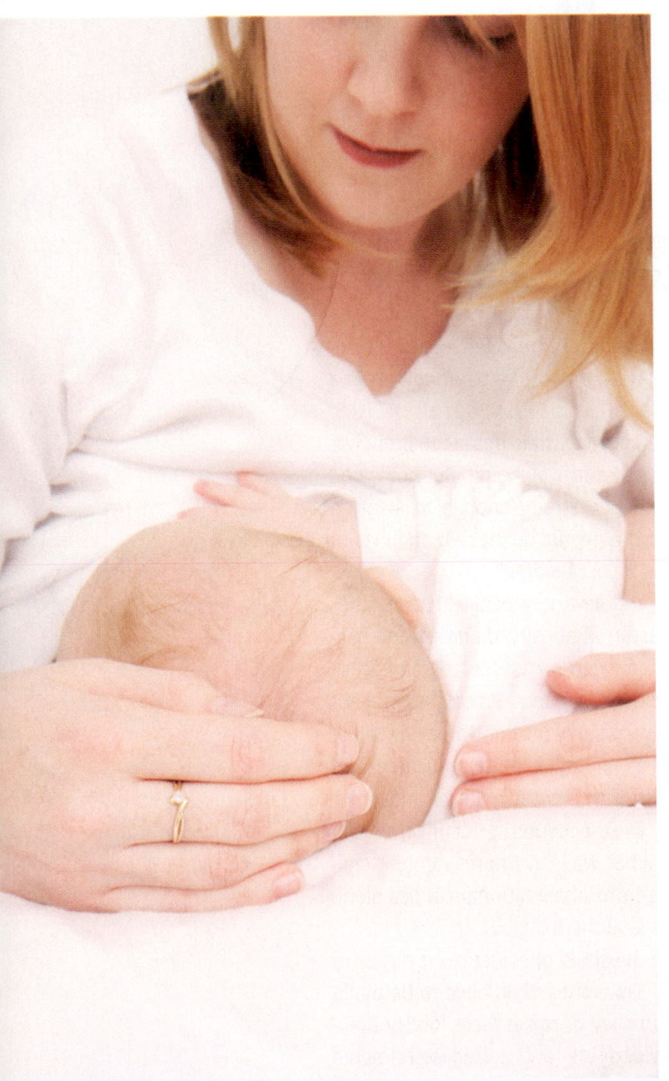

Are mothers who don't breast-feed risking their babies' health?
Source: iStockphoto.com/hidesy.

Rational Model of Policy

Weimer and Vining (2010) describe the steps of a rational model of policy analysis in which research plays a central role. To evaluate alternative solutions, they explain, the policy analyst must "[predict] impacts of alternatives" by "identifying and organizing relevant data, theories and facts" (Weimer & Vining, 2010, p. 257). Weimer and Vining also stress the importance of *cost-benefit analysis* to make the best use of limited resources, and they point out that research *evidence* about comparative effectiveness is needed to do cost-benefit analysis. Further illustrating how important they consider research to be in policy making, they provide an appendix that describes how to conduct focused secondary and (to a lesser extent) primary research. For example, they suggest looking for a past natural experiment (not their term) that raised parking fees to help predict the effects of proposed changes.

This kind of rational ideal of the role of research in the policy-making process is a useful place to start because it raises several important issues and questions—even before introducing politics, interests, values, ethics, and other real-world complexities into the picture.

Statistical Significance

To become a basis for a policy or administrative action, most would agree that the evidence should be statistically significant—not just a one-off fluke. But as we discussed in Chapter 9, the reality is more complex. First, we don't want to treat a p value of .05 as some magical mark to be applied too rigidly. In some contexts, p values of .10 or perhaps more can be enough evidence to act. Remember also that statistical power is important as well: We don't want to miss out on policies that really work, or overlook a potentially deadly risk factor, just because we have too small a sample size or too tough a standard for our p values. In other cases, however, we might want to be very sure that a program or intervention works and therefore require a lower p value, despite the lower power that it implies. Statistical significance should always be considered, but thoughtfully. And it should be considered in combination with practical significance, discussed next, for example, by the use of confidence intervals in addition to (or even in place of) significance tests.

Practical Significance

We have stressed the importance of presenting and understanding causal effects in terms that allow them to be practically evaluated. Is the magnitude of the effect big enough to be worth implementing? This is the question of practical, as opposed to purely statistical, significance. Measures of effect size are sometimes used to evaluate practical significance, but this is still only a first step. A program with a small effect size might be worth implementing—if it still beats the alternatives or it is combating an important or costly problem. Cost-benefit analysis, as mentioned above, is often a useful framework for gauging the practical significance of a demonstrated effect.

Evidence of Causation

One of the most difficult challenges involved in making policy or taking administrative action based on research is determining if the evidence of causation is good enough. Statistical and even practical significance alone can never establish causation. Therefore, before implementing a program to achieve a desired outcome, we need to establish that an effect is actually causal and that our estimate of the magnitude of the effect is not biased.

But good causal estimates are very hard to get, as we have seen in previous chapters. On real-world topics, policy makers and practitioners will almost always have to act before or even without getting definitive causal evidence.

For example, when the National Breastfeeding Campaign was initially launched, evidence of the causal effect of breast-feeding on child outcomes was weak, yet some evidence suggested the possibility of big effects. Public health practitioners decided to promote a policy based on statistical and practical significance, because they believed it to be valuable and they could not wait for conclusive causal evidence that might never come. Since then, yet more evidence has emerged, although the results are still not clear and continue to be debated (see Box 16.1). The real world cannot always wait for definitive evidence, and sometimes a clear answer will never emerge.

BOX 16.1
The Effects of Breast-Feeding: Many Studies

The National Breastfeeding Campaign began in 2003 (as the National Breastfeeding Awareness Campaign) without the benefit of many recent studies of the effects of breast-feeding. Breast-feeding was associated in observational data with many good outcomes for children. Some outcomes had highly plausible mechanisms, while others did not. Many studies with control variables had been performed before the campaign was launched, but important unmeasured variables were still unaccounted for. In Chapter 13, we discussed at length the Der, Batty, and Deary (2006) study that found no effect of breast-feeding on child cognitive skills after controlling for mother's own aptitude. We have already discussed the possible weaknesses of observational studies, even those with control variables.

The best new evidence comes from results of a cluster-randomized experiment. Kramer, Chalmers, and colleagues (2001b) designed a study that randomized maternal hospitals and associated polyclinics in Belarus to either a breast-feeding promotion arm or a control group. Mothers in the breast-feeding promotion arm did in fact breast-feed more often and longer, allowing the researchers to measure a causal effect of breast-feeding on a long list of child outcomes. To date, the evidence is mixed: Some outcomes (e.g., respiratory infections, asthma, obesity, dental cavities) show no effect, while others (cognitive skills, infant gastrointestinal infections, atopic eczema) do (Kramer, Aboud, et al., 2009; Kramer, Chalmers, et al., 2001a, 2001b; Kramer, Matush, et al., 2007, 2009; Kramer, Vanilovich, et al., 2007).

(Continued)

(Continued)

Moreover, cluster-randomized designs result in weaker evidence of causation than an ordinary randomized trial. Consequently, both significant and insignificant outcomes carry caveats or have been challenged. For example, the finding of no effect on asthma was challenged because the cluster design made the two arms somewhat unbalanced. In particular, the treatment arm had a higher family history of allergies and asthma, raising the possibility that the treatment arm was at an initial disadvantage (Mamabear, 2007). The effects on cognitive skills, which were strong enough to be practically significant, may have been due to the fact that the researchers doing the cognitive assessments were not blinded and so knew which children were in the treatment or control arm (Kramer, Aboud, et al., 2009; Kramer, Martin, et al., 2009). However, later research found that for a subset of children whose cognitive skills were measured by blinded evaluators, the correlation of cognitive skills measured by the unblinded assessors was between .58 and .67, suggesting that practically and statistically significant cognitive effects would remain with blinded evaluators (Kramer, 2010). Other challenges could include the generalizability of the results to both poorer and richer countries and the legitimacy of statistical significance tests for so many outcomes in one trial, although the outcomes were specified before the experiment began. Of course, such challenges in no way invalidate the research, but rather, they illustrate how hard it is to do definitive research even with a rigorous research design.

Recent new natural experiment studies have also emerged. Two studies make use of differences between siblings in breast-feeding, based on the idea that all other factors driving outcomes are the same among siblings and so the effect of breastfeeding can be isolated (Evenhouse & Reilly, 2005; Rees & Sabia, 2009). Each study showed effects on some outcomes, such as physical health, mental health, cognitive skills, and education. But both studies found that most observational estimates (even with control variables) are biased. As in most natural experiments, the premise that all other relevant factors are the same among siblings could be challenged. In particular, one wonders why one sibling was breast-fed and not the other. In fact, in a later study, Fletcher (2011) found that breast-fed siblings were favored by their parents in other ways and that differences in educational outcomes were eliminated when only comparing siblings otherwise treated equally. Baker and Milligan (2008) use the natural experiment of an increase in mandated maternity leave in Canada that raised breast-feeding. They found no effects on most child health measures. This study, too, could be challenged for several reasons, particularly that a government maternity leave policy had only a small effect on Canadian mothers' breast-feeding.

These many recent breast-feeding articles illustrate two important points. First, real-world policy decisions must often be made with incomplete evidence. Second, evidence is often contradictory.

How Many Studies?

Replication is a central principle of research. It inhibits researchers from cherry-picking, or manipulating their results, helping to ensure that the evidence is more trustworthy. But replication of the same or similar studies is often not enough to provide evidence to justify action. Instead, having different kinds of studies helps because of the various strengths and weaknesses of, for example, observational studies in comparison with natural or quasi experiments.

Consider again the example in Chapter 2 about the effects of divorce on children. Many observational studies showed that divorce is associated with poor outcomes for children but provided little evidence that divorce caused those outcomes. Gruber (2004) used a natural experiment, provided by the fact that states changed their divorce laws at different times, to come up with stronger evidence of causation—but only of no-fault divorce and only on limited outcomes. Collectively, however, the various studies of the issue made the case that divorce could causally affect many of the correlated outcomes, including hard-to-measure psychological ones not in the Gruber study.

Dealing With Uncertainty, Costs, and Benefits

In applying research to make policy, two kinds of uncertainty must be considered. First, there is the statistical question of whether there is a real difference or just a fluke or chance difference. Second, even if there is a statistically significant difference, there is the question of whether, and to what extent, the difference reflects a causal effect. As we saw in Chapter 11 in the opening example about family dinners and drug use, there often can be alternative theories that might explain a relationship or difference—meaning there is uncertainty as to which causal explanation represents the truth.

What do we do when we don't know? Obviously, looking for more evidence is a good choice. But what do we do while we wait? And what if there is no doable study that can answer the question?

Because policy often must be made with only limited research, the available evidence must be weighed against other factors. The cost of acting, including, but certainly not limited to, the financial cost, is a central consideration. If a program is not expensive, is not time-consuming, and carries few risks or side effects, then it is probably worth implementing even if the evidence is weak. Programs with much higher costs—in terms of money, time, or risk—require stronger evidence of their benefits.

Consider again an individual mother deciding whether or not to breast-feed. If she can breast-feed with little cost in terms of her personal finances or comfort, then it makes good sense. Why not? It could be highly beneficial, or at least somewhat beneficial. For those mothers who find other benefits of breast-feeding, such as bonding, the decision is clear. But what about mothers—for example, working mothers or single mothers with other children to care for—who may suffer financial costs, stress, or major logistical inconveniences by trying to breast-feed? How big do the benefits have to be, and how good does the evidence need to be for them? And how much of the evidence should they know? Few mothers will read even a small part of the voluminous research literature. They depend on government agencies and other groups to inform them. We return later to the difficult ethical questions this raises for those in charge of informing the public.

QUESTION 

What are some criteria you should use to evaluate the utility of research for policy and practice?

Pathways of Influence

Having considered issues that arise even when following a rational ideal of policy making, we now turn to the ways research actually does influence policy. We will start off with some of the official pathways of influence.

Official Pathways

The use of research is procedurally, and sometimes even legislatively, built into the policy-making process. For example, the government sometimes requires, as part of legislation, an evaluation of a program, particularly a new or controversial program. For example, the U.S. Congress mandated an evaluation of the State Children's Health Insurance Program. The U.S. Department of Health and Human Services oversaw the contract to researchers from Mathematica and the Urban Institute, highly regarded research organizations, who published a final report to Congress (Wooldridge, Kenney, & Trenholm, 2005).

Many government agencies conduct both research and analysis ranging from performance measurement to extensive analysis by teams of experienced full-time researchers. Some specialized agencies, such as the Government Accountability Office or the Congressional Research Service, are specifically charged with doing independent research and analysis. And many agencies responsible for data gathering, such as the Bureau of the Census and the Bureau of Labor Statistics, do methodological research to sustain their data gathering and other, substantive research. Many of these and other government agencies have scientific advisory boards to ensure that their research and analyses are well done. Examples include the Census Advisory Committee, the Financial Research Advisory Committee, and the AIDS Research Advisory Committee, among many others.

The various national academies of science also collect and synthesize research to play a role in the policy process. For example, the Institute of Medicine conducted a 3-year study on the lack of health insurance and its implications. Six subcommittees produced a report each, synthesizing research on topics such as societal costs of uninsured populations (Institute of Medicine Committee on the Consequences of Uninsurance, 2003). To ensure balance, all subcommittees contained experts with a variety of disciplinary backgrounds and political affiliations.

"Like Water Falling on Limestone"

For much research, the pathway to policy is slow and indirect. Walt (1994) (quoting Bulmer quoting Thomas) said that "the pattern of influence [of research on policy] can be likened to water falling on limestone: The water is absorbed, but there is no knowing what route it will take . . . or where it will come out" (p. 234). This metaphor suggests that a lot of research knowledge is produced and eventually, through some unknown pathways, some of it gets used.

Many researchers are also teachers at universities, and as such they train their students about bodies of research in their fields of expertise. Eventually, some of those students become legislative staff, advisers, heads of agencies, and so on, where the research they learned as students influences their actions.

Some research does influence policy through this route, but often, nonresearchers play a more active role. That role can be illustrated with the example of taxing cigarettes.

High Cigarette Taxes: The Power of Ideas and of Advocacy[1]

Starting in the early 1980s, as we saw in Chapter 13, university researchers published studies on how sensitive cigarette consumption is to the price of cigarettes (e.g., Lewit & Coate, 1982). The research happened to come out at a time when government revenues were particularly needed and public opinion was turning against smoking. The research was picked up and promoted by various antismoking advocates, in both the United States and Canada. The Canadian advocates were the first to succeed in getting higher cigarette taxes, and rates of smoking in the country began to fall (confirming the causal predictions of the academic studies). Advocates in the United States then pushed for higher cigarette taxes in California and other states and, eventually, at the federal level as well.

The cigarette tax example illustrates how advocacy groups and think tanks pick up on research findings and try to inform a much broader public of their significance. For that process to succeed, the research must strike some chord and fit in with the values or politics of the moment. The luck of timing, or window of opportunity, can also influence whether someone decides to champion the research in the first place. But to be credible, the research has to be methodologically sound so that it stands up to scrutiny and convinces those who are not already committed to the issue.

Politics and Other Barriers

We have discussed what research ought to influence policy and how research often does influence policy, both directly and indirectly. But valuable research often fails to influence policy. We now turn to the barriers research faces in influencing policy.

[1]This section is based on Kennedy School of Government (1993).

Time and Timeliness

Policy is often made quickly, in response to pressing practical or political circumstances and opportunities that cannot wait. Unfortunately, the research process is often slow, and policy makers have no choice but to form policy without research or with only preliminary or ambiguous findings.

Certain forms of research, such as randomized field experiments with long-term outcomes, can be especially slow. For example, final results from the Moving to Opportunity experiment took 15 years from the time the study was initiated (and even more time since it was a glimmer in someone's eye). Besharov (2009) lists that example and many others when describing how high-quality evidence from randomized field trials often arrives after policies have already been made and formulated. Consequently, he also advocates research studies that can be done comparatively quickly, even if the evidence produced is not as definitive. On the other hand, it is important that policy makers do not bounce forever from policy to policy without even getting convincing evidence. The best strategy is probably a combination of longer-term research that produces convincing causal evidence and more rapid research that does the best possible job in a short amount of time.

Cultural and Moral Values

Sometimes, research does not influence policy because attitudes toward the policy are driven by cultural and moral values and not by evidence. For example, some individuals may oppose educating teenagers about birth control because they feel that it is simply wrong. In that case, their policy positions do not depend on the results of studies comparing the effects of different forms of sex education on teenage pregnancy and sexually transmitted diseases. The death penalty provides another example: Many people are simply opposed to the idea on moral grounds, regardless of whatever evidence there might be regarding the deterrent effect of the death penalty on murder rates.

Researchers should understand that the values held by individuals and societies can legitimately trump research when making policy. The democratic process must work out conflicts about values. The role of research is to provide information. The mechanisms through which values can legitimately affect the policy process and restrict the influence of research are many: legal mandates, rights, and fairness procedures (Pannell & Roberts, 2009).

But we should distinguish values about what ought to be from potentially false beliefs about what is. If political positions are based on false beliefs about what is, then ideally, research could play a role. Unfortunately, people may not be open to evidence that contradicts what they believe. In the sex education example, one can believe that educating teenagers about birth control is wrong and oppose it on moral grounds. It is a different matter to refuse to consider evidence that educating teenagers about birth control reduces teen pregnancies.

Distrust of Researchers

Sometimes research cannot influence policy because the public or politicians do not trust researchers. They believe that the research results are driven by the values and biases of the researchers—and sometimes they are right. Values certainly shape the questions that researchers ask and often shape which results researchers pay attention to and which they ignore. And unfortunately, a few researchers sometimes deliberately manipulate or suppress research to support their agenda. Ethics dictate that researchers try their best to be open-minded and react to research results based on the quality of the evidence.

Politics and Interest Groups[2]

Interest groups support policies that benefit them, even if research shows that the policies are inefficient or ineffective. Politicians support policies that benefit their own constituencies or political interests as well. And

[2]We thank Karl Kronebusch for his help with this section.

frequently, interest groups successfully make politicians' interests coincide with their own. In such situations, all these groups may ignore, suppress, or distort research to pursue their own interests and objectives.

Interest groups and politicians sometimes try to prevent research if they worry that the findings might hurt their cause. Jamieson (2013) describes how lobbying from the National Rifle Association (NRA), a pro-gun ownership rights group in the United States, practically eliminated federal funding for research on gun violence from 1996 through 2013. Following the mass shooting at Sandy Hook Elementary School, and responding to an open letter from many researchers (University of Chicago Crime Lab, 2013), federal funding for research on gun violence was reinstated by executive order of the president (Plummer, 2013). However, the more than 15-year ban on funding such research has limited our knowledge about gun violence in the United States, including even basic descriptive research about the prevalence of gun ownership.

It is important to note, however, that some believe that research has a very limited role to play in politics, or simply that politics has a life of its own, independent of scientific facts. For example, Stone (1997) describes politics as a paradox in which causation is really more about stories that groups agree on than evidence about real causes that research could prove or disprove. Kingdon (1995) describes a similar view but with more of a role for research, in which the political process of creating policy is a soup with three separate ingredients: problems, policies, and politics. These ingredients can be combined or separated as circumstances vary. For example, the policy of public transport was put forward to combat first the problem of congestion, then the energy crisis, and most recently global warming. Politics determines which problems get attention, which policies get paired with which problems, which policies get implemented, and how and when. Within this soup of varied ingredients, research can play a role by documenting new problems and evaluating proposed policies.

A Failure to Move From Research to Policy: The U.S. Poverty Definition

As the emphasis on research and evidence has grown, measurement, particularly performance measurement, has grown in importance. As a result, performance measures influence the careers of politicians and senior managers, often leading them to become less concerned about accurate measurement or the substance of what is supposed to be measured and instead focused only on making their numbers or meeting their targets. For example, in the television series *The Wire,* this tendency was both dramatized and satirized by showing politicians and government officials doctoring both crime and education statistics, "juking the stats," so that success could be claimed (Sheehan & Sweeney, 2009, p. 3).

Despite its inaccuracies, changing the out-of-date poverty measure is politically difficult.
Source: © iStockphoto.com/BrandyTaylor.

Even when government officials do not try to doctor measures, they may be reluctant to improve their accuracy if it could make things look worse on their watch. This is one of the reasons that the U.S. poverty measure, widely viewed as seriously flawed, has remained as it is for so long. In Chapter 4, we described the shortcomings in the official U.S. poverty measure, and we saw that two main problems stand out. First, the income or resources counted in the measure of poverty do not include any in-kind benefits, such as food stamps, public housing, or tax credits (such as the Earned Income Tax Credit). Second, the income threshold was based on three times a basic expenditure on food in 1966, updated for inflation. Since the relative price of food has dropped while the relative prices of other essentials, such as housing, have risen, this threshold is now considered inadequate for essentials or, at the very least, calculated in an arbitrary way unrelated to the prices of essentials. Some have referred to the poverty data as "nonsensical numbers" (Blank, 2008, p. 236).

And yet, despite fairly widespread agreement that the official poverty measure is flawed, it has proven difficult to change it, and (as of this writing) it has not been changed. Rebecca Blank, an economist, has had extensive involvement in political efforts to reform the poverty measure, including being on the Council of Economic Advisers to the Clinton administration during its failed attempts to reform the measure. In her 2007 address to the Association for Public Policy Analysis and Management (APPAM), she described the political barriers (Blank, 2008).

First, according to Blank, many benefits are tied to the poverty definition. Consequently, a major reform could increase the number of people entitled to benefits, resulting in either a major increase in expenditures or an outcry of unjustly denied benefits. No politician wants to have such budgetary or public opinion difficulties.

Even if the new poverty definition were calibrated to keep the poverty rate constant, the distribution of beneficiaries would change, with some losing benefits while others gained. For example, the recommendations of an expert panel on how to reform the poverty measure would result in more working families being identified as "poor" and fewer families with large in-kind benefits being deemed poor. And, as Blank (2008) notes,

> Both increases and decreases in the number of poor among a group could provoke concern. . . . What president wants to announce that poverty has gone up on his watch? But decreases in poverty counts . . . [appear] to minimize economic need among groups that . . . garner political attention. (p. 241)

Second, a variety of other government programs allocate funds in ways tied to poverty rates, such as mandates that Medicaid cover pregnant women with incomes up to 133% of the poverty level. If the poverty level were changed, many other funding formulas would need to be redone, opening up new political fights.

Third, the main group that was interested in having accurate measures of poverty consisted of economists and statisticians; it was not a major political interest group. Without politically influential groups that can fight for a reformed poverty measure, the costs of reform loomed too large.

Recognizing these difficulties, Blank and other statisticians and economists have developed a supplementary poverty measure that addresses the official measure's weaknesses. But the new measure is not intended to replace the official poverty measure, only to supplement it for purposes of research and analysis (Short, 2011).

How Can Research Have More Influence?

QUESTION

What are the different ways that research influences policy? What factors interfere with research influencing policy?

We have described many barriers to research influencing policy, including time, cultural values, and politics. Is there a way to legitimately increase the influence of research? Walt (1994) suggests that researchers need to better understand power and the political process so that information can be strategically deployed to target audiences in the most effective way. He suggests paying attention to timing and making greater efforts with communication. Pannell and Roberts (2009) echo those suggestions and add others, stating that researchers should try harder to "understand the policy-maker's perspective, practice excellent communication, be solution oriented, find a champion, avoid appearances of vested interest, and be simple, patient, persistent, resilient, responsive and timely." Thus, researchers can and should try harder to make their research known and relevant. But importantly, policy makers and administrators also need to make efforts to find and interpret research findings that relate to their areas of policy and practice.

We turn next to the production of research, including research funding and institutions, and how these forces shape the priorities and activities of researchers.

The Production of Research

In addition to being a method of inquiry, research is also a major social and economic activity involving billions of dollars in spending and employing many thousands of people. The various sources of research funding, as well as the different kinds of research institutions, are important components of a complete understanding and interpretation of research.

Who Funds Research?

Various government agencies, foundations, and private companies fund research around the globe. In the United States, for example, basic science research is funded by the National Science Foundation (NSF), which spends about $7 billion annually (NSF, 2013). Basic biomedical research is funded by the National Institutes of Health (NIH), which spends about $31 billion each year (NIH, 2013). These agencies also fund some policy research as well as basic research. For example, the NIH includes the National Institute on Drug Abuse, which does research on many social and policy issues. And the NSF includes a social science section that funds some applied social research. But other government agencies fund most of the applied research. For example, the Institute of Education Sciences within the U.S. Department of Education sponsors research on education and learning. The Justice Department, the Environmental Protection Agency, the Labor Department, the Department of Transportation, the Department of Housing and Urban Development, the Department of Homeland Security, and the Department of Agriculture, to name a few, all sponsor research and evaluations of new or existing programs or issues, either to respond to a congressional mandate or for their own strategic management purposes. The U.S. Bureau of the Census (housed in the U.S. Department of Commerce) spends about $1 billion annually for collecting and disseminating social and demographic data of various kinds, and over $12 billion alone for the last decennial census in 2010 (Office of Inspector General, U.S. Department of Commerce, 2013). In addition, state and local governments support applied research related to their own policy priorities and concerns.

Private foundations also spend a significant amount of money to support research of various kinds. The Bill & Melinda Gates Foundation, the Ford Foundation, the Robert Wood Johnson Foundation, the Andrew W. Mellon Foundation, the John D. and Catherine T. MacArthur Foundation, and many others provide a total of billions in research funding in many areas, including public health, education, criminal justice, and policy research. There are also nonprofit, fund-raising, and advocacy organizations that support research on specific issues or diseases, such as the American Cancer Society, the American Heart Association, the American Foundation for the Blind, and the Public Health Foundation, again just to name a few.

We have been listing mostly U.S. sources of funding, but of course, governments and private foundations in many other countries around the world spend considerable resources on research as well. For example, the European Research Council (ERC), the research funding arm of the European Commission, spends about $2 billion a year on research of various kinds across the natural sciences, social sciences, and humanities (ERC, 2013).

Requests for Proposals (RFPs)

When government agencies, foundations, or other funders have research they wish to commission or support, they often put out **requests for proposals** (**RFPs**). These describe the aims of the research funding program, including what research questions the funders want answered and, sometimes, the preferred methodology of the proposed research. The RFPs also describe the amount of time and money available. Researchers apply for funding by submitting proposals that describe their research plans as well as their qualifications and experience. Typically, governments and foundations establish committees—often made up of other researchers in the field (peers)—to review, rate, and rank the proposals and decide which ones will receive funding awards.

Competitive funding awards tend to go to well-defined research questions with a high likelihood of success. This makes it hard, sometimes, for researchers to do more innovative, risky research. Indeed, some researchers complain that to win a grant they must have already done most of the work, demonstrating the potential success.

Unfunded Research

Although external funding is essential for many studies, not all research depends on it. Sometimes research can be relatively inexpensive, for example, when a sole researcher analyzes publicly available data sets using desktop software. Such research is often (but not always) **unfunded**, meaning that no specific **grant** or contract was provided to support it. College and university professors, who also devote time to teaching and administrative activities, do most of this kind of unfunded research. Strictly speaking, of course, the institutions that employ these professors and provide them with salaries, office space, technology, libraries, and other resources provide important internal, indirect funding.

Some organizations, particularly government agencies, think tanks, interest groups, and international agencies, have staff researchers. These researchers may occasionally compete for external grants and contracts, but much of the research they do is part of their ordinary job duties.

How Time and Cost Shape Research

Research, like all human endeavors, is shaped by constraints of time and cost. For example, a long and expensive randomized field experiment might provide a really definitive answer to a particular question, but if no one is willing to fund it (internally or externally), then the research won't be done. And researchers are limited by their other obligations. If a research project would take 50 hours a week, over several years, a professor who teaches six classes a year won't do that research project and will choose a less time-consuming one.

Sometimes, researchers or observers lament the fact that time and cost constraints shape research, but these constraints are often legitimate. Resources, including an individual's time, always have other uses—"opportunity costs," in the jargon of economists. A particular piece of research should only be done if its expected value is greater than the next best use of the time and other resources.

However, some constraints are a bit artificial. Young researchers at colleges and universities often hope to get tenure, a strong form of job security. To do so, they must have a substantial body of published work by the time they come up for tenure, which is usually less than 7 years after starting as an assistant professor. Projects that require a long start-up and a long data-gathering stage, such as a prospective longitudinal study, are generally avoided by untenured professors. Even tenured faculty and researchers in nonacademic settings have time deadlines—periods of time during which a substantial amount of work is expected to be completed.

All funders of research—government agencies, not-for-profit organizations, and private companies—seek value for money. They have their own budget constraints. Therefore, large-scale, long-term, or labor-intensive research is difficult to fund. Time and cost constraints inevitably affect both choice of research question and choice of research methods.

Where Is Research Conducted?

Social and policy research is conducted in a variety of institutional and organizational settings. Understanding these settings is important, because they shape the focus and methods of a study—and determine what questions researchers ask, or ignore.

Universities and Colleges

Doing research, both basic and applied, is essential to the mission of most universities and colleges. Even many colleges that once only focused on teaching now also emphasize research. Still, only a few hundred of the several thousand higher education institutions in the United States are considered research universities with high levels of research activity, according to the Carnegie classification (Carnegie Foundation for the Advancement of Teaching, 2009). These universities emphasize the training of doctoral students, and they tend to require less teaching—and more research—from their faculties. But good research also comes from many smaller, more specialized colleges and universities as well.

Universities are just one of the settings in which social and policy research occur.

Source: © iStockphoto.com/Pgiam.

The quantity and quality of research have become major criteria in the rankings of universities and colleges, in the hiring and promotion of university faculty, and in the awarding of tenure. Thus, university and college departments and professors have a major incentive to produce research and to demonstrate its quality by publishing their work in top-rated journals or books. This incentive leads to much good and useful research, but it can also lead to the proliferation of what sometimes seems to be rather restricted, highly specialized, and even arcane research that only relates to fairly narrow academic questions or concerns.

The professional schools—such as schools of public affairs, education, public health, or criminal justice—generally focus more on applied research, while arts and sciences departments (sociology, economics, psychology, political science, etc.) do more basic research. But this division is far from universal, and much applied social research is done in arts and sciences departments.

Government

Some research is performed at government research institutes. In the United States, the NIH and the Centers for Disease Control and Prevention (CDC) are important examples, although less social research than biological or physical science research is conducted in government institutes. In continental Europe, government research institutes play a relatively larger role in the direct production of research than they do in the United States. Examples include France's *Centre National de la Recherche Scientifique* and Spain's *Consejo Superior de Investigaciones Científicas.*

In the United States, many government agencies whose primary role is not research nonetheless conduct significant amounts of research. A noteworthy example is the Federal Reserve (central bank), but the Department of Agriculture, the Census Bureau, and many other administrative agencies produce research. Obviously, the research is applied and meant to serve the needs of the agency. The research is typically conducted within units devoted to policy analysis or program evaluation.

Think Tanks

Research is also done in foundations and think tanks, which are not-for-profit organizations with some kind of public interest mission. Some prominent public policy think tanks in the United States include the Brookings Institution, the American Enterprise Institute, the Heritage Foundation, the Aspen Institute, the Council on Foreign Relations, the Center on Budget and Policy Priorities, the Economic Policy Institute, and the Hoover Institution, among many others. Some of these think tanks are associated with certain political or ideological perspectives. The Heritage Foundation, for example, is a conservative think tank, while the Center on Budget and Policy Priorities is a liberal think tank.

Contract Research Organizations

Policy research is often produced under government contract by organizations such as the RAND Corporation, the Urban Institute, the Research Triangle Institute (RTI), Mathematica Policy Research, the Manpower Demonstration Research Corporation (MDRC), Abt Associates, Westat, and others. These organizations may be not-for-profit or for-profit entities. They tend to be quite large and to have the technical capability as well as the organizational capacity to carry out large, complex research projects, including large national surveys or major randomized policy experiments. The clients of these firms are usually large government agencies, although they also do research work for nonprofit and for-profit private organizations.

There are also research companies that focus more on serving the private sector, such as polling and market research firms. Some examples include Gallup, Harris Interactive, Ipsos, Edison Research, and Knowledge Networks. But these firms do research work for government agencies, universities, and other nonprofit clients as well.

Advocacy Organizations

Advocacy organizations are primarily consumers of research, secondarily commissioners of research, and only thirdly conductors of research. But there are advocacy organizations that focus more directly on conducting their own research, such as the various public interest research groups (PIRGs) in many U.S. states and Canadian provinces. Often advocacy studies resemble investigative journalism more than scientific research, although important and sophisticated studies are done by advocacy organizations.

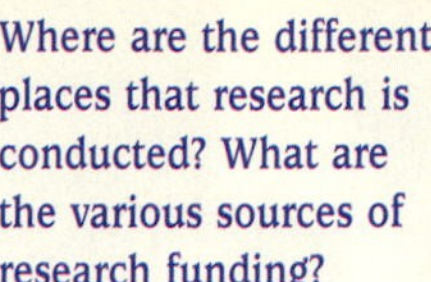

Where are the different places that research is conducted? What are the various sources of research funding?

The lines between think tanks, **contract research organizations**, and advocacy organizations are not clear-cut, as much depends on the mission of the organization and on the particular configuration of clients and research activities, which can change over time. Some organizations cross categories, such as the Urban Institute, which operates as both a think tank and a contract research organization.

The growing accessibility of data and computers makes performing research within reach of far more organizations and individuals of all kinds than was once possible. For example, some journalists have begun to do original quantitative analysis that was once only possible for full-time professional researchers (Institute for Analytical Journalism, n.d.).

Research Cultures and Disciplines

Researchers have a culture of their own, just as all occupations do. Researchers tend to value curiosity, insight, and even cleverness. An article that is widely read becomes a status symbol, as are publications in prestigious journals, invitations to speak at important conferences and seminars, and so on. While money has some status, status among researchers is more divorced from money than it is in many other professions.

The culture of researchers is also fragmented. Particular disciplines have their own cultures. For example, economists are known for their aggressive questioning in seminars. Applied social research cultures are also defined by the policy domain or content of study, so education research and health services research have specific cultures. And the different settings have their own cultures. In research organizations supported by external funding, the culture values the ability to bring in grants. In academic settings, publication in highly ranked journals is paramount.

Which Research Questions Should Be Studied?

As we have seen, political, economic, social, and institutional factors have significant influence over which research questions get addressed. Some of that influence is right and good: The interests of society should drive which research questions society spends scarce resources addressing. Some of that influence, however, can reflect narrow interests and idiosyncrasies of the political process as well as institutional features of how research is conducted. Even when research questions are chosen to best reflect society's interests, the process is difficult, dealing with innate complexity and balancing many concerns.

In applied research, the questions usually come from pressing issues or problems facing policy makers or practitioners. For example, an analyst working in a child services agency might be asked to determine whether a new procedure for responding to first-time child abuse reports does a better job of accurately assessing whether abuse is taking place than the established procedure. The usual keys for formulating research questions, discussed in Chapter 2, still apply. For example, the applied researcher should determine if the question is descriptive or causal. In this example, the question is causal—the *effect* of the new reporting procedure. Unfortunately, as we have seen in previous chapters, getting a definitive causal answer is difficult. If the agency implemented the new policy all at once, and there is no comparison group, it will be difficult to disentangle the effect of the new procedure from other changes in the program and its context.

The inability to definitively determine causation is just one of many ways in which a doable research question often falls short of the original question confronting policy makers or practitioners. Another shortfall often occurs in attempts at measurement: how to measure whether "abuse is taking place," for example. There may be no fully accurate measure, so we turn to the best available proxy. In these ways, real-world policy and practice questions are often challenging to address through research. Moreover, applied researchers often have tight time frames and sometimes very limited resources, such as when an administrative

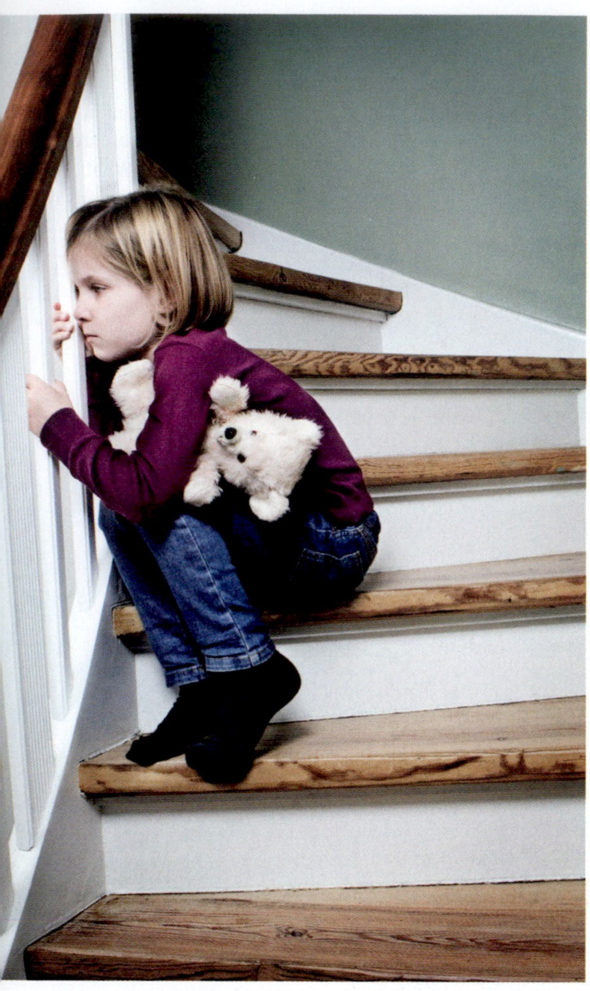

Many methods are needed to determine the effects of divorce on children.
Source: © iStockphoto.com/ClarkandCompany.

agency, service organization, or business does its own research in-house. But they should be honest and clearly describe how the questions they can answer differ from the original policy or practice questions they set out to answer. Pretending to have better answers will only make the decision-making process less effective.

Some researchers, like university professors or think tank scholars, have much more leeway to choose their own research questions and follow their own research agendas. In doing so, they are often guided by a desire to increase basic knowledge and to fill gaps in theories. But academic researchers can also be motivated by specific policy or practice questions, even though they are not working directly for or with policy makers and practitioners. Consider the studies on the impact of divorce on children. Real-world legal, political, cultural, and even personal discussions illustrate how many people want to know the answer to this question. To find such questions, academic researchers might read trade journals and newspapers and talk to those working in the area. But good researchers don't stop with what those in the field say they want to know, because sometimes those caught up in the details and struggles of implementing policy fail to see the forest for the trees. It is important to focus on theory and speculate: What could be causing what? Why do couples get divorced? What happens to them and their children after they get divorced? What would happen if they did not divorce? Why do some stay in bad marriages? And so on. Such thinking can result in new questions that someone should be asking but no one is.

In addition to having their own cultures, as we saw earlier, academic disciplines have their own theories and tools that shape how specific questions are framed and answered—and even shape which questions are asked and which ones are ignored. Consider this analogy:

One night someone sees a friend looking around under a lamppost.

"What are you looking for?" the first friend asks.

"My keys," the searching friend says.

"Did you lose them here beneath the lamppost?"

"No. But this is where the light is."

Disciplines have their own methodological tools, their own kinds of light. So they tend to address questions that can be answered with the tools commonly used in their discipline—even if these are not the most important questions. Like the friend who lost his keys, they tend to look where they have light, even if it is not where the keys are.

Another limitation in how academics choose research questions is letting the ideal of the perfect research study become the enemy of doing good research. Scheiber (2007), writing for a general audience, complained that economists have become too focused on finding really good natural experiments that definitively determine causal effects, "crowd[ing] out some of the truly deep questions we rely on economists to answer." Unfortunately, journal and grant reviewers sometimes favor research that definitively answers a less important question over research that only partially or imperfectly answers a more important question. It is another feature of the "lamppost problem"—looking only where there is light.

Making Research Ethical

The broad principles of ethical research—beneficence, no harm, justice—were introduced in Chapter 1. In subsequent chapters, we discussed the ethical issues of different research methods, treating ethics as an integral part of each method. Some of the most important discussions included

- the historical development of ethical principles and procedures (Chapter 1);
- informed consent in qualitative research (Chapter 3), in surveys (Chapter 7), in randomized experiments (Chapter 14), and in quasi experiments (Chapter 15);
- not overburdening research subjects with long questionnaires (Chapters 4 and 7) or pushing too hard for responses (Chapter 5);
- protecting the confidentiality and privacy of individuals when using administrative data (Chapter 6), public use microdata (Chapter 6), primary qualitative data (Chapter 3), and secondary qualitative data (Chapter 6), as well as when making primary survey data public (Chapter 7);
- protecting minors and other vulnerable populations being surveyed (Chapter 7);
- intrinsic ethical limitations of experiments (Chapter 11) and the particular ethical issues of randomization (Chapter 14);
- ensuring that all subjects benefit in randomized experiments (Chapter 14); and
- the ethical issues of manipulating treatments and programs people receive in randomized field experiments and strong quasi experiments that take place in real-world settings and have high-stakes outcomes (Chapters 14 and 15).

But some ethical issues cross methods or make sense to consider only after exposure to the various methods of research and the ethical challenges that they raise. We begin with the formal processes that have been established for having research officially approved by ethical review boards.

The Ethical Review Process

In many countries, there is an official process to ensure that all research involving human subjects gets done ethically. In this section, we describe how that process works in the United States, and in the next section, we discuss how the process is similar or different in other countries.

In the United States, almost every university, college, hospital, health agency, school system, and research organization now has an **institutional review board (IRB)**. If the organization receives federal money of any kind, then a government regulation known as 45 CFR Part 46 requires an IRB and specifies its composition and procedures. If you are doing research in one of these settings, you will likely need to get IRB approval for your study, even if it is unfunded. Even student research comes under the IRBs. Research done in more than one location, whether within the United States or in other countries, typically requires the approval of the ethical oversight bodies in each location.

The first step is to be aware of the process—find out about your institution's ethical review body and its policies. Many provide training in human subjects protection that you can attend. As **principal investigator** (PI), the lead person responsible for a study, or as a member of a research team, you may need to become certified in the protection of human subjects. Typically, one becomes certified by completing training and by passing a test about research ethics and related regulations. Much of this training and testing is now done online.

Is It Research on Human Subjects?

According to U.S. federal regulations, IRBs are only required to review research on human subjects. Some studies on social and policy topics may not be research—and others may not involve human subjects. The regulations define research as "a systematic investigation, including research, development, testing and evaluation designed to develop or contribute to *generalizable* knowledge" (45 CFR § 46.102). This definition refers largely to primary research; secondary research—summarizing what others have found—is thus not considered research for purposes of the IRB. Many IRBs do not insist on reviewing program evaluations when such studies are used only for internal or organizational purposes. But if the evaluations are intended to be published, then the studies will often be considered research that an IRB must approve. When in doubt, check with your IRB.

The federal legislation defines a human subject as a living individual about whom an investigator conducts research to obtain either data through an interaction with the individual or identifiable private information. If there are living humans being studied in some way, then the research is almost always considered to be on human subjects. (A possible exception occurs when you interview or survey an individual but only collect information about his or her organization.) Analysis of publicly available data, which are completely de-identified (no personal identifiers and publicly recognized as having insufficient detail to enable identification), is also not usually considered human subjects research. When in doubt, it is possible to apply to an IRB as a precaution to get its determination on the status of your research.

The IRB Process

For all human subjects research, you must submit your research plan to the IRB for review *before* beginning the research. You will need to complete a form and provide a narrative describing your study, including procedures for recruiting participants and obtaining their consent as well as the details of the research design, measurement instruments, qualitative methods, and data management procedures that will be used in your study.

Your study will fall into one of the following three categories of review, depending on the level of risk to human subjects:

- **Exempt review**—meaning there is only minimal risk to human subjects and the study meets one of several criteria:
    - Research in educational settings employing tests used in ordinary practice
    - Surveys, tests, interviews, and public observation, provided that the topics are not sensitive or private and the information collected will not make identification possible
    - Collection and analysis of existing data, documents, or records without personally identifying information
    - Many (although not all) observational social science studies fall into this category.
- **Expedited review**—the study presents only minimal risks, but it does not meet the exempt requirements. Often, these are experimental or medical studies in which the treatments, or measurements, pose no more than minimal risks. They also include many interviews and focus groups, provided the topics are not disturbing or highly personal.
- **Full IRB review**—the study does not qualify for either exempt or expedited review, often because there is more than a minimal risk to subjects, or because the subjects are children, prisoners, pregnant women, cognitively impaired persons, or another of several specially protected groups. This category includes most of the many clinical trials used in testing new drugs or potentially risky medical procedures as well as psychological experiments that cause discomfort or potential harm (such as sleep deprivation studies) or involve deception. Comparatively little social and policy research requires full IRB review, but if the research topic is sufficiently sensitive (like domestic violence) or the population sufficiently vulnerable (such as children), even an anonymous survey may require full IRB review. The full IRB meets to discuss these studies as a committee before granting approval.

As well as obtaining approval before beginning your research, you must report any adverse events that occur during the study (such as any complaints from or injuries to participants) and file a final report at the end of your study. While federal rules about grants create a certain amount of uniformity of IRB rules and procedures, there is still a great deal of variation within the United States (Abbott & Grady, 2011; Sieber & Tolich, 2013, pp. 7–8).

BOX 16.2
Template for Informed Consent Form

INSTITUTION NAME <*e.g., University of Nearby*>

Department of <*e.g., Applied Social Science*>

CONSENT TO PARTICPATE IN A RESEARCH PROJECT

Project Title: <*Enter title of study*>

Principal Investigator: <*Enter name of principal investigator*> <*Enter PI's title, campus affiliation, full office address, telephone number, e-mail*>

Faculty Advisor: <*If PI is a student, enter faculty advisor's title, campus affiliation, full office address, telephone number, e-mail*>

Site Where Study Is to Be Conducted: <*Enter location of study; e.g., Nearby University Building 1A Room 001, Small Town Community Hospital, Big Town High School*>

Introduction/Purpose: You are invited to participate in a research study. The study is conducted under the direction of <*Enter PI name, title, affiliation*>. The purpose of this research study is to <*Explain purpose of study; e.g., better understand how . . . , examine different ways in which . . .*>. The results of this study may <*Explain what you expect to be the outcome of this study; e.g., aid in the development of rehabilitative strategies . . . , improve teaching methods . . . , increase awareness of . . .*>. <*Are you using audio, video, or digital recordings? If so, state for what purposes*>.

Procedures: Approximately <*Enter approximate number of subjects*> individuals are expected to participate in this study. Each subject will participate in <*Provide type of activity; e.g., one survey, one interview, a series of questionnaires*>. The time commitment of each participant is expected to be <*Enter expected duration of participation; e.g., over a span of 2 hours, 30 minutes, 1 hour per week for 4 weeks*>. Each session will take place at <*Enter location information including name of institution (if applicable) and address*>.

Possible Discomforts and Risks: Your participation in this study may involve <*Explain what risks the subject may encounter; e.g., breach of confidentiality, fall, embarrassment, anxiety, stress*>. <*Will there be any physical discomfort? If so, state this and explain*>. To minimize these risks, <*Explain how risks will be minimized*>. If you are <*bothered, troubled, upset*> as a result of this study, you should <*Provide contact information or resources that the subject can utilize*>.

Benefits: There are <*Enter either "no direct benefits. However, participating in the study may increase general knowledge of . . ." or "direct benefits" (and explain what those might be).*>

Alternatives: <*If applicable, state the alternatives to participation in this study.*>

Voluntary Participation: Your participation in this study is voluntary, and you may decide not to participate without prejudice, penalty, or loss of benefits to which you are otherwise entitled. If you decide to leave the study, please contact the principal investigator <*Enter PI's name*> to inform <*him/her*> of your decision.

Financial Considerations: <*If applicable*> Participation in this study will involve <*Enter cost to the subject, if any. What are the costs? And why are there costs? Who will be responsible for the*

(Continued)

(Continued)

costs?>. For your participation in this study, you will receive <*Enter the object or amount of compensation you will give the subject, when it will be provided (after one session, after completion of the study, 6 weeks after one session, etc.), method of distribution (check, cash)*>.

Confidentiality: The data obtained from you will be collected via <*video, audio, digital, photographs, written document*>. The collected data will be accessible to <*State who will have access to the data; e.g., IRB members and staff must be included here*>. The researcher will protect your confidentiality by <*coding the data, securely storing the data*>. The collected data will be stored <*State how the data will be stored. Will it be kept in paper format, on a computer, or in encrypted files, or will consent be kept separate from data? If using audio, digital, or visual recordings, what will the recordings be used for, and how will you protect the subjects from breach of confidentiality?*>

or

<*Are you asking for permission to bypass confidentiality and use the participant's identity, voice, or image? If so, you must do so here with Yes and No checkboxes next to each response.*>

<*Example: I give permission to the researcher to use my (identity, photograph, voice recording) in published materials:* ☐ *Yes* ☐ *No*>

Contact Questions/Persons: If you have any questions about the research now or in the future, you should contact the principal investigator, <*Enter name, phone, e-mail*>. If you have any questions concerning your rights as a participant in this study, you may contact <*Enter your campus IRB administrator's name, phone, e-mail*>.

Statement of Consent:

"I have read the above description of this research, and I understand it. I have been informed of the risks and benefits involved, and all my questions have been answered to my satisfaction. Furthermore, I have been assured that any future questions I may have will also be answered by the principal investigator of the research study. I voluntarily agree to participate in this study.

"By signing this form, I have not waived any of my legal rights to which I would otherwise be entitled. I will be given a copy of this statement."

______________	______________________	______________
Printed Name of Subject	Signature of Subject	Date Signed
______________	______________________	______________
Printed Name of Person Explaining Consent Form	Signature of Person Explaining Consent Form	Date Signed
______________	______________________	______________
Printed Name of Investigator	Signature of Investigator	Date Signed

Source: Adapted from *Consent Form Sample—Adults* of the Baruch Human Research Protection Program (HRPP) Office (formerly IRB), available at http://www.baruch.cuny.edu/hrpp/forms.htm

How to Write an Informed Consent Form

One of the most important documents that an IRB typically requires for a research project directly gathering data from people is an *informed consent form.* A template for an informed consent form, adapted from the template form for the City University of New York, is shown in Box 16.2. Most U.S. universities and organizations have similar templates, or at least similar expectations. Notice how the form closely mirrors the *Belmont Report* principles, for example requiring description of risks and benefits.

When You Don't Need an Informed Consent Form

Human subjects research always requires informed consent, meaning that subjects have been fully informed about the research, have understood its risks and benefits, and freely agree to participate. Informed consent, however, does not always require a signed informed consent *form.* In fact, under certain circumstances, an informed consent form can be less ethical. For example, when interviewing or surveying individuals who are political opponents to an oppressive regime, the identifying information on an informed consent form puts subjects at risk. In other circumstances, a form is impractical. For telephone surveys, verbal agreement by research subjects after having been told the relevant information is usually sufficient.

QUESTION

What are some of the main elements of an informed consent form?

Research Ethics Procedures: It Depends Which Country You're In

The international conventions on human subjects research, particularly the Declaration of Helsinki, focus primarily on biomedical research. The rules, infrastructure, and procedures governing *social* and *policy* research have evolved with much more variation across countries. In fact, the same social research project may be treated quite differently in different countries (Edwards et al., 2012). While Canada and the United Kingdom specifically require that all social science research go through formal review, Sweden, Denmark, and the Netherlands, for example, do not (Edwards et al., 2012; Sieber & Tolich, 2013, p. 9).

Even where formal ethical review of social research is not uniformly mandated, certain research subjects, methods, or questions often demand greater scrutiny, specifically vulnerable populations, sensitive data, and privacy concerns. But such convergence masks differences in how such terms are defined (Edwards et al., 2012). A further source of variation across countries is whether or not research that is exempt from review must nonetheless be submitted to a review committee to be deemed exempt. While countries vary substantially in their treatment, several factors—multinational research projects, rules of granting agencies in other countries, and the rules of peer-reviewed journals—are forces that constrain such variation and steer it toward convergence (Edwards et al., 2012).

Most developing countries focus their ethical reviews on biomedical research and provide little or no oversight of social research (Macklin, 2012, p. 243). Still, foreigners doing social research in developing countries need approval by their home countries' ethical review boards. But as Macklin (2012, chaps. 11–12) points out, some home-country ethical review boards can be unreasonably insistent about their usual procedures and ignorant of the country in which research is conducted. For example, a U.S. IRB required that the consent form in a study in Bangladesh inform participants that they should telephone the university research office (collect) with any questions or concerns. But making international calls was not at all practical in many poor areas of Bangladesh. In a study of coercive sexual behavior in Latin America, a U.S. IRB wanted the protocol to mandate that all rapes revealed during the course of research be reported to the police. But in some parts of Latin America, the police have a reputation for humiliating and even abusing rape victims. Researchers involved in international research need to be aware of the cultural and political context of their proposed studies and communicate (even insistently) such knowledge to their ethical review committees.

How to Keep Data Anonymous or Confidential

Sometimes researchers can keep data *anonymous,* which means they never record or even know their subjects' identities. For example, a survey may involve mailing questionnaires to households whose members then answer and return the surveys without putting their name, address, or other identifying information on the questionnaire. Or people may visit a website and complete an online questionnaire, again without providing their name, e-mail address, or other identifying information. But be careful: Sometimes people will put their name and address on the return envelope out of habit, or sometimes web survey software will automatically record someone's IP address (which is a form of identification). Additional procedures, such as discarding envelopes or deleting IP addresses from the data file, may be needed to maintain anonymity.

But more often researchers aim only to keep data *confidential,* meaning they know their subjects' identities or record identifying information but do not reveal it. Data confidentiality is a major concern for IRBs, particularly if the data cover private or sensitive matters. The practicalities of maintaining confidentiality vary depending on the form of data and type of research. As we described in Chapter 3, examples of qualitative data, such as quotes, may inadvertently reveal someone's identity—even when such identifying information is not requested.

But there are some standard practices that can help keep data confidential. A locked filing cabinet is a traditional means of protecting data on paper or audio or video tapes. For data in electronic files on computers, password protection of the folders or drives is a recommended step, although technologically sophisticated individuals might still gain access. A more secure approach is to store all confidential electronic data (including video and audio recordings) on a specially designated hard drive, which can be both password protected and put under lock and key. Another basic, important step is to separate the storage of identifying information, such as names or addresses, from the substantive data, such as the answers to survey questions. This can be done by using two different pages or forms, or electronically by keeping identifying information in a separate data file, with an ID number or code used to link to the substantive data later, if needed. Because consent forms contain names and other identifying information, it is important to separate these from the substantive data and to keep them confidential as well.

With data mining and the explosion of information available about individuals on the Internet, it has become increasingly difficult to ensure anonymity and confidentiality because of the ability to link various kinds of data from multiple sources. Once the data set contains many characteristics about individuals, it can become possible to identify them. For this reason, researchers need to be especially cautious about what information they make available publicly and what assurances they give to participants.

Ethical Authorship and Collaboration

Thus far we have focused on ethical treatment of research subjects—those being investigated. This is where abuses have been greatest and thus where review processes have focused. But research subjects are not the only people involved in research. Since many relevant ethical issues, such as how to treat employees or subordinates, are not specific to research, this is not the place to discuss them. But some ethical issues are specific to research collaboration.

Who gets to be an author of a publication? When are other forms of credit needed or appropriate? A publication's authors should include everyone who contributed substantively to the study—and no one who did not. Although the problems of not giving authorship and thus credit are more obvious and salient, it is also unethical to give authorship credit to someone who played little or no role in the actual research. Someone who helped facilitate the research administratively or financially should receive an acknowledgement but not authorship, unless they also participated substantively in the research.

But what constitutes a substantive contribution? Should the person who created the data set (used for another project) get authorship? What about someone who implemented relatively standard statistical procedures, if the procedures were chosen by someone else? Rules and conventions differ between fields. Medical and health research is fairly inclusive: Performing analysis that is chosen and directed by someone else can be sufficient for authorship. In contrast, in economics, only those individuals who contribute creatively in some relatively original fashion are usually given authorship. Because of the problems of inappropriate authorship, some medical and health journals now require that all papers describe in the published article each author's role and contributions. Even if not required by the journal, a good ethics test for authorship is whether everyone would be comfortable honestly describing each author's role and contributions in the published paper.

Additional Issues in Research Ethics

It is not always obvious how to conduct research ethically. How does one balance properly compensating poor people for their time and effort—and yet not coerce them into participating in the research just because they badly need the incentive money? How does one balance documenting informed consent with protecting individuals' privacy? Like many ethical questions in life, the right course of action is not always clear-cut. And the ethical dilemmas don't stop with doing research, but continue with decisions about how to present and disseminate the research results.

Ethics of Research Dissemination and Presentation

We saw at the beginning of this chapter that when the National Breastfeeding Campaign was started in 2003, the group issued dire warnings about the consequences of not breast-feeding, even though there was little evidence that the positive measured effects of breast-feeding were causal (Wolf, 2007). Because causal evidence is so hard to obtain, public health officials and others in charge of disseminating research do face a genuine problem. The epidemiology and public health literatures illustrate how researchers have struggled with these issues (e.g., Sandman [1991], and other citations in Wolf [2007]).

But the ethical dilemmas are not limited to public health information campaigns. Researchers and those who use research in all applied areas, including criminal justice, housing, education, and others, must decide how to present research, as well as when and how to disseminate it. Clearly, manipulating or cherry-picking results is unethical. But how much ambiguity and complexity should be presented? Some summary and simplification of the results must be done, yet knowing where to draw the line can be difficult. It is certainly important in all research to openly and honestly discuss the limitations of the research, such as when it is inappropriate to draw firm cause-effect conclusions or when caution should be used in applying the results to other settings or participants (the generalizability issue).

An important check on how research is presented is a clear and complete description of the methods and results of the research so that others may assess the researcher's conclusions—and draw their own. Transparency is thus key to the ethical presentation of research.

Life-Saving Research, Limited Access, and Peer Review

Much valuable and even life-saving research is published in journals that are not freely available without purchasing a subscription. When such research could benefit people, is it unethical to limit its availability? For this reason, certain articles, particularly in medical journals, are published with open access.

A similar issue arises when apparently life-saving research is tied up in a lengthy peer-review process. On the one hand, peer review is used to help ensure that research results are really true and is needed to protect the public against false claims. On the other hand, a lengthy review process can mean that those who might benefit remain in ignorance about a potentially life-saving treatment. Ethics dictate that the review process should be sensitive to these issues.

Doing Research in Less Developed Countries

Whenever researchers are more educated or financially better off than their research subjects, differences in culture and power raise ethical issues, as we saw for informed consent. When researchers are from richer countries and the research subjects are (poor people) from poorer countries, these problems are exacerbated. Biomedical research on drugs and treatments that can benefit richer countries but that is carried out in poorer countries has been an area of particular concern. The *Belmont Report* states that research subjects should not consist significantly of groups who are unlikely to benefit from the subsequent applications of the research. Testing AIDS drugs in African countries, the majority of whose citizens will not be able to afford the experimental drugs, would seem to violate that principle (Macklin, 2012, chap. 11). Concerns focus on situations where the research might well have been done in a wealthier country and the main motivation to go to a poor country is lower costs and/or fewer ethical regulations.

Such concerns are much less likely to apply to social and policy research, where the findings are unlikely to generalize to very different economic and cultural contexts. Thus, for social and policy research, the local country is a likely beneficiary of the research findings. But that may not always be true, particularly if the social research reflects political, economic, or strategic interests of the wealthier country. Moreover, other ethical concerns, such as confidentiality and informed consent, can arise when doing research in a foreign culture, as we saw earlier.

Sham Surgery

Ethics can be particularly difficult—and important—with experiments that involve major interventions. Consider the issue of sham surgery (Gerber & Patashnik, 2006). When people receive a treatment of any kind, they experience the placebo effect: The expectation of a benefit itself causes a benefit. The placebo effect is not limited to pills, and in fact, the placebo effect of surgery appears to be quite strong. As a result, some have pushed for those in the control arm of a surgical intervention to receive sham surgery—a real operation but one that actually does nothing (other than cut the patients open and sew them up again). Many view sham surgery as ethically unacceptable. Surgery always carries some risks, although they can be quite small. How can people be subjected to those risks with no prospect of any real benefit? On the other hand, sham surgery may be the only way to demonstrate that a surgical procedure believed to be effective is, in fact, not effective after all. Such knowledge could help prevent unnecessary pain and discomfort, or even save lives, down the road. But such abstract benefits are likely to be of little comfort to those subjected to the sham surgery. Regulations about informed consent and no harm done can help address such dilemmas, but they do not eliminate them. Often there are no easy answers.

Deception

Informed consent means that research subjects are fully informed about the research before agreeing to participate. But in certain circumstances, some deception is necessary for research purposes. For example, many behavioral economics experiments examine how the framing of an offer affects financial decision making. If the experimental purpose was explained, the research subjects would be aware of the framing, and its natural effect could not be determined. Sieber and Tolich (2013, chap. 8) describe hurdles that research with deception (or nondisclosure) should meet, including that there are no effective alternative research designs and that the research has benefits for society. And of course, the research should not harm the subjects. Importantly, there need to be clear and careful debriefing processes that can eliminate false feedback and ensure that research subjects are not upset by the deception.

Is Approved Research Always Ethical—and Is Ethical Research Always Approved?

Several commentators believe that the fear of lawsuits and the desire of institutions to protect themselves largely drive IRB policies and decisions (Israel & Hay, 2006; Sieber & Tolich, 2013). As a result, sometimes ethical—and valuable—research may be blocked by IRBs fearful of controversy or blame. Some allege that the ethical review procedures developed for biomedical research are being inappropriately applied to social and policy research, to the detriment of the public interest. Denmark, for example, decided not to have formal ethical review committees for social research, because the country did not want research that is useful to policy formation to be constrained by ethical process demands (Israel & Hay, 2006, p. 54).

The review process and related bureaucratic rules can substantially slow down research, delaying the search for potentially useful answers to pressing problems. For example, researchers may not be able to conduct interviews of political protesters during an uprising, something that journalists can readily do. While academics may (or may not!) be able to conduct interviews later, the gap in time changes what can be learned. The very divergent rules and procedures for judging the ethics of journalism and academic research are largely due to the history of each profession (Sieber & Tolich, 2013, chap. 4).

It Should Be Ethical, Even If Not Subject to Review

Research done for internal managerial reasons, within a for-profit, nonprofit, or government organization, is not required to undergo IRB approval. Most commercial market research or political polling is not subject to IRB approval either. Indeed, many applied research studies fall outside the formal review requirements that apply to academic or government research. But still such research should be undertaken in an ethical manner, even if a formal ethical review is not required. Research ethics are not only—and not primarily—about jumping through the hoops required by regulations and IRBs. Ethics imply an effort to take ethical issues seriously—to pay attention to the harms and benefits to people, to equity issues, and to the autonomy and dignity of the people who participate in research.

Conclusion

In this chapter, you learned how research fits into the broader political context and the policy-making process, including the pathways to as well as barriers against research influencing policy and practice. You also found out about how research is produced, including the different sources of research funding and the types of institutions that conduct research. You learned about the formal rules and procedures that have been established to protect participants in research—and learned some of the dilemmas and problems that persist despite those procedures.

This chapter may have discouraged some of you who hope to use research to improve policy. But realize that the world of policy and practice must take into account a wide array of influences and interests and that research-based knowledge is only a part of the picture.

Chapter Resources

Key Terms

- Contract research organization
- Exempt review
- Expedited review
- Full IRB review
- Grant
- Institutional review board (IRB)
- Principal investigator (PI)
- Requests for proposals (RFPs)
- Unfunded research

Exercises

Research in the Policy Process

16.1. Pick a policy issue that is currently being debated in the news or in your field of study. How does research form part of the policy debate? What advocates, or sides of the debate, are promoting research findings? What other considerations, including values and political interests, also matter in the debate?

Public Information Campaigns Based on Research

16.2. Find a recent public information campaign to change a behavior, similar to the National Breastfeeding Campaign. What research evidence do you think lies behind the campaign? (You may find a summary and references on the website of the organization sponsoring the campaign.) Does the research being cited meet the standards of statistical significance, practical significance, and evidence of causation? In your judgment, is the campaign to change people's behavior ethical? Why, or why not?

Where Does Research Come From?

16.3. Look at a journal in your field or area of interest and pick out an article that looks relevant to you. Answer the following questions:

- Where was the research done? At a university or a college? If so, what kind of school or department? Or was the research done by a government agency, think tank, or contract research organization?
- Was the research funded, or unfunded? (All external funding should be acknowledged in research articles, sometimes in the footnotes or acknowledgments.) How costly and time-consuming do you think the research was to complete?

Ethical Issues in Your Own Research

16.4. Think about a simple piece of research you might do involving, say, a small survey of people in your community or workplace. What ethical issues would you need to consider? How would you ensure informed consent, voluntary participation, no harm to subjects, and beneficence?

Researchers Deceiving Researchers

16.5. In a *Chronicle of Higher Education* article, "Academe Hath No Fury Like a Fellow Professor Deceived," Basken (2010) describes a research project by two researchers:

> [They] wanted to find out if people are more likely to act admirably when given more time to do so. And so they sent fake e-mail messages to 6,300 professors nationwide, pretending to be a graduate student seeking a few minutes of the professors' time. . . . The professors contacted by [the researchers] were divided into two groups, with some told by

> their fictional graduate student that he or she wanted a 10-minute meeting that same day, and others asked by the fake student for a meeting in a week.
>
> [One professor], among those asked by her bogus e-mail sender for an immediate meeting, wrote back saying she would be available during her regular office hours from 10 to 11 A.M. that day. The researchers sent out immediate cancellation messages to those who accepted, explaining what they did and why, but [that professor] didn't find that follow-up e-mail message until after sitting in anticipation the full hour.

That professor and many others were angry about being deceived and having their time wasted. Do you think that this research was unethical due to the deception? Could the research have been accomplished in some other way? What if the researchers had sent a debriefing e-mail making the case for the value of their research and the case that no alternatives would work?

Student Study Site

Visit the Study Site at **www.sagepub.com/remler2e** to

- test your knowledge with the self-quiz
- check your understanding of key terms with the eFlashcards
- explore helpful resources that relate directly to this chapter

Research can be found in many sources.
Source: © iStockphoto.com/Tobias Ackeborn.

Overview: This chapter will help you find studies on a topic of interest in research journals, government reports, books, and other electronic and print sources. A wealth of empirical research can be found on many important topics, if you know where to look. The chapter also provides some guidance for how to present, write about, and perhaps publish your own research. Doing good research is important, of course, but it is just as important to communicate research clearly and effectively to various audiences that can use it to decide policy or improve practice.

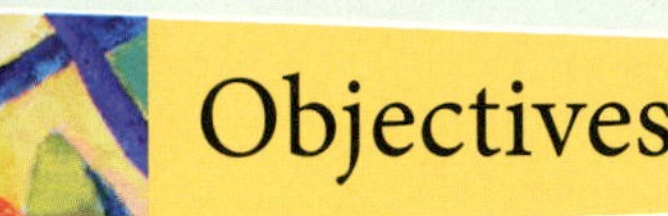

Objectives

Learning Objectives

After reading this chapter, you should be able to

- Find research studies relevant to your own interests
- Write a literature review on a topic of interest and appropriate to the review's purpose
- Write and present your own research clearly and appropriately to an audience

17 How to Find, Review, and Present Research

We have given lots of examples of research in this book, and we have covered ways to understand and assess various research strategies. But we have not said much about where to find a study (or studies) on a topic of interest to you. This chapter introduces you to the various outlets where research is published or presented and to some tools for finding relevant studies. And after you find a collection of studies on a topic, you may need to produce a written review of their main findings. This chapter will give you some guidance on how to write a good literature review.

When you do your own research, you will need to communicate the findings to others, either in a presentation or in a written report. There are standard formats for presenting or writing about research that you need to be aware of, as well as good practices for creating tables and figures to display your findings. The last sections of this chapter cover the presentation and communication of your own research results, including how to publish in a journal.

Where to Find Research

To read or hear research on a topic of interest, you must first find it—in journals, books, reports, conference presentations and proceedings, and other outlets. So let's begin by considering the major outlets for publishing, presenting, and disseminating research.

Journals

You are likely to find much of the available research on a given topic in **journals** (also called **scholarly** or **research journals**), which are published periodically (quarterly, semimonthly, monthly, or even weekly). This might make the task of finding research seem somewhat manageable—until you realize the sheer number of journals now in existence. One estimate came up with more than 40,000 academic or scholarly journals worldwide, including more than 20,000 peer-reviewed journals (Tenopir, 2004).

Journals are organized by traditional academic discipline (e.g., economics, psychology, sociology, political science), by applied field or practice area (e.g., public administration, public health, education, criminal justice, management), or by topic area (e.g., traffic safety, human resources administration, drug abuse, early childhood education). Thus, one of the challenges in finding relevant research on a topic of interest is to recognize that it may appear in any one of these types of journals.

A search on the topic of "teenage pregnancy," for example, will turn up articles in journals of public health, family planning, child development, obstetrics and gynecology, sociology, law, psychology, pediatrics, and political economy. Teenage pregnancy is a multifaceted problem, so it makes sense in many ways that research on this topic would appear in so many different types of journals. So when searching for research, be open to searching in journals outside of just one or two fields.

Peer Review and Prestige

If an article is peer reviewed, outside experts—called **reviewers** or **referees**—evaluate the quality and value of a research paper before it is accepted for publication. Reviewers are generally experts in the specific topic of the article, not just any researcher in the general field. Peer review is considered the main guarantor of research quality and integrity. But it is far from perfect. Reviewers cannot redo the analysis and must take the researchers' word on the details of the study. Groups of experts can also collectively fail to see a particular research weakness, with such weaknesses even becoming standard practice. Nonetheless, experienced outside reviewers devote many hours of careful thought to the papers they review and provide the bedrock of quality control in academic journals.

Some journals are very prestigious, with many researchers submitting papers to them in hopes of being published. These first-tier journals typically are known for having a rigorous and demanding review process and for accepting only a small fraction of submitted articles for publication. Articles published in these top-tier journals tend to be of higher quality, although you should always judge for yourself. The most prestigious journals in the world tend to focus on the natural and health sciences, such as *Science, Nature,* and the *Proceedings of the National Academy of Sciences (PNAS)*, but both *Science* and *PNAS* publish some articles from the social sciences as well.

To find out what journals are prestigious in your field, ask around and notice which journals get cited the most. One formal measure of a journal's prestige is the **impact factor**, which is the average number of citations (in other journals) per published article. Depending on which journals (and other types of publication) are counted for citations and for how long after publication citations are counted, a journal's impact factor can vary. Table 17.1 gives a few examples of top journals in selected fields from the website Eigenfactor.org, which is freely accessible and provides an article influence (AI) score that is similar to the impact factor. (Note that the results are sensitive to how fields are defined and which journals are included in which fields.)

The journals listed in Table 17.1 are just a few of the top publications in each field—there are many prestigious, selective journals in these fields, especially the larger ones (e.g., economics or psychology). Some journals are known as the top journal in a particular subfield, such as labor economics. There are also many other, less selective journals that accept a much higher percentage of the papers submitted for publication.

Knowing a journal's prestige factor provides a preliminary indication of the quality of its articles and their methodologies. But it is just an indicator, and you should judge for yourself. Moreover, the most relevant research for your interests may be in more specialized or narrowly focused journals, which tend to have lower-impact factors simply because they are more specialized and have a smaller audience. *Ulrich's periodicals directory* has extensive information, including information about journals with small circulations.

Types of Journal Articles

Journals focus primarily on peer-reviewed **original research articles** (or **original contributions**), which are reports of primary research. Most original research articles are empirical, but some may present a new theory or methodology. Journals also publish **review articles**, which provide a review and assessment of many related research studies on a topic in an effort to synthesize the results and reach broader conclusions. A review article is a good place to start when exploring a new topic. Most fields have an annual journal that specializes in review articles, such as the *Annual Review of Sociology* or the *Annual Review of Public Health*. **Book reviews** also appear in journals. Some applied journals also contain comments or opinion essays that are not peer reviewed and contain little or no primary research. Some journals act more like professional magazines, publishing only these kinds of essays or opinion articles and not original studies. The fact that a publication is called a "journal" does not necessarily mean that it contains peer-reviewed research; sometimes you have to look closely at the editorial statement (near the title page or at the end of the issue) or visit the journal's webpage to find out for sure.

Table 17.1 Some Top Journals in Selected Fields, as Measured by Eigenfactor.org Impact Factors

Field	Top Five Journals by 2011 Article Influence (AI) Score (Excludes Review Journals)
Criminology	*Criminology; Journal of Research in Crime and Delinquency; Trauma, Violence, and Abuse; Journal of Quantitative Criminology; Crime and Delinquency*
Education	*Journal of Educational and Behavioral Statistics; American Educational Research Journal; Scientific Studies of Reading; Sociology of Education; Educational Evaluation and Policy Analysis*
Economics	*Quarterly Journal of Economics; Journal of Economic Literature; Journal of Political Economy; Econometrica; The Review of Economic Studies*
Health care sciences and services	*Milbank Quarterly; Health Affairs; Health Technology Assessment; Journal of Health Economics; Medical Care*
Planning and development	*World Bank Economic Review; Research Policy; Journal of the American Planning Association; World Development; Economic Development and Cultural Change*
Political science	*Political Analysis; American Political Science Review; American Journal of Political Science; Quarterly Journal of Political Science; Journal of Conflict Resolution*
Psychology, applied	*Journal of Applied Psychology; Research in Organizational Behavior; Personnel Psychology; Organizational Research Methods; Organizational Behavior and Human Decision Processes*
Public administration	*Philosophy and Public Affairs; Journal of Policy Analysis and Management; Journal of Public Administration Research and Theory; Journal of European Public Policy; Governance*
Public health	*International Journal of Epidemiology; Epidemiology; American Journal of Epidemiology; Bulletin of the World Health Organization; Environmental Health Perspectives*
Social work	*Trauma, Violence, and Abuse; Child Maltreatment; Child Abuse and Neglect; American Journal of Community Psychology; Social Service Review*
Sociology	*American Sociological Review; American Journal of Sociology; Sociological Methodology; Population and Development Review; Social Networks*

Source: www.eigenfactor.org (accessed July 11, 2013).

Open-Access and e-Journals

Most journals are commercially published and require a paid subscription, either to receive the journal in the mail or to gain access to it online. Often, subscription to a journal accompanies membership in a professional association. For example, members of the American Society for Public Administration receive *Public Administration Review.* Universities as well as other organizations often subscribe to full-text journal databases that may give you access to commercially published journals if you are affiliated with the subscribing institution.

But with the possibilities of the Internet, there is now a movement toward "open access" journals—journals published entirely online and open to free public use. There is a Directory of Open Access Journals, at www.doaj.org, that lists nearly 10,000 online journals (as of November 2013). Many open-access journals aim to serve readers in parts of the world beyond the United States and Europe, especially developing countries, and many open-access

Source: © wonderlandstock / Alamy.

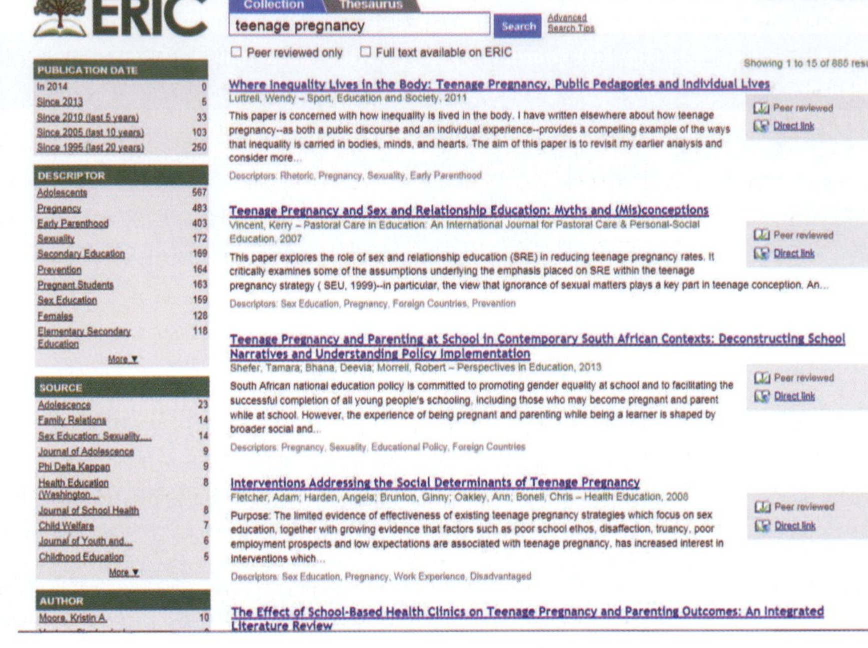

Research materials can be found both in the library and online.

Source: http://eric.ed.gov/.

journals are published in languages other than English. Thus, open-access journals fill a need for research in parts of the world, as well as within small institutions, that cannot afford commercially published journals.

But unfortunately, you need to be increasingly wary of open-access journals these days: Some of them are scams set up by unscrupulous publishers just to collect processing fees from authors (which is the predominant business model for open-access journals). Scholarly Open Access, a website run by University of Colorado librarian Jeffrey Beall, maintains a list of these predatory open-access publishers (see ScholarlyOA.com). If you have any doubts about a publication's legitimacy, either when looking for studies on a topic or when submitting your research for possible publication, you should consult Beall's list and ask professors or colleagues knowledgeable about your field.

Books

In some fields—such as history, anthropology, and qualitative sociology—books are the preferred format for the publication of important primary research. Books are the main form of publishing in-depth case studies, ethnographies, and historical studies. But in many other fields, including applied social and policy research, books serve another purpose. For researchers in these fields, books provide a medium to summarize a line of research and make it accessible to a more general audience. Like review articles, such books are a good place to start secondary research on a new topic.

Attending Conferences and Seminars

Research is often disseminated at research conferences or seminars. Each year, thousands of conferences are held all around the world in many fields and on various special research topics or issues. Governments sponsor research conferences to promote knowledge and inform practice. And professional associations hold research conferences for their members. Universities often have seminar series, some of which are open to the public. So there are many opportunities to hear and learn about research firsthand. A research conference is a bit like a menu tasting: You get to try little bits of research and see what you like. If you find a study interesting, you can ask the researcher for the paper or find the researcher's published work.

Because it typically takes a year or more after a research paper is written before it is reviewed, revised, and available in the pages of a journal (or online), conferences and seminars provide early access to research findings. Some conferences publish some or all of the studies presented in the form of proceedings of a research conference or post papers presented on a conference website. The practice varies by discipline, and accessing proceedings is sometimes difficult if you are not registered for the conference or a member of the sponsoring organization.

Reports

Government agencies, think tanks, advocacy groups, and other organizations put out many research reports. Most such reports are not peer reviewed, although some government reports go through an advisory board or other review process. Check to see if the report was reviewed, and by whom. With nongovernmental research reports, much depends on the aims and qualifications of the sponsoring organization. Does the organization have a reputation for producing honest, impartial information? Does it have an advocacy agenda, or even an axe to grind? It is also important to look at the qualifications of the researcher or consultant who produced the report. Organizations often hire someone to do the research and write the report, and some hired researchers are more independent than others. In general, it is more difficult to trust the findings of a research report that has not been peer reviewed. The value of the results depends on the quality of the methodology.

Working Papers

Various academic departments, institutes, and organizations publish **working papers**—research papers that are, in a sense, works in progress. Some of the most influential in policy research are the working papers of the National Bureau of Economic Research, available at www.nber.org. Many other research organizations post working papers on their websites. We suggest that you regularly consult the websites of research organizations in your area. Another good source is the Social Science Research Network, available at www.ssrn.com, which publishes working papers and also abstracts of published papers on a wide range of topics.

In some disciplines, work-in-progress manuscripts are distributed even more informally, accompanying a seminar or simply on the researcher's webpage. Working papers can be spread in increasingly diverse ways, including by electronic newsletters, blogs, and social networking sites. Such papers have not undergone peer review and should be treated as preliminary (often authors explicitly caution against using or citing the paper). But they do provide an up-to-date picture of what is happening in a field.

The News Media and Blogs

Although not a formal source of research findings, the news media often cover interesting new studies or scientific breakthroughs. So it can be helpful to search the news for stories about research on your topic or area of interest. There are also magazines dedicated to covering scientific research, such as in the general sciences *Scientific American* or *Discover*, in the social sciences *Pacific Standard* (PSmag.com), or in statistics *Significance* (SignificanceMagazine.org).

Blogs increasingly mention research. Some blogs are written by researchers mostly for other researchers (e.g., Statistical Modeling, Causal Inference, and Social Science at AndrewGelman.com). Such blogs do discuss specific research studies but more often focus on methodological issues or even theories. Other blogs that focus on research are meant to be read by broader audiences; they may be written by researchers (e.g., TheMonkeyCage.org; TheIncidentalEconomist.com) or by nonresearchers who follow research. Blogs often link to working papers.

QUESTION

Think of a topic of interest to you. Where is research on this topic likely to be found?

How to Search for Studies

Having reviewed the various outlets for publication and dissemination of research, we turn now to the tools available to help you search for and retrieve studies.

Google Scholar

We begin with Google—the search tool people use for just about everything these days. Google Scholar (beta) is Google's search engine designed especially for research journals, books, and reports, as well as some more journalistic pieces that are cited in research papers (see Box 17.1). It works very well for finding relevant research on most topics, although it has some gaps and should not be considered a compete listing. There are many other important abstract and full-text databases to consider as well in your search—which we will discuss shortly. But Google Scholar is certainly a good, readily available place to start.

Conducting a search using the basic form of Google Scholar is just like conducting a search with any other search engine: Keywords are entered, and the search engine's algorithms find relevant information. And just like using other search engines, specific words can be excluded (using –), whole phrases can be searched by putting the phrases in quotes (" "), fragments can be searched using the wildcard (*), and either of two or any of several words can be searched using "OR." Google Scholar can also be used in "Advanced Scholar Search" mode, which provides more search options tailored to scholarly fields and topics. While Google Scholar provides information about the scholarly literature, gaining access to the articles in non-open-access journals is best done through your university or organization's website to make use of its subscriptions.

BOX 17.1
What Is Google Scholar?

Google Scholar provides a simple way to broadly search for scholarly literature. From one place, you can search across many disciplines and sources: articles, theses, books, abstracts and court opinions, from academic publishers, professional societies, online repositories, universities and other web sites. Google Scholar helps you find relevant work across the world of scholarly research.

Features of Google Scholar

- Search all scholarly literature from one convenient place
- Explore related works, citations, authors, and publications
- Locate the complete document through your library or on the web
- Keep up with recent developments in any area of research
- Check who's citing your publications, create a public author profile

How Are Documents Ranked?

Google Scholar aims to rank documents the way researchers do, weighing the full text of each document, where it was published, who it was written by, as well as how often and how recently it has been cited in other scholarly literature.

Source: www.scholar.google.com

Electronic Resources: Indexes, Full-Text Databases, and Aggregators

Beyond Google, there are many important electronic resources: databases of research abstracts, often called indexes; databases of full-text articles and reports; and databases that combine both. Very recently, electronic access to books has started to become available. And sometimes a library will combine all the electronic databases to which it has access to form an *aggregator*. Because of all the innovation and mergers, the general term *electronic resources* is used to refer to all these new tools for finding research.

To search electronic resources, one must specify some or all of the available *fields*, which are specific types of information. Available fields generally include author, title, year of publication, language, type of publication, source, and so on. Such searches are more specific than those of a typical search engine where the keyword's role is not specified.

Although the lines between databases are blurring due to aggregators and mergers, we will discuss the different types of databases and provide some examples. We begin with those sponsored by government or nonprofit organizations that are freely available to the public.

> ERIC (Education Resources Information Center; U.S. Department of Education) at www.eric.ed.gov: An online, digital library of education research and information, including full-text publications from the U.S. government and other sources.

> GPO Access (U.S. Government Printing Office) at www.gpoaccess.gov: Provides free electronic access to most U.S. government reports and publications.

> JSTOR at www.jstor.org: A nonprofit organization that archives full-text scholarly articles across the humanities, social sciences, and sciences. (JSTOR does not include articles published in the last one to five years, depending on the journal.)

> NCJRS (National Criminal Justice Reference Service; U.S. Department of Justice) at www.ncjrs.gov: A federally funded resource offering access to publications on justice, crime, public safety, substance abuse, and related issues.

> PubMed Central (National Institutes of Health) at www.pubmedcentral.nih.gov: A free digital archive of journal literature in the biomedical and life sciences.

Major international organizations, such as the United Nations, the World Bank, the World Health Organization, and the Organisation for Economic Co-operation and Development provide some (though not all) of their books and periodicals online for free public use.

In addition to these government and nonprofit databases, a number of commercial services compile research literature across many journals—and even compile across multiple bibliographic databases. These services include EBSCO, IngentaConnect, OCLC, Ovid, ProQuest, and others. More general commercial databases that focus on news, such as Lexis/Nexis, can be useful for seeing how research influences policy. These commercial services require subscription, which is typically done through universities or other institutions and made available to affiliated students or employees. Although they are all very comprehensive in their content, and there is some overlap in coverage, no one service provides access to all the published studies and articles that are available. The electronic publishing industry is evolving and changing rapidly, with companies merging or forming alliances and new companies entering the field.

The broad reach of many of these electronic resources, both public and private, is obviously of tremendous value. However, sometimes it is also useful to use a more specific resource, such as EconLit, that includes more specialized or low-circulation journals that represent a particular field or disciplinary perspective.

Portals and Library Services

Technology and practice in finding research is evolving rapidly, so some of what we discuss here may have changed by the time you are reading this. You can discover recent approaches to finding research through the first screen in your library's catalog or information center, also known as its portal. All universities and many research organizations, large commercial and not-for-profit organizations, and public libraries have services that help you conduct a search, such as *Ask a Librarian* or *Text a Librarian*.

Wikipedia

In a very short period of time, *Wikipedia,* an online encyclopedia that can be edited by anyone, has emerged as a remarkable resource. Its content continues to grow rapidly and is generally very up-to-date, if often uneven in its coverage and quality. Box 17.2 contains Wikipedia's own description of itself.

While anyone can edit Wikipedia, its policy is that all statements should be backed up with good sources and citations. Various editors search pages to note where citations or sources are needed and to remove biased or unsupported information. Wikipedia benefits from the so-called *wisdom of crowds* in which the aggregated contributions of many people increase accuracy. (James Surowiecki coined the term in 2004.) In the context of Wikipedia, the idea is that false or dubious information, as well as important omissions, are spotted and fixed by the many Wikipedia users all over the world. Nonetheless, the open nature of Wikipedia means that it can contain unreliable and even false information. To address these concerns, Wikipedia's policies remain in rapid flux, with some increasing restrictions on the open editing policy.

Because of the potential for unreliability, Wikipedia cannot normally be used as an academic citation. Indeed, many academics eschew its use entirely. However, we would still recommend Wikipedia as at least a place to start secondary research, particularly due to its extensive and up-to-date coverage. But it is *only* a place to start and should not itself be a citation. You should move on to sources of information cited in the Wikipedia article you are reading and use the primary research articles or other sources. And you should also employ other initial entry points to a subject, such as a scholarly index search or a review article, as described earlier.

BOX 17.2
What Is Wikipedia?

Wikipedia is a free encyclopedia, written collaboratively by the people who use it. It is a special type of website designed to make collaboration easy, called a wiki. Many people are constantly improving Wikipedia, making thousands of changes per hour. All of these changes are recorded in article histories and recent changes. For a more detailed account of the project, see About Wikipedia.

How You Can Contribute

Don't be afraid to edit—*anyone* can edit almost any page, and we are encouraged to **be bold**! Find something that can be improved and make it better—for example, spelling, grammar, rewriting for readability, or removing non-constructive edits. If you wish to add new facts, please try to provide references so they may be verified, or suggest them on the article's discussion page. Changes to controversial topics and Wikipedia's main pages should usually be discussed first.

Remember—you can't break Wikipedia; all edits can be reversed, fixed or improved later. Wikipedia is allowed to be imperfect. So go ahead, edit an article and help make Wikipedia the best information source on the Internet!

Source: http://en.wikipedia.org/wiki/Wikipedia:Introduction (accessed November 22, 2013).

Browsing and Following Citation Trails

Once you have found a few relevant research studies or overviews through the various means described above, you should look at the reference lists at the end of the articles for more ideas about articles or other publications to search out. Following a **citation trail** in this way can be a very effective approach to finding research of interest. *One hint:* Begin with the newest articles first, as these will have the most up-to-date reference lists.

Browsing bookshelves provides another useful approach. Not so long ago, researchers and others looking to find published research browsed library stacks of books and journals, searching for research. With so many resources available electronically, and some only published online, this kind of physical browsing has become much less common. It is, however, still valuable at times to go into the stacks (especially when searching for older books or journal volumes).

Bibliographic Citation Software

As you search for studies, it is a good idea to keep track of the references you find with **bibliographic citation software**, also known as reference management software. Such software will not only make it easy to collect and remember references but will also make it much easier to add references to your finished paper—and change the reference format to meet the requirements of various journals. Examples of bibliographic citation software include EndNote, RefWorks, Zotero, and others. Zotero is free, works inside Mozilla Firefox or as a stand-alone program, and is capable of capturing not only bibliographic information from websites but many other forms of web content as well (see www.zotero.org). No doubt these products and others will continue to evolve and improve.

We have tried to be up-to-date in this section on how to search for research, but technology and practice in these areas are evolving rapidly. You should consult your library or information center, as well as colleagues, about new resources and practices.

QUESTION

Think of a topic of interest to you. How would you begin your search for published studies on this topic?

How to Write a Literature Review

After finding studies on a topic, you may next need to write a review of the literature. A **literature review** can be done as a stand-alone project in order to summarize and assess published research on a topic (such as hot-spot policing, negative political ads, distracted driving, organizational commitment, or small-school reform). Policy makers or executives may ask for a literature review in order to make or support an important decision, especially when there is little time for original research. In many fields, you can find an "annual review" journal dedicated to publishing reviews of the scientific literature in a discipline or field (such as the *Annual Review of Political Science* or the *Annual Review of Public Health*). But often you will be required to do a literature review as part of presenting your own research, perhaps as part of a thesis or research project. What does reviewing the literature entail?

What a Literature Review Should Not Do

It is instructive to begin with a few points about what a literature review is not—because writers often start out with misconceptions of the task.

First, a literature review is not an inventory or demonstration of how much reading you have done on the topic. Although you may have spent many days or even weeks slogging through countless studies (many dry or obscure), you should not make your reader suffer through the same experience. And do not discuss everything you've read just to make the point that you've read it. Rather, you need to be selective and use judgment. Sort out the wheat from the chaff, as it were, and focus your writing on the studies or findings that matter most. Often a batch of related studies of lesser importance can be referenced in just one sentence: for example, *Early observational studies of [your topic], relying on survey data, have found that [x] and [y] are strongly associated (Elephant, 1998; Giraffe, 1995; Hippopotamus, 1999; Zebra, 2000).* Your job is to make it easy for the reader to make quick sense of the literature and get to the main points.

Second, a literature review is not a series of strung-together quotes or excerpts—it is not a montage of the literature. In fact, you should probably try to avoid using quotes as a general rule. One reason is that quoting is frequently a rather inefficient way to summarize someone else's study or findings. In a literature review, it is your job to explain the evidence and its meaning, not to rely on other authors to do this job for you. In addition, quotes often do not make complete sense out of context, and providing context would mean quoting at length. Ultimately, nobody really enjoys reading a lot of quotations.

Finally, a literature review is not an opinion piece or polemic. It is not a platform for you to express your views or argue with the big names in the field about the proper perspective to take on, say, negative political campaigns or small-school reforms, although it is fine to acknowledge policy debates. Rather, the literature review is primarily about empirical findings and theoretical analyses. It should, of course, include relevant *scholarly* debates. And although you need to exercise judgment, such effort should focus on the nature and strength of the evidence, not on whether you support or oppose various normative claims or positions.

What a Literature Review Should Do

So what should a literature review do? Simply put, it should summarize the research literature on a given topic—with an emphasis on the words *summarize* and *research*. Much of the challenge in doing a good literature review is boiling things down, stripping away the unnecessary clutter, and focusing the reader on the key points. Use your own words and provide the reader with an organized view of the lay of the land. At the same time, it is important to cite the many sources that you are reviewing, even if you refer to studies in only a sentence or two or just a parenthetical reference. The reference list at the end of a review essay is critical: It needs to contain nearly all (if not all) of what you have found on the topic.

It is perhaps worth pointing out that, in reviewing the literature, you do not have to read every study word for word. Begin by reading the abstract, which will help you figure out if it is worthwhile to dig deeper. Government or other reports typically have executive summaries that provide an even more extensive overview of the study and its findings. Even when you decide to dig deeper, it often makes sense to first scan the body of the article or report, with particular attention to the methods used and the key findings presented in the tables and figures. If it looks like a good study, with important findings on your topic, then read away.

A review should focus foremost on real research, not opinions or unsubstantiated claims. Just because something is published does not make it a fact. In some areas, there are many things written and published but many fewer empirical findings. Take the example of negative political campaigning: Hundreds of essays, journal articles, and books have been published on negative campaigning and its ruinous effect on our fragile democracy. But the bulk of what has been published provides little in the way of evidence about, say, how widespread negative campaigning has really become, or what effects it really has on voters. Are things today actually worse than they were 50 or even 100 years ago? Has anyone tried to look at this systematically, rather than just claiming it is so? Does negative political advertising really affect voters, and if so how? What evidence shows this? Frequently, a good literature review ends up revealing that certain widely held assumptions are supported by surprisingly little if any good evidence.

But not all evidence is the same or of equal weight. In particular, it is important in a literature review to distinguish evidence of mere correlation from more solid evidence of causation. For example, management researchers over the years have looked at how a worker's organizational commitment influences outcomes such as job turnover and productivity. The vast majority of these studies come from cross-sectional surveys of workers in various industry and organizational settings, with organizational commitment, as well as outcomes like turnover intentions and productivity, measured by self-reporting. It might be tempting in a literature review to conclude that *"many studies confirm that organizational commitment influences turnover and productivity on the job (Elephant, 2000; Giraffe, 2005; Hippopotamus, 2009; Zebra, 2012)."* But this makes too large a leap, from correlation to causation. It is a bit like the childhood game of human telephone: "Jane's mother went to the ballet" becomes "Jane's mother was in the ballet" and finally "Jane's mother was a famous ballerina." It's important when translating evidence from an article or a report into your literature review not to allow it to morph into something more certain and definitive than what it really is. Again, just because something was published does not make it an established fact. Indeed, a convenient way of organizing or classifying the studies in a literature review about a causal effect is by the strength of the causal evidence.

Literature Review as Context for Your Own Study

If you conduct and write up your own study, you will need a literature review to provide background and context for your research. In addition to what we've said above, a literature review for your own study needs to accomplish some additional objectives. To begin with, it needs to explain the *motivation* for your particular study—why you chose to do the research you did. Try to avoid the facile "gap in the literature" argument, which typically goes something like this: *My comprehensive review of the literature in the field suggests that, surprisingly, no one before has looked at whether kite flying is associated with a person's religiosity. In order to fill this gap in the literature, my study will look at . . .* Sometimes gaps exist for a reason. Instead, give a real and meaningful explanation for why your study matters, either in terms of the social or policy issue it addresses or in terms of the theory it tests.

Your literature needs to move from the more general to the more specific, ending with the research question or hypothesis your study will examine. It helps to think about the shape of your literature review, if it had one, as being like an inverted triangle. For example, say your study is a survey experiment in which you randomly allocated respondents to view either a positive or a negative political ad in order to probe the influence of the ads on people's self-reported trust of government. The shape of your literature review might look something like Figure 17.1.

Figure 17.1 General Outline of a Literature Review, From the Broader Context to the More Specific

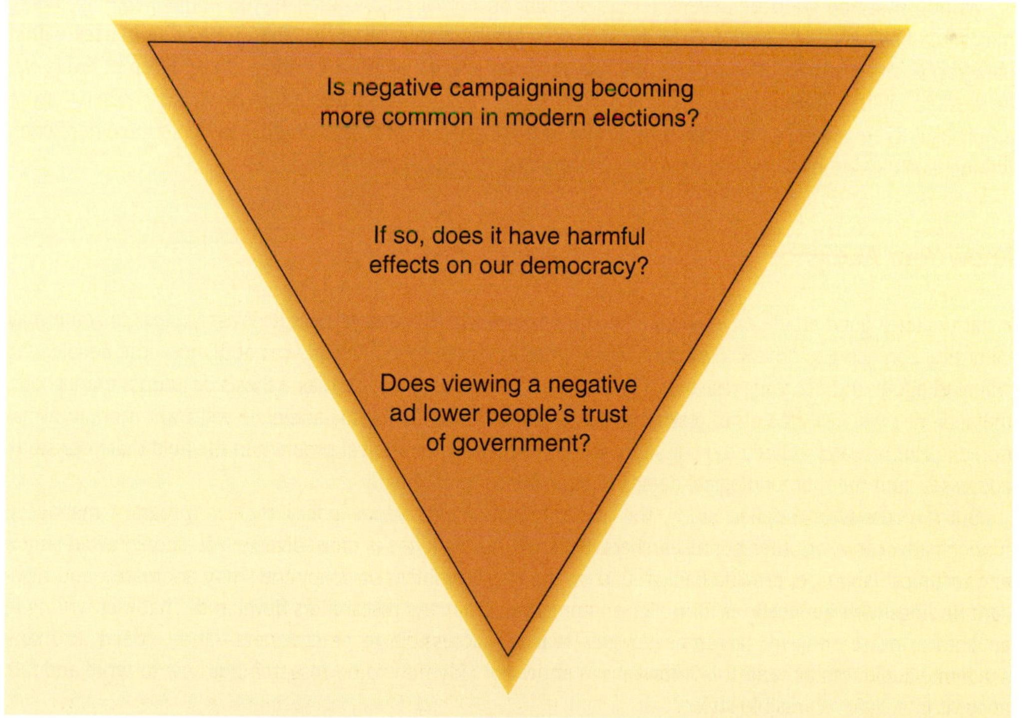
Is negative campaigning becoming more common in modern elections?
If so, does it have harmful effects on our democracy?
Does viewing a negative ad lower people's trust of government?

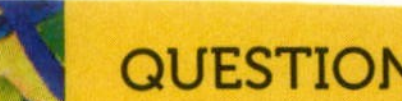

QUESTION

What should you try to do in a literature review? What should you not do?

Another way to put this is that, even if your study is focused on a rather small or limited empirical question, make sure the reader understands its broader context. Psychologist and behavioral economist Dan Ariely and colleagues published an article that captures this point: "Man's Search for Meaning: The Case of Legos" (Ariely, Kamenica, & Prelec, 2008). The study involved asking volunteers to build Lego figures for wages (a cash payment for each completed figure) under a "meaningful" condition, in which each completed figure was kept on the table, and a "meaningless" condition, in which each completed figure was disassembled and handed back to be rebuilt again. Regardless of being paid the same, people in the meaningful condition built 10.6 figures on average compared with just 7.2 figures in the meaningless condition. The broader significance of the study, as the title suggests, is that people search for meaning in their lives and will work harder when a job is seen as having a purpose, regardless of economic incentives. This was not just a study about Legos.

How to Communicate Your Own Research

To be useful to others, your research must be communicated in the form of a written report or a presentation. Care and effort need to go into the report, because people only know about your research through what you write or say about it. So it is important to allow sufficient time and resources for this stage of the research project.

The Importance of Rewriting

Research is often complicated. Therefore, writing and speaking clearly about it is not an easy task. It takes practice—even for those with a lot of experience. It is important not to put off writing until the end, but rather to begin writing as you conduct your research. The process of writing itself will help you clarify your ideas and may reveal flaws in your thinking and in the design of your research. In your initial writing up of your research methods, you may discover alternatives to or variations on your original research plans.

Writing must be good on several levels: overall conceptual organization of the entire piece, including major headings and subheadings; the order of paragraphs within headings; the order of sentences within paragraphs; the structure of sentences; and the choice of specific words. Of course, these different levels can be worked on in different drafts. This is not the place for a detailed discussion of writing, other than to emphasize its importance. You can consult any of the excellent resources on how to do serious, nonfiction writing, such as Joseph M. Williams's *Style: Toward Clarity and Grace* (1995).

Know Your Audience

What makes a good article or presentation depends on who will read or hear it. What is clear to some may be utterly confusing to others. Therefore, when writing, always keep in mind your audience—the people who will read about and use your research. If yours is an academic study, such as a thesis or journal manuscript, the audience will likely be other researchers or students in the field. This audience will want more information on prior research related to your study, the conceptual or theoretical problem in the field that your study addresses, and the methodological details of importance to the field.

But if yours is an applied study, the audience will likely include policy makers, program managers, funders, advocates, or other nonresearchers. Because this audience is more diverse, you should avoid jargon and technical language, provide background on the social problem or policy the study addresses, and highlight findings with implications for policy and practice. Too many researchers develop the habit of writing in an obtuse, passive-voiced, jargon-heavy style that is inaccessible to practitioners—and, indeed, to many academic audiences as well. It is important to know not only how to do research but how to write and talk about it in a clear, accessible style.

As much as possible, try out your writing or presentation on a target audience. Give drafts of your writing to others for feedback, or practice giving your presentations to a friend or colleague. You will learn a lot in this way about how to match your writing to your audience.

We turn next to the organization of a research report or article.

Organization of a Research Report

There is a standard six-part organization for writing or presenting research: Give an abstract, provide the context, state the objectives (research questions), describe the methods, present the findings, and discuss conclusions or implications. Although the specific parts vary somewhat by discipline and type of study, most research articles or reports essentially follow this organization. We review each of these parts in turn.

Abstract: The Essentials in Brief

It helps to write this first part of the manuscript last—but you should not overlook the importance of an abstract. As mentioned earlier, readers of research often search and assess studies based solely on abstracts. Indeed, databases of abstracts exist for this purpose (such as the Applied Social Sciences Index and Abstracts). An unclear, inaccurate, or poorly written abstract hurts the chances that your study will be found and read by its intended audience.

Context: Giving the Necessary Background

Although you are immersed in the problems and issues that motivated your research, your audience may not be. And even if most people have heard something about a major social problem, such as drug trafficking on the U.S.-Mexico border or AIDS in southern Africa, they probably do not know the actual trends or scope of the problem. So it is necessary to give your audience sufficient context to fully appreciate your research.

- What is the problem or issue your research addresses—what is its main outcome of interest?
- Where is the problem happening—is it local, regional, national, or international?
- How big is the problem—how many people are affected? Is the problem getting better or worse?
- What are the political or policy responses to the problem?
- What prior research has been done—what have been the main findings of prior research?
- What conceptual or theoretical problems surround the topic of your study?

This section usually contains the theory that drives the empirical research, although sometimes a separate theory section is added after the background (but before the empirical analysis) when there is a need for more in-depth discussion of theoretical issues. The background section also usually contains the review of the relevant scholarly literature, separate or interwoven with the other background material. But some articles contain a separate literature review section. So depending on the discipline and topic, there are various ways to organize this part of the manuscript.

Objectives: Stating the Research Questions

Having given the context, the next step in writing or presenting research is to clearly state your objectives or research questions. What exactly is the research question your study aims to answer? If the study has explicit or formal hypotheses, these should be stated also. This section can and often should be concise.

It should be noted that stating the research questions or hypotheses concisely and clearly is something that should happen *before* you begin your research. Indeed, this is an essential step for ensuring that the research is worth doing and that the methods are well chosen. Even for exploratory research, a clear question or focus is essential at the outset. Of course, research questions can evolve as discoveries are made, but if so they should be rewritten—clearly and concisely—at the time.

Methods: Explaining How the Study Was Conducted

Novice writers and presenters of research tend to skip over the methods and jump to the findings. But it will be difficult for an audience to make sense of findings, even simple charts, without knowing how the study was conducted. Also, much of the validity of a study—its integrity and worth—lies in the logic and quality of its methodology. Indeed, that has been our theme throughout much of this book. Thus, it is very important to clearly explain *how* the study was conducted.

The kind of information needed in the methods section depends, of course, on the methods used. A complicated analysis of secondary data will need to provide different information than open-ended interviews to address an exploratory research question. The *Critical Questions to Ask* lists, given at the end of earlier chapters, can be used to think about the kind of information you may need to include when describing your particular method to an audience.

Despite the variation in describing different methods, most research reports should address the following general points:

- What is the setting of the study—what locations or institutions were included? When were the data collected—or obtained?
- Who are the participants in the study—how were they sampled or recruited? Is the entire sample, or a subsample with particular characteristics, included in the study?
- What is the key outcome measure (dependent variable), and what are the other variables? How were these variables measured? What are the units?
- What is the design of the study—is it a survey, an experiment, a natural or quasi experiment (and if so, what kind), a qualitative study, an analysis of secondary data, or something else?
- How were the data analyzed? What calculations were performed? Were further approximations or assumptions made?

When the analysis of data is fairly involved, the methods section is usually broken into separate "data" and "analysis" sections, or even multiple analyses sections.

The methods section should not present or discuss findings—you must hold off on this for the time being. However, it is appropriate to present basic descriptive statistics for your variables—such as the range, mean, and standard deviation. A table of descriptive statistics can serve as a concise way of defining and describing your variables—but not in an article in which the main results are descriptive statistics. Presenting baseline comparisons may be appropriate in some studies, for example, to show that treatment and control groups are indeed comparable—or if not, how they differ (and thus what control variables need to be taken into account).

Results: Presenting the Findings

In this section, you present your findings in the form of a narrative, tables, or figures (charts). Focus in this section on *presenting* the findings and interpreting them in straightforward ways, not on drawing conclusions—that is the work of the final section. The reason for this is that your readers or audience members must first grasp *what* you found before they can fully appreciate its implications. For example, in this section, you should present treatment effects directly provided from the analysis and interpret those findings in understandable units and contexts, but you should not compare the effects with those of other programs. Those comparisons belong in the final section.

Introduce tables and figures and explain what they show. Even assuming that the tables and figures are clearly labeled and largely self-explanatory, as they should be, the text or presentation should still walk the audience through each table and figure. Beyond orienting readers or audience members to what they are looking at, the text or presentation should call attention to overall patterns as well as any unusual values or outliers. The direction as well as the magnitude of key relationships or effects should be described. Results should be presented in such a way that readers can place them in a relevant context.

Conclusions: Providing Interpretations and Implications

In this final section, you make interpretations and conclusions based on your findings as well as discuss policy or practice implications. If your aim was to test specific hypotheses or predictions, did your findings support or refute those hypotheses? How strong was the evidence? If the research question was more descriptive or exploratory, what is your interpretation of the main findings? What insights do your findings provide?

An important part of this section is to acknowledge and discuss methodological *limitations* and how they might have influenced the results. Were there difficulties in measuring some of the variables? Are there variables that could not be measured but that might have been important? Were there limitations in the sampling or selection of participants? If the study was an experiment, was there any contamination or problem in administering the treatment? If it was a natural or quasi experiment, how comparable were the groups, and how exogenous was the treatment? Acknowledging and discussing such limitations helps your audience judge the meaning and implications of your research, and also it is the ethical thing to do.

This section should also describe how your results add to the existing knowledge base. Return to the issues in the broader context and focus on any policy or practice implications. What has been learned from the study? How should the results alter policy or practice? Do these results suggest other research?

Writing About Numbers

Most of us have had plenty of experience with writing since grade school, but we may not have written very much about numbers. And research, particularly quantitative research, requires us to write a lot about numbers. Some advice can help with this task.

To begin with, it's important to realize that written prose is often not the most efficient or effective way to present numerical information. Especially if there are lots of numbers to present, tables or figures often work much better. Then you can save your prose writing (or oral presentation) for a discussion of what is in the tables or figures, pointing out the patterns or highlights but not giving all the numbers in the text.

But when presenting or discussing just a few numbers, it may help to include them in your written or spoken sentences or paragraphs. How should you do this?

In her comprehensive books on writing about numbers, Jane Miller (2004, 2005) suggests these seven principles for good quantitative writing:

1. Establish the context for the number (the who, what, when, and where) as well as the units the number is in (dollars of annual income, years of age, etc.).

   For example, don't just write, *The income of the state was $58,000.*

   Instead, provide the relevant context: *According to data compiled by the U.S. Census Bureau, the median annual income of households in California in 2007 was $58,000, $8,000 above the median for all U.S. households.*

2. Use examples, analogies, or comparisons to help your audience interpret the number.

   For example, don't just write, *California's unemployment rate was 12.2% in August.*

   Instead, use a comparison to give the number more meaning: *California's unemployment rate was 12.2% in August, the highest level seen since the end of the Great Depression.*

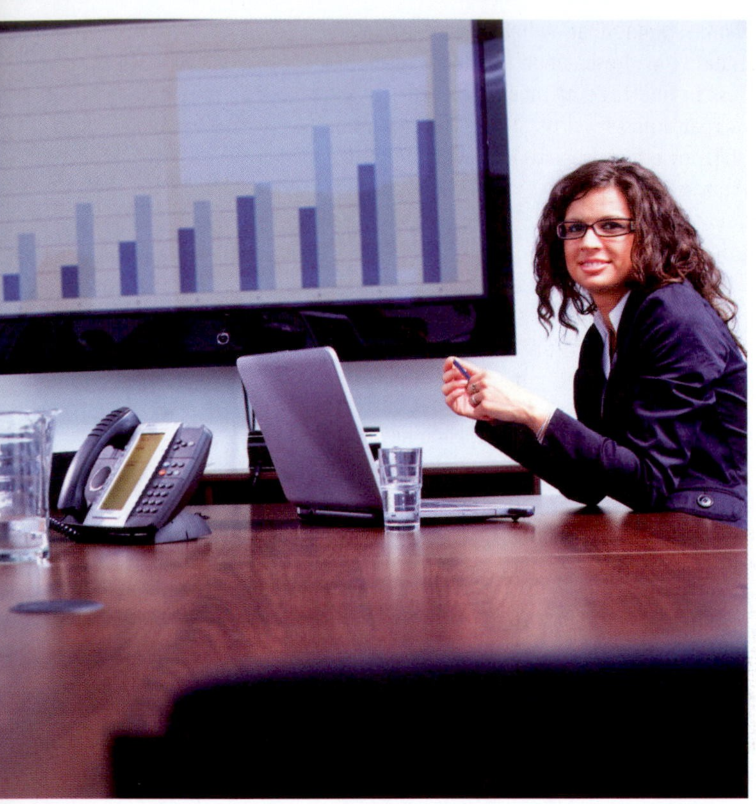

Charts are often the best way to communicate quantitative information.
Source: © iStockphoto.com/nyul.

3. Select the right tool to present the numbers—text, tables, or figures (charts).

   We will have more to say about this shortly, but consider this example of a sentence that tries to give too much numerical information (better suited to a table): *California is the most populous state in the United States, with 36.8 million residents, followed by Texas with 24.3 million residents, New York with 19.5 million, Florida with 18.3 million, Illinois with 12.9 million, Pennsylvania with 12.4 million, Ohio with 11.5 million, and Michigan with 10.0 million.*

4. Define your terms, and avoid research or professional jargon (especially for a more general audience).

   Avoid writing like this: *According to our OLS model, state public educational spending has a significant positive coefficient on NAEP math scores, controlling for student SES and demographic variables.*

   Instead, help your audience by spelling out acronyms and using more ordinary language: *Using regression analysis to adjust for the socioeconomic and demographic characteristics of students, we found that states that spend more on public education have higher average math scores on the National Assessment of Educational Progress.*

5. Interpret numbers in the text—numbers do not speak for themselves.

   To continue with a previous example, do not just write, *California's unemployment rate was 12.2% in August.*

   Instead, help your audience interpret this number: *California's unemployment rate was 12.2% in August, up from 11.9% in July, and representing 2.2 million state residents who are now unemployed. This is the highest rate of unemployment seen in California since the end of the Great Depression.*

6. Specify the direction and magnitude of a relationship.

   It is not enough just to write, *Our analysis suggests that education spending by the states is related to average math scores on the National Assessment of Educational Progress.*

   Instead, specify the direction and help the reader understand the magnitude of the relationship: *Our analysis suggests that an additional $1,000 per pupil in state spending on education is associated with a 10-point advantage in average math scores on the National Assessment of Educational Progress, which has a 0 to 500 scale.*

7. Summarize patterns in the data.

   When numbers appear in tables or figures, as we will soon see, it becomes important to use the text to summarize the patterns in the data: Is there a trend or relationship? Are there outliers? What is the overall message to take away from the numbers?

Miller (2005) recommends paying special attention to writing about causality (i.e., causation), statistical significance, and substantive significance (i.e., practical significance). We agree. Be sure to explain whether the numbers aim to estimate a causal relationship or simply describe an association. If a causal relationship is the focus, be sure to address and try to explain the causal mechanism—the causal theory of the relationship. And be sure to consider the strength of the causal evidence. For example, in an observational study, judge the plausibility of reverse causation or whether important common causes have not been controlled for. As the author of the study, you've given these issues much more thought than an initial reader (or hopefully so), and you should share your considerations and interpretations with your readers.

When writing about statistical significance tests, be sure to understand what they mean in a given context and do not overinterpret them (readers tend to do this enough as it is). In most cases, statistical significance tests simply rule out chance as an explanation of an observed difference or relationship; they do not prove causation or even that an effect is important. Miller (2005) suggests that, for nontechnical audiences, significance tests should be used simply to decide which results to present and discuss. More technical audiences, however, will want to know details such as the standard errors, confidence intervals, or p values.

Last, and perhaps most important, be sure to discuss the policy or practical significance of the results—how large is the effect, and what does it mean, in the real world? To do this, the results must be presented in a way that allows for interpretation in a real-world context. For example, a logistic regression coefficient has no meaning to most readers and can only be interpreted if converted to an odds ratio or marginal effect.

QUESTION

What are the main parts of a research report or manuscript?

Tables and Figures

As we noted earlier, prose is often not the best way of communicating numbers—especially when you have lots of numbers to present. Tables and figures (charts or graphs) often help organize or display data more efficiently and effectively. A table gives exact numerical values and organizes the numbers into columns and rows so that the reader can find and compare them more easily. A figure presents the data in the form of a graph or chart that displays the overall pattern visually, typically using bars, lines, or other graphical symbols. But figures do not convey precise values.

We will provide some specific tips on producing good tables and figures shortly. But first, there are a few guidelines that apply to both tables and figures:

- *Make your table or figure largely self-explanatory.* Give your table or figure to friends or colleagues to test this out. Can they make sense of what it says on their own? How much additional explanation is required before the meaning comes into focus? How could you incorporate this additional information into the title, headings, or notes to the table or figure to make it more self-explanatory?
- *Number your tables and figures* in the order in which they are mentioned in the text. Some tables or figures require more explanation and discussion than others, but you must always reference a table or figure in the text of the paper (e.g., "As Table 1 shows . . .").
- *Title your table or figure carefully and completely.* Novice writers or presenters frequently make the mistake of giving their table a vague title or no title at all (e.g., just "Table 1"). Often, it is better to err on the side of a longer, more descriptive title than a short, cryptic one. With survey data, it can help to use some version of the wording of the question in the title.
- *Avoid just cutting and pasting the tables and figures* from statistical software packages (such as SPSS, Stata, or SAS). Consider reformatting, or even re-creating the table or figure, using a spreadsheet or specialized graphing software to make it more presentable. Statistical software packages increasingly have commands capable of producing tables and figures suitable for publication, but you must use the specialized commands and features and not the standard output.

Let's turn now to more specific advice and examples, beginning with tables.

Tips for Creating Good Tables

When you need to present more than a few numbers, or to compare numbers across groups or categories, you will likely need to prepare a table. Tables are also useful for presenting multivariate results such as coefficients and related statistics from a multiple regression analysis.

A good table requires careful and creative editing and formatting. Include only the essential information your audience needs to make sense of the results—do not overload the table with nonessential numerical detail. The aim should be to make the table as clear and simple as possible so that your readers can make sense of it.

The information for your table will most often come from statistical software, but don't just cut and paste software output into your report or presentation. Table 17.2 shows raw output in SPSS using data from the 2005 World Values Survey, and you can see that it is not that easily interpreted. You will need to reformat this output, cutting extraneous numbers and clarifying the labeling and formatting of the table.

Table 17.3 presents the same results in a cleaner, simpler format that audiences can more readily read. Notice that only the column percentages were included because these provided the meaningful results to be interpreted, as discussed in Chapter 8. Counts do not mean very much when the data are from a sample. (Of course, you must present the total sample size, and any important subgroup sample sizes, usually in the notes.) When presenting any results, particularly complex ones, think about what points are to be made and construct the table layout to facilitate the audience's understanding of those points. It takes some time, effort, and practice to make good tables.

Table 17.2 Unformatted Computer Output (From SPSS)

V248 Are you the chief wage earner in your house * V235 Sex Crosstabulation					
			V235 Sex		Total
			1 male	2 female	
V248 Are you the chief wage earner in your house	1 yes	Count			
			17371	7299	24670
		% within V235			
			66.5%	28.2%	47.4%
		Sex			
	2 no	Count	8750	18626	27376
		% within V235			
			33.5%	71.8%	52.6%
		Sex			
Total		Count	26121	25925	52046
		% within V235			
			100.0%	100.0%	100.0%
		Sex			

Source: World Values Survey (2005).

Table 17.3 Reformatted Table Using Clearer, Simpler Layout

Are you the chief wage earner in your house?			
	Male	Female	Total
Yes	66.5%	28.2%	47.4%
No	33.5%	71.8%	52.6%
Total	100.0%	100.0%	100.0%

Note: N = 52,046 respondents in 57 countries.

Source: World Values Survey (2005).

Good resources for advice on preparing tables include the style guides put out by the American Psychological Association (2009), the American Medical Association (JAMA & Archives Journals, 2007), and the University of Chicago (2003), as well as the books by Miller (2004, 2005) and Booth, Colomb, and Williams (2008).

Tips for Creating Good Figures

Figures are typically graphs or charts that use bars, lines, or other graphical symbols to show data. Figures work better than tables at presenting the overall pattern in the data, but they do not work as well for conveying precise numerical values. Because figures allow for many options of scale, shape, color, and other stylistic elements, they can require more time and effort to produce.

Again, the aim is to keep the figure as clear and as simple as possible so that an audience can make sense of it. Avoid distracting colors, textures, and chart junk (such as pictures or symbols) that add little to an understanding of the data.

As with tables, the information for the chart will most often come from statistical software, but again, do not just take what the computer spits out and paste it into your report or presentation. Figure 17.2, for example, shows a simple bar chart from SPSS using 2005 World Values Survey data. By devoting some effort to reformatting, this figure can be made much clearer and simpler, as shown in Figure 17.3. The rotation of the axis provides more space for the full value labels, and the categories are reordered by frequency (rather than just by accepting the order of categories in the raw output). These kinds of changes will help your audience more readily grasp the meaning of your data.

Figure 17.2 Unformatted Statistical Graph (From SPSS)

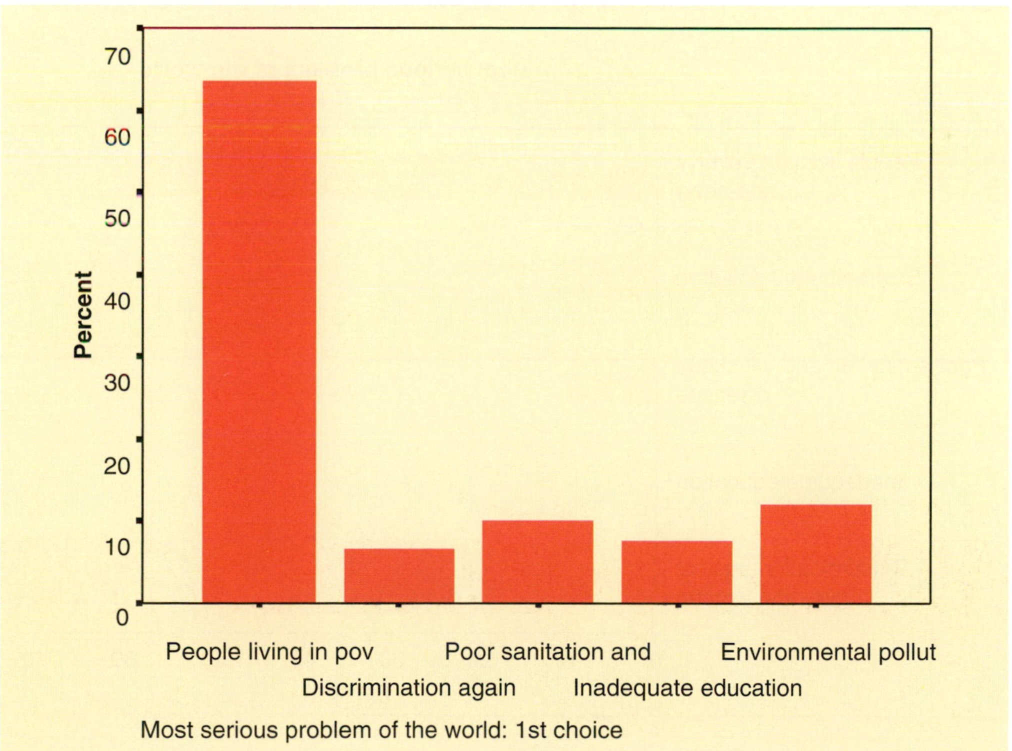

Source: World Values Survey (2005).

QUESTION

What kind of information would you present in a table, and what kind of information would you present in a figure?

The science and art of graphing data is a big topic that we can only touch on here. Excellent resources for developing this important skill include Tufte's (2001) *The Visual Display of Quantitative Information,* Cleveland's (1994) *The Elements of Graphing Data,* and Henry's (1994) *Graphing Data.* Particularly when presenting for a broader audience, this is a rapidly evolving and innovative field. See the Information Is Beautiful website (www.informationisbeautiful.net) for an example.

How to Write About Qualitative Research

Writing about qualitative research is different in many ways. The information you will be presenting comes mostly in the form of language, texts, images, and qualitative observations of behavior, not numbers or statistics. And it is not possible to write about all the information gathered from in-depth interviews or case studies—there is just too much of it, in most cases. Writing about qualitative research, therefore, requires you to make many subtle decisions about what and how to present.

In his book on qualitative inquiry, Creswell (2006) identifies several rhetorical issues to consider in the writing of a qualitative research report:

- *Reflexivity and representation:* Who are you, as the researcher-writer, and what is your relationship to the participants? How does your perspective, either as an outsider or an insider (say, in the case of full participation), influence your interpretation of the data? Because qualitative research and analysis are inherently more subjective, it is important to reflect on your own perspective in your writing.

Figure 17.3 Reformatted and Annotated Graph to Improve Presentation

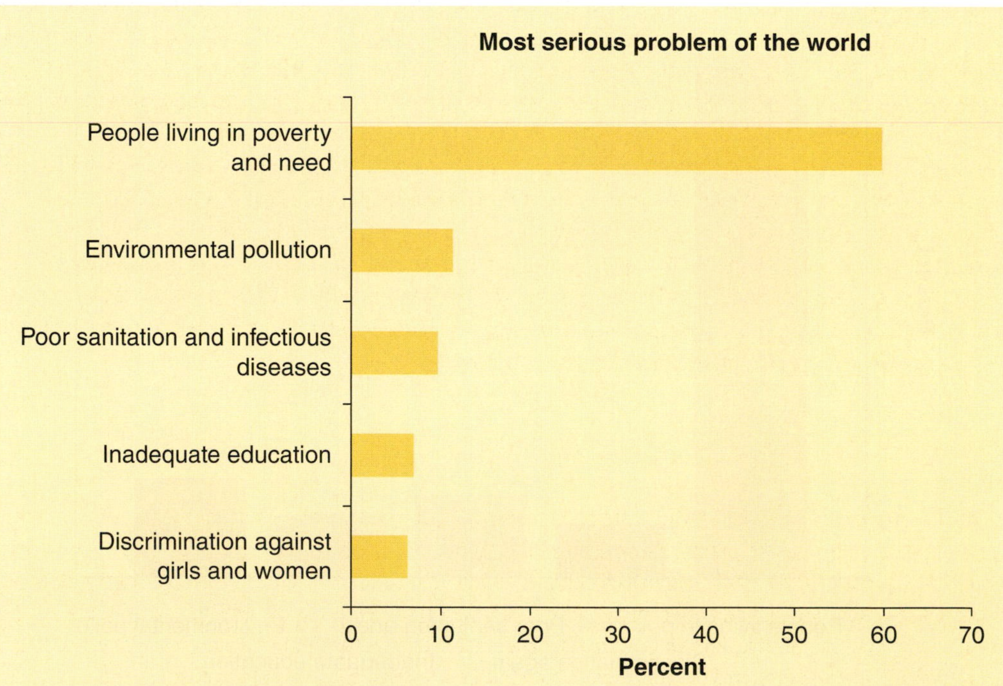

Note: N = 55,941 respondents in 57 countries.

Source: World Values Survey (2005).

- *Audience:* For whom are you writing this report? We discussed this issue earlier with respect to how much technical detail or terminology to use in writing about numbers, but the issue is a bit different in qualitative research. An important point here is to provide your audience with enough information on the context, background, and culture of participants to fully interpret the qualitative evidence.
- *Encoding:* What language or style will you use in your report? This issue is related to the audience question, but it refers more specifically to the style of presentation. Will you write in an informal, journalistic style or a more formal, academic manner? Will you write with a focus on conceptual or theoretical ideas, or with more attention to public policy or practice implications?
- *Quotes:* What quotes or other examples of your data will you present? You can use extended quotes or dialogue (e.g., from an in-depth interview), or embed shorter quotes that appear in your own narrative interpretation. It is always important to frame the quote in sufficient context about the participant and the situation for it to make sense to your readers. It is also important to give a sense of how representative, or unique, the quote is in relation to all the data (which you are not quoting).

Although writing about qualitative research presents unique challenges, you should be aware that the general standards for presenting research still apply. In particular, you still must tell your audience about the methodology of your study: How many people did you interview or observe? How did you choose (sample) the people or settings in the study? Whom did you leave out, or who did not agree to participate? What questions did you ask or issues did you focus on? What instruments (such as interview guides, observation forms, and audio or video recorders) did you use? How many visits did you make, and how much time did you spend in the setting? How did you summarize or reduce the qualitative data (e.g., by coding, content analysis, or using qualitative software)? Journal editors and reviewers, policy makers, funders, and other readers of your report will expect and deserve answers to these basic methodological questions.

If you coded and content-analyzed your qualitative data, most likely you will have some numerical tables or figures in your report as well. For example, you may want to show the overall frequency of codes, or you may count codes across settings or analytical categories. To this extent, the prior advice about preparing good tables and charts still applies. Be sure to give quotes or other evidence of the actual content and meaning of codes, however, as the code labels alone are often ambiguous and too abstract.

Finally, many studies these days involve *mixed methods,* with both qualitative and quantitative findings to report. You will then need to blend the approaches and advice we have suggested thus far. If initial qualitative methods (such as focus groups) were used to develop a later quantitative effort (such as a survey), it is helpful to present and interpret them in this sequence. The same applies, of course, to qualitative investigation that comes after quantitative findings (such as follow-up interviews with survey respondents). If the qualitative and quantitative methods ran concurrently, however, you should describe each method separately but perhaps interpret them in a more integrated manner (Creswell, 2006).

Presenting: How It Is—and Is Not—Like Writing

Most of our suggestions about how to write about research apply equally to a presentation or talk, which are ways of presenting research orally to an audience in attendance. But presentations do bring up a few special issues. Unlike readers of an article, those listening to and watching a presentation cannot go back and reread if they missed something, and they cannot go more slowly (or quickly) than the presenter does. So pacing is critical. And because of that, knowing what your audience will, or will not, understand becomes especially important. Also, most oral presentations are much shorter, in terms of the number of words, than a written report and somewhat less formal in style. So a presentation must be much more concise and often less technical. One advantage of a presentation, however, is that the audience may ask questions and engage in a dialogue with the researcher.

Most presenters today accompany their talk with some kind of slide show, such as PowerPoint or PDF slides. You should put enough—but not too much—information into your slides. Figures and tables belong in slides, but be aware that tables with too many numerical details are difficult for an audience to read on a screen and make sense of. Figures often work better if you have a choice. When presenting tables, select a small portion of any large tables, the portion with the most important results that you will discuss verbally. And highlight the most important results on that table by using different colored lettering or circles around the numbers. Background or commentary is often more effective when it simply comes from the speaker—so don't overly script yourself or bore your audience with too many talking points on slides.

Another form of presentation found at research conferences is a poster presentation. In a poster presentation, the researcher prepares a large poster board with a summary of the study, including key tables and figures. Each researcher stands next to his or her poster board, spaced out in a conference room, and the audience strolls from poster to poster, engaging the researcher with questions and discussion. Such poster sessions not only accommodate a large number of studies, but also give the audience members direct access to the researcher and flexibility in attending only to studies that interest them.

How to Publish Your Research

As we saw earlier in the chapter, research in both applied and academic fields gets out to the world largely through publication in peer-reviewed journals. So if you've worked on a research project for class or as part of your job, and certainly if you're planning a career as a researcher, you should consider publishing your work. Of course, research communication takes other forms as well, such as reports and presentations. But even so, you may still want to publish your study later as a journal article so it enters a wider array of search engines and has enhanced reputation from passing peer review.

Where should you publish your study? In most applied and academic fields, you can find a range of journals to consider. To learn about different journals' reputations, notice what is highly cited and speak with advisers and others in the field. An important issue in choosing is fit: What journal would be most interested in your study? Consider the journals you came across most often in your literature review, as these are likely to be outlets that might be interested in your work. Indeed, if you submit to a journal but do not cite the journal, you may receive a cool reception from reviewers or editors. An important consideration is audience: Who reads the journal? Whom do you want to reach—specialists or generalists, practitioners or academics? Answering these questions can help you select a journal—and, importantly, it also influences the perspective you take and the audience you should imagine as you write. Finally, some journals are more prestigious and selective than others, so much depends on how strong or important you think your study is. Although it is tempting to aim high, you also want your paper to have at least a chance of making it through the peer-review process. One advantage of aiming high, however, is the valuable criticisms and suggestions from reviewers that can help you improve your study.

Preparing a research manuscript involves all of the writing and presentation skills that we have already discussed in this chapter. And the manuscript should also follow the general outline we described earlier: abstract, context (or background, including theory and literature review), objectives, methods, results, and conclusions (or discussion). The names for these sections differ, depending on discipline and on the type of study, but this overall structure is a fairly standard one across the natural and social sciences. A big difference between a report and a journal article for publication is length: Manuscripts for journals typically have strict page limits, often not more than 20 to 30 pages (including tables, figures, and references). These page limits reflect the costs of publishing, but they also aim to make the article more efficient for readers. Before preparing the manuscript, you should consult the website for your chosen journal and look for its instructions for authors (or guidelines for preparing a manuscript). These instructions will tell you what the journal expects not only in terms of page length but also in terms of the required format for references, writing style guidelines, the number of tables or figures allowed, and other aspects of formatting the manuscript. Most journals these days use online submission and peer-review management software, such as ScholarOne, which allows you to upload your manuscript and track it online as it goes through peer review.

The peer review process is the most important and often challenging step. The editor or managing editor of the journal will first assess your manuscript and decide whether it should even go to peer review, and if so which reviewers it should be assigned to. Sometimes the editor will decide at the outset that the article should be rejected, either because of quality concerns or because it is not a good fit for the journal. If it goes out for peer review, the editor will identify reviewers with substantive or methodological interests in the area of your study. Peer reviewers are mostly academics, as well as some full-time and published researchers in government institutes and other settings. But journals in applied fields will also use experienced practitioners as reviewers.

Journals typically aim to get three reviews back, although sometimes you may get as many as four or even five reviews or as few as two. Frequently, editors will look at what authors you've cited in your paper and use them as a guide for finding appropriate reviewers. Depending on the journal and the number of submissions, editors may select at least one reviewer from their editorial board as well. The reviewers receive your paper as an anonymous manuscript, and they are asked to complete their review in about 15 to 90 days (depending on the journal's policy), but reviewers unfortunately may take longer. The editor then assembles and transmits the reviews to you, along with the editor's own comments and a decision to accept the paper, reject it, or ask for a revision and resubmission. The requested revisions could be relatively minor or rather substantial, involving new analysis and major rewriting. Journals may give you only one chance to revise the paper, so it is worth making a concerted effort. The revised manuscript is again uploaded to the journal submission website, along with a critical additional document: your point-by-point response to each reviewer's comments and concerns. This response can sometimes be more important even than the revised manuscript itself, since it is where you highlight specific changes or perhaps rebut the criticisms leveled by the reviewers. The editor may make the final decision based on these reviews or may go back to the original reviewers. After another period of weeks or a few months, you will hear back from the editor. Most often you will get a final decision—accept, accept conditional on further changes, or reject. But sometimes the journal may request a further round of modifications without a guarantee of eventual publication.

QUESTION

What are the main steps involved in publishing a journal article?

If accepted, your paper will go into production, and after a period of time, you will be asked to review and correct page proofs, which show how your article will actually look in the pages of the journal. Altogether—from the time you first submit your paper to its appearance in the pages of a journal—the publication of an article in a peer-reviewed journal can easily take between a year and two years, sometimes more. Publishing research is a long process, so you must be persistent.

Conclusion

In this chapter, you have learned where to find research of interest to you and how to write a literature review. And you have picked up some tips related to writing up or presenting your research to others. These are all important how-to skills, and in the end, they require practice to master. So we encourage you to get out there and find studies to read or talks to attend, try your hand at reviewing the literature, and practice writing up or presenting the results of your own research activities.

In doing all of this, we encourage you to keep in mind the broad issues and ideas that we have covered in previous chapters on the strategies for description and for assertions about causation. You will find that understanding the logic and limitations of research methods helps a great deal in reading studies of interest to you, focusing your research question, and presenting your own research. The more you grasp the big picture, the better able you will be to do these tasks.

Chapter Resources

Key Terms

- Bibliographic citation software
- Book reviews
- Citation trail
- Impact factor
- Journal (scholarly journal, research journal)
- Literature review
- Original research article (original contribution)
- Review article
- Reviewers (referees)
- Working paper

Exercises

Find a Research Article of Interest

17.1. Think of a topic of interest and search for recent research papers about it using some of the search tools discussed in this chapter. After examining paper titles, authors, and abstracts, pick one of particular interest. Which search methods were most useful? How did the abstract influence which paper you settled on? How did the writing and presentation quality influence your choice? What other factors influenced your choice?

17.2. Using what knowledge you have about libraries and technology in the past, think about what your search experience above would have been like had you been searching in 1980, 1990, and even 2000. It might help to talk with someone who was studying or doing research at the time.

Reviewing the Literature

17.3. Using the article you found in the first exercise (or another journal article of interest to you), read and consider carefully the literature review section(s) of the paper (which may be labeled "Background," "Context," or something similar). These are the section(s) of the article that come after the abstract or introduction but before the methods of the study are described. In the literature review, notice how the author discusses and cites previous studies. Does the author move from more general issues to more narrow, focused research questions? Does the author distinguish empirical findings in the literature from ideas, opinions, or hypotheses? Does the author distinguish evidence of causation in the literature from mere correlation? Does the literature review give you a clear sense of the author's motivation for conducting the study?

17.4. Try your hand at doing a literature review. Begin with a collection of articles or reports on a topic of interest to you. Read the abstracts or executive summaries, and decide which articles are worth reading fully and which are less important (and perhaps only worth skimming). Write a 5- to 7-page (double-spaced) review of this literature that organizes and evaluates the various studies, giving your reader an overview of the main findings as well as gaps or inconsistencies in the literature. Use parenthetical citations with at least one reference to each study (including the lesser studies) and attach a complete reference list.

Parts of a Research Article

17.5. Using a research article that you find, identify the parts of the research article. Are they the same as the standard six parts outlined in this chapter? If not, in what way do they vary? What do you learn from each part about the study?

Tables and Figures

17.6. Find a research article that presents quantitative research in tables and figures. What tables and figures does the paper use? Could they be largely understood on their own? Why or why not? Could the results have been presented more clearly another way?

Writing About Numbers

17.7. Again find and read a research article of interest, one with numerical results. Do you think that the text should have contained more or less discussion of the quantitative results? If there are statistical significance tests, how are the results presented (stars, *p* values, other methods)? Is the practical significance of the results discussed, either explicitly or implicitly?

Publishing Your Research

17.8. Find the website of a journal in your field or practice area that is of interest to you. Look for the editorial aims or mission statement and read the guidelines for submitting to the journal. What would you need to do, or change, about one of your own papers or projects to submit it to the journal?

Student Study Site

Visit the Study Site at **www.sagepub.com/remler2e** to

- test your knowledge with the self-quiz
- check your understanding of key terms with the eFlashcards
- explore helpful resources that relate directly to this chapter

Glossary

Activities: Training, counseling, marketing, and other tasks that make up the work of implementing a program and that are described in implementation-oriented logic models. See also *inputs, outputs,* and *outcomes.*

Adjusted *R*-squared: An adjusted version of *R*-squared that takes into consideration the number of independent variables. Technically, an unbiased estimator of the population *R*-squared—the proportion of the dependent variable variance explained by all the independent variables in the population. See also R-*squared.*

Aggregate data: Data summarized as a mean, proportion, count, or other statistic at a higher unit of analysis, such as a geographic area or institutional unit (such as a school). Also called *ecological data.* Contrasts with *microdata.*

Aggregate matching: A form of matching in which groups (aggregates) of the individuals or cases (the unit of analysis) are matched. Also called *group-level matching.*

Aggregation problem: The fact that relationships that hold at one unit of analysis may not hold at more aggregated levels.

Alternative hypothesis: A negation of the null hypothesis; usually the hypothesis researchers would like to test but cannot do so directly. Contrasts with *null hypothesis.*

Anonymity: When the researchers themselves do not know the identities of people in their study. Contrasts with *confidentiality.*

ANOVA: A statistical analysis that compares the means across groups, normally used in analysis of experimental data.

Antecedent: A variable that causally comes *before* both independent and dependent variables, and thus is viewed as a potential common cause.

Antipositivism: A term applied to social research that rejects the traditional scientific method, empiricism, and the notion of a single knowable reality and instead emphasizes interpretive methods and the socially constructed nature of reality. Contrasts with *positivism.*

Applied research: Pursuit of knowledge to help in some practical problem or need.

Arms of an experiment: The groups in an experiment that are each exposed to different treatments or control conditions.

Attrition: The problem of participants dropping out of a study.

Audit studies: A form of randomized experiment in which matched pairs of race- or gender-discordant auditors apply for a job, a loan, or other services to test for discrimination.

Average treatment effect: The average of the various individual effects that the treatment had on each subject in the experiment.

Bar chart: A graph for displaying categorical data with bars representing each category.

Basic research: Pursuit of basic scientific knowledge that has no immediate practical application.

Bayesian inference: Statistical inference approach that starts with a prior probability about the parameter, which is adjusted based on study data to produce a posterior probability. See also *frequentist inference, posterior probability*, and *prior probability.*

Before-after study: A study that compares outcomes before and after a treatment occurs to determine the treatment's effect. Also called *one-group pretest-posttest* or *pre-post comparison.*

Beneficence: Ethical research norm that dictates that people who participate in research are not harmed and that they should benefit from the research.

Between-subjects experiment: An experiment in which subjects are randomly assigned to groups and remain in the groups, so that the comparison is *between* subjects or units in the groups.

Bias: A systematic error (distortion) in an estimate from a study that can happen in measurement, sampling, causal estimation, or other aspects of the study.

Bias (in a causal estimate): A systematic error (distortion) in the strength or even sign of an estimate of a causal effect.

Bias (in measurement): Systematic error (distortion) in the measurement of some trait or construct. Also called *systematic measurement error.*

Bibliographic citation software: Software that stores all the fields of references, enabling management, easy insertion into articles, and changing of reference format.

Big Data: A general term referring to the gathering, merging, and creative use of very large data sets, often from electronic records or online sources, to solve problems

Blind experiments: Experiments in which subjects do not know if they are in the treatment or control group. See also *double-blind experiments*.

Book reviews: Articles in scholarly journals that review books but do not contain original research and are not peer reviewed.

Bootstrapping: A computer simulation approach to calculate sampling distributions, particularly standard errors, by repeatedly resampling—with replacement—from the original sample itself and calculating the point estimate of interest each time.

Case: An individual, group, or institution that is the focus of qualitative research.

Case (in a case control study): Those with a condition (often rare) in a case-control study.

Case-control study: A study in which individuals who experience an outcome, such as a particular disease or injury (the cases), are compared with other, similar individuals who did not experience this same outcome (the controls).

Case study: Research that focuses on a single complex case, applying multiple qualitative and sometimes quantitative methods.

Categorical variables: Variables that refer to categories and not to actual quantities. Contrasts with *quantitative variables.*

Causal mechanism: A detailed causal process that produces an outcome. Called *mechanism* for short.

Causal relationship: A relationship (correlation or association) due to causation. When one variable changes, another one changes as a consequence. Contrasts with *noncausal relationship.*

Causal research: Research to answer "What if?" questions. Contrasts with *descriptive research.*

Causality: When change in one variable produces change in another variable. Also called *causation*.

Causation: When change in one variable produces change in another variable. Also called *causality*.

Census: Every member of a population. Contrasts with *sample.*

Chi-square test: Statistical test most commonly employed to see if two categorical variables are related.

Citation trail: A method for finding resources on a topic by examining references in a recent research study or overview article, and then tracing references in those studies.

Closed-ended question: Question that may be answered only with a limited set of predetermined response categories. Contrasts with *open-ended question.*

Cluster randomization: Randomization of convenient and natural clusters of individuals (e.g., classrooms) rather than randomization of individuals (e.g., students). See also *random assignment*.

Cluster sampling: A probability sampling method in which more aggregated units (clusters) are sampled before sampling individuals.

Codebook: Documentation that describes the variables in a data set, layout of a data file, and how data were collected, coded, and weighted.

Code-recode reliability: The consistency of coding qualitative data.

Coding: The process of tagging or organizing qualitative data using a system of categories or codes.

Coefficient of the independent variable (in regression): The number that multiplies a given independent variable in a regression. Also known as the slope.

Coefficient of variation: A measure of spread equal to the standard deviation divided by the mean.

Cognitive pretesting: Survey questionnaire development stage in which the wording and meaning of the questionnaire are probed carefully through a process of debriefing respondents right after completing the questionnaire or interview or by having them "talk aloud" as they complete the questionnaire. See also *field pretesting* and *pretesting.*

Cohen's d: The ratio of the effect or difference in means to the standard deviation, a measure of effect size.

Cohort study: Study in which a defined group at a particular time is followed over time. See also *prospective cohort study*.

Common cause: A variable that is a cause of both the presumed dependent variable (or outcome) and the presumed independent variable (or cause).

Comparative case study: A case study with two or more cases that are compared.

Comparison group: Group in a quasi experiment that does not receive the treatment and serves to estimate the counterfactual. Similar to a control group in a randomized experiment.

Complete observer: A researcher in participant observation who attempts to remain unobtrusive and does not interview or engage with people in the setting.

Complete participant: The role of a researcher in a participant observation study involving full or complete participation.

Complex survey sampling: Probability sampling methods that are more complex than simple random sampling, such as cluster sampling, stratified sampling, and disproportionate sampling.

Composite measure: A measure composed of multiple items, such as a scale or an index.

Computer-assisted personal interviewing (CAPI): In-person interviewing done on a computer so that software controls the flow of questions and data are entered in electronic form.

Computer-assisted self-interviewing (CASI): Interview provided to subjects on a computer so that software controls the flow of questions and data are entered in electronic form.

Computer-assisted telephone interviewing (CATI): Telephone interviewing done on a computer so that software controls the flow of questions and data are entered in electronic form.

Conceptualization: Stage in the measurement process in which the construct (or concept) to be measured is carefully and fully defined.

Concurrent validity: The extent to which a measure concurs or agrees with other established classifications or measures taken at the same time.

Confidence interval: A range of values in which we have a defined level of confidence (e.g., 95%) that the true value of the statistic being estimated lies. See also *margin of error.*

Confidentiality: When the identity of people in a study is known to researchers but not revealed in publications or presentations of the study's findings. Contrasts with *anonymity.*

Confirmatory factor analysis: Factor analysis in which theory is used to specify both the number of factors and which variables load onto each factor. Contrasts with *exploratory factor analysis*.

Confounder: A variable that causes (directly or indirectly) both the dependent variable and the independent variable of interest and leads to bias. Also called *lurking variable* or *omitted variable.* See also *common cause*.

Confounding: When the causal relationship is biased due to a common cause that is not accounted for. Also called *omitted variable bias*.

Constant (in regression): The predicted value of the dependent variable when the independent variables are zero in a regression. Also called *intercept*.

Construct: The concept or trait that a measure is trying to capture. Also called *trait*.

Construct validity: The extent to which a measure correlates with other variables or behaves in a statistical model in a way that would be expected, based on theory and prior research.

Contact rate: Share who are reached from those sampled from the sampling frame. See also *cooperation rate* and *response rate.*

Contamination: Something that interferes with the integrity and logic of an experiment, such as when the treatment (or elements of the treatment) is taken up by the control group.

Content analysis: The analysis of the content of qualitative data, such as texts or images, usually involving a process of coding.

Content validity: How well a measure captures all the important dimensions of a construct.

Contextual variables: Higher level or more aggregate variables in a multilevel analysis.

Contingency table: A method to describe the relationship between two categorical variables. Also called *cross-tabulation* or *two-way table*.

Contingent: Limited to certain times, places, or contexts.

Contract research organizations: Organizations (both nonprofit and for-profit) that produce research on a contract basis, often for government.

Control (in a case-control study): Those without a condition, compared with those with a condition, in a case-control study. See also *case-control study.*

Control group: Group that does not receive the treatment being tested in a randomized experiment or sometimes a quasi experiment. See also *comparison group*.

Control variable: A variable representing a common cause that is used to stratify or statistically adjust the data to better estimate a causal effect, often with observational data.

Convenience sample: A nonprobability sample that was chosen for reasons of convenience, such as proximity.

Convergent validity: The extent to which a measure correlates with other closely related measures in the same data set.

Cooperation rate: Share who cooperate with a survey request from among those contacted. See also *contact rate* and *response rate.*

Correlation: A measure of the strength and direction of a relationship between two variables.

Correlation coefficient: The expected standard deviation change in one variable if the other variable changes by one standard deviation. Also called *Pearson r* or simply *r*.

Cost-effectiveness: The outcome obtained by a program relative to its cost.

Counterfactual: The world as it would be without the cause present but everything else the same.

Covariate: A variable that is correlated (covaries) with both x and y and is included in the analysis.

Coverage bias: Bias in a survey that occurs when members of the sampling frame are systematically different from the target population in a way related to the measures.

Criterion-related validity: The extent to which a measure relates, empirically, to various criteria that can demonstrate its validity.

Cronbach's alpha (α): The average of all possible split-half correlations; a measure of the internal consistency of a multi-item scale.

Crossover experiment: An experiment in which subjects get exposed to one condition, then cross over to another condition. See also *within-subjects experiment* and *repeated-measures experiment*.

Cross-sectional data: Measurements of many individuals, organizations, or places at a single point in time.

Cross-sectional variation: Variation across individuals, organizations, or places at a single point in time.

Cross-tabulation: A method to describe the relationship between two categorical variables. Often shortened to *cross-tabs*. Also called *contingency table* or *two-way table.*

Data: Unprocessed or unaggregated observations—raw data.

Data archive: A place where data and related documentation from various surveys and studies are stored and made publicly available for research.

Data cleaning: Process of verifying, correcting, coding, and reformatting data to make them suitable for analysis.

Debriefing: Writing down or recording impressions and ideas, immediately following an interview, focus group, or period of participant observation.

Deduction: A process of scientific reasoning in which theories lead to hypotheses (predictions) that are compared with data (observation).

Dependent variable: The effect, outcome, prediction, or response from a cause or independent variable—the variable the researcher is trying to explain. Contrasts with *independent variable*.

Descriptive research: Research to describe how the world is. Contrasts with *causal research.*

Design effect: The loss of (or gain in) precision due to a particular complex survey sampling design. See also *effective sample size.*

Difference-in-differences study: A study that compares the difference between the before-after differences of a treatment and comparison group. Also called *diff-in-diff* for short. See also *pre-post study with a comparison group.*

Dimension: A facet of a multifaceted construct. Also called *domain.*

Direct effect: When the independent variable influences the dependent variable directly and not through intervening variables. Contrasts with *indirect effect*.

Discriminant validity: Extent to which a measure is independent of (not correlated with) other measures in the same data set that it does not logically relate to.

Disproportionate sampling: A variation on stratified sampling in which some strata are sampled at different rates. Also called *oversampling*.

Distribution: The pattern of values spread out over a variable's categories or numeric range, illustrating which values are taken on and how often.

Domain: A facet of a multifaceted construct. Also called *dimension*.

Dose-response relationship: A relationship describing how the effect of the experiment varies as the dosage of the treatment increases.

Double-blind experiment: An experiment in which both the subjects and the research workers who interact with the subjects, or make measurements, do not know who was assigned to the treatment or control groups. See also *blind experiment*.

Dummy variables: Categorical variables that have only two values, 0 and 1, where 1 indicates being in the category named by the variable and 0 indicates not being in it. Also called *indicator variables*.

Ecological data: Data summarized as a mean, proportion, count, or other statistic at a higher unit of analysis, such as a geographic area or institutional unit (such as a school). Also called *aggregated data*. Contrasts with *microdata*.

Ecological fallacy: A directional relationship that appears at an aggregated level but does not exist, or has the reverse sign, at the individual level.

Effect coding: Coding a set of dummy variables for a multicategory independent variable so that the regression coefficients are differences relative to the grand mean (the mean of the means of each category).

Effect size: A standardized way of measuring the effect of a treatment, usually the ratio of the effect or difference to the standard deviation.

Effective sample size: The comparable sample size from a simple random sample; it expresses the design effect (often a loss) due to complex sampling. See also *design effect*.

Endogeneity: A phenomenon that occurs when the independent variable is caused by variables or processes that also affect the dependent variable—or by the dependent variable itself. Contrasts with *exogeneity*.

Endogenous: A condition of the independent variable of interest that occurs when it is caused by variables or processes that also affect the dependent variable—or by the dependent variable itself. Contrasts with *exogenous*.

Epistemology: Theory of knowledge, or ways of knowing.

Establishment survey: A survey that aims to measure the characteristics of organizations, not individuals.

Ethnography: Qualitative research method to describe and understand the culture of a group of people, often using participant observation.

Evaluation research: Research to determine the impact of a program or intervention.

Exempt review: Research that poses only minimal risk to human subjects and meets certain requirements, so that it receives a more limited review by an IRB. Contrasts with *expedited review* and *full IRB review*.

Exogeneity: A phenomenon that occurs when the independent variable of interest is not caused by variables or processes that also affect the dependent variable—or by the dependent variable itself. Contrasts with *endogeneity*.

Exogenous: A condition of the independent variable of interest when it is not caused by variables or processes that also affect the dependent variable—or by the dependent variable itself. Contrasts with *endogeneous*.

Expedited review: Research that poses minimal risks to human subjects but does not meet the requirements for exempt review. Contrasts with *exempt review* and *full IRB review*.

Experimental control: Holding constant factors that could affect an outcome.

Experimental subjects (units): The people or other units that participate in an experiment.

Experimentation: The act of manipulating a treatment (presumed cause) to observe an effect—a causal effect. Contrasts with *observational study*.

Exploratory factor analysis: Factor analysis in which the number of factors and how items correlate with factors are discovered by the procedure rather than specified in advance by the researcher. Contrasts with *confirmatory factor analysis*.

External validity: The extent to which the results generalize to a wider group or reality, external to the study. Also called *generalizability*.

Extraneous variable: A variable that is extraneous (not of substantive interest) to the investigation of the relationship between independent and dependent variables, but nevertheless needs to be taken into account in order to reduce bias. See also *control variable.*

Face validity: On the face of it, how well a measure captures what it is supposed to measure—the extent to which a measure makes intuitive sense.

Factor analysis: Multivariate method that groups many variables (indicators) into a smaller set of clusters or underlying factors. See also *confirmatory factor analysis* and *exploratory factor analysis*.

Factor loadings: Correlations between the observed variables and the underlying and unobserved factors. See also *factor analysis*.

Factorial design: Experimental design that allows for the estimation of two or more treatment effects, along with interaction effects, through arms representing all possible combinations of treatments.

Factorial experiment: An experiment that examines the effect of two or more treatments, called *factors*, and how they interact with one another.

Factors (in an experiment): The independent variables tested in an experiment, which can have main effects as well as interaction effects.

Field experiment: An experiment that takes place in the real world or in a real social setting, rather than in a lab.

Field pretesting: Survey development stage in which the complete survey procedures—the contact procedures, the questionnaire or interview, the technology, and any follow-up procedures—are tested on a small sample of the population. See also *cognitive pretesting* and *pretesting*.

Flat file: Two-dimensional data structure generally used by statistical software with variables represented in columns and rows representing the unit of analysis.

Focus group: A qualitative group interviewing procedure that involves typically 6 to 12 participants, seated around a table, and a moderator who asks questions and guides the discussion.

Forecasting: Using data from time series in the past to predict future values of the dependent variable(s).

Frequency distribution: The distribution of a categorical variable showing the count or percentage in each category.

Frequentist inference: The most common approach to inference, it views each study as one realization of a sampling process from a great many possible samples that could have been drawn. Contrasts with *Bayesian inference*.

Full IRB review: Research that poses more than minimal risk to human subjects and receives the full level of IRB scrutiny. Contrasts with *exempt review* and *expedited review*.

General equilibrium effects: Long-run effects of policy changes that include the reactions by all relevant parties as they respond to the policy, and to each other, over time.

Generalizability: The extent to which the results of a study project to a wider group or context of interest. Also called *external validity.*

Grand theory: Comprehensive theory or framework covering all aspects of the human experience. Also called *theoretical paradigm*. Contrasts with *middle-range theory*.

Grant: Funding to perform a research study or related studies.

Grounded theory: A theory that emerges from observations made in a qualitative study and is grounded in the specific setting.

Group-level matching: A form of matching in which groups (aggregates) of the individuals or cases (the unit of analysis) are matched. Also called *aggregate matching*.

Group self-administered surveys: Mode of survey research in which self-administered questionnaires are distributed in group settings.

Haphazard randomization: An informal procedure that mimics true random assignment.

Hawthorne effect: How people in a study change their behavior when they know they are being studied or observed.

Hermeneutics: A method of interpretation applied to texts and other qualitative data.

Heterogeneous treatment effects: Treatment effects that vary systematically with the characteristics of individuals.

Hierarchical data: Data that combine variables with different units of analysis. Also called *multilevel data.*

Hierarchical models: Models that describe relationships between variables at different units of analysis. Also called *multilevel models*.

Histogram: A graph showing the distribution of a quantitative variable.

Household interview survey: Survey conducted by visiting and interviewing people in their homes.

Human research subject: A living human being about whom a researcher obtains private identifiable information or about whom a researcher obtains information through intervention or interaction.

Hypothesis: A prediction of what will happen if a theory is correct.

Hypothesis test: A test to see if a result is unlikely to be due to chance. Used to test whether relationships or group differences are statistically significant. Also called *significance test*.

Impact factor: The average number of recent citations in a journal's articles, a measure of a journal's prestige.

Incidence: The rate at which new cases of a disease or condition appear in a population.

Independent variable: The variable whose effect is of interest—the cause, the explanatory variable, the treatment, or the predictor. Contrasts with *dependent variable*.

Index: A composite measure composed of multiple items, which may be selected for different reasons.

Indicator: Some observable measure that reveals information about a factor or latent trait.

Indicator variables: Categorical variables that have only two values, 0 and 1, where 1 indicates being in the category named by the variable and 0 indicates not being in it. Also called *dummy variables*.

Indirect effect: When the independent variable influences the dependent variable through its causal effect on one or more intervening variables. Contrasts with *direct effect*.

Individual-level matching: A form of matching in which individuals or cases, the unit of analysis, are matched.

Induction: A process of scientific reasoning in which systematic observation leads to the development of theory and hypotheses.

Inference: Using samples to learn about the population, or using evidence to identify a causal relationship.

Informed consent: Research subjects being fully informed about the research, including risks and benefits and voluntarily consenting to participate.

Inputs: The financial, human, and material resources required by the program described in more implementation-oriented logic models. See *also activities, outputs,* and *outcomes*.

Institutional review board (IRB): Board that reviews research in the United States to ensure that it meets the required ethical guidelines.

Instrument (of instrumental variables): A variable that causes the independent variable to change but does not affect the outcome in any way, other than through the independent variable. See also *instrumental variables (IV) study*.

Instrument (of measurement): A tool that helps measure something, such as a survey instrument.

Instrument bias: Refers to results that are inaccurate or distorted by a faulty or uncalibrated scientific or other instrument.

Instrumental variables (IV) study: A method that estimates a causal effect through the use of a variable that causes the independent variable to change but does not affect the outcome in any way, other than through the independent variable. See also *instrument (of instrumental variables)*.

Intent to treat (ITT): Analysis of randomized experiments in which everyone is kept in their original randomized group—treatment or control—irrespective of compliance or attrition. Contrasts with *treatment of the treated (TOT)*.

Interaction effect: An effect of both factors together that is more (or less) than the sum of the two main effects. See also *moderator variable*.

Interaction variable: A variable defined as the product of two other variables, usually used to empirically measure an interaction. See also *moderator variable*.

Intercept interview survey: Mode of survey research in which people are stopped (intercepted) in public places and asked questions.

Intercoder reliability: The consistency with which codes are applied to qualitative data.

Internal consistency: Refers to the intercorrelation of the items or indicators of a multi-item scale. See also *Cronbach's alpha* and *split-half reliability*.

Internal validity: Strength of causal evidence provided by a study.

Internet access panel: An opt-in e-mail list of people recruited to participate in online research.

Internet survey: Mode of survey research that uses web-based forms or questionnaires to gather responses. Also called *online survey* or *web survey*.

Interpretivism: Approach to social research and theory that focuses on the interpretation of the meanings and intentionality of human action, rather than deterministic explanations. See also *antipositivism*.

Interrater reliability: How similar the scores of different raters or interviewers are when they measure the same person or object.

Interrupted time series: A study that uses a series of periodic measurements interrupted by an event or treatment.

Intersubjectivity: The notion that language allows us to stand in someone else's shoes and see the world from the other's perspective.

Interval measure: A quantitative measure in which the size of a difference—an interval—has meaning, but there is no meaningful zero. Contrasts with *ratio measure*.

Intervening variable: A variable along a causal pathway. Also called *mediator*.

Intervention: An action taken to try to make something happen in the world, rather than just watch it happen, and thus to probe for causation. See also *treatment*.

Interview guide: A set of open-ended questions, sometimes accompanied by probes, that help guide or structure the discussion in a semistructured interview.

Interviewer effects: When responses to an interview are influenced by the interviewer's gender, ethnicity, age, and other characteristics.

Interviewer or observer bias: Distortions or systematic bias attributable to the particular interviewer or observer who is collecting the data.

Intraclass correlation: Similarity of elements within a cluster. Also referred to as *rho*—the rate of homogeneity.

Item: A variable that comes from a single question on a questionnaire or test. See also *indicator*.

Item response theory: An approach to trait measurement based on the idea that responses to items depend on both difficulty and trait strength.

Journal: Publications, published periodically, that contain research and scholarship, usually peer reviewed. Also called *research journal* or *scholarly journal*.

Justice (in research ethics): Requires consideration of equity among subjects and fairness in regard to who in society becomes a research subject.

Lab experiment: An experiment that takes place in a specialized facility or location, rather than in the real world. Contrasts with *field experiment*.

Latent construct: A construct or trait that is not directly observable. Contrasts with *manifest construct*.

Layered cross-tabs: Separate cross-tabs stratified (layered) with a categorical control variable.

Level of confidence: The area—usually 95%—of the sampling distribution that is the basis for a *confidence interval*.

Level of measurement: The distinction between quantitative and categorical variables, or "ladder of measurement": nominal, ordinal, interval, and ratio.

Likert response format: Possible responses to a statement to which respondents are asked the extent to which they agree or disagree.

Likert scale: A composite measure (named after the psychometrician Rensis Likert, who introduced this response format) made up of multiple items, using an agree-disagree response format.

Limited dependent variable: A dependent variable that is truncated or constrained in terms of the values it can take on.

Linear probability model: Ordinary least squares regression model in which the dependent variable is a dummy variable and predicted values of the dependent variable are interpreted as probabilities.

Literature review: An article or portion of an article that summarizes and assesses the published research on a topic.

Logic model: Model (usually a diagram) that communicates the underlying theory or mechanism of how a program will work. See also *path model*.

Logistic (logit) regression: Regression model used to predict a dichotomous (dummy) dependent variable, from one or more independent variables, in which the estimation is based on a logistic function. Can be used to estimate log odds. See also *probit regression*.

Longitudinal data: Data gathered over time.

Longitudinal variation: Variation over time.

Lurking variable: A variable that lurks (unseen) in the background and thus potentially biases the estimated causal relationship between x and y. Also called *confounder*, *omitted variable*.

Mail self-administered survey: Mode of survey research in which forms are mailed to respondents along with instructions to complete and return the forms.

Main effect: The average effect of one factor across all levels of the other factors in an experiment. See also *simple main effect*.

Manifest construct: A construct or trait that is directly observable. Contrasts with *latent construct*.

Marginal effect: The predicted difference in the probability due to a specified change in the relevant independent variable.

Margin of error: The amount added to the point estimate in both directions to create the confidence interval. See also *confidence interval*.

Matching: A study in which individuals in the comparison group are chosen so that the values of their matching variables are as close as possible to those in the treatment group.

Mean: The average of a quantitative variable—the sum of all observations divided by the number of observations.

Measure: The score or result produced by a measurement process.

Measurement: The process of systematically observing some feature or characteristic of the world and then recording it in the form of a number or category.

Measurement error: Errors in a measure or how it differs from the true construct to be measured. Consists of noise and bias.

Mechanism: Detailed causal process that produces an outcome. Also called *causal mechanism*.

Median: The value at the point that splits the distribution into two halves, the 50th percentile in the distribution of a quantitative variable.

Mediator: A variable along a causal pathway. Also called an *intervening variable*.

Meta-analysis: A method for pooling together multiple smaller studies to get a much bigger, combined study.

Metadata: Data providing information about the data.

Microdata: Data at its most basic level of observation—or unit of analysis—often of individual people or households. Contrasts with *aggregate data* and *ecological data*.

Middle-range theory: A logical description of how a particular corner or aspect of the world works. Contrasts with *grand theory*.

Minimal detectable effect: The smallest effect that would still have statistical significance in a study with a particular sample size and design, often chosen to perform sample size calculations.

Mixed-method study: Research approach that combines both quantitative and qualitative research techniques.

Mixed-mode survey: Survey using more than one mode of data collection.

Model: A diagram or equation or other representation that serves to articulate and communicate a theory.

Moderator (of a focus group): The person who guides a focus group. Also called a facilitator.

Moderator variable: A variable that changes the magnitude of the effect of another variable. See also *interaction*.

Moderator's guide: A script for the facilitator or moderator of a focus group, containing open-ended questions and sometimes accompanied by probes, that helps guide or structure the discussion.

Modifiable variable: An independent variable of interest that can be changed, or influenced, by policy or practice. Contrasts with *nonmodifiable variable*.

Multicollinearity: Phenomenon in which an independent variable is a linear combination of two more of the other independent variables.

Multilevel data: Data that combine variables with different units of analysis. Also called *hierarchical data*.

Multilevel models: Models that describe relationships between variables at different units of analysis. Also called *hierarchical models*.

Multiple comparison correction: Correction applied to a statistical significance test when it is one of many statistical tests carried out in the same study, because one of the many tests could be significant by chance.

Multiple regression: The best linear predictor of a dependent variable using more than one independent variable. Contrasts with *simple regression*. See also *regression*.

Multistage sampling: A probability sampling method in which more aggregated units (clusters) are sampled and then sampling occurs within the aggregates.

Multivariate statistics: Statistics examining the relationships between multiple (more than two) variables at the same time.

Mystery shopping method: Participant observation method in which a researcher plays the role of a customer to experience service quality.

Natural experiment: Situation in which the treatment (the independent variable of interest) varies through some naturally occurring or unplanned event that happens to be exogenous to the outcome (the dependent variable of interest).

Negative (−) relationship: Relationship in which the two related variables move in the opposite direction. Contrasts with *positive relationship*.

Noise: Errors—deviations from the true construct in a measure—that are not systematic and average out to zero. Also called *random measurement error.* Contrasts with *bias, systematic measurement error*.

Nominal categorical variables: Categorical variables that have no intrinsic order. Contrasts with *ordinal categorical variables*.

Nomological validity: The extent to which a measure behaves as it should in a system or network of other variables.

Noncausal relationship: A relationship (correlation or association) between two variables in which neither is a direct cause of the other. Contrasts with *causal relationship*. See also *spurious relationship*.

Noncompliance: Subjects in an experiment who do not take or follow the treatment.

Nonidentifiable: Not containing information that identifies who an individual is or enables identification through indirect means.

Nonmodifiable variable: An independent variable of interest that cannot be changed or influenced by policy or practice. Contrasts with *modifiable variable*.

Nonreactive measures: Measures that occur naturally or routinely or otherwise do not disturb the subjects in an experiment. Also called *unobtrusive measures.*

Nonresponse bias: Bias in survey results that occurs when those who do not respond are systematically different from those who do respond in a way related to what the survey aims to measure.

Normal distribution: A theoretical distribution that is bell-shaped and symmetrical, and that has many useful properties in statistics.

Normative (statement or theory): A statement or theory that describes how things should be. Contrasts with *positive*.

Null hypothesis: In hypothesis testing, the hypothesis that is directly tested, typically resulting in no difference or no effect. Contrasts with *alternative hypothesis*.

Observational study: Study in which researchers do not attempt to change or manipulate variables to test their effects; they simply observe or measure things as they are in the natural, unaltered world. Contrasts with *experimentation*.

Observer as participant: Researcher in participant observation who visits the setting, typically only on one or just a few occasions, to conduct interviews with people and make observations.

Odds: For an outcome that has only two possibilities, the ratio of one outcome (e.g., success) to the other possible outcome (e.g., failure).

Odds ratio (OR): Ratio of the odds of an outcome for one group to the odds of the outcome for another group.

Omitted variable: A variable, often an unmeasured variable, not used as a control, in a control variable study, whose omission causes a biased estimate of a causal effect. Also called *confounder, lurking variable*. See also *omitted variable bias*.

Omitted variable bias: When the causal relationship is biased due to a common cause, including a complex common cause, that is not accounted for. Also called *confounding*.

***One-group pretest-posttest*:** A study that compares outcomes before and after a treatment occurs to determine the treatment's effect. Also called *before-after study, pre-post comparison*.

Online data analysis tool: Software that allows users to directly analyze public data on the web.

Online survey: Mode of survey research that uses web-based forms or questionnaires to gather responses. Also called *Internet survey* or *web survey.*

Open-ended question: A question that cannot be answered with a limited set of possible answers and gives the person answering the opportunity to choose what information to provide. Contrasts with *closed-ended question.*

Operationalization: The process of devising or identifying an empirical measure.

Ordinal categorical variables: Categorical variables that can be put in a meaningful order. Contrasts with *nominal categorical variables*.

Original contribution: Report of primary research, published in a scholarly journal. Also called *original research article*. Contrasts with *review article*.

Original research article: Report of primary research, published in a scholarly journal. Also called *original contribution*. Contrasts with *review article*.

Outcome: The response of interest to a program. See also *activities, inputs, outputs*, and *dependent variable*.

Outliers: Extreme scores or observations that stand out in a distribution.

Outputs: Immediate products of activities, such as people trained, brochures distributed, or citations issued, described in implementation-oriented logic models. See also *activities, inputs*, and *outcomes*.

Out-of-sample extrapolation: Making a prediction using a fitted model (particularly regression) far from the data used to fit the model.

Oversampling: A variation on stratified sampling in which some strata are sampled with probability greater than their population share. Also called *disproportionate sampling*.

***p* value:** The probability of observing our sample estimate (or one more extreme) if the null hypothesis about the population is true. See also *statistical significance*.

Panel data: Repeated measures on the same individuals (or group or entity) over time.

Panel survey: Survey in which the same respondents are tracked and repeatedly surveyed over time, sometimes over many years. See *panel data*.

Parallel forms reliability: The extent to which two forms of a test or measure are really the same.

Parameter: The characteristic or feature of a population that a researcher is trying to estimate.

Participant as observer: A researcher in a participant observation who spends significant time in the setting, joining in important activities or events, but does not assume an actual role as such.

Participant observation: A qualitative research method in which the researcher participates in and observes his or her subjects.

Path analysis: Method that estimates the pattern of relationships between variables in a presumed causal structure.

Path diagram: A diagram showing causal relationships (represented by arrows) between variables (represented by circles). Also called *path model*.

Path model: A model showing causal relationships between variables. Also called *path diagram*.

Pearson *r*: The expected standard deviation change in one variable if the other variable changes by one standard deviation. It is the most common measure of correlation. Also called the *correlation coefficient*.

Peer review: Process in which studies or proposals are reviewed and approved (or rejected) by a group of peers—other researchers in the same field—who render a judgment on the methodology and worth of the paper or proposal.

Percent change: Change relative to the starting base, expressed as percentage. Contrasts with *percentage point change*.

Percentage point change: The change of a variable measured in its own units when it is a percentage. Contrasts with *percent change*.

Performance measurement: The process in which an organization collects information to measure and report on how well it is doing, usually with the goal of managing to improve its performance.

Phenomenology: Philosophy that prioritizes subjective experience and seeks to carefully describe and explain the structure and flow of consciousness.

Pie chart: A graph showing percentages among categories, shown as segments of a circle.

Placebo: A false or ineffective treatment used with the control group in an experiment, usually to blind participants as to whether they are getting the treatment or not.

Placebo effect: The fact that people often respond to any kind of treatment, even a completely phony or useless one.

Point estimate: The statistic calculated from the sample that is inferred to be the best guess as to the value of the parameter (the truth about the population).

Pooled cross sections: Repeated independent cross sections over time.

Population of interest: The population the study aims to investigate. Also called *universe*.

Positive (statement or theory): A statement or theory that describes how things really are. Contrasts with *normative*.

Positive (+) relationship: Relationship in which the two related variables move in the same direction. Contrasts with *negative relationship*.

Positivism. A term generally applied to social research that patterns itself after the traditional scientific method of the natural sciences, and more narrowly a movement in science that argues for a strict form of empiricism (such as behaviorism in psychology).

Poster presentation: Method of presenting a research study on a large poster board, used at conferences.

Posterior probability: Conclusions about a parameter from analyzing a study's data using Bayesian inference methods, an update to the prior probability. See also *Bayesian inference* and *prior probability*.

Poststratification adjustment: Adjustment of sample statistics to ensure that each stratum's share of the sample represents its share in the population. Used to correct samples that do not reflect the characteristics of the population. Also called *poststratification weighting*.

Poststratification weighting: Adjustment of sample statistics to ensure that each stratum's share of the sample represents its share in the population. Used to correct samples that do not reflect the characteristics of the population. Also called *poststratification adjustment*.

Posttest: Outcome measured after the intervention. Contrasts with *pretest*.

Power: In statistics, the ability to recognize that the null hypothesis is false; related to sample size.

Practical significance: The extent to which an effect or relationship's magnitude (if true) would be important or relevant in the real world.

Precision: Refers to the amount of random variability in the results of a sample (the less variability, the more precision). See also *sampling variability.*

Predictive validity: The extent to which a measure predicts logically related outcomes or behaviors in the future.

Pre-post comparison: A study that compares outcomes before and after a treatment occurs to determine the treatment's effect. Also called *before-after study, one-group pretest-posttest*.

Pre-post study with a comparison group: A study that compares the difference between the before-after differences of a treatment and comparison group. See also *difference-in-differences study*.

Pretest: A measure of the outcome variable, such as a test score, taken at baseline or prior to a treatment or intervention. Contrasts with *posttest*.

Pretesting: A measure of the outcome (dependent variable of a study) before the study intervention occurs. See also *cognitive pretesting* and *field pretesting.*

Prevalence: The number or share of the population that has a particular disease or condition.

Primary data: Collecting new data to provide a description or explanation of the world. Contrasts with *secondary data*.

Primary research: The original collection or analysis of data to answer a new research question or to produce new knowledge.

Principal investigator: The lead person responsible for a study; the person responsible for overseeing a grant when research is funded by a grant.

Prior probability: Guess about a parameter prior to analyzing a study's data, used in Bayesian inference, and often in the form of a distribution. See also *Bayesian inference* and *posterior probability*.

Probability proportional to size (PPS) sampling: Sampling in which elements, such as businesses or communities, are selected with a probability proportional to their size.

Probability sampling: A method of sampling that uses chance to select people (or elements) from a population. Also called *random sampling.*

Probit regression: Regression model used to predict a dichotomous (dummy) dependent variable, from one or more independent variables, in which the estimation is based on a cumulative normal distribution. See also *logistic (logit) regression.*

Proceedings: Publication in a scholarly journal of studies presented at a conference.

Propensity score matching: A matching method that employs multivariate statistics to match along many variables at the same time.

Propensity to respond: Likelihood of responding to a survey or survey question.

Prospective cohort: Group of study subjects followed longitudinally over time. See also *panel study*.

Prospective study: Study in which researchers look ahead—they decide to do the study in advance and then track and measure subjects over time. See *prospective cohort*. Contrasts with *retrospective study*.

Protocols: Carefully specified procedures for using the instruments properly in measurement.

Proxy: A measure that substitutes for another unavailable measure.

Proxy reporting: Situation in a survey in which a person who responds provides information about someone else.

Proxy respondent: A person who responds to a survey providing information about someone else.

Psychometrics: The field that deals with the measurement of latent traits or constructs, primarily using instruments such as scales or tests composed of multiple items or questions, and related statistical techniques.

Public use microdata: Individual-level data collected and made available to the public.

Purposive sampling: Subjects or cases of research are chosen for a purpose, not to provide a sample that is representative of a population, for qualitative research. See also *theoretical sampling*.

Qualitative data: The raw data from qualitative research, which can take the form of field notes, interview transcriptions, video or audio recordings, or documents, among others.

Qualitative data analysis: The organization and interpretation of qualitative data, which may or may not be aided with software.

Qualitative research: Research that involves language, images, and other forms of expressing meaning that researchers then interpret—research that does not involve numbers or quantification.

Quantiles: Points taken at regular intervals (such as every quarter or tenth) in a distribution.

Quantitative data: Information that is recorded, coded, and stored in numerical form.

Quantitative research: Any research involving the statistical analysis of quantitative data—including both quantitative and categorical variables.

Quantitative variables: Variables that take the form of numbers that refer to actual quantities of something. Contrasts with *categorical variables*.

Quasi experiment: A study of a planned or intentional treatment that resembles a randomized field experiment but lacks full random assignment.

Question order bias: Responses influenced by the form or content of preceding questions.

Question wording bias: Responses that are distorted by how the question is worded.

Quota sampling: A nonprobability sampling approach in which people (or units) are recruited to fill quotas that match known demographic or other subgroups of the population.

Random assignment: A procedure in which the one who receives the treatment under investigation and the one who is in the control group are determined randomly. See also *random experiment*.

Random digit dialing (RDD): A telephone survey method that gives both listed and unlisted numbers an equal chance of being selected by replacing random digits at the ends of listed residential telephone numbers.

Random measurement error: Errors—deviations from the true construct in a measure—that are not systematic and average out to zero. Also called *noise*. Contrasts with *bias, systematic measurement error*.

Random sampling: A method of sampling that uses chance to select people (or elements) from a population. Also called *probability sampling*.

Randomization: A procedure in which the one who receives the treatment under investigation and the one who is in the control group are determined randomly. Also known as *random assignment*.

Randomized clinical trial: A randomized experiment of medical treatment, including drugs. See also *randomized controlled trial (RCT)* and *randomized experiment*.

Randomized controlled trial (RCT): Experiment in which subjects are randomly assigned to conditions (or treatments) in order to test causal relationships. Also called *randomized experiment*.

Randomized experiment: Experiment in which subjects are randomly assigned to conditions (or treatments) to test for causal relationships. Also called *randomized controlled trial (RCT)*.

Randomized field experiment: A randomized experiment conducted in an actual social or policy setting—the field.

Rate: The share of a population with a particular characteristic, which is expressed relative to some base size population. See also *risk*.

Rate of change: How rapidly a variable changes.

Ratio measure: A quantitative measure in which there is a meaningful zero and the size of a difference, an interval, has meaning. Contrasts with *interval measure*.

Referee: Expert on the topic of a research article submitted to a peer-reviewed journal, who carefully evaluates the quality and importance of the research. Also known as a *reviewer*.

Regression: Any method for predicting a dependent variable with one or more independent variables, including simple and multiple regression, as well as more advanced models. See also *simple regression, multiple regression*.

Regression discontinuity: A regression analysis study in which the assignment to treatment is based on a cut point for a single quantitative assignment variable.

Relational database: Database structure composed of various tables of information that are linked and work together.

Relationship: How two different variables covary or are related. See also *correlation*.

Relative risk: Ratio of the risk of two groups.

Reliability: Consistency of a measure.

Repeated-measures experiment: An experiment used for observational studies that take repeated measures of the same individuals over time. Also called *within-subjects experiment*. See also *crossover experiment*.

Replication: Repeating a study with a different sample; in a different place, time period, or policy context; or with a different study design.

Requests for proposals (RFPs): Notices distributed by government agencies, foundations, or other funders providing notification of and describing research they wish to commission or support.

Research journal: Publications, published periodically, which contain research and scholarship, usually peer reviewed. Also called *journal, scholarly journal*.

Research methods: Techniques and procedures that produce research evidence.

Research personnel: The technicians, interviewers, trained observers, and other personnel who implement research protocols.

Research question: The practical or theoretical question that motivated a researcher to do a study.

Residual: The error in a regression—the difference between the actual value of the dependent variable and the predicted value.

Respect for persons (in research ethics): Dictates that people used as the subjects of research provide informed consent and are not coerced into participating in research.

Respondent-driven sampling: Method of sampling based on respondent contacts, like snowball sampling, but with a statistical foundation. See also *snowball sampling*.

Response bias: A broad term that refers to various ways in which respondents alter their answers because of the format or context of the study.

Response format: The categories or range people are given in order to register their response to a question or statement.

Response rate: Share who respond to a survey from among those sampled from a sampling frame. See also *contact rate* and *cooperation rate*.

Retrospective study: Study in which researchers look back—they find subjects and gather data about past events. Contrasts with *prospective study*.

Reverse causation: A situation when the presumed dependent variable (or outcome) is actually the cause of the presumed independent variable (or cause).

Review article: A type of article in a scholarly journal that discusses many research studies, synthesizing the results and reaching broader conclusions. Contrasts with *original research article*.

Reviewer: Expert on the topic of a research article submitted to a peer-reviewed journal, who carefully evaluates the quality and importance of the research. Also called a *referee*.

Risk: The share of a population with a particular condition or disease, which is expressed relative to some base size population. See also *rate*.

Robustness: When multiple models and varying assumptions produce consistent results.

***R*-squared:** In a regression, the proportion of the variation in the dependent variable predicted by variation in the independent variables.

Sample: A subset of people or elements selected from a population. Contrasts with *census*.

Sample size calculation: A calculation done before a study or survey to determine the sample size needed to get a certain level of precision or to be able to detect certain differences.

Sampling: Process of selecting people or elements from a population for inclusion in a research study.

Sampling bias: When results of a study differ systematically from the population because of shortcomings in the sampling process. See also *coverage bias* and *nonresponse bias*.

Sampling distribution: The distribution of statistics estimated from many repeated samples.

Sampling error: Error in sample statistics due to random chance of who ends up in a sample. See also *sampling variability*.

Sampling frame: A list, map, or other representation of a population used for purposes of drawing a sample.

Sampling variability: Variability in sample statistics, across different samples, due to random chance of who ends up in a sample. See also *sampling error*.

Saturation: The point in the process of collecting qualitative data when few new issues or questions arise that have not already been discovered.

Scale: A composite measure composed of multiple items and thought to reflect a single latent construct.

Scatterplot: A graph illustrating the values two quantitative variables take on in data.

Scholarly journal: Publications, published periodically, that contain research and scholarship, usually peer reviewed. Also called *journal, research journal*.

Scientific method: A way of knowing that is based on systematic observation, logical explanation, prediction, openness, and skepticism.

Scientific realism: A view of social science that favors empiricism and applying the scientific method to social phenomena, based on the view that the social world is part of an objective and comprehensible reality.

Secondary data: Data collected by others, such as existing government surveys, administrative records, or transcripts. Contrasts with *primary data*.

Secondary research: The search for published sources describing the results of research or information provided by others.

Secret (or mystery) shopping method: A participant observation method in which a researcher plays the role of a customer to experience service quality.

Self-reporting: When survey respondents are asked to report their own behaviors or characteristics.

Self-selection: A phenomenon occurring when the individuals studied, or someone acting on their behalf, choose their category or level of the independent variable of interest.

Semistructured interview: A qualitative research method that involves interviewing with an interview guide, including a planned set of open-ended questions.

Significance level: The cutoff to which the *p* value of a statistical significance test is compared, to determine statistical significance, often set at .05.

Significance test: A test to see if a result is unlikely to be due to chance. Used to test whether relationships or group differences are statistically significant. Also called *hypothesis test*.

Simple main effect: The effect of an independent variable on a dependent variable, before or without its moderation by another variable (interaction).

Simple random sampling: Selecting of people (or elements) from a population in such a way that each individual has an equal chance, or probability, of selection.

Simple regression: A best-fit straight line for describing how one quantitative variable—the independent variable—predicts another quantitative variable—the dependent variable. Contrasts with *multiple regression*. See also *regression*.

Simultaneity bias: Bias in an estimate of a causal effect due to reverse causation.

Skewness: Characteristic of a distribution that is not symmetrical and has one tail longer than the other.

Snowball sampling: Method of sampling or finding study subjects in which interviewees are asked to refer people they know to the researcher for inclusion in the sample. See also *respondent-driven sampling*.

Social desirability bias: The tendency of respondents to a survey or interview to provide answers that make themselves look good or that are socially acceptable.

Specifications: Different versions of a multiple regression analysis with the same (or related) dependent variable and independent variable of interest but different control variables or functional forms.

Split-ballot survey: Survey experiments designed to test different versions of a question or questionnaire. Also called *survey experiment*.

Split-half reliability: A measure of reliability of a composite measure such as a scale based on dividing the items randomly into two halves and then looking at the correlation between the two halves.

Spurious relationship: When two correlated variables are presumed to be causally related but in fact are not and the correlation is entirely due to a common cause.

Standard deviation: Common measure of variability of a quantitative variable.

Standard error: The precision of the estimate—how good a job we expect it to do, on average.

Standardized score: A variable converted to standard deviation units and shifted to mean zero. Also called a *z* score.

Statistical control: Statistical method of analyzing data, usually to estimate a causal effect, that involves holding variables constant in the analysis, often using multiple regression.

Statistical equivalence: The result of random assignment, it refers to the fact that the treatment and control groups are equivalent, *on average*, on both measured and unmeasured variables.

Statistical inference: Formal procedure that uses facts about the sampling distribution of statistics from a sample to infer the unknown parameters of a population.

Statistical significance: The extent to which a difference or a relationship exists, judged against the likelihood that it would happen just by chance alone. See also *p value*.

Strata: Exhaustive and mutually exclusive subgroups of a target population. See also *stratified sampling*.

Stratification: Breaking the data into exhaustive and mutually exclusive groups, sometimes as an approach to implementing control variables, also called conditioning in that context. See also *strata*.

Stratified sampling: Probability sampling method in which a sample is drawn separately from each group—each stratum—and the population is divided into exhaustive and mutually exclusive strata. See also *strata*.

Stratify: To break the data into exhaustive and mutually exclusive groups. See also *strata*.

Structural equation modeling (SEM): Multivariate method for estimating models in which observed indicators represent latent variables and also latent variables are related to each other in a presumed causal (structural) manner similar to path analysis.

Structuralists: Researchers who insist that social research start with strong theories and test these with empirical predictions (deduction).

Student* t *distribution: A probability distribution with thicker tails than the normal (*Z*) distribution and used for many statistical tests, especially with small samples. Also called t *distribution*.

Subject: The units, such as individuals or families, studied in an experiment. See also *experimental unit*.

Survey: A method of gathering primary data by asking structured questions of respondents.

Survey experiment: An experiment that is embedded in the design of a survey questionnaire, often used to test variations in question wording or other information. Also called *split-ballot survey*.

Survey mode: The method or modality used to administer the questionnaire and collect the survey data, such as telephone, mail, or Internet.

Survival analysis: Method to predict the length of time until some event.

Systematic measurement error: Errors—or deviations from the true construct—in a measure that are systematic and do not average out to zero. Also called *bias*. Contrasts with *noise*, *random measurement error*.

Systematic sampling: Probability sampling method in which individuals or elements are sampled at even intervals—every *k*th individual for some integer *k*.

Tailored design method (TDM): Method for conducting self-administered mail surveys, which emphasizes the importance of all components of the mail survey, including the initial contacting materials, the survey layout and design, the timing and tone of the follow-up requests, and the use of multiple contacts and modes of communication.

t distribution: A probability distribution with thicker tails than the normal (*Z*) distribution and used for many statistical tests, especially with small samples. Also called *student* t *distribution*.

Telephone interview survey: Survey conducted by telephone, usually based on random digit dialing.

Test-retest reliability: An approach to determining reliability based on measuring the same thing twice.

Test statistic: A statistic used for significance testing (or hypothesis testing), calculated using data.

Theoretical sampling: Sampling in which people or cases are chosen to generate theory, and the number of people or cases is necessarily limited, for qualitative research. It does not produce a representative sample. See also *purposive sampling.*

Theory: A logical description of how a particular corner or aspect of the world works.

Time series: Completely aggregated or single-measure data over time.

Trained observation: A method of data collection that involves training research workers to systematically observe and record conditions or behaviors, typically using an observation rating form.

Trait: Concept, construct, or characteristic of which the measurement is sought. See also *construct*.

Treatment: The program whose effect is of interest—the cause, the independent variable, the explanatory variable, or the predictor. See also *intervention*.

Treatment group: Group in a randomized experiment that is assigned to receive the treatment under investigation.

Treatment of the treated (TOT): An analysis of a randomized experiment that provides an estimate of the effect of the treatment on those who were actually exposed to it. Contrasts with *Intent to Treat (ITT)*.

Treatment selection bias: A misleading comparison between treatment and control groups because of how people were selected into groups, usually when not based on random assignment.

Triangulation: The use of multiple methods or analyses to confirm a finding.

True sample: All the people or elements originally selected from the sampling frame, regardless of whether they are contacted or respond.

Two-way table: A method to describe the relationship between two categorical variables. Also called *contingency table* or *cross-tabulation*.

Type I error: The rejection of a true null hypothesis.

Type II error: The acceptance of a false null hypothesis.

Unfunded research: Research with no specific grant or contract to support it. Contrasts with *grant*.

Unit: The precise meaning of the numbers in quantitative variables—how many of what the numbers refer to. Also called *unit of measurement*.

Unit of analysis: The objects, individuals, or things described by the variables or theory.

Units of measurement: The units that define the numbers in quantitative variables—how many of what that numbers refer to. Also called simply *units*.

Unit of observation: The objects (what or who) being described by the data being collected. See *unit of analysis.*

Universe: The population the study aims to investigate. Also called *population of interest*.

Unmeasured variables: Variables that are not measured in the current data, particularly common causes that cause omitted variable bias because they are not used as control variables.

Unobtrusive measures: Measures that occur naturally or routinely, or otherwise do not disturb the subjects in an experiment. Also called *nonreactive measures*.

Unstructured interview: A qualitative research method that involves interviewing with no predetermined set of questions.

Validity (of a measure): How well a measure represents the construct of interest.

Variable: Something that can take on different values or different attributes.

Variance: A measure of spread of a quantitative variable, the square of the standard deviation.

Voluntary sample: A sample consisting of volunteers.

Volunteer bias: Bias in a study that occurs when volunteers differ from a more representative sample of the population in ways that influence the findings of the study.

Web survey: Mode of survey research that uses web-based forms or questionnaires to gather responses. Also called *Internet survey* or *online survey.*

Weighting (or weighting the sample): Analyzing data so that some of the individuals in the data count more in the analysis, while others count less, often due to disproportionate sampling or to ensure that the data from a sample better represent the population.

Within-subjects experiment: Experimental conditions are varied *within* each person or unit, so that each gets exposed to both the treatment and control conditions. Also called *repeated measures experiment*. See also *crossover experiment*.

Working paper: A scholarly article that has not been published and may still be in progress.

***z* score:** A variable converted to standard deviation units and shifted to mean zero. Also called a *standardized score*.

References

AAPOR Cell Phone Task Force. (2010). *New considerations for survey researchers when planning and conducting RDD telephone surveys in the U.S. with respondents reached via cell phone numbers.* Retrieved from http://www.aapor.org/Cell_Phone_Task_Force_Report.htm

Abbott, Andrew. (2004). *Methods of discovery*. New York: Norton.

Abbott, Lura, & Grady, Christine. (2010). A systematic review of the empirical literature evaluating IRBs: What we know and what we still need to learn. *Journal of Empirical Research on Human Research Ethics, 6*(1), 3–19.

Abraham, Jean, Feldman, Roger, & Carlin, Caroline. (2004). Understanding employee awareness of health care quality information: How can employers benefit? *Health Services Research, 39,* 1799–1816.

Abrams, Laura S., Shannon, Sarah K., & Sangalang, Cindy. (2008). Transition services for incarcerated youth: A mixed methods evaluation study. *Children and Youth Services Review, 30*(5), 522–535.

Agence France-Presse. (2012). *Eurozone jobless rate hits new record of 11.7 percent*. Retrieved from http://www.france24.com/en/20121130-eurozone-jobless-unemployment-rate-record-11-7-percent

Agger, Ben. (2006). *Critical social theories* (2nd ed.). Boulder, CO: Paradigm Publishers.

Agresti, Alan. (2007). *An introduction to categorical data analysis* (2nd ed.). Hoboken, NJ: Wiley-Interscience.

Allen, Arthur. (2007). Vaccines and autism? In *Vaccine: The controversial story of medicine's greatest lifesaver*. New York: Norton.

Allen, Mary J., & Yen, Wendy M. (1979). *Introduction to measurement theory*. Belmont, CA: Wadsworth.

American Psychological Association. (2009). *Publication manual of the American Psychological Association* (6th ed.). Washington, DC: Author.

Angrist, Joshua D., & Krueger, Alan B. (2001). Instrumental variables and the search for identification: From supply and demand to natural experiments. *Journal of Economic Perspectives, 15*(4), 69–85.

Angrist, Joshua, & Pischke, Jorn-Stefan. (2009). *Mostly harmless econometrics*. Princeton, NJ: Princeton University Press.

Ariely, Dan. (2010). *Predictably irrational, revised and expanded edition: The hidden forces that shape our decisions*. New York: HarperCollins.

Ariely, Dan, Kamenica, Emir, & Prelec, Drazen. (2008). Man's search for meaning: The case of Legos. *Journal of Economic Behavior & Organization, 67*(3–4), 671–677.

Associated Press. (2008). *Poll finds support for teacher raises.* Retrieved from www.kten.com/Global/story.asp?S = 7836551

Babylon. (2013). Theoretical. In N. Porter (Ed.), *Webster's revised unabridged dictionary (1913).* Retrieved from http://dictionary.babylon.com/theoretical

Badger, Emily. (2013). Nine questions about gun violence we may now be able to answer. *The Atlantic Cities.* Retrieved from http://www.theatlanticcities.com/politics/2013/01/9-questions-researchers-may-now-be-able-answer-about-urban-gun-violence/4418/

Baicker, Katherine, Taubman, Sarah L., Allen, Heidi L., Bernstein, Mira, Gruber, Jonathan H., Newhouse, Joseph P., . . . Finkelstein, Amy N. (2013). The Oregon experiment: Effects of Medicaid on clinical outcomes. *New England Journal of Medicine, 368*(18), 1713–1722.

Baker, Michael, & Milligan, Kevin. (2008). Maternal employment, breastfeeding, and health: Evidence from mandated maternity leave. *Journal of Health Economics, 27,* 871–887.

Banerjee, Abhijit V., & Duflo, Esther. (2011). *Poor economics: A radical rethinking of the way to fight global poverty*. New York: Public Affairs.

Baron, Reuben M., & Kenny, David A. (1986). The moderator-mediator variable distinction in social psychological research: Conceptual, strategic and statistical considerations. *Journal of Personality and Social Psychology, 51,* 1173–1182.

Basken, Paul. (2010). Academe hath no fury like a fellow professor deceived. *Chronicle of Higher Education*, May 9. Retrieved from http://chronicle.com/article/Academe-Hath-No-Fury-Like-a/65466/

Bauman, Zygmunt. (2010). *Hermeneutics and social science: Approaches to understanding* (Routledge revivals). New York: Routledge.

Becker, Gary, & Becker, Guity. (1998). *The economics of life: From baseball to affirmative action to immigration, how real-world issues affect our everyday life.* New York: McGraw-Hill.

Beecher, Henry K. (1966). Ethics and clinical research. *New England Journal of Medicine, 274*(24), 1354–1360.

Belle, Gerald van. (2008). *Statistical rules of thumb* (2nd ed.). Hoboken, NJ: Wiley-Interscience.

Belli, Robert F., Moore, Sean E., & VanHoewyk, John. (2006). An experimental comparison of question forms used to reduce vote overreporting. *Electoral Studies, 25*(4), 751–759.

Berk, Robert A., & Freedman, David A. (2003). Statistical assumptions as empirical commitments. In *Law, punishment and social control: Essays in honor of Sheldon Messinger* (2nd ed., pp. 235–254). Hawthorne, NY: Aldine de Gruyter.

Bernard, H. Russell. (1996). Qualitative data, qualitative analysis. *Cultural Anthropology Methods Journal, 8*(1), 9–11.

Bernheim, B. Douglas. (1998). Comment on Deaton and Paxson's "Measuring poverty among the elderly." In D. A. Wise (Ed.),

Inquiries in the economics of aging. Chicago: NBER/University of Chicago Press.

Besharov, Doug. (2009). Presidential address: From great society to continuous improvement government: Shifting from "does it work?" to "what would make it better?" *Journal of Policy Analysis and Management, 28*(2), 199–220.

Best, Roger. (2008). *Employee satisfaction, firm value and firm productivity* (Working paper). Warrensburg: University of Central Missouri, Department of Economics & Finance. Retrieved from http://ideas.repec.org/p/umn/wpaper/0806.html

Blalock, Hubert M. (1961). *Causal inferences in nonexperimental research*. New York: Norton.

Blank, Rebecca M. (2008, Spring). Presidential address: How to improve poverty measurement in the United States. *Journal of Policy Analysis and Management, 27*(2), 233–254.

Bloom, Dan, Hendra, Richard, Kemple, James J., Morris, Pamela, Scrivener, Susan, & Verma, Nandita (with Adams-Ciardullo, Diana, Seith, David, & Walter, Johanna). (2000). *The family transition program: Final report on Florida's initial time-limited welfare program*. New York: Manpower Demonstration Research Corporation. Retrieved from www.mdrc.org/publications/20/overview.html

Bloom, Howard S. (1995). Minimum detectable effects: A simple way to report the statistical power of experimental designs. *Evaluation Review, 19*(5), 547–556.

Bloom, Howard S. (Ed.). (2005). *Learning more from social experiments*. New York: Russell Sage Foundation.

Bloom, Howard S., Thompson, Saskia Levy, & Unterman, Rebecca. (2010). Transforming the high school experience: How New York City's new small schools are boosting student achievement and graduate rates. *MDRC*, June. Retrieved from http://papers.ssrn.com/sol3/papers.cfm?abstract_id = 1786966

Blundell, Richard, & Stoker, Thomas M. (2005). Heterogeneity and aggregation. *Journal of Economic Literature, 43*(2), 347–391.

Bogardus, Emory S. (1933). A social distance scale. *Sociology and Social Research, 17*, 265–271.

Bollinger, Bryan, Leslie, Philip, & Sorensen, Alan. (2011). Calorie posting in chain restaurants. *American Economic Journal: Economic Policy, 3*(1), 91–128.

Booth, Wayne C., Colomb, Gregory G., & Williams, Joseph M. (2008). *The craft of research* (3rd ed.). Chicago: University of Chicago Press.

Bowen, William C., Chingos, Matthew M., Lack, Kelly A., & Nygren, Thomas I. (2012). Interactive learning online: Evidence from randomized trials (Report). *ITHAKA S + R*, May 22. Retrieved from http://www.sr.ithaka.org/research-publications/interactive-learning-online-public-universities-evidence-randomized-trials

Bradburn, Norman M., Sudman, Seymour, & Wansink, Brian. (2004). *Asking questions: The definitive guide to questionnaire design—For market research, political polls, and social and health questionnaires*. San Francisco: Jossey-Bass.

Branstetter, Lee G., Chatterjee, Chirantan, & Higgins, Matthew. (2011). *Regulation and welfare: Evidence from Paragraph IV generic entry in the pharmaceutical industry* (Working paper 17188). Cambridge, MA: National Bureau of Economic Research.

Braunsberger, Karin, Wybenga, Hans, & Gates, Roger. (2007). A comparison of reliability between telephone and web-based surveys. *Journal of Business Research, 60*(7), 758–764.

Bronzaft, Arline L., & McCarthy, Dennis P. (1975). The effect of elevated train noise on reading ability. *Environment and Behavior, 7*(4), 517–527.

Brown, Steven R., & Melamed, Lawrence E. (1990). *Experimental design and analysis*. Newbury Park, CA: Sage.

Buckley, Cara. (2010). To test housing program, some are denied aid. *New York Times*, December 8.

Bulmer Martin. (Ed.). (1986). Social science and social policy. London: Allen and Unwin.

Bunge, Mario. (1993). Realism and antirealism in social science. *Theory and Decision, 35*(3), 207–235.

Bunge, Mario. (2011). *Causality and modern science* (3rd rev. ed.). Mineola, NY: Dover Publications.

Burkhauser, Richard V. (2009). Deconstructing European poverty measures: What relative and absolute scales measure. *Journal of Policy Analysis and Management, 28*(4), 715–724.

Burnham, Gilbert, Lafta, Riyadh, Doocy, Shannon, & Roberts, Les. (2006). Mortality after the 2003 invasion of Iraq: A cross-sectional cluster sample survey. *Lancet, 368*, 1421–1428.

Cabinet Office. (2013). *What works: Evidence centers for social policy*. Retrieved from https://www.gov.uk/government/publications/what-works-evidence-centres-for-social-policy

Caminer, Colin, Loewenstein, George, & Prelec, Drazen. (2005). Neuroeconomics: How neuroscience can inform economics. *Journal of Economic Literature, 43*(1), 9–64.

Campbell, Donald. T. (1969). Reforms as experiments. *American Psychologist, 24*(4), 409–429.

Campbell, Donald T., & Stanley, Julian. (1963). *Experimental and quasi-experimental designs for research* (1st ed.). Belmont, CA: Wadsworth.

Card, David. (1999). The causal effect of education on earnings. In O. Ashenfelter & D. Card (Eds.), *Handbook of labor economics* (Vol. 3A, pp. 1801–1863). Amsterdam: Elsevier.

Carmines, Edward G., & Zeller, Richard A. (1979). *Reliability and validity assessment*. Newbury Park, CA: Sage.

Carnegie Foundation for the Advancement of Teaching. (2009). *Basic classification tables*. Stanford, CA: Author. Retrieved from www.carnegiefoundation.org/classifications/index.asp?key = 805

CBS News. (2005). *Poll: Katrina response inadequate, public says response to Katrina too slow; confidence in Bush drops*. Retrieved from www.cbsnews.com/stories/2005/09/08/opinion/polls/main824591_page2.shtml

Center for Spatially Integrated Social Science. (2009). *Spatial resources for the social sciences*. Retrieved from www.csiss.org

Centers for Disease Control and Prevention. Youth Risk Behavior Survey. (n.d.). Retrieved from http://www.cdc.gov/HealthyYouth/yrbs/index.htm.

Centers for Disease Control and Prevention. (2008). *BRFSS: Summary data quality reports—Technical information and data*. Retrieved from www.cdc.gov/brfss/technical_infodata/quality.htm

Centers for Disease Control and Prevention. (2009a). *Malaria facts: CDC malaria*. Retrieved from www.cdc.gov/malaria/facts.htm

Centers for Disease Control and Prevention. (2009b). *NHANES dietary web tutorial: Dietary data overview: History of dietary data collection*. Retrieved from www.cdc.gov/nchs/tutorials/dietary/SurveyOrientation/SurveyDesign/Info1.htm

Centers for Disease Control and Prevention. (2013a). *Behavioral Risk Factor Surveillance System: 2011 summary data quality report* (Version 5, revised February 4, 2013). Retrieved from http://www.cdc.gov/brfss/pdf/2011_Summary_Data_Quality_Report.pdf

Centers for Disease Control and Prevention. (2013b). *Smoking and tobacco use: Trends in state and federal cigarette tax and retail price—United States, 1970–2011*. Retrieved from http://www.cdc.gov/tobacco/data_statistics/tables/economics/trends/index.htm

Centers for Disease Control and Prevention. (2013c). *What you should know for the 2012–2013 influenza season*. Retrieved from http://www.cdc.gov/flu/about/season/flu-season-2012-2013.htm

Centers for Disease Control and Prevention, Division for Heart Disease and Stroke Prevention. (n.d.). *State program, evaluation guides: Developing and using a logic model*. Atlanta, GA: Author. Retrieved from www.cdc.gov/DHDSP/state_program/evaluation_guides/logic_model.htm

Chang, Linchiat, & Krosnick, Jon A. (2009). National surveys via RDD telephone interviewing versus the Internet comparing sample representativeness and response quality. *Public Opinion Quarterly, 73*(4), 641–678.

Chew, Cynthia, & Eysenbach, Gunther. (2010). Pandemics in the age of Twitter: Content analysis of Tweets during the 2009 H1N1 outbreak. *PLoS ONE, 5*(11), e14118. doi:10.1371/journal.pone.0014118

China launches nationwide AIDS prevention program. (2008). *China Daily*, March 28. Retrieved from www.chinadaily.com.cn/china/2008-03/28/content_6574756.htm

Christensen, Michael C., & Remler, Dahlia K. (2009). Information and communications technology in U.S. health care: Why is adoption so slow and is slower better? *Journal of Health Politics Policy and Law, 34*(6), 1011–1034.

Citro, Constance F., & Michael, Robert T. (Eds.). 1995. *Measuring poverty: A new approach*. National Research Council of the National Academy of Sciences. Washington, DC: National Academies Press.

City of Fort Collins. (2005). *Garbage and recycling survey*. Prepared by Corona Research, Inc. Retrieved from http://www.fcgov.com/talkingtrash/

City of New York. (2008). *Mayor's office of operations: Scorecard*. Retrieved from www.nyc.gov/html/ops/html/scorecard/scorecard.shtml

City of New York. (2013). *Department of Sanitation percent of acceptably clean streets* (Fiscal 1975–2012). Retrieved from http://www.nyc.gov/html/ops/html/data/street_scorecard.shtml

Cleveland, William S. (1994). *The elements of graphing data* (2nd ed.). Lafayette, IN: Hobart Press.

Coalition for Evidence-Based Policy. (2009). *Increasing government effectiveness through rigorous evidence about "What Works."* Retrieved from http://coalition4evidence.org/wordpress

Cohen, Jacob. (1992). A power primer. *Psychological Bulletin, 112*(1), 155–159.

Colman, Silvie, Joyce, Ted, & Kaestner, Robert. (2008). Misclassification bias and the estimated effect of parental involvement laws on adolescents' reproductive outcomes. *American Journal of Public Health, 98*(10), 1881–1885.

Communications New Brunswick. (2004, March 25). *Minister unveils literacy initiative as part of Quality Learning Agenda*. Fredericton, New Brunswick, Canada: Author. Retrieved from www.gnb.ca/cnb/news/edu/2004e0357ed.htm

Converse, Jean M., & Presser, Stanley. (1986). *Survey questions: Handcrafting the standardized questionnaire*. Beverly Hills, CA: Sage.

Cook, Royer F., Bernstein, Alan D., Arrington, Thadeus L., & Andrews, Christine M. (1997). Assessing drug use in the workplace: A comparison of self-report, urinalysis, and hair analysis. In Lana Harrison & Arthur Hughes (Eds.), *NIDA research monograph: Vol. 167. The validity of self-reported drug use: Improving the accuracy of survey estimates* (HIH Publication No. 97-4147). Rockville, MD: National Institute on Drug Abuse.

Cook, Thomas D., Shadish, William R., & Wong, Vivian C. (2008). Three conditions under which experiments and observational studies produce comparable causal estimates: New findings from within-study comparisons. *Journal of Public Analysis and Management, 27*(4), 724–750.

Cook, Thomas D., & Steiner, Peter M. (2010). Case matching and the reduction of selection bias in quasi-experiments: The relative importance of covariate choice, unreliable measurement and mode of data analysis. *Psychological Methods, 15*(1), 56–68.

Cooper, Michael, & Sussman, Dalia. (2013). Poll shows school shooting sways views on guns. *New York Times*, January 17. Retrieved from http://www.nytimes.com/2013/01/18/us/poll-shows-school-shooting-sways-views-on-guns.html

Corbin, Juliet, & Strauss, Anselm. (2007). *Basics of qualitative research: Techniques and procedures for developing grounded theory* (3rd ed.). Thousand Oaks, CA: Sage.

Costello, E. Jane, Compton, Scott N., Keeler, Gordon, & Angold, Adrian. (2003, October). Relationships between poverty and psychopathology: A natural experiment. *Journal of the American Medical Association, 290*(15), 2023–2028.

Creswell, John W. (2006). *Qualitative inquiry and research design: Choosing among five approaches* (2nd ed.). Thousand Oaks, CA: Sage.

Creswell, John W., & Plano Clark, Vicki L. (2006). *Designing and conducting mixed methods research*. Thousand Oaks, CA: Sage.

Davies, Huw T. O., Nutley, Sandra M., & Smith, Peter C. (2000). *What works? Evidence-based policy and practice in public services*. Bristol, UK: Policy Press.

Davis, James A. (1985). *The logic of causal order*. Newbury Park, CA: Sage.

Davis, John M., Chen, Nancy, & Glick, Ira D. (2003, June). A meta-analysis of the efficacy of second-generation antipsychotics. *Archives of General Psychiatry, 60*(6), 553–564.

Deaton, Angus. (2010). Instruments, randomization, and learning about development. *Journal of Economic Literature, 48*(2), 424–455.

Der, Geoff, Batty, G. David, & Deary, Ian J. (2006). Effect of breast feeding on intelligence in children: Prospective study, sibling pairs analysis, and meta-analysis. *British Medical Journal, 333*(7575), 945–955.

De Souza Briggs, Xavier, Popkin, Susan J., & Goering, John. (2010). *Moving to opportunity: The story of an American experiment to fight ghetto poverty*. New York: Oxford University Press.

DeVellis, Robert F. (1991). *Scale development: Theory and applications*. Thousand Oaks, CA: Sage.

Dillman, Don A. (2007). *Mail and Internet surveys: The tailored design method, 2007 update*. Hoboken, NJ: Wiley.

Draper, Steven W. (2008). *The Hawthorne, Pygmalion, placebo and other expectation effects: Some notes*. Retrieved from www.psy.gla.ac.uk/~steve/hawth.html

Drews, Frank A., Yazdani, Hina, Godfrey, Celeste N., Cooper, Joel M., & Strayer, David L. (2009). Text messaging during simulated driving. *Human Factors: The Journal of the Human Factors and Ergonomics Society, 51*(5), 762–770.

Dubner, Stephen J., & Levitt, Steven D. (2005). Why vote? *New York Times*, November 6. Retrieved from http://www.nytimes.com/2005/11/06/magazine/06freak.html

Duflo, Esther, Banerjee, Abhijit, Glennerster, Rachel, & Kinnan, Cynthia G. (2013). *The miracle of microfinance? Evidence from a randomized experiment* (Working paper 18950). Cambridge, MA: National Bureau of Economic Research.

Duncan, George T., Jabine, Thomas B., & de Wolf, Virginia A. (1993). *Private lives and public policies*. Washington, DC: National Academies Press. Retrieved from http://www.nap.edu/openbook.php?isbn=0309047439

Duncan, Otis Dudley. (1984). *Notes on social measurement: Historical and critical*. New York: Russell Sage Foundation.

Dupas, Pascaline. (2009). What matters (and what does not) in households' decision to invest in malaria prevention. *American Economic Review: Papers and Proceedings, 99*(2), 224–230.

Edwards, Nancy, Viehbeck, Sarah, Hamalainen, Riitta-Maija, Rus, Diana, Skovgaard, Thomas, Goor, Ien van de, . . . Aro, Arja R. (2012). Challenges of ethical clearance in international health policy and social sciences research: Experiences and recommendations from a multi-country research programme. *Public Health Reviews, 34*(1). Retrieved from http://www.publichealthreviews.eu/upload/pdf_files/11/00_Edwards.pdf

Egan, Patrick J.,& Sherrill, Kenneth. (2005). Neither an in-law nor an outlaw be: Trends in Americans' attitudes toward gay people. *Public Opinion Pros*. Retrieved from http://www.publicopinionpros.norc.org/features/2005/feb/sherrill_egan.asp

Elbel, Brain, Gyamfi, Joyce, & Kersh, Rogan. (2011). Child and adolescent fast-food choice and the influence of calorie labeling: A natural experiment. *International Journal of Obesity, 35*(4), 493–500.

European Commission. (2007). *The European emergency number 112*. Retrieved from http://ec.europa.eu/public_opinion/flash/fl_228_sum_en.pdf2

European Commission Directorate-General for Employment, Social Affairs & Inclusion. (2011). *The measurement of extreme poverty in the European Union*. Brussels: European Commission.

European Research Council. (2013). *Facts and figures*. Retrieved from http://erc.europa.eu/about-erc/facts-and-figures

European Social Survey. (n.d.). *ESS1-2e02 variable documentation list*. Retrieved from www.europeansocialsurvey.org

Evans, William N., & Ringel, Jeanne. (1999, April). Can higher cigarette taxes improve birth outcomes? *Journal of Public Economics, 72*(1), 135–154.

Evenhouse, Erik, & Reilly, Siobhan. (2005). Improved estimates of the benefits of breastfeeding using sibling comparisons to reduce selection bias. *Health Services Research, 40*(6, Pt. 1), 1781–1802.

Faden, Ruth R., & Beauchamp, Tom L. (1986). *A history and theory of informed consent*. New York: Oxford University Press.

Farrell, Dan, & Petersen, James C. (2010). The growth of Internet research methods and the reluctant sociologist. *Sociological Inquiry, 80*(1), 114–125.

Federal Reserve Bank of St. Louis. (2013). *FRED graph*. Civilian Unemployment Series. Retrieved from http://research.stlouisfed.org/fred2/graph/

Ferryman, Kadija S., Souza Briggs, Xavier de, Popkin, Susan J., & Rendón, María. (2008). *Do better neighborhoods for MTO families mean better schools?* (Metropolitan Housing and Communities Center Policy Brief No. 3). Washington, DC: Urban Institute Press.

Fetterman, David M., Kaftarian, Shakeh, & Wandersman, Abraham. (1995). *Empowerment evaluation: Knowledge and tools for self-assessment and accountability* (1st ed.). Thousand Oaks, CA: Sage.

Feuer, Alan. (2013). The mayor's geek squad. *New York Times*, March 23.

Finkelstein, Amy, Taubman, Sarah, Wright, Bill, Bernstein, Mira, Gruber, Jonathan, Newhouse, Joseph P., . . . Oregon Health Study Group. (2012). The Oregon Health Insurance Experiment: Evidence from the first year. *Quarterly Journal of Economics, 127*(3), 1057–1106.

Fisher, Gorden M. (1992). The development and history of the poverty thresholds. *Social Security Bulletin, 55*(4), 3–14. Retrieved from www.ssa.gov/history/fisheronpoverty.html

Fletcher, Jason M. (2011). Long-term effects of health investments and parental favoritism: The case of breastfeeding. *Health Economics, 20*(11), 1349–1361.

Fowler, Floyd J. (1995). *Improving survey questions: Design and evaluation*. Thousand Oaks, CA: Sage.

Fowler, Floyd J. (2008). *Survey research methods* (4th ed.). Thousand Oaks, CA: Sage.

Frattaroli, Shannon, & Teret, Stephen P. (2006). Understanding and informing policy implementation: A case study of the domestic violence provisions of the Maryland Gun Violence Act. *Evaluation Review, 30*(3), 347–360.

Freedrnan, David A. (1991). Statistical models and shoe leather. *Sociological Methodology*, *21*, 291–313.

Fried, Joseph P. (2004). Following up. *New York Times*, February 8. Retrieved from http://www.nytimes.com/2004/02/08/nyregion/following-up.html

Frieden, Thomas R., Mostashari, Farzad, Kerker, Bonnie D., Miller, Nancy, Hajat, Anjum, & Frankel, Martin. (2005). Adult tobacco use levels after intensive tobacco control measures: New York City, 2002–2003. *American Journal of Public Health, 95*(6), 1016–1023.

Friedman, David, Pisani, Robert, & Purves, Roger. (2007). *Statistics* (4th ed.). New York: Norton.

Friedman, Michael S., Powell, Kenneth E., Hutwagner, Lori, Graham, LeRoy M., & Teague, W. Gerald. (2001). Impact of changes in transportation and commuting behaviors during the 1996 Summer Olympic Games in Atlanta on air quality and childhood asthma. *Journal of the American Medical Association, 285*(7), 897–905.

Fund for the City of New York. (2010). *Computerized neighborhood environment tracking: ComNET.* Retrieved from http://venus.fcny.org/cmgp/comnet.htm

Furr, R. Michael, & Bacharach, Verne R. (2008). *Psychometrics: An introduction*. Thousand Oaks, CA: Sage.

Gelman, Andrew, Hill, Jennifer, & Yajima, Masanao. (2012). Why we (usually) don't have to worry about multiple comparisons. *Journal of Research on Educational Effectiveness, 5*, 189–211.

George, Alexander L., & Bennett, Andrew. (2005). *Case studies and theory development in the social sciences*. Cambridge, MA: MIT Press.

Gerber, Alan S., & Green, Donald P. (2012). *Field experiments: Design, analysis, and interpretation*. New York: Norton.

Gerber, Alan S., Karlan, Dean, & Bergan, Daniel. (2009). Does the media matter? A field experiment measuring the effect of newspapers on voting behavior and political opinions." *American Economic Journal: Applied Economics, 1*(2), 35–52.

Gerber, Alan S., & Patashnik, Eric M. (2006). *Sham surgery: The problem of inadequate medical evidence* (Working paper). Charlottesville: Miller Center of the University of Virginia. Retrieved from http://millercenter.org/scripps/archive/colloquia/detail/1959

Gilgun, Jane. (2011). *Analysis in qualitative research: Identifying and tracking webs of meaning*. Kindle edition.

Ginsberg, Jeremy, Mohebbi, Matthew H., Patel, Rajan S., Brammer, Lynnette, Smolinski, Mark S., & Brilliant, Larry. (2009). Detecting influenza epidemics using search engine query data. *Nature, 457*, 1012–1014.

Glaser, Barney G., & Strauss, Anselm. (1967). *The discovery of grounded theory: Strategies for qualitative research*. Piscataway, NJ: Aldine Transaction.

Glennerster, Rachel. (2012). The power of evidence: Improving the effectiveness of government by investing in more rigorous evaluation. *National Institute Economic Review, 219*, R4–R14.

Glied, Sherry, Remler, Dahlia, & Graff Zivin, Joshua. (2002, December). Inside the sausage factory: Understanding and improving estimates of the effects of health insurance expansion proposals using a reference case approach. *Milbank Quarterly, 80*(4), 602–636.

Godfrey-Smith, Peter. (2003). *Theory and reality: An introduction to the philosophy of science* (1st ed.). Chicago: University of Chicago Press.

Gold, Raymond L. (1958, March). Roles in sociological field observations. *Social Forces, 36*(3), 217–223.

Gordis, Leon. (2000). *Epidemiology* (2nd ed.). Philadelphia: Saunders.

Graff Zivin, Joshua, & Neidell, Matthew. (2012). Impact of pollution on worker productivity. *American Economic Review, 102*(7), 3652–3673.

Gray-Little, Bernadette, Williams, Valerie S. L., & Hancock, Timothy D. (1997). An item response theory analysis of the Rosenberg Self-Esteem Scale. *Personality and Social Psychology Bulletin, 23*(5), 443–451.

Grazer, Frederick M., & Jong, Rohrich H. de. (2000). Fatal outcomes from liposuction: Census survey of cosmetic surgeons. *Plastic and Reconstructive Surgery, 105*(1), 436.

Grbich, Carol. (2012). *Qualitative data analysis: An introduction* (2nd ed.). Thousand Oaks, CA: Sage.

Green, Elizabeth. (2009). New York's annual math tests are repeating themselves. *GothamSchools*, June 12. Retrieved from http://gothamschools.org/2009/06/12/new-yorks-annual-math-tests-are-repeating-themselves/

Greenberg, David, Shroder, Mark, & Onstott, Matthew. (1999). The social experiment market. *Journal of Economic Perspectives, 13*(3), 157–172.

Grieco, Elizabeth M., & Cassidy, Rachel C. (2001). *Overview of race and Hispanic origin: Census 2000 brief* (Census Report CENSUS-C2KBR/01-1). Washington, DC: U.S. Census Bureau. Retrieved from www.census.gov

Groves, Robert M. (2006). Nonresponse rates and nonresponse bias in household surveys [Special issue]. *Public Opinion Quarterly, 70*(5), 646–675.

Groves, Robert M., Fowler, Floyd J., Jr., Couper, Mick P., & Lepkowski, James M. (2004). *Survey methodology*. Malden, MA: Wiley-Interscience.

Gruber, Jonathan. (2004). Is making divorce easier bad for children? The long-run implications of unilateral divorce. *Journal of Labor Economics, 22*(4), 799–833.

Guo, Shenyang, & Fraser, Mark W. (2010). *Propensity score analysis: Statistical methods and applications*. Thousand Oaks, CA: Sage.

Gurley-Calvez, Tami, Gilbert, Thomas J., Harper, Katherine, Marples, Donald J., & Daly, Kevin. (2009). Do tax incentives affect investment? An analysis of the new markets tax credit. *Public Finance Review, 37*, 371.

Hamilton, Anita. (2009). What Facebook users share: Lower grades. *Time*. Retrieved from http://www.econ.ucdavis.edu/graduate/dvdng/principles/face.pdf

Hardy, Melissa A. (1993). Regression with dummy variables. *Quantitative Applications in the Social Sciences, 93*. Newbury Park, CA: Sage.

Harpster, Tracy, Adams, Susan H., & Jarvis, John P. (2009). Analyzing 911 homicide calls for indicators of guilt or innocence: An exploratory analysis. *Homicide Studies, 13*(1), 69–93.

Harris, Katherine M., & Remler, Dahlia K. (1998). Who is the marginal patient? Understanding instrumental variables estimates of treatment effects. *Health Services Research, 31*(5, Pt. 1), 1337–1360.

Harris Interactive. (2008). *The Harris Poll: Majority in U.S. favors stricter gun control but gun control is not likely to be much of an issue in upcoming presidential election*. Retrieved from www.harrisinteractive.com/harris_poll/index.asp?PID = 471

Harvard Business Press. (2009). *Measuring performance*. Boston: Author.

Hatry, Harry P. (2007). *Performance measurement: Getting results* (2nd ed.). Washington, DC: Urban Institute Press.

Heckathorn, Douglas D. (1997). Respondent-driven sampling: A new approach to the study of hidden populations. *Social Problems*, pp. 174–199.

Heckman, James J. (2000). Causal parameters and policy analysis in economics: Twentieth century retrospective. *Quarterly Journal of Economics, 115*, 45–97.

Heckman, James J., & Smith, Jeffrey A. (1995). Assessing the case for social experiments. *Journal of Economic Perspectives, 9*(2), 85–110.

Henry, Gary T. (1990). *Practical sampling*. Newbury Park, CA: Sage.

Henry, Gary T. (1994). *Graphing data: Techniques for display and analysis* (Illustrated ed.). Thousand Oaks, CA: Sage.

Herman, Dena R., Harrison, Gail G., Afifi, Abdelmonem A., & Jenks, Eloise. (2008). Effect of a targeted subsidy on intake of fruits and vegetables among low-income women in the special supplemental nutrition program for women, infants, and children. *American Journal of Public Health, 98*(1), 98–105.

HighScope Educational Research Foundation. (2005). *HighScope Perry preschool study lifetime effects: The HighScope Perry preschool study through age 40*. Retrieved from www.highscope.org/Content.asp?ContentId = 219

Hillier, Sharon, Cooper, Cyrus, Kellingray, Sam, Russell, Graham, Hughes, Herbert, & Coggon, David. (2000). Fluoride in drinking water and risk of hip fracture in the UK: A case-control study. *Lancet, 355*(9200), 265–269.

Holzer, Marc, & Yang, Kaifeng. (2004). Performance measurement and improvement: An assessment of the state of the art. *International Review of Administrative Sciences, 70*(1), 15–31.

Howell, David C. (2007). Multiple comparisons among treatment means. In D. C. Howell (Ed.), *Statistical methods for psychology* (6th ed., chap. 12). Belmont, CA: Thomson Wadsworth.

How the poll was conducted. (2009). *New York Times*, October 23. Retrieved from www.nytimes.com/2009/11/02/technology/02mbox.html?_r = 1

Human Development Reports. (n.d.) *The Human Poverty Index*. Retrieved from http://hdr.undp.org/en/statistics/indices/hpi/

Humphreys, Laud. (1975). *Tearoom trade: A study of homosexual encounters in public places*. New York: Aldine.

Huston, Aletha C., Miller, Cynthia, Richburg-Hayes, Lashawn, Duncan, Greg, Eldred, Carolyn, Weisner, Thomas S., . . . Redcross, Cindy. (2003). *New hope for families and children: Five year results of a program to reduce poverty and reform welfare*. New York: MDRC.

Huurre, Taina, Junkkari, Hanna, & Aro, Hillevi. (2006). Long-term psychosocial effects of parental divorce: A follow-up study from adolescence to adulthood. *European Archives of Psychiatry and Clinical Neuroscience, 256*(4), 256–263.

Iezzoni, Lisa. (2002). Using administrative data to study persons with disabilities. *Milbank Quarterly, 80*(2), 347–379.

Imbens, Guido W., & Angrist, Joshua D. (1994). Identification and estimation of local average treatment effects. *Econometrica, 62*(2), 467–475.

Institute for Analytic Journalism. (n.d.). *Welcome to the IAJ*. Retrieved from http://www.analyticjournalism.com/2005/03/14/welcome-to-the-iaj/

Institute of Medicine Committee of the Consequences of Uninsurance. (2003). *Hidden costs, value lost: Uninsurance in America*. Washington, DC: Institute of Medicine.

Intergovernmental Panel on Climate Change. (2007). *Climate change 2007: Synthesis report*. Retrieved from www.ipcc.ch/publications_and_data/publications_ipcc_fourth_assessment_report_synthesis_report.htm

The Internet Party: Second Amendment. (2008). Retrieved from www.theinternetparty.org/comments/index.php?cid = pol20051201000

Israel, Mark, & Hay, Iain. (2006). *Research ethics for social scientists*. Thousand Oaks, CA: Sage.

Iyengar, Radha. (2009). Does the certainty of arrest reduce domestic violence? Evidence from mandatory and recommended arrest laws. *Journal of Public Economics, 93*, 85–98.

Iyengar, Sheena S., & Lepper, Mark R. (2000). When choice is demotivating: Can one desire too much of a good thing? *Journal of Personality and Social Psychology, 79*, 995–1006.

Jackson Public Schools. (2004). *Class-size reduction grant program*. Retrieved from www.jackson.k12.ms.us/departments/curriculum/class_reduction/class_reduction.htm

Jacobsen, Steven J., Goldberg, Jack, Miles, Toni P., Brody, Jacob A., Stiers, William, & Rimm, Alfred A. (1990). Regional variation in the incidence of hip fracture: US white women aged 65 years and older. *Journal of the American Medical Association, 264*(4), 500.

JAMA & Archives Journals. (2007). *AMA manual of style: A guide for authors and editors* (10th ed.). New York: Oxford University Press.

Jamieson, Christine. (2013). Gun violence research: History of the federal funding freeze. *Psychological Science Agenda*. Retrieved from http://www.apa.org/science/about/psa/2013/02/gun-violence.aspx

Jones, James H. (1993). *Bad blood: The Tuskegee syphilis experiment*. New York: Free Press of Simon & Schuster.

Jorgensen, Danny L. (1989). *Participant observation: A methodology for human studies*. Newbury Park, CA: Sage.

Kahneman, Daniel. (2011). *Thinking, fast and slow*. New York: Farrar, Strauss & Giroux.

Kalton, Graham. (1983). *Introduction to survey sampling*. Newbury Park, CA: Sage.

Kaplan, Robert S., & Harvard Business School. (2009). *Measuring performance: Expert solutions to everyday challenges*. Boston, MA: Harvard Business Press.

Kaplan, Sue A., & Garrett, Katherine E. (2005). The use of logic models by community-based initiatives. *Evaluation and Program Planning, 28,* 167–172.

Katz, Lawrence F., Kling, Jeffrey R., & Liebman, Jeffrey B. (2001). Moving to opportunity in Boston: Early results of a randomized mobility experiment. *Quarterly Journal of Economics, 116,* 607–654.

Kellett, Mary, & Nind, Melanie. (2001). Ethics in quasi-experimental research on people with severe learning disabilities: Dilemmas and compromises. *British Journal of Learning Disabilities, 29,* 51–55.

Kelling, George L., & Wilson, James Q. (1982). Broken windows. *The Atlantic*, March. Retrieved from http://www.theatlantic.com/magazine/archive/1982/03/broken-windows/304465/3/

Kennedy, Peter. (2003). *A guide to econometrics* (5th ed.). Cambridge, MA: MIT Press.

Kennedy School of Government. (1993). *From research to policy: The cigarette excise tax* (Kennedy School of Government Case C16-93-1233.0). Cambridge, MA: Harvard University Press.

Kiecolt, K. Jill, & Nathan, Laura E. (1985). *Secondary analysis of survey data*. Beverly Hills, CA: Sage.

Kifner, John. (2001). Scholar sets off gastronomic false alarm. *New York Times*, September 8. Retrieved from http://www.nytimes.com/2001/09/08/nyregion/scholar-sets-off-gastronomic-false-alarm.html

Kim, Jae-On, & Mueller, Charles W. (1978). Introduction to factor analysis: What it is and how to do it. *Quantitative Applications in the Social Sciences, 13.* Newbury Park, CA: Sage.

King, Gary, Keohane, Robert O., & Verba, Sidney. (1994). *Designing social inquiry*. Mahwah, NJ: Princeton University Press.

Kingdon, John W. (1995). *Agendas, alternatives, and public policies* (2nd ed.). New York: HarperCollins.

Kirby, Douglas. (2007). *Emerging answers 2007: Research finding on programs to reduce teen pregnancy and sexually transmitted diseases*. Washington, DC: The National Campaign to Prevent Teen and Unplanned Pregnancy. Retrieved from www.thenationalcampaign.org/EA2007/EA2007_sum.pdf

Koepsell, Thomas, McCloskey, Lon, Wolf, Marsha, Vernez Moudon, Anne, Buchner, David, Kraus, Jess, & Patterson, Matthew. (2002). Crosswalk markings and the risk of pedestrian-motor vehicle collisions in older pedestrians. *Journal of the American Medical Association, 288*(17), 2136–2143.

Korenman, Sanders, & Neumark, David. (1991). Does marriage make men more productive? *Journal of Human Resources, 26*(2), 282–307.

Korenman, Sanders, & Remler, Dahlia. (2013). *Rethinking elderly poverty: Time for a health inclusive poverty measure?* (Working paper 18900). Cambridge, MA: National Bureau of Economic Research.

Koretz, Daniel. (2005). Alignment, high stakes, and the inflation of test scores. *Yearbook of the National Society for the Study of Education, 104*(2), 99–118.

Kowalski, Alex. (2010). Michigan Consumer Sentiment Index decreased in October. *Bloomberg*, October 29. Retrieved from http://www.bloomberg.com/news/2010-10-29/u-s-michigan-consumer-sentiment-index-falls-more-than-estimated-to-67-7.html

Kozinets, Robert V. (2009). *Netnography: Doing ethnographic research online*. Thousand Oaks, CA: Sage.

Kramer, Fredrica D., Finegold, Kenneth, & Kuehn, Daniel. (2008, April). *Understanding the consequences of Hurricane Katrina for ACF service populations: A feasibility assessment of study approaches*. Washington, DC: Urban Institute Press.

Kramer, Michael S. (2010). "Breast is best": The evidence. *Early Human Development, 86,* 729–732.

Kramer, Michael S., Aboud, Frances, Miranova, Elena, Vanilovich, Irina, Platt, Robert W., Matush, Lidia, . . . Shapiro, S. (2009). Breastfeeding and child cognitive development: New evidence from a large randomized trial. *Archives of General Psychiatry, 65*(5), 578–584.

Kramer, Michael S., Chalmers, Beverly, Hodnett, Ellen D., Sevkovskaya, Zinaida, Dzikovich, Irina, Shapiro, Stanley, . . . Helsing, Elisabet, for the PROBIT Study Group. (2001a). A breastfeeding intervention increased breastfeeding and reduced GI tract infections and atopic eczema. *Evidence-Based Nursing, 4,* 106.

Kramer, Michael S., Chalmers, Beverly, Hodnett, Ellen D., Sevkovskaya, Zinaida, Dzikovich, Irina, Shapiro, Stanley, . . . Helsing, Elisabet, for the PROBIT Study Group. (2001b). A Promotion of Breastfeeding Intervention Trial (PROBIT): A randomized trial in the Republic of Belarus. *Journal of the American Medical Association, 285*(4), 413–420.

Kramer, Michael S., Martin, Richard M., Sterne, Jonathan A. C., Shapiro, Stanley, Dahhou, Mourad, & Platt, Robert W. (2009). The double jeopardy of clustered measurement and cluster randomization. *British Medical Journal, 339,* b2900.

Kramer, Michael S., Matush, Lidia, Vanliovich, Irina, Platt, Robert, Bogdanovich, Natalia, Sevkovskaya, Zinaida, . . . Mazer, B. (2007). Effect of prolonged and exclusive breastfeeding on risk of allergy and asthma: Cluster randomised trial. *British Medical Journal, 335*(7624), 815–820.

Kramer, Michael S., Matush, Lidia, Vanilovich, Irina, Platt, Robert W., Bogdanovich, Natalia, Sevovskaya, Zinaida, . . . Shapiro, S. (2009). A randomized breast-feeding promotion intervention did not reduce child obesity in Belarus. *Journal of Nutrition, 139*(2), 417S–421S.

Kramer, Michael S., Vanilovich, Irina, Matush, Lidia, Bogdanovich, Natalia, Zhang, Xiang, Shishko, Gyorgy, . . . Platt, Robert W. (2007). The effect of prolonged and exclusive breast-feeding on dental caries in early school-age children. *Caries Research, 41*(6), 484–488.

Krueger, Alan B., & Kuziemko, Ilyana. (2013). The demand for health insurance among uninsured Americans: Results of a survey experiment and implications for policy. *Journal of Health Economics, 32*(5), 780–793. doi:10.1016/j.jhealeco.2012.09.005

Kruschke, John. (2010). *Doing Bayesian data analysis: A tutorial with R and BUGS*. Burlington, MA: Academic Press, Elsevier.

Kuhn, Thomas S. (2012). *The structure of scientific revolutions: 50th anniversary edition* (4th ed.). Chicago: University of Chicago Press.

Kunz, Tanja, & Fuchs, Marek. (2012). Improving RSS call phone samples, evaluation of different pre-call validation methods. *Journal of Official Statistics, 28*(3), 373–394.

Lacy, Rebecca. (2009). Are people with health insurance healthier than those without? *The Oregonian*, April 23. Retrieved from www.oregonlive.com/news/index.ssf/2009/04/oregon_health_study_tries_to_d.htm

Lamont, Michele, & White, Patricia. (Eds.). (2005). *Workshop on interdisciplinary standards for systematic qualitative research: Report*. Washington, DC: National Science Foundation. Retrieved from www.nsf.gov/sbe/ses/soc/ISSQR_workshop_rpt.pdf

Lancer Julnes, Patria de, & Holzer, Marc. (2008). *Performance measurement: Building theory, improving practice*. Armonk, NY: M. E. Sharpe.

Langbein, Laura, & Felbinger, Claire. (2006). *Public program evaluation: A statistical guide*. Armonk, NY: M. E. Sharpe.

Laudan, Larry. (1977). *Progress and its problems: Towards a theory of scientific growth*. Berkeley: University of California Press.

Layard, Richard. (2005). *Happiness: Lessons from a new science*. New York: Penguin Books.

Lemert, Charles. (2004). *Social theory: The multicultural and classic readings* (3rd ed.). Nashville, TN: Westview Press.

Leonard, Carl, Bourke, Sid, & Schofield, Neville. (2002). *Student quality of school life: A multilevel analysis*. Paper presented at the Annual Conference of the Australian Association for Research in Education, Brisbane, Queensland, Australia, December. Retrieved from www.aare.edu.au/02pap/le002063.htm

Lewis-Beck, Michael S. (1980). *Applied regression: An introduction*. Beverly Hills, CA: Sage.

Lewit, Eugene M., & Coate, Douglas. (1982). The potential for using excise taxes to reduce smoking. *Journal of Health Economics, 1*, 121–145.

Lijphart, Arend. (1971). Comparative politics and the comparative method. *The American Political Science Review, 65*(3), 682–693.

Lincoln, Yvonna, & Guba, Egon G. (1985). *Naturalistic inquiry*. Beverly Hills, CA: Sage.

Lind, Torbjorn, Lonnerdal, Bo, Stenlund, Hans, Gamayanti, Indira L., Ismail, Djauhar, Seswandhana, Rosadi, & Persson, Lars-Åke. (2004). A community-based randomized controlled trial of iron and zinc supplementation in Indonesian infants: Effects on growth and development. *American Journal of Clinical Nutrition, 80*(3), 729–736.

Lipsey, Mark W., & Wilson, David B. (2001). *Practical meta-analysis*. Thousand Oaks, CA: Sage.

Lohr, Sharon L. (2009). *Sampling design and analysis* (2nd ed.). Pacific Grove, CA: Duxbury Press.

Long-Sutehall, Tracy, Sque, Madi, & Addington-Hall, Julia. (2010). Secondary analysis of qualitative data: A valuable method for exploring sensitive issues with an elusive population? *Journal of Research in Nursing, 16*(4), 335–344.

Ludwig, Jens, Liebman, Jeffrey B., Klin, Jeffrey R., Duncan, Greg J., Katz, Lawrence F., Kessler, Ronald C., & Sanbonmatsu, Lisa. (2008). What can we learn about neighborhood effects from the Moving to Opportunity experiment? *American Journal of Sociology, 114*(1), 144–188.

Luhrmann, Tanya Marie. (2008). The street will drive you crazy: Why homeless psychotic women in the institutional circuit in the United States often say no to offers of help. *American Journal of Psychiatry, 165*(1), 15–20.

Luke, Douglas A. (2004). *Multilevel modeling* (1st ed.). Thousand Oaks, CA: Sage.

Macklin, Ruth. (2012). *Ethics in global health: Research, policy and practice*. New York: Oxford University Press.

Macklin, Ruth. (2013). Ethical quandaries raised by cluster randomized trials. *The Doctor's Tablet*, March 21. Retrieved from http://blogs.einstein.yu.edu/ethical-quandaries-raised-by-cluster-randomized-trials/

Malhotra, Neil, & Krosnick, Jon A. (2007). The effect of survey mode and sampling on inferences about political attitudes and behavior: Comparing the 2000 and 2004 ANES to Internet surveys with nonprobability samples. *Political Analysis, 15*(3), 286–323.

Mamabear. (2007). *Feeling a little paranoid? You will after this* [Blog entry]. San Antonio, TX: The International Breastfeeding Symbol. Retrieved from http://www.breastfeedingsymbol.org/2007/09/24/feeling-a-little-paranoid-you-will-after-reading-this/

Manski, Charles F. (1995). *Identification problems in the social sciences*. Cambridge, MA: Harvard University Press.

Mayer-Schonberger, Viktor, & Cukier, Kenneth. (2013). *Big Data: A revolution that will transform how we live, work, and think*. New York: Houghton-Mifflin-Harcourt.

McClellan, Mark, McKethan, Aaron N., Lewis, Julie L., Roski, Joachim, & Fisher, Elliott S. (2010). A national strategy to put accountable care into practice. *Health Affairs, 29*(5), 982–990.

McDowall, David, McCleary, Richard, Meidinger, Errol E., & Hay, Richard A. (1980). *Interrupted time series analysis* (1st ed.). Beverly Hills, CA: Sage.

McFadden, Daniel. (1974). The measurement of urban travel demand. *Journal of Public Economics, 3,* 303–328.

McGonagle, Katherine A., & Schoeni, Robert F. (2006). *The panel study of income dynamics: Overview and summary of scientific contributions after nearly 40 years*. Ann Arbor: University of Michigan, Institute for Social Research.

McIntyre, Alice. (2007). *Participatory action research* (1st ed.). Thousand Oaks, CA: Sage.

McIver, John P., & Carmines, Edward G. (1981). *Unidimensional scaling*. Beverly Hills, CA: Sage.

McKee, Rosie, Mutrie, Nanette, Crawford, Fiona, & Green, Brian. (2007). Promoting walking to school: Results of a quasi-experimental trial. *Journal of Epidemiology and Community Health, 61*(9), 818–823.

Mead, Margaret. (1971). *Coming of age in Samoa*. New York: Harper Perennial.

Melloni, Chiara, Berger, Jeffrey S., Wang, Tracy Y., Gunes, Funda, Stebbins, Amanda, Pieper, Karen S., . . . Newby, L. Kristin. (2010). Representation of women in randomized clinical trials of cardiovascular disease prevention. *Circulation: Cardiovascular Quality and Outcomes, 3*(2), 135–142.

Merton, Robert K. (1967). *On theoretical sociology*. New York: Free Press.

Meyer, Bruce D. (1995). Natural and quasi-experiments in economics. *Journal of Business and Economics Statistics, 13,* 151–161.

Miguel, Edward, & Kremer, Michael. (2004). Worms: Identifying impacts on education and health in the presence of treatment externalities. *Econometrica, 72*(1), 159–217.

Miguel-Tobal, Juan José, Vindel, Antonio Cano, Iruarrízaga, Iciar, González Ordi, Héctor, & Galea, Sandro. (2005). Psychopathological repercussions of the March 11 terrorist attacks in Madrid. *Psychology in Spain, 9,* 75–80.

Miles, Matthew B., & Huberman, Michael. (1994). *Qualitative data analysis: An expanded sourcebook* (2nd ed.). Thousand Oaks, CA: Sage.

Milgram, Stanley. (1974). *Obedience to authority: An experimental view*. New York: HarperCollins.

Miller, D. W. (2001). Poking holes in the theory of "Broken Windows." *The Chronicle of Higher Education*, February 9.

Miller, Jane E. (2004). *The Chicago guide to writing about numbers*. Chicago: University of Chicago Press.

Miller, Jane E. (2005). *The Chicago guide to writing about multivariate analysis*. Chicago: University of Chicago Press.

Miller, Nancy K., Verhoef, Maria, & Cardwell, Kelly. (2008). Rural parents' perspectives about information on child immunization. *International Electronic Journal of Rural and Remote Health Research, Education, Policy and Practice, 863.* Retrieved from www.rrh.org.au/articles/subviewnthamer.asp?ArticleID = 863

Mills, C. Wright. (1959). *The sociological imagination*. Oxford: Oxford University Press.

Mills, Mary Alice, Edmondson, Donald, & Park, Crystal L. (2007, April). Trauma and stress response among Hurricane Katrina evacuees. *American Journal of Public Health, 97*(1), S116–S123.

Mohr, Lawrence B. (1995). *Impact analysis for program evaluation*. Thousand Oaks, CA: Sage.

Moldova. (2009, October 30). In *Wikipedia, The Free Encyclopedia*. Retrieved from http://en.wikipedia.org/w/index.php?title = Moldova&oldid = 322953548

Mooney, Christopher Z., & Duval, Robert D. (1993). *Bootstrapping: A nonparametric approach to statistical inference*. Newbury Park, CA: Sage.

Moore, David S. (2009). *The basic practice of statistics* (5th ed.). New York: W. H. Freeman.

Morgan, Stephen L., & Winship, Christopher. (2007). *Counterfactuals and causal inference: Methods and principles for social research*. Cambridge, UK: Cambridge University Press.

Mortensen, Erik Lykke, Michaelsen, Kim F., Sanders, Stephanie A, & Reinisch, June M. (2002). The association between duration of breastfeeding and adult intelligence. *Journal of the American Medical Association, 287*(18), 2365–2946.

MSNBC News Report. (2007, November 1). *Support for birth control: Sixty-seven percent of parents support giving contraceptives to teenagers*. Retrieved from http://msnbcmedia2.msn.com/i/msnbc/Components/ArtAndPhoto-Fronts/HEALTH/071101/AP_BIRTH_CONTROL.gif

Muller, Andreas. (2004). Florida's motorcycle helmet law repeal and fatality rates. *American Journal of Public Health, 94*(4), 556–558.

Mutz, Diana C. (2011). Population-based survey experiments. New Brunswick, NJ: Princeton University Press.

Muzzio, Douglas, & Van Ryzin, Gregg G. (2001). *Satisfaction with New York City Services 2001*. New York City Council, Office of Oversight and Investigation.

Nagourney, Adam, & Thee-Brenan, Megan. (2009). Outlook on economy is brightening, poll finds. *New York Times*, April 6. Retrieved from www.nytimes.com/2009/04/07/us/politics/07poll.html

Napoli, Anthony R., & Hiltner, George J., III. (1993). An evaluation of developmental reading instruction. *Journal of Developmental Education, 17*(1), 14.

National Center for Chronic Disease Prevention and Health Promotion, Division for Heart Disease and Stroke Prevention. (2013, August 1). *Developing and using a logic model*. Retrieved from http://www.cdc.gov/dhdsp/programs/nhdsp_program/evaluation_guides/logic_model.htm

National Center for Education Statistics. (2006). *Comparing private and public schools using hierarchical linear modeling* (NCES 2006-461). Washington, DC: U.S. Department of Education.

National Center for Education Statistics. (2009). *NAEP 2008: Trends in academic progress in reading and mathematics (1973–2008)*. Retrieved from http://nces.ed.gov/pubsearch/pubsinfo.asp?pubid = 2009479

National Center for Education Statistics. (2013). *National Education Longitudinal Study of 1988* (NELS:88) Overview. Retrieved from http://nces.ed.gov/surveys/nels88/index.asp

National Center for Health Statistics. (2007). *FASTATS: Illegal drug use*. Atlanta, GA: Centers for Disease Control and Prevention. Retrieved from www.cdc.gov/nchs/fastats/druguse.htm

National Center for Health Statistics. (2011). *Health, United States, 2011: With special feature on socioeconomic status and health*. Huntsville, MD: Author.

National Diabetes Information Clearinghouse, National Institutes of Health. (n.d.). *National diabetes statistics, 2007: General information*. Bethesda, MD: Author. Retrieved from http://diabetes.niddk.nih.gov/DM/PUBS/statistics/#y_people

National Institutes of Health. (2009). *The NIH Almanac: Appropriations*. Retrieved from www.nih.gov/about/almanac/appropriations/part2.htm

National Institutes of Health. (2013). *NIH budget*. Retrieved from http://www.nih.gov/about/budget.htm

National Science Foundation. (2009). *NSF congressional highlight: Congress passes FY09 omnibus bill*. Arlington, VA: Author. Retrieved from www.nsf.gov/about/congress/111/highlights/cu09_0310.jsp

National Science Foundation. (2013). *NSF-OLPA congressional affairs/congressional update—April 9, 2013*. Retrieved from http://www.nsf.gov/about/congress/113/highlights/cu13_0409.jsp

Newhouse, Joseph P., & Insurance Experiment Group. (1993). *Free for all: Lessons from the RAND health insurance experiment*. Cambridge, MA: Harvard University Press.

O'Connor, A. (2003). Rise in income improves children's behavior. *New York Times*, October 21. Retrieved from www.nytimes.com/2003/10/21/health/rise-in-income-improves-children-s-behavior.html?scp = 1&sq = O%E2%80%99Connor,%20A.%20(2003,%20October%2021).%20Rise%20in%20income%20improves%20children%E2%80%99s%20behavior.%20New%20York%20Times&st = cse

OECD.Stat Extracts ALFS Summary Tables. (2013). Retrieved from http://stats.oecd.org/Index.aspx?DatasetCode = STLABOUR

Office of Inspector General, U.S. Department of Commerce. (2011). *Census 2010: Final report to Congress, June 27, 2011*. Retrieved from http://www.oig.doc.gov/Pages/Census-2010-Final-Report-to-Congress.aspx

Offit, Paul A. (2013). Don't take your vitamins. *New York Times*, June 8. Retrieved from http://www.nytimes.com/2013/06/09/opinion/sunday/dont-take-your-vitamins.html

Orr, Larry, Feins, Judith D., Jacob, Robin, Beecroft, Erik, Sanbonmatsu, Lisa, Katz, Lawrence, . . . Kling, Jeffrey R. (2003). *Moving to Opportunity for Fair Housing Demonstration project: Interim impacts evaluation*. Washington, DC: U.S. Department of Housing and Urban Development.

Ostrom, Charles W. (1990). *Time series analysis: Regression techniques* (2nd ed.). Newbury Park, CA: Sage.

Palmer, Richard E. 1969. *Hermeneutics*. Evanston, IL: Northwestern University Press.

Pampel, Fred C. (2000). *Logistic regression: A primer. Quantitative Applications in the Social Sciences, 132*. Thousand Oaks, CA: Sage.

Pannell, David J., & Roberts, Anna M. (2009). Conducting and delivering integrated research to influence land-use policy: Salinity policy in Australia. *Environmental Science and Policy*. Retrieved from www.sciencedirect.com/science?_ob = ArticleURL&_udi = B6VP6-4VDSJTG-2&_user = 10&_rdoc = 1&_fmt = &_orig = search&_sort = d&_docanchor = &view = c&_searchStrId = 1112684737&_rerunOrigin = google&_acct = C000050221&_version = 1&_urlVersion = 0&_userid = 10&md5 = 270d0ea80bf195080a9cfb4efac1b257

Parker-Pope, Tara. (2010). She works. They're happy. *New York Times*, January 22. Retrieved from http://www.nytimes.com/2010/01/24/fashion/24marriage.html?pagewanted = all

Patton, Michael Quinn. (2002). *Qualitative research and evaluation methods* (3rd ed.). Thousand Oaks, CA: Sage.

Pearl, Judea. (2009). *Causality: Models, reasoning and inference* (2nd ed.). Cambridge, UK: Cambridge University Press.

Peffley, Mark, & Hurwitz, Jon. (2007, October). Persuasion and resistance: Race and the death penalty in America. *American Journal of Political Science, 51*(4), 996–1012.

Petrella, Margaret, Biernbaum, Lee, & Lappin, Jane. (2007). *Exploring a new congestion pricing concept: Focus group findings from Northern Virginia and Philadelphia*. Cambridge, MA: Volpe Center, U.S. Department of Transportation.

Pew Research Center for the People and the Press. (2012a). *Assessing the representativeness of public opinion surveys*. Retrieved from http://www.people-press.org/2012/05/15/assessing-the-representativeness-of-public-opinion-surveys/

Pew Research Center for the People and the Press. (2012b). *Young voters supported Obama less, but may have mattered more*. Retrieved from http://www.people-press.org/2012/11/26/young-voters-supported-obama-less-but-may-have-mattered-more/

Pew Research Center for the People and the Press. (2013). *Majority now supports legalizing marijuana* (released April 4). Retrieved from http://www.people-press.org/2013/04/04/majority-now-supports-legalizing-marijuana/

Pew Research Center for the People and the Press. (n.d.). *Cell phone surveys*. Retrieved from http://www.people-press.org/methodology/collecting-survey-data/cell-phone-surveys/

Plumer, Brad. (2013). Gun research is allowed again. So what will we find out? *Washington Post*, January 17. Retrieved from http://www.washingtonpost.com/blogs/wonkblog/wp/2013/01/17/gun-research-is-allowed-again-so-what-will-we-find-out/

Poister, Theodore H. (2003). *Measuring performance in public and nonprofit organizations* (1st ed.). San Francisco: Jossey-Bass.

PollingReport.com. (2009). *Terrorism*. Retrieved from www.pollingreport.com/terror.htm

PollingReport.com. (2013a). *Direction of country*. Retrieved from http://www.pollingreport.com/right.htm

PollingReport.com. (2013b). *Guns: Gallup poll*. Retrieved from http://www.pollingreport.com/guns.htm

Popper, Karl R. 1959. *The logic of scientific discovery*. New York: Basic Books.

Project on Human Development in Chicago Neighborhoods. (2008). *Systematic social observation*. Retrieved from www.icpsr.umich.edu/PHDCN/descriptions/sso.html

Ragin, Charles C. (2008). *Redesigning social inquiry: Fuzzy sets and beyond*. Chicago: University of Chicago Press.

Rampell, Catherine. (2011). About that 99 percent . . . *New York Times*, October 10. Retrieved from http://economix.blogs.nytimes.com/2011/10/10/about-that-99-percent/

RAND Corporation. (2013, May 9). *36-item short form survey from the RAND Medical Outcomes Study.* Retrieved from http://www.rand.org/health/surveys_tools/mos/mos_core_36item.html

RAND Corporation. (n.d.). *The Health Insurance Experiment: A classic RAND study speaks to the current health care reform debate*. Retrieved from www.rand.org/pubs/research_briefs/RB9174/index1.html

Ravallion, Martin. (2011). *On multi-dimensional indices of poverty* (Working paper 5580). Washington, DC: World Bank.

Rees, Daniel I., & Sabia, Joseph J. (2009). The effect of breast feeding on educational attainment: Evidence from sibling data. *Journal of Human Capital, 3*(1), 43–72.

Remler, Dahlia K., Graff Zivin, Joshua, & Glied, Sherry A. (2004). Modeling health insurance expansions: Effect of alternate approaches. *Journal of Policy Analysis and Management, 23*(2), 291–314.

Roberts, Les, Lafta, Riyadh, Garfield, Richard, Khudhairi, Jamal, & Burnham, Gilbert. (2004). Mortality before and after the 2003 invasion of Iraq: Cluster sample survey. *Lancet, 364,* 1857–1864.

Robinson, William S. (1950). Ecological correlations and the behavior of individuals. *American Sociological Review, 15*(3), 351–357.

Rolston, Howard, Geyer, Judy, & Locke, Gretchen. (2013). *Evaluation of the Homebase Community Prevention Program: Final report*. Cambridge, MA: Abt Associates. Retrieved from http://www.abtassociates.com/Reports/2013/Evaluation-of-the-Homebase-Community-Prevention-Pr.aspx

Rosen, Sherwin. (1981). The economics of superstars. *American Economic Review, 17*(5), 845–858.

Rosenbaum, Paul R. (2002). *Observational studies* (2nd ed.). New York: Springer.

Rosenbaum, Paul R., & Rubin, Donald B. (1985). Constructing a control group using multivariate matched sampling methods that incorporate the propensity score. *The American Statistician, 39*(1), 33.

Rosenberg, Alexander. (2012). *Philosophy of social science* (4th ed.). Boulder, CO: Westview Press.

Rosenberg, Morris. (1965). *Society and the adolescent self-image*. Princeton, NJ: Princeton University Press.

Rosenzweig, Mark R., & Wolpin, Kenneth I. (2000). Natural "natural experiments" in economics. *Journal of Economic Literature, 38*(4), 827–874.

Rosnow, Ralph L., & Rosenthal, Robert. (1997). *People studying people: Artifacts and ethics in behavioral research*. New York: W. H. Freeman.

Rossi, Peter H., Lipsey, Mark W., & Freeman, Howard E. (2003). *Evaluation: A systematic approach* (7th ed.). Thousand Oaks, CA: Sage.

Rothman, Kenneth. (1990). No adjustments are needed for multiple comparisons. *Epidemiology, 1*(1), 43–46. Retrieved from www.jstor.org/stable/20065622

Rubin, Donald B. (2005). Causal inference using potential outcomes: Design, modeling, decisions. *Journal of the American Statistical Association, 100,* 322–331.

Rubin, Donald B. (2007). The design versus the analysis of observational studies for causal effects: Parallels with the design of randomized trials. *Statistics in Medicine, 26,* 2–36.

Salkind, Neil J. (2010). *Statistics for people who (think they) hate statistics* (4th ed.). Thousand Oaks, CA: Sage.

Sampson, Robert J., & Raudenbush, Stephen W. (1999). Systematic social observation of public spaces: A new look at disorder in urban neighborhoods. *American Journal of Sociology, 105*(3), 603–651.

Sanbonmatsu, Lisa, Ludwig, Jens, Katz, Lawrence F., Gennetian, Lisa A., Duncan, Greg J., Kessler, Ronald C., . . . Lindau, Stacy Tessler. (2011). *Moving to Opportunity for Fair Housing Demonstration project: Final impacts evaluation.* Cambridge, MA: National Bureau of Economic Research. Retrieved from http://www.huduser.org/publications/pdf/MTOFHD_fullreport_v2.pdf

Sandman, Peter M. (1991). Emerging communication responsibilities of epidemiologists. *Journal of Clinical Epidemiology, 44*(Suppl. 1), 41–50.

Savas, E. S. (2007). *Slow train to better service*. Retrieved from www.nytimes.com/2007/12/16/opinion/nyregionopinions/16CIsavas.html

Scheiber, Noam. (2007). Freaks and geeks: How Freakonomics is ruining the dismal science. *The New Republic*, April 2. Retrieved from www.tnr.com/article/freaks-and-geeks-how-freakonomics-ruining-the-dismal-science?page=0,0

Schemo, Diana Jean, & Fessenden, Ford. (2003). A miracle revisited: Measuring success; gains in Houston schools: How real are they? *New York Times*, December 3. Retrieved from www.nytimes.com/2003/12/03/us/a-miracle-revisited-measuring-success-gains-in-houston-schools-how-real-are-they.html?scp=1&sq=gains+in+Houston+schools%3A+How+real+are+they%3F+&st=nyt

Schmitz, Connie C., & Parsons, Beverly A. (1999). *Everything you wanted to know about logic models but were afraid to ask*. Boulder, CO: InSites. Retrieved from www.insites.org/documents/logmod.htm

Schwartz, J. (1994, January). Air pollution and daily mortality: A review and meta analysis. *Environmental Research, 64*(1), 36–52.

Schwartz-Shea, Peregrine, & Yanow, Dvora. (2012). *Interpretive research design: Concepts and processes*. New York: Routledge.

Scola, Nancy. (2012). Why it's going to be hard for Republicans to match the Big-Data advantage Democrats have built. *The Atlantic*, November 8. Retrieved from http://www.theatlantic.com/politics/archive/2012/11/why-its-going-to-be-hard-for-republicans-to-match-the-big-data-advantage-democrats-have-built/264929/

Seawright, Jason, & Gerring, John. (2008). Case selection techniques in case study research: A menu of qualitative and quantitative options. *Political Research Quarterly, 61*(2), 294–308.

Seidman, Steven. (2012). *Contested knowledge: Social theory today* (5th ed.). Malden, MA: Wiley-Blackwell.

Seron, Carroll, Van Ryzin, Gregg, & Frankel, Martin. (2001). Impact of legal counsel on outcomes for poor tenants in New York City's housing court: Results of a randomized experiment. *Law & Society Review, 35*, 419.

Shadish, William R., Clark, M. H., & Steiner, Peter M. (2008). Can nonrandomized experiments yield accurate answers? A randomized experiment comparing random to nonrandom assignment. *Journal of the American Statistical Association, 103*, 1334–1343.

Shadish, William R., Cook, Thomas D., & Campbell, Donald T. (2002). *Experimental and quasi-experimental designs for generalized causal inference*. Boston: Houghton Mifflin.

Sheard, Laura, & Tompkins, Charlotte. (2008). Contradictions and misperceptions: An exploration of injecting practice, cleanliness, risk, and partnership in the lives of women drug users. *Qualitative Health Research, 18*(11), 1536–1547.

Sheehan, Helena, & Sweeney, Sheamus. (2009). *The Wire* and the world: Narrative and metanarrative. *Jump Cut: A Review of Contemporary Media, 51*. Retrieved from www.ejumpcut.org/currentissue/

Sherman, Lawrence W., & Berk, Richard A. (1984). The specific deterrent effects of arrest for domestic assault. *American Sociological Review, 49*(2), 261–272.

Short, Kathleen. (2011). *The research supplemental poverty measure (SPM): 2010*. Current Population Reports P60-241, U.S. Census Bureau, November. Retrieved from https://www.census.gov/hhes/povmeas/methodology/supplemental/research/Short_ResearchSPM2010.pdf

Sieber, Joan E., & Tolich, Martin B. (2013). *Planning ethically responsible research* (2nd ed.). Thousand Oaks, CA: Sage.

Silver, Nate. (2012a). Do presidential polls break toward challengers? *FiveThirtyEight*, July 22. Retrieved from http://fivethirtyeight.blogs.nytimes.com/2012/07/22/do-presidential-polls-break-toward-challengers/?_r = 0

Silver, Nate. (2012b). Which polls fared best (and worst) in the 2012 presidential race. *FiveThirtyEight*, November 10. Retrieved from http://fivethirtyeight.blogs.nytimes.com/2012/11/10/which-polls-fared-best-and-worst-in-the-2012-presidential-race/

Simon, Steve. (2008). *Odds ratio vs. relative risk*. Retrieved from www.childrensmercy.org/stats/journal/oddsratio.asp

Skocpol, Theda, & Somers, Margaret. (1980). The uses of comparative history in macrosocial inquiry. *Comparative Studies in Society and History, 22*(02), 174–197.

Sloman, Steven A. (2009). *Casual models: How people think about the world and its alternatives*. Oxford, UK: Oxford University Press.

Small, Mario Luis. (2009). "How many cases do I need?" On science and the logic of case selection in field-based research. *Ethnography, 10*(1), 5–38.

Smith, Jonathan A., Flowers, Paul, & Larkin, Michael. (2009). *Interpretative phenomenological analysis: Theory, method and research*. Thousand Oaks, CA: Sage.

Smith, Robert. (2005). *Mexican New York: Transnational lives of new immigrants*. Berkeley: University of California Press.

Sokolowski, Robert. 1999. *Introduction to phenomenology*. Cambridge, UK: Cambridge University Press.

Spector, Paul. (1992). *Summated rating scale construction: An introduction*. Newbury Park, CA: Sage.

Spencer, Elizabeth A., Appleby, Paul N., Davey, Gwyneth K., & Key, Timothy J. (2007). Validity of self-reported height and weight. *Public Health Nutrition, 5*(4), 561–565.

Staley, Oliver. (2011). Chicago economist's crazy idea wins Ken Griffiths backing. *Bloomberg.com*. Retrieved from http://www.bloomberg.com/news/2011-02-23/chicago-economist-s-crazy-idea-for-education-wins-ken-griffin-s-backing.html

Steiner, Peter M., Cook, Thomas D., Shadish, William R., & Clark, M. H. (2010). The importance of covariate selection in controlling for selection bias in observational studies. *Psychological Methods, 15*(3), 250–267.

Stone, Deborah. (1997). *Policy paradox: The art of political decision making*. New York: Norton.

Stringer, Ernest T. (2007). *Action research* (3rd ed.). Thousand Oaks, CA: Sage.

Struyk, Michael, & Fix, Raymond J. (1993). *Clear and convincing evidence: Measurement of discrimination in America*. Lanham, MD: University Press of America.

Sullivan, Ryan S., & Dutkowsky, Donald H. (2012). The effect of cigarette taxation on prices: An empirical analysis using local-level data. *Public Finance Review, 40*, 687.

Surowiecki, James. (2004). *The wisdom of crowds: Why the many are smarter than the few and how collective wisdom shapes business, economies, societies and nations*. New York: Doubleday of Random House.

Taubes, Gary, & Mann, Charles C. (1995). Epidemiology faces its limits. *Science, 269*(5221), 164–169.

Tenopir, Carol. (2004). Online databases—Online scholarly journals: How many? *Library Journal*, February 1. Retrieved from www.libraryjournal.com/article/CA374956.html

Teresi, Jeanne A., Ramirez, Mildred, Remler, Dahlia, Boratgis, Gabriel, Silver, Stephanie, Lindsey, Michael, Kong, Jian, Eimicke, Jian, & Dichter, Elizabeth. (2013). Dissemination of evidence-based best practices in nursing homes: Effects on falls, quality-of-life and costs. *International Journal of Nursing Studies, 50*(4), 448–463.

Thaler, Richard H., & Sunstein, Cass R. (2008). *Nudge: Improving decisions about health, wealth, and happiness*. New Haven, CT: Yale University Press.

Time-sharing experiments for the social sciences. (n.d.). *Welcome*. Retrieved from http://tess.experimentcentral.org

Treloar, Carla, Laybutt, Becky, Jauncey, Marianne, van Beek, Ingrid, Lodge, Michael, Malpas, Grant, & Carruthers, Susan. (2008). Broadening discussions of "safe" in hepatitis C prevention: A close-up of swabbing in an analysis of video recordings of injecting practice. *International Journal of Drug Policy, 19*(1), 59–65.

Trochim, William. (2001). *The research methods knowledge base*. Cincinnati, OH: Atomic Dog.

Tufte, Edward R. (2001). *The visual display of quantitative information* (2nd ed.). Cheshire, CT: Graphics Press.

Turner, Charles F., Ku, Leighton, Rogers, Susan M., Lindberg, Laura D., Pleck, Joseph H., & Sonenstein, Freya L. (1998). Adolescent sexual behavior, drug use, and violence: Increased reporting with computer survey technology. *Science, 280*(5365), 867–873.

Turney, Kristin, Clampet-Lundquist, Susan, Edin, Kathryn, Kling, Jeffery R., & Duncan, Greg J. (2006). Neighborhood effects on barriers to employment: Results from a randomized housing mobility experiment in Baltimore. In G. Burtless & J. R. Pack (Eds.), *Brookings-Wharton papers on urban affairs* (pp. 137–187). Washington, DC: Brookings Institution Press.

United States Elections Project. (2012, March 31). *2008 general election turnout rates*. Retrieved from http://elections.gmu.edu/Turnout_2008G.html

University of Chicago. (2003). *The Chicago manual of style* (15th ed.). Chicago: University of Chicago Press.

University of Chicago Crime Lab. (2013). *Open letter to Vice President Joseph Biden*. http://crimelab.uchicago.edu/sites/crimelab.uchicago.edu/files/uploads/Biden%20Commission%20letter_20130110_final.pdf

University of Michigan. (2009). *Surveys of consumers. Questionnaire*. Ann Arbor, MI: Survey Research Center, Institute for Social Research. Retrieved from http://www.sca.isr.umich.edu/fetchdoc.php?docid=24776

U.S. Bureau of Justice Statistics. (2013, March 6). *Number of rape/sexual assaults, robberies, aggravated assaults, and simple assaults, 2007–2011*. Generated using the NCVS Victimization Analysis Tool at www.bjs.gov.

U.S. Census Bureau. (2009a). *Annual survey of manufactures: How the data are collected*. Retrieved from www.census.gov/manufacturing/asm/how_the_data_are_collected/index.html

U.S. Census Bureau. (2009b). *The 2009 statistical abstracts. Incomes, expenditures, poverty and wealth* (Table 687). Retrieved from www.census.gov/compendia/statab/tables/09s0687.pdf

U.S. Census Bureau. (2009c). *The 2009 statistical abstracts. Law enforcement, courts, & prisons: Crimes and crime rates*. Retrieved from www.census.gov/compendia/statab/tables/09s0301.pdf

U.S. Census Bureau. (2012a). Table 312. Homicide trends: 1980 to 2008. *Statistical Abstract of the United States: 2012*. Retrieved from http://www.census.gov/compendia/statab/2012/tables/12s0312.pdf

U.S. Census Bureau. (2012b). Table 709. Individuals and families below poverty level—number and rate by state: 2000 and 2009. *Statistical Abstract of the United States: 2012*. Retrieved from http://www.census.gov/compendia/statab/2012/tables/12s0709.pdf

U.S. Census Bureau. (2013a). "American FactFinder—Community Facts." Retrieved from http://factfinder2.census.gov/faces/nav/jsf/pages/community_facts.xhtml

U.S. Census Bureau. (2013b). *USA QuickFacts from the U.S. Census Bureau*. Retrieved from http://quickfacts.census.gov/qfd/states/00000.html

U.S. Department of Health and Human Services. (2009). *Women's Health.gov. Ad Council Materials*. Retrieved from www.womenshealth.gov/breastfeeding/programs/nbc/adcouncil/#b

U.S. Department of Housing and Urban Development. (n.d.). *Moving to opportunity for fair housing*. Retrieved from www.hud.gov/progdesc/mto.cfm

U.S. Department of Labor, Bureau of Labor Statistics. (2009). *News: The employment situation—August 2008*. Retrieved from www.bls.gov/news.release/archives/empsit_09052008.pdf

U.S. Federal Bureau of Investigation. (2010, March 29). Reported crime by locality (city, county), state, and nation. *Uniform Crime Reporting Statistics*. Retrieved from http://www.ucrdatatool.gov/Search/Crime/Crime.cfm

U.S. Federal Bureau of Investigation. (2013a). Table 1: Crime in the United States by volume and rate per 100,000 inhabitants. *Crime in the United States: 2011*. Retrieved from http://www.fbi.gov/about-us/cjis/ucr/crime-in-the-u.s/2011/crime-in-the-u.s.-2011/tables/table-1

U.S. Federal Bureau of Investigation. (2013b). Table 8: Offenses known to law enforcement by state by city, 2011. *Crime in the United States: 2011*. Retrieved from http://www.fbi.gov/about-us/cjis/ucr/crime-in-the-u.s/2011/crime-in-the-u.s.-2011/tables/table_8_offenses_known_to_law_enforcement_by_state_by_city_2011.xls/view

U.S. Global Change Research Program. (2009). *Global climate change impacts in the United States*. Washington, DC: Author. Retrieved from www.globalchange.gov/usimpacts

USA Today. (2008). Quick question: How many firearms do you own? *On Deadline: USATODAY.com*. Retrieved from http://blogs.usatoday.com/ondeadline/2008/06/quick-question.html

Valverde, Maria de la Luz, & Hassan Tajalli. (2006). *The City of Austin citizen survey 2006*. Retrieved November 10, 2009, from www.ci.austin.tx.us/budget/06-07/downloads/citizensurvey2006.pdf

Van Ryzin, Gregg G. (1996). The impact of resident management on residents' satisfaction with public housing: A process analysis of quasi-experimental data. *Evaluation Review, 20*(4), 485–506.

Van Ryzin, Gregg G. (2008). Validity of an on-line panel approach to citizen surveys. *Public Performance & Management Review, 32*(2), 236–262.

Van Ryzin, Gregg G. (2009, October 1–3). *Outcomes, process, and citizens' trust of the civil service*. Paper presented at the 2009 conference of the Public Management Research Association, Columbus, Ohio.

W. K. Kellogg Foundation. (2004). *Logic model development guide*. Retrieved from www.wkkf.org/Pubs/Tools/Evaluation/Pub3669.pdf

Walt, Gill. (1994). How far does research influence policy? *European Journal of Public Health, 4*, 233–235.

Ware, John E., & Cathy Donaldson Sherbourne. (1992). The MOS 36-Item Short Form Health Survey (SF-36): I. Conceptual framework and item selection. *Medical Care, 30*(6), 473–483.

Wasunna, Beatrice, Zurovac, Dejan, Goodman, Catherine A., & Snow, Robert W. (2008). Why don't health workers prescribe ACT? A qualitative study of factors affecting the prescription of artemether-lumefantrine. *Malaria Journal, 7*(1), 29.

Webb, Eugene J., Campbell, Donald T., Schwartz, Richard D., & Sechrest, Lee. (1999). *Unobtrusive measures* (Rev. ed.). Thousand Oaks, CA: Sage.

Webb, Theresa, Jenkins, Lucille, Browne, Nickolas, Afifi, Abdelmonen A., & Kraus, Jess. (2007). Violent entertainment pitched to adolescents: An analysis of PG-13 films. *Pediatrics, 119*(6), e1219–e1229.

Webster, Daniel W., Bulzacchelli, Maria T., Zeoli, April M., & Vernick, John S. (2006). Effects of undercover police stings of gun dealers on the supply of new guns to criminals. *Injury Prevention, 12*(4), 225–230.

Weimer, David L., & Vining, Aidan R. (2010). *Policy analysis concepts and practice* (5th ed.). Upper Saddle River, NJ: Prentice Hall.

Weiss, Carol H. (1997). *Evaluation* (2nd ed.). Upper Saddle River, NJ: Prentice Hall.

Weiss, Robert S. (1994). *Learning from strangers: The art and method of qualitative interview studies*. New York: Free Press of Simon & Schuster.

Whitehead, Nicole. (2004). The effects of increased access to books on student reading using the public library. *Reading Improvement, 41*(3), 165.

Williams, Joseph M. (1995). *Style: Toward clarity and grace*. Chicago: University of Chicago Press.

Williamson, Elizabeth, Morley, Ruth, Lucas, Alan, & Carpenter, James. (2012). Propensity scores: From naïve enthusiasm to intuitive understanding. *Statistical Methods in Medical Research, 21*(3), 273–293.

Willis, Bob. (2008). *U.S. Michigan Consumer Sentiment Index falls in June*. Bloomberg, June 27. Retrieved from www.bloomberg.com/apps/news?pid = 20601103&refer = news&sid = aQAloSZDtBuo

Wolf, Joan B. (2007). Is breast really best? Risk and total motherhood in the national breastfeeding awareness campaign. *Journal of Health Politics, Policy and Law, 32*(4), 595–635.

Woodward, James. (2003). *Making things happen: A theory of causal explanation*. Oxford, UK: Oxford University Press.

Wooldridge, Jeffrey. (2009). *Introductory econometrics: A modern approach* (4th ed.). Florence, KY: SouthWestern Cengage Learning.

Wooldridge, Judith, Kenney, Genevieve, & Trenholm, Christopher (with Lisa Dubay, Ian Hill, Myoung Kim, Lorenzo Moreno, Anna Sommers, & Stephen Zuckerman). (2005). *Congressionally mandated evaluation of the state children's health insurance program* (Final Report to Congress). Cambridge, MA/Washington, DC: Mathematica Policy Research/Urban Institute Press.

World Health Organization. (2009). *Malaria fact sheet*. Retrieved from www.who.int/mediacentre/factsheets/fs094/en/index.html

World Values Survey. (2005). Retrieved from www.worldvaluessurvey.org/

Yanovski, Jack A., Yanovski, Susan Z., Sovik, Kara N., Nguyen, Tuc T., O'Neil, Patrick M., & Sebring, Nancy G. (2000). A prospective study of holiday weight gain. *New England Journal of Medicine, 342*(12), 861–867.

Yeager, David S., Krosnick, Jon A., Chang, LinChiat, Javitz, Harold S., Levendusky, Matthew S., Simpser, Alberto, & Wang, Rui. (2011). Comparing the accuracy of RDD telephone surveys and Internet surveys conducted with probability and non-probability samples. *Public Opinion Quarterly, 75*(4) (November 1), 709–747.

Yin, Robert K. (2008). *Case study research: Design and methods* (4th ed.). Thousand Oaks, CA: Sage.

Zaller, John R. (1992). *The nature and origins of mass opinion*. New York: Cambridge University Press.

Zengerle, Jason. (2008, December 31). Going under: A doctor's downfall, and a profession's struggle with addiction. *The New Republic*, p. 21.

Zheng, Hang, Liu, Yanyou, Li, Wei, Yang, Bo, Chen, Dengbang, Wang, Xiaojia, . . . Halberg, Franz. (2006). Beneficial effects of exercise and its molecular mechanisms on depression in rats. *Behavioural Brain Research, 168*(1), 47–55.

Ziliak, Stephen T., & McCloskey, Deirdre N. (2008). *The cult of statistical significance*. Ann Arbor: University of Michigan.

Author Index

Subject Index

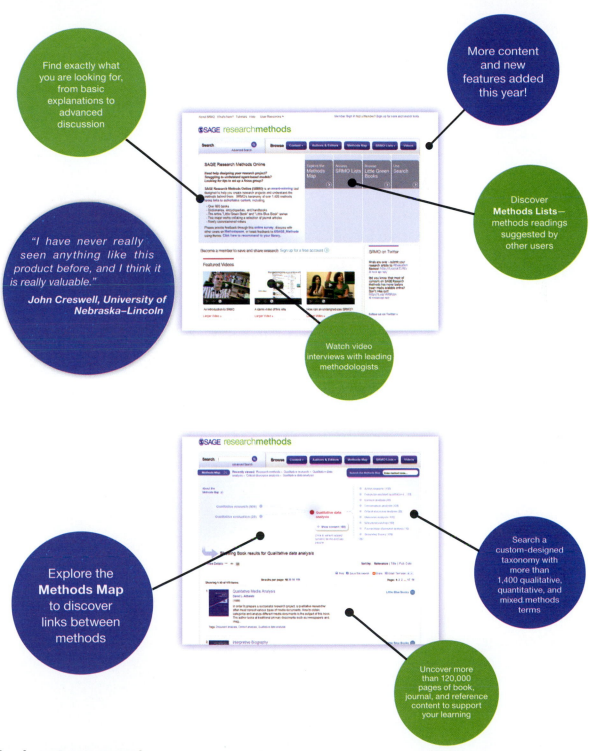